RENAISSANCE & BAROQUE BRONZES IN THE FRICK ART MUSEUM

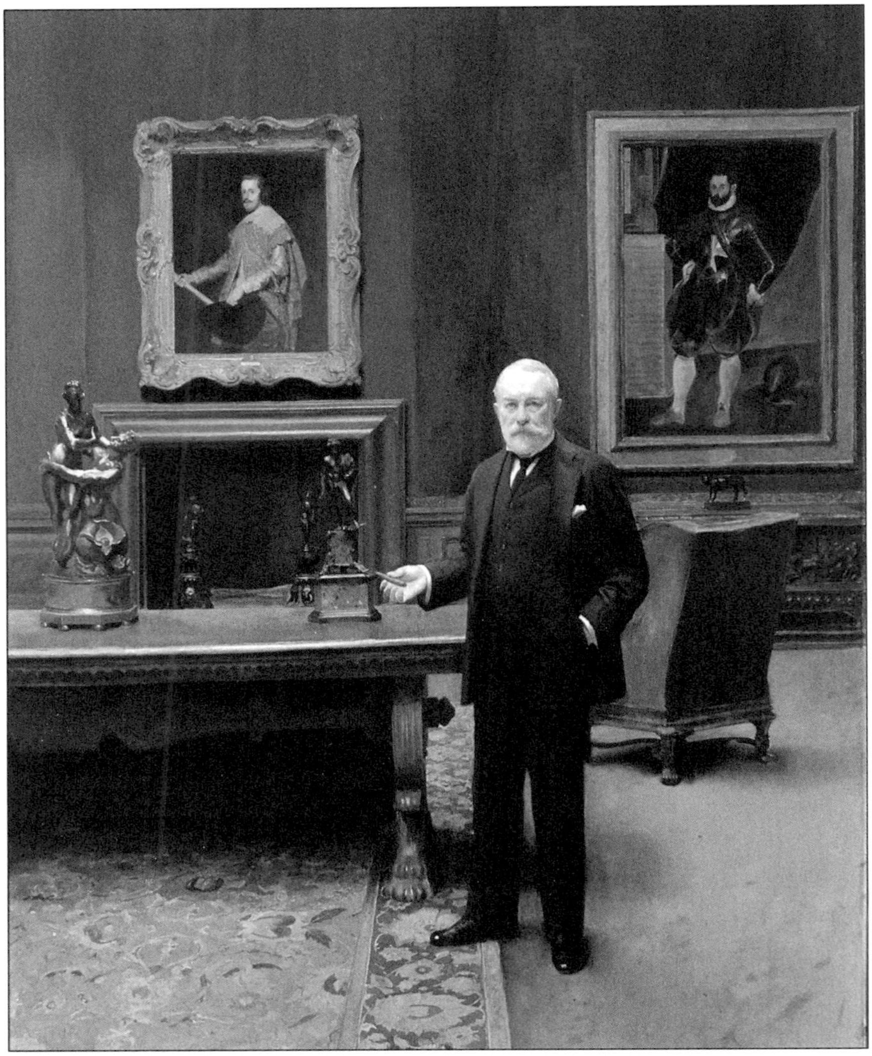

Portrait (post humous) of Henry Clay Frick in the West Gallery, One East 70th Street, New York; Sir Gerald F. Kelly, (British, 1879–1972); 1925, oil on canvas
Private Collection

RENAISSANCE & BAROQUE BRONZES IN THE FRICK ART MUSEUM

Charles Avery

The Frick Art &
Historical Center

Pittsburgh

1993

Library of Congress Catalog Card Number 93-073993
ISBN 1-881-403-02-5

Designed by Landesberg Design Associates
Photography of exhibition pieces by Lockwood Hoehl
Typeset by Esprit Graphics
Printed by Hoechstetter Printing Company

Set in Garamond No. 49

Cover illustration: *Venus with Apple*, attributed to Severo Calzetta of Ravenna, (active 1496–1525); Italian, early 16th century; gilt bronze statuette; FAM 1991.2

This catalogue is dedicated to
Hon. J. William Middendorf II,
connoisseur, collector and artist, friend of
The Frick Art Museum and of the Author.

Foreword and Acknowledgements

If Helen Clay Frick had a particular attachment (over and above vigorous loyalty to her father's interests) to the thirty-nine bronze statuettes left in her custody once Henry Clay Frick's famous art collection had been divided among The Frick Collection and the individual legatees, the fact is not recorded. Her own interest in sculpture centered on Houdon, several of whose works she acquired and about whom she published two scholarly articles.

Miss Frick, nonetheless, preserved her share of her father's collection of bronzes intact and passed this legacy on to The Frick Art Museum, mainly in 1970 and 1973. Three decades earlier, in 1940, twenty-six statuettes were recorded as being at "Eagle Rock," the huge Georgian-revival summer house at Prides Crossing, Massachusetts, that held many of the objects eventually given to The Frick Art Museum. Undated archival photographs show cat. Nos. 3 & 4, the *Neptune* inkstands from the workshop of Severo, resting symmetrically on the Carlin writing table in the Music Room; cat. No. 13, *Mars*, here attributed to Segala, standing on a commode in the same room, paired with what appears to be the Antico *Hercules* that Miss Frick later donated to The Frick Collection; cat. No. 14, the *Inkstand Supported on Three Putti*, and cat. No. 22, *Old Man Riding on a Goat* (here attributed to Ferdinando Tacca), in a casual but deliberate arrangement on the long table in the marble-columned Living Hall; and, in a photograph possibly of later date, cat. No. 39, the problematic *Charging Bull*, resting atop a *desserte* in the Breakfast Room.

Other statuettes not shown in the interior photographs of "Eagle Rock" bear small labels underneath their bases revealing how they were placed about the house: cat. Nos. 1, 6, 19, 23, 28, & 35 stood on the Library bookcase; cat. No. 10, the *Lamp in the Form of a Satyr's Head*, perched on the Library mantel; and cat. No. 5, the beautiful gilt bronze *Venus* here attributed to Severo, resided peacefully by a ". . . window near [the] Terrace." Fragmentary labels underneath still others suggest that they, too, had their designated places.

It would appear that along with many furnishings, the bronzes at "Eagle Rock" were removed in the mid 1960s; the house was pulled down toward the end of the decade. The Frick Art Museum opened in Pittsburgh on October 10, 1970, with the most important of the thirty-three statuettes that Miss Frick had donated prominently on exhibition; the rest were kept in the museum's storage. Four others, which in 1970 had been held back for repair, entered the museum in 1973.

A slight mystery surrounds the route traveled by cat. Nos. 5 & 28, the Severo *Venus* and the *Bronze Candlesticks*. These arrived at The Frick Art Museum only after Miss Frick's death in 1984, when they appeared among the large quantity of furnishings, household objects and personal items delivered to the premises from a storage warehouse by order of Miss Frick's executors. The *Candlesticks* may be those recorded as stored on Miss Frick's behalf at The Frick Collection as of July, 1977, but of the *Venus* there is no mention until November 20, 1981, when it appears on a handwritten list of items shipped to Pittsburgh from Miss Frick's office on the sixth floor of The Frick Art Reference Library. It is tempting to conclude that in the 1960s, when the first shipment of bronzes was dispatched to Pittsburgh, Miss Frick retained the exquisite *Venus* in her inner sanctum for the enjoyment of her friends and herself, although proof of this has yet to surface.

Not until several years after Miss Frick's death was serious thought given to studying the bronzes. This effort originated rather casually in a remark to Ambassador J. William Middendorf II, himself a discerning collector of bronzes (and much else), that The Frick Art Museum possessed a small collection of distinguished provenance that had not been examined thoroughly in decades. In his usual enthusiastic fashion, Ambassador Middendorf offered to put the museum into contact with just the right scholar — Charles Avery.

To Ambassador Middendorf, then, we owe warm thanks for forging the crucial link between collection and expert. Charles Avery proved every bit as willing and as capable as Ambassador Middendorf suggested he would be; he has carried catalogue and exhibition every step of the way, not merely undertaking all details of scholarship and writing an erudite and lively text, but directing the efforts of a dedicated, yet small and inexperienced, museum staff, and cheerfully educating all around him in the history and aesthetics of bronze sculpture and producing a very model of a beautiful and useful publication. The Frick Art Museum's gratitude to Dr. Avery will be as permanent as this catalogue itself.

Dr. Avery benefited from earlier and sensible efforts — recorded in the museum files — to re-assess the collection in the light of modern scholarship, which were made in the late 1960s by David Owsley of Pittsburgh and Anthony Radcliffe of the Victoria & Albert Museum, London.

First to Alan R. Fausel, curator of The Frick Art Museum 1989–91, then to Nadine Grabania, assistant curator, fell responsibility for organizing materials and providing support for Dr. Avery's research. In the early stages of the project, they were assisted by Manu Schuck, Catherine R. Kiefer and Jeanne Brown. Later, as Ms. Grabania coordinated production with her usual careful attention to detail, administrative support was provided by Michele Karnack.

Under Dr. Avery's supervision, each object in the collection was expertly cleaned by Bruce Christman of the Cleveland Museum of Art, then patiently photographed by Lockwood Hoehl to maximize clarity of (in some cases, newly revealed) detail. Providing a suitable framework for Dr. Avery's text and Mr. Hoehl's photographs is a graphic design that displays the customary sensitivity of its author, Rick Landesberg and Mr. Landesberg's associate, Caroline Zellers Mengon, to artistic subject matter.

For their generous assistance in tracking details of the whereabouts of the Frick bronzes during the many decades of Miss Frick's ownership, we are most thankful to Helen Sanger, Andrew W. Mellon Librarian of The Frick Art Reference Library; to Edgar Munhall and Bernice Davidson, curator and research curator, respectively, of The Frick Collection; and to Helen Clay Chace and Julia B. Egan.

For granting permission to reproduce photographs and for suggestions helpful to research, we are particularly grateful to Ruth Blumka and to Robert Kashey and David Wojciechowski of Shepherd Gallery Associates. Anne Bertrand, intern at The Frick Art Museum, and Ray Anne Lockard, librarian of the Frick Fine Arts Library, University of Pittsburgh, lent assistance in obtaining photographs, as did Bernice Davidson and Deborah Charlton of The Frick Collection. Also generous with assistance in photographic research were Dr. David Ekserdjian of the Department of Sculpture, Christie's (London), and Elizabeth Wilson, senior director, European Works of Art, Sotheby's (London).

The following individuals and museums graciously lent works of art to the exhibition: Mrs. Ruth Blumka; the Glass family; the Los Angeles County Museum of Art (James E. Clark Bequest and the Collection of Mary Stansbury Ruiz); the National Gallery of Art, Washington (Samuel H. Kress Collection); The Toledo Museum of Art (Gift of Edward Drummond Libbey); The Walters Art Gallery, Baltimore; and an anonymous private collector.

Finally, the staff of The Frick Art & Historical Center and The Frick Art Museum wishes to thank Dr. Henry Clay Frick, II, chairman, and the Individual Trustees of The Helen Clay Frick Foundation for their understanding and support of the entire enterprise represented by this publication.

DeCourcy E. McIntosh
Executive Director
The Frick Art & Historical Center
Pittsburgh, Pennsylvania
October, 1993

TABLE OF CONTENTS

Introduction

Bronzes in the Collection of The Frick Art Museum

The Frick Art Museum possesses the residue of the famous collection of bronze statuettes originating mainly, though not exclusively, from the Italian Renaissance, which was formed by John Pierpont Morgan in London around the beginning of the century. The collection was lent to the Victoria & Albert Museum for exhibition between 1901 and 1912. It was brought to the United States in July 1912 and lent to the Metropolitan Museum after Morgan's death in 1913. In 1916 the bulk of Morgan's collection was negotiated by Duveen, mostly to Henry Clay Frick, though some signal pieces were acquired by Henry E. Huntington and are in the art gallery founded by him in San Marino, California. A few other less important pieces also failed to find their way into Frick's hands, possibly by deliberate selection, or simply by accident: one or two may have been casually disposed of since the family owned them.

Mr. Frick thus acquired at a stroke a major collection, which equalled many an old noble family holding in Europe, and outshone most by its diversity and range. Furthermore it had been catalogued by the renowned Director of the Kaiser Friedrich Museum in Berlin, Dr. Wilhelm von Bode, the founding father of the modern understanding and appreciation of Renaissance bronze statuettes. The catalogue was privately printed in a deluxe folio edition which is today an extremely rare and valuable book.

What were then perceived, and in most cases still are recognized, as the masterpieces were to find a fitting place integrated with illustrious paintings and fine furniture, amidst the grand reception halls and panelled rooms of the mansion on Fifth Avenue, now known internationally as The Frick Collection. This has been catalogued by great specialists over the course of many years.

What is less well known is that Miss Helen C. Frick kept a substantial number of bronze statuettes in her summer residence, "Eagle Rock," at Prides Crossing, Massachusetts. She gave most of them to The Frick Art Museum when it was opened in 1970; they have been displayed sporadically and in varying quantities over the years since. Upon the demise of Miss Frick, a most notable statuette was bequeathed to the museum, the gilt *Venus* by Severo Calzetta from Ravenna (No. 5), which evidently Miss Frick displayed in her office at the Frick Art Reference Library and which has proved to be the star of the collection now foregathered, which numbers in all thirty-nine pieces: this Venus thus has an accession number as recent as 1991, and has since been expertly cleaned, for display and photography, to provide a worthy cover plate for the present catalogue.

There is no indication of the reasons for the particular selection that was made for The Frick Collection, New York, though common sense suggests that the more obviously magnificent objects, and those associated with greater sculptors, would have been chosen; duplicates (for instance the two inkstands by Severo showing *Neptune* on a Dragon (Nos. 3, 4)) were relegated to other locations, as perhaps were the very few controversial pieces. Under these circumstances, it is evident that The Frick Collection would have a majority of the best examples, but not a monopoly. Ten of the bronzes (i.e., over a quarter of the total) in Pittsburgh are of masterly quality and constitute a significant addition to the *corpus* of such pieces that are now distributed worldwide. These include the *Circular Inkstand,* by Riccio (No. 1), small and hard to "read" in detail when in a vitrine but fully illustrated here; the gorgeous *Venus* by Severo (No. 5), the *Leaping Hound* (No. 20), recently recognized as a fine example of animal sculpture by Giovanni Bandini, and close cousin of his great group of *Meleager* in the Treasury of the Prado Museum in Madrid (Fig. 20.1); the Baroque bronze of *Diana* by the Florentine Ferdinando Tacca (No. 21) and the library-sized bust of *Pope Innocent X,* after Algardi (No. 32), which has gained in beauty and aesthetic appreciation since its cleaning: and, finally, the two — very rare — representatives of the Renaissance in Southern Germany — Peter Vischer's *Athlete as a Candelabrum* (No. 36), whose twin is in the Walters Art Gallery, Baltimore (Fig. 36.1), and the solidly cast half-length of *Hippocrates* (No. 37) bearing his classic epigram, most appropriate in the context of a private collection, "Ars longa, Vita brevis" (*Art is long-lasting, though life is short*).

Others of the bronzes, of distinctly less aesthetic appeal, nevertheless open up fascinating avenues for scholarly investigation of their origins — the *Bust of a Humanist* perhaps M.A. Passeri (No. 12); the *Rearing Horseman* (No. 31); or the *Satyr* (No. 38), here connected with Adrian de Vries. One bronze acquired as "Flemish, 17th century," has been known for some years to be a deceptively re-mounted group of a *Hunter and his Dog* (No. 35) by the celebrated Welsh Neo-Classical sculptor who worked in Rome in the following of Canova, John Gibson! Even so, there are only two other bronze reductions known at present. Finally a *Charging Bull* (No. 39), commonly regarded as Flemish 17th century, has had to be notionally demoted (along with all other known versions), under suspicion of being a later pastiche that was indifferently modelled, virtually mass produced, and rather crudely finished.

Charles Avery

The Bronze Statuette in the Renaissance

1. Technique

Bronze is produced by alloying copper and tin in the proportion of roughly nine parts to one: silver, zinc and lead may also be added in small amounts, while trace elements also appear in historical statuettes, owing to imperfect refining techniques and the use of older scrap metal. A high copper content makes the alloy more workable once it has solidified, allowing the sculptor to add more incisive details or to alter the texture of the surface. Casting in two-part sand moulds was appropriate for straightforward objects such as reliefs, medals or simple figures. But for any human figure, quadruped or action group with limbs projecting freely or with complex undercutting (e.g. between the legs) it was necessary to use the process called 'lost-wax' (*cire perdue* in French). This involves making the basic form in clay and coating it with a wax skin as thick as the bronze is required to be (this is determined by a compromise between the need for durability and for avoiding flaws, and the desire to economize with the expensive metal alloy and to keep the statuette relatively light to handle). The beauty of this process lies in the fact that it permits the sculptor to model on the surface of the wax the most minute details and varied textures, which — all being well — will be exactly reproduced in bronze, once the item is cast.

Specialist foundrymen were normally employed to carry out the preparation for casting of the sculptor's clay and wax model, by adding wax rods at appropriate points on the surface, all leading to an inverted cone of solid wax: when encased in an outer coat of plaster (the investment) and after the wax was melted out these rods would provide hollow tubes through which metal might enter ('runners') and hot gases escape ('risers') from the mould and a funnel through which the molten alloy could be poured in. After cooling, the outer mould was broken off, and the metal runners and risers were cut off where they touched the surface of the sculpture, leaving little rough areas that needed tooling to match their surroundings. The sculptor himself might intervene again at this state, to do the tooling and to freshen up with a burin any details that had become blurred in the casting process, and to add a final polish where he wished. A statuette that is finished by the master in this way is defined as 'autograph,' whereas one that does not appear to have enjoyed his personal attention is normally called a 'workshop' cast.

Once the cast has been cleaned and polished it has the bright, coppery gold colour of a new penny, and it will in the course of time oxidize naturally to a brown hue, just as the coin does. A lacquer may be applied to preserve the original golden colour, or the surface may be mercury gilded with gold leaf (see No. 5). Other colours may be induced by treating the cast with acid (e.g. green with sulfuric acid, which imitates the after-effects of long burial in the ground, and thus of an antiquity, see No. 34).

Finally, other hues could be obtained by applying a coloured varnish to the surface — e.g. the bituminous black that was evidently favored in Padua during the Renaissance (see Nos. 6, 7, 10), or the translucent reddish lacquer that was preferred at the end of the 16th century and in the early 17th century (see Nos. 20–22). Even clear lacquers darken with age, and so the majority of old bronzes have a darker appearance than was perhaps intended originally: statuettes are normally shown in contemporaneous paintings as golden, but this does not necessarily mean that they were conceived of as gilded.

A commercially important refinement of the lost-wax technique was developed towards the end of the 15th century in north Italy, whereby piece-moulds would be taken in plaster from the original model. When re-assembled, these could be used to reproduce a number of identical replicas in wax, which could then each be cast in bronze (see Nos. 3, 4). Variations in the positions of limbs or hands could be introduced in these intermediary wax casts, and particular attributes could be added or subtracted, before casting them into metal: thus slight variants could be readily produced from only one master-model. Pieces could also be 'personalized' by the application in wax of particular coats-of-arms, names or other devices: this was much used on domestic artifacts such as bells and mortars, to label their ownership indelibly on them.

Broadly speaking, earlier bronzes were heavily cast (for safety's sake, and owing to lack of technical expertise) in a coppery alloy, and were unique ('one-off'); while later bronzes have thinner walls of metal, and so are lighter. Casting technology was more advanced, and could be relied upon to convey a surface accurately, so that a minimum of after-working would be required, and an alloy with more zinc, and thus akin to brass, was used, e.g. in 18th-century Rome, and later all over Europe (see Nos. 34, 35, 39).

II. Origins, Cultural Background and Subject-Matter

Bronze statuettes and functional artifacts had originated with the Bronze Age itself and featured in all the great cultures of the ancient world, Egypt, Greece, Etruria and Rome. Statuettes were mostly produced for cult purposes, and with the advent of monotheism and Christianity became anathema to believers — idols of pagan gods fit only for destruction. A number of mostly Christian subjects were manufactured in the Byzantine world, but relatively few were produced during the Middle Ages in Western Europe. Candlesticks, incense-burners, and water pitchers (aquamaniles) were cast in bronze or brass, but figures were rare — an equestrian statuette of the Emperor Charlemagne cast in Metz in the 9th century (Louvre Museum, Paris) is the most famous.

Early in the 15th century, the revival of interest in all things Greek and Roman which was the essence of the Italian Renaissance led to a revaluation of ancient bronze statuettes and artifacts: their durability had allowed them to survive in relatively good condition, and they began to be collected by the early humanists, along with coins, gems and cameos. This encouraged imitation by contemporary sculptors, either legitimately, to supply gaps in certain collections, or as fakes suitably patinated and produced to deceive the more gullible collectors, who had few means of checking the authenticity of things that looked 'old.'

From its dubious inception, therefore, the bronze statuette was a 'collectable': it did not have a distinct function, except to inform, inspire or delight the beholder, unlike its ancient and medieval prototypes, which had a religious purpose. A new range of subjects emerged, mostly with a distinctly classical — and hence pagan — flavor: copies on a reduced scale of monuments (e.g. Filarete's *Marcus Aurelius,* Grünes Gewölbe, Dresden) or on the same scale of ancient cult statuettes (see Nos. 24, 25). The importance of astrology to Renaissance life found expression in miniatures of signs of the zodiac, e.g. *Aquarius* the water-carrier, (Staatliche Museen, Berlin); *Taurus* the bull (No. 25), and *Cancer,* the crab. These could be used as meaningful paperweights on one's desk.

Examples of classical nudity were also treasured for their aesthetic and intellectual appeal; Venus (No. 5), *Juno* (No. 29) and *Diana* (No. 21) were favorite goddesses, while *Neptune* (god of the sea, Nos. 3, 4) and *Mercury* (god of commerce, No. 23) often appeared alongside the supremely masculine subjects of *Hercules* or *Mars* (No. 13). Nude athletes were also admired, as far afield as Germany (No. 36).

Classical literature, especially Ovid's *Metamorphoses,* provided fascinating accounts of mythological monsters such as the sphinx (Nos. 2, 19), the satyr (No. 10) and the centaur. Portrait busts of ancient philosophers also featured in the repertoire (No. 37), and the form was re-used for serious-minded contemporaries (No. 12), and even for Christian subjects, such as Christ, his saints, and the popes (No. 32).

While ideally the statuette is defined as an image standing free from any context, in practice, many were associated with functioning domestic artifacts such as inkstands (Nos. 1, 3, 4, 6, 7, 8b, 14); lamps (No. 2); candlesticks (No. 36), or door-knockers. The collection in The Frick Art Museum provides a good and representative cross-section of the range of subjects that was treated from the Renaissance until the end of the Neo-Classical period (c. 1800).

III. *History*

The great sculptors in bronze of the early Renaissance in Florence, Ghiberti and Donatello, are not credited nowadays with having created any actual free-standing statuettes, though both were clearly capable of having done so. One need look no further than the figures in cartouches that flank Ghiberti's *Gates of Paradise* (c. 1425–50) or the child-musicians by Donatello that crown the font in Siena, (c. 1427) or the infant shield-bearers who inhabit the knop of the crozier held by his gilt-bronze statue of *St. Louis of Toulouse*. Except for being ensconced in an architectural setting, these are in essence statuettes, albeit with vaguely religious themes. However it is from the workshop of Donatello, apparently, that the earliest free-standing and pagan statuette emerged in Florence — *A putto standing on a tortoise* (formerly Pierpont Morgan collection, now with John Abbott and Peter Guggenheim in New York). One of the earliest plaquettes of the Renaissance, showing *Cavorting Putti*, is also Donatellesque in character, and is represented in the collection at Pittsburgh, on all three sides of a triangular inkstand (No. 8b). There is reason to believe that the composition dates from 1465 or before, and therefore from the lifetime of the great master.

Several of the earliest significant statuettes of the Renaissance reproduce on a reduced scale monumental statues that survive in Rome: Filarete made a model of the equestrian *Marcus Aurelius* (Grünes Gewölbe, Dresden) while he was there in the 1440s producing in bronze the great doors of St. Peter's (still *in situ),* and Donatello's associate Bertoldo (1420–1491) used bronze to create in miniature a proposed restoration as *Bellerophon and Pegasus* (Kunsthistorisches Museum, Vienna) of one of the famous marble groups showing *Horse-tamers* on the Piazza del Quirinale, Rome. Bertoldo also created for an overmantel in the Medici Palace in Florence a *Battle-scene* (now Bargello Museum) with a multitude of figures in such deep relief and so undercut that they are virtually statuettes: these provide a repertory of types by which other, independent statuettes may be reliably attributed to this apparently quite prolific sculptor of bronze on a small scale. Also indebted to Donatello was Antonio Pollaiolo (1431–1498), who specialized in statuettes of male figures in conflict, such as *Hercules*, in order to demonstrate his knowledge of anatomy. In Siena, Donatello's work of the 1420s and visit of the 1450s inspired native sculptors of great importance, Vecchietta (1412–1480) and Francesco di Giorgio, who exploited the freedom of modelling and surface texture inherent in lost-wax casting.

Most influential of all was Donatello's decade of residence in Padua (1443–1453), where he built up a team of skilled assistants and founded a tradition of fine-art casting that was to survive in the Veneto for some two centuries. Bartolommeo Bellano was to become famous for his dramatic bronze reliefs (St. Antonio, Padua) and his statuettes, though most were still of Christian subjects, (e.g. *David*, Philadelphia Museum of Art). Bellano in turn inspired Severo Calzetta from Ravenna (active 1496–1525) and Andrea Briosco, called Il Riccio (c. 1460–1532). Their thematically interrelated oeuvres have only recently been disentangled: a plethora of bronze saints (No. 8), satyrs (No. 10), classical gods (Nos. 3–5), candlesticks, hanging lamps, inkstands and door-knockers all emanated from Severo's workshop, which seems to have resorted to serial production, and to have survived him by a generation or more.

Riccio preferred a slightly more elevated range of subjects and a more poetic interpretation of classical themes inspired by the humanist intellectuals of Padua University: complex allegories (No. 1), handsome nudes, nymphs and shepherds, Roman warriors, satyrs (benignly interpreted as symbols of the animal side of human nature), as well as grotesque lamps (No. 2) and masks. All were imbued with a nervous vivacity conveyed by his subtle modelling in the original wax models, conscientious chasing of detail and painstaking hammering of exposed surfaces, which gives a vibrant effect. The dark bituminous lacquer that he employed then softened their appearance into an almost Leonardesque *sfumato* effect.

A completely different interpretation of Antiquity was meanwhile being given at the court of the Gonzaga in Mantua, (who were also famous for employing Mantegna) by a bronze sculptor who was nicknamed L'Antico on account of his penchant for making direct copies of classical statuary (by contrast with the free 'modern' variations wrought by Riccio). Antico (1460–1528) used to polish the smooth, nude surfaces of his figures, darken them artificially, and pick out details with gilding or silver inlay (e.g. in the eyes). These luxury products appealed to his princely patrons such as Isabella d'Este. In the present collection nearest to Antico in style is the miniature *Cupid Shooting* (No. 24).

In Venice, a great center of bronze-founding in order to equip its fleet with cannon etc., the first great sculpture produced in bronze was the equestrian monument to Colleoni, modelled by Verrocchio, but cast only after his death in 1488 by Leopardi. The latter went on to produce three splendid pedestals for the flagpoles in front of St. Mark's. Camelio, Desiderio da Firenze and

Antonio Lombardi also made excellent statuettes in bronze there during the High Renaissance.

Thereafter, Venice replaced Padua as the greatest center of bronze sculpture in northern Italy. Tuscan influence was introduced by Jacopo Sansovino, when he arrived from Rome in 1527: employed by the city as chief architect, bronze offered him the principal means of continuing his career as a sculptor, for he needed only to produce the wax models, and could delegate the rest of the work to skilled craftsmen — sculptors such as Tiziano Minio (see Jacopo's signed group of the *Virgin and Child* in the Cleveland Museum of Art). His greatest follower, who also produced some superb statuettes (e.g. *St. Sebastian,* Metropolitan Museum of Art, New York), was Alessandro Vittoria (1525–1608), with whom Girolamo Campagna (1552–1623) from Verona shared the laurels during the latter part of the 16th century: neither is represented in Pittsburgh. However, the Venetian school also comprised other highly qualified sculptors in bronze whose styles may be appreciated in this exhibition: Niccolo Roccatagliata (active 1593–1636), a Genoese, is accredited with the *Inkstand* (No. 14) and Francesco Segala (c. 1535–1592) with the heavier statuette of *Mars/Perseus* (No. 13). The latter is roughly and massively cast, which suggests that it was a crowning figure from one of the great firedogs (andirons) which were a typical product of the Venetian foundries, along with door-knockers and -handles, candlesticks and inkstands, bells and mortars.

In Tuscany meanwhile, Michelangelo's distaste for bronze as a medium for sculpture discouraged younger artists until well after he had left Florence in 1534. Then, in the 1540s both Bandinelli and Cellini revived the tradition of Donatello and Pollaiolo with a number of statuettes of mythological characters (Bargello Museum, Florence). The next generation all mastered the art of the small bronze, in order to purvey statuettes to the Medici Grand-Dukes and their courtiers, as well as their international contacts. The *locus classicus* was the celebrated *Studiolo* of Francesco I de'Medici created around 1570 in the government palace in Florence: eight large statuettes to fill niches on the walls and symbolizing the four elements were commissioned from different sculptors, providing the ideal opportunity to compare their styles and talents. Among them were two sculptors who are represented in The Frick Art Museum collection: Giambologna (1529–1608), a Flemish immigrant, by a later reduction of his famous figure of *Mercury* (No. 23), and Giovanni Bandini (1540–1599) by a *Leaping Hound*, which has been recognized as his only in the course of research for the present catalogue and exhibition (No. 20). Previously held to be Flemish, this hound is a close cousin of one who attacks a boar in a documented masterpiece of a bronze group by Bandini showing *Meleager hunting,* (Fig. 20.1).

Giambologna became court sculptor and dominated Florentine, and indeed European, sculpture for half a century between around 1560 and his death in 1608. His suave, eye-catching compositions assured him international success, and this was achieved by the wide dissemination all over Europe of statuettes, either as diplomatic gifts or by way of commerce. As his popularity grew, Giambologna was forced to delegate their production to a specialist, Antonio Susini. He also employed many younger aspiring sculptors from the north, like himself, and among them was Adrian de Vries. To him is tentatively attributed a flawed and unfinished cast of a *Satyr* (No. 38) in this collection.

Another of Giambologna's principal colleagues, as he grew older, and his successor as sculptor to the Grand-Dukes, was Pietro Tacca, and he passed on in due course the stylistic tradition of the workshop to his own son, Ferdinando. The latter is credited with two of the best statuettes in Pittsburgh, a large one of *Diana* with her hound, (No. 21), and a smaller group of an *Old Man Riding a Goat* (No. 22), an enigmatic subject probably connected with witchcraft.

While the Italians tended to dominate the European scene in the production of bronze statuettes, as is evident in this typical collection, other countries also made contributions, notably France, in the style of the School of Fontainebleau derived from Primaticcio and Cellini, with sculptors such as Pilon, Ponce Jacquiot and Prieur — none of whom is represented here. In Germany the strong traditions of the Meuse valley and elsewhere in producing decorative and ecclesiastical metalwork in brass, which tended to retain Gothic traits of style until well into the 16th century, was combined in the southern cities of Nuremberg and Augsburg with influences from the neighboring northern parts of Italy. The prolific draftsman Albrecht Dürer was in great part responsible for importing knowledge of the classical revival which was being effected in Venice after a visit there. The father and more particularly the son Peter Vischer (1487–1528) adapted the tradition of bronze craftsmanship in Nuremberg to the exigencies of High Renaissance design. The figure of a *Man as a Candelabrum* (No. 36) originated in this exciting artistic environment, and demonstrated a more than adequate understanding of anatomy and the principles of harmonious design. The small but massively cast bust of the philosopher *Hippocrates* (No. 37) also displays an appreciation of the calm dignity of Graeco-Roman portrait busts. These are two of the masterpieces in The Frick Art Museum.

The Roman Baroque school is represented only by one item, the miniature bust of *Pope Innocent X* after an over life-size portrait by Algardi (No. 32). The later bronze foundrymen of Rome resorted once again as a commercial expedient to reproducing famous antiquities on a domestic scale, for visiting

Grand Tourists, many of them from Great Britain: whole garnitures for one's mantlepiece could be purchased inexpensively from a shop such as that of Francesco Righetti, typical of whose work is *Meleager and the Calydonian Boar* (No. 34).

After the lifetime of Canova, for whom Righetti also cast sculpture, and during the second quarter of the 19th century, the nature of society changed, and bronze statuettes tended to be directed towards the less elevated tastes of the emerging bourgeoisie, rather than those of intellectuals or aristocrats, as had been traditional. They were brilliantly cast and reproduced in great quantities by Parisian foundries using the technique of sand-casting that had been modernized to meet the needs of the Industrial Revolution.

Catalogue

Note for Readers:

In view of the fact that Dr. Wilhelm von Bode's pioneering *Catalogue of the Pierpont Morgan Collection: Bronzes of the Renaissance*, privately printed in Paris in 1910 in a deluxe edition, is today very rare and valuable, and hence relatively inaccessible to students, it was decided to quote verbatim his titles and entries at the head of the text of each entry here.

In view of Bode's pre-eminence in the connoisseurship and study of statuettes, this procedure is valid also from the point of view of the historiography of bronze statuettes. In the case of a few pieces, the present author has felt unable to add significantly to Bode's conclusions, and has therefore chosen not to discuss them further, to avoid muddying the waters of scholarship by otiose speculations.

The entries have been arranged in a topographical order, which respects as far as possible the broad, chronological sequence. An attempt has been made at a comprehensive survey of the literature and of other examples of each item, but particularly in the latter respect omissions may have occurred, as is inevitable when dealing with serially produced works of art.

All full page illustrations are of bronzes in The Frick Art Museum, while the marginal figures show comparative material.

PLATE I
Circular Tripod Inkstand
Bronze inkstand

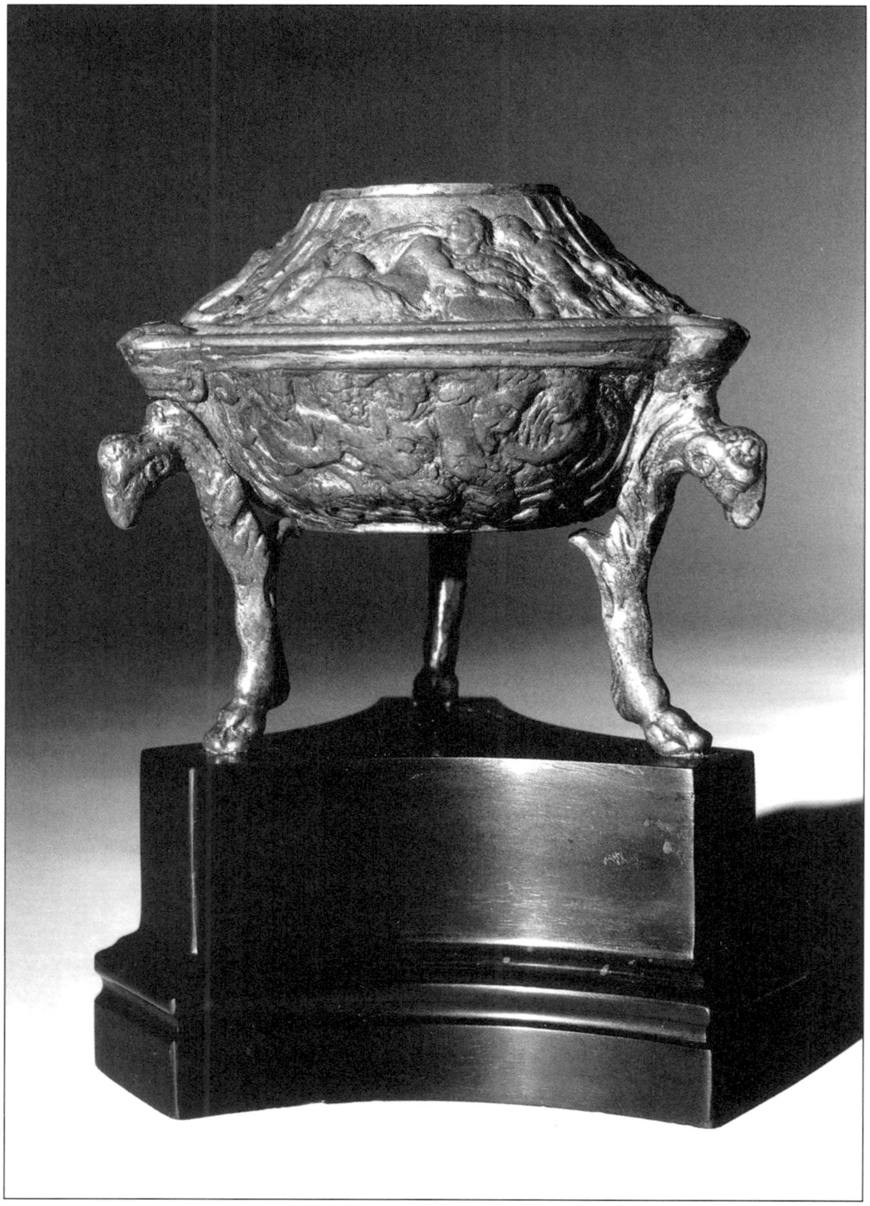

I

Circular Tripod Inkstand

Bronze inkstand

ITALIAN, PADUA, EARLY 16TH CENTURY

Andrea Briosco, called Il Riccio (c. 1470–1532)

3⅛ x 3¾ in. (8 x 9.5 cm); diam. of bowl 3½ in. (8.8 cm)

Central aperture above: diam. 1¼ in. (3 cm)

Circular rebate underneath: diam. 1¾ in. (4.5 cm)

1970.105

Gift of Miss Frick, 1970. Once kept in the library bookcase of "Eagle Rock," Prides Crossing, Massachusetts.

CONDITION

The lid and bowl are soldered together with lead. The central aperture has a vertical flange, over which probably fitted a conical lid with a finial, possibly a figurine. The three legs are cast in a brassier metal, and are soldered on: they are not very detailed.

PROVENANCE

Henry Joseph Pfungst Collection, London
Durlacher, London
J. P. Morgan Collection, New York
Duveen
Frick 1916
Helen Clay Frick

EXHIBITED

London, Victoria & Albert Museum, 1901–12, no. 297, lent by J. Pierpont Morgan

LITERATURE

Bode, 1897, p. 299, no. 237
Pfungst, 1899, no. 46
Bode, 1910, I, no. 46, plate XXX, fig. on p. 13, Introduction, p. XVI
Nicodemi, 1920/21, p. 473
Pope-Hennessy, 1965, p. 130, no. 481
Radcliffe, 1972, p. 38

OTHER EXAMPLES

Brescia, Museo Cristiano
Washington, DC, National Gallery of Art (1957.14.66: Kress Collection, Inv. no. A 219.60c)
Washington, DC, National Gallery of Art (1942.9.150: Widener Collection, Inv. no. A 1472)

Spherical in form, with narrow circular opening above, supported on three slender legs terminating in projecting ram's heads and claw feet. Round the body of the inkstand are two bands of ornaments with classical subjects. — BODE, 1910: WORKSHOP OF RICCIO, *Inkstand.*

There are six scenes in relief, three on the lid and three on the bowl:

Lid

(1) A recumbent, half-draped figure wearing a diadem amidst luxuriant hair, probably female (unless e.g. Bacchus). She is leaning with her right elbow on a tree-stump with two projecting branches on which stand two flasks. In the crook of this elbow is a rod, the end of which seems to encircle the trunk of the

Lid (1)

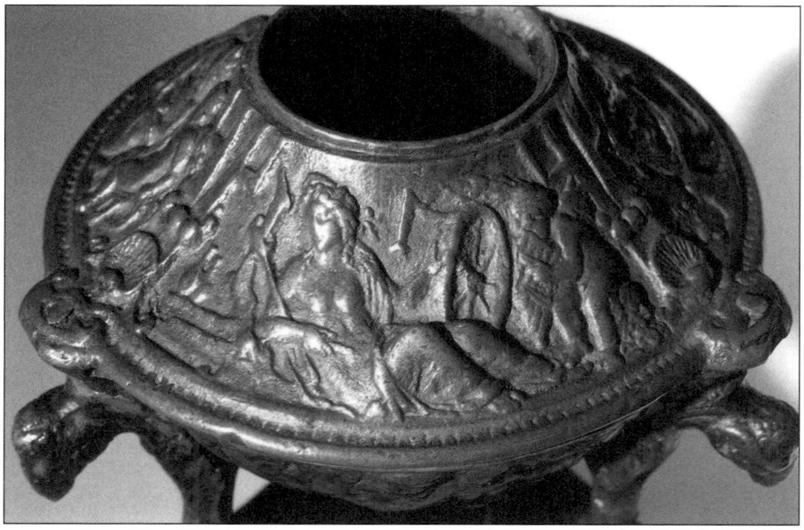

Lid (2)

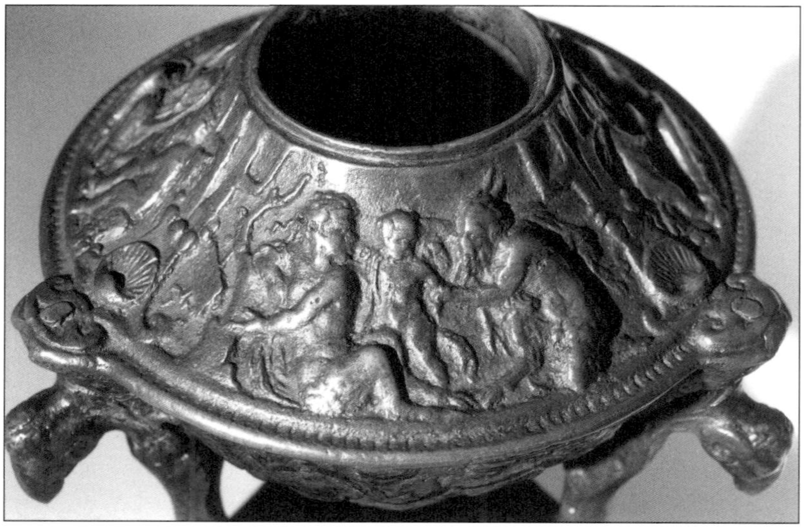

Lid (3)

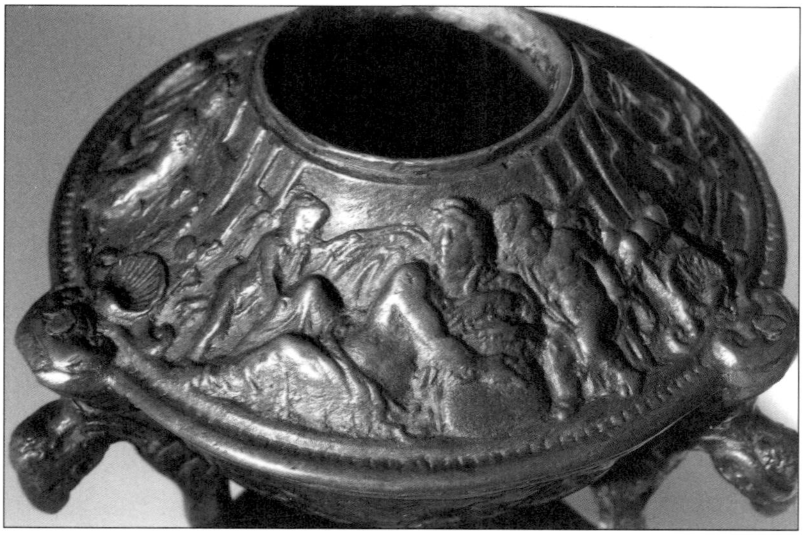

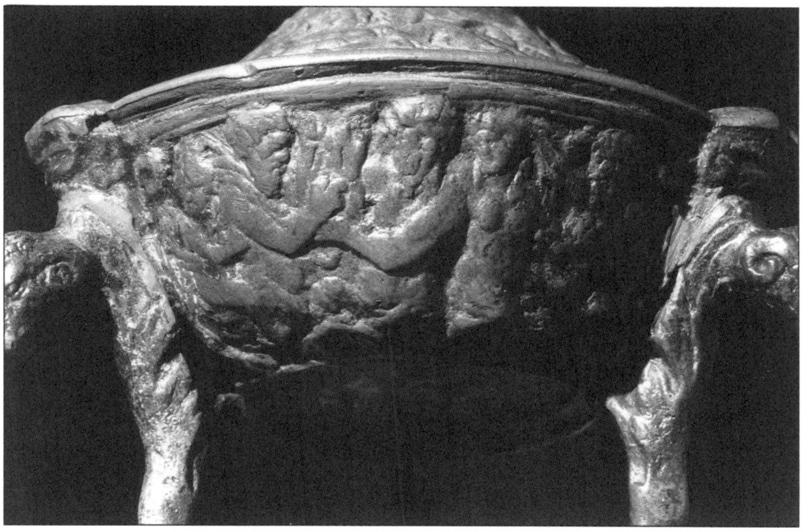

Bowl (1)

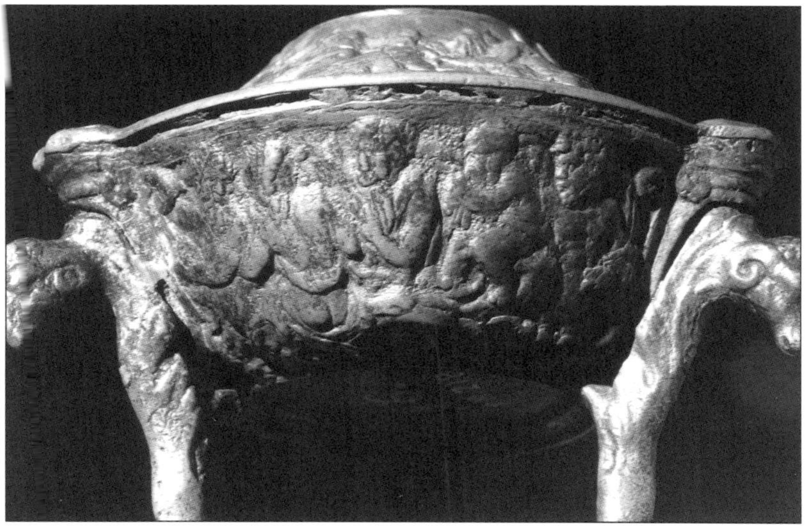

Bowl (2)

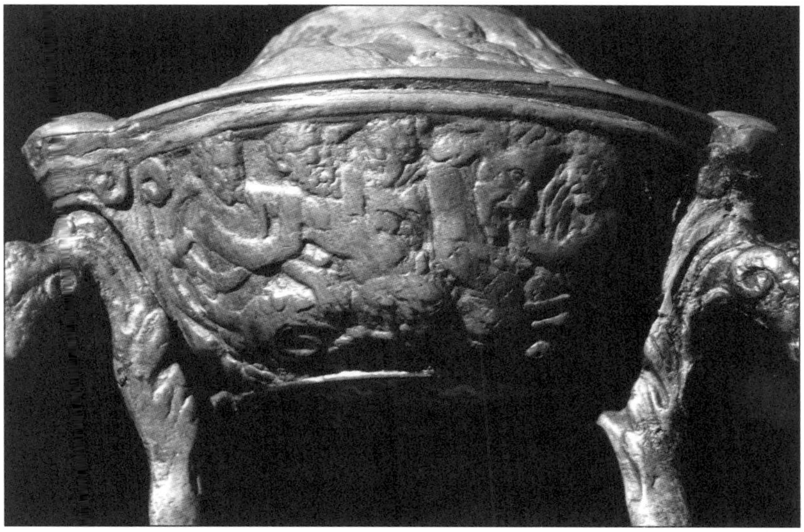

Bowl (3)

tree half way up. With her left hand she holds a wheel that is attached by a cord to a central stick (unless this represents a handle), and so she may be Fortune. To the right Cupid, seated on a bearded old man's (or lion's?) head, is playing on a *syrinx* (panpipes) with his left hand, while his right one is extended upwards over the wheel.

(2) A satyress(?) seated on the ground against a withered tree stump points across her body with her left hand towards a tablet hanging from the far side of the tree. In the center is a boy (Cupid, if to his right it is a wing that shows against the background), whose left arm is grasped by a kneeling bearded satyr, with a lion's skin over his far shoulder.

(3) A recumbent lightly-draped woman points with her right hand to a scroll that she holds open with her left forearm. She is flanked by two cupids, the one on the left holding the flowing end of her garment (unveiling her), while the one on the right is seated on a decorated stool and holds her shoulders with his right arm, while looking off-stage to the right.

Figure 1.1
Three-wick lamp with Bacchic Scenes, (Andrea Briosco, called) Riccio; c. 1500
©1992, National Gallery of Arr, Washington; Samuel H. Kress Collection (1957.14.66 [A-219.60c])

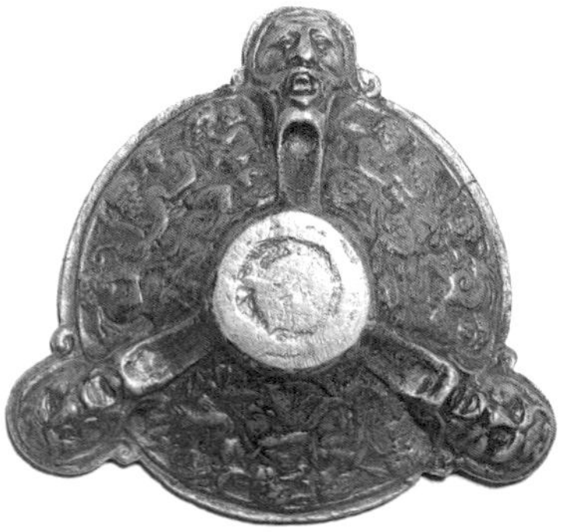

The scenes are separated by curious forked motifs ('bidents'?), which are bound with pearls and rise from cockle-shells below.

Bowl

(1) A *thiasos* (marine bacchanale). At the left two male ichthyocentaurs (a monster composed of sea-horse body and human torso) meet and both play upon a lyre held in mid-air. One is ridden by Cupid (?) and the other by a nude nymph, while to the right another ichthyocentaur with raised right arm approaches.

(2) An ichthyocentaur swims to the left, turning his head backwards to behold a nymph seated upon his back, with her back to the spectator. In the center, another ichthyocentaur approaches them, playing a lyre in mid-air: Cupid sits on his upturned tail, blowing into panpipes. At the right another ichthyocentaur swims towards the spectator and rightwards, but looks back over his shoulder into the scene.

(3) An elderly satyr, astride a sea-monster (with a 'Green Man' mask for a face) that is swimming to the right, is dismounted by two tritons, while another triton with flowing, windswept drapery arrests the monster's progress at the right hand edge.

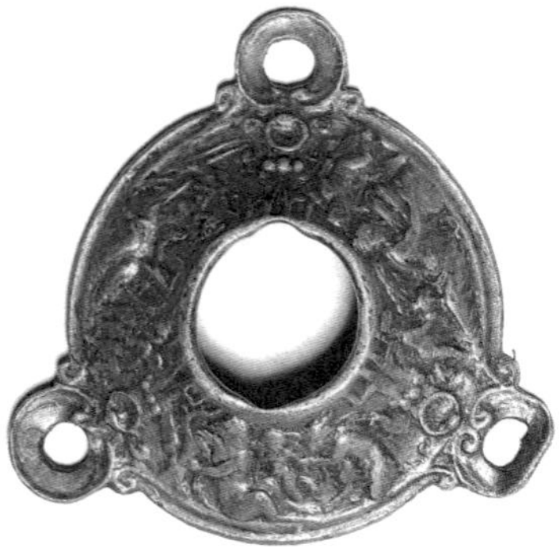

Figure 1.2
Three-wick lamp with Bacchic Scenes, (Andrea Briosco, called) Riccio; c. 1500
©1992, National Gallery of Art, Washington; Samuel H. Kress Collection (1957.14.66 [A-219.60c])

Described by Bode as an inkstand, this model is closely related to a circular oil lamp with three nozzles for wicks, of which an example in its complete form, standing on three naturalistic animal legs terminating above in goat's heads (as here), is in Brescia (Fig. 1.4). A cast of bowl and lid alone is in the Kress Collection (Figs. 1.1; 1.2), while another, also in the National Gallery of Art, but from the Widener collection, is a poor aftercast (surmoulage) taken from the Kress piece, probably in the 19th century (Fig. 1.3).

Bode (1897) ascribed the latter, poor example, to Riccio, but called the present, Frick piece 'Paduan, end of 15th century.' Its then owner, Mr. Pfungst, described it in his catalogue as 'School of Caradossa (sic), Paduan work, end of 15th century,' but pencilled in his own copy 'Bode thinks by Riccio himself.' Pope-Hennessy (1965) included the Kress example under the heading of 'Riccio,' but in the entry qualified this as 'workshop.' Radcliffe (1972) concurred, relating the scenes in relief to those on a lamp in the Fortnum Collection, now in the Ashmolean Museum, Oxford; and the masks under the nozzles to one under the nozzle of a cognate oil lamp, formerly in Berlin, both of which are generally accepted as by Riccio.

The Frick version is more crisply cast than the Kress one, and is therefore arguably nearer to Riccio's own hand. It differs in various respects: notably, the three apertures for wicks, carefully modelled with scrolling cartouches on the Kress lamp, are here substituted by minor decorative protrusions on the lid, so that wicks could not be inserted. Correspondingly, on the bowl underneath, the three elderly male masks with moustaches of the Kress example are omitted. This deliberate alteration was perhaps made to change the function from that of a lamp into that of an inkstand (as in Bode's 1910 description).

While the three segmental reliefs on the lid are identical to those of the Kress example, those below are quite different, though they also depict scenes from a battle of sea-monsters, à la Mantegna.

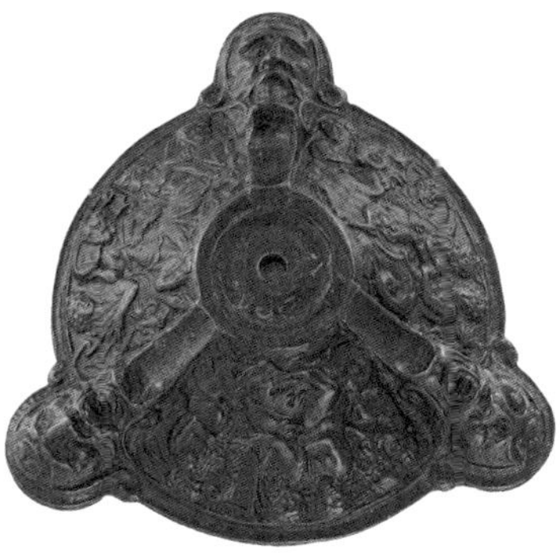

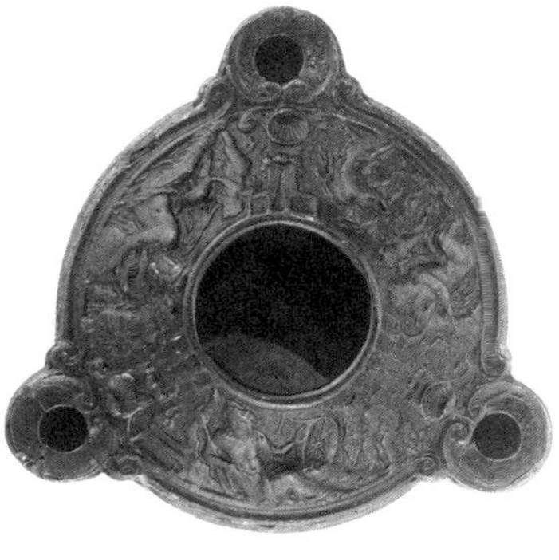

Figure 1.3
Three-wick lamp with Bacchic Scenes, after (Andrea Briosco, called) Riccio; c. 1800/1899
©1992, National Gallery of Art, Washington; Widener Collection (1942.9.150 [A 1472])

Figure 1.4
Three-wick lamp with Bacchic Scenes
By kind permission of the Civici Musei d'Arte e Storia, Brescia

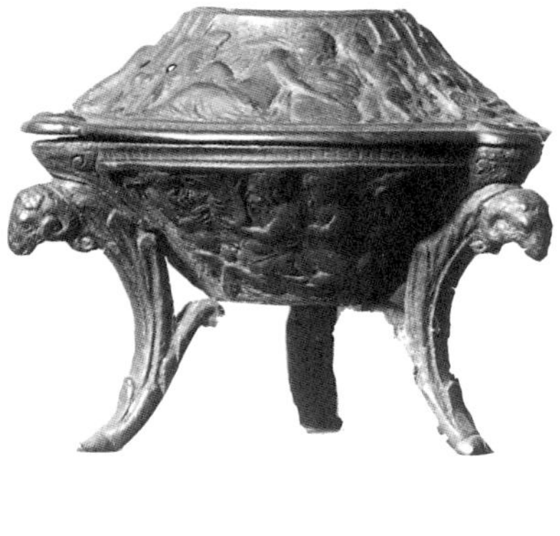

PLATE 2

Bronze Lamp in the Form of a Grotesque Sphinx

Bronze oil lamp

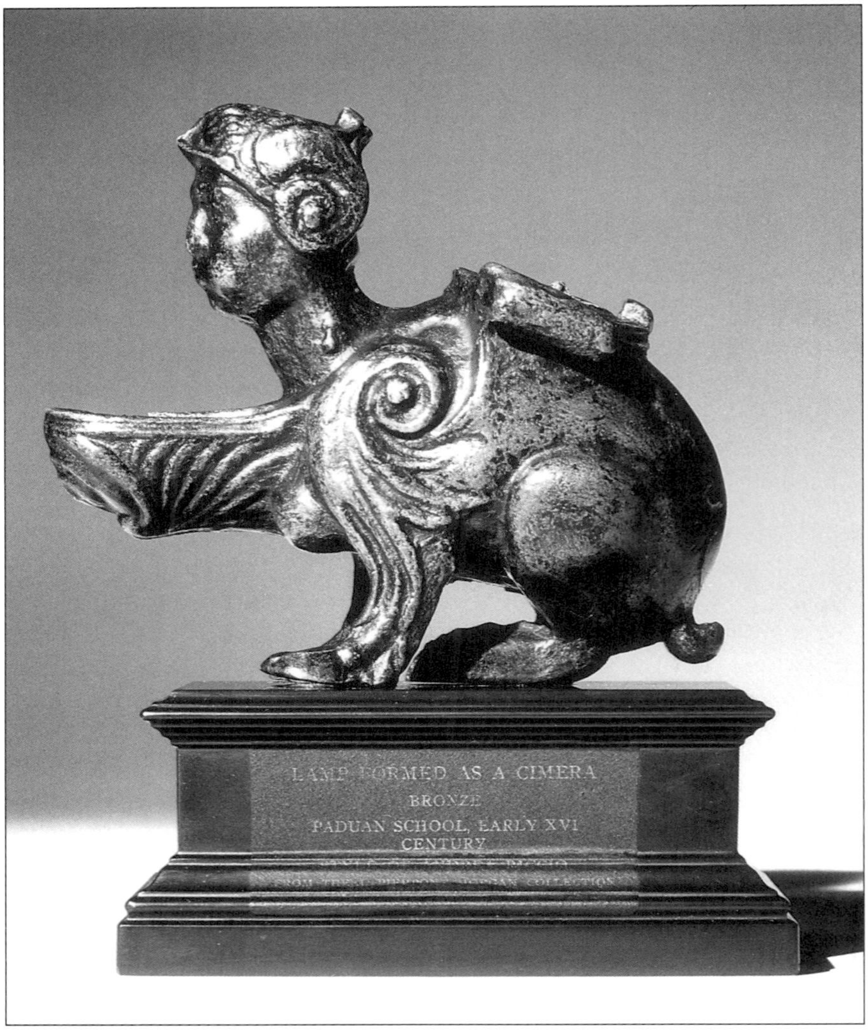

2

Bronze Lamp in the Form of a Grotesque Sphinx

Bronze oil lamp

ITALIAN

After a model by Andrea Briosco, called Il Riccio (c. 1470–1532)

4¾ x 5¾ in. (12.1 x 14.6 cm)

1970.106
Gift of Miss Frick, 1970

CONDITION
This is an unpleasing, sandy aftercast of a well-known model. The hinged, oval copper lid in its back is a replacement.

PROVENANCE
J. P. Morgan Collection, New York
Duveen
Frick 1916
Helen Clay Frick

EXHIBITED
London, Victoria & Albert Museum, 1901–12, no. 419, lent by J. Pierpont Morgan

LITERATURE
Montfaucon, 1719, V, pl. 145
Bode, 1910, no. 56, pl. XXXVIII
Planiscig, 1927, pp. 380–81, 489, cat. no. 188, pls. 478–79
Sheard, 1978, no. 125
Radcliffe, 1982, p. 418f. (note 47 refers to the present example)
Frankfurt, 1986, no. 222
Banzato & Pellegrini, 1989, no. 25

OTHER EXAMPLES
Chicago, The Art Institute (formerly Vienna, Emil Weinberger Collection; 13 cm high)
Florence, Bargello (13 cm high)
The Hague, formerly Bachstitz Gallery (ex-Hollitscher Collection Berlin; 12 cm high)
Naples, Museo Nazionale di Capodimonte (10.590)
New York, Metropolitan Museum (11.38.2; 12.4 cm high; ex-von Beckerath Collection)
Padua, Museo Civico (inv. no. 107; 12 cm high)
Paris, Louvre (15 cm high)
Paris, Adda Collection (sold Palais Galliera, Paris 29 Nov.–3 Dec. 1965, lot 305; repro. Radcliffe 1982, fig. 23)
Troppau, Landesmuseum

Seated figure of a monster, with the head of a woman covered with a helmet, and the body of a beast. The burner is affixed to the chest; the body forms the receptacle for the oil and is pierced for this purpose in the center of the back. — BODE, 1910: PADUA, BEGINNING OF 16TH CENTURY, STYLE OF ANDREA RICCIO, *Lamp in the form of a Sphinx.*

This oil lamp is cunningly modelled in the shape of a monster, which has some of the features of a sphinx, but with additional grotesque elements. The sphinx should have the body of a lion and the head and chest of a human female. Here, in contrast with the full breasts below, the head is distinctly masculine: its brow is furrowed with effort, its lips pursed and its cheeks deflated, as though puffing at the real flame of the wick, which would have projected up in front of it from the curving nozzle projecting out of the chest below.

It is not made clear whether the spiralling ram's horns are an organic part of the beast, or an appurtenance of the helmet, though the former seems more probable. The rear legs are conjoined into one, so that the creature is literally a tripod. Its tail is truncated, unlike a lion's one. The shoulders are covered with scrolls of acanthus ornament, the spiral centers of which are also joined by a three-dimensional S-shaped scroll to the furled wings of strapwork. These flank an oval hole with a hinged lid modelled as a snail-shell (Paduan example), through which oil could be poured into the hollow-cast body, which functions as a container.

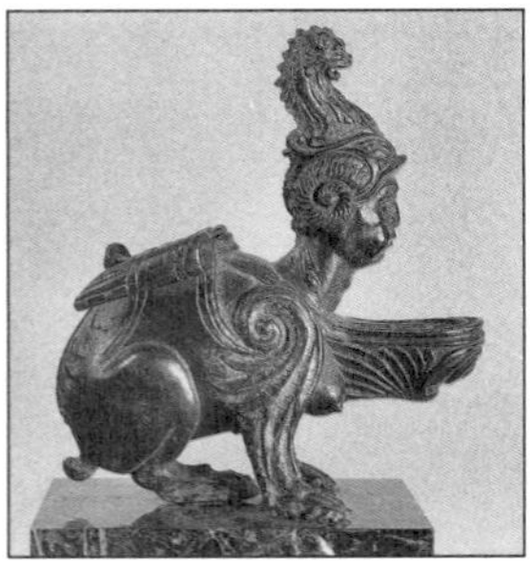

Figure 2.1
Lamp in the Form of a Sphinx Oil Lamp, Riccio; bronze
©1993 ARS, New York/SPADEM, Paris (Louvre)

The lamps exist in three variant designs, analyzed by Radcliffe (1982), of which the Frick one is an aftercast of the first type. The best and most complete example (in the Louvre, Fig. 2.1), also has another hinged lid on the top of its head, which is modelled as a crest to the helmet in the form of a lion's head. Its sinuous contour flows up smoothly from the helmet, and elegantly counterpoints the spiral of the ram's horns. All the weird, organic mouldings, e.g. the snail-shell and radiating leaf pattern beneath the projecting nozzle and the wing-like motif on the shoulders, are sharply chased out, and not blunt as here. The minute striations made with a stylus in the original wax casting model, which are characteristic of Riccio, appear on e.g. the lamps in the Louvre, in Chicago, and formerly in the Adda Collection (Planiscig, pls. 478–79; Radcliffe 1982, fig. 23), but are lacking in the Frick aftercast version.

This functional bronze monster is connected with Riccio owing to its thematic relationship with the four (much larger and more canonical) sphinxes on his *Paschal Candelabrum* in St. Antonio, Padua (1507–16); and the other set of four that support the sarcophagus of the *Monument to the della Torre* in Verona (Planiscig, 1927, pls. 471–72). This was executed probably between 1516 and 1521. The latter have elongated necks like the present sphinx.

As Radcliffe wrote (1982, p. 423):

> There can be little doubt that, as a concept at least, the lamps originated with Riccio. The skillful combinations of human elements with various animal elements, shell-forms (here both snail and cockle), semi-vegetal ornaments and inorganic decorative forms such as scrolls, volutes, bands and strapwork to produce a plausible hybrid creature is typical of him, and the parentage of the sphinxes in the Candelabrum is clear.

It is therefore likely that the model originated as a by-product of Riccio's great commissions in the second decade of the 16th century.

Two other variant types exist as well. Furthermore, the number of surviving examples with minor differences of detail or handling indicates that the model was quite popular among the humanists, and probably remained in production from moulds kept in the foundry for the better part of the 16th century.

Latterly, it was to be revamped in the style of the second school of Fontainebleau (see Radcliffe, 1982, p. 424, figs. 25, 28 for discussion of a unique example in the Victoria & Albert Museum).

As Sheard wrote in 1978:

> This amusing oil lamp demonstrates the Renaissance delight in and fascination with the grotesque. Hybrids like this sphinx which draw upon the forms of rediscovered Roman first century A.D. painting were increasingly favored as decoration. In north Italy, Andrea Riccio's inventions in bronze revealed the rich gamut of his fantasy, by turns whimsical, classical, and romantic, inspiring the many decorative objects employing antique motifs as novelties.

The strongly classical flavor of this type of lamp even persuaded scholar-connoisseurs, like Fortunio Liceto in Padua in 1652, and in the 18th century a Frenchman, Montfaucon, that it was a genuine antiquity and the latter included it, naively as it now appears, in his great tome *L'Antiquité expliquée* of 1719. No classical prototype in fact exists.

The author of the Frankfurt exhibition catalogue (1986, no. 222) attempted to rationalize the curious subject-matter of the lamp by explaining that the sphinx originated in ancient Egyptian religion as a protective deity. The iconography is developed in the present instance into the idea of Fortuna or Destiny, with power over life (light) and death (darkness), symbolized expressly by the gesture of blowing on the real flame of the wick, and hence kindling or extinguishing it at will.

3
Neptune and Sea-monster with Shell
Bronze inkstand

ITALIAN, PADUA, EARLY 16TH CENTURY
Workshop of Severo Calzetta of Ravenna, (active 1496–1525)
8¼ x 8¼ in. (21 x 21 cm); Neptune alone: 6¾ in. (17 cm) high

1970.107
Gift of Miss Frick, 1970

CONDITION
Plate on underside of monster added later.

PROVENANCE
J. P. Morgan Collection, New York
Duveen
Frick 1916
Helen Clay Frick

EXHIBITED
London, Victoria & Albert Museum, 1901–12, no. 1076, lent by J. Pierpont Morgan

LITERATURE
Bode, 1910, no. 21, plate XVIII
Planiscig, 1924, no. 21, pp. 16–17, plate 12
Planiscig, 1927, p. 112, plate 109
Planiscig, 'Severo da Ravenna (Der 'Meister des Drachens'),' *Jahrbuch der Kunsthistorischen Sammlungen in Wien,* N.F. IX, 1935, pp. 75–86
Meyer, 1935, pp. 75–86, ' "Neptune on a Dragon" by Severo da Ravenna, the "Master of the Dragons," ' *Detroit Institute of Arts Bulletin,* vol. 38, no. 2, 1958–59, pp. 24–25 (ill.)
The Museum of Fine Arts, Houston, Texas, "The Lively Arts of the Renaissance," exhibition catalogue, 1960, no. 112
Smith College, Mass., *Renaissance Bronzes in American Collections,* 1964, no. 8, (Dragon, signed *O. SEVERI. RA.* with Mrs. Ruth Blumka, New York)
Pope-Hennessy, 1965, pp. 132–33, nos. 487–88, figs. 484–85
E. Munhall, 'Severo Calzetta, called Severo da Ravenna,' exhibition catalogue, The Frick Collection, New York, 1978, nos. 1, 11, 13, 16, 17
Avery & Radcliffe, 1983
Frankfurt, 1986, no. 139
De Winter, 1986, pp. 93–96, 116, figs. 37–39, 42, 45–47, 110
Masterpieces from the Detroit Institute of Arts, Bunkamura Museum of Art, Tokyo, 1989, cat. no. 6, (ill.)

OTHER EXAMPLES
Detroit, Institute of Arts (58.36)
Florence, Museo Nazionale del Bargello
London, Sotheby's, 17 April 1980, lot 19
London, Christie's, 15 May 1984, lot 123
Melbourne, National Gallery of Victoria (I N 4003)
New York, Metropolitan Museum of Art, (25.142.7)
New York, Mrs. Ruth Blumka Collection (signed)

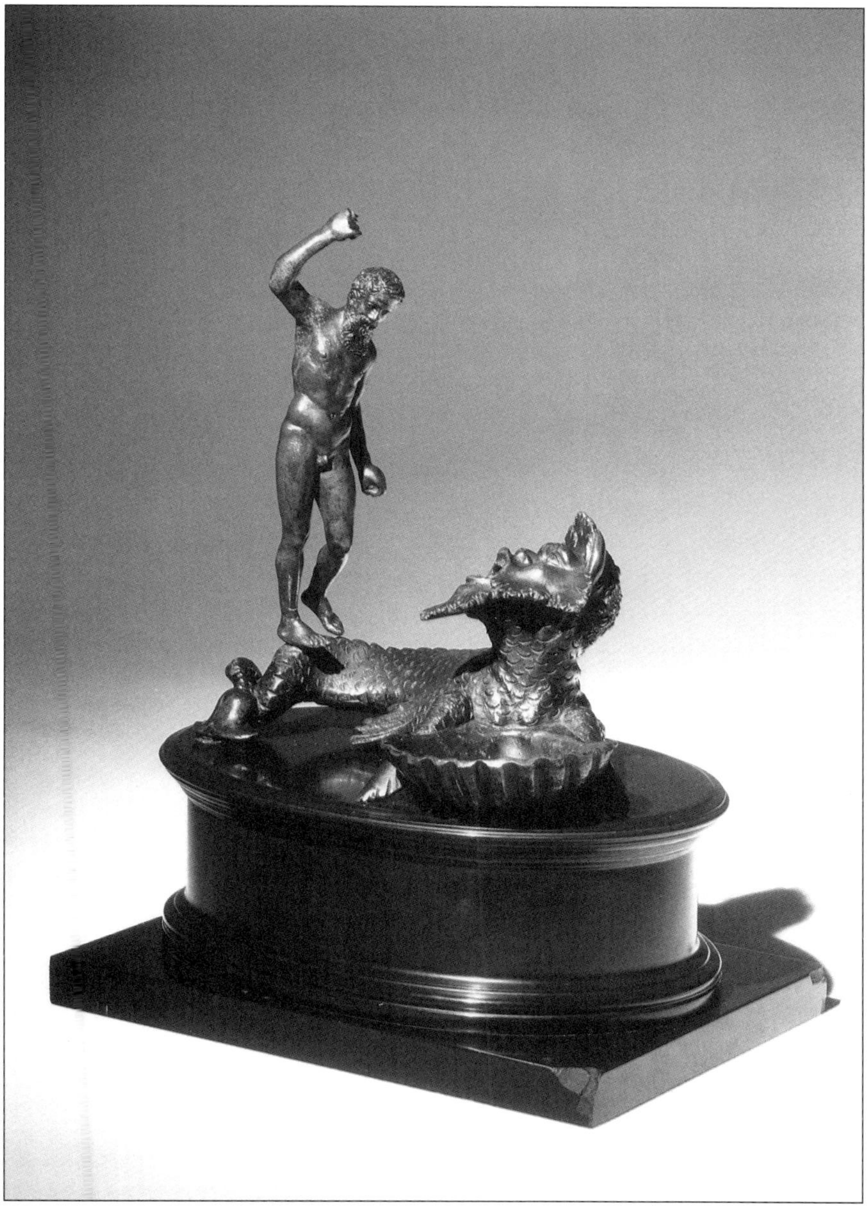

PLATE 3
Neptune and Sea-monster with Shell
Bronze inkstand

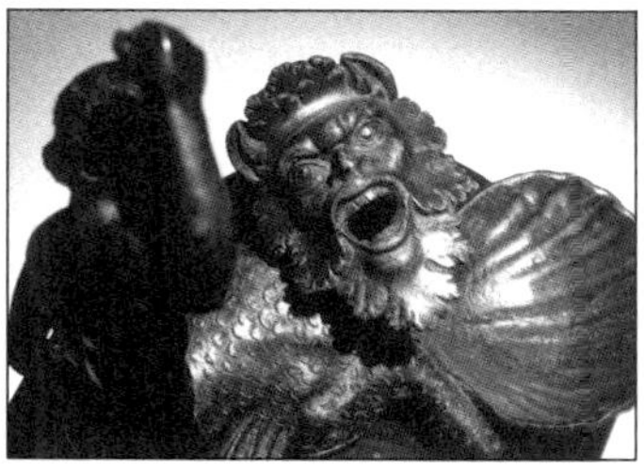

Full-length nude, standing with one foot on the tail of a human-headed sea-monster; the other foot poised with the toes resting upon the creature's back. The right arm is raised above the head; the left hangs down, the clenched hand must originally have held the trident. The head which is seen nearly in full face, is bent forward slightly and looks down. The features are benevolent in expression and the lips are parted as if speaking. The monster holds a shell between its fins and turns its head appealingly to Neptune. — BODE, 1910: FREE COPY AFTER BELLANO, *Neptune and Sea-Monster.*

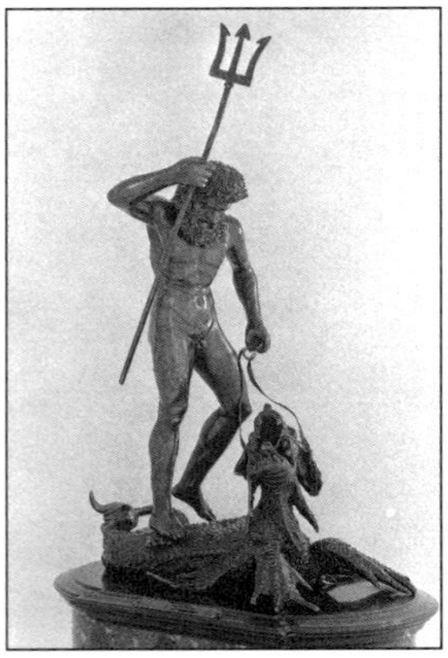

Figure 3.1
Neptune on a Sea-Monster, Severo da Ravenna
COPYRIGHT THE FRICK COLLECTION, NEW YORK (16.2.21)

The Frick Art Museum possesses two examples of this favorite product of the sculptor who used to be called after its theme 'The Master of the Dragons,' but who has long since been identified as Severo Calzetta of Ravenna, who set up a sculptural practice in Padua in 1500 (Avery & Radcliffe, 1983, p. 118).

The dragon is indebted to the sea-monsters in Mantegna's famous engraving of a *Battle of Seamonsters*, having a similar face, and long, spiny fins on its fore-legs and underside, as well as a sinuous, lashing tail ending in a foliate motif. It looks up, with its mouth opening into the hollow-cast interior, probably to accommodate a quill pen. In some cases (as here) it has a scallop-shell between its fins, to hold the ink, or some sand for blotting. In others (as in Catalogue No. 4) the scallop-shell is absent.

On the rump, the dragon often has a flattened circular area with a screw-threaded hole, into which may be screwed a separately cast shell (or other container) to hold ink (Frankfurt, 1986, nos. 234, 235), or (as here) a statuette of Neptune, who attempts to tame the monster with his raised trident (usually missing, as it would have been separately fashioned from a metal rod).

The prime example of the dragon (Figs. 3.2; 3.3; New York, Blumka Collection) is signed *O. SEVERI. RA.* (= the work of Severo of Ravenna): it was the discovery of this piece in 1935 that permitted the correct identification of 'The Master of the Dragons' (see Avery & Radcliffe, 1983; De Winter, 1986).

Strangely enough, the prime version of the present subject, *Neptune on a Sea-Monster* (Fig. 3.1; The Frick Collection, New York, no. 16.2.21: Pope-Hennessy & Radcliffe 1970, pp. 126–35), and one nearly as good in Washington DC (National Gallery of Art, Widener Collection, Inv. no. A-98; De Winter 1986 fig. 47) are actually quite different in respect of both Neptune and the sea-monster from the type of our Catalogue Nos. 3, 4 (Munhall 1978, nos. 1, 13).

Figure 3.2
Dragon, Severo da Ravenna
The Ruth Blumka Collection, New York

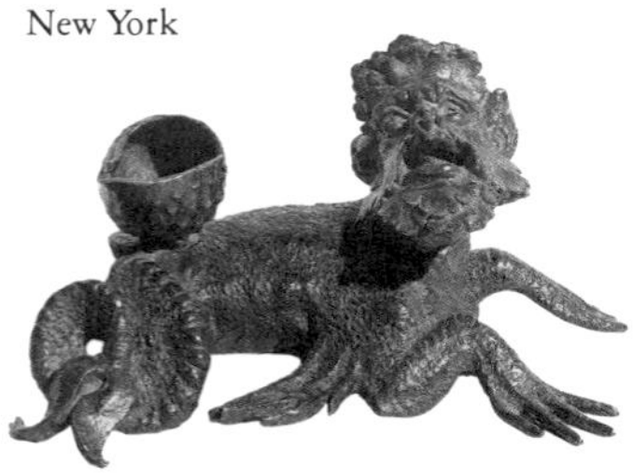

The present bronzes are far smaller (8¼ in. high as against 13⅜ and 13⅞ in. respectively for the Frick and Washington groups). Their dragons' heads are anthropoid rather than canine in appearance, while the figure of Neptune, though clearly derived in pose from the larger one, has a less impressively modelled body and less strikingly characterized head, lacking the wild hair and beard. Indeed, the anatomy of the smaller Neptunes looks 'wobbly' and 'knobbly,' in a shorthand derivative of Severo's true style of figure composition which seems to have characterized his, or his followers,' workshop: it went on producing his models serially, well into the 16th century (see De Winter, 1986, for a survey of its typical products, and compare our Catalogue Nos. 7–9).

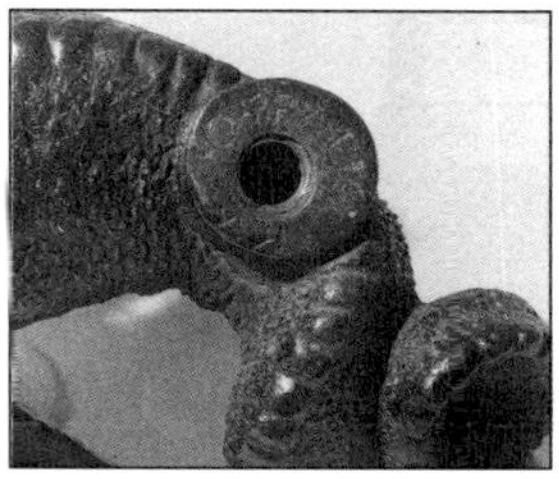

Figure 3.3
Dragon, (detail, the signature), Severo da Ravenna
The Ruth Blumka Collection, New York

4
Neptune and Sea-monster
Bronze inkstand

ITALIAN, PADUA, EARLY 16TH CENTURY
Workshop of Severo Calzetta of Ravenna, (active 1496–1525)
8¼ x 7 in. (21 x 17.8 cm); Neptune alone: 7⅛ in. (18 cm) high

1973.17
Gift of Miss Frick, 1973

CONDITION
Rich reddish-brown patina, with traces of black lacquer.

PROVENANCE
Henry Joseph Pfungst Collection, London
Durlacher, London
J. P. Morgan Collection, New York
Duveen
Frick 1916
Helen Clay Frick

EXHIBITED
London, Victoria & Albert Museum, 1901–12, no. 328, lent by J. Pierpont Morgan

LITERATURE
Pfungst, 1899, no. 29 (as 'Paduan, end of 15th century')
Bode, 1910, no. 20, plate XVI
Hovey, 1975, p. 113, ill. p. 112

For further references, other examples, and discussion, see Catalogue No. 3.

Full-length nude, seen in profile, standing upon the tail of a human-headed sea-monster, his right arm upraised in a threatening attitude. The monster turns its head and looks at Neptune as if imploring mercy. — BODE, 1910: FREE COPY AFTER BELLANO, *Neptune on a Sea-Monster.*

PLATE 4
Neptune and Sea-monster
Bronze inkstand

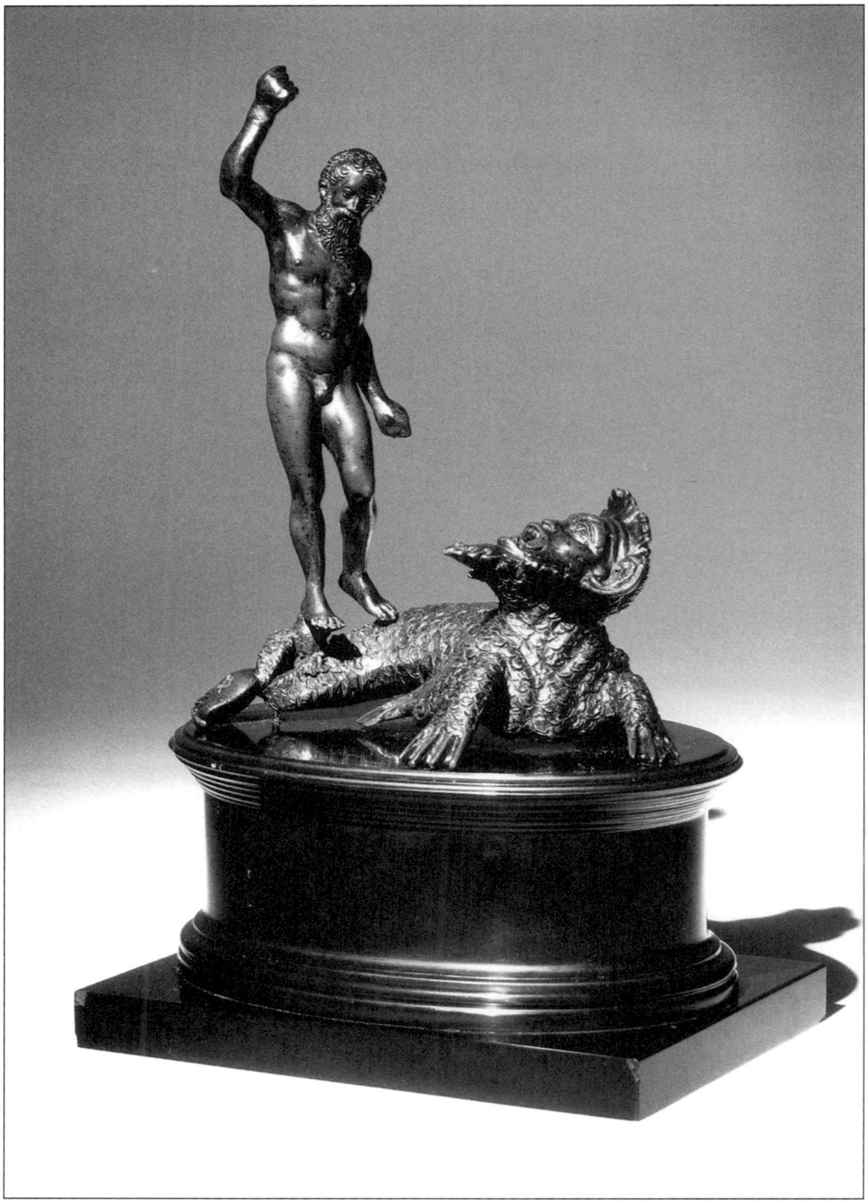

The 'Green Man' mask of the face does not have extra leaves protruding beneath the ears, as in Catalogue No. 3. Its lateral fins are transformed into acanthus leaves and the tail is fringed with nicks. The scales are carefully incised into the wax before casting and the tongue is shown resting on the lower lip. Neptune is slightly more generously modelled, while his hair and face are better chased.

5

Venus with Apple

Gilt bronze statuette

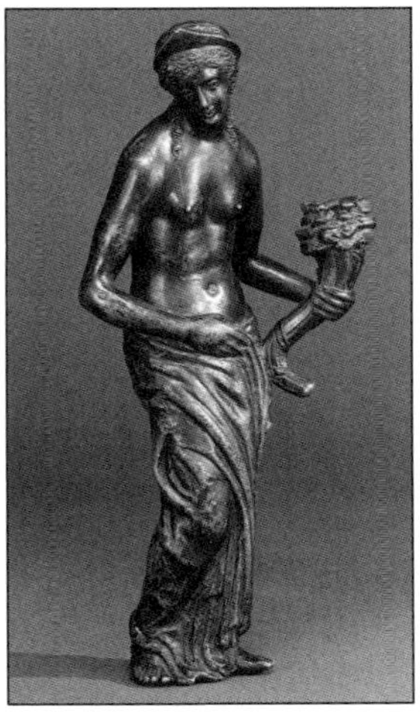

Figure 5.1
Venus, Severo da Ravenna
By kind permission of Sotheby's, New York (Lot #92, 23/24 November, 1984)

ITALIAN, PADUA, EARLY 16TH CENTURY

Attributed to Severo Calzetta of Ravenna, (active 1496–1525)

10¼ in. (26 cm)

1991.2
Bequest of Miss Frick, 1984

CONDITION

The hair is carefully cast and chased, though her cap is not. Venus's left hand is quite separate from her stomach and her inner palm is partially modelled, while her knuckles are striated and finger nails retroussé. The drapery is not given a texture. The apple is cast separately and attached to her open palm.

PROVENANCE

Charles Mannheim Collection, Paris
J. P. Morgan Collection, New York
Duveen
Frick 1916
Helen Clay Frick

EXHIBITED

London, Victoria & Albert Museum, 1901–12, no. 140, lent by J. Pierpont Morgan

LITERATURE

Molinier, 1898, no. 140, pl. 41
Bode, 1910, I, no. 23, pl. XX
Sheard, 1978, no. 37
Lloyd, 1980, no. 11
Frankfurt, 1986, no. 118

OTHER EXAMPLE

Oxford, Ashmolean Museum (Fortnum Bequest, F411)

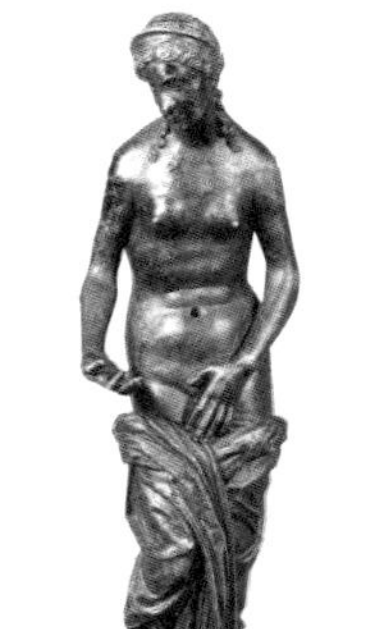

Figure 5.2
Statue of Venus (Fortnum Venus), Severo da Ravenna; bronze
Ashmolean Museum, Oxford

Full-length standing figure, the upper part of the body nude, the lower draped to the feet. She holds the apple in her right hand and turns her head looking down at it. Her hair, adorned with a small diadem, is rolled back from her face and gathered into a knot at the back; a ringlet on either side of her face falls to the shoulders. She stands on a small circular base, her bare feet are visible below the folds of the drapery. The modelling of the hands, fingers, and the treatment of the folds of the drapery, are characteristic. — BODE, 1910: BARTOLOMEO BELLANO, *Venus.*

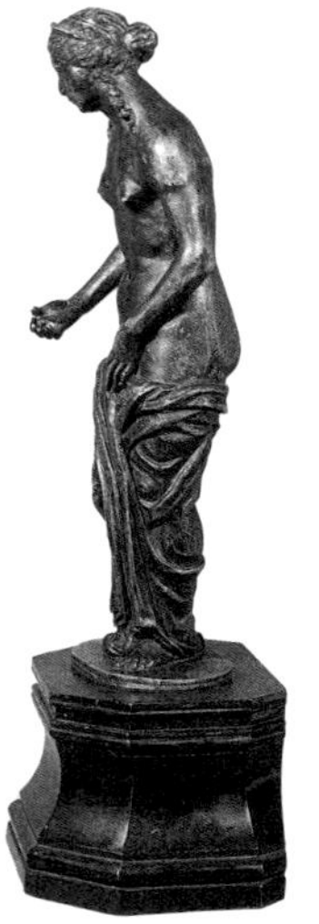

Figure 5.3
Statue of Venus (Fortnum Venus), Severo da Ravenna; bronze
Ashmolean Museum, Oxford

This statuette is virtually identical with a more widely known one in Oxford (Fig. 5.2; 5.3). Formerly attributed by Molinier to the Paduan School, late 15th century, and not illustrated in his catalogue of the Mannheim Collection; by Bode to Bellano; and, more recently, to Riccio (Sheard 1978); these beautiful figures in fact have the quality of autograph works by Severo.

There is not much modelling in their backs, but they have the same suave, well-rounded forms and delicately modelled hands as a female nude of similar size representing *Queen Tomyris with the Head of Cyrus* (Fig. 5.4; Frick Collection, New York, no. 16.2.25; 10⅝ in. (27.1 cm) high), which was also attributed by Bode to Bellano, or to a follower, but has recently been established as an autograph work of Severo's (Pope-Hennessy & Radcliffe, 1970, pp. 136–40).

The 'crinkly' treatment of folds in the drapery, which emphasizes realism at the expense of linear elegance, may be recognized as Severo's by comparison with the robe of his statuette of *St. John the Baptist* in Oxford (Avery & Radcliffe 1983, pls. 17, 19).

While the attribution to Severo of these particular statuettes of *Venus* has not appeared in print, it has been correctly applied to a cognate figure of *Venus* holding her drapery and a cornucopia in either hand (Fig. 5.1; Sotheby's, New York, 23–24 November 1984, lot 92, 9¾ in. (25 cm) high, formerly in the A. E. Ganz Collection, see E. Tietze-Conrat, 'A Bronze Statuette by Andrea Riccio,' in *Arte Veneta*, 1959–60, figs. 273–74).

The carefully modelled open hands, bent slightly at the knuckles, with incisions to render the tiny folds of skin and inside the palm to define different areas of flesh, are also a distinguishing feature of Severo's autograph bronzes, appearing on the signed *Kneeling Satyr* (Zurich, private collection), *St. John the Baptist* (Oxford, Ashmolean Museum), *Corpus Christi* (Cleveland Museum of Art), and *St. Sebastian* (Paris, Louvre) (see Avery & Radcliffe, 1983, for illustrations of all these).

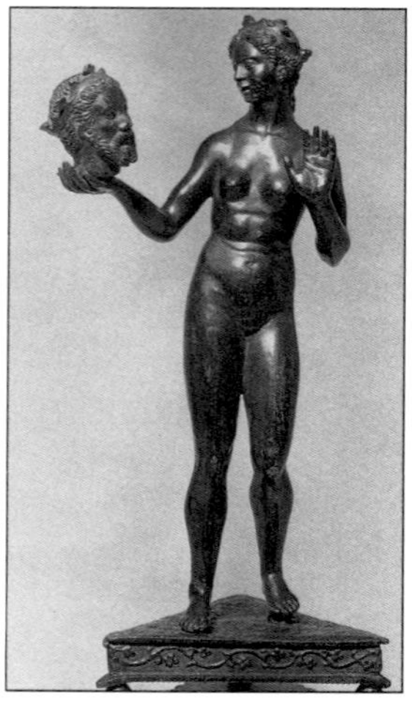

Figure 5.4
Queen Tomyris with the Head of Cyris, Severo da Ravenna; bronze
COPYRIGHT THE FRICK COLLECTION, NEW YORK

There has been much speculation over the source of this obviously classical image of Venus, under two main headings: the type of the figure if she were totally nude, and the type actually showing her with drapery around her thighs. Sheard (1978) noted the general dependence on ancient literary descriptions (Pliny, Lucian) of the celebrated *Venus of Cnidus* by Praxiteles, which was sensuously nude.

As far as visual sources go, the now well-known Capitoline and Medici marble statues of *Venus* were not known until far later than Severo's lifetime. Even so, several statues of *Venus Pudica* ('Modest Venus,' with her hands covering her bosom and thighs) were available as early as the 14th and 15th centuries in

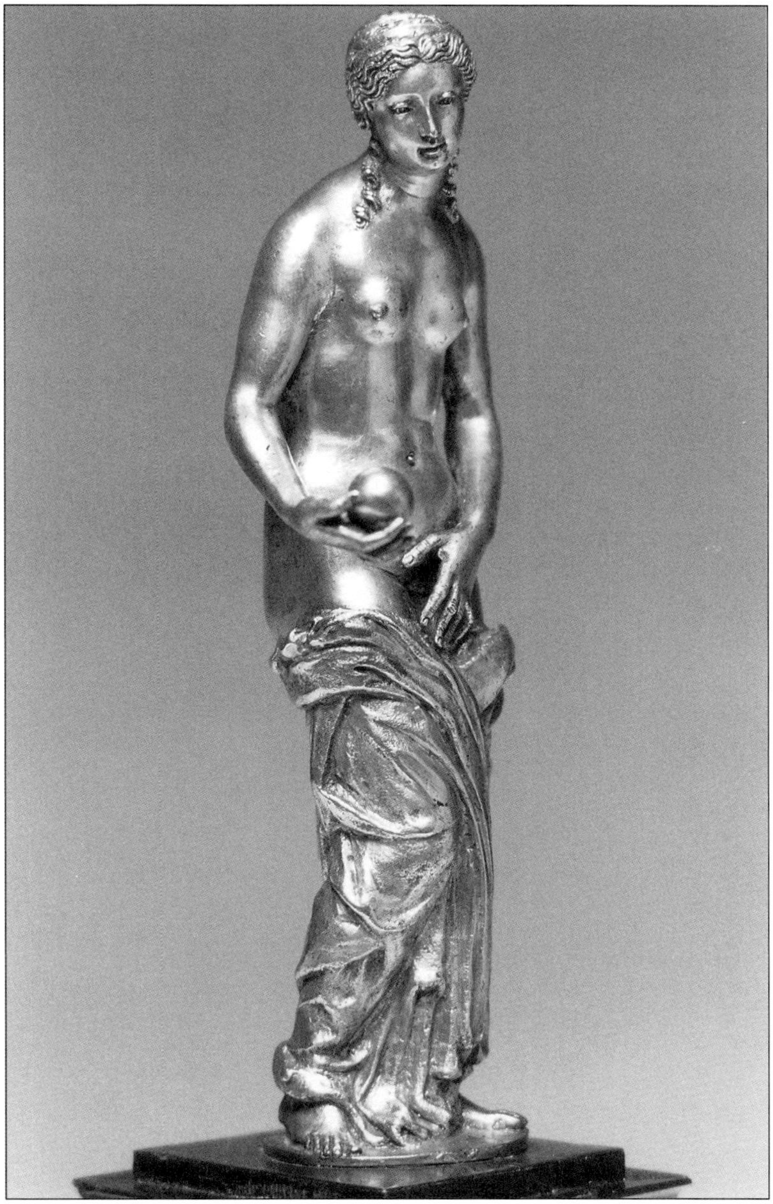

PLATE 5
Venus with Apple
Gilt bronze statuette

Tuscany: one in Florence was described about 1390 by Benvenuto da Imola; another which (until its deliberate destruction in 1357) existed in Siena, was known to the sculptor Ghiberti through a drawing by Ambrogio Lorenzetti (this probably inspired his rendering of Eve in the *Creation* panel of his 'Gates of Paradise' c. 1430). One of these, or another, was sketched by Gentile da Fabriano in the early Quattrocento. In the Louvre (Fig. 5.5, Baron Davillier Bequest) there is a bronze statuette of a *Venus Pudica*, described as 'Paduan, end of the 15th century,' and illustrated by Migeon (1904, no. 57). This may also be by Severo.

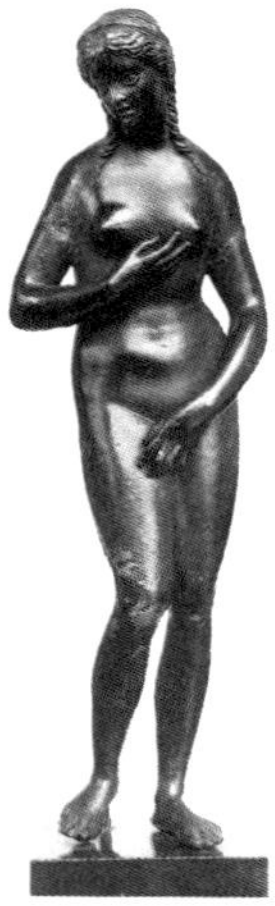

Figure 5.5
Venus pudique, Paduan, 15th century; bronze
cliché REUNION DES MUSEES NATIONAUX, Paris

Ghiberti recorded in his *Commentaries* that he had seen *in Padua* another statue of Venus, with drapery over the hips, which had come from Florence (R. Krautheimer, *Lorenzo Ghiberti*, Princeton, 1970, p. 287, note 17). This partially draped statue was presumably of the classical type of draped Venus best known to us from the *Venus de Milo* (Paris, Louvre, excavated only in 1820) or, which would be more relevant to the present case, from the *Celestial Venus* (Florence, Uffizi Gallery: Haskell & Penny, 1981, no. 85), which may have been available in Rome by the 16th century. In the latter, the goddess makes a creditable attempt with her left arm to hold her drapery up in front of her private parts, as it slips off her thighs. The direction of her arm and the general play of folds of tumbling drapery conform with those in the present *Venus*, though Severo has his goddess imprudently let go of the drapery and hold her hand out free, as in the standard pose of the fully nude *Venus Pudica* type.

That the classical original may actually have held up, or at least touched, the drapery is suggested by this very gesture in another statuette in Berlin (24.4 cm high), which has also correctly been related to the present model by Bode (1930, p. 12, no. 50, pl. 18). Giovanni Antonio da Brescia engraved a *Venus*, with slipping drapery, labelled as 'recently discovered in Rome,' around 1513 (example in the Art Institute of Chicago).

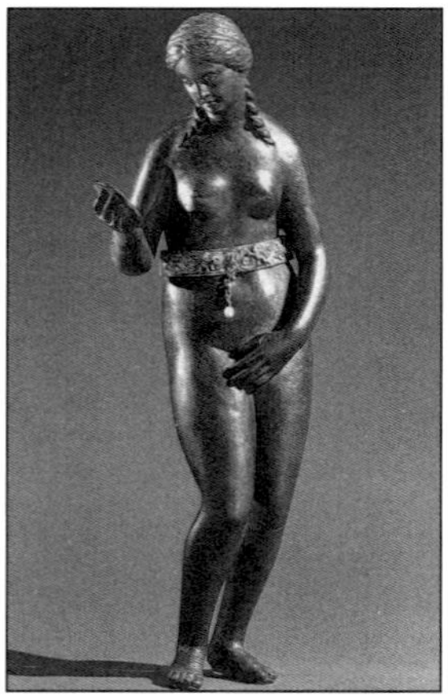

Figure 5.6
The Amerbach Venus, Paduan or Venetian, c. 1500; bronze
Copyright Historisches Museum, Basel

Ancient bronze statuettes may also have served to convey the model with draped thighs, and to inspire sculptors to make copies on the same scale for humanist patrons, such as abounded in the university of Padua and in Venice nearby: indeed a similar bronze figure of Venus features on a shelf in Carpaccio's deliberately humanist, painted rendering of *St. Augustine in his study* (Venice, Scuola di St. Giorgio degli Schiavoni).

In The Frick Art Museum version, Venus has a separately cast golden apple screwed into the palm of her hand, but her fingers do not grasp it convincingly: in fact, had she been intended to hold an apple (the prize awarded to her in preference to Juno and Minerva by Paris in the mythological episode of the *Judgement of Paris*) it would have been more sensible and practical to cast it in one with the fingers closed around it, as in a similar, though nude, statuette in

Berlin (Sheard, 1978, no. 379). The Oxford version holds nothing in her open hand, but it is clear from the direction of her downturned head, lowered eyes and glance that Venus *was* looking at something held in her hand, at right-angles to her line of vision.

The vital clue to what this was is supplied by another celebrated bronze statuette, the *Amerbach Venus*, which was probably produced in Padua or Venice around 1500: it closely reflects the present work by Severo in pose, although it is nude and holds a small round *mirror* up in its hand (Fig. 5.6; Basel, Historisches Museum no. 1909.243, h 26.5 cm; Frankfurt, 1986, no. 314). Basilius Amerbach, a noted Swiss German humanist and collector, who created a special *Kunstkammer* (Art-cabinet) in Basel, purchased his *Venus* from a French nobleman in 1578, probably believing her to be a real antiquity. He loved her so much that he had a silver-gilt girdle with a pendant pearl made to go around her waist! The *Amerbach Venus* admittedly holds the mirror up at chest level to view her features, while the Frick and Oxford *Venuses* by Severo appear to have been more long-sighted.

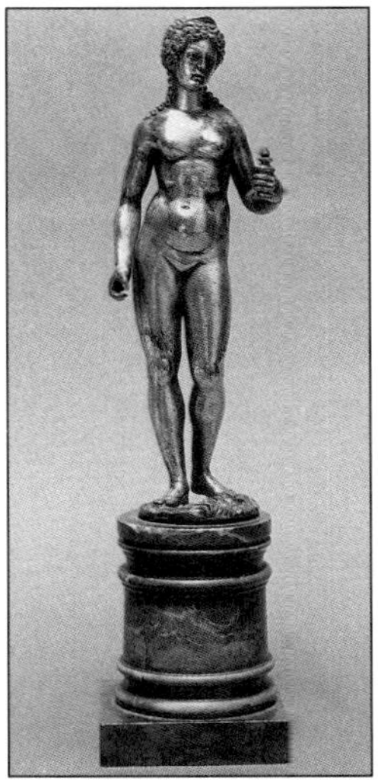

Figure 5.7
Venus Prudentia, attributed to Tullio Lombardo, (c. 1455–1532); Venetian
The Cleveland Museum of Art, John L. Severance Fund (48.171)

Interest in bronze statuettes of Venus was high in north Italy around the year 1500, at the moment of birth of the High Renaissance. An interesting comparison may be drawn between Severo's draped statuette and another gilt-bronze, but nude, statuette of *Venus* of a similar size attributed to a famous sculptor-contemporary, Tullio Lombardo (c. 1455–1532) (Fig. 5.7; Cleveland Museum of Art, no. 48.171; 18.3 cm high: see Wixom 1975, no. 109; Sheard 1978, no. 38; Frankfurt 1986, no. 119).

Antico, a great sculptor in bronze who specialized in reproducing antiquities on a small scale, with a high finish, also produced a *Venus-Charity* around 1500 in Mantua, which was almost a mirror-image of Tullio's one (Fig. 5.8; Baltimore, Walters Art Gallery, no. 54.1027; 45.6 cm high; Frankfurt, 1986, no. 116); while presumably at much the same period in Padua, a sculptor from the close circle of Andrea Riccio modelled both a *Venus Pudica* (Vienna, Kunsthistorisches Museum, nos. 5693 and 5687, 21.4 cm high; Frankfurt, 1986, no. 110) and a *Venus Abundance*, with apple and cornucopia (London, Victoria & Albert Museum, no. A 6-1971, 21 cm high; Frankfurt 1986, no. 109).

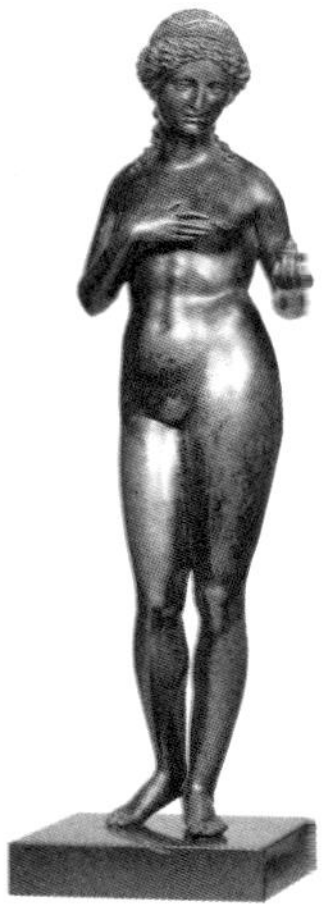

Figure 5.8
Statuette, Venus, Antico; Italian, 16th century
Walters Art Gallery, Baltimore

It appears therefore that all the major specialists in bronze statuettes, Severo, Tullio, Antico, and Riccio, were vying with each other to produce the most ravishing image of the goddess of Love for the humanist or noble patrons, who, in the newly liberated atmosphere of the High Renaissance, were clamoring for such sensuous, nude statuettes of classical deities.

6

Boy Carrying a Shell

Bronze statuette

ITALIAN, PADUA, 16TH CENTURY

Workshop of Severo Calzetta of Ravenna, (active 1496–1525)

8 x 3¼ in. (20.3 x 8.3 x 7.6 cm)

1970.78

Gift of Miss Frick, 1970. Once kept in the library bookcase at "Eagle Rock," Prides Crossing, Massachusetts.

CONDITION

The cast is hollow right down through the shell and into the head and body. Brassy metal with black lacquer. The base has metal hammered over at center with acanthus leaves radiating around it. Two large and one small hole in base, irregularly placed (casting hole in left buttock).

PROVENANCE

J. P. Morgan Collection, New York
Duveen
Frick 1916
Helen Clay Frick

EXHIBITED

London, Victoria & Albert Museum, 1901–12, no. 309, lent by J. Pierpont Morgan

LITERATURE

Bode, 1910, I, no. 49, pl. XXXV

Figure of a boy, partially clad in a short garment of skins, striding forward and bearing on his head the lamp, in the form of a shell, which he holds with both hands. — BODE, 1910: WORKSHOP OF RICCIO, *Lamp: Boy with a Shell.*

The boy has protruding buttocks, curly hair and heavy-lidded eyes which connect him with the models of Severo.

This rare model inspired a later Venetian bronze sculptor, possibly Campagna or Roccatagliata, to produce a closely similar model, though with the torn goat-skin modified into Michelangelesque bands of drapery across the chest and loins (formerly Eduard Simon Collection Berlin; Bode/ed Draper, 1980, pl. CCIV, 1).

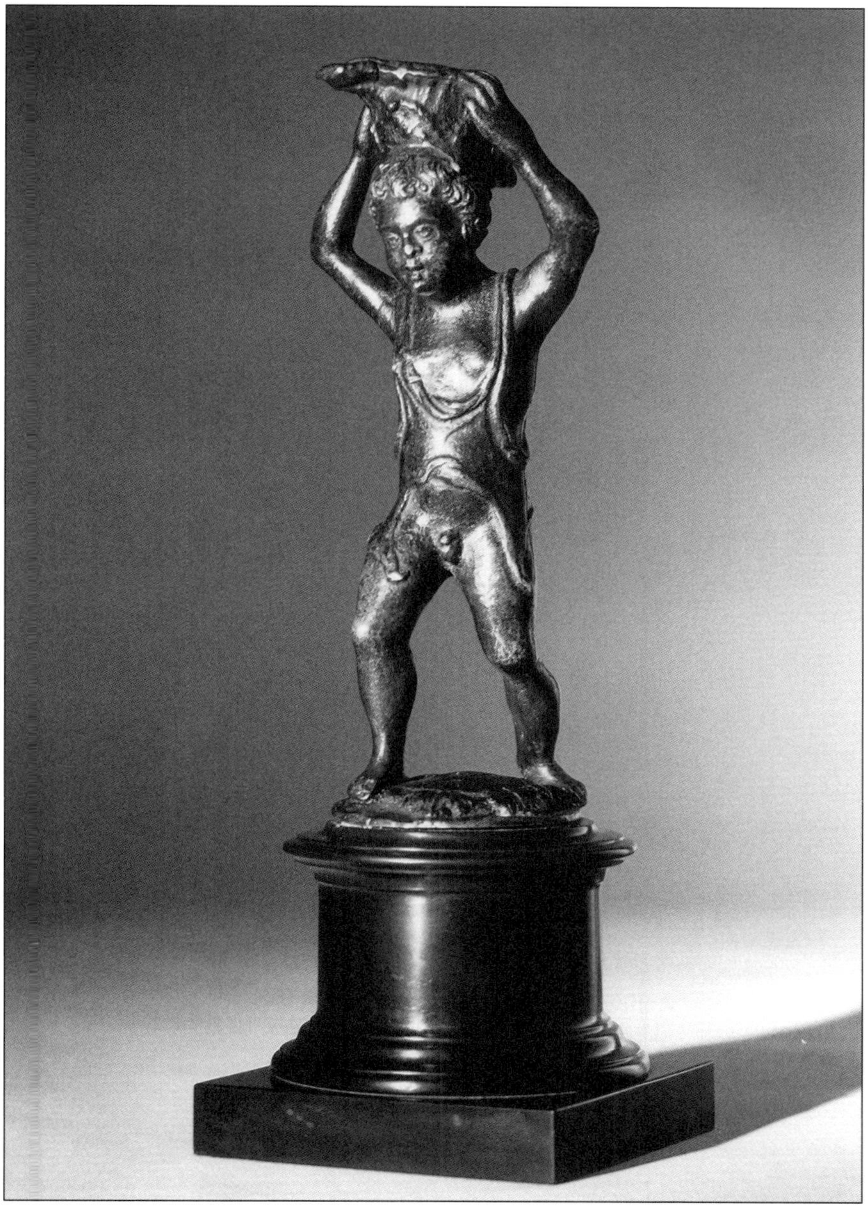

PLATE 6
Boy Carrying a Shell
Bronze statuette

7

Boy Supporting a Shell

Bronze inkwell

ITALIAN, PADUA, EARLY 16TH CENTURY

Workshop of Severo Calzetta of Ravenna, (active 1496–1525)

Formerly attributed to the workshop of Andrea Riccio

4½ in. (11.4 cm)

1973.19
Gift of Miss Frick, 1973

PROVENANCE

Henry Joseph Pfungst Collection, London
J. P. Morgan Collection, New York
Duveen
Frick 1916
Helen Clay Frick

EXHIBITED

London, Victoria & Albert Museum, 1901–12, no. 315, lent by J. Pierpont Morgan

LITERATURE

Pfungst, 1899, no. 31 (as 'School of Verrocchio, early 16th century,' but pencilled in his own copy 'Bellano nach Bode')
Bode, 1910, no. 45, plate XXXV
Planiscig, 1927, pp. 200–1, 481
Bode, 1930, pp. 15–16, no. 66, pl. 24
Pope-Hennessy, 1965, p. 129, no. 476, fig. 498
De Winter, 1986, p. 104, fig. 68: p. 134, note 56

OTHER EXAMPLES

(1) Belgium, Château de Laarne, 1967, exhibition catalogue, p. 56, no. 36 (aftercast)
(2) Berlin, Staatliche Museen, Skulpturengalerie, Inv. 2287, 11.5 cm high
(3) Hamburg Museum für Kunst und Gewerbe, Inv. 1953.68, H.11.1 cm (*Bildführer II*, Hamburg, 1964, no. 61; Frankfurt 1986, p. 536, no. 259)
(4) London, Sotheby's, 30 June 1969, lot 37, sold to Cyril Humphris Ltd, 13.1 cm high
(5) London, Christie's, 5 December, 1972, lot 19, 11.5 cm high
(6) London, Victoria and Albert Museum, Inv. A 65–1956
(7) Paris, formerly Miller von Aicholz/Marquis de Ganay-Ridgway Collection
(8) Paris, Musée du Louvre (Inv OA 6414; illustrated in De Winter, 1986, fig. 68)
(9) Switzerland, private collection (including a triangular base) 19 cm high (reproduced in *Art venitien en Suisse et au Liechtenstein*, exhibition catalogue, Pfaffikon, Seedamm-Kulturzentrum; Geneva, Musée d'art et d'histoire (Zurich: Fondation Suisse pro Venezia, Milan, 1978), p. 218, no. 224, entry by Mauro Natale)
(10) Vienna, formerly Castiglioni Collection
(11) Washington, National Gallery of Art, Kress Collection, Inv. A.188.26C, 11.6 cm high

Full-length figure of a boy clad in a short garment. He supports the shell on his back with both arms, bending his head to the right. His weight is thrown on to his left leg, his right is raised as though about to step forward. — BODE, 1910: WORKSHOP OF RICCIO, *Boy carrying a Shell.*

The boy is wearing the ancient Greek working garment known as the *Exomis*, and supports on his shoulders a disproportionately large shell (*Murex brandaris* (Linnaeus)), which is probably a nature cast. The idea may have been inspired

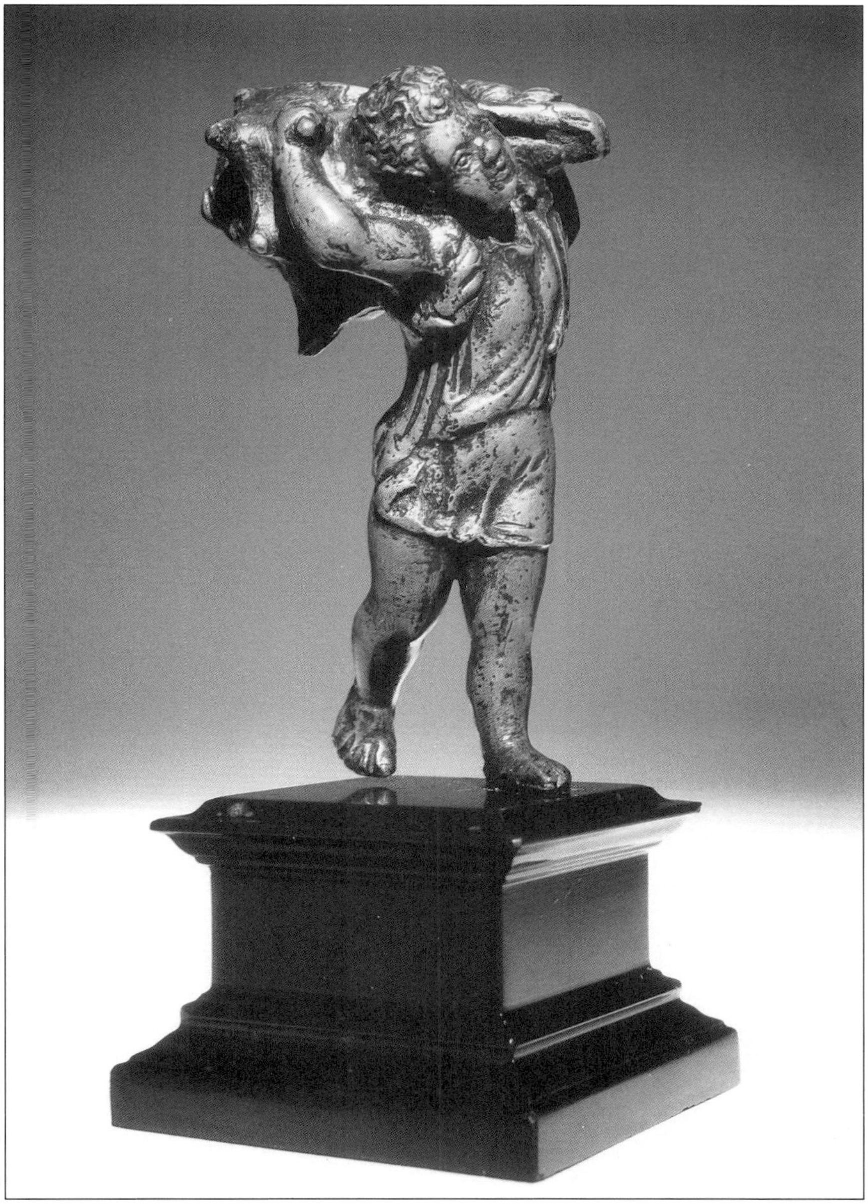

PLATE 7
Boy Supporting a Shell
Bronze inkwell

by a famous ancient Roman relief in San Vitale, Ravenna, showing *putti* carrying the attributes of Neptune. One of them is balancing in a closely similar way an over life-size snail-shell (B. Degenhardt and A. Schmitt, 'Gentile da Fabriano und die Anfange des Antikenstudiums,' in *Münchner Jahrbuch für Bildende Kunst,* F III, XI, 1960, p. 59f. no. 10, pl. 76; De Winter, 1986, fig. 69).

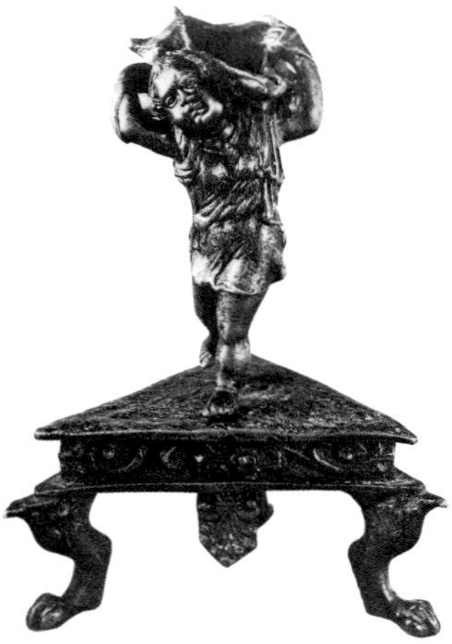

Figure 7.1
Boy Supporting a Shell, Severo da Ravenna
Switzerland, private collection; photograph supplied by the author

The statuette was probably originally mounted (by means of a screw projecting downward from its standing leg) on to a triangular base from Severo's workshop, as in another example, no. 9 listed above (Fig. 7.1). Other sand-boxes, candle-nozzles or pen-holders could have been screwed on near it *au choix*, to make a complete writing set, as on no. 7 listed above, formerly in the Miller von Aicholz/Marquis de Ganay-Ridgway Collection (see C. Dreyfus, in *Les Arts*, no. 96, December, 1909, pp. 26, 30).

The combination of a classical boy with a life-cast shell is reminiscent of a writing-utensil formerly in the Bode-Museum, Berlin (Frankfurt 1986, p. 198, fig. 123), which shows a similarly clad infant reaching up from a naturalistic base to a gnarled tree.

The present model was popular, judging from the large number of surviving examples.

8a

Figurine of Judith with the Head of Holofernes

Bronze figurine (associated with a triangular bronze sand-box in a wooden frame with double-baluster colonnettes at the angles)

ITALIAN, PADUA, EARLY 16TH CENTURY
Workshop of Severo Calzetta of Ravenna, (active 1496–1525)
4⅞ in. (12.4 cm) high

CONDITION
The sword blade fractured, its tip possibly replaced. Black patina. According to a previous owner, Mr. Pfungst, 'Unfortunately, the surface and the "Patina" of the Bronze have been injured by the effects of fire, the little figure having been found amongst the debris remaining in a room in Florence, the contents of which were destroyed by fire.'

8b

Triangular sand-box, its sides formed of three identical plaquettes of cavorting putti

ITALIAN, MIDDLE THIRD OF THE 15TH CENTURY

From the circle of Donatello

Each side 1¾ x 3¾ in. (4.5 x 8.5 cm) high

1970.74
Gift of Miss Frick, 1970

PROVENANCE
Henry Joseph Pfungst Collection, London
Durlacher, London
J. P. Morgan Collection, New York
Duveen
Frick 1916
Helen Clay Frick

EXHIBITED
London, Victoria & Albert Museum, 1901–12,

LITERATURE
(The whole assemblage)
Pfungst, 1899, no. 39A
Bode, 1910, I, no. 64, plate XL
(The figurine of Judith)
Pfungst, 1899, no. 39
De Winter, 1986, pp. 106–7, fig. 75
(The triangular inkstand)
Goldschmidt, 1914, no. 249
Bange, 1922, no. 299, pls. 32, 42
(The plaquette)
Molinier, 1886, no. 79
Maclagan, 1924, p. 17
Planiscig, 1927, pp. 309, 312, 491, cat. no. 217, pl. 357
Pope-Hennessy, 1965, no. 361
Panvini Rosati, 1968, p. 67, Plachette, no. 1

OTHER EXAMPLES
(The complete triangular inkstand)
Berlin, Staatliche Museen (Inv. 1026)
New York, Pierpont Morgan Library (sold Christie's, London, 11 December, 1979, lot no. 198)
(The plaquette)
Florence, formerly Stefano Bardini Collection
Florence, Museo Nazionale del Bargello
London, British Museum (TWG 173, and another)
Naples, Museo Nazionale di Capodimonte
Paris, formerly Picard Collection
Rome, Doria Gallery
Trento
Venice, Museo Correr
Washington, DC, National Gallery of Art (Kress Collection, A 289.12B)

Triangular in form, supported at the angles by slender columns and resting on lion's claw feet. The sides are decorated in low relief with a frieze representing cupids at play one of whom wears a large mask in order to scare the others, a subject borrowed from classical art. This example has been subsequently adapted as the socle for a figure of

PLATE 8A
Figurine of Judith with the Head of Holofernes
Bronze figurine

PLATE 8B
Triangular sand-box, its sides formed of three identical plaquettes of cavorting putti

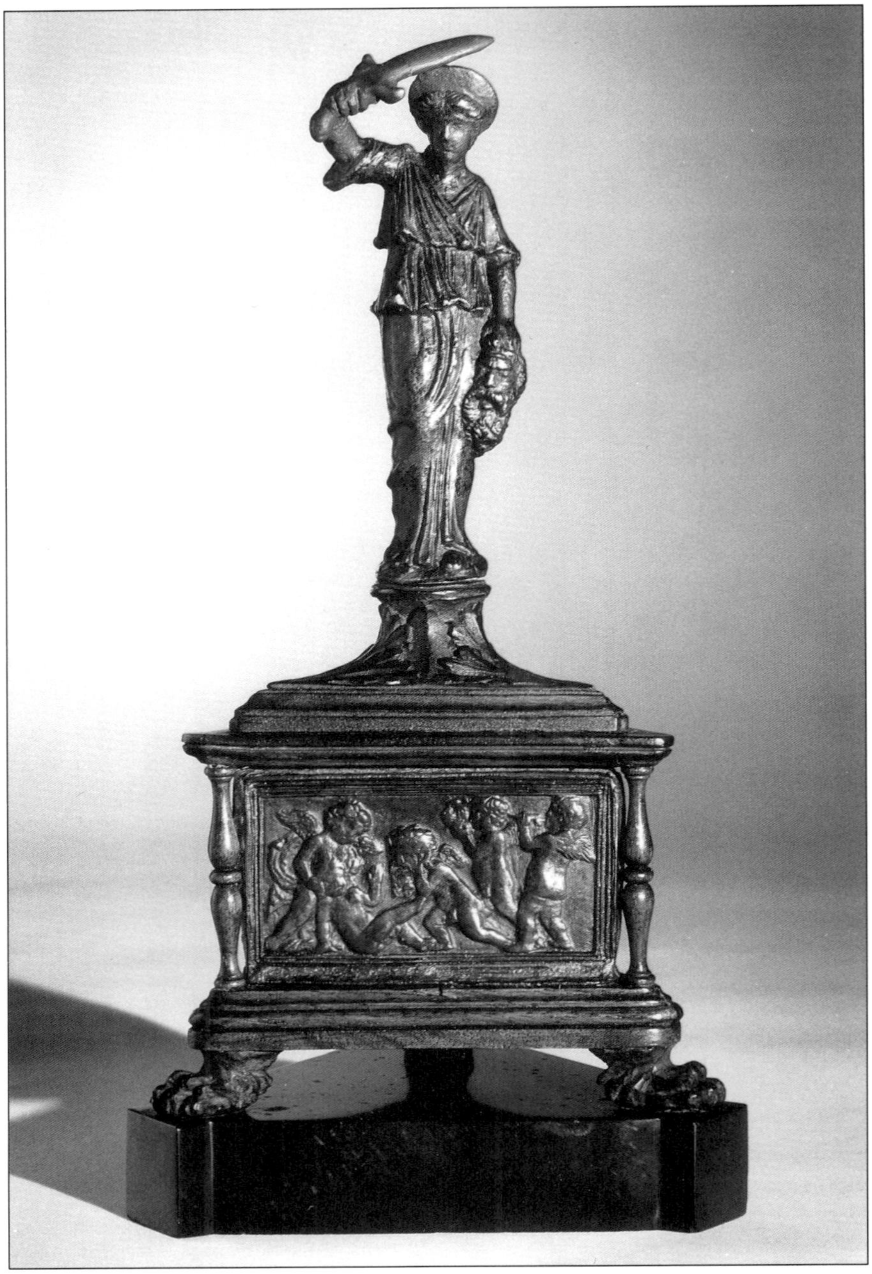

Judith holding the head of Holofernes in her left hand and the sword in her uplifted right; she rests the blade against her head. — BODE, 1910: PADUAN SCHOOL, LATE 15TH CENTURY, *Inkstand with Judith holding the Head of Holofernes.*

8a

The bronze figurine is of a type associable with the workshop of Severo, and may once have formed the handle of a table-bell, to which its vertical shape is better adapted. De Winter (1986) reproduced a slightly larger and differently posed *Judith* (Sotheby's, London, 30 June 1969, lot 24), of which he listed two other, inferior, examples in his note 60. A similar, larger *Judith,* 19 cm high, was sold at Christie's, London, 4 July 1989, lot 136; while a miniature *Judith* was mounted on a lamp in the Robert Straus collection (sold Christie's, London, 3 May 1977, lot 64).

Its former owner, Mr. Pfungst, described it as follows in his catalogue: 'This little figure is a sketch in "Cire perdu" (*sic*), either for or after the large group of *Judith and Holofernes* in the Loggia dei Lanzi in Florence by Donatello, and inspired by the master.' Presumably the thematic association with Donatello encouraged him (or whoever he had purchased it from) intelligently to mount it on the Donatellesque triangular inkstand, in imitation of the triangular pedestal of the monumental group of Judith, which also is decorated with plaques of cavorting putti.

8b

The triangular inkstand is one of only three known examples, the others being in Berlin and formerly in the Morgan Library, New York. Numerous individual examples of the rectangular plaquette forming its sides are known (Maclagan, 1924, p. 17; Pope-Hennessy, 1965, no. 361). Formerly attributed on the basis of its subject matter of cavorting putti to Donatello (Molinier, Bode, Bange, Maclagan), and later to Riccio (Planiscig, 1927, p. 309, fig. 357), the plaquette was regarded by Middeldorf, Pope-Hennessy and Panvini Rosati as 'North Italian late 15th century.'

A terracotta mould (matrix) for the plaquette survives in Rome, Museo di Palazzo Venezia (4.5 x 8.5 cm; P.V. no. 10419; Santangelo, 1954, p. 23, fig. 20; Cannata, 1982, pp. 36–37, no. 4). This great rarity was excavated in 1876 from the foundations of Palazzo Venezia, together with some medals of 1465 of the Venetian Pope Paul II Barbo (a year after his election to the papacy). They were in one of the terracotta money-boxes which were deliberately placed in commemoration all around the foundations of the palace. Paul's death in 1471 gives an ultimate *terminus ante quem* for the existence of the matrix, while the date of the particular medals in 1465 suggests that the matrix may well have been created before then.

This would place its origins just within the lifetime of Donatello (d. 1466), and so his authorship should not be excluded. The motif of putti frightened by one of their number hiding behind a mask is classical, and the location of the find points to Rome as a possible place of production, rather than north Italy. Donatello was not in Rome after 1432 as far as we know, and so if it were his work it would have to have been made in Florence or Padua, and obtained by the avid collector, Pope Paul II, and prized by him precisely on account of its authorship. Failing this it may be by an unidentified Roman.

Santangelo's idea of assigning the authorship of the matrix, and hence of the plaquette, on the basis of the letter 'G' inscribed on its reverse, to Giovanni Gavino (or Cavino) the reviver (or forger) of classical coins does not have much to recommend it.

9

St. Michael Weighing Souls

Bronze finial

ITALIAN, PADUA, EARLY 16TH CENTURY

Workshop of Severo Calzetta of Ravenna, (active 1496–1525)

4½ x 1¾ x 2¼ in. (11.4 x 4.4 x 5.7 cm)

1970.91
Gift of Miss Frick, 1970

CONDITION

There is a screw hole in the center of the base for attachment. The strings of the pans of the scales, and the dragon's tongue, are all very waxy. The wings are perfectly plain, and were cut out of a sheet of wax and dabbed on to the back of the original model. The tip of the sword is missing, probably owing to a casting failure. There is very little, if any, chasing on the surface.

PROVENANCE

Henry Joseph Pfungst Collection, London
Durlacher, London
J. P. Morgan Collection, New York
Duveen
Frick 1916
Helen Clay Frick

EXHIBITED

London, Victoria & Albert Museum, 1901–12, no. 338, lent by J. Pierpont Morgan

LITERATURE

Pfungst, 1899, no. 34 (as 'Florentine, latter half 15th century')

The saint's short skirt, tucked up around the waist, is like that on the boy *David with the Head of Goliath* by Severo.

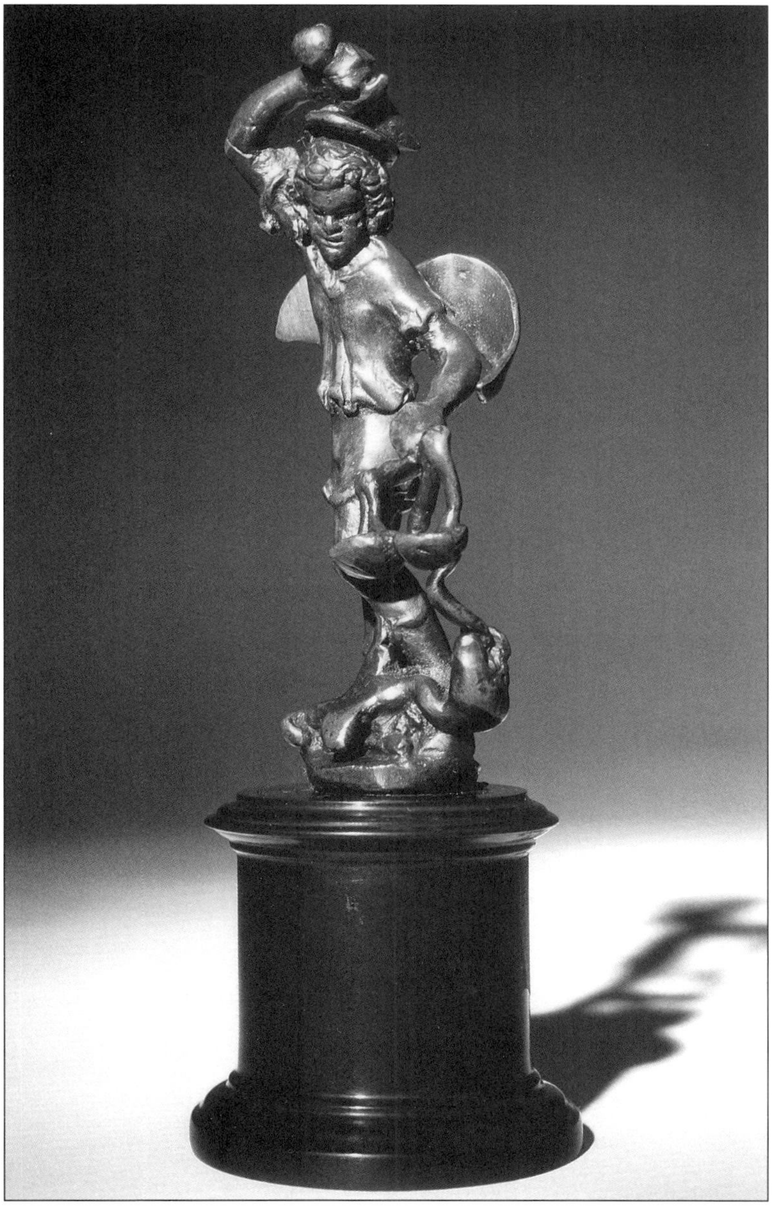

PLATE 9
St. Michael Weighing Souls
Bronze finial

10

Lamp in the Form of a Satyr's Head

Bronze oil lamp

ITALIAN, PADUA, EARLY 16TH CENTURY

Workshop of Severo Calzetta of Ravenna, (active 1496–1525)

3½ x 4 x 1¾ in. (9 x 10 x 4.5 cm)

1970.90

Gift of Miss Frick, 1970. Once kept on the library mantel at "Eagle Rock," Prides Crossing, Massachusetts.

CONDITION

Lateral drill hole in top curl (or stylized bird), to accommodate a loop for suspension. Tongue cast inside the mouth to support the wick.

PROVENANCE

Henry Joseph Pfungst Collection, London
Durlacher, London
J. P. Morgan Collection, New York
Duveen
Frick 1916
Helen Clay Frick

EXHIBITED

London, Victoria & Albert Museum, 1901–12, no. 311, lent by J. Pierpont Morgan

LITERATURE

Pfungst, 1899, no. 10 (as 'North Italian, late 15th century')
Bode, 1910, I, no. 58, plate XXXIX

OTHER EXAMPLES

Berlin, Kunstgewerbe Museum, (Pechstein 1968, no. 75: as 'Workshop of Riccio')
Rome, Museo di Palazzo Venezia (Santangelo, 1954, p. 33: as 'Workshop of Riccio')
Vienna, Kunsthistorisches Museum, (Planiscig, 1924, no. 56, as 'Venetian, mid-16th century')
Turin, Museo Civico.

The wide-open jaws form the burner, the neck is surrounded with leafage, the handle curls over from the back of the head and rests upon the forehead. — BODE, 1910: WORKSHOP OF RICCIO, *Lamp in the form of a Satyr's Head.*

The bug-eyeballs, with drilled pupils, and the nicely relieved details (e.g. of oak leaves around the beard) are typical of a good quality product from Severo's shop. Only the example in Berlin appears to be virtually identical, while the others cited above show minor variations in facial features and ornaments.

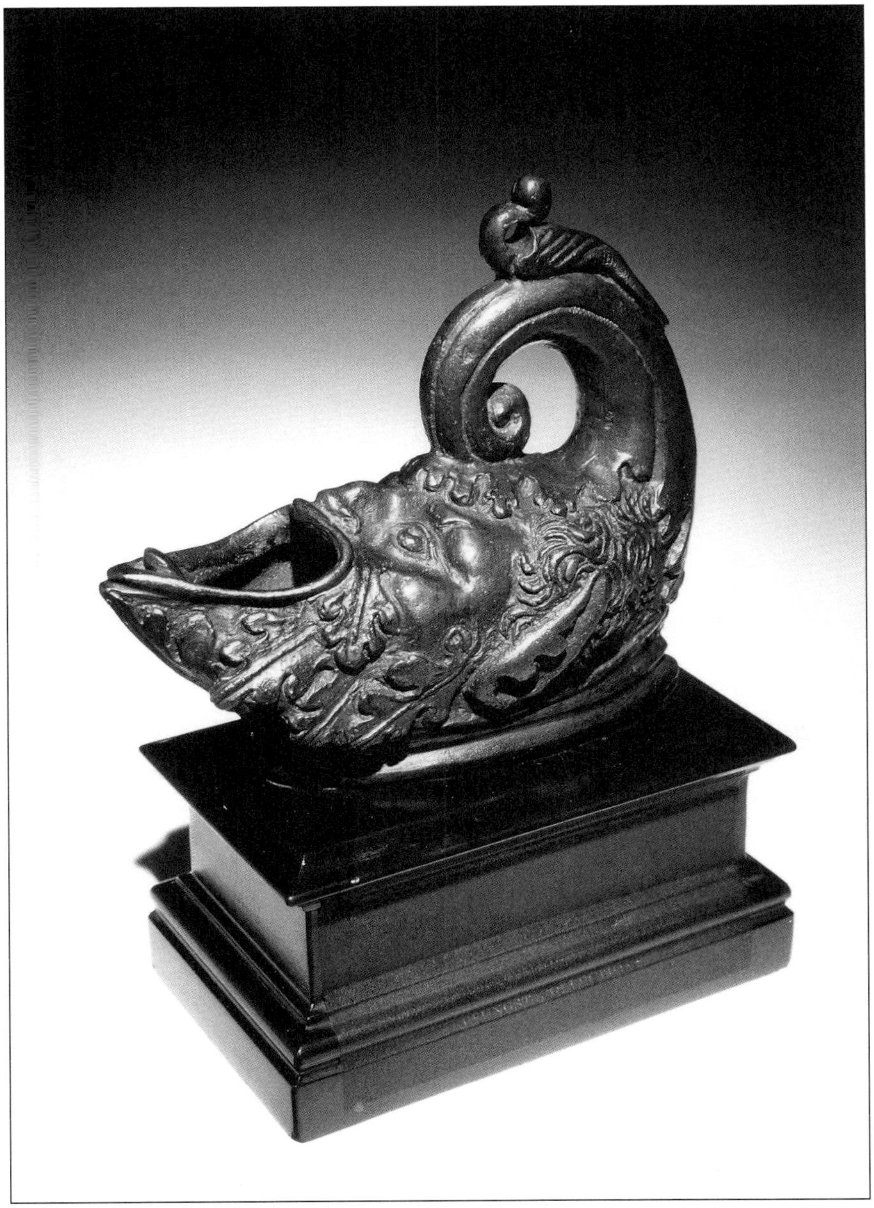

PLATE 10
Lamp in the Form of a Satyr's Head
Bronze oil lamp

PLATE II
Butting Goat
Bronze statuette

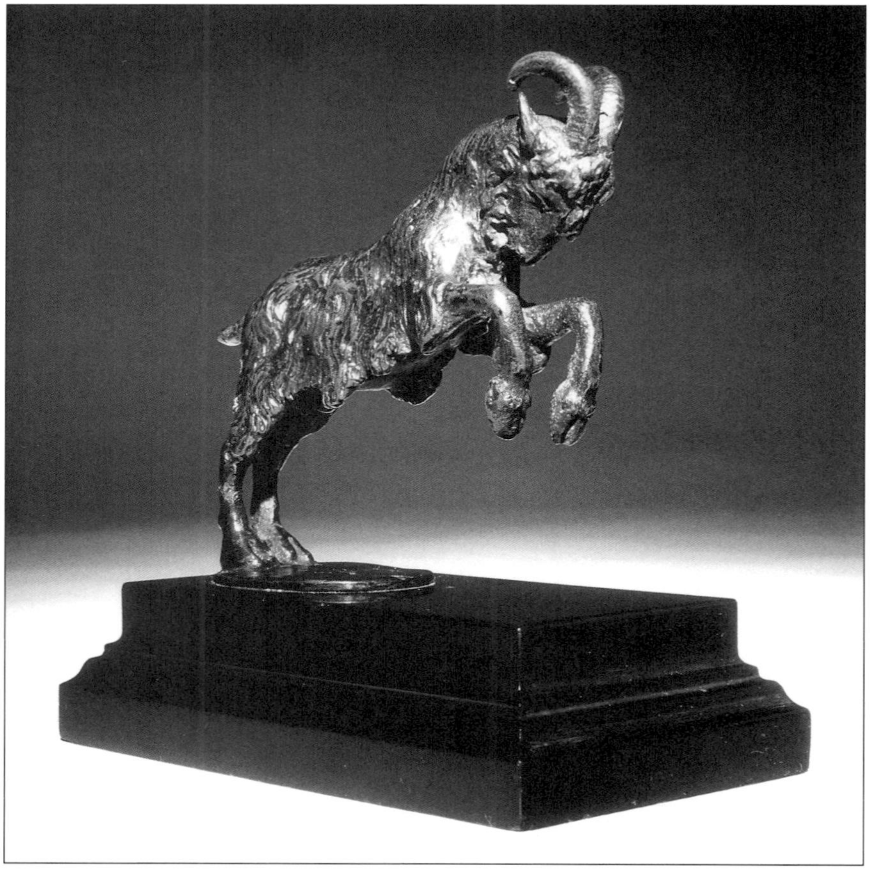

11

Butting Goat

Bronze statuette

ITALIAN, PADUA, EARLY 16TH CENTURY

3⅜ x 1 x 3¾ in. (8.6 x 2.5 x 9.5 cm)

1970.75
Gift of Miss Frick, 1970

CONDITION
Brownish metal with black lacquer on integrally cast(?), roughly oval, base-plate.

PROVENANCE
Henry Joseph Pfungst Collection, London
Durlacher, London
J. P. Morgan Collection, New York
Duveen
Frick 1916
Helen Clay Frick

EXHIBITED
London, Victoria & Albert Museum, 1901–12, no. 343, lent by J. Pierpont Morgan

LITERATURE
Pfungst, 1899, no. 47 (as 'Florentine, early 16th century')
Bode, 1910, , no. 71, fig. on p. 20
Bode/ed. Draper, 1980, p. 45, 86, fig. 48 (as 'Possibly North Italian 16th century, unlocated')

OTHER EXAMPLE
Vienna, Kunsthistorisches Museum, (?)

A goat springing forward; its head bent, its fore-legs raised in the air. — BODE, 1910: WORKSHOP OF RICCIO, PADUAN, 16TH CENTURY, *Goat.*

This type of small goat has traditionally been associated with Riccio. It was subsequently believed to have been made by the Roman bronze-founder and goldsmith, Luigi Valadier (1726–85), and to be derived from ancient marble goats in the Sala degli Animali in the Vatican Museums. One appears on the frame for a classical cameo in the Louvre, which is documented to Valadier. Valadier's may be a slightly different model, however, with the head turned distinctly to the goat's left flank (e.g. Berlin, Dahlem, Staatliche Museen (Bode/ed. Draper, 1980, pl. CXIII, as 'Probably Netherlandish, late 16th-early 17th century').

However, the present example is smaller and better than the standard Valadier type, and the brown colour of the metal, with black lacquer, is typically Paduan. It has beautifully modelled curly hair around the face, and appears to be an early bronze (see Bode/ed. Draper 1980, where described as 'Possibly North Italian, XVI century').

12

Portrait of a Man, said to be Marcantonio Passeri, (1491–1565)

Bronze bust

ITALIAN, VENICE, EARLY 16TH CENTURY

16 x 13½ x 12 in. (40.6 x 34.3 x 30.5 cm)

1970.93
Gift of Miss Frick, 1970

CONDITION

This is a very thin-walled cast, with fractures and casting flaws around its edge. There are small (2–3 mm) holes at the right side of the mouth and in the left nostril. The bust is pitted at the back of the bald head, and the ears are not undercut behind. The beard was modelled in the wax with a stylus. There is some hammering over the eyebrows, and there is a very waxy texture to the edge of the shirt and tie in front.

It is covered with thick layers of lacquer and paint. P M 324 in red paint. There is an old paper label pasted inside, with a printed number 1501, corresponding with that of the J. P. Morgan loan to the Victoria & Albert Museum.

PROVENANCE

J. P. Morgan Collection, New York
Duveen
Frick 1916
Helen Clay Frick

EXHIBITED

London, Victoria & Albert Museum, 1901–12, no. 1501, lent by J. Pierpont Morgan

LITERATURE

Bode, 1910, I, no. 114, plate LXXIX
Planiscig, 1924, pp. 26–27, no. 40; pp. 94–95, no. 165
Hovey, 1975, p. 100, ill. p. 103
Pollard, J. G., *Medaglie Italiane del Rinascimento nel Museo Nazionale del Bargello*, Florence, 1985, III, pp. 1318–19, no. 768
Boucher, 1991, II pp. 370–71, nos. 114–16, figs. 390–92

Bust almost life-size, with bald head and square-shaped beard; the robe is fastened in front by a ribbon. The treatment is simple and life-like. — BODE, 1910: PADUAN, 16TH CENTURY, PROBABLY BY ANDREA RICCIO, *Portrait bust of Marcantonio Passeri.*

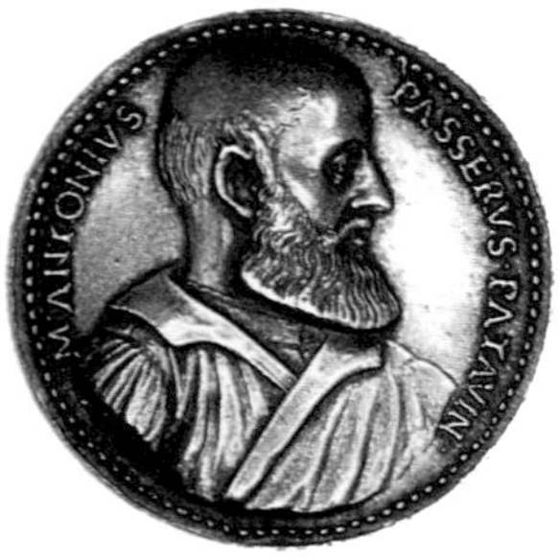

Figure 12.1
Giovanni dal Cavino, *Marcantonio Passeri*; Paduan, 16th century; bronze medal
(Reproduced by kind permission of Bonham's, London)

According to Bode, Marcantonio Passeri was a Fleming who lived in Venice in the mid-16th century, but elsewhere he is described as Paduan, and a Professor of Philosophy at the University there. His likeness is known from a medal (Fig. 12.1) by Giovanni dal Cavino (1500–1570), of which there is an example in the Bargello, Florence (see Pollard, op. cit.). While the profiles of the actual faces are similar, they are not totally identical, and there seem to be differences in the shape of the head, the bust having a squarer — and balder — back to the cranium and a distinct bull-neck.

Catalogued by Bode as 'probably by Andrea Riccio'; Hovey suggested a relationship with the work of Danese Cattaneo (1509–1573); while Pope-Hennessy in December 1979 suggested an attribution to Bartolomeo Bellano (1434–

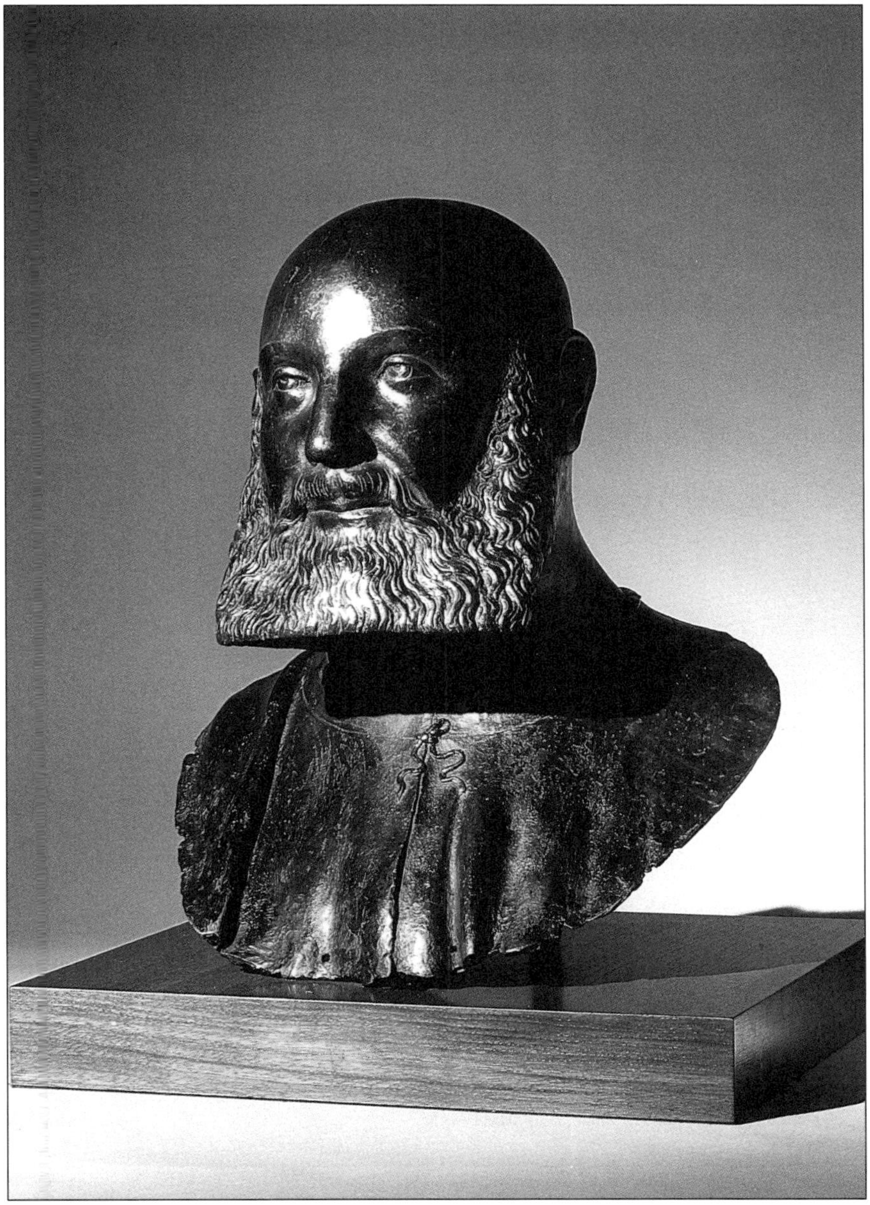

PLATE 12
Portrait of a Man, said to be Marcantonio Passeri, (1491–1565)
Bronze bust

1496). All three attributions have been rejected by various other scholars, most authoritatively (though only on the evidence of photographs) by Dr. M. Leithe-Jasper of the Kunsthistorisches Museum, Vienna, an acknowledged expert on Venetian sculpture and bronzes (letter of 15 October 1991): he also confessed to reservations even as to the authenticity of the Frick bust, while mentioning possible similarities with portrait medals by Maffeo Olivieri.

The present writer, from personal examination, finds no particular reason to doubt the authenticity of the bust: indeed, the rather poor, flawed casting seems typical of several other busts of apparently the same general period and place of origin — the beginning or middle of the 16th century in the Veneto — though *not* of the products of Padua in the late 15th or early 16th centuries (which rules out the authorship of Bellano and Riccio). In any case, neither this bust, nor anything remotely similar, appears in the recent, authoritative monograph on Bellano (V. Krahn, *Bartolommeo Bellano*, Munich, 1988).

The tentative connection made by Hovey with Danese Cattaneo was probably based on generic similarities with Cattaneo's bronze bust of *Lazzaro Bonamico* (Bassano, Museo Civico), and one purportedly of *Girolamo Fracastoro* (Vienna, Kunsthistorisches Museum), which was attributed to him (on the basis of alleged similarities with the Bonamico portrait) by Planiscig (1924).

The closest parallel for the distinctively square cut of the beard in a Venetian context (apart from Cavino's undated medal of Passeri) is on a medal by Fra Antonio da Brescia showing Simone Michele Contarini as Canon of Treviso, a post to which he was appointed in 1510 (Hill, 1930, p. 125, no. 472). This medal is also close in style to those by Maffeo Olivieri (active c. 1520–30), which were cited by Leithe-Jasper as possibly analogous with the bust.

A dating to earlier in the century than has been traditional is also corroborated by a comparison of the image with that in a bronze bust supposedly representing *Marcantonio della Torre*, a Paduan who died in 1510 (Vienna, Kunsthistorisches Museum; Planiscig, 1924 — an analogy kindly suggested by Dr. Douglas Lewis and Dr. Alison Luchs of the National Gallery of Art, Washington, DC). The direct, unflinching, gaze of the subject, and the austere, self-consciously classicizing, and slightly abstract, treatment of the shapes of cranium, facial features and neck are indeed similar (though the casting apparently is not, for the della Torre looks in photographs more solidly made).

In the present state of knowledge about this field of sculpture, it appears safest to dismiss all attempts to connect the bust with an identifiable sculptor, and to revert to the judicious position of 'knowing that one knows not.'

To give a name would imply a degree of certainty that is not warranted by any of the evidence adduced so far. The same stance has been adopted recently by Bruce Boucher in his monograph on Jacopo Sansovino (1991) with regard to a series of replicated bronze portraits of Girolamo Giustinian and his wife Agnesina Badoer (Fig. 12.2), which appear to the present writer to resemble the Frick bust in general type, feeling, and facture. Boucher concludes his rejection of them from the catalogue of Sansovino's oeuvre as follows: 'all of the bronzes appear to date from the sixteenth century and represent the kind of serial reproduction of family portraits that great Venetian families like the Giustinian and Cornaro enjoyed. Bode's conclusion, that they were by a 'Venetian — of the beginning of the sixteenth century,' seems chronologically more accurate and prudent.'

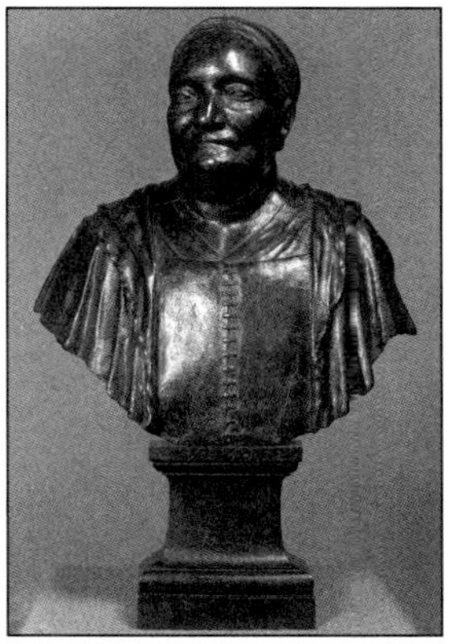

Figure 12.2
Agnesina Badoer Giustinian, Venetian, c. 1542; bronze
©1992, Widener Collection, National Gallery of Art, Washington; (1942.9.146 [A-139]SC)

13

Mars, or Perseus

Bronze

ITALIAN, PADUA OR VENICE, LATE 16TH CENTURY

Attributed to Francesco Segala (c. 1535–1592)

16½ x 7 x 4⅞ in. (41.9 x 17.8 x 12.4 cm)

1970.79
Gift of Miss Frick, 1970

CONDITION

Heavily cast in a coppery alloy, with dark lacquer. There is not much chasing, but only a roughcast metallic surface, with occasional flaws. The plume crest on helmet is broken off, and the visor is fractured. Chestnut brown colour on exposed parts of metal surfaces, with thick black lacquer in the hollows.

PROVENANCE

Henry Joseph Pfungst Collection, London
Durlacher, London
J. P. Morgan Collection, New York
Duveen
Frick 1916
Helen Clay Frick

LITERATURE

Pfungst, 1899, no. 2 (as 'School of Michael Angelo, first half of 16th century')
Bode, 1910, I, no. 138, plate XCIX
Planiscig, 1921, pp. 569–70, pl. 626
Pope-Hennessy & Radcliffe, 1970, III, pp. 183–84
Mariacher, 1971, p. 40, figs. 169–70
Royal Academy, 1983, p. 385, no. S34
Banzato & Pellegrini, 1989, pp. 86–88, nos. 62–63 (with earlier literature)

OTHER EXAMPLE

Venice, Museo Correr

PLATE 13
Mars, or Perseus
Bronze

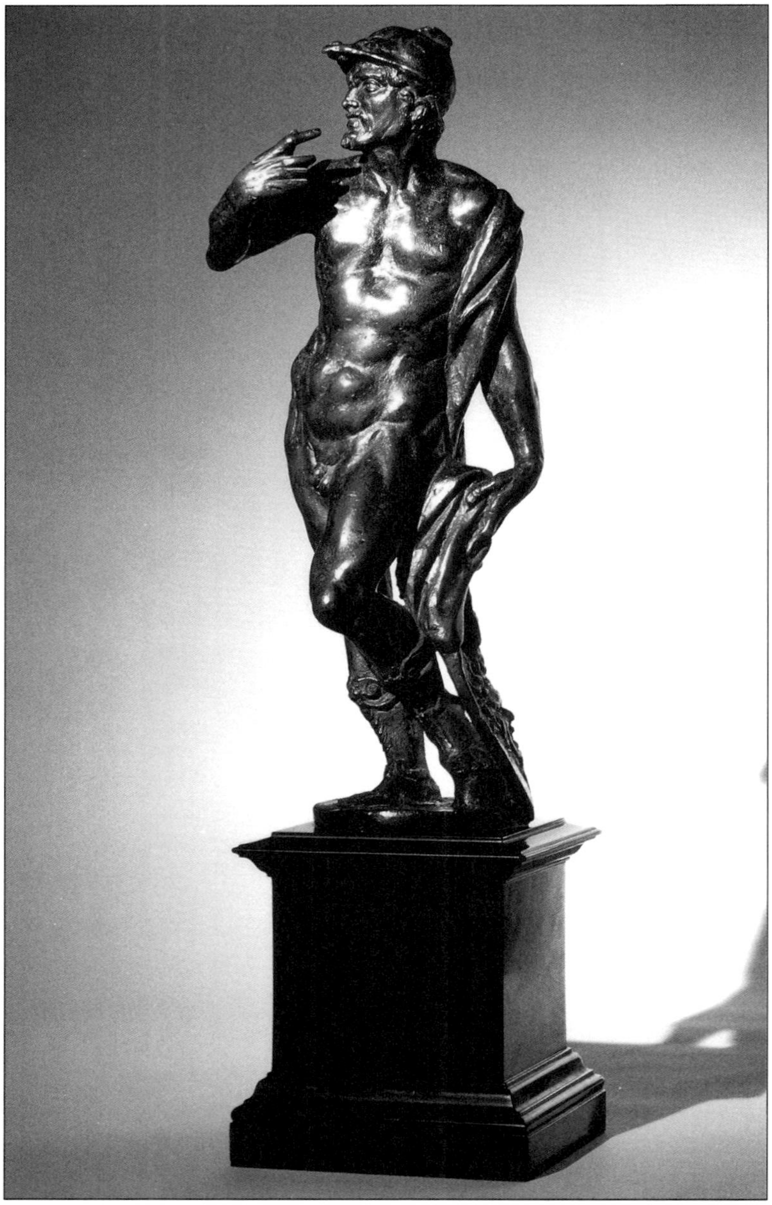

Full-length nude; a drapery falls over his left shoulder and covers the top of his shield which he holds with his left hand. His right foot planted firmly, his left with bent knee slightly raised. He wears a helmet and turns his head to the right; raising his right arm and bending the elbow, his legs are cased in leather, the feet bound with thongs. On the shield a gorgon's head. — BODE, 1910: ITALIAN, LATE 16TH CENTURY, *Mars.*

There is a wonderful Medusa head on the shield, which may indicate that the subject is *Perseus*, as Mr. Pfungst described it, rather than *Mars*, as it has since been described.

The figure patently comes from the top of an andiron (fire-dog), as can be surmised from its scale, heavy casting, generalized surface, and circular base-plate, with a hole at the center to accommodate the iron bolt which normally secures such bronzes to the pyramidal stand below.

A relationship in subject and pose with a statuette of *Mars* crowning an andiron in The Frick Collection, New York (16.2.56), which is by Tiziano Aspetti, does not justify an attribution to that master. The anatomy is far heavier and physically broader (unlike Aspetti's lithe figure), and the surface is handled in a more painterly fashion, with rippling surfaces and glancing highlights. These characteristics are to be found in the work of the Paduan sculptor Francesco Segala, a follower of Jacopo Sansovino and a contemporary of Campagna and Vittoria.

The present *Mars/Perseus* is related in style and facture to a pair of large bronze statuettes (c. 72 cm high) depicting *Hercules* and *Omphale* which are now normally attributed to Segala, on the basis of comparisons with his documented sculpture, e.g. a *St. Catherine* of 1564 in St. Antonio, Padua. *Hercules* and *Omphale* exist as a pair in the Kunstgewerbe Museum, Berlin, attached to andirons, and in the Museo Civico, Padua, as statuettes; while another separated pair is known too: Cologne, Kunstgewerbemuseum, *Omphale* alone; Christie's, London, 15 May, 1984, lot 138; *Hercules* alone: our Fig. 13.1).

There was probably once a pendant to this figure depicting *Venus,* or *Andromeda*, which has not yet been identified.

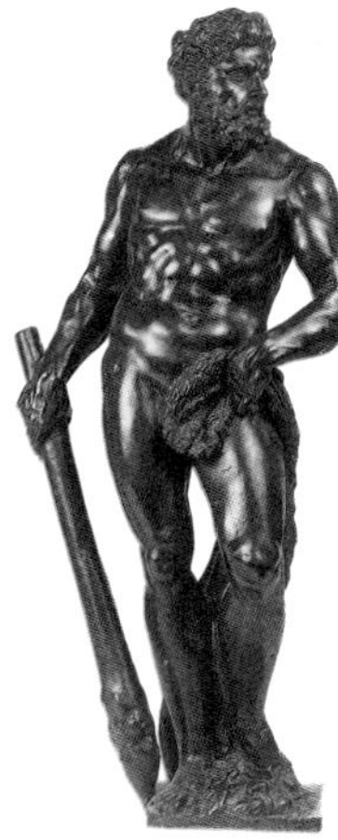

Figure 13.1
Hercules, Attributed to Francesco Segala
Courtesy of Christies', London

PLATE 14
Inkstand Supported on Three Putti
Bronze inkstand

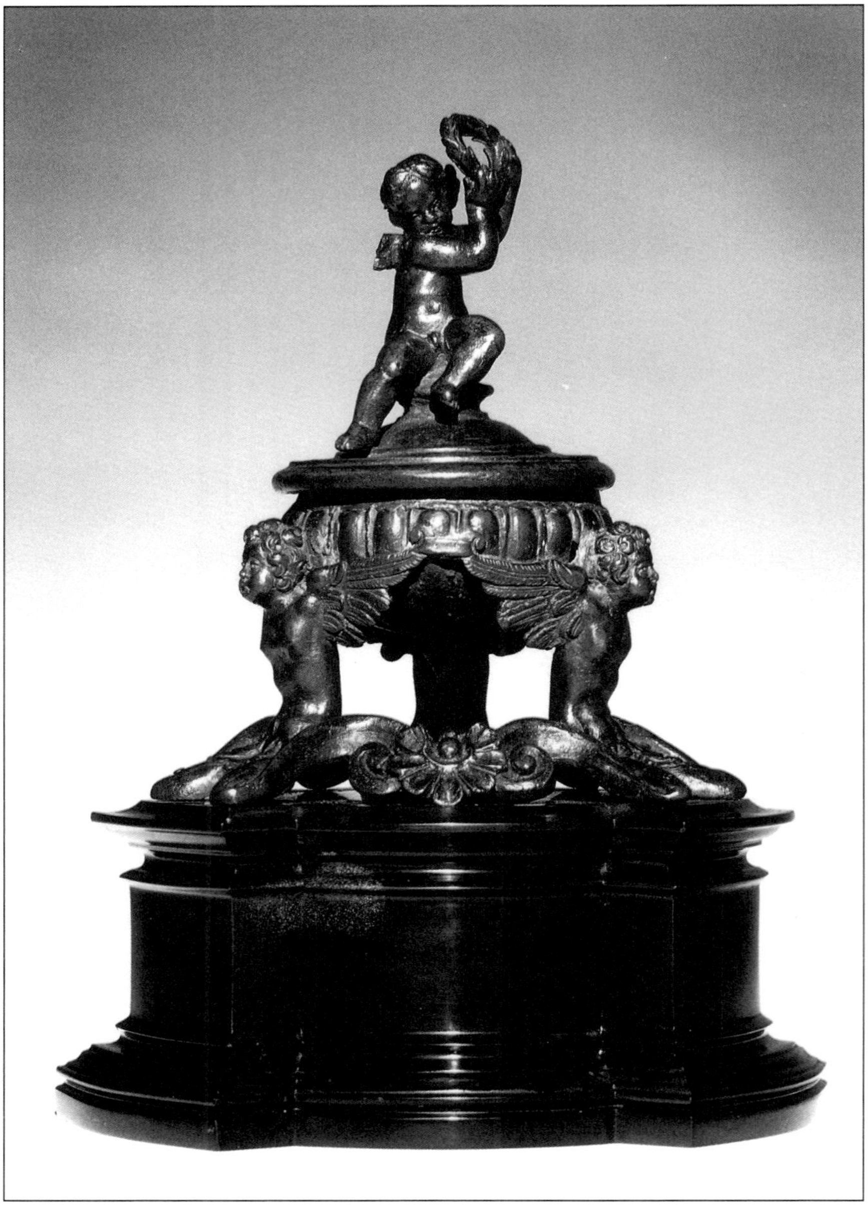

14

Inkstand Supported on Three Putti

Bronze inkstand

ITALIAN, VENICE OR VERONA,
LATE 16TH OR EARLY 17TH CENTURY

Workshop of Niccolo Roccatagliata, (active between 1593 and 1636), or Giuseppe de Levis (active between 1552 and 1611/14)

8¼ in. (21 cm) high; 7 in. (17.7 cm) diameter

1970.76
Gift of Miss Frick, 1970

CONDITION

The bowl has an upright brass rim lead-soldered on to its gadrooned shoulder, to adjust its diameter to fit under the rim of the later lid. The lid is very roughly cast, probably from a 17th century model.

PROVENANCE

Henry Joseph Pfungst Collection, London
Durlacher, London
J. P. Morgan Collection, New York
Duveen
Frick 1916
Helen Clay Frick

EXHIBITED

London, Victoria & Albert Museum, 1901–12, no. 350, lent by J. Pierpont Morgan

LITERATURE

Pfungst, 1899, no. 16 (as 'Venetian, late 16th century')
Bode, 1910, II, no. 196, plate CXXVIII
Pechstein, 1968, no. 90
Avery, 1981, p. 66, pl. 9

In the form of a gadrooned vase on a slender stem supported by three demi-figures of winged children united at the base by scroll-work. The cover is surmounted by a seated figure of a cupid holding up a wreath with both hands on his left side; his head and body are inclined to his right, he looks in front of him with a downward glance. — BODE, 1910: SCHOOL OF ALESSANDRO VITTORIA, *Inkstand supported on three putti, seated putto with wreath on lid.*

The bowl of the inkstand is characteristic of Venetian or Veronese products of around 1600. Such pieces have been traditionally associated with Roccatagliata, because of analogies with putti on some of his signed reliefs and statues (e.g. Berlin, Kunstgewerbemuseum; Pechstein, 1968, no. 90). Similar inkstands were however also produced in the foundry of Giuseppe (Joseph) de Levis and his relations in Verona. A cognate *Inkstand*, formerly (1938) in the collection of Sir John Martin-Harvey, was evidently signed (see Avery, 1981, p. 66, fig. 9): there, however, the tripod supports were harpies, rather than winged putti.

The volutes of strapwork that spring from the legs of the putti and curl around sideways to frame a floral motif figure frequently in Venetian functional bronzes such as andirons, but are also found in the work of de Levis (e.g. an *Inkstand with the Three Graces*, in the Metropolitan Museum: Avery, 1981, p. 59, pl. 11).

15

Equestrian Figure of Alberico Suardi

Bronze statuette

NORTH ITALIAN, MIDDLE OF THE 15TH CENTURY (OR MID-19TH CENTURY?)

Inscribed: MAGNUS ALBERICUS SUARDUS, in intaglio Lombard script running around three sides of the base

8⅞ x 6¾ x 3 in. (22.6 x 17.1 x 7.7 cm)

1970.104
Gift of Miss Frick, 1970

CONDITION

Coppery red metal with a black/green lacquer. The horse is cast separately from the base. Light is visible below the standing forehoof. The surfaces are all chiselled. The rear right leg of the horse has been broken and repaired with lead, or cast separately with a stepped joint.

PROVENANCE

Collection of Count Marenzi, Castello/Villa Secco Suardo, Lurano, near Bergamo
J. P. Morgan Collection, New York
Duveen
Frick 1916
Helen Clay Frick

EXHIBITED

London, Victoria & Albert Museum, 1901–12, no. 288, lent by J. Pierpont Morgan
London, Burlington House, Burlington Fine Arts Club, *Catalogue of a Collection of Italian Sculpture and Other Plastic Art of the Renaissance*, 1913, p. 65, no. 27, pl. XXXVIII

LITERATURE

Bode, 1910, I, no. 8, plate V, Introduction, pp. V–VI
Hovey, 1975, p. 114, ill. p. 115

Clad in a long loose garment with a close-fitting cap on his head and mounted on a small sturdy horse; he holds the reins in his left hand; his right rests upon his horse's neck. His name is inscribed on the pedestal in Gothic letters. — BODE, 1910: NORTH ITALIAN, ca. 1450 (ONE OF THE EARLIEST WORKS OF ITS KIND), *Equestrian figure of Alberico Suardi.*

The rider is clad in a long, flowing robe, with a wide collar and embroidered edging. It is held together by a button at the throat and then hangs freely down, opening to fall either side of the horse. He is wearing a floppy cap with a tassel. He is seated on a small 'U'-shaped saddle, which is visible under his coat-tails, and this is set on a large, oval, fringed saddle-cloth. There are two girths, at the front and back of the saddle, and horse brasses on either side of the rump, one being a rosette and the other like a plume (or inverted flame).

The rider is holding the end of a baton (which is broken off) in his right hand. His stirrups are formed with a hollow square below the sole of the foot.

The horse is not at all classical, but resembles those found on late medieval aquamaniles. It has a rather miserable tail, which may have been truncated from a casting sprue. It has a leather cap on its head, which is held on by a strap, and its ears protrude through holes. This curious feature may be a misinterpretation by the maker of the statuette of the prominent forelock of the horse that is shown on the medieval relief which served as his model.

Bode wrote in 1910 that this bronze, highly unusual for its presumably early date, was a 'free copy' of a relief from the front of a monument of the Gothic period to Alberico Magno de' Suardi in Santo Stefano, Bergamo, dating from the year of his death, 1309 (Fig. 15.1). Attributed to Ugo da Campione, this is preserved in the chapel ('chiesetta') of Castello Secco Suardo at Lurano outside Bergamo, which has been transformed into a villa, and in Bode's day belonged to a descendant, Count Marenzi. In his Introduction (pp. V–VI) he set out the circumstances and argued his attribution as follows:

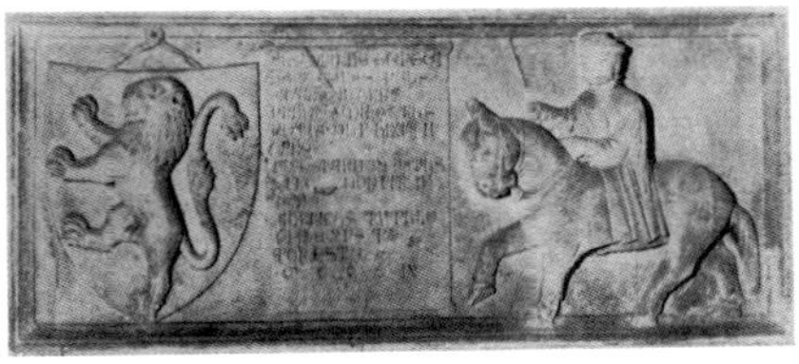

Figure 15.1
Tomb Relief, Ugo da Campione
Castello Secco Suardo at Lurano, Bergamo; photograph supplied by the author

> Totally different in character is another bronze in the collection, a small equestrian figure of semi-gothic style — the antique appearance being due to the fact that it is a free copy of a monument of the Gothic period. As the inscription on the base shows, the horseman is Alberico Magno de' Suardi. A monument was erected to this Bergamesque noble in S. Stefano at Bergamo in the year 1309. Only the front of the tomb is preserved; it is in a villa at Lurano near Bergamo belonging to a descendent of the family, Count Marenzi, who was also the former owner of this small bronze horseman. A relief on the tomb by the hand of the sculptor Ugo de' Campione (according to A.G. Meyer) represents Alberico and in composition closely resembles the bronze statuette; but the conventional Gothic style of the relief has vanished in the statuette, and in its place is seen a fresher and more naive naturalism which proves that the statuette undoubtedly belongs to the Quattrocento. Some equestrian monuments of this period and from the same neighborhood are preserved to us; they are almost life-size, in high relief, and altogether akin in character; one, dated 1436, is in the museum at Verona; the other, also from Verona, is now in the Berlin Museum. Like the small equestrian of Alberico, both depict a horseman in travelling garb, ambling along on a sturdy little steed. In simple and sane naturalism as well as in the absence of any exaggerated sentiment, these equestrian figures approach the contemporary compositions of the great Veronese, Antonio Pisano, without however equalling Pisano in power and delicate observation of nature. We see from the unskilled casting, as well as from the rough chisel-

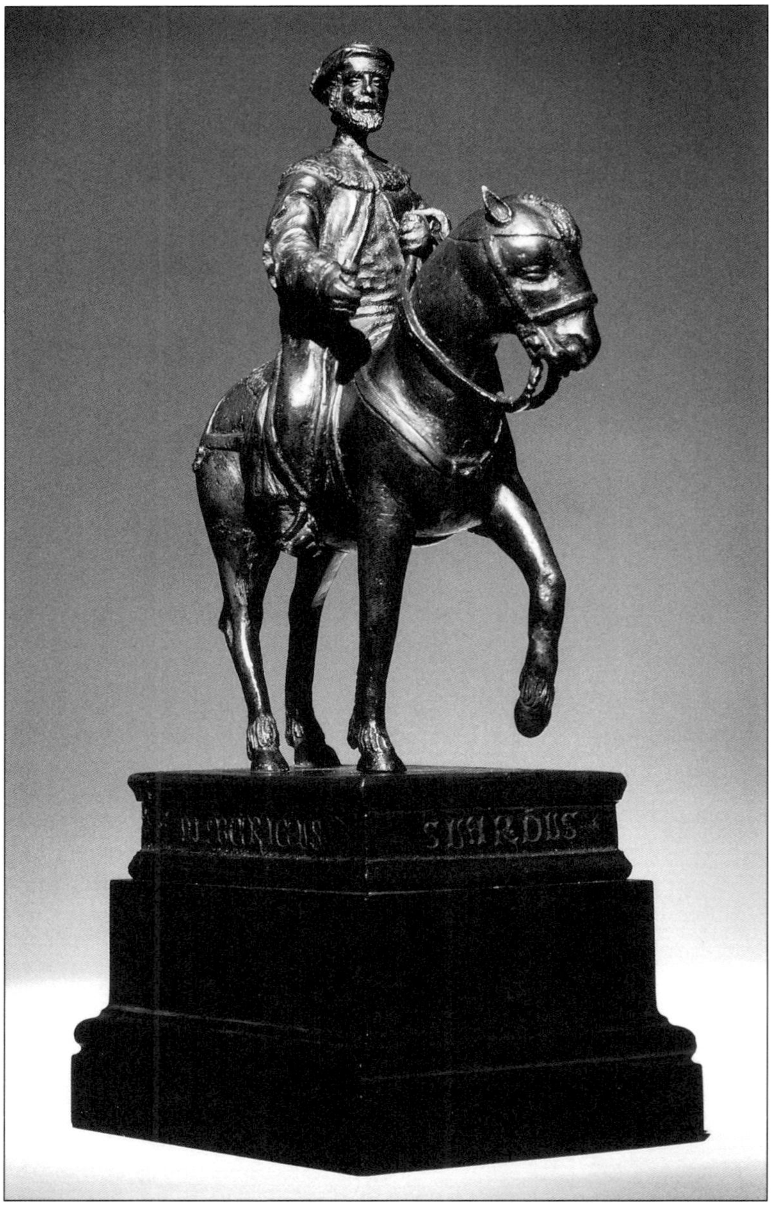

PLATE 15
Equestrian Figure of Alberico Suardi
Bronze statuette

ling, that this bronze statuette belongs to the earliest work of the kind in Northern Italy; we should ascribe it to about the year 1450.

Alberico Suardo was a prominent figure in Bergamo at the turn of the 13th/14th centuries. He was appointed Podestà of the city of Pavia in 1295. In the following year he was involved in violent riots between the Ghibelline faction that he headed and the Guelphs under the Colleoni family. The latter were defeated and exiled. He was subsequently appointed Consul of Justice and one of the Captains of the Società del Popolo di Bergamo, an internal peace-keeping force that was set up in the city to prevent a renewal of internecine feuding between its citizens.

His tomb front is carved with the following Latin inscription:

Moribus egregius constans probus notus in urbe
Prudens dilectus potens dum vixit in orbe.
Prole Suardorum natus nunc dormit in isto
Albericus tumulo cuius Christe memor esto. MCCCIX.
(Bortolo Belotti, *Storia di Bergamo* . . . , Bergamo, 1959, II, pp. 64–69, 77 note 48)

This may be roughly translated: '(He was) outstanding in behaviour, loyal, upright and well known in the city; and prudent, well-loved and powerful while he lived on earth. Born of the Suardo stock, Alberico now sleeps in this tomb. May Christ remember him. 1309.'

The inscription does not apply to Alberico the adjective *Magnus* (the Great) which is engraved on the base of the bronze statuette, though the list of virtues implies that he might be so regarded.

The statuette is an enigma. The image on the subject's tomb has been available ever since it was carved, and could have been copied at any time. Bode and others assumed that this took place in the 15th century, presumably in Bergamo, or at any rate in North Italy, where there was a tradition of bronze casting adequate to its production from a technical point of view.

However, the idea of a historical-revival statuette referring to a hero from the recent Middle Ages, and not from antiquity, would be unique among Renaissance bronzes. Parallels for the slightly unsure treatment of the horse may be seen on the reverses of some of Pisanello's bronze medals. Even so, the neatly classical architectural lines of the pedestal and the uncertain epigraphy and spacing of the inscription do lead to certain doubts as to its authenticity.

An origin in the mid-19th century, in the Romantic period of historical revival, cannot be ruled out. If this is the case, Wilhelm von Bode was evidently taken in, perhaps encouraged by the seemingly impeccable provenance from descendants of the subject, and fascinated by the art-historical interest of its dependence on the earlier image.

16
Fantastic Composition, with a Cockerel, a Lion, and a Snake

Bronze group

NORTH ITALIAN or SOUTH GERMAN,
POSSIBLY 17TH–19TH CENTURY

4 x 4¼ x 4 in. (10 x 10.8 x 10 cm)

1970.85
Gift of Miss Frick, 1970

CONDITION

There are holes into the hollow bodies of lion and cockerel. The animals are matt-punched, even underneath, with feathers and scales obsessively inscribed.

PROVENANCE

J. P. Morgan Collection, New York
Duveen
Frick 1916
Helen Clay Frick

EXHIBITED

London, Victoria & Albert Museum, 1901–12, no. 384, lent by J. Pierpont Morgan

LITERATURE

Bode, 1910, I, no. 66, fig. on p. 19

A cock, a lion and a serpent, on a heavy marble base. The cock and the lion placed side by side, the serpent between them coiled around the two bodies; its head turned towards the lion with its deadly fangs exposed. It appears to have just attacked the beast who raises its head, turning it in a contorted attitude with an expression of mortal terror and agony. — BODE, 1910: WORKSHOP OF RICCIO, *Fantastic Composition.*

The bronze is hard to fault in terms of facture and patina, *but* what was it for? And what did it mean? If it *is* old, it is presumably of Venetian or South German origin, dating from 1580–1620.

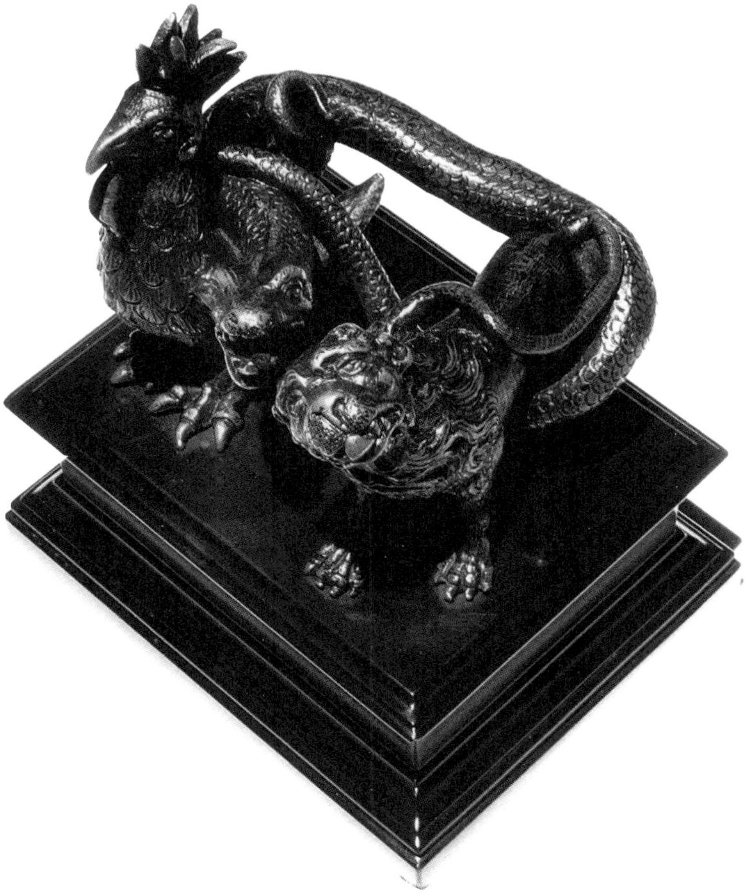

PLATE 16
Fantastic Composition, with a Cockerel, a Lion, and a Snake
Bronze group

PLATE 17
An Allegory of Winter, a Bearded Man with Vulture and Serpents
Bronze group

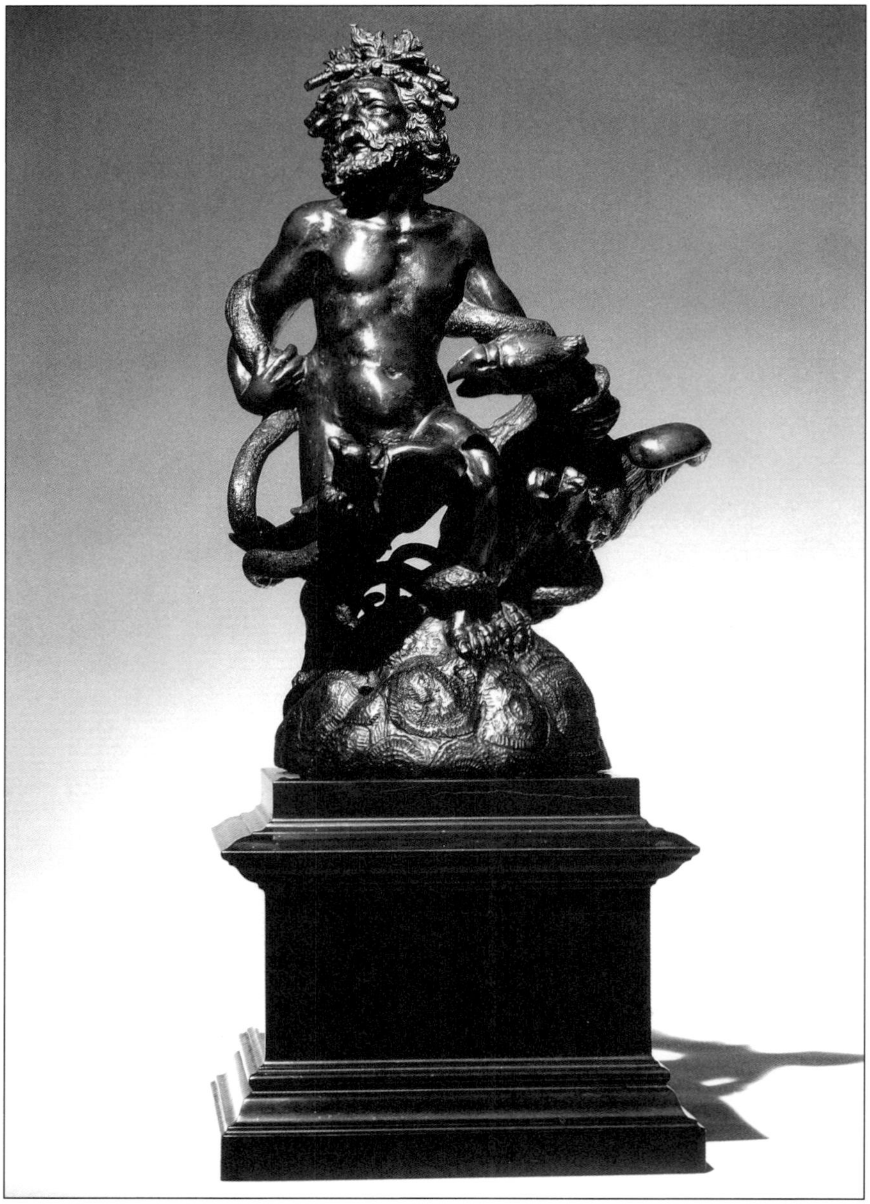

17

An Allegory of Winter, a Bearded Man with Vulture and Serpents

Bronze group

NORTH ITALIAN or GERMAN, LATE 16TH OR EARLY 17TH CENTURY

11¼ x 5½ x 5½ in. (28.6 x 14 x 14 cm)

1970.97
Gift of Miss Frick, 1970

CONDITION
There is heavy matt-punching over the base, to represent ground. The modelling of the figures is 'lumpy,' with rather crude details e.g. thumb nails.

PROVENANCE
J. P. Morgan Collection, New York
Duveen
Frick 1916
Helen Clay Frick

LITERATURE
Bode, 1910, I, no. 207, plate CXLIV

Nude figure of a man standing on a rock, his head turned towards his right shoulder. He grasps with his left hand the neck of a vulture which stands beside him; serpents are coiled around the bird and around the body of the man who grasps the coils of one of the reptiles with his right hand. The figure of the man is grotesque in drawing, the stunted body being surmounted by a head of massive proportion with thick hair and beard. In the hair are tongues of flame while the brow of the figure is adorned with a garland of reeds or small branches partly consumed by the flames. This figure probably represents one of the elements, i.e. Fire. — BODE, 1910: VENETIAN, 16TH CENTURY, *Bearded man with vulture, serpents.*

18

An Allegory of Autumn, a Child with Vulture and Serpents

Bronze group

NORTH ITALIAN or GERMAN, LATE 16TH OR EARLY 17TH CENTURY

11¼ x 5½ x 5½ in. (28.6 x 14 x 14 cm)

1970.99
Gift of Miss Frick, 1970

CONDITION
There is heavy matt-punching over the base, to represent ground. The modelling of the figures is 'lumpy' with rather crude details e.g. thumb nails.

PROVENANCE
J. P. Morgan Collection, New York
Duveen
Frick 1916
Helen Clay Frick

LITERATURE
Bode, 1910, II, no. 208, plate CXLV
Pendant to Catalogue No. 17 (1970.97)

He grasps the Vulture's neck with his right hand and the coils of the serpents with his left. His head, which is wreathed with fruit, flowers and foliage is thrown back and slightly inclined to the left shoulder. This figure, if its pendent represents the element 'Fire,' should be designated 'Earth.' — BODE, 1910: VENETIAN, 16TH CENTURY, *Child with vulture and serpents.*

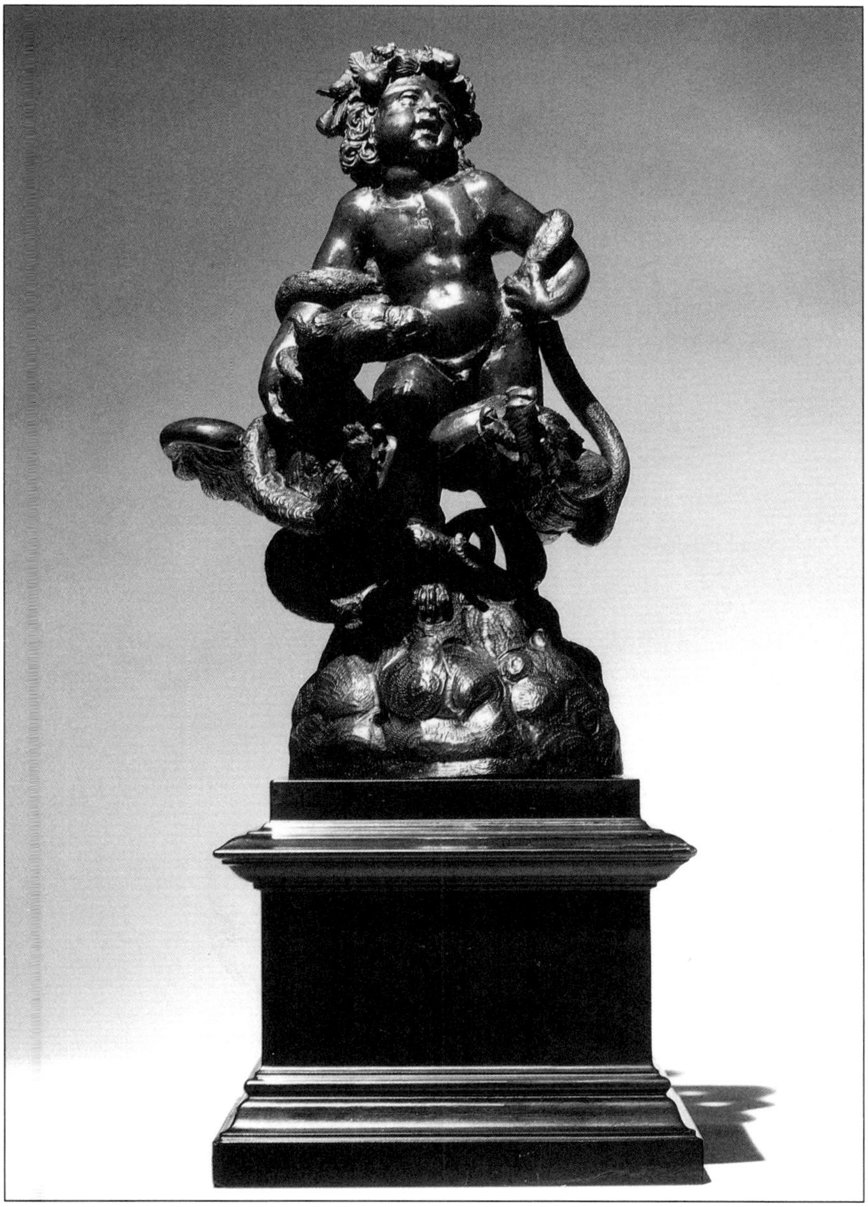

PLATE 18
An Allegory of Autumn, a Child with Vulture and Serpents
Bronze group

PLATE 19
Sphinx
Bronze statuette

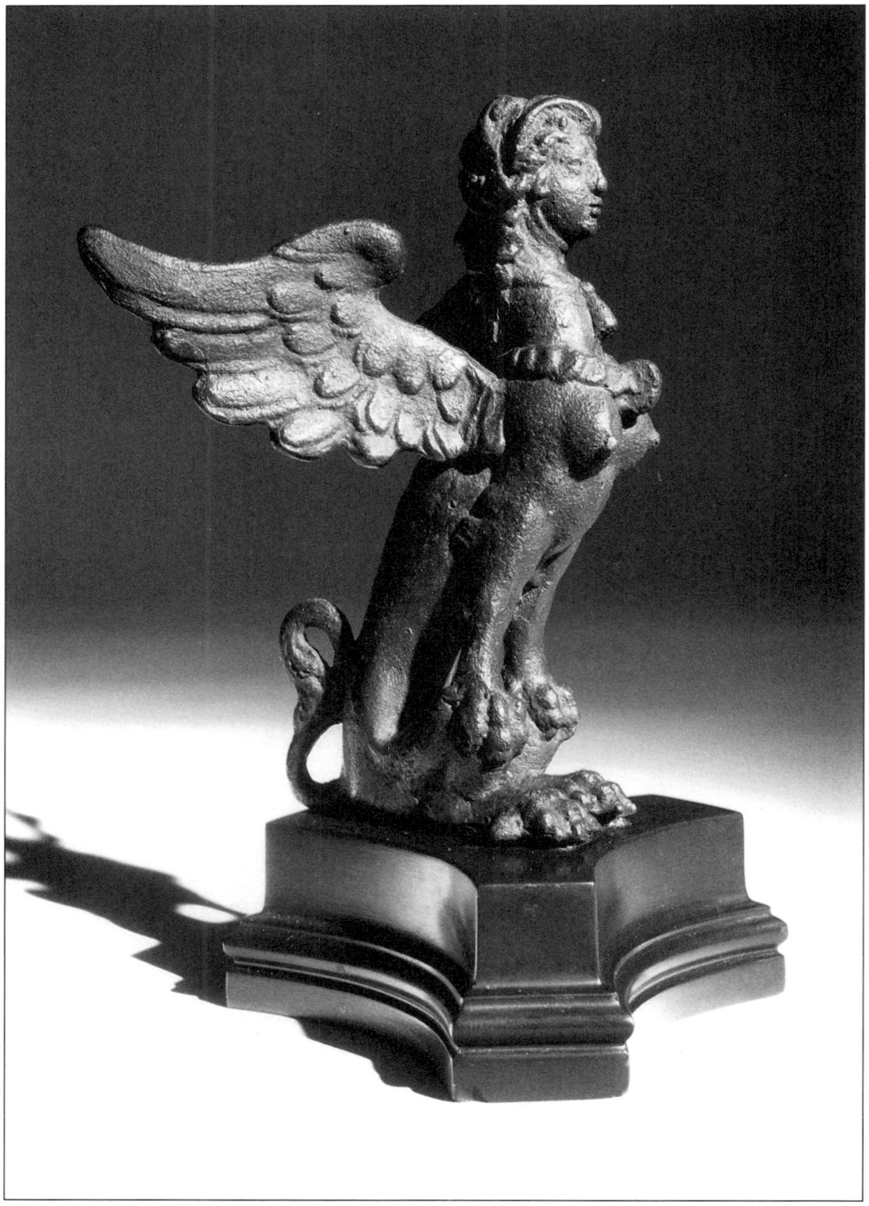

19

Sphinx

Bronze statuette

ITALIAN, FLORENCE, 16TH CENTURY (OR LATER)

Formerly attributed to Benvenuto Cellini (1500–1572)

4¾ x 3⅞ x 3¼ in. (12 x 9.8 x 8.2 cm)

1970.86

Gift of Miss Frick, 1970. Once kept in the library bookcase at "Eagle Rock," Prides Crossing, Massachusetts.

CONDITION

The bronze has a uniformly plastery/sandy surface with no chasing, which suggests that it is an aftercast. There are flaws in stomach. The wings are plain behind.

P M 169 in red paint

34.1953 in red paint

PROVENANCE

S. Bardini Collection, Florence

J. P. Morgan Collection, New York

Duveen

Frick 1916

Helen Clay Frick

EXHIBITED

London, Victoria & Albert Museum, 1901–12, no. 342, lent by J. Pierpont Morgan

LITERATURE

Bode, 1910, I no. 122, fig. on p. 5, vol. II

Foot or support for a coffer or cabinet in the form of a female-headed griffin with outspread wings; around the neck is a bell suspended from a thin chain. Similar to the feet of the casket ascribed to Cellini in the Galitzin Collection. — BODE, 1910: BENVENUTO CELLINI, FLORENTINE SCHOOL, *Sphinx.*

Bode's identification of the monster as a griffin is inaccurate for it should have an eagle's head combined with the lion's body: the human female head defines it as a classic sphinx.

There is no reason to associate the model with Cellini, and though it appears to date from the 16th century, it may not even be from Florence, for the wings look Venetian. In any case, in view of the indifferent quality of casting, which suggests that this is a late aftercast (surmoulage), it is impossible to define the origins of the lost original. It may well have served as a support at the corner of a casket or cabinet, or as a corner finial, and could also have been cast in precious metal rather than bronze.

20

Leaping Hound

Bronze statuette

ITALIAN, FLORENCE, LATE 16TH CENTURY

Giovanni Bandini (1540–1599)

7⅝ x 3¼ x 12⅛ in. (19.4 x 8.3 x 30.8 cm)

1970.71
Gift of Miss Frick, 1970

CONDITION

Heavily cast, if not solid. Smooth, compact, flawless surface. Brownish patina, with dark lacquer in hollows. Plugs in back and belly. Tip of tail docked.

PROVENANCE

Hoentschel Collection, Paris
J. P. Morgan Collection, New York
Duveen
Frick 1916
Helen Clay Frick

LITERATURE

Bode, 1910, II, no. 218, plate CLV, Introduction, p. XLI
Middeldorf, 1929, pp. 481–518; reprinted 1979/80, pp. 77–92
Pope-Hennessy, 1963/1968, pp. 193–94
Hovey, 1975, pp. 26–27
Firenze e la Toscana dei Medici nell' Europa del Cinquecento *Palazzo Vecchio: committenza e collezionismo medicei 1537–1610*, Florence, 1980, no. 712
Blanco and Lorente, 1981, no. 265, pp. 191–92, pl. 18

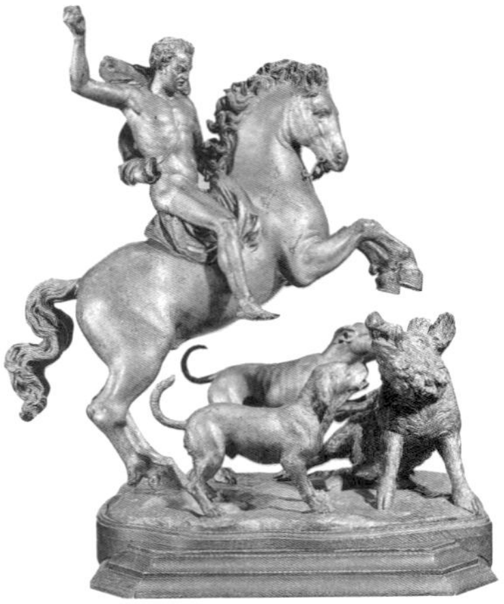

Figure 20.1
Meleager Hunting the Boar, Giovanni Bandini; bronze
Prado Museum, Madrid

Its forepaws in the air, its tail stiffened, ears thrown back and jaws open, about to make a spring. — BODE, 1910: FLEMISH, 17TH CENTURY, *A Hound.*

Previously regarded as 'Flemish 17th century,' the *Leaping Hound* has been recognized by the author as a work by the celebrated sculptor Giovanni Bandini of Castello (near Florence). It is virtually identical in composition with one of the two hounds in a bronze group showing *Meleager hunting the Boar* which is now in the Prado Museum, Madrid (having descended from the Spanish Royal Collection in the Real Palacio).

That magnificent group (Fig. 20.1; 30¾ in. (78 cm) high) shows Meleager on a rearing horse, and the boar seated at bay (as in the ancient marble sculpture of the Uffizi Gallery). It was perceptively recognized by the late Professor Ulrich Middeldorf as being identical with one described by Raffaello Borghini in his book *Il Riposo* (Florence, 1584, pp. 639–40) as being in production by Bandini for the Duke of Urbino at the time of writing: "(Giovanni Bandini) di presente, prepara di gitar di bronzo una figura, que essendo sopra un cavallo, que salta, ferisce un cinghiale, e vi sono due cani l'uno que presa la fiera per un'orechio, e l'altro in atto di abbaiare: la qual si spera che sera bellisima . . ." ('who at present is preparing to cast into bronze a figure

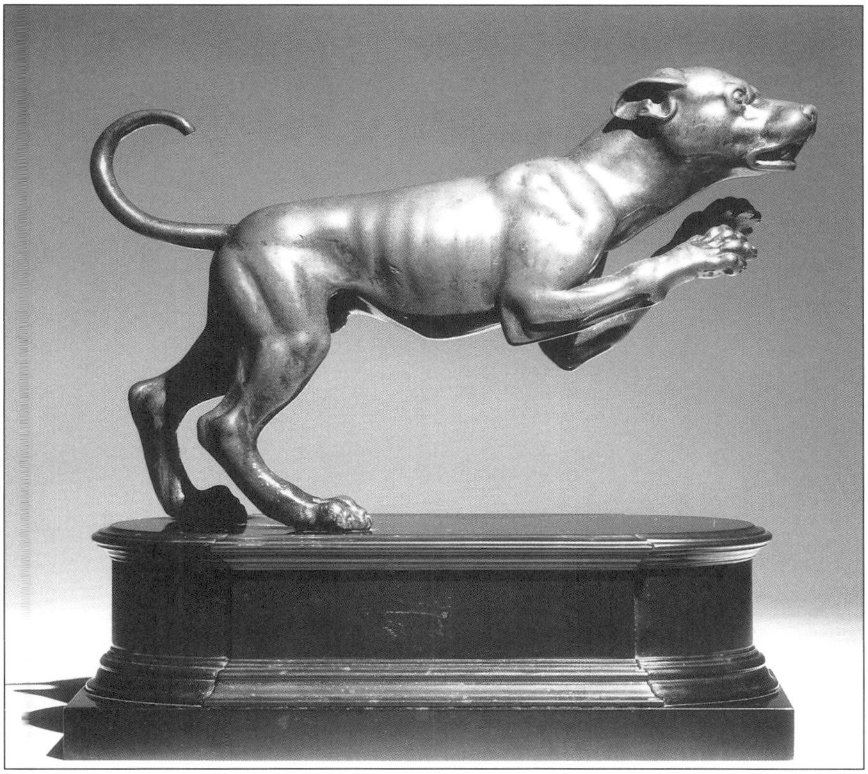

PLATE 20
Leaping Hound
Bronze statuette

mounted on a rearing horse who is attacking a boar, and there are two hounds, one catching the beast by its ear, and the other in the act of barking; it is hoped that it will turn out to be very beautiful').

The present hound is a duplicate of the first one described by Borghini, which is unfortunately barely visible in the standard photograph of the group in Madrid, as it is on the far side, and masked by the boar. It is approximately one third smaller, and comes from a similar group of a hunt, presumably, though not necessarily, with a boar as its prey.

The attribution to Bandini is corroborated by the appearance of a similar, boldly modelled, hound seated beside a marble statue of Meleager, which is signed and dated 1598 (recently on the art market in London, with Colnaghi's in 1982 and Cyril Humphris in 1990).

21

Diana

Bronze statuette

ITALIAN, FLORENCE, SECOND HALF OF 17TH CENTURY

Ferdinando Tacca (1619–1686)

15¾ x 5½ x 3½ in. (39.4 x 14 x 8.9 cm)

1970.84
Gift of Miss Frick, 1970

CONDITION

The base-plate and pyramidal block are cast integrally. Diana and the hound are attached mechanically. The bronze is a yellowish alloy with thin black lacquer.

PROVENANCE

Alphonse Kann Collection, Paris
J. P. Morgan Collection, New York
Duveen
Frick 1916
Helen Clay Frick

EXHIBITED

London, Victoria & Albert Museum, 1901–12, no. 1153, lent by J. Pierpont Morgan

LITERATURE

Bode, 1910, II, no. 166, plate CXV
Hovey, 1975, p. 59, ill. p. 59
Radcliffe, 1976, p. 23 note 21

OTHER EXAMPLES

Formerly in the Hermitage, St. Petersburg (Leningrad), then in the collection of Baron Hatvany, London (sold Christie's, 25 June 1980, lot 24)

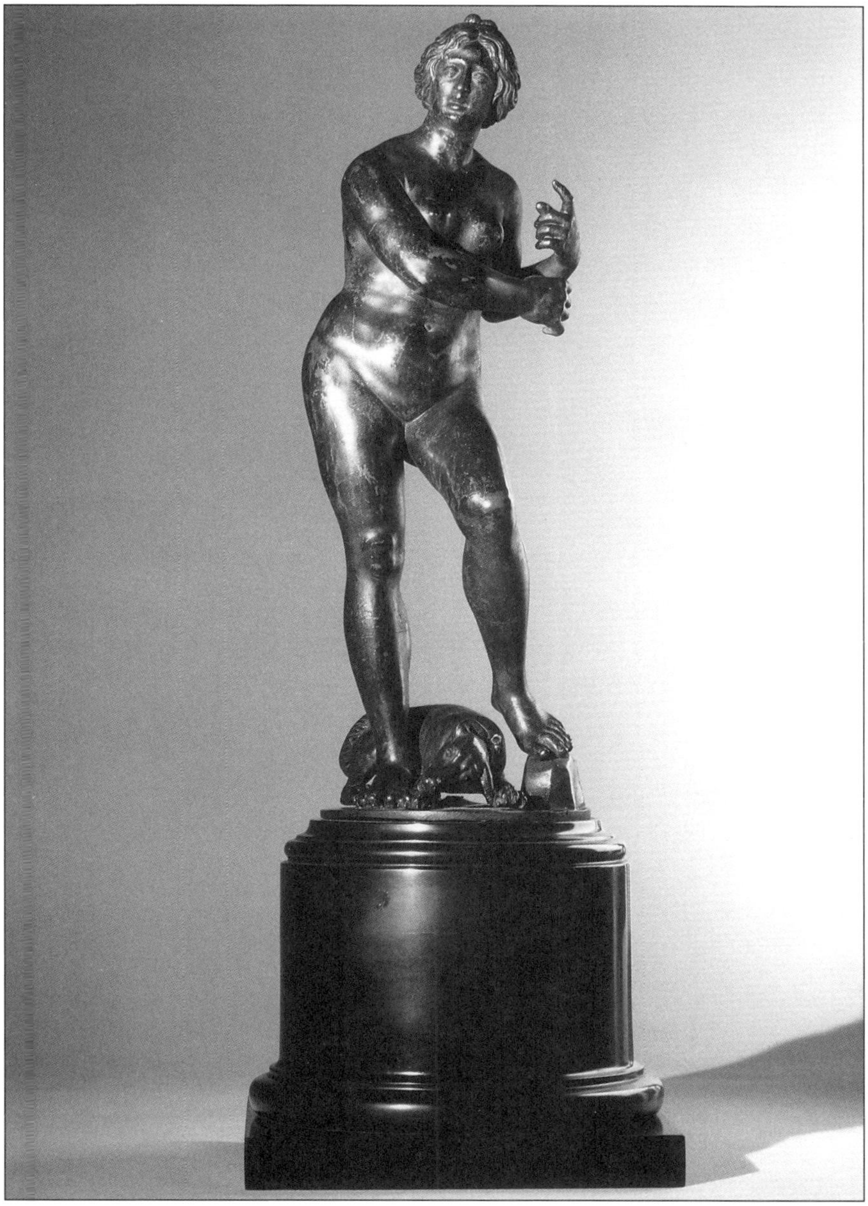

PLATE 21
Diana
Bronze statuette

Full-length standing nude figure of a woman of fleshy form, seen in full face and characterized as Diana by the hound which crouches beside her right foot. The upper part of the body slightly turned to the left, the head follows the inclination of the body; she looks straight before her with parted lips and down-ward glance of the eyes. The thick hair, waved over the temples, covers the ears and is gathered high at the back of the head in a small knot. The left hand is raised and supported by the right arm which is crossed over the body at the waist. The left foot rests upon a low support set in the small round base upon which the figure is placed. — BODE, 1910: FLEMISH, C. 1650, *Diana.*

The model forms a pair with an *Apollo* (15⅝ in. high) formerly in the collection of David Daniels, New York, and now in the Los Angeles County Museum of Art (The Minneapolis Institute of Arts, *Sculpture from the Daniels Collection*, Exhibition Catalogue, 1979–80, no. 25, entry by A. F. Radcliffe; our Fig. 21.1).

Bode's description as 'Flemish, c. 1650' reflects the ignorance that has been general until recently about bronzes produced in Florence during the early Baroque period: the date he suggested is, however, creditably accurate.

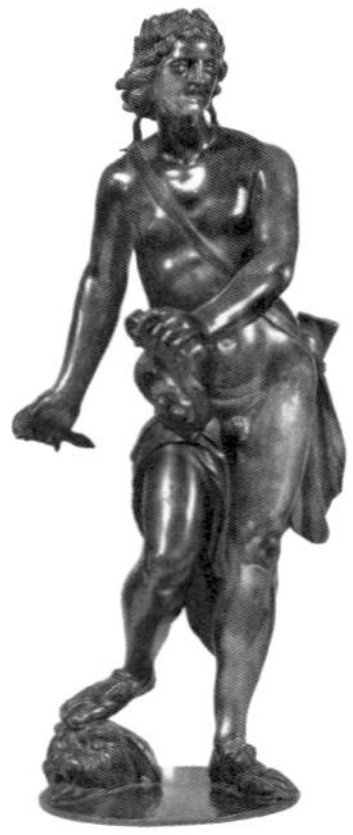

Figure 21.1
Apollo, Ferdinando Tacca; Italian, 16th century; bronze
James E. Clark Bequest, Los Angeles County Museum of Art (M.87.119.25)

These figures of both female and male nudes are absolutely characteristic of the work of Ferdinando Tacca, a second generation follower of Giambologna and Francavilla. He was in the habit of developing their very serpentine compositions into more frontal and pictorial poses.

A distant, but perceptible, influence from Venetian bronze statuettes off fire-dogs, which are of about the same size, is also to be felt, and this is a reflection of the arrival in the Florentine ambiente of Tiziano Aspetti in 1599, and his work there until his death in Pisa in 1606.

22

Old Man Riding a Goat

Bronze statuette

ITALIAN, FLORENCE, MIDDLE OF THE 17TH CENTURY
Attributed to Ferdinando Tacca (1619–1686),
formerly attributed to Pietro Tacca (1578–1640)
6½ x 5⅜ in. (16.5 x 13.5 cm)

1973.18
Gift of Miss Frick, 1973

CONDITION
The cast is in raw coppery metal, naturally oxidated. The right horn of the goat is broken off. Its hair is heavily matt-punched.

PROVENANCE
Henry Joseph Pfungst Collection, London
Durlacher, London
J. P. Morgan Collection, New York
Duveen
Frick 1916
Helen Clay Frick

EXHIBITED
London, Victoria & Albert Museum, 1901–12, no. 292, lent by J. Pierpont Morgan

LITERATURE
Pfungst, 1889, no. 53 (as 'French or North Italian (Verona), late 16th or early 17th century')
Bode, 1910, II, no. 157, fig. on p. 14, vol. II, Introduction, p. XXXIII
Hovey, 1975, p. 114, ill. p. 114

The animal prances forward; the old man holds its left horn and presses his knees against its flanks. He turns his head and glances to the left, laughing. A small round cap rests on his long hair. His legs and the upper part of his body are bare; a loose drapery falling from his left shoulder and passing around his waist, touches the ground on the off side of the goat. — BODE, 1910: PIETRO TACCA, FLORENTINE SCHOOL, *Old Man Riding a Goat.*

In his Introduction (p. XXXIII) Bode wrote of this group as follows:

> Among Gian Bologna's numerous pupils and assistants Pietro Tacca was the one prominently associated with the artist in his last works, and in consequence was himself entrusted with the execution of different great monuments. He is credited with a number of small bronzes of fantastic figures which are often unpleasing and spasmodic in effect, though sometimes designedly so, for these small groups, which are mostly met with singly, appear to depict a great Witches' Sabbath; emaciated witches, tailors and other lean figures, who gallop wildly on goats accompanied by demons. One such group, in the Pierpont Morgan Collection, has always been set down to Pietro Tacca; and the fantastic masks on his bronze fountains in the Piazza dell'Annunziata in Florence render this attribution probable.

PLATE 22
Old Man Riding a Goat
Bronze statuette

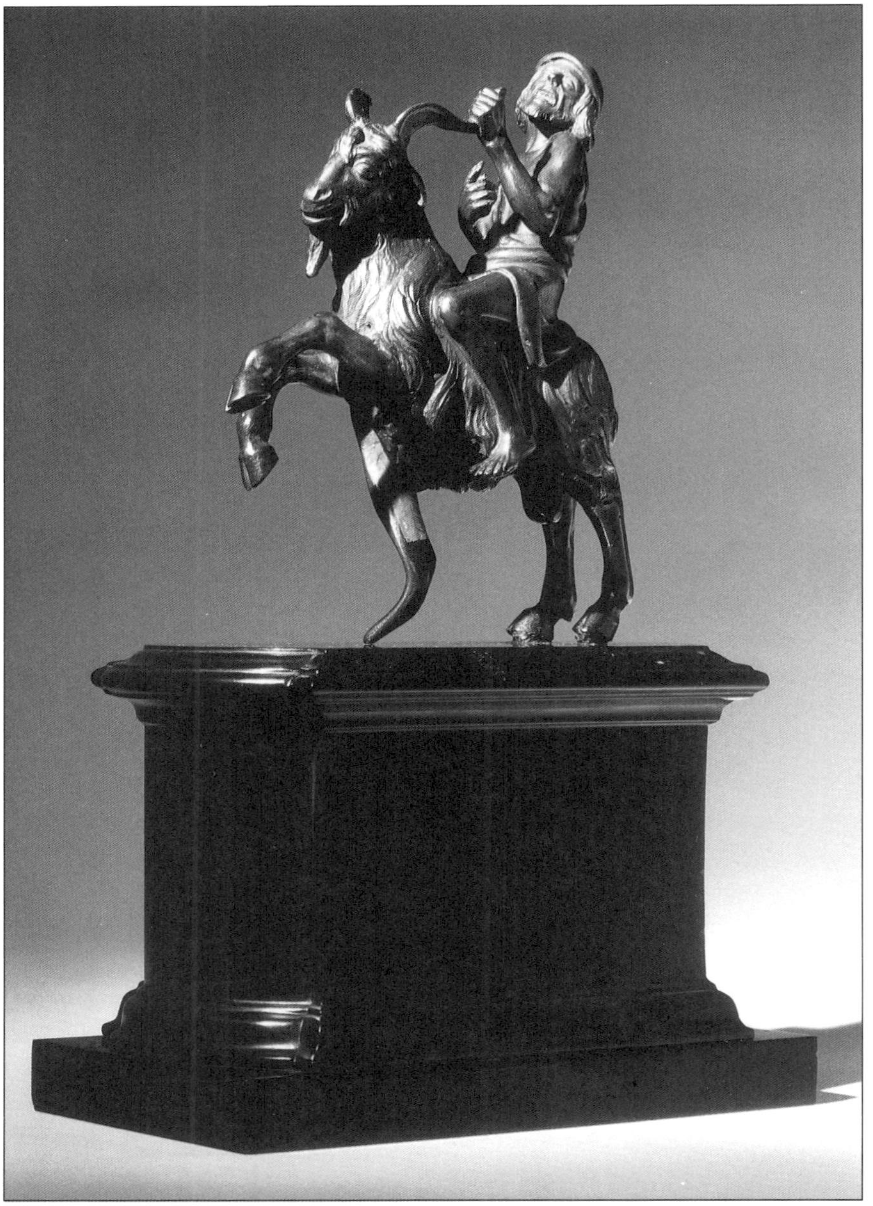

This bronze statuette is related in its bizarre subject and style to one sold from the Hon. Hanning Phillips collection (Christie's, London, 15 December 1982, lot 21[illegible]), which was accompanied by a couple of cavorting devils (Fig. 22.1).

Formerly attributed to Pietro Tacca (Bode, 1910, and Lewy, 1929), with whom such bizarre figures were traditionally associated, they were expunged from his oeuvre by Lo Vullo Bianchi (1931) and Torriti (1975, p. 75). They were first given to Pietro's son Ferdinando by the present author in the Christie's catalogue entry of 1982:

> The attribution of these extraordinary bronzes to Ferdinando Tacca is based on stylistic comparisons with recently attributed equestrian groups including various animals: a *Bull-hunt* and *Boar-hunt* in Budapest (J. Balogh, *Katalog der Ausländischen Bildwerke des Museums der Bildenden Kunste in Budapest*, Budapest, 1975 nos. 242–3: there attributed incorrectly to Fanelli); and a similar *Bull-hunt* paired with a *Lion-hunt* in Chatsworth, other individual examples of which are known. Of these, the *Lion-hunt* was first specifically associated with Ferdinando in the catalogue of the Giambologna exhibition in Vienna (1978–9, no. 166).
>
> The vivacious rearing goat is ultimately derived from Giambologna's animal sculptures and is closely analogous to the fleeing boar in the Budapest group, as is its rider with those in Budapest and Chatsworth. Other analogies for the figures are to be found in Ferdinando's published *oeuvre*, from the *Martyrdom of St. Stephen* in Florence, to the *Diana and a Satyr* in Minneapolis (A. F. Radcliffe, 'Ferdinando Tacca, the Missing Link in Florentine Baroque Bronzes,' in *Kunst des Barock in der Toskana*, Munich, 1976, pp. 14–23, especially figs. 1, 9). A 'landscaped' base characteristic of Ferdinando would have served to relate the three components to one another in a sensible narrative sequence.

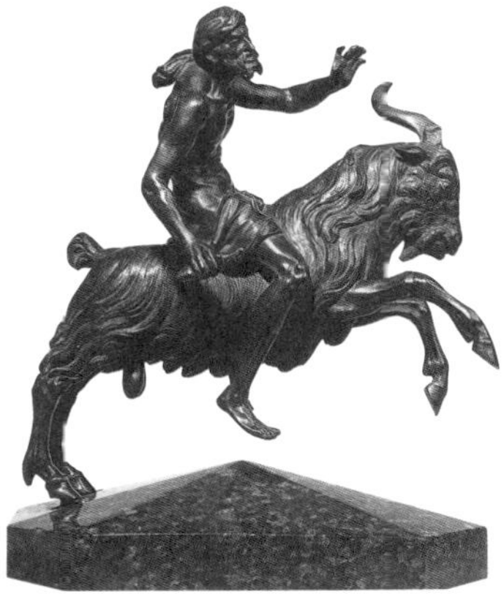

Figure 22.1
Man Riding a Goat, Florentine, Middle of 17th century; bronze
Courtesy of Christies', London (15 December, 1982)

The bizarre subject of both groups has overtones of witchcraft, and recalls an engraving currently thought to have been designed by Giulio Romano, called in Italian, *Lo Stregozzo* (Fig. 22.2; Bruce Davis, *Mannerist Prints: International Style in the 16th Century*, Los Angeles County Museum of Art, 1951, pp. 110–13). This shows a frightening scene of a witches' sabbath, set in a marsh, with a trumpeting boy riding on a leaping goat, and two crouching elderly figures riding skeletons of quadrupeds. It is characteristic of the generation of Ferdinando Tacca to refer to pictorial sources for their narrative groups, or to create compositions that are pictorial, in the sense of being spread out across a single plane, rather than to be viewed from all angles, as had been the aim of his predecessor, Giambologna.

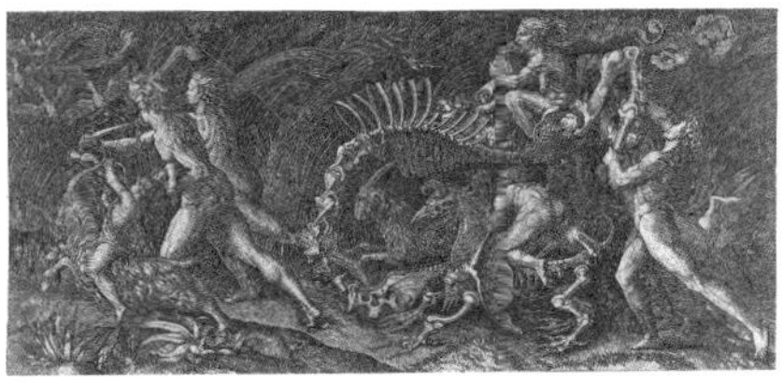

Figure 22.2
Lo Stregozzo, Marcantonio Raimondi; Engraving
Collection of Mary Stansbury Ruiz, Los Angeles County Museum of Art (M.88 91.36)

PLATE 23
Mercury
Bronze

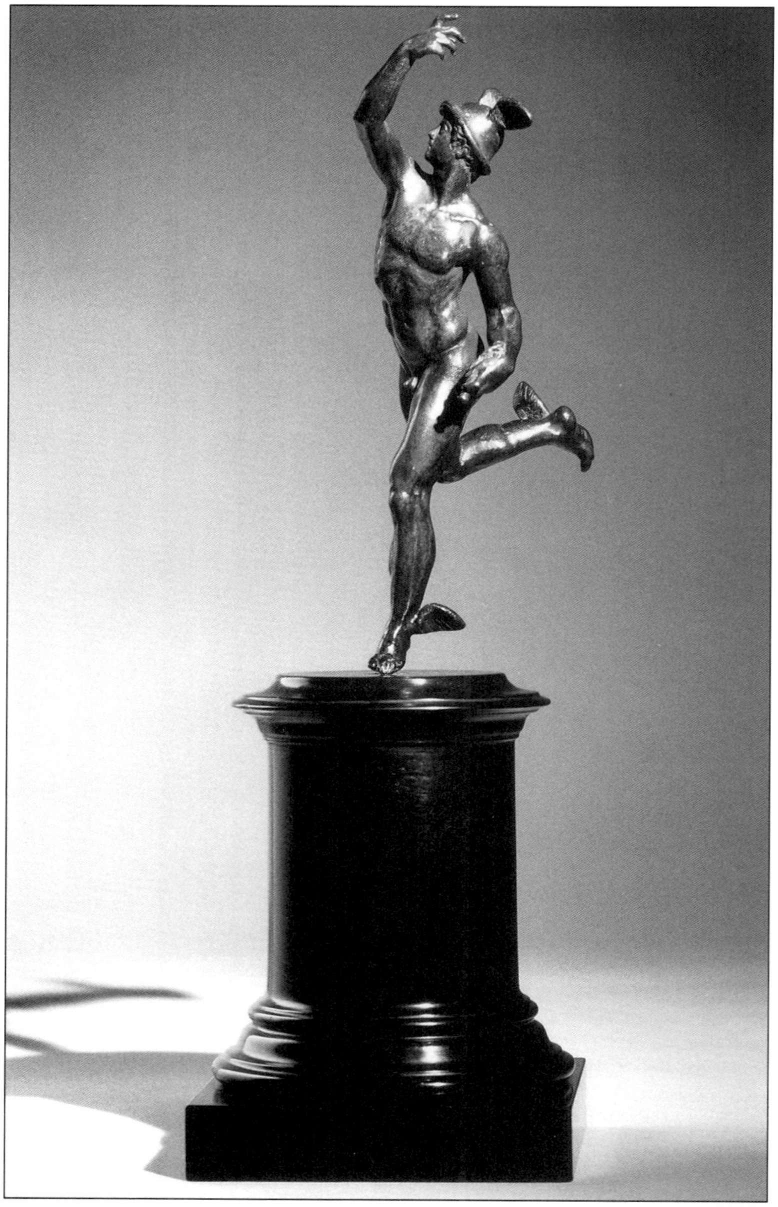

23

Mercury

Bronze

ITALIAN, FLORENCE or ROME, 18TH CENTURY

After Giovanni Bologna (1529–1608)

7 13/16 x 2 x 5½ in. (19.8 x 5.1 x 14 cm)

1970.80
Gift of Miss Frick, 1970. Once kept in the library bookcase at "Eagle Rock," Prides Crossing, Massachusetts.

CONDITION
Fair quality in details, possibly an 18th-century cast. The *caduceus* is broken off.

PROVENANCE
J. P. Morgan Collection, New York
Duveen
Frick 1916
Helen Clay Frick

EXHIBITED
London, Victoria & Albert Museum, 1901–12, no. 398, lent by J. Pierpont Morgan

LITERATURE
Bode, 1910, II, no. 154, plate CX
Dhanens, 1956, pp. 129–30, catalogue no. XV
Keutner, 1984, pp. 27–34, no. 5
Avery, 1987, p. 256, catalogue no. 34, pls. 14, 15, 121, 124, 238

OTHER EXAMPLES
too numerous to cite

Full-length nude, the head seen in profile turned to the right, wearing the winged helmet. The right arm raised above the head, the left foot poised lightly on the ground supporting the weight of the body; the right leg, with knee bent, raised high in the air. The feet are winged, the pose is indicative of a rapid forward movement. — BODE, 1910: FLORENTINE, 17TH CENTURY, AFTER GIAN BOLOGNA, *Mercury.*

This statuette is a reduction from Giambologna's famous composition, the *Medici Mercury*, the original bronze statue (1.70 m high) of which was cast in 1580

It was sent to Rome as the centerpiece of a fountain in the gardens of Villa Medici It was returned to Florence in 1780, and so would have been available to Roman sculptors throughout the period when this particular cast was probably produced. Casts (50.5 cm high) were made for example by the Roman foundryman Giacomo Zoffoli (c. 1731–1785) and they date from c. 1763.

24
Cupid Shooting
Bronze statuette

ITALIAN, 16TH CENTURY
After the Antique
3½ x 1½ x 13/16 in. (8.9 x 3.8 x 2.2 cm)

1970.87
Gift of Miss Frick, 1970

CONDITION
Bow and arrow and fingers of left hand now missing. Black lacquer.

PROVENANCE
Henry Joseph Pfungst Collection, London
Durlacher, London
J. P. Morgan Collection, New York
Duveen
Frick 1916
Helen Clay Frick

EXHIBITED
London, Victoria & Albert Museum, 1901–12, no. 337, lent by J. Pierpont Morgan

LITERATURE
Pfungst, 1899, no. 23 (as 'Attributed to Donatello, Florentine, middle 15th century')
Bode/Draper, 1908/80, p. 7, fig. 8 (as 'Handle of a bell. After Donatello')
Bode, 1910, II, no. 178, fig. on p. 20, vol. II

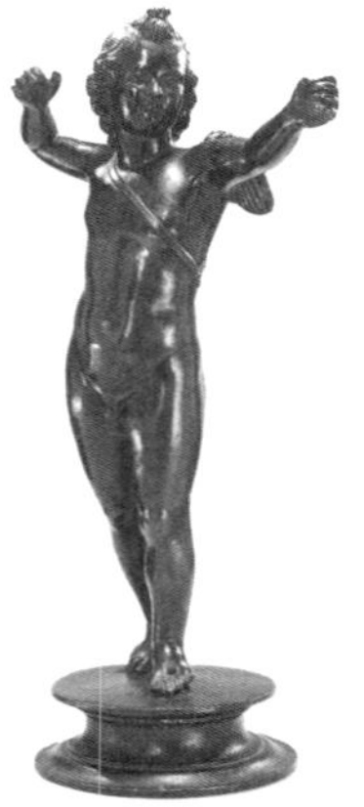

Figure 24.1
Cupid Drawing his Bow, Studio of Pier Jacopo Alari Bonacolsi, named Antico; first quarter of 16th century; bronze, black lacquer patina
Collection of Rijksmuseum, Amsterdam (RBK 1693b, catalogue nr. 663)

Nude standing winged figure, the head thrown back and turned towards the left shoulder. The left arm raised, the right bent at the elbow. From the position of the arms it is evident that the figure originally held the bow and was about to let fly the arrow. Found upon a composition by Donatello. — BODE, 1910: ITALIAN, 17TH CENTURY, *Cupid.*

The excellently modelled and rotund anatomy reminds one of Antico (Fig. 24.1) or the Mantuan school of pseudo-Antiquities. The facial features are delicately modelled. It has a similar motif to a statuette in the Victoria and Albert Museum, but is slimmer and more elegant. It is not particularly 'Donatellesque.'

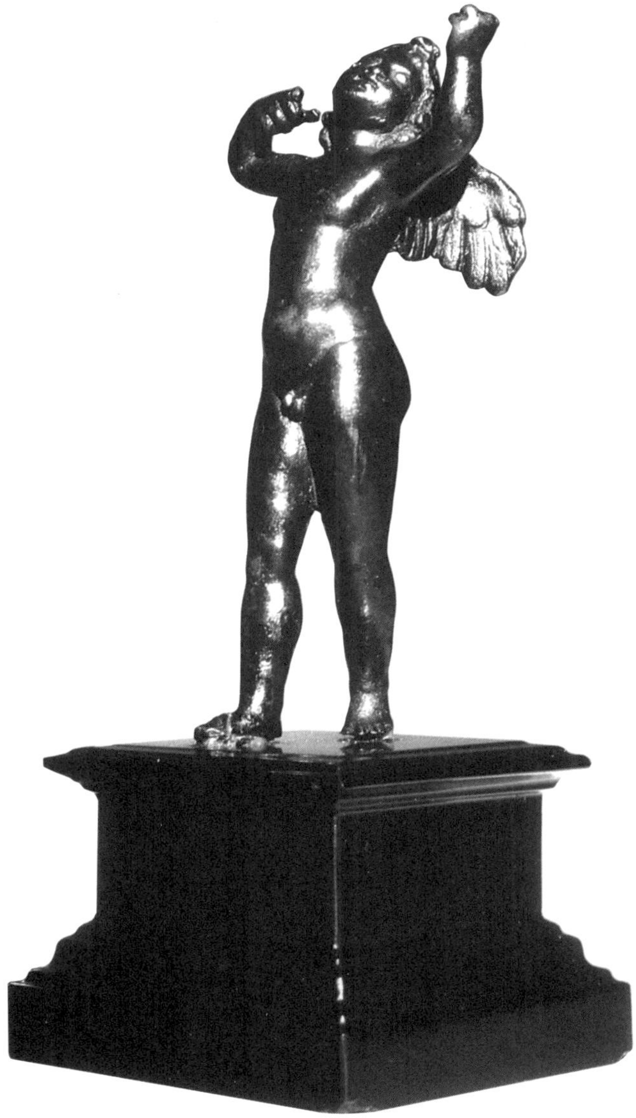

PLATE 24
Cupid Shooting
Bronze statuette

PLATE 25
Bull
Bronze

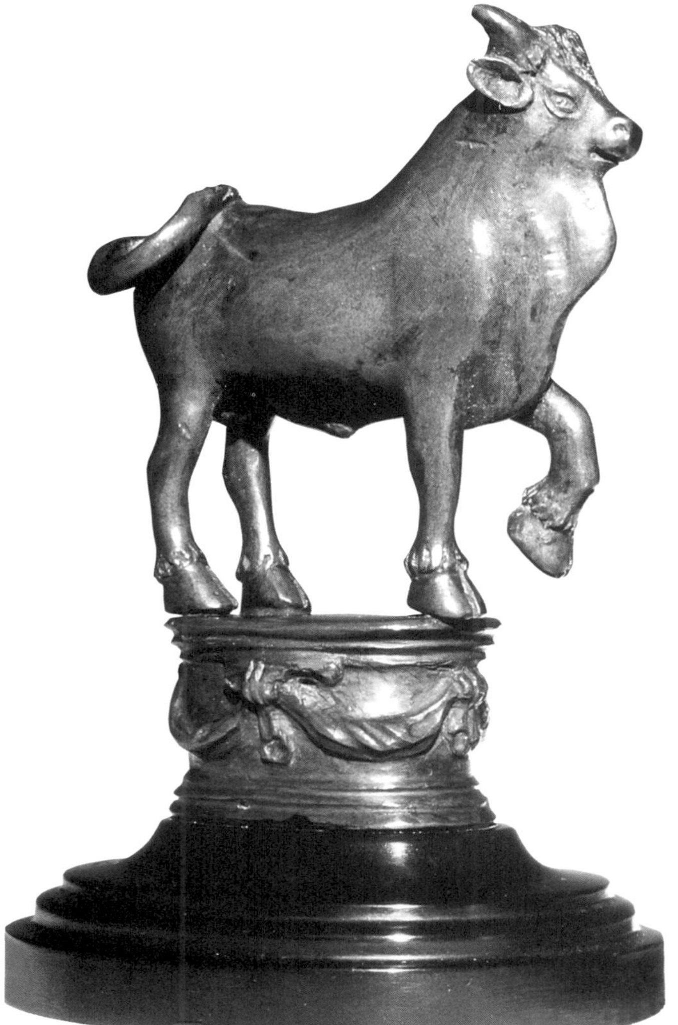

25

Bull

Bronze

ITALIAN, 16TH CENTURY

After the Antique

4⅛ in. (10.5 cm)

The bull: 3 in. (7.5 cm)

1973.20

Gift of Miss Frick, 1973

PROVENANCE

J. P. Morgan Collection, New York

Duveen

Frick 1916

Helen Clay Frick

EXHIBITED

London, Victoria & Albert Museum, 1901–12, no. 293, lent by J. Pierpont Morgan

LITERATURE

Bode, 1910, I, no. 74, fig. on p. 21

A bull standing on a small oval pedestal ornamented with festooned drapery; the fore off-leg raised, the tail curled over the back. The neck short; the dewlap abnormally developed. — BODE, 1910: ITALIAN, 16TH CENTURY, AFTER THE ANTIQUE, *Figure of a Bull.*

A figurine of a *Bull* (11 cm) nearer in type to Giambologna's larger *Walking Bull* (Avery, 1987, no. 144) is in the Museo Correr, Venice (Inv no. XI, 1277: see Frankfurt, 1985/86, no. 287). Others are in the Staatliche Museen, Berlin-Dahlem (See Bode, 1930, nos. 110, 111, plate 31): they are 10.3 and 11.4 cm high respectively, and are based on ancient Roman prototypes, as too the present example may be.

PLATE 26
Tigress
Bronze model

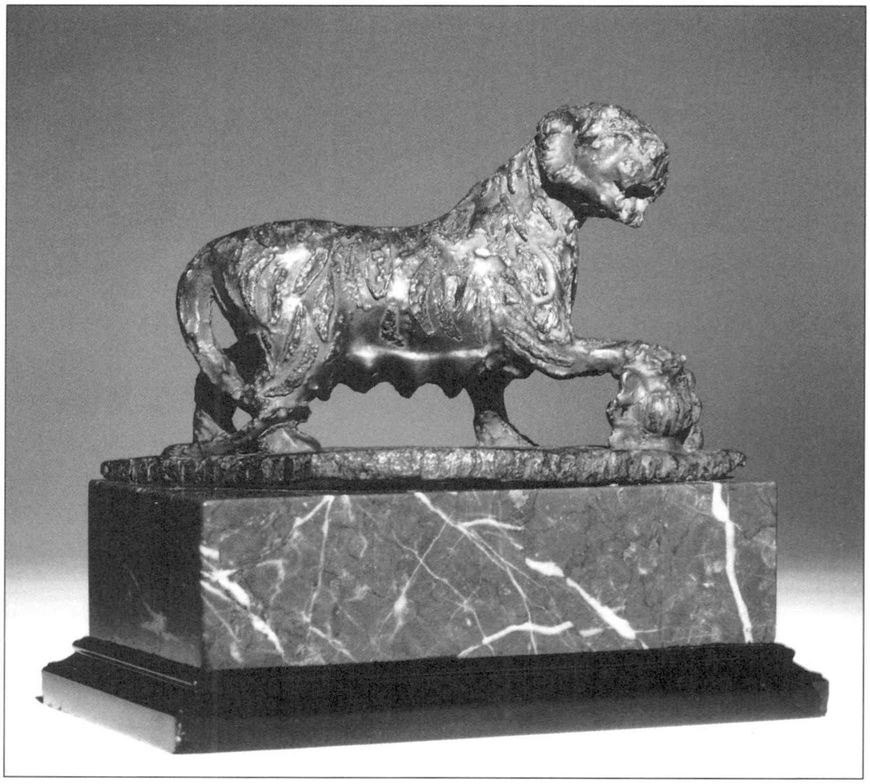

26

Tigress

Bronze model

ITALIAN, 16TH CENTURY (?)

4⅞ x 7¼ x 4 in. (12.4 x 18.4 x 10.2 cm)

1970.83
Gift of Miss Frick, 1970

CONDITION

There are traces of rust all over it, perhaps from traces of iron in the alloy. The striping in relief is deliberate. The curved part of the base has a flange, but the two straight sides at the rear do not, i.e. it was cut out of a larger, oval base, perhaps with various other animals attached. There is a large rectangular opening into its chest behind. Much of the surface is waxy-looking, and it seems to be a raw casting that has not been chased.

PROVENANCE

J. P. Morgan Collection, New York (?)
Duveen (?)
Frick 1916 (?)
Helen Clay Frick

EXHIBITED

London, Victoria & Albert Museum, 1901–12, no. 1271, lent by J. Pierpont Morgan

LITERATURE

Not mentioned in Bode

PLATE 27
Boy Balancing on a Ball
Bronze statuette

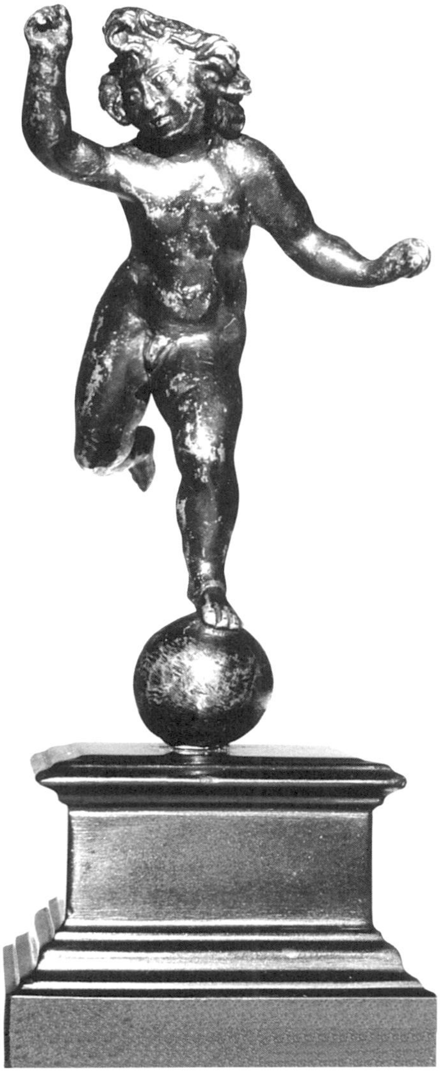

27

Boy Balancing on a Ball

Bronze statuette

ITALIAN, 16TH CENTURY

3¾ x 2⅛ x 2½ in. (9.5 x 5.3 x 6.3 cm)

1970.89
Gift of Miss Frick, 1970

CONDITION
Coppery colour with black lacquer. There is a large flaw in the crutch. The hands are drilled to hold things (a bow and arrows?). There is a hole at center of back, possibly to screw on a pair of wings.

PROVENANCE
J. P. Morgan Collection, New York
Duveen
Frick 1916
Helen Clay Frick

EXHIBITED
London, Victoria & Albert Museum, 1901–12, no. 413, lent by J. Pierpont Morgan

LITERATURE
Bode, 1910: II, no. 183, fig. on p. 21, vol. II

Full-length nude, his left foot is poised on a ball, the right is lifted high in the air. His right arm and hand are raised, his left extended. His head, with thick hair resting in a heavy curl upon his forehead is slightly inclined to the right shoulder. — BODE, 1910: ITALIAN, END OF 16TH CENTURY, *Boy Balancing on a Ball.*

PLATE 28
A Pair of Candlesticks
Bronze

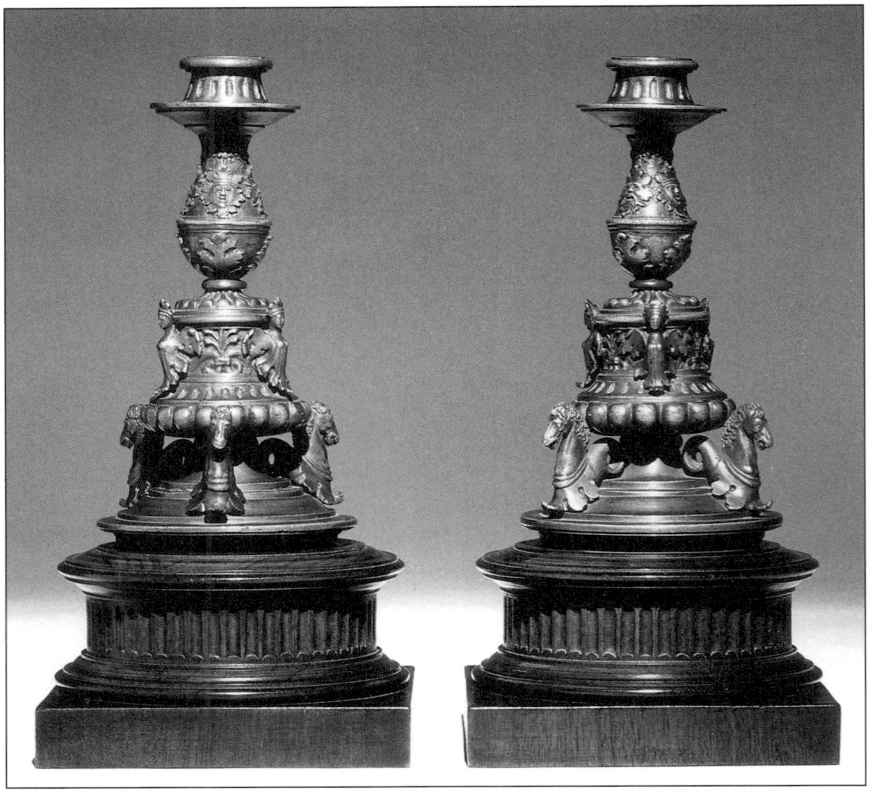

28

A Pair of Candlesticks

Bronze

ITALIAN, 19TH CENTURY

In the Renaissance style

4⅞ in. (12.4 cm) high

6⅞ in. (17.5 cm); diam. 3¾ in. (9.5 cm)

1991.1 a,b

Bequest of Miss Frick, 1984. Once kept in the library bookcase at "Eagle Rock," Prides Crossing, Massachusetts.

CONDITION

They have no patination. They are cast in sections and are held together by a central screw.

PROVENANCE

Collection of Prince Canonica (Rome?)
J. P. Morgan Collection, New York
Duveen
Frick 1916
Helen Clay Frick

EXHIBITED

London, Victoria & Albert Museum, 1901–12, no. 895–6, lent by J. Pierpont Morgan

LITERATURE

Bode, 1910, II, no. 199, pl. CXXXVI

Circular base, the baluster-shaped stem divided into two tiers: the lower rests on sea-horses and is adorned with sphinx-like figures; from this rises the upper tier with gadrooned base, decorated with acanthus leaves, foliated masks and garlands. — BODE, 1910: VENETIAN, FIRST HALF OF 16TH CENTURY, *Pair of Candlesticks.*

29

Juno with Peacock

Bronze statuette

ITALIAN, LATE 16TH OR EARLY 17TH CENTURY

5¾ in. (14.6 cm)

1970. 103
Gift of Miss Frick, 1970

CONDITION

There are traces of gilding and a hole in the base for attachment and a plug in the rump.

PROVENANCE

Charles Mannheim Collection, Paris
J. P. Morgan Collection, New York
Duveen
Frick 1916
Helen Clay Frick

EXHIBITED

London, Victoria & Albert Museum, 1901–12, no. 402, lent by J. Pierpont Morgan

LITERATURE

Bode, 1910, I, no. 141, pl. CII

Full-length nude figure, looking towards her right, her right hand on her breast, her left hanging by her side, holds a small drapery and touches the head of the peacock which stands beside her. Her hair parted in the center is drawn over her ears and gathered together at the back. — BODE, 1910: ITALIAN, LATE 16TH CENTURY, *Juno with Peacock.*

Probably off a cabinet.

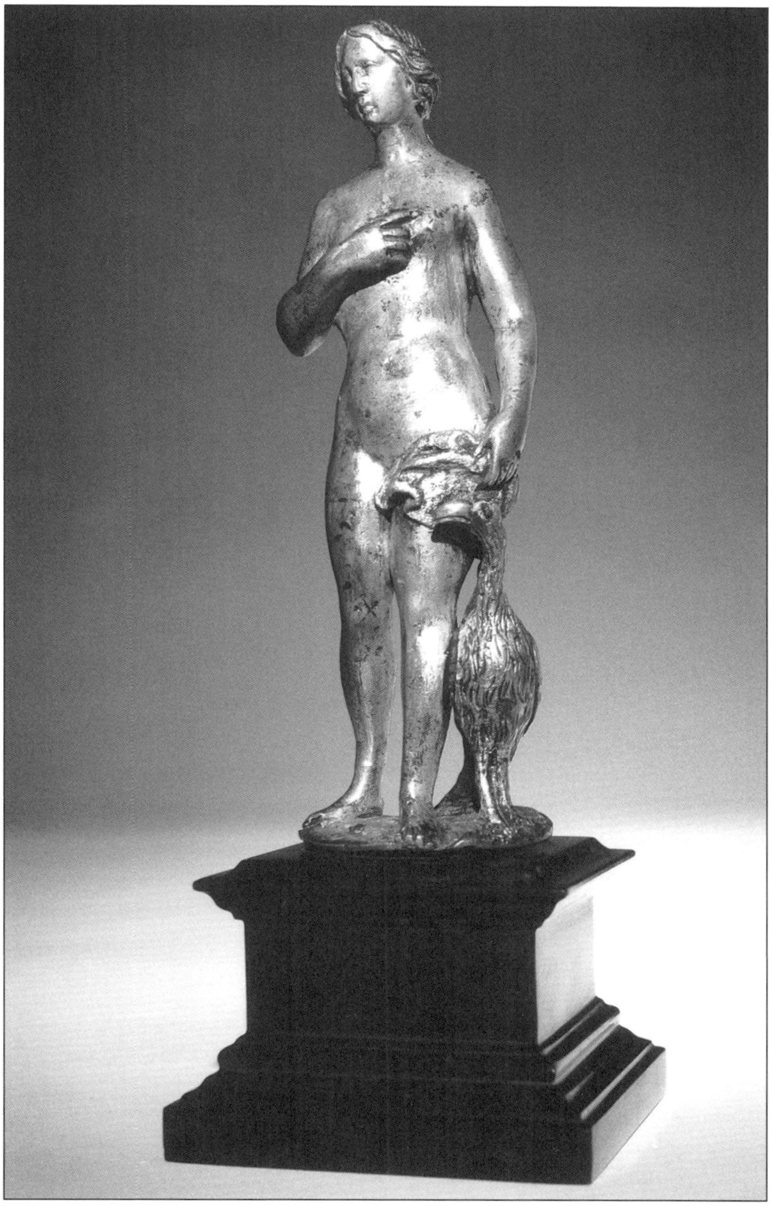

PLATE 29
Juno with Peacock
Bronze statuette

30

Seated Pensive Cupid

Bronze statuette

ITALIAN, EARLY 17TH CENTURY

2½ x 1¼ x 2¾ in. (6.4 x 3.2 x 7 cm)

1970.88
Gift of Miss Frick, 1970

CONDITION
The surface is roughish, being lightly rasped, but not polished or much chased. The wings are feathered inside and outside. The quiver is cast separately and pinned on. His left hand is pierced vertically, probably to accommodate a bow. Blackish lacquer.

PROVENANCE
J. P. Morgan Collection, New York
Duveen
Frick 1916
Helen Clay Frick

EXHIBITED
London, Victoria & Albert Museum, 1901–12, no. 407, lent by J. Pierpont Morgan

LITERATURE
Bode, 1910, II, no. 184, fig. on p. 22, vol. II

He sits cross-legged upon an oblong base, his right hand supporting his head, which is turned to the left looking upwards in a contemplative attitude. His body is bent forward and his left arm is supported on the left thigh. His quiver, in an upright position, is fastened by a strap to the waist. — BODE, 1910: ITALIAN, BEGINNING OF THE 17TH CENTURY, *Seated Cupid.*

The type of chubby infant is not unlike those of Francesco Fanelli. This may have formed a finial, or a handle on the lid of a bronze box.

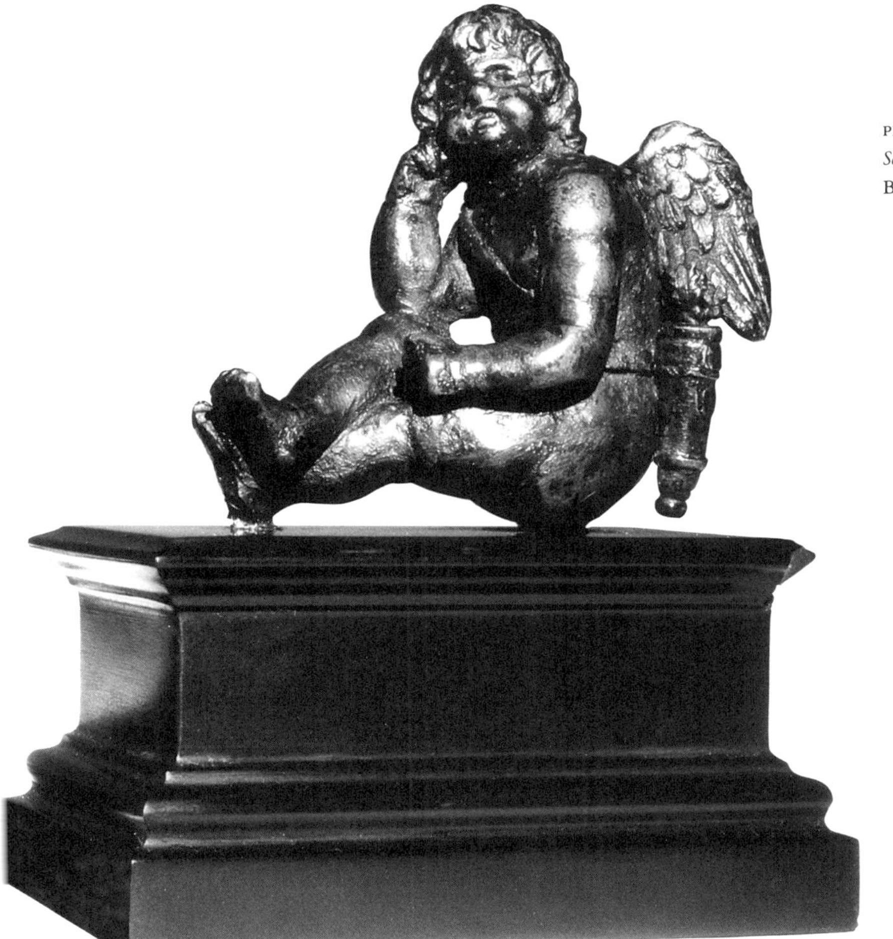

PLATE 30
Seated Pensive Cupid
Bronze statuette

31

Equestrian Figure

Bronze

ITALIAN, EARLY 18TH CENTURY (OR LATER)

11¾ x 10⅞ in. (29.8 x 27.6 cm)

The horse alone: 10¾ in. (11.3 cm)

1970.95

Gift of Miss Frick, 1970

CONDITION

The group is cast in a brassy alloy with a thin, darkish patina, and has a nasty, generalized plastery or sandy surface. The rider is separately cast, and attached by a screw through his left forearm into the mane of the horse — all improvised. There is a flaw in the horse's tail, probably where an iron armature rod protruded from the interior of the casting.

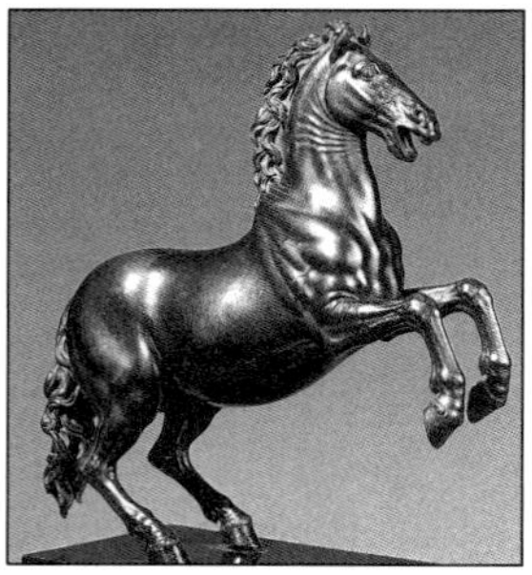

Figure 31.1
Rearing Horse, Giambologna
Courtesy of Christies', London

PROVENANCE

Henry Joseph Pfungst Collection, London
Durlacher, London
J. P. Morgan Collection, New York
Duveen
Frick 1916
Helen Clay Frick

EXHIBITED

London, Victoria & Albert Museum, 1901–12, no. 290, lent by J. Pierpont Morgan

LITERATURE

Pfungst, 1899, no. 6 ('Dr. Bode pronounces this to be the work of an unknown Venetian master of circa 1520')
Bode, 1910, I, p. xxv, no. 100, plate LXVII
Schottmüller, F., 'An equestrian statuette of the Renaissance,' in *Art in America*, XIII, no. 2, 1925, pp. 63–72, pl. 2
Leeuwenberg & Halsema-Kubes, 1973, pp. 394–95, no. 676
Hovey, 1975, p. 59, ill. p. 59

OTHER EXAMPLES

Amsterdam, Rijksmuseum (N.M. 13152): Schottmüller, *loc cit*, as 'by Tiziano Aspetti'; exhibited Detroit, *Decorative Arts of the Italian Renaissance*, 1958–9, p. 106, no. 252, as 'Gianfrancesco Rustici'; London 1961, no. 175, as 'Venetian, mid 16th century'; Amsterdam, 1961–2, no. 178 as 'Lombard, second half of the 16th century'
Dresden, Grünes Gewölbe, (first listed without provenance in sculpture inventory of 1726, as no. 141.)
Another version reproduced by Montfaucon, *Antiquité Expliquée*, supp. IV, p. 12, as 'Antique.'
For German versions in silver see Amsterdam, *De Triomf van het Manierisme* 1955, no. 428

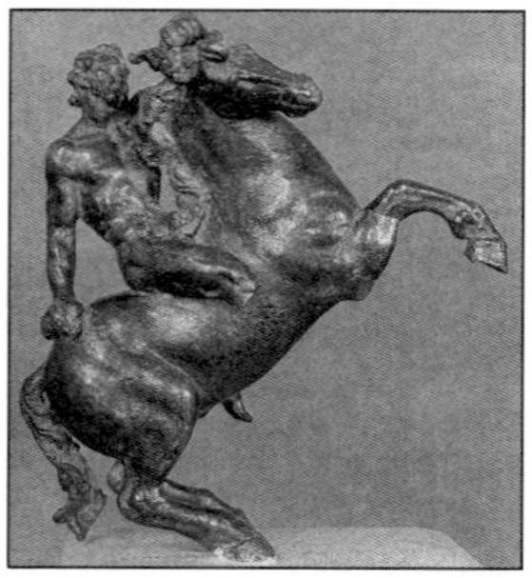

Figure 31.2
Man on a Rearing Horse, Italian, Lombardy; bronze
Collection of Rijksmuseum, Amsterdam (13152)

Nude male figure, barebacked on a prancing horse. His head, turned almost in full face, is inclined to the left shoulder, his body is thrown back slightly, his legs pressed against the flanks. His right hand is clenched above the horse's hip, his left grasps its mane. — BODE, 1910: PADUAN, END OF THE 16TH CENTURY, *Equestrian Figure*

Bode regarded this puzzling group as 'Paduan, late 16th century.' However, it has recently emerged that the horse is simply an indifferent aftercast of a *Rearing Horse* by Giambologna (see Phillips, London, 21 November 1978, lot 126; Sotheby's, New York, 16 May 1985, lot 184; and Christie's, London, 6 December 1988, lot 211; our Fig. 31.1).

This discovery, made since the attribution of the group was last considered, completely alters one's attitude to the piece, and to the question of its authenticity.

The low quality of the horse and the diverse character of the separate male figure rule out any connection with Giambologna or his followers. The man seems to have been modelled later to fit on the back of the horse, which was not originally designed to have a rider at all.

The face of the man is strongly modelled and his anatomy is suavely rendered, in a style which is typical of the end of the 16th century.

The rider is a 'cousin' of those mounted (similarly bare-back) on a *different* rearing horse, in equestrian groups in the Rijksmuseum (Fig. 31.2) and in the Grünes Gewölbe, Dresden (Fig. 31.4). These are also enigmatic and not by any means identical, though less suspect. That in the Rijksmuseum has had a chequered history of attributions. It reminded Schottmueller of the Venetian, Tiziano Aspetti, and of the Frick version she commented: 'A weaker copy is found in the J. Pierpont Morgan Collection. Weaker, because all the details are generalized and the contrasts in motion are simplified. Here the subject has the effect of a pose and the representation loses the power of convincing.'

Subsequently the name of Gianfrancesco Rustici, the sculptor-associate of Leonardo da Vinci, has been introduced into the discussion (on account of its relationship with some of Leonardo's drawings of equestrian subjects). Currently, the Amsterdam bronze is more plausibly catalogued as 'Lombard, second half of the 16th century,' and an association with Annibale Fontana may be in order.

Figure 31.3
Cavalier, B. de Montfaucon *L'Antiquité Expliquée et representée en figures*; supplement, Vol. IV, Paris, 1724, p. 23, pl. XII; photograph supplied by the author

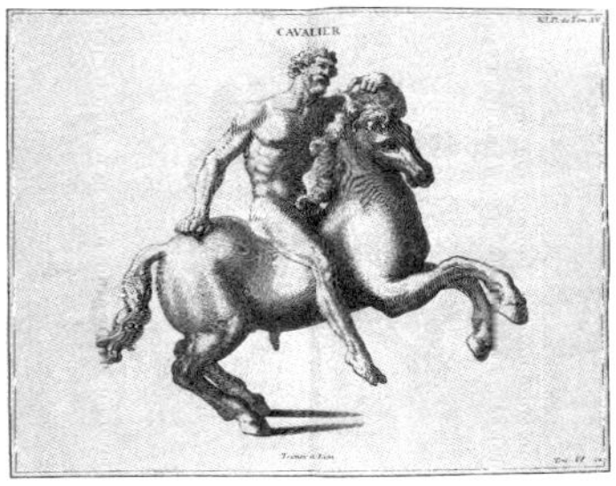

The group in Dresden shows the rider holding horizontally in his lowered right hand a club, and is therefore probably to be interpreted as Hercules. It was regarded by the late Professor Weihrauch as a South German aftercast from a North Italian model, on account of its having served as a prototype for Augsburg goldsmiths in the 17th century. The present curator in Dresden, Dr. Martin Raumschussel (to whom we are grateful for a helpful letter of 3 August 1992), has stated that he would not exclude a French origin, c. 1600, on account of the facture and light yellowish-brown lacquer patination. The group first appeared in an inventory of 1726 under no. 141, but without provenance. Many of the other bronzes in Dresden had been purchased in Paris a few years earlier, in 1699 and 1715, and are mostly French (W. Holzhausen, 'Die Bronzen Augusts des Starken in Dresden,' in *Jahrbuch der Preussischen Kunstsammlungen*, LX, 1939, pp. 157–86).

PLATE 31
Equestrian Figure
Bronze

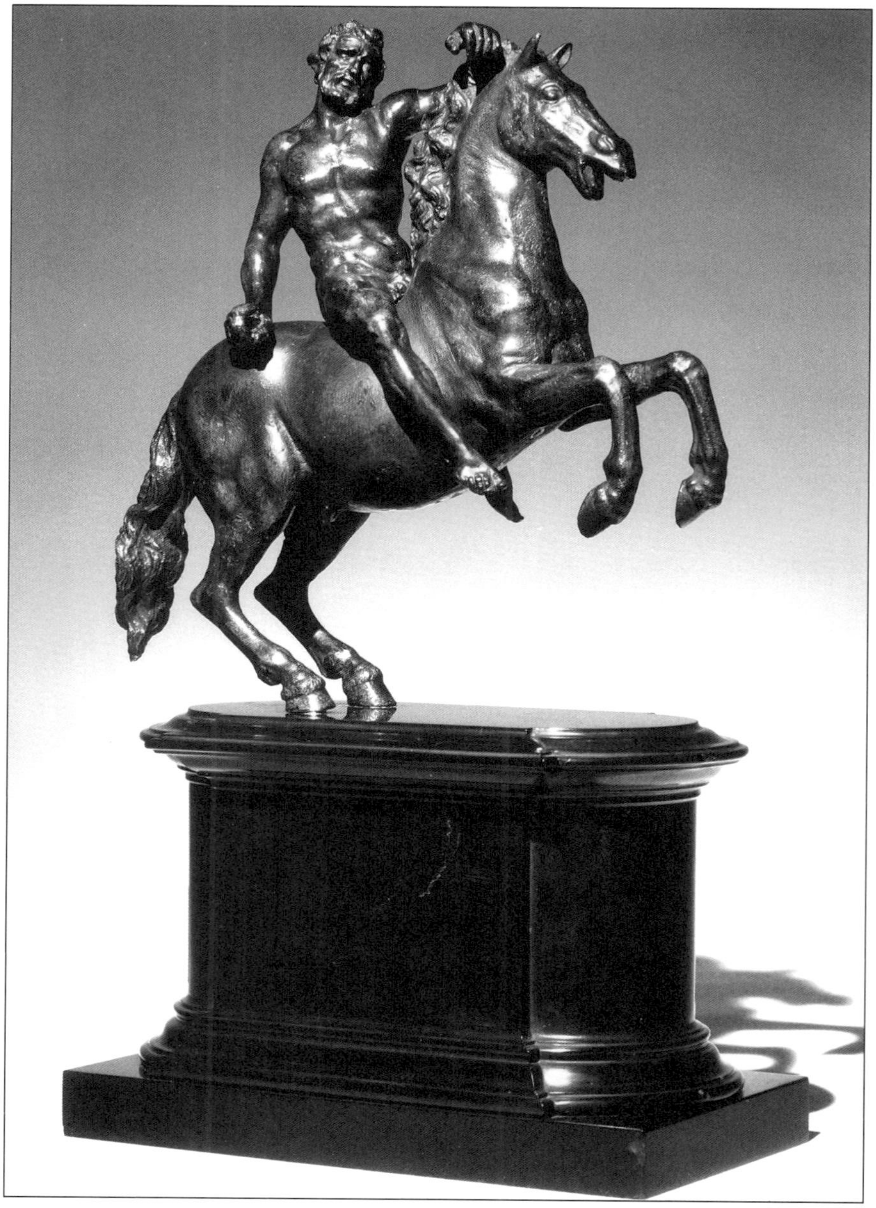

While the poses of the riders are similar, they are not identical, and this proves that the present figure was deliberately adapted to bestride the Giambologna-type horse.

The equestrian group in the Rijksmuseum, or another cast of it, stated to have been *excavated* (!) at Lyon, was apparently the model for an engraving in B. de Montfaucon's great survey of ancient art, *L'Antiquité Expliquée et representée en figures* (supplement Vol. IV, Paris, 1724, p. 23, pl. XII; our Fig. 31.3). This suggests that it already looked 'old' at the time, perhaps because of its unchased, rough surface, and also the addition of a deceptive 'antique' patina. Montfaucon, convinced of its antiquity, discussed it only in terms of subject matter, refusing to believe with others that it represented Marcus Curtius, and preferring the idea that it was a Gaulish chieftain, who had won a prize in a race.

The suggestion of Marcus Curtius was probably a reflection of its chance similarity in pose to the monumental equestrian statue of King Louis XIV by Bernini that had recently (1702) been transformed into one of Marcus Curtius, and relegated to the bottom of the gardens at Versailles (S. Hoog, *Le Bernin: Louis XIV, une statue deplacée*, Paris 1989).

In the engraving, the horse is not rearing back on its haunches as much as in the Amsterdam bronze, nor is its tail touching the ground. Its body is shown more horizontal, and hence that of the rider is more upright, even leaning slightly forward.

The rider's right leg is extended forward with its big toe outstretched, as in the Frick version (the Amsterdam leg being broken below the knee). The rider is pointing with his left index finger, and not quite touching the flying lock of the horse's mane.

The rider in the Frick group is probably an aftercast from either the one in Amsterdam, or, if it was indeed a different piece, that excavated at Lyon and illustrated by Montfaucon.

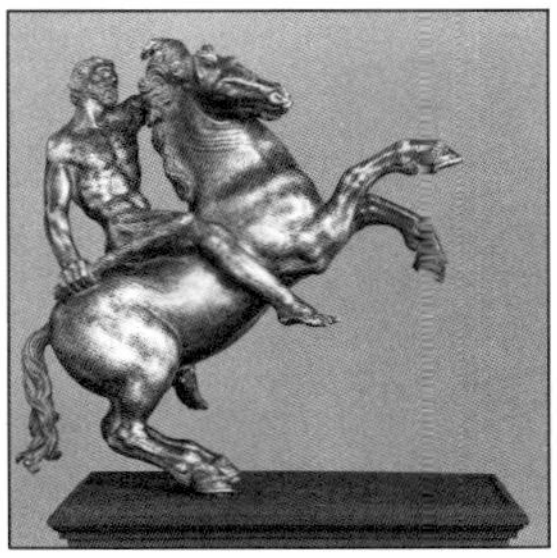

Figure 31.4
Hercules (?) on Horseback, bronze
Grünes Gewölbe, Staatliche Kunstammlungen, Dresden, Skulpturensammlung (Inv. No. IX 47)

32

Portrait Bust of Pope Innocent X (Giovanni Battista Pamphili, 1574–1655)

Bronze bust

ITALIAN, ROME, MIDDLE OF THE 17TH CENTURY

Reduction from a model by Alessandro Algardi (1598–1654)

11½ x 9½ x 3½ in. (29.2 x 24.1 x 8.9 cm)

1970.96
Gift of Miss Frick, 1970

CONDITION

The bust is integrally cast with its base, on which it is supported behind by twin flanges. Several casting sprues and screwed plugs are visible inside the bust. Its surface is very carefully worked with abrasives. The stole, its cord, the top button and the base are partially gilt.

PROVENANCE

Charles Mannheim Collection, Paris
J. P. Morgan Collection, New York
Duveen
Frick 1916
Helen Clay Frick

EXHIBITED

London, Victoria & Albert Museum, 1901–12, no. 149, lent by J. Pierpont Morgan

LITERATURE

Molinier, 1898, no. 149, p. 42 (incorrectly identified as 'Pope Gregory XIII,' and so dated late 16th century)
Bode, 1910, II, no. 164, plate CXIII
Hovey, 1975, p. 116, ill. p. 116
Amherst College, *Five College Roman Baroque Festival; Roman Baroque Sculpture*, Smith College Museum of Art, 1974, no. 22
Pope-Hennessy, 1964, no. 660 (and p. 625)
Heimburger-Ravalli, 1973, p. 118, cat. no. 36a
Montagu, 1985, II, p. 429, no. R.44 (cf. nos. 154f)

OTHER EXAMPLES

Christie's, London, 15 May 1984, lot 127 (32.5 cm high)
Sir Brinsley Ford Collection, London

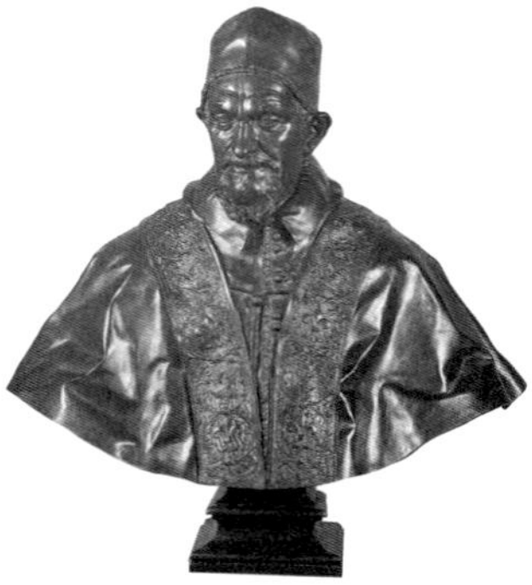

Figure 32.1
Bust of Pope Innocent X (Giovanni Battista Pamfili, 1572–1655), Algardi, Allesandro (1595–1654), after; middle 17th century; bronze
The Metropolitan Museum of Art, Rogers Fund, 1908 (08.49)

Bust seen in full face. The pope wears a mozzetta, *and a stole embroidered with the dove and fleur-de-lys, charges from the arms of the Pamphili. His head is covered by a* camauro. *The stole and base are gilded.* — BODE, 1910: ITALIAN, 17TH CENTURY, POSSIBLY ALESSANDRO ALGARDI, *Portrait of Pope Innocent X.*

The reduction is considerably simplified (on account of its much smaller scale) from the original, life-size busts designed by Algardi, and closely copied after his demise by Domenico Guidi (e.g. the bronze cast in the Metropolitan Museum of Art, New York, no. 08.49; our Fig. 32.1).

Neither of the other examples is as well chased, nor are they parcel-gilt. Of the Frick example, Montagu writes '. . . (it) derives ultimately from Algardi's image, but is too far from his style in the working of the head and the more

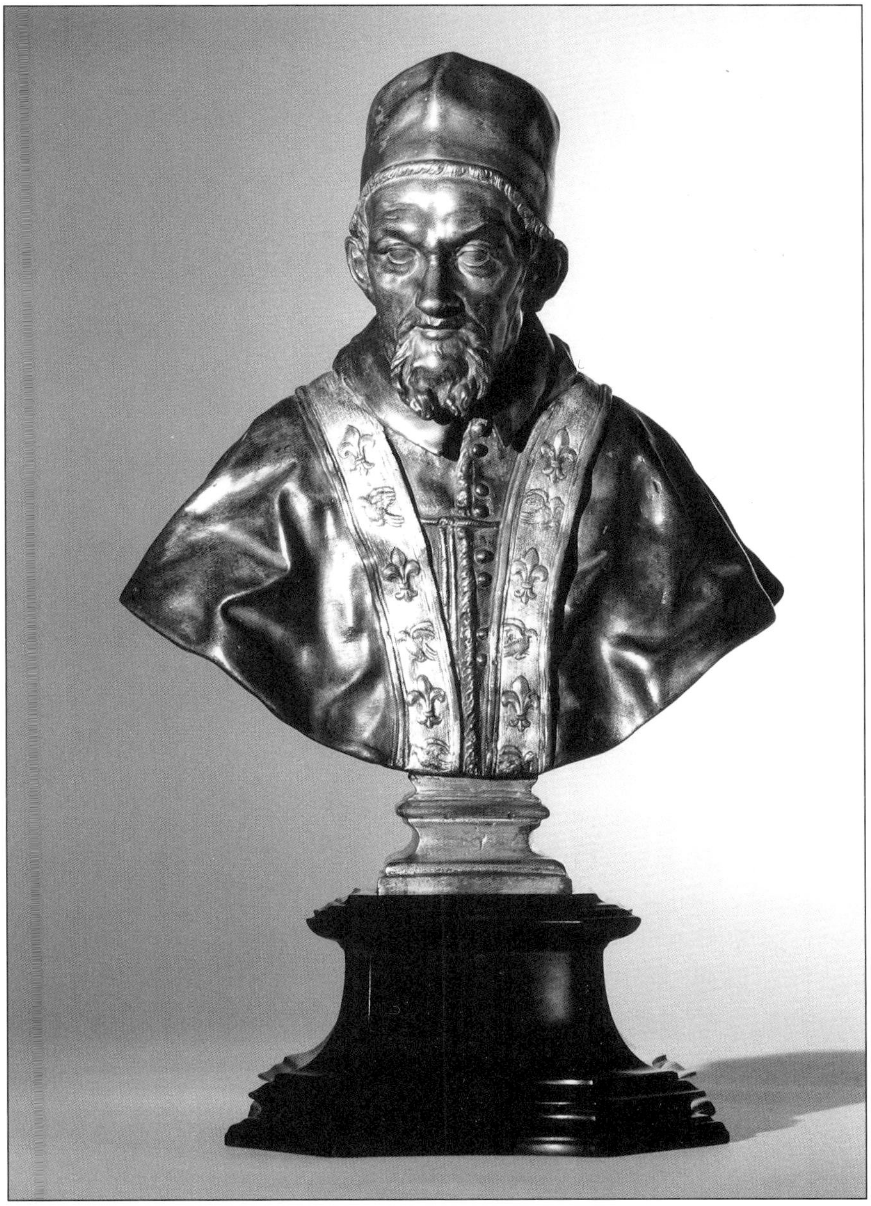

PLATE 32
Portrait Bust of Pope Innocent X (Giovanni Battista Pamphili, 1574–1655)
Bronze bust

agitated *mozzetta* to warrant an attribution to him, or even his immediate circle. Another cast, without gilding and with less after-work, is in the collection of Brinsley Ford in London.[7]

Nevertheless, the Frick bust is a creditable example of mid-17th-century Roman bronze craftsmanship, and, in view of the superior chiselling and parcel gilding, it must have been destined for an important recipient.

An inferior variant of this bust appeared at Christie's, London, in 1984 (Fig. 32.2).

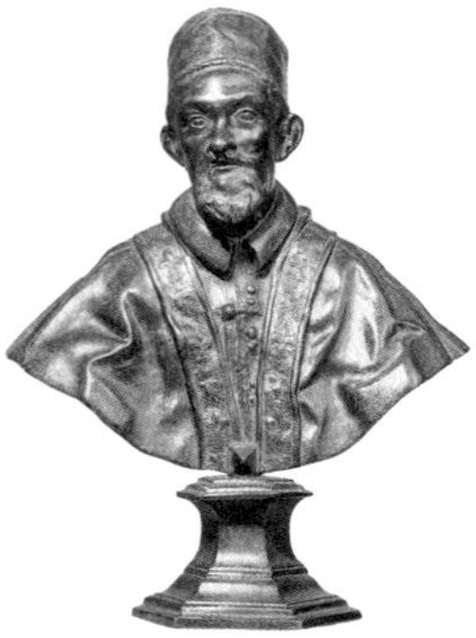

Figure 32.2
Bust of Pope Innocent X (Giovanni Battista Pamfili, 1572–1655)
Courtesy of Christies', London, 1984

33

Saturn Devouring One of his Children

Bronze statuette

ITALIAN, ROME, MIDDLE OF 17TH CENTURY
6 x 8 x 2 in. (15.2 x 20.3 x 5.1 cm)

1970.92
Gift of Miss Frick, 1970

CONDITION
This is a thin, flawed cast, rasped, but not polished, and with a dark lacquer. The right hand is drilled to accommodate a scythe.

PROVENANCE
J. P. Morgan Collection, New York (?)
Duveen (?)
Frick 1916 (?)
Helen Clay Frick

LITERATURE
Not mentioned in Bode, 1910

The composition is very Baroque, with its flowing hair, beard, and swirling drapery, and so it must post-date the early work of Bernini.

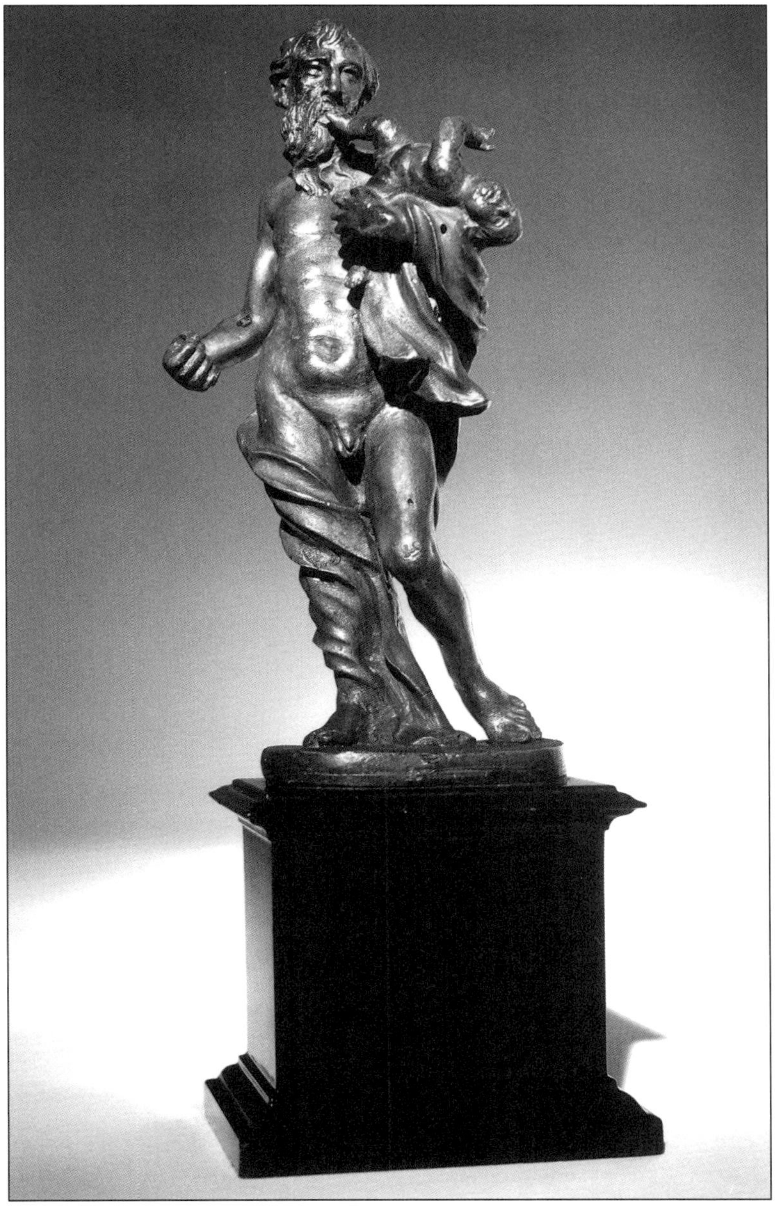

PLATE 33
Saturn Devouring One of his Children
Bronze statuette

34

Meleager with the Calydonian Boar

Bronze statuette

ITALIAN, ROME, LATE 18TH CENTURY

Attributed to Francesco Righetti (1749–1819), after the Antique statue in the Vatican Museum

16⅝ x 8½ x 4½ in. (42.2 x 21.6 x 11.4 cm)

1970.100
Gift of Miss Frick, 1970

CONDITION

The bronze is cast in a coppery alloy, with black lacquer. It has a wedge-shaped sub-base to tilt the group backwards, for balance. On the hand behind his back there remains a bar across the fingertips from the casting process, which has not been removed.

PROVENANCE

J. P. Morgan Collection, New York
Duveen
Frick 1916
Helen Clay Frick

LITERATURE

Bode, 1910, no. 102, plate LXVIII
Hovey, 1972, p. 6, fig. 8
Hovey, 1975, p. 119, ill. p. 120
Haskell and Penny, 1981, pp. 263–65, no. 60, fig. 137

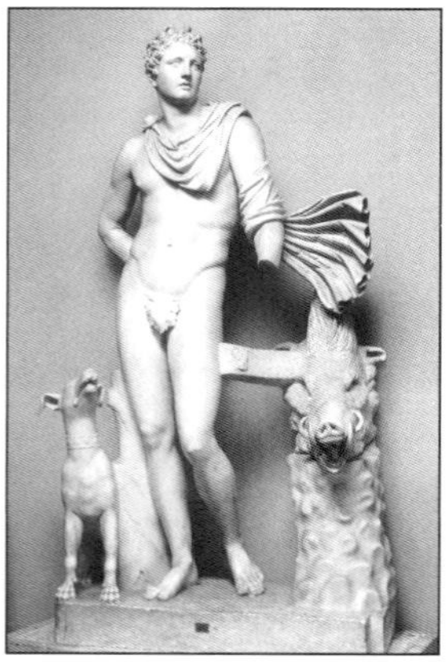

Figure 34.1
Meleagro (Meleager with the Calydonian Boar), anonymous; marble
Museo Pio Clementino, The Vatican (inv. 490, XXXI.75.12)

Full-length standing nude, a small drapery fastened on the right shoulder falls over the left and is wound around the arm above the elbow. He leans over slightly to the left, turning his head and resting one hand upon the hound's head, which is seated beside him, looking up at his master. — BODE, 1910: ITALIAN, LATE 16TH OR EARLY 17TH CENTURY, *Meleager.*

The original, classical statue was recorded in 1546 in the house of the papal doctor, Francesco Fusconi, and it remained in the possession of his heirs until 1770, when it was bought by Pope Clement XIV for his new museum in the Vatican (Fig. 34.1). It was installed in the Room of the Animals in the Museo Pio-Clementino by 1792.

In 1546 it was regarded as one of the most beautiful statues in Rome, and it was engraved in 1555. It was ranked among the seven most famous antiquities in the world.

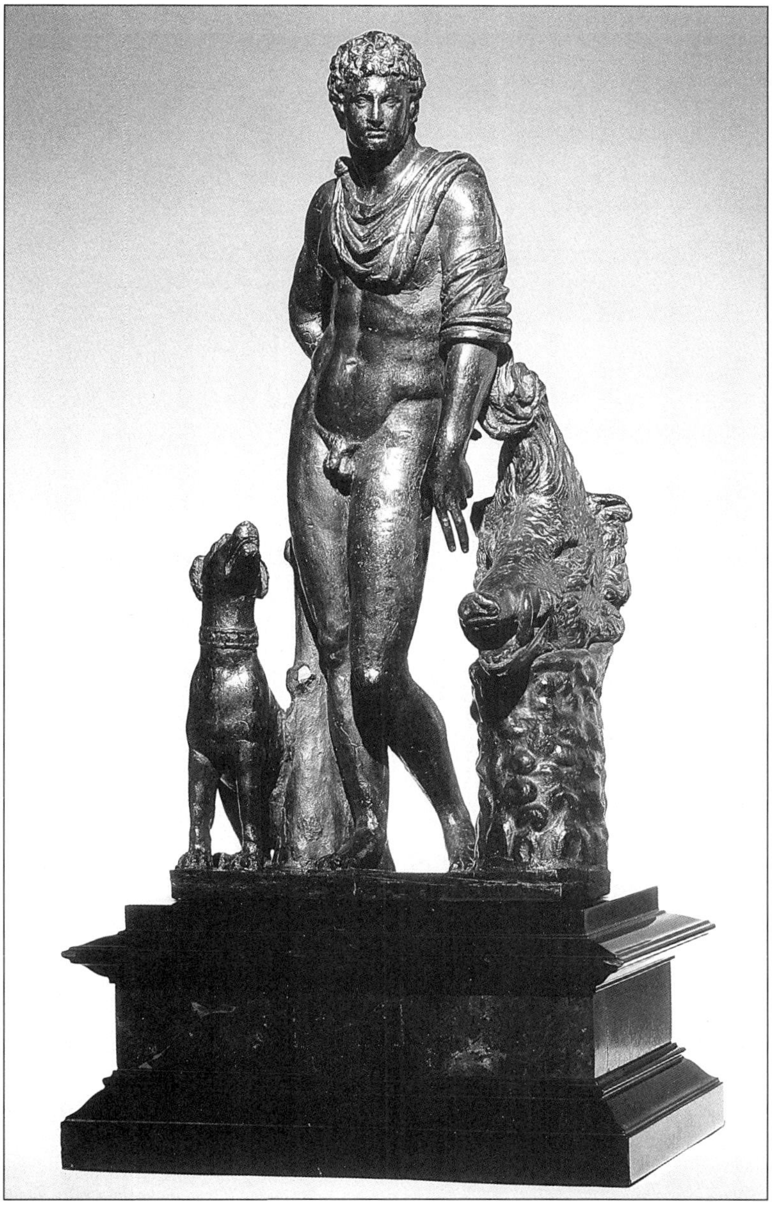

PLATE 34
Meleager with the Calydonian Boar
Bronze statuette

Reduced sized casts in bronze were produced by Francesco Righetti, in Rome, and listed in his catalogue of 1794 (Fig. 34.2). This is probably one of them, for its scale, brassy alloy, and greenish-black patination are typical of Righetti's productions.

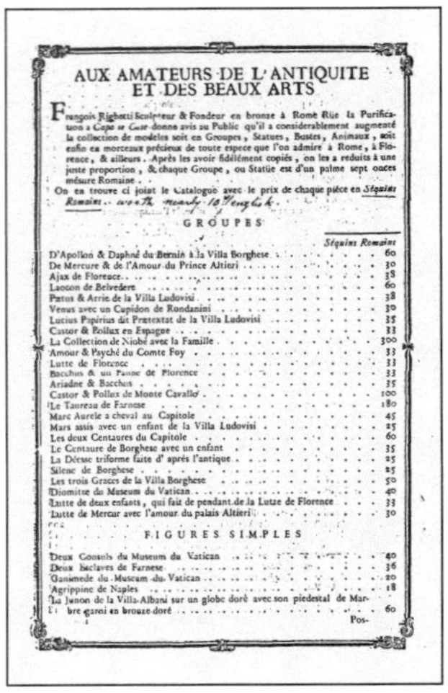

AUX AMATEURS DE L'ANTIQUITE ET DES BEAUX ARTS

François Righetti Sculpteur & Fondeur en bronze à Rome Rüe la Purification a Capo le Case donne avis au Public qu'il a considerablement augmenté la collection de modeles soit en Groupes, Statues, Bustes, Animaux, soit enfin en morceaux précieux de toute espece que l'on admire à Rome, à Florence, & ailleurs. Après les avoir fidélément copiés, on les a reduits à une juste proportion, & chaque Groupe, ou Statüe est d'un palme sept onces mésure Romaine.

On en trouve ci joint le Catalogue avec le prix de chaque piéce en Séquins Romains.

GROUPES

	Séquins Romains
D'Apollon & Daphné du Bernin à la Villa Borghese	60
De Mercure & de l'Amour du Prince Altieri	30
Ajax de Florence	38
Laocon de Belvedere	60
Pætus & Arrie de la Villa Ludovisi	38
Venus avec un Cupidon de Rondanini	30
Lucius Papirius dit Prætextat de la Villa Ludovisi	35
Castor & Pollux en Espagne	33
La Collection de Niobé avec la Famille	300
Amour & Psyché du Comte Foy	33
Lutte de Florence	33
Bacchus & un Faune de Florence	33
Ariadne & Bacchus	35
Castor & Pollux de Monte Cavallo	100
Le Taureau de Farnese	180
Marc Aurele a cheval au Capitole	45
Mars assis avec un enfant de la Villa Ludovisi	25
Les deux Centaures du Capitole	60
Le Centaure de Borghese avec un enfant	35
La Déesse triforme faite d' aprés l'antique	25
Silene de Borghese	25
Les trois Graces de la Villa Borghese	50
Diomitte du Museum du Vatican	40
Lutte de deux enfants, qui fait de pendant de la Lutte de Florence	33
Lutte de Mercur avec l'amour du palais Altieri	30

FIGURES SIMPLES

Deux Consols du Museum du Vatican	40
Deux Esclaves de Farnese	36
Ganimede du Museum du Vatican	20
Agrippine de Naples	18
La Junon de la Villa-Albani sur un globe doré avec son piedestal de Marbre garni en bronze doré	60

Pos-

Figure 34.2
Aux Amateurs de L'Antiquité et des Beaux Arts, Francesco Righetti Catalogue, Rome, 1794; photograph supplied by the author

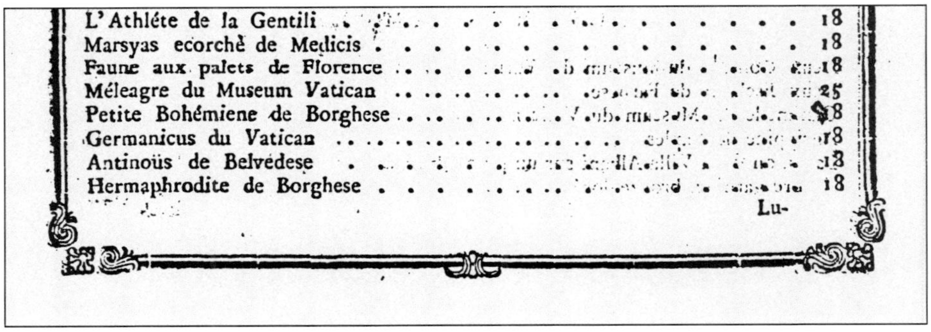

L'Athléte de la Gentili	18
Marsyas ecorché de Medicis	18
Faune aux palets de Florence	18
Méleagre du Museum Vatican	25
Petite Bohémiene de Borghese	18
Germanicus du Vatican	18
Antinoüs de Belvédese	18
Hermaphrodite de Borghese	18

Lu-

35

Hunter and his Dog

Bronze

ITALIAN, ROME or ENGLISH, LONDON,
SECOND HALF OF 19TH CENTURY

Cast from a model by John Gibson R A (1790–1866)

11½ x 8 x 3½ in. (29.2 x 20.3 x 8.9 cm)

1970.98

Gift of Miss Frick, 1970. Once kept in the library bookcase at "Eagle Rock," Prides Crossing, Massachusetts.

CONDITION

The two figures have been removed from a naturalistic, oval bronze base, on which other examples are mounted (see Fig. 35.2). The hunter has a fig-leaf over his genitals which appears to have been cast in originally, rather than added later. His clenched left hand has been drilled to hold a missing spear (⅜ in. diam). The dog is separately cast and pinned to the inside of the calf of the hunter's left leg. The tip of its tail is missing, and the joint in its collar is now loose. The surface of the bare metal is greenish, with the remains of a fugitive, brownish-black lacquer.

PROVENANCE

J. P. Morgan Collection, New York
Duveen
Frick 1916
Helen Clay Frick

LITERATURE

Lady Eastlake, *Life of John Gibson R A*, London 1870, p. 249
Bode, 1910, II, no. 216, plate CLIII, Introduction, p. XLI
T. Matthews, *The Biography of John Gibson R A, Sculptor, Rome*, London, 1911, pp. 96–7, 242, pls. opp. pp. 98, 100
R. Gunnis, *Dictionary of British Sculptors 1660–1851*, London, n. d., pp. 171–73
Weihrauch, 1967, p. 379 (as 'c. 1600')

OTHER EXAMPLES

R. Kashey and M. Reymert, *Catalogue of Western European Bronzes of the 19th Century*, Shepherd Gallery, New York, 1973, no. 13
Agnew's, London, *Sculpture and Works of Art*, London, 1981, p. 26, no. 20

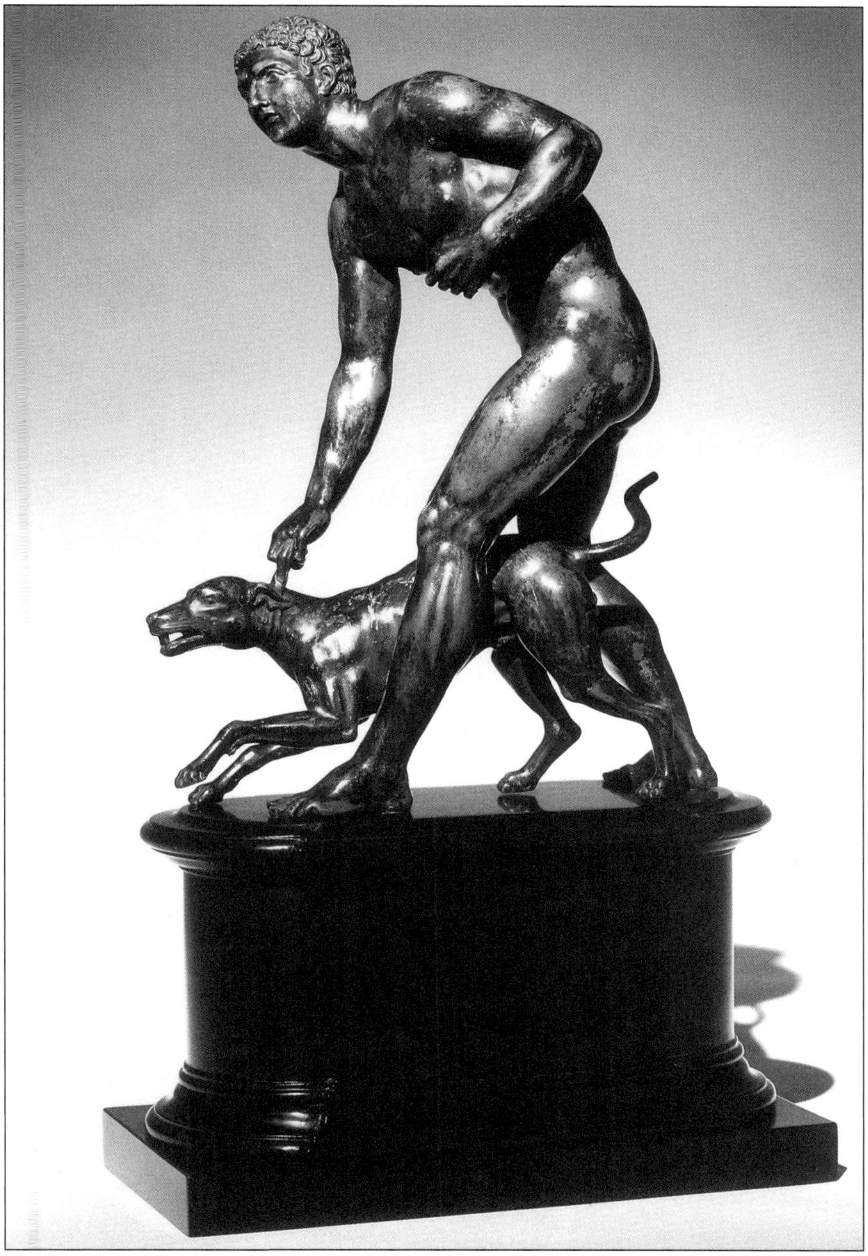

PLATE 35
Hunter and his Dog
Bronze

Full-length nude male figure bending down and holding the hound by a ring attached to its collar. His left foot is advanced, his left arm bent across his chest. His head covered with crisply curled hair leaving the ear visible, is slightly thrown back, he glances upwards. — BODE, 1910: FLEMISH, 17TH CENTURY, *Hunter with Hound.*

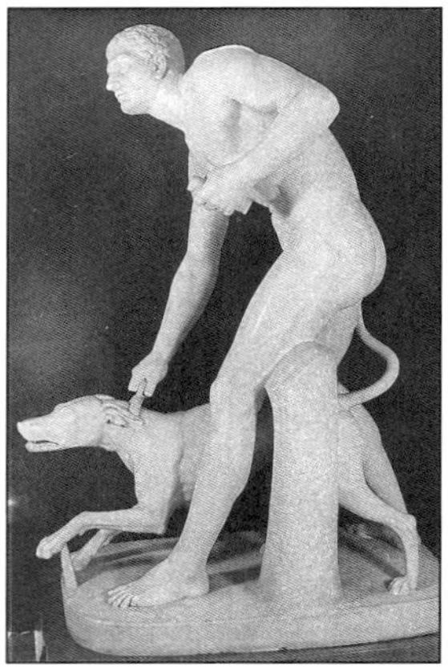

Figure 35.1
Hunter with Hound, John Gibson
Usher Art Gallery, Lincoln; photograph supplied by the author

Thought by Bode to be 'Flemish, 17th century' though he evinced suspicion of its facture, etc. (see Catalogue No. 39), the composition is in fact by John Gibson, a British admirer of Canova, who spent much of his career in Rome. The model in marble was commissioned by Henry Sandbach for Hafod-un-nos in Wales in 1838. A replica, also in marble, was commissioned by the Earl of Yarborough, and is now in the Usher Art Gallery, Lincoln (Fig. 35.1); while a third also exists (until recently on loan to the National Museum of Wales).

Gibson wrote of the original commission as follows:

> In the year 1838 came to Rome Mr. Henry Sandbach and his Lady . . . One subject became the favourite of Mr. Sandbach as well as of his Lady. It was a *Hunter and his Dog.* The idea was caught from an incident in the street. I observed a big lad holding a dog by the collar at the moment of flying at some object, when he let him off. This caught my eye in a moment. I saw a composition which impressed me. I carried the whole of it in my memory and made my small model in clay. It was ordered by Mr. Sandbach in marble the size of life. This is a statue which I studied with great care and ambition to make it my best work. It is at Mr. Sandbach's house on his estate in North Wales . . . When I was modelling the *Hunter and Dog*, I had then a very fine model in the prime of his youth, and his proportions correct; besides having this young man, I went often to contemplate the casts from the Elgin marbles at the Academy of St. Luke's.

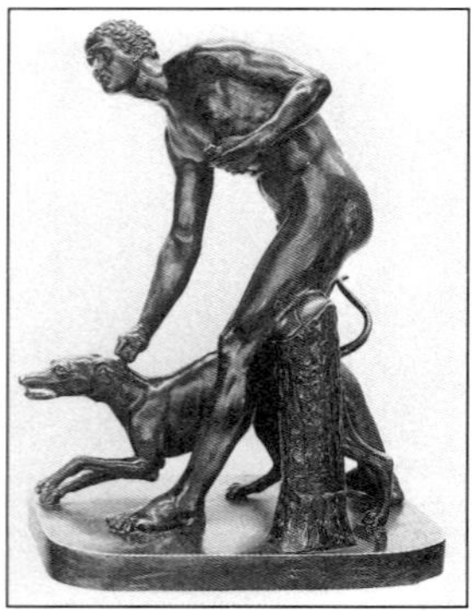

Figure 35.2
Nude Male with Greyhound, John Gibson RA (1790–1866); bronze
Photography courtesy of Shepherd Gallery, Associates, New York

The present bronze reduction is one of only three known. They may have been copied from Gibson's original working clay model (which might have been at much the same size), or scaled down by the use of a reducing machine from one of the marble versions.

The present figures of hunter and dog have been deliberately detached from the separately cast, oval bronze base with which both other examples are furnished, in order to make them appear older, and therefore more valuable. It is a tribute to Gibson's powers of classicizing invention, that this commercial subterfuge succeeded in deceiving the successive owners, and even a great connoisseur like von Bode!

One of the other casts differs in including a tree-stump for support, which bears the signature *J. GIBSON FECIT ROMA* (see Fig. 35.2). This proves that at least two separate editions were cast, possibly one in Rome, where Gibson resided, and the other in London, where his fame was great.

36

Figure of a Man as a Candelabrum

Bronze candelabrum

GERMAN, NUREMBERG, FIRST THIRD OF THE 16TH CENTURY

Attributed to Peter Vischer the Younger (1487–1528) or to Peter Flötner (1486/95–1546)

14 x 6 x 9¾ in. (35.5 x 15.2 x 24.8 cm)

The man (head to toe): 9 1/16 in. (23 cm)

Base: 4¼ x 5⅞ (10.8 x 13.6 cm)

1970.73
Gift of Miss Frick, 1970

CONDITION

A waxy-looking cast, not chased. The figure shows on its surface the joints of piece-moulds, which have not been chiselled off. There are other excrescences on the surface. The holder in his left hand has a hole with a screw thread to attach the nozzle, while the other is a modern replacement.

PROVENANCE

J. P. Morgan Collection, New York
Duveen
Frick 1916
Helen Clay Frick

LITERATURE

Felix, 1880, p. 20, pl. IX.2
Felix, 1882, no. 413, pl. IX.2
Bode, 1910, II, no. 205, Introduction, pp. XXXIX-XL
Stafski, 1962, figs. 4–11, 76–77, 88–90
Weihrauch, 1967, pp. 277, 281, fig. 329
Pilz, 1970, pp. 71–72
E. P. Bowron, *Renaissance Bronzes in the Walters Art Gallery*, Baltimore, 1978, ill. p. 16
Smith, 1983, no. 118
Metropolitan Museum, 1986, nos. 194, 248

OTHER EXAMPLES

Baltimore, Walters Art Gallery, (Inv. no. 54.29)
Leipzig, Eugen Felix Collection (formerly), no. 413 (ex-Pulsky Collection)

Full-length nude figure of a bearded man seen in full face; his arms extended and grasping in each hand a sickle-like object designed as a candleholder. He stands on a small circular base raised upon a three-legged pedestal which is adorned with shells, serpents, cherubs' heads and other decorative ornaments; the legs supporting the stand end in claw feet. — BODE, 1910: PETER VISCHER THE YOUNGER, SCHOOL OF NUREMBERG, *Figure of a Man as a Candelabrum Bearer.*

The tripod base is symmetrical, apart from a tiny lizard cast on top of the leaf-moulding to mark the front, and a corresponding blank cartouche behind. The face of the mature, bearded athlete is well characterized.

PLATE 36
Figure of a Man as a Candelabrum
Bronze candelabrum

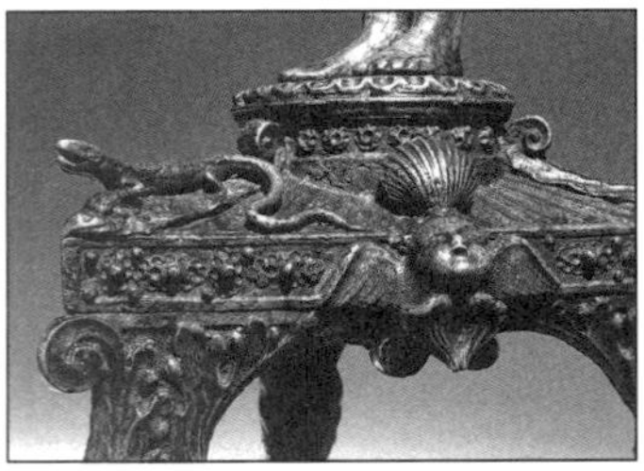

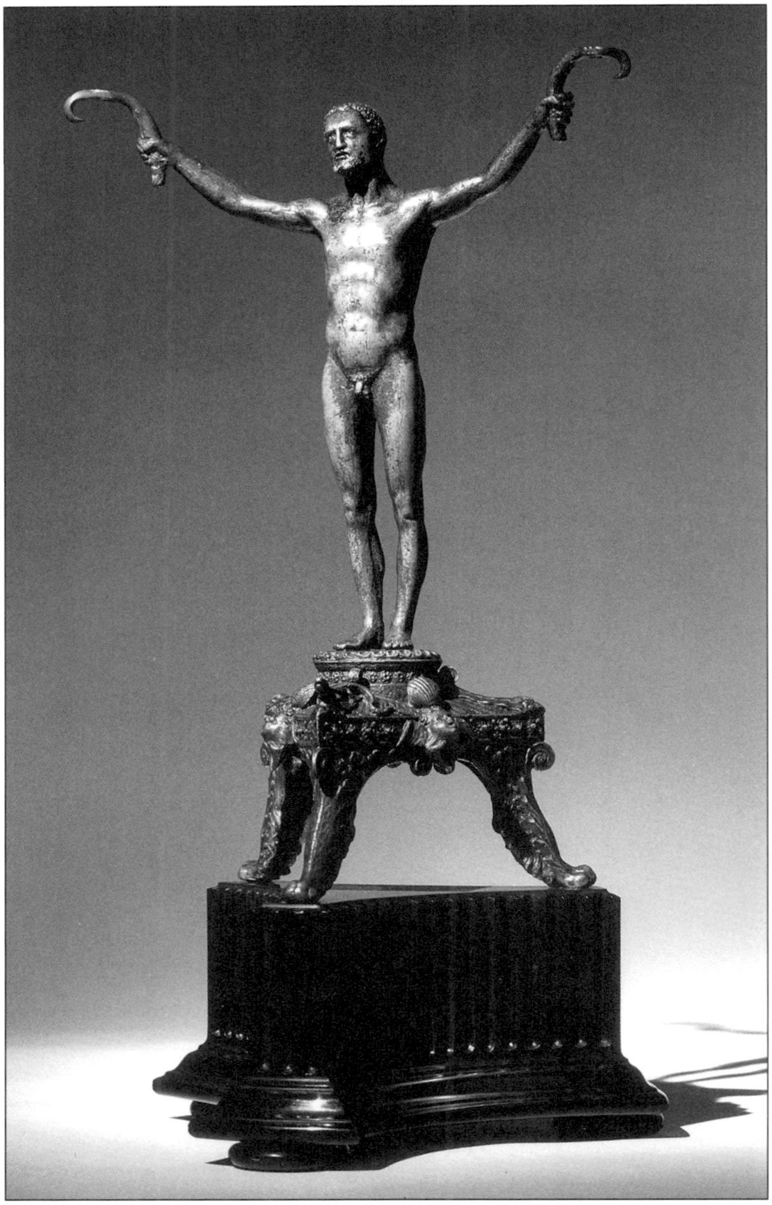

This model is known in two other casts. One in the Walters Art Gallery, (Fig. 36.1) which is more finished and has been gilded, was recently catalogued in an exemplary manner for an exhibition in Austin, Texas (Smith, 1983):

> This candlestick of a slender yet athletic nude male supporting two candle holders in his out-stretched arms is one of the very few first-rate Nuremberg bronzes in the United States. It probably once adorned the desk of a scholar or a humanistically educated patrician. The figure with its symmetrical posture and lack of contraposto is based on contemporary German, not classical or north Italian, models. As Weihrauch has correctly observed, the statue immediately recalls the oeuvre of Peter Vischer the Younger, whose nudes tend to be rather elongated, with thin, muscular legs and a taut torso emphasizing the anatomical structure of the chest. Like the apostles on the *Tomb of St. Sebaldus*, the candle-bearer possesses a relaxed demeanor and characteristic upturned tilt to the head that imparts a sense of detachment or even hauteur. He is closest in spirit to the figures of *Sts. Peter, James the Minor*, and *Simon*, which Pilz attributed to Peter the Younger, or *Judas Thaddeus*, by Peter or the workshop. The beard and moustache types reflect current tastes and again may be found on the tomb figures or on the nude Hercules in Peter's *The Dream of Hercules* drawing in Berlin. This statue was done by Peter the Younger sometime after the completion of the *Tomb of St. Sebaldus* in 1518–1519.

In his Introduction, Bode perceptively attributed the figure as follows:

> Another smaller figure undoubtedly owes its origin to the elder brother of Hans — Peter Vischer the Younger. It is the nude figure of a man of Herculean proportions, with both arms outstretched and holding in each hand a sickle-shaped object in which a candle was originally inserted. The type of head and formation of the figure are equally characteristic of the younger Peter Vischer.

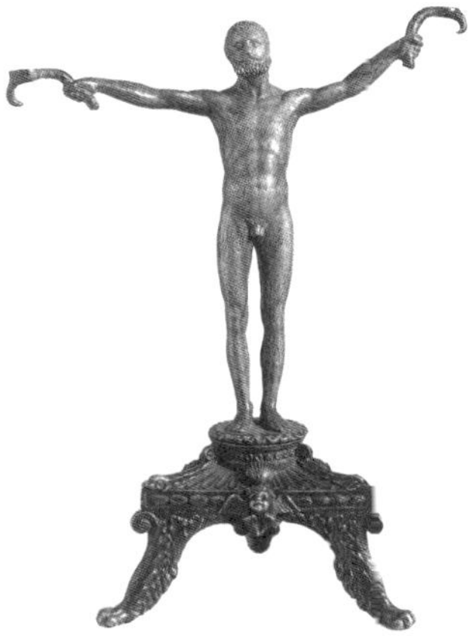

Figure 36.1
Candlestick, An Athlete, Peter Vischer (1487–1528); German, 16th century; bronze
Walters Art Gallery, Baltimore (54.29)

To this excellent summary may be added the fact noted by Smith (p. 219) in his biography of Peter Vischer the Younger that the sculptor probably learned the art of casting by the lost-wax process from Andrea Riccio, when he visited Padua around 1512: this permitted the production of pieces with fine detail, such as the present bronze, which in its less than finished state betrays signs of the wax model from which it was originally piece-moulded.

The idea of a free-standing statuette, with a humanist subject, such as a classical nude male as here, and with a functional aspect too (i.e. here a candelabrum), was also derived from Paduan precedents, from the workshops of Riccio and Severo Calzetta (see Catalogue Nos. 3,4,6,7,8,10). The repertory of ornament on the foot — shells, cherubim, lion's paw feet with acanthus motifs — is also of Paduan derivation, though the combination of circular base with tripod foot is effected rather awkwardly.

The suave treatment of male anatomy also recalls the figure of Orpheus in a plaquette with Eurydice by Peter Vischer the Younger, bearing his device (Fig. 36.2; Hamburg, Museum für Kunst und Gewerbe, 1887.265).

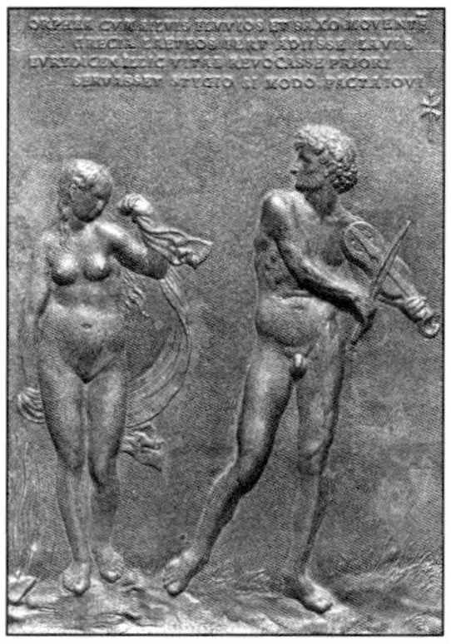

Figure 36.2
Orpheus Redeeming Eurydice, Peter Vischer the Younger; about 1516; brass, cast after a wax model
Museum für Kunst und Gewerbe, Hamburg (1887.265)

The subject gives the impression of a mature classical athlete holding up palms of victory (though the elements he holds also resemble the *strigil*, with which, in the ancient world, one scraped oneself after bathing). The arms are not held quite level in the Walters example (perhaps due to an accident in casting, or to later damage), while the figure formerly in Leipzig (reproduced by Weihrauch 1967, fig. 329) inclines its head slightly to the spectator's right, unlike the Walters and Frick ones, where the heads lean slightly to the left. The Leipzig candelabrum might therefore have formed a pair with one of the other two, probably the Frick one, in view of the fact that it was not gilded.

While the stylistic and morphological analogies remarked heretofore with the work of Peter Vischer the Younger are convincing, it should be noted that the athletic nudity, slim proportions and rather small head also find parallels in a celebrated bronze figure of *Apollo* dated 1532, (Fig. 36.3; Germanisches Nationalmuseum, Nuremberg). This crowns a bronze fountain commissioned by the Archers' Guild for their shooting range in Nuremberg (Metropolitan Museum 1986, no. 248). Its base also consists of an agglomeration of basically Paduan, Riccioesque ornamental motifs — shells, masks, putti — similar to those on the present tripod.

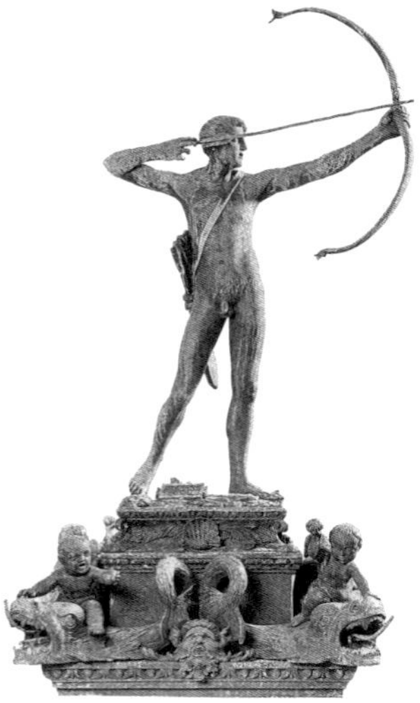

Figure 36.3
Apollo, Peter Flötner; bronze fountain figure
Germanisches Nationalmuseum, Nuremberg, Germany (Pl.O.3146)

Still more significant is the fact that the angles are marked out, as in the present instance, by curving serpent-like creatures, with their curling tails towards the centre and facing outward, so that their noses exactly meet the corners of the architectural moulding below.

The fountain and a related drawing of 1531 are not signed, and were formerly ascribed to Peter Vischer the Younger, but are now believed to be designed by Peter Flötner (1486/95–1546), and the bronze actually cast by Pancraz Labenwolf. Both artists were in any case closely associated with the Vischer workshop. Flötner may also therefore be borne in mind as a candidate for the authorship of the athletic candelabra.

37

Bust of Hippocrates, the Greek Physician (d. 361 BC)

Bronze half-length figure in deep relief

GERMAN, Probably NUREMBERG, EARLY 16TH CENTURY
8⅞ x 9¾ x 3½ in. (22.5 x 24.8 x 8.9 cm)
Base: 2 13/16 x 11¼ x 7 in. (7.4 x 28.6 x 17.7 cm)

1970.77
Gift of Miss Frick, 1970

CONDITION

Very thick casting, open behind and with traces of the original wax being brushed into the mould. Two holes in flange behind, one with an old screw thread. Light brown patinated metal with dark lacquer. Cape and scroll matt-punched. Behind is pasted an old paper label: *'ON LOAN FROM: H. Willett Esq, May 1865*, and *Exhibition of Italian Art, no. 79'* (?). A printed paper label no. *909* corresponds with that of the J. P. Morgan loan to the Victoria & Albert Museum. The associated carved walnut base, which could be 16th-century French, has the name *Aristophanes* written in ink on its upper surface.

PROVENANCE

H. Willett Collection
J. P. Morgan Collection, New York
Duveen
Frick 1916
Helen Clay Frick

EXHIBITED

London, Victoria & Albert Museum, 1901–12, no. 909, lent by J. Pierpont Morgan

LITERATURE

Bode, 1910, II, no. 204, plate CXL, Introduction, p. XXXIX
Meller, 1926–37, pp. 23–24, plate 61
Hovey, 1975, pp. 113–14

Half-figure of a bearded man, wearing a garment with long sleeves tied in at the waist and a cowl-like cap covering his long hair. He looks to the right, resting his right hand on an open book which is set up on end; his left hand holds an hour-glass with a scroll inscribed with the legend: "Vita Brevis." On the cover of the book is inscribed: "Ars Lunga." The whole rests upon a low wooden pedestal decorated with cornucopiae, fruit and foliage. This bust has always been traditionally known as Aristophanes, *but the motto "Life is short and Art is long" points to its being Hippocrates.* — BODE, 1910: GERMAN, 16TH CENTURY, *Half-length figure: Aristophanes.*

There can be little doubt that this distinguished and unusual bust is South German in origin, owing to the general appearance of the subject and garments, as well as to technical features such as the heavy, flawless casting and the smooth, but robust, finish.

The emergence of humanism in northern Europe in the first quarter of the 16th century provides the background for this Germanic treatment of an

PLATE 37
Bust of Hippocrates, the Greek Physician (d. 361 BC)
Bronze half-length figure in deep relief

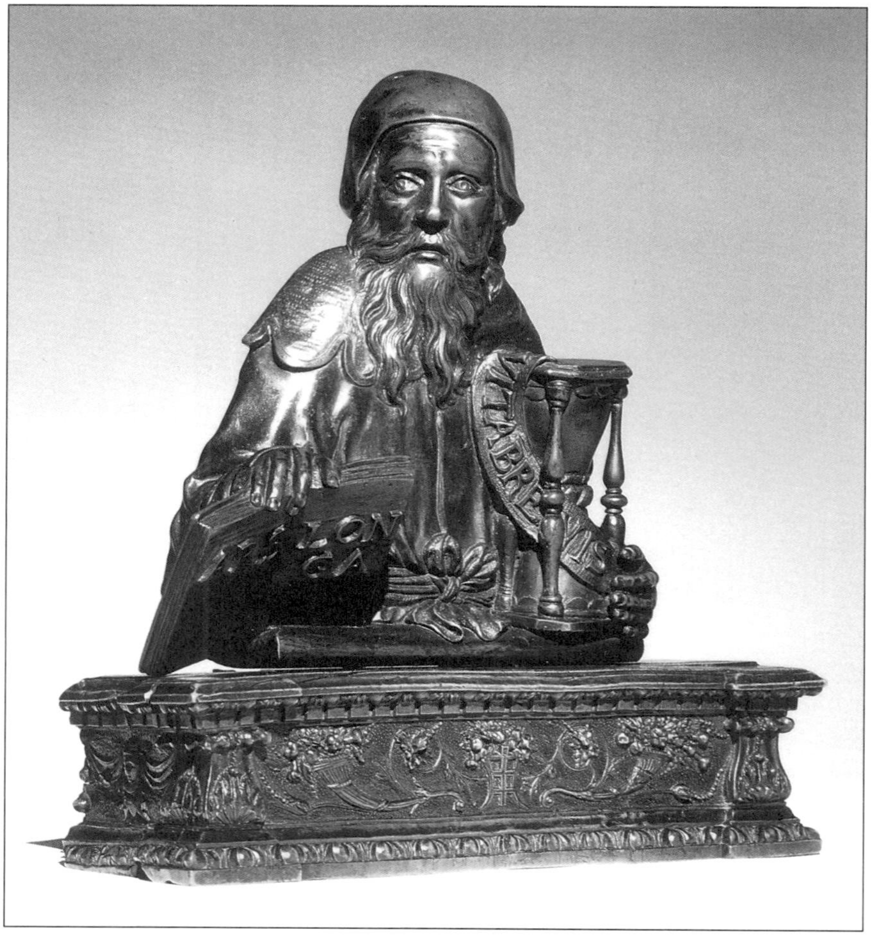

image that is careful to proclaim its classical respectability by the 'learned' motto in Latin: what is more, it is cast in unrealistically large letters and in relief (as opposed to more normal and simpler method of incising such an inscription), surely in order to emphasize its significance.

The waist-length image, including both arms, and with the hands holding distinguishing attributes, resembles a German alabaster bust of the Elector Ottheinrich of the Palatinate, which was carved in Mainz around 1556–58 (Paris, Louvre; 16 cm. high: see T. Mueller, *Deutsche Plastik der Renaissance . . .*, 'Die Blauer Buecher,' Koenigstein im Taunus, 1963, pl. 47).

The image is also reminiscent of the upper part of the self-portrait statuette of *Peter Vischer the Elder*, on the Shrine of St. Sebaldus in Nuremberg (Weihrauch, 1967, plate 322). However, the modelling and chasing are different, as noted by Bode (Introduction, p. XXIX): '. . . a bust of Aristophanes, which is considered to be the work of the elder Vischer, is not by him nor is it a product of his workshop.' Several analogies may be found: most indicative may be those between the typology of the elderly, bearded sage and the treatment of his hands, and a bronze statuette of a *Pilgrim* once in the Imperial Treasury in Vienna (Fig. 37.1; Kunsthistorisches Museum: Bange, 1949, p. 118, no. 58). This is currently attributed to Peter Vischer's eldest son, Hermann Vischer the Younger (1486–1517), who spent some time in Siena and Rome around 1515. Hermann might well have conceived just such a classicizing image after his visit to Italy, and had time to realize it before his premature death two years later.

The sinuous, rippling folds of the thick material of Hippocrates' tunic also recall those around the hem of the dress worn by *Elisabeth of Austria*, one of the great bronze statues of Habsburg ancestors that stand around the tomb of the Emperor Maximilian I in the Hofkirche in Innsbruck (Mueller, 1963, pls. 48–49): this was made in 1516 by Gilg Sesselschreiber. The modelling of the hands, with carefully separated and almost geometrically bent fingers, separating the pages of an open book, is also rather like. This serves at least to corroborate the probable date of the bust of Hippocrates in the second or third decade of the 16th century, if not its authorship.

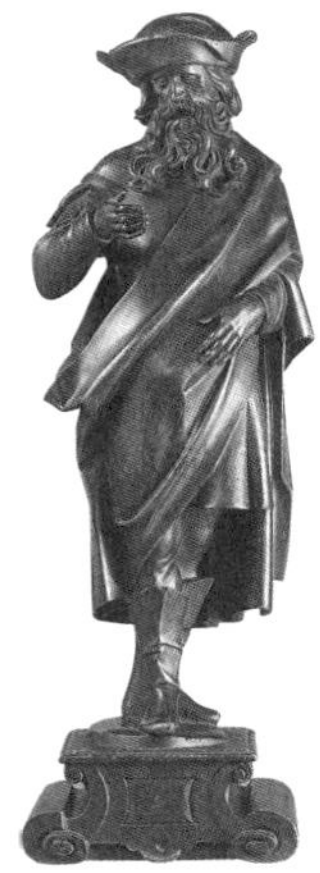

Figure 37.1
Pilgrim, Hermann Vischer the Younger (1486–1517); bronze statuette
Courtesy Kunsthistorisches Museum, Wien, Kunstkammer (INV 6026)

38

Satyr Standing by a Tree Stump

Bronze statuette

DUTCH, EARLY 16TH CENTURY

Attributed to Adrian de Vries (1545–1626)

14½ x 11 x 9 in. (36.9 x 27.9 x 22.9 cm)

1970.81

Gift of Miss Frick, 1970

CONDITION

The bronze is porous over the breast and neck of the figure, and especially on its back. The flaws have been roughly filled in, sometimes with suitably tinted wax, resulting in a poor surface. There are traces of four sprues cut off on the base, and three on the tree stump. In the right hand of the satyr are the remains of a substantial, but unidentifiable object, possibly the hilt of a knife.

PROVENANCE

J. P. Morgan Collection, New York
Duveen
Frick 1916
Helen Clay Frick

LITERATURE

Bode, 1910, II, no. 139, plate C
Larsson, 1967
Arts Council, 1978, nos. 69, 71, 72

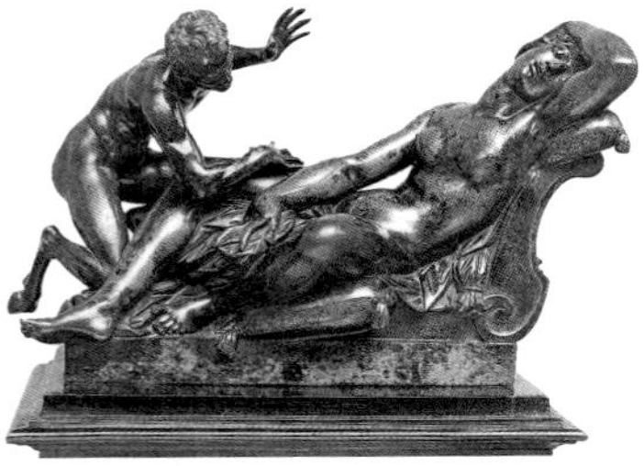

Figure 38.1
Faun and Nymph, Giambologna; bronze
Grünes Gewölbe, Staatliche Kunstammlungen, Dresden, Skulpturensammlung (Inv. No. IX.34)

Full-length nude, bending forward and leaning his left hand upon the stump of a tree. He looks down smiling and rests his right arm upon his left thigh, bending the wrist and holding a piece of wood broken from the tree stump. — BODE, 1910: ITALIAN, 16TH CENTURY, *Satyr standing by a tree.*

The satyr's left hand on top of the stump is well modelled, with cocked joints on the fingers and squarish nails. The bronze was probably abandoned in its present state owing to the severe flawing.

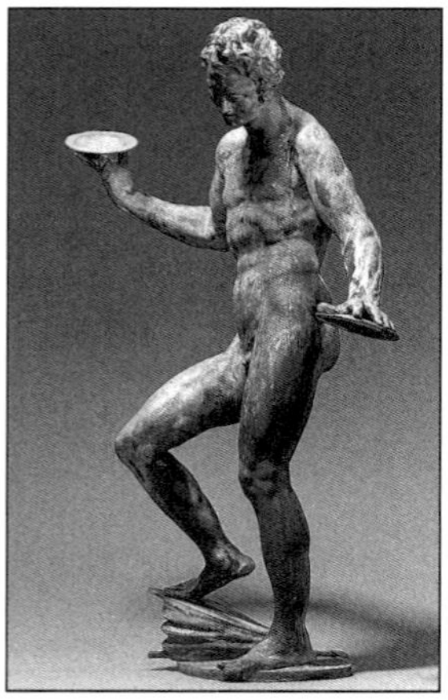

Figure 38.2
Dancing Faun, Adrian de Vries
By kind permission of Sotheby's, London (Lot #65, 7/12/89), now in the J. Paul Getty Museum

This is an unfinished cast of an interesting, sophisticated spiralling composition, with multiple points of view. Regarded by Bode as 'Italian, 16th century,' it is reminiscent of the satyr in Giambologna's group with a sleeping nymph, and it is from this tradition that this bronze comes (Fig. 38.1). However, the looser modelling points to his Dutch follower, Adrian de Vries, who, after working in Augsburg, became court sculptor in Prague to the Emperor Rudolf II.

There are significant points of comparison with works by de Vries from throughout his mature career, particularly with the many large bronze statues that he made for gardens and fountains, most of which are now in Drottningholm Palace near Stockholm. They are normally nude, male mythological figures, as is the case with the Frick *Satyr*, and because of their intended

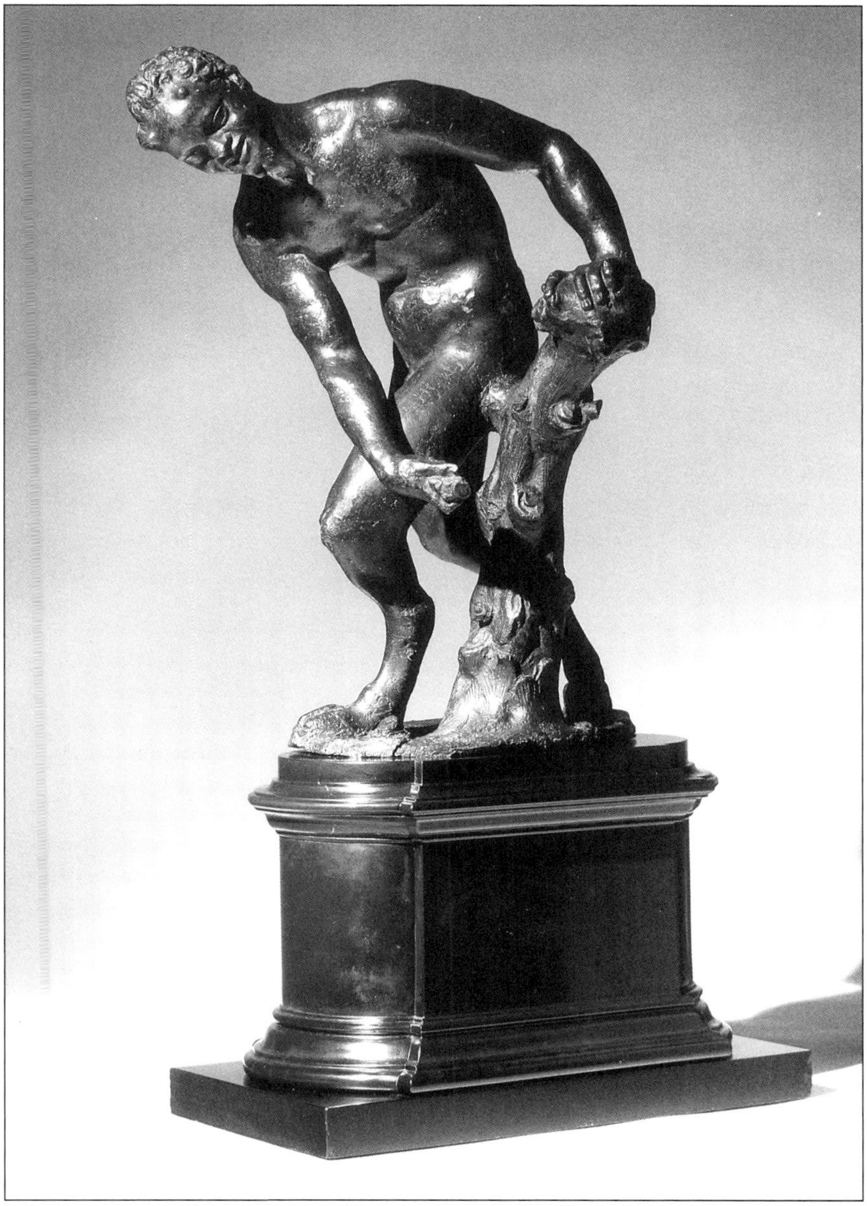

PLATE 38
Satyr Standing by a Tree Stump
Bronze statuette

locations many look downwards. Their limbs are contorted in vigorous action, and are frequently so composed that they touch each other (as the *Satyr's* right forearm touches his left thigh), for this gives the statue added strength, and also serves, during the casting process, to facilitate the flow of molten metal to all the extremities.

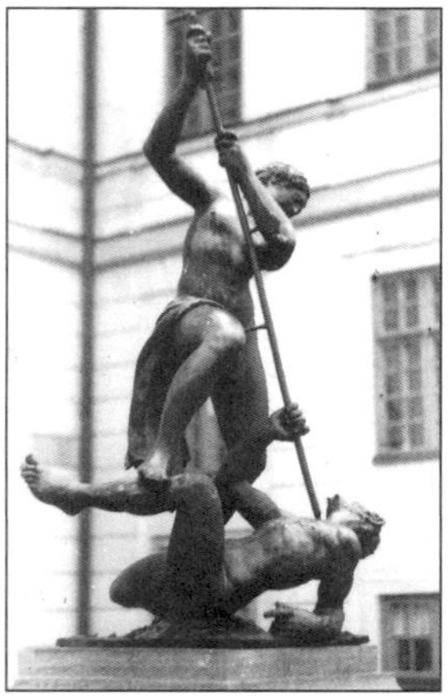

Figure 38.3
Virtue Triumphing over Vice, Adrian de Vries
Drottningholm, Stockholm, Sweden; photograph supplied by the author

The subject of fauns or satyrs was frequent in the oeuvre of de Vries, and their facial types are similar to that of the Frick bronze: the *Faun dancing in front of a Nymph* (Dresden, Grünes Gewölbe: Larsson, 1967, pls. 7–8; Metropolitan Museum of Art, *Splendors of Dresden*, exhibition catalogue, 198, no. 51; Baltimore, Walters Art Gallery, 54.468; Royal Ontario Museum L974.1.86); the Satyr accompanying *Bacchus finding Ariadne* (Amsterdam, Rijksmuseum; Larsson, 1967, pl. 97); and the faun with abandoned panpipes seated on the ground of the *'Farnese Bull'* (Gotha, Schlossmuseum; Larsson, 1967, pl. 163); and with the *Dancing Faun*, now in the J. Paul Getty Museum (Fig. 38.2; sold London, Sotheby's 7 December 1989, lot 65).

The facial type, with a high curly forelock and a forked beard is also frequent on ordinary male figures: notable examples occurring in the defeated male nude figure in the monumental group of *Virtue triumphing over Vice* (Fig. 38.3; Drottningholm, Larsson, 1967, pl. 177); and in both of the *Wrestlers* (Drottningholm, Larsson, 1967, pls. 198–200). Similar, rather summarily modelled, though perfectly convincing, musculature features on the *Seated Tritons* at Drottningholm (Larsson, 1967, pls. 131–33). The gnarled tree-stump modelled integrally with the naturalistic ground of the base, and with its bark indicated, finds analogies in those on which the three *Tritons* on the *Fountain of Neptune* from Frederiksborg Castle rest their ornamental ewers (now at Drottningholm, Larsson, 1967, pls. 142–44).

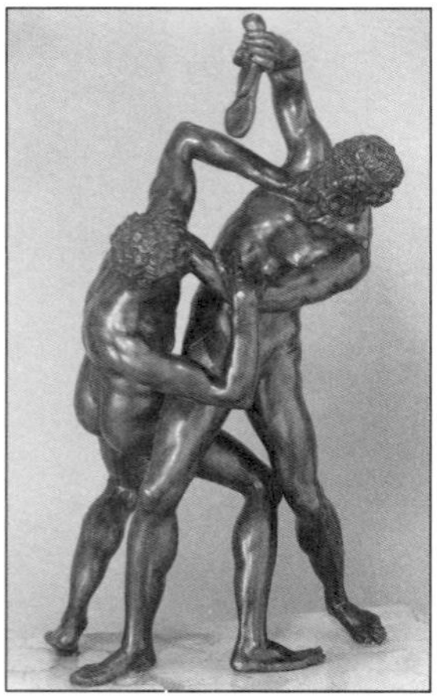

Figure 38.4
Samson and the Philistine, Follower of Giovanni da Bologna; bronze
The Toledo Museum of Art; Purchased with funds from the Libbey Endowment, Gift of Edward Drummond Libbey (1951.383)

The crouching pose, with the head turned downwards may be paralleled in a relief showing *The Forge of Vulcan* (Munich, Bayerisches Nationalmuseum no. 69/57).

In the very waxy-looking, and slightly flawed casting, and in the lack of attention to the chasing of details, and hence in the putative relationship with de Vries, the Satyr bears some resemblance to a bronze group of *Samson slaying a Philistine* also in the United States (Figs. 38.4; 38.5; Toledo Museum of Art, no. 51.383). The treatment of the hands, especially of the Philistine's right one, wrestling with Samson's left elbow, is also very like that of the *Satyr's* left hand resting on the top of the tree-stump. The composition of the Toledo group shows many resemblances with the *Wrestlers* in Drottningholm mentioned above, and with a statue of *Hercules* by de Vries (Prague, Castle; Larsson, 1967, pl. 202).

Mr. Alan Fausel has noted a similarity in this composition with the classical statue by Myron of a *Discus-thrower (Discobolus)*: one fragmentary marble torso of such a figure was known in the 16th century, but was not recognized for what it was, being regarded simply as a gladiator (now Rome, Capitoline Museum; see Haskell & Penny, 1981, pp. 199–202, pl. 104). It could however have served to inspire the creator of the present *Satyr*, and if he is indeed de Vries, a fascination with classical prototypes is a constant feature, e.g. in the case of the *Dancing Faun* (Fig. 38.2), which is a variation on a classical statue in the Uffizi Gallery.

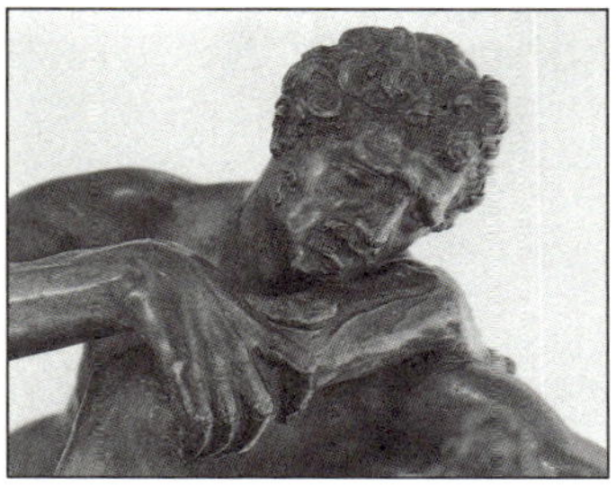

Figure 38.5
Samson and the Philistine (detail), Follower of Giovanni da Bologna; bronze
The Toledo Museum of Art; Purchased with funds from the Libbey Endowment Gift of Edward Drummond Libbey (1951.383)

39
Charging Bull
Bronze statuette

FLEMISH, 17TH CENTURY (OR LATER?)
7 x 12⅜ in. (17.8 x 31.5 cm)

1970.72
Gift of Miss Frick, 1970

CONDITION
Good

PROVENANCE
Woronzoff Collection, location unknown
J. P. Morgan Collection, New York
Duveen
Frick 1916
Helen Clay Frick

LITERATURE
Bode, 1910, II, no. 217, plate CLIV, Introduction, p. XLI
Weihrauch, 1956, no. 209
Auriti Collection catalogue, 1964, p. 29, p. XXXIX
Château de Laarne, 1967, no. 97
Weihrauch, 1967, p. 379
Leeuwenberg & Halsema-Kubes, 1973, no. 208
Hovey, 1975, p. 27
Hunter Stiebel, 1985, no. 45

OTHER EXAMPLES
Amsterdam, Rijksmuseum (RBK 16426)
Belgium, private collection (exhibited Château de Laarne, 1967, no. 97)
Boston, Museum of Fine Arts (52.281: ex-Eugene L. Garbaty, lent since 1946)
Florence, Elia Volpi Collection (sale catalogue 1910, lot 611, pl. XXVII)
The Hague, with Cramer (Supplement catalogue 10, 1964)
London, Christie's, 11 February 1972, lot 86
London, Heim Gallery (Autumn Exhibition 1967, no. 80, ill.)
Moscow (?)
Munich, Bayerisches Nationalmuseum (50/119)
New York, Michael Hall Fine Arts Inc. (1985)
Rhineland, private collection
Rome, Museo di Palazzo Venezia (Auriti Collection)

PLATE 39
Charging Bull
Bronze statuette

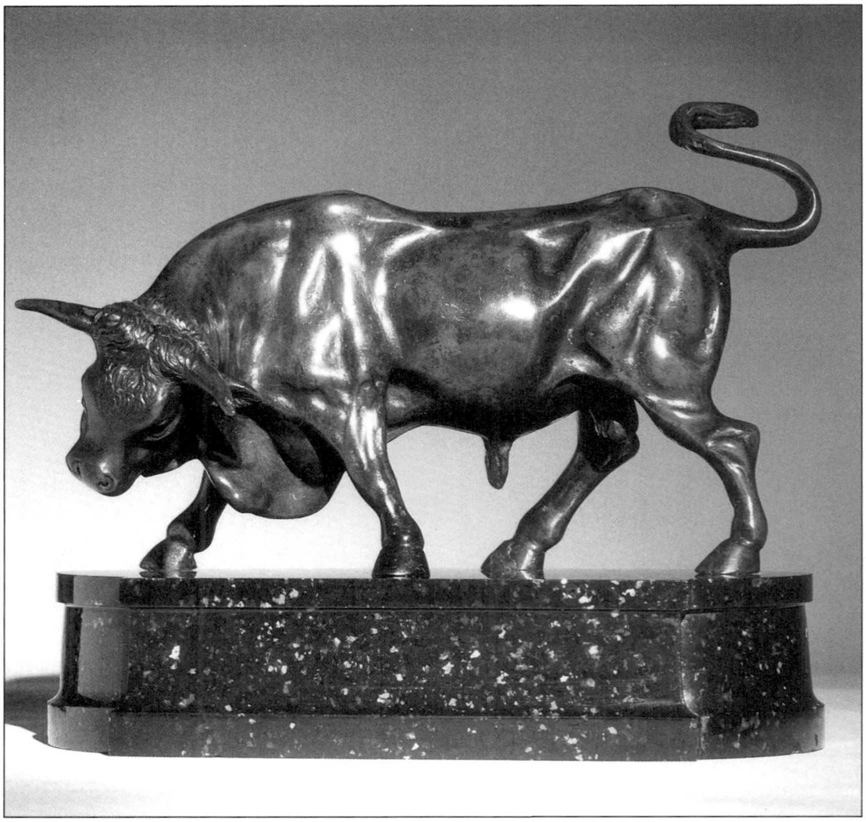

Of powerful build with head bent down preparing to dash forward, its tail lashing the air. — BODE, 1910: FLEMISH, 17th century, *Figure of a bull.*

This *Charging Bull* is a well known model, of which at least a dozen examples are recorded. They vary slightly in size, though this may be accounted for partly by the difficulty of measuring accurately and consistently such an item, with its extensions in various directions, and partly by relatively minor differences in the positions of the head and horns, and of the lashing tail, caused by original variations in casting and repairing, or subsequent accidental damages. It may also however, reflect the fact that some examples are after-casts (see below).

The model was regarded by Bode and Weihrauch as Flemish, 17th century, and this has been accepted with minor permutations by most other writers. In the present instance Bode associated it tentatively, but incorrectly, as it now emerges, with the *Leaping Hound* (Catalogue No. 20) and the *Hunter and his Dog* (Catalogue No. 35), which appeared to be of the same origin; Introduction, p. XLI:

> As Flemish works of the seventeenth century showing a very decided strain of Italian feeling, I should designate three bronzes which must originally have belonged to a large group composed of many figures, principally animals and representing a bull-fight. The figures are coarse and unpleasing in conception and in the treatment of form.

How right Bode was, at least as regards the present *Bull*!

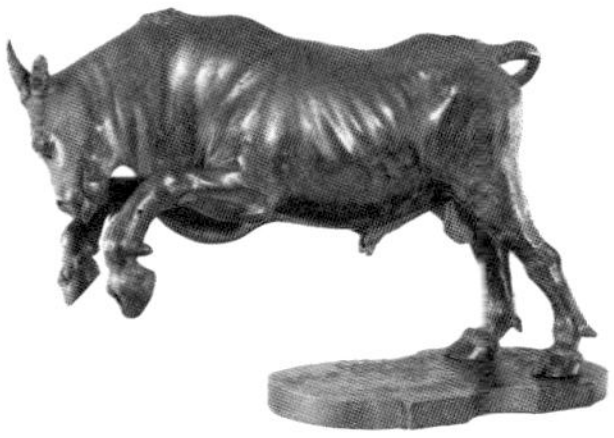

Figure 39.1
Bull, Italian
Formerly Garbaty Collection, Berlin; photograph supplied by the author

The bull is not to be connected with an extended group forming a *Bull Hunt* and including horsemen, huntsmen on foot and hounds (Fig. 39.1; formerly Garbaty Collection, Berlin; with Leopold Blumka, New York, c. 1968; on loan to the Bayerisches Nationalmuseum, Munich, c. 1973): that group is different in facture and style, and is now attributed to a master active in Venice, Rome, or Naples.

The model is generically based on bulls by Giambologna and by Dutch or Flemish sculptors parallel with, or inspired by, him, as well as earlier mid-16th-century South German naturalistic renderings of bulls on fountains (e.g. those from the fountain formerly in Schloss Hessen, which Duke Julius von Braunschweig-Lüneberg ordered in Augsburg, now in the Herzog Anton Ulrich-Museum, Braunschweig (Bro 225); our Fig. 39.2); or the bellowing ones now in the Rijksmuseum, Amsterdam (Leeuwenberg & Halsema-Kubes, 1973, no. 240) and in the Bayerisches Nationalmuseum, Munich (Weihrauch, 1956, no. 209).

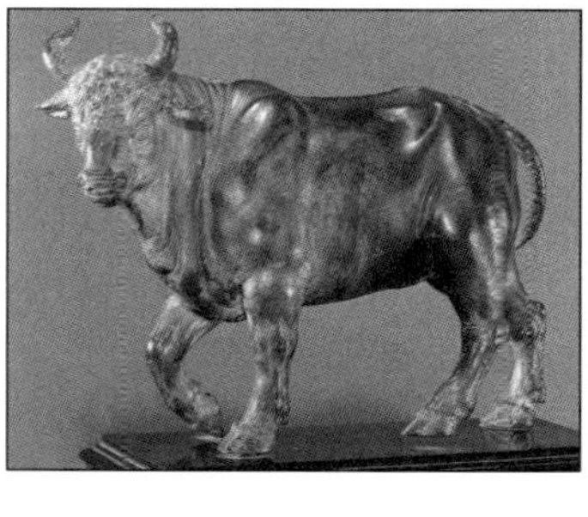

Figure 39.2
Walking Bull, South German, middle 16th century
Photograph courtesy Herzog Anton Ulrich-Museum, Braunschweig (Bro 225)

All of these are much more carefully modelled, detailed and characterized than any example of the present model. Careful comparison only serves to emphasize in the present bronze an unpleasantly schematized rendering of the bones and musculature, chiselling all over the body that makes the surface too bland, and perfunctory and uncomprehending chasing of details, e.g. in the curly hair of the forehead and the tuft at the tip of the tail, the folds of skin around the neck and dewlap.

It should be pointed out that no example with a provenance dating from before the late 19th century exists, and no corresponding references have so far been discovered in earlier archives, nor is it shown in any of the 17th-century Flemish paintings of gallery interiors, some of which illustrate other bronzes of bulls that were popular in that area and period (e.g. *Interior of Rubens' Studio*, attributed to Corneille de Bailleur in Palazzo Pitti, Florence: see S. Speth-Holterhoff, *Les peintres flamands des cabinets d'amateurs au XVIIe siècle*, Brussels, 1957, p. 119, pl. 49).

The present model is therefore open to suspicion of being a pastiche of comparatively recent, 19th-century, date. Or also, if the model itself is authentic, as has always been assumed, most of the examples in circulation seem to be recent aftercasts (*surmoulages*): it may be no coincidence that the examples in the Rijksmuseum and in the Bayerisches Nationalmuseum were purchased in Lucerne in the same year, 1950.

Biographies of Sculptors Represented

ALGARDI, ALESSANDRO (1598, Bologna–1654, Rome) — No. 32
Algardi was one of a triumvirate of sculptors, along with Bernini and Duquesnoy, who constituted the Baroque school in Rome during the first half of the 17th century. Most of his creations were on the large scale predicated by grandiose environments in churches and palaces of popes, cardinals and their relatives, but a number of statuettes were cast to his designs in precious metals, or bronze, with or without gilding, and mostly on Christian themes (*Virgin and Child; Charity; Flagellation of Christ).* He was also a gifted portraitist.

ASPETTI, TIZIANO (1559, Padua–1606, Pisa)
Aspetti belonged to a Paduan family with a tradition of bronze-casting over three generations. He was associated with two of the greatest names in Venetian sculpture from the second half of the 16th century, Girolama Campagna and Alessandro Vittoria, whose styles he amalgamated. At the end of the century he cast a pair of bronze reliefs of *Episodes from the Life of St. Daniel* for the crypt of St. Anthony's, Padua (signed duplicates now in the Metropolitan Museum of Art, New York): these are peopled with vigorous muscular figures in dramatic poses and with stylized drapery. He is credited with a large number of statuettes and artifacts, attributed on the basis of style and not documents. From 1599 to 1602 he worked in Tuscany, and there seem to have been reciprocal influences with the style of Giambologna and his followers there.

BANDINI, GIOVANNI (1540, Florence–1599, Florence) — No. 20
Bandini was apprenticed to Bandinelli, the court sculptor of the Medici Grand-Duke, and after his master's death in 1560 completed the long series of marble reliefs of single figures for the choir surround of Florence Cathedral. He was well thought of, being elected a member of the Academy of Design in 1563 and playing an important part in the sculpture for the catafalque and later the marble tomb of Michelangelo (d. 1564). He made statues of saints for the Cathedral, several excellent portraits of the Medicean rulers, and contributed a bronze statuette of Juno to the Studiolo of Francesco I in 1573. In 1582 he was recruited as court sculptor by the Duke of Urbino, again producing several good portraits, and a number of ambitious religious and mythological statues. A highly competent animal sculptor, his masterpiece was a bronze group with *Meleager Hunting the Boar* (1583-84: see Fig. 20.1).

FLÖTNER, PETER — No. 36
(Between 1486 and 1495, Thurgau [Switzerland] — 1546, Nuremberg)
A specialist in small scale sculpture, and especially reliefs, Flötner worked in Augsburg and on the Fugger Chapel there until 1522, when he became a citizen of Nuremberg. Before then, and again in 1529, he went to Italy, hence absorbing, like Albrecht Dürer before him, strong influence from Renaissance sources. This is reflected in his masterpiece in bronze, the *Fountain of Apollo* in Nuremberg Town Hall of 1531–33: the lithe nude god reflects a classical statue, the *Apollo Belvedere,* while its base, animated by putti astride sea-monsters, recalls the world of the Paduan bronze foundries. His interest in designing plaquettes also shows an awareness of their popularity in northern Italy: Flötner was also closely associated with Peter Vischer the Younger, another specialist in bronze sculpture.

GIAMBOLOGNA, (JEAN BOULOGNE)
(1529, Douai [France]–1608, Florence) — No. 23
Trained in his native Flanders until 1550, Giambologna, as he became known in Italy, went to Rome and then Florence, where he became court sculptor to successive Medici Grand-Dukes. A great admirer of ancient Graeco-Roman sculpture and of Michelangelo, Giambologna could turn his hand to all sorts of sculpture: monumental statues in bronze or marble; a multitude of subjects on the smaller scale of statuettes in bronze; and reliefs, often on Christian themes. His most famous tour-de-force was the marble group of the *Rape of a Sabine Woman,* with three figures carved out of a single block (1583, Loggia dei Lanzi, Florence). His statuettes were brilliantly calculated evocations of an ideal world of pagan gods and goddesses, among which his *Flying Mercury* (Messenger of the gods) was such a strong image that it is still in use today to symbolize speedy courier services worldwide. Giambologna was the premier sculptor of Europe during the second half of the 16th century, and his busy workshop was a fertile training ground for aspiring sculptors, both Italian, like Ferdinando Tacca (Nos. 21, 22), and northerners, like Adrian de Vries (No. 38).

GIBSON, JOHN (1790, Conway [Wales]–1866, Rome) — No. 35
Welsh by birth, Gibson moved as a child to Liverpool, where he was apprenticed to a firm of statuaries. He was patronized by William Roscoe and the Blundell family. He then went briefly to London, perhaps working under Nollekens, but soon proceeded to Rome (1817), where he was to spend most of his career. He was helped by both Canova and Thorwaldsen, the two leading lights of the Neo-Classical school of sculpture, and continued to produce work for British patrons, often commissioned during their visits on the Grand Tour. He exhibited work at the Royal Academy in London between 1816 and 1864, becoming an Academician in 1838. In 1844, and again in 1850, Gibson

revisited England to carve statues of Queen Victoria. He revived the ancient Greek idea of adding touches of colour to marble statuary, most famously on his *Tinted Venus,* and this outraged contemporary taste. Gibson was a fulfilled and prolific sculptor, who enjoyed life in Rome and produced much mythological work of high quality, in a style redolent of Canova and Thorwaldsen, but adapted to the predilections of his respectable British patrons.

RICCIO (ANDREA BRIOSCO, CALLED IL RICCIO)
(1470, Trent [Italy]–1532, Padua) — Nos. 1, 2
Generally known by his nickname, Riccio was the greatest sculptor of bronze statuettes ever known. Their subjects were influenced by the revival of interest in ancient mythology among the humanist professors of Padua University. Riccio also worked in terracotta and bronze on a larger scale, though there his themes tended to be Christian, rather than pagan. Although trained as a goldsmith, Riccio soon turned to sculpture, which he learned from Bellano, Donatello's associate, and so he became indirectly a follower of Donatello, through the example of his statuary in the Basilica of St. Anthony. Riccio completed Bellano's series of narrative panels of Old Testament themes in the Basilica, but he introduced a suaver, distinctly more classical style, influenced by Mantegna. His masterpiece was the twelve foot high *Paschal Candlestick* in the Basilica: commissioned in 1507, its completion was interrupted by hostilities until 1516. It is an extraordinarily rich compendium of Christian and pagan themes (used allegorically), expressed in reliefs and attached statuettes, which provide a touchstone for attributing to him undocumented statuettes and domestic artifacts.

RIGHETTI, FRANCESCO (1749, Rome–1819, Rome) — No. 34
Righetti learned his craft under Luigi Valadier, the prominent Roman silversmith and designer, and founded a dynasty of bronze foundrymen. A member of the Congregazione dei Virtuosi, his first major commission came in 1781, with the casting of twelve life-size statues after Antique and modern originals. In 1794 he was in a position to supply a whole range of subjects chosen from the most famous ancient statues in Rome, as well as a few by Renaissance sculptors (e.g. Giambologna's *Medici Mercury*), and he published a priced catalogue in French to advertise his works. Roughly one foot high, many of his statuettes bore signatures and dates, as did those by his predecessors and rivals in the business of reproductions, the Zoffoli. Righetti also cast in bronze statues by Canova, such as the nude Napoleon for the courtyard of the Brera Gallery, Milan, and the equestrian King Charles III for Naples.

ROCCATAGLIATA, NICCOLO
(b. Genoa, active Venice, 1593–1636, Venice) — No. 14

Trained as a goldsmith in Genoa, Roccatagliata moved to Venice, supposedly learning to carve stone. However, all his documented or signed works are cast in bronze. In 1593 he received a commission for a pair of large statuettes of *Sts. George and Stephen* and some candlesticks and brackets for San Giorgio Maggiore, Venice. Between 1598 and c. 1630 Roccatagliata returned to Genoa, but in 1633 he signed (together with his son and the foundrymen) a magnificent bronze altar-frontal (*antependium*) showing *God the Father* for the Venetian church of San Moise. Roccatagliata's figure style and technique of rapid modelling, with most of the detail defined in the original wax casting models, was derived from the painterly technique of Jacopo Sansovino, and the work of his major contemporary, Alessandro Vittoria. A vast range of domestic artifacts from the Venetian school, with figurative decoration often including chubby cherubs (*'putti'*), is grouped under his name, without much substantiating evidence.

SEGALA, FRANCESCO (active 1559, Padua–1592, Padua) — No. 13

The earliest document records Segala's marriage in 1559, and by then he must have finished his apprenticeship, possibly under A. Zoppo or Tiziano Minio. Of middle-class background, Francesco was in the circle of Alvise Cornaro, who introduced him to other patrons in Venice. His first documented sculpture was a bronze statuette of *St. Catherine* in the Basilica of St. Anthony in his native Padua (1564), closely followed by a bigger commission for a series of statues of saints in stucco for the Oratory of San Prosdocimo in Santa Giustina, Padua. By 1565 he received a major commission for St. Mark's in Venice, to cast a *St. John the Baptist* for the font. Segala continued to work in Padua, producing a number of portrait busts, some on a miniature scale and in coloured wax. On the basis of stylistic and morphological comparisons with his documented *St. Catherine,* a pair of large statuettes for firedogs (of which several examples are known) is attributed to Segala: they show *Hercules* and *Omphale,* and have thick-set, muscular bodies, quite unlike the more lithe figures of Aspetti (See No. 13, Fig. 13.1)

SEVERO DA RAVENNA (SEVERO CALZETTA)
(active 1496, Ravenna–active 1525, Ravenna) — Nos. 3–10

Severo's bronze sculpture has been disentangled from that of Bellano and of his closer contemporary, Il Riccio, only recently. His first documented work was a marble statue of *St. John the Baptist* for the chapel of St. Anthony in the Basilica at Padua (signed and dated 1500), and he worked in that city probably until its occupation by hostile troops in 1509, when he returned to his native Ravenna for the remainder of his career. Several bronze statuettes of religious figures may be associated with the marble *St. John* of 1500, but the majority of Severo's oeuvre was of pagan subject-matter, notably of dragons (see Nos. 3, 4) and satyrs (see No. 10) in various combinations. In this he preceded Andrea Riccio. They were usually associated with functional attributes and served as inkstands, lamps and candlesticks. Shells and pots to contain ink, or sand for blotting, were fitted by means of projecting screw threads into holes on geometrically shaped stands, alongside the statuettes. This meant that the components were interchangeable, and so could be assembled in various combinations to suit a client's taste. Workshops in Padua or Ravenna continued to reproduce Severo's designs in increasingly debased casts for a generation or more. Severo himself was highly praised by a learned young friend, Pomponius Gauricus, in his treatise *De Sculptura,* published in Padua in 1504.

TACCA, FERDINANDO (1619, Florence–1686, Florence) — Nos. 21, 22
Ferdinando was son of Pietro Tacca, the Grand-Ducal sculptor who had succeeded Giambologna. First documented in Madrid supervising the installation of Pietro's equestrian statue of King Philip IV of Spain, Ferdinando undertook other important commissions for the Spanish crown that have since been lost. In 1641 Ferdinando succeeded his father as court sculptor and returned to Florence in 1642, subsequently also becoming the First Architect and First Engineer. After completing the colossal bronze statue of *Ferdinando I* for the Cappella dei Principi in San Lorenzo, Florence, Ferdinando Tacca concentrated on producing bronzes: notably an altar frontal with the *Martyrdom of St. Stephen* (1656) for Santo Stefano al Ponte. The various strongly projecting and vigorously posed figures, about one foot or more high, in this scene provided touchstones for the attribution to Ferdinando of a number of independent and undocumented statuettes and groups of mythological and Renaissance literary figures. Ferdinando evolved away from Giambologna's spiralling compositions toward a more pictorial, relief-like approach, concentrating the action and interest in a frontal plane, with less interesting subsidiary views.

VISCHER, PETER THE YOUNGER
(1487, Nuremberg–1528, Nuremberg) — No. 36
The sculptor-foundryman belonged to the third generation of a family that had been practicing its craft in Nuremberg since 1455, but probably came originally from the Low Countries. His father, also called Peter (1460–1529), oversaw the casting of the great ornamental bronze *Tomb of St. Sebaldus,* in his church in Nuremberg, designed in 1488, and executed between 1507 and 1519 — in virtually the same span of years as the *Paschal Candlestick* by Riccio in St. Anthony's, Padua. In fact this is no casual connection, for Peter the Younger and his brother Herman the Younger had both been in north Italy, to further their knowledge of the Renaissance, following in the footsteps of their fellow countryman, Albrecht Dürer. This younger pair of sculptor-foundrymen may have been responsible for introducing many very Italian

motifs on the *Tomb of St. Sebaldus,* e.g. nude figures of Hercules, harpies holding candlesticks, monsters, and natural creatures such as snails. Several independent statuettes, some mounted as inkstands (Ashmolean Museum, Oxford), are reliably attributed to Peter the Younger, and their imaginative and technical qualities place him on a par with his Paduan counterparts.

VRIES, ADRIAN DE (c. 1545, The Hague–1626, Prague) — No. 38
This Dutch sculptor first appeared in Giambologna's workshop in Florence in 1581, described as a goldsmith and chasing the surface of a crucifix. Eventually he transmitted Giambologna's style to the whole of central Europe. In 1588 he was appointed court sculptor to the Duke of Savoy in Turin, but by 1593 he was in the employ of the Emperor Rudolf II in Prague. After briefly visiting Rome (1595) he worked for some years in Augsburg creating two magnificent public fountains: they were crowned respectively with bronze statues of *Mercury* and of *Hercules* (1596–1602). He next moved to Prague, upon his appointment as court sculptor to Rudolf (1602), and worked there for most of the remainder of his career. De Vries evolved an exciting and idiosyncratic style by adapting the free technique that Giambologna used in his models to finished work, even when on a monumental scale. He exploited his expertise in casting to avoid the necessity for much afterworking of the cold metal, and so was able to produce a larger than average number of monumental statues. They comprise impressively muscular and sinuous figures in complex poses. Many of them were plundered in the Thirty Years War and still decorate the gardens of the Swedish royal palace of Drottningholm.

Bibliography

Arts Council, 1978

Arts Council of Great Britain, *Giambologna, Sculptor to the Medici, 1529–1608*, exhibition catalogue, ed. Avery C. and Radcliffe, A., London, 1978.

Avery, 1981

Avery, C., *Studies in European Sculpture*, London, 1981.

Avery, 1987

Avery, C., *Giambologna: The Complete Sculpture*, Oxford, 1987 (paperback, London/San Francisco, 1993).

Avery, 1988

Avery, C., *Studies in European Sculpture — II*, London, 1988.

Avery and Radcliffe, 1983

Avery, C. and Radcliffe, A., 'Severo Calzetta da Ravenna: New Discoveries' in *Studien zum europäischen Kunsthandwerk: Festschrift Yvonne Hackenbroch*, Munich, 1983, pp. 107–22 (reprinted in Avery, 1988, pp. 50–61).

Bange, 1949

Bange, E. F., *Die Deutschen Bronzestatuetten des 16. Jahrhunderts,* Berlin, 1949.

Bange, 1922

Bange, E. F., *Die italienischer Bronzen der Renaissance und des Barock, II: Reliefs und Plaketten*, Staatliche Museen zu Berlin, 1922.

Banzato and Pellegrini, 1989

Banzato, D. and Pellegrini, F., *Bronzi e placchette dei Musei Civici di Padova*, Padua, 1989.

Bode, 1897

Bode, W. von, *Die Sammlung Oscar Hainauer*, Berlin, 1897.

Bode, 1910

Bode, W. von, *Bronzes of the Renaissance: Catalogue of The Pierpont Morgan Collection*, Paris, 1910.

Bode, 1930
Bode, W. von. Staatliche Museen zu Berlin, *Bildwerke des Kaiser-Friedrich Museums. Die italienischen Bildwerke der Renaissance und des Barock, II.*

Bode, 1930
Bode, W. von, *Bronzestatuetten, Büsten und Gebrauchsgegenstände*, 4th edition, Berlin/Leipzig, 1930.

Bode/Draper, 1980
Bode, W. von, *The Italian Bronze Statuettes of the Renaissance*, London, 1908/12, 2nd edition, ed. J.. D. Draper, New York, 1980.

Cannata, 1982
Cannata, P., *Rilievi e placchette dal XV al XVIII secolo*, exhibition catalogue, Museo de Palazzo Venezia, Rome, 1982.

Château de Laarne, 1967
Association royale des demeures historiques de Belgique, *Catalogue de l'exposition Bronzes de la Renaissance de Donatello à François Duquesnoy conserves dans les collections privées belges*, Château de Laarne, Belgium, 1967.

De Winter, 1986
De Winter, P. M., 'Recent Accessions of Italian Renaissance Decorative Arts. Part 1: Incorporating Notes on the Sculptor Severo da Ravenna,' *The Bulletin of the Cleveland Museum of Art*, vol. 73, no. 3, March, 1986, p. 75f.

Dhanens, 1956
Dhanens, E., *Jean Boulogne, Giovanni Bologna Fiammingo*, Brussels, 1956.

Felix, 1880
Eye, A. von, and Boerner, P. E., *Die Kunstsammlung von Eugen Felix in Leipzig, Katalog. Atlas*, Leipzig, 1880.

Felix, 1883
Eye, A. von, and Boerner, P. E., *Zierstücke des älteren Deutschen, Französichen ünd Italienischen Kunstgewerbes, zumeist aus den Sechzehnten Jahrhunderts*, Leipzig, 1883.

Frankfurt, 1986
Liebieghaus Museum Alter Plastik, *Natur und Antike in der Renaissance*, exhibition catalogue, Frankfurt am Main, 1986.

Goldschmidt, 1914
Goldschmidt, F., *Die italienischen Bronzen der Renaissance und des Barock, II pt. 1: Büsten, Statuetten und Gebrauch-gegenstände*, Konigliche Museen, Berlin, 1914.

Haskell and Penny, 1981
Haskell, F. and Penny, N., *Taste and the Antique*, New Haven/London, 1981.

Heimburger-Ravalli, 1973
Heimburger-Ravalli, M., *Alessandro Algardi scultore*, Rome, 1973.

Hill, 1930
Hill, G. F., *A Corpus of Italian Medals of the Renaissance before Cellini*, London, 1930.

Hovey, 1975
Hovey, W. R., *Treasures of The Frick Art Museum*, Pittsburgh, 1975.

Keutner, 1984
Keutner, H., *Giambologna e il Mercurio Volante*, Florence, 1984.

Larsson, 1967
Larsson, L. O., *Adrian de Vries*, Vienna, 1967.

Leeuwenberg and Halsema-Kubes, 1973
Leeuwenberg, J. and Halsema-Kubes, W., *Beeldhouwkunst in het Rijksmuseum*, The Hague/Amsterdam, 1973.

Lewis, 1983
Lewis, D., 'The Sculptures in the Chapel of the Villa Giustinian at Roncade . . .,' *Mitteilungen des Kunsthistorischen Institutes in Florenz*, XXVII, 1983 pp. 307–52.

Lewy, 1929
Lewy, E., *Pietro Tacca*, Cologne, 1929.

Lloyd, 1980
Lloyd, C. H., *Renaissance Bronzes in the Ashmolean Museum*, Oxford, 1980.

Lo Vullo Bianchi, 1931
Lo Vullo Bianchi, S., *'Note e documenti su Pietro e Ferdinando Tacca,' Rivista d'arte*, XIII, 1931, pp. 137–213.

Maclagan, 1924
Maclagan, E., *Catalogue of Italian Plaquettes, Victoria and Albert Museum*, London, 1924.

Mariacher, 1971
Mariacher, G., *Bronzetti veneti del Rinascimento*, Vicenza, 1971.

Meller, 1926/1937
Meller, S., *Die Deutschen Bronzestatuetten der Renaissance*, Munich, 1926 (2nd edition, translated into Italian, Milan, 1937, used here).

Metropolitan Museum, 1986

Gothic and Renaissance Art in Nuremberg: 1300–1550, exhibition catalogue, Metropolitan Museum of Art, New York, 1986.

Migeon, 1904

Migeon, G., *Catalogue des Bronzes et Cuivres . . .*, Musée National du Louvre, Paris, 1904.

Molinier, 1886

Molinier, E., *Les plaquettes: catalogue raisonné, Paris,* 1886.

Molinier, 1898

Molinier, E., *Collection Charles Mannheim*, Objets d'Art, Paris, 1898.

Montagu, 1985

Montagu, J., *Alessandro Algardi*, London, 1985.

Montfaucon, 1719

Montfaucon, B. de, *L'Antiquité expliquée en figures*, Paris, 1719.

Nicodemi, 1920/21

Nicodemi, G., 'Bronzi veneti del rinascimento del Museo dell'Era Cristiana a Brescia,' in *Dedalo*, I 1920/21, p. 473.

Panvini Rosati, 1968

Panvini Rosati, F., *Medaglie e placchette italiane del Rinascimento al XVIII secolo*, exhibition catalogue, Rome, 1968.

Pechstein, 1968

Pechstein, L., *Kataloge des Kunstgewerbemuseums Berlin: Band III. Bronzen und Plaketten vom ausgehenden 15. Jahrhundert bis zur Mitte des 17. Jahrhundert*, Berlin, 1968.

Pfungst, 1899

Pfungst, H. J., *Descriptive Catalogue of a small collection principally of XVth and XVIth Century Bronzes*, London (only 20 copies privately printed), 1989.

Planiscig, 1921

Planiscig, L., *Venezianische Bildhauer der Renaissance*, Vienna, 1921.

Planiscig, 1924

Planiscig, L., *Die Bronzeplastiken: Statuetten, Reliefs, Geräte und Plaketten*, Kunsthistorisches Museum, Vienna, 1924.

Planiscig, 1927

Planiscig, L., *Andrea Riccio*, Vienna, 1927.

Pope-Hennessy, 1963/1968
Pope-Hennessy, J., *Italian High Renaissance and Baroque Sculpture*, London, 1963 (2nd edition, 1968).

Pope-Hennessy and Lightbown, 1964
Pope-Hennessy, J. and Lightbown, R. W., *Catalogue of Italian Sculpture in the Victoria & Albert Museum*, London, 1964.

Pope-Hennessy, 1965
Pope-Hennessy, J., *A Catalogue of Renaissance Bronzes from the Samuel H. Kress Collection*, London, 1965.

Pope-Hennessy and Radcliffe, 1970
Pope-Hennessy, J. and Radcliffe, A., *The Frick Collection: An Illustrated Catalogue, vol. III: Sculpture Italian*, New York, 1970.

Radcliffe, 1972
Radcliffe, A., 'Bronze oil lamps by Riccio' in *Victoria and Albert Museum Yearbook*, 1972, pp. 29–58.

Radcliffe, 1982
Radcliffe, A., 'Ricciana: III The Riddle of the Sphinx,' *Burlington Magazine*, CXXIV, 1982, pp. 418–24.

Royal Academy, 1904
Royal Academy of Arts, *Exhibition of works by the Old Masters . . . and also a collection of sculptures and bronzes, Winter Exhibition, 35th year*, London, 1904.

Royal Academy, 1983
Royal Academy of Arts, *The Genius of Venice 1500–1600*, exhibition catalogue, London, 1983.

Santangelo, 1954
Santangelo, A., *Catalogo delle sculture*, Museo di Palazzo Venezia, Rome, 1954.

Sheard, 1978
Sheard, W. S., *Antiquity in the Renaissance*, exhibition catalogue, Smith College Museum of Art, Northampton, Mass., 1978.

Smith, 1983
Chipps Smith, J., *Nuremberg: A Renaissance City 1500–1618*, A. M. Huntington Art Gallery, University of Texas, Austin, Texas, 1983.

Stafski, 1962
Stafski, H., *Der Jungere Peter Visscher*, Nuremberg, 1962.

Torriti, 1975
Torriti, P., *Pietro Tacca de Carrara*, Genoa, 1975.

Weihrauch, 1956
Weihrauch, H. R., *Die Bildwerke in Bronze und in anderen Metallen*, Bayerisches Nationalmuseum, Munich, 1956.

Weihrauch, 1967
Weihrauch, H. R., *Europäische Bronzestatuetten 15–18 Jahrhunderts*, Braunschweig, 1967.

Wixom, 1975
Wixom, W., *Renaissance Bronzes from Ohio Collections*, Cleveland Museum of Art, Cleveland, Ohio, 1975.

365 blagues

Tome 1

pour les enfants à partir de 7 ans

Éditions Hemma

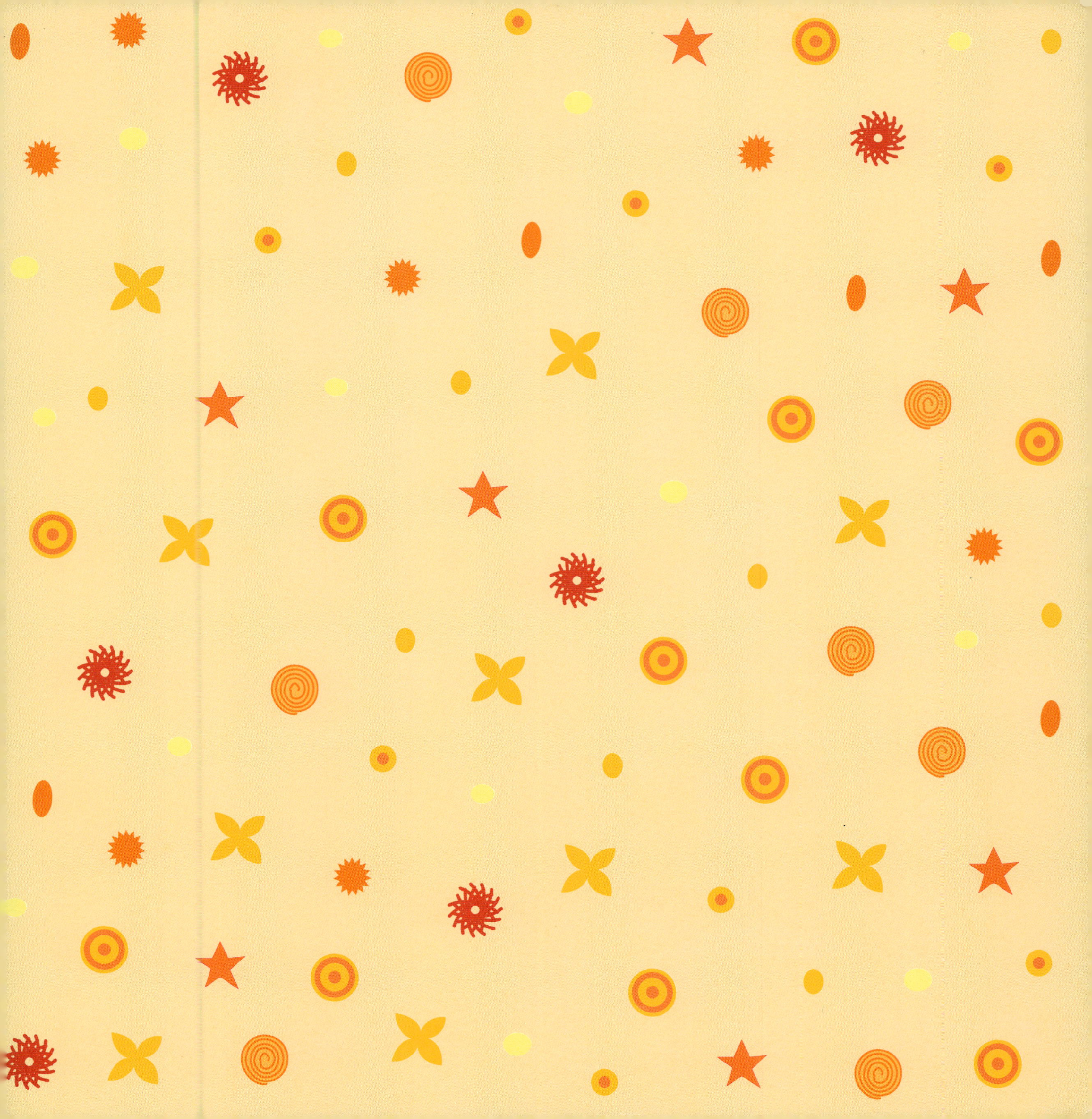

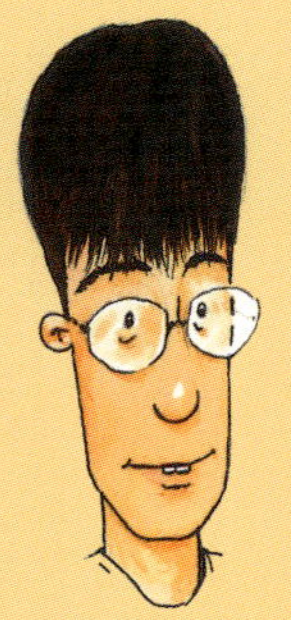

Aussi incroyable que cela puisse paraître, Fabrice Lelarge est instituteur ! Ses élèves, habitués à ses blagues et à ses farces, sont sans aucun doute les enfants les plus souriants de toute l'école ! Auteur chez Hemma depuis 1999, ses récits sont toujours emprunts d'humour et de tendresse...

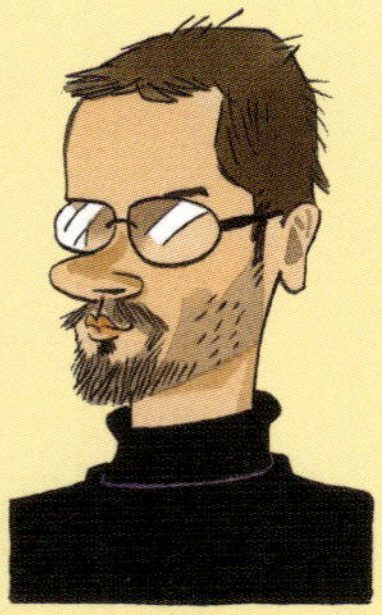

Enfant, Étienne Jung rêvait de dessiner pour Walt Disney. Après l'atelier des Arts Décoratifs de Strasbourg, il illustre principalement des journaux pour enfants et des bandes dessinées.

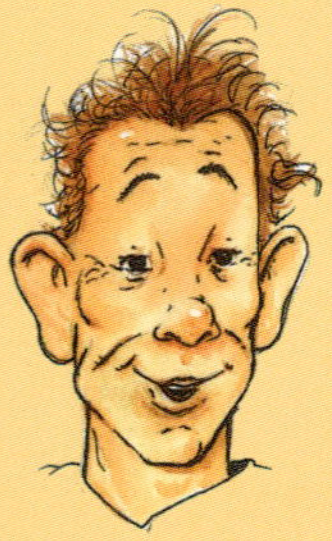

Quand on ne sait rien faire, on se met par dépit à dessiner.
C'est ce que François Ruyer fit très tôt. Déjà tout petit, il griffonnait dans les marges de son cahier, au grand désespoir de ses maîtres. Depuis bientôt douze ans qu'il sévit dans l'univers impitoyable du livre, combien d'enfants a-t-il fait rêver ?

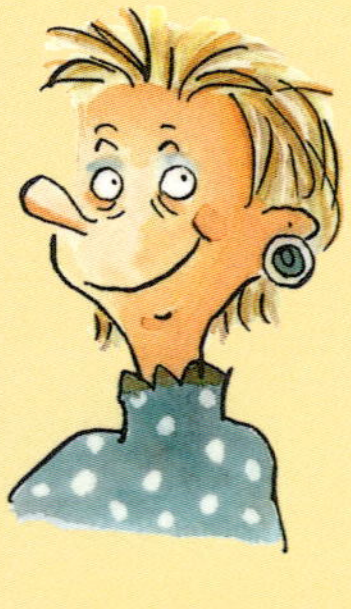

Son désir de mener une carrière artistique poussa tout naturellement Pascale Mugnier à faire des études scientifiques ! Quand elle en eut assez d'observer des insectes, des microbes et autres petites bêtes au microscope, elle se mit à les dessiner. Et aujourd'hui, elle en dessine encore...

365 blagues
Tome 1

pour les enfants à partir de 7 ans

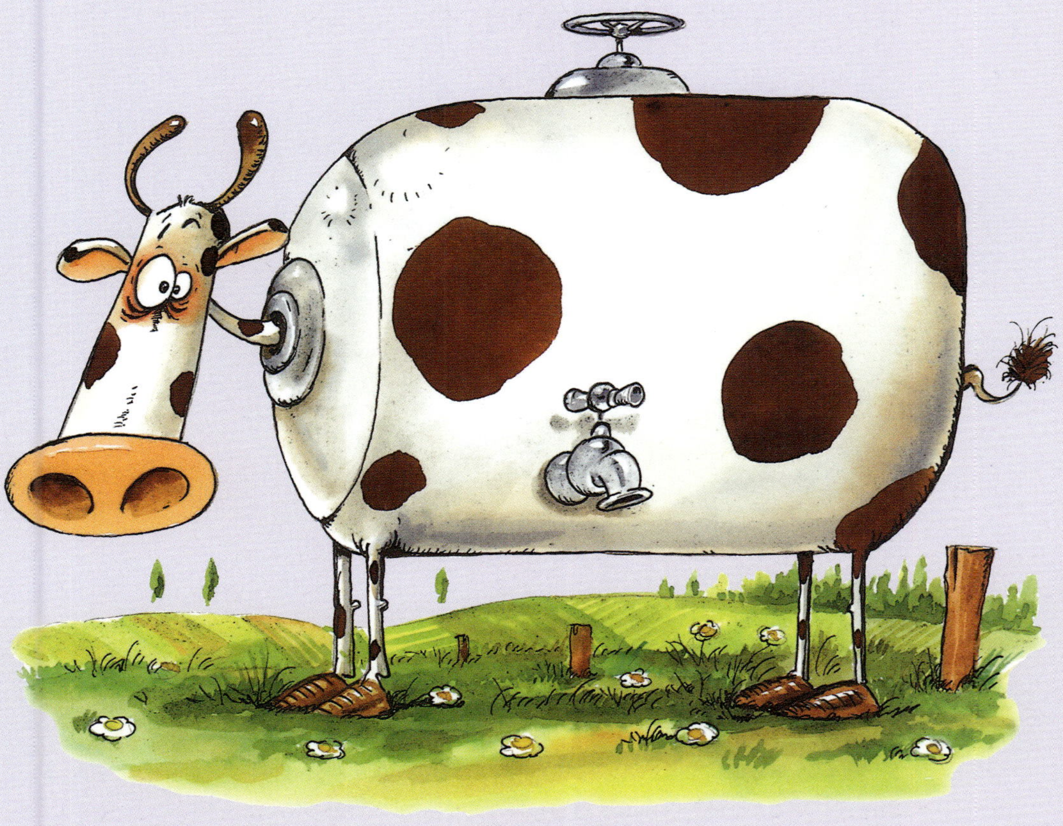

Éditions Hemma

La maîtresse donne la consigne :

- Pour votre rédaction, vous écrirez brièvement les effets d'une énorme tempête de neige.

Les enfants commencent à plancher, et une minute plus tard, une élève rend sa copie.

- C'est tout, Mélanie ? s'étonne la maîtresse.

- Oui.

L'institutrice regarde la copie, qui contient une seule phrase :

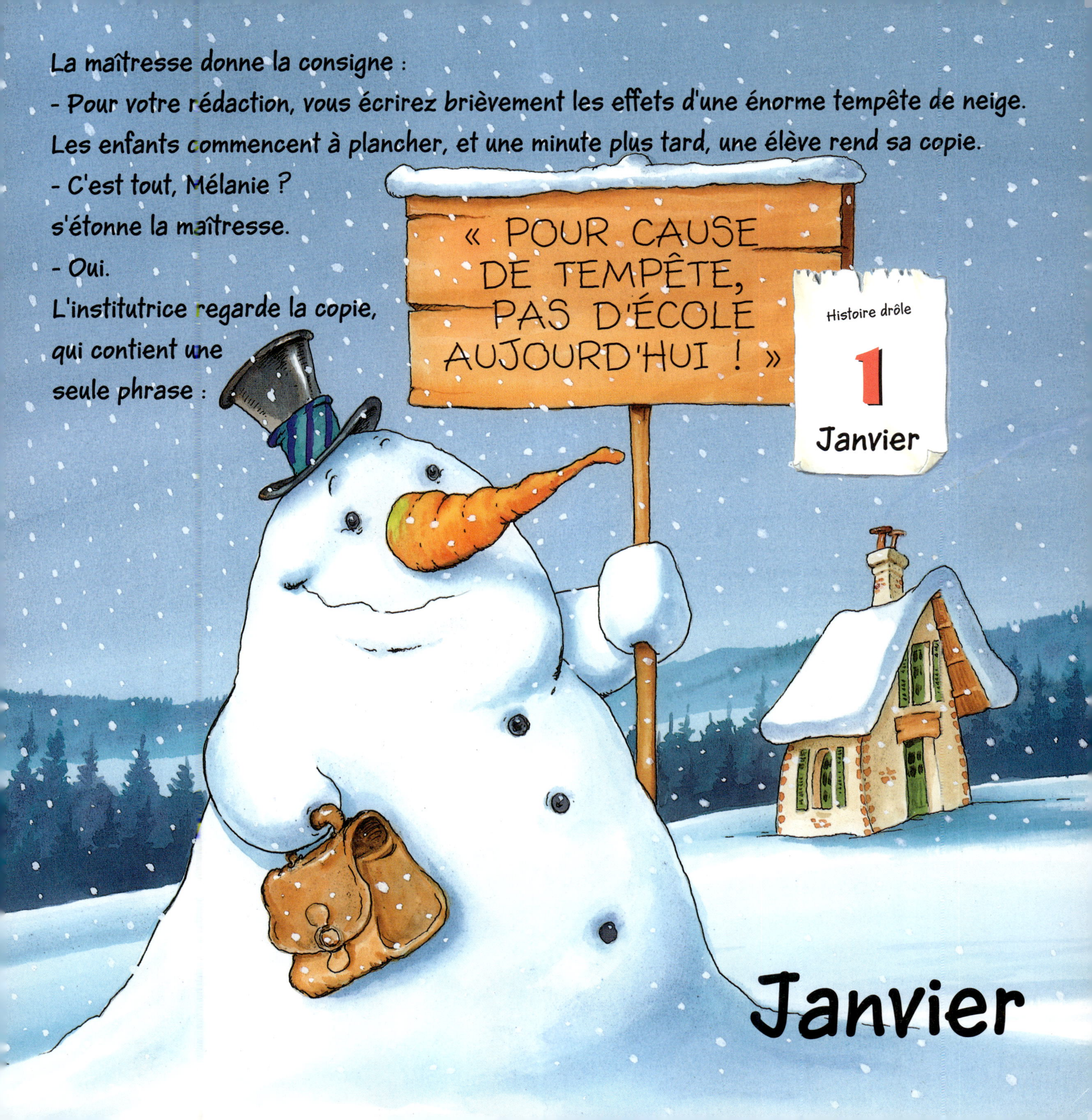

Petite annonce

2 Janvier

Mois de janvier excédé échange trente « Bonne année » contre un « Joyeux Noël ».

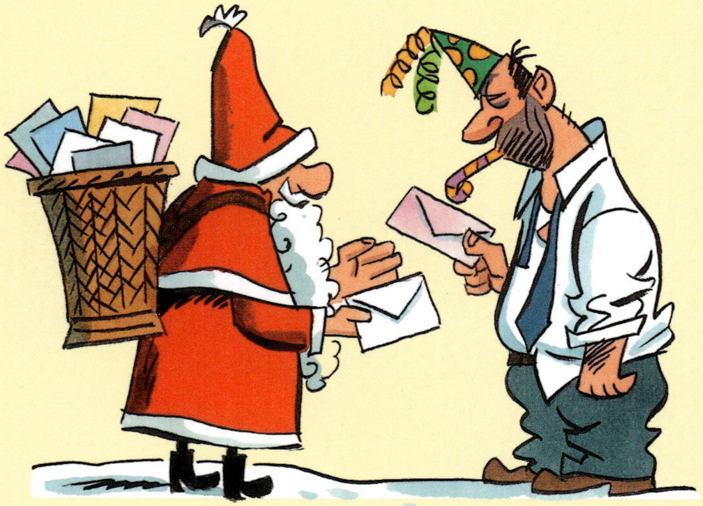

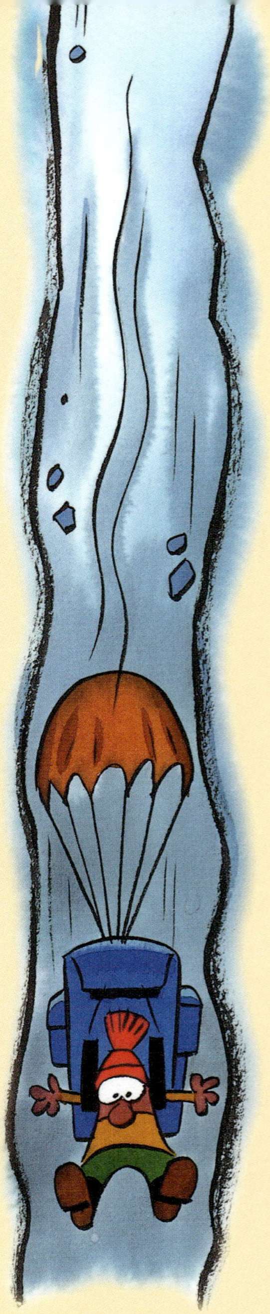

Histoire drôle

3 Janvier

Deux alpinistes escaladent une montagne, quand l'un d'entre eux tombe dans une crevasse.

L'autre lui crie :

- Est-ce que ça va ? Tu as mal ?

- Non, non ! répond une voix lointaine.

- Tu as pourtant l'air d'être tombé très bas ! Tu es sûr que tu n'as pas mal ?

- Non, répond la voix encore plus lointaine. Mais c'est parce que je n'ai pas encore fini de tomber !

Petite annonce

4 Janvier

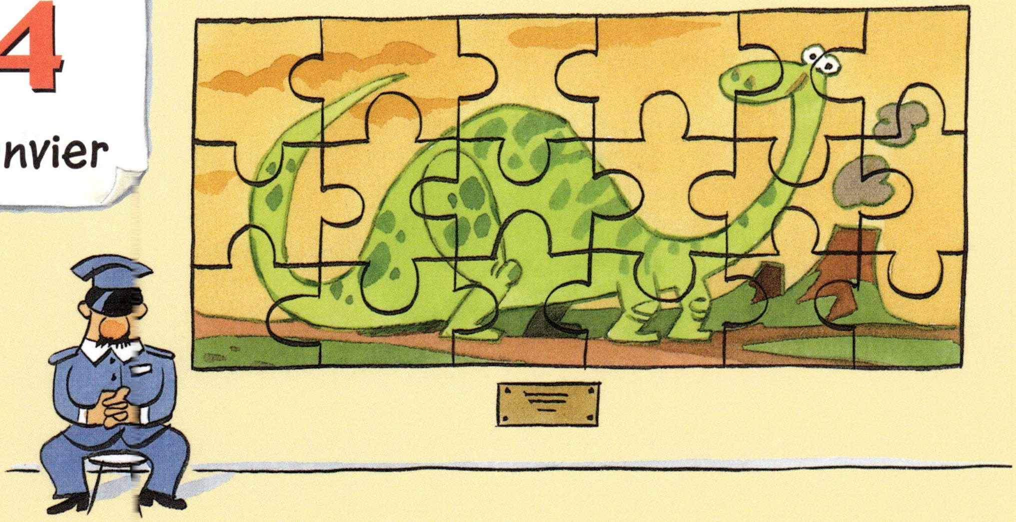

LOISIRS : vieux dinosaure prête son squelette à champion de puzzle contre une place de musée.

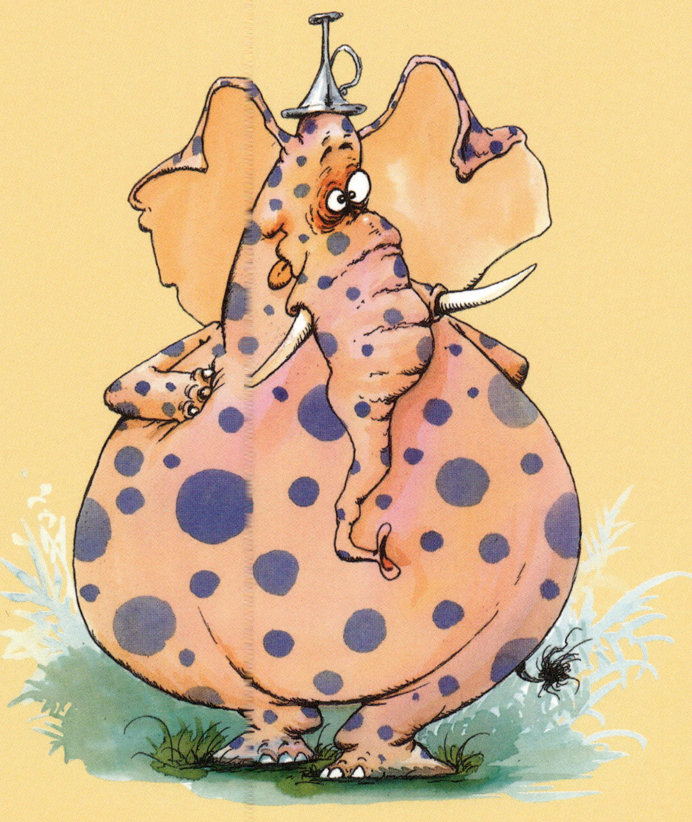

Comment capturer un éléphant vert ?
(réponse : avec un piège à éléphant vert.)
Comment capturer un éléphant jaune ?
(réponse : avec un piège à éléphant jaune.)
Comment capturer un éléphant rouge ?
(réponse : on le peint en jaune et on utilise un piège à éléphant jaune.)
Comment capturer un éléphant à pois bleus ?
(réponse : vous avez déjà vu des éléphants à pois bleus, vous ? Soyons sérieux deux minutes !)

Derinette

5 Janvier

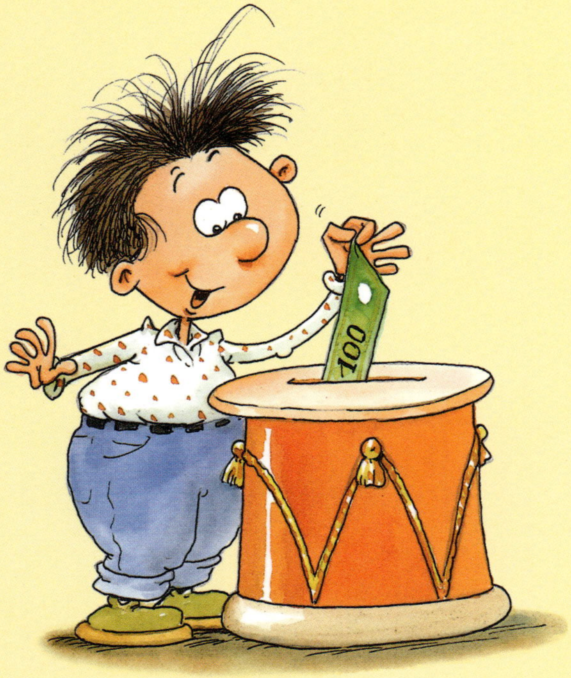

Histoire drôle

6

Janvier

Deux enfants dans la cour :

- Qu'est-ce que tu as eu à Noël ? demande l'un.

- Le plus beau cadeau du monde : un tambour ! répond son copain en souriant.

- Bof ! un tambour, c'est pas un très beau cadeau.

- Si, c'est génial ! Depuis Noël, maman me donne 100 euros par semaine pour que je n'en joue pas !

Deux fous se promènent dans la rue.

L'un d'eux ramasse un morceau de miroir. Il le regarde un instant, voit son visage et s'exclame :

- Hé ! La tête de ce type me dit quelque chose !

L'autre prend le miroir et le regarde à son tour.

- Pas étonnant ! C'est moi !

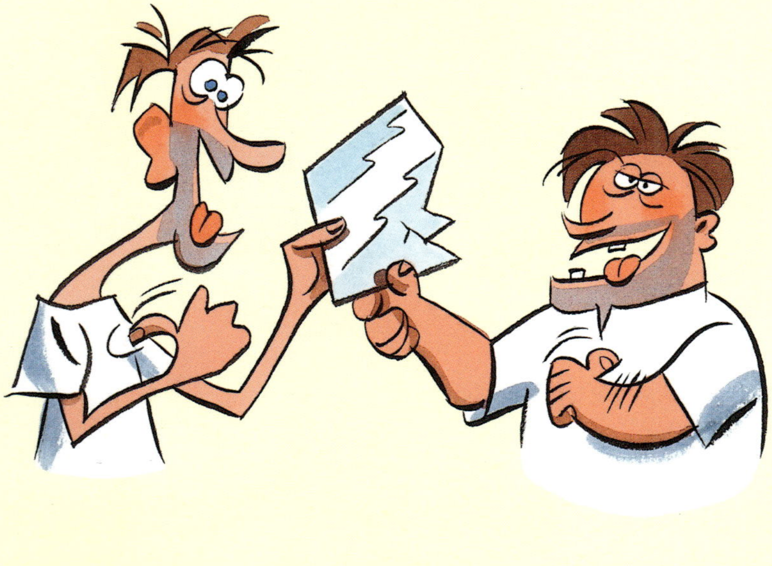

Histoire drôle

7

Janvier

Histoire drôle

8 Janvier

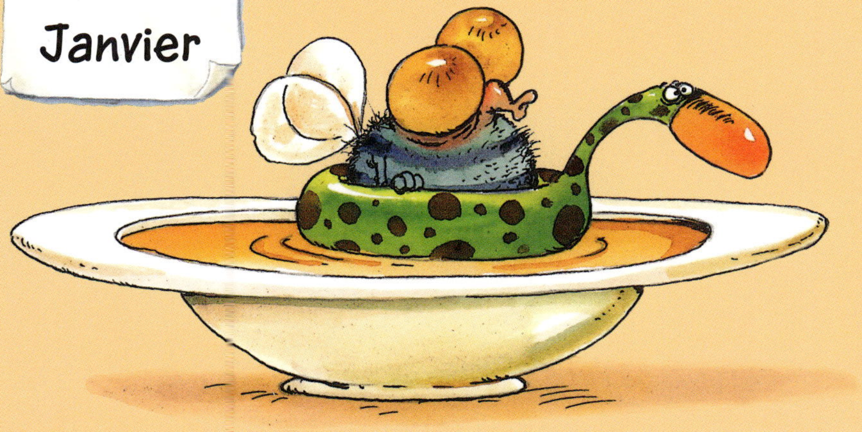

Un monsieur au restaurant :

- Garçon ! Il y a une mouche noyée dans ma soupe ! C'est inadmissible !

Le garçon arrive, regarde l'assiette de soupe et dit :

- Vous avez raison : d'habitude, les mouches ont pied !

Un monsieur dans un restaurant :

- Garçon ! Il y a une mouche dans ma soupe ! C'est inadmissible ! Enlevez-moi ça tout de suite !

Le serveur lui amène deux minutes plus tard une araignée vivante et la jette dans la soupe.

- Mais... Mais... que faites-vous ? s'indigne le monsieur.

- Ne vous inquiétez pas : l'araignée, c'est pour manger la mouche.

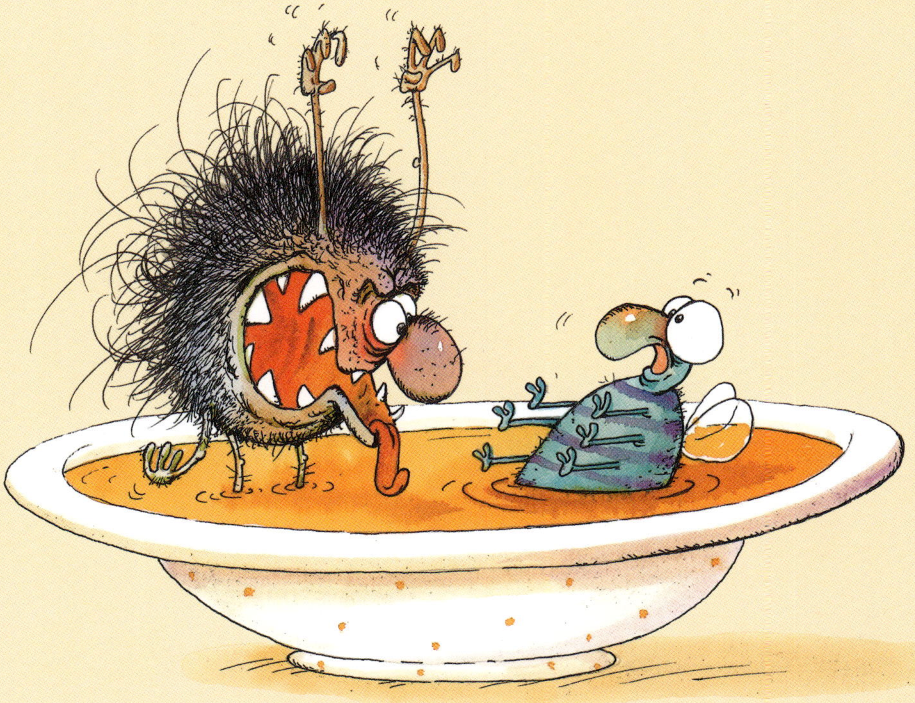

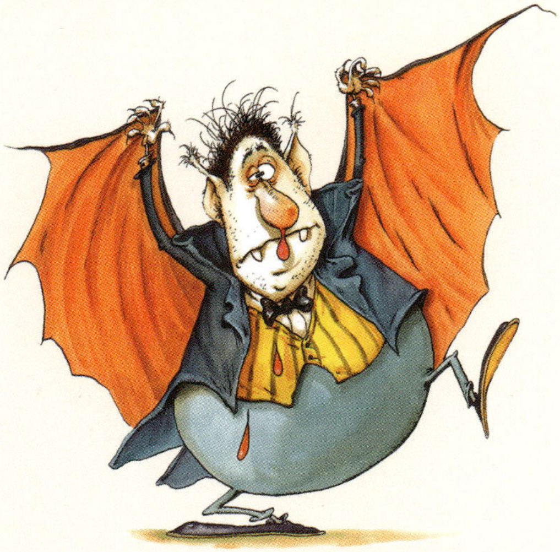

La nuit tombe. Deux vampires s'éveillent.
- Je vais chercher du sang, dit l'un.
Il sort du château un instant et revient, la figure pleine de sang.
- Que s'est-il passé ? demande celui qui est resté.
- Tu vois la sortie du château ?
- Oui, je vois.
- 'Y a une rue, puis une pharmacie, tu vois ?
- Oui, oui, je vois.
- à côté de la pharmacie, il y a un poteau, tu vois ?
- Oui, oui, oui, je vois.
- Bah, moi, je l'ai pas vu !

Histoire drôle
9
Janvier

Histoire drôle
10
Janvier

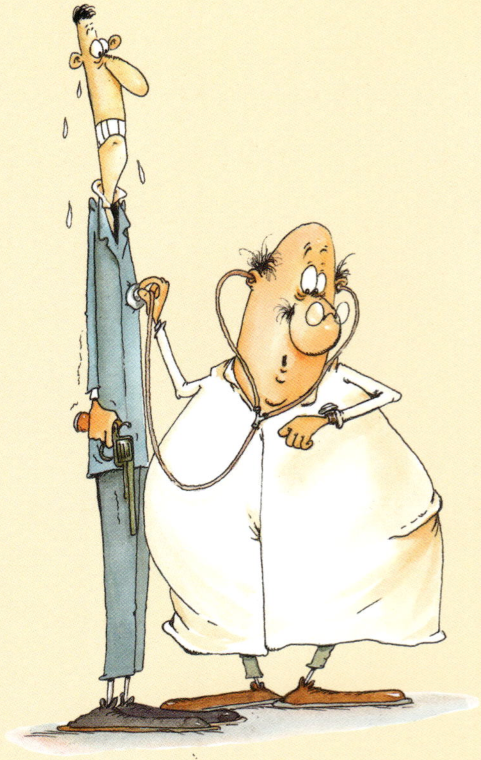

Un gros homme est jugé dans un tribunal.
- J'ai tendance à grossir, explique-t-il au juge. Je suis allé voir un médecin pour qu'il me donne un régime. Le premier jour, il m'a supprimé le pain. Le second, il m'a supprimé le sel. Le troisième, il m'a supprimé le beurre et l'huile. Le quatrième, il m'a supprimé la viande, les œufs, le lait, l'alcool et les plats en sauce. Le cinquième jour, il m'a supprimé les pâtes et les patates.
- Et le sixième jour ? interroge le juge.
- Le sixième jour, j'ai supprimé le médecin.

Histoire drôle

11

Janvier

Un martien entre dans une boulangerie sur sa planète.

- Bonjour, monsieur, je voudrais un ouihishnu au chocolat s'il vous plaît.

Le boulanger le regarde d'un drôle d'air.

- Un ouihishnu à quoi ?

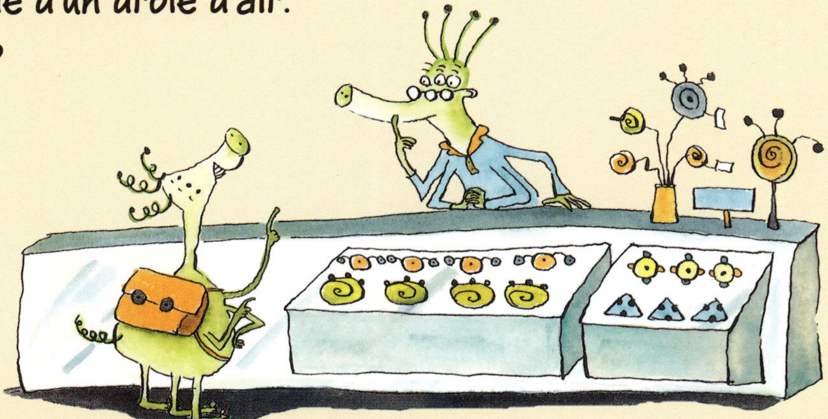

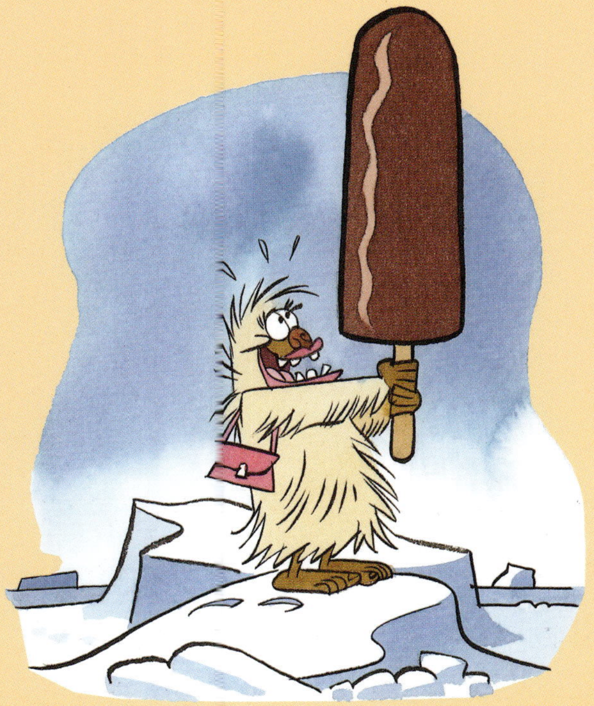

CARNET ROSE : esquimau géant voudrait rencontrer abominable femme des neiges pour briser la glace.

Petite annonce

12

Janvier

Petite annonce

13

Janvier

RETARD : le soleil de minuit arrivera à une heure du matin seulement. Sa montre s'est arrêtée.

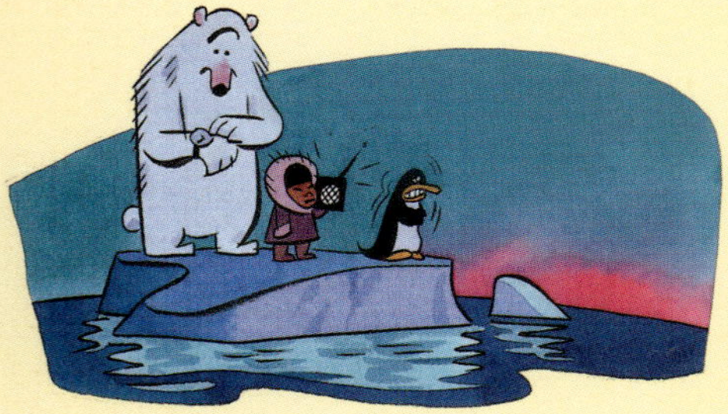

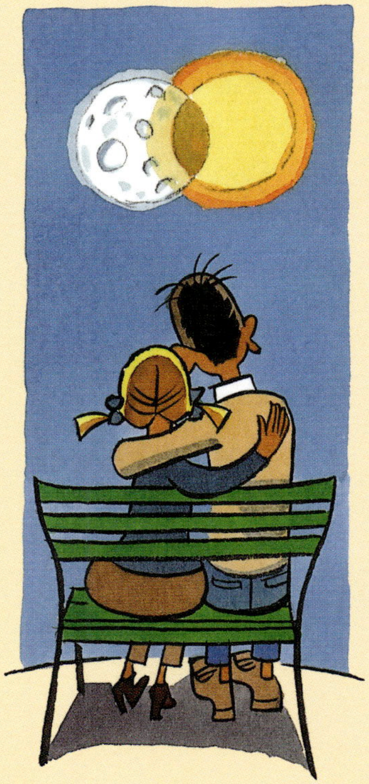

RENCONTRE : soleil de minuit rencontrerait lune matinale.

Petite annonce

14

Janvier

Petite annonce

15

Janvier

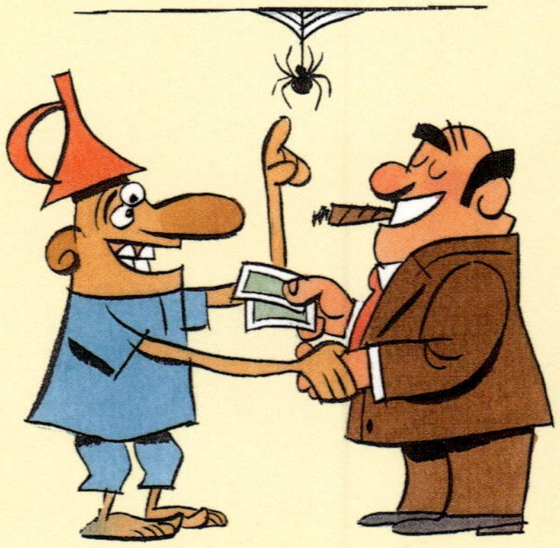

BONNE NOUVELLE : fou guéri vend araignée au plafond.

Un citadin, en visite à la campagne, tombe dans une mare cachée derrière des roseaux.

- Oh ! je suis vraiment désolé, s'excuse le paysan. J'ai oublié de vous signaler qu'il y avait cette mare derrière chez moi.

- Ce n'est rien, répond le citadin tout trempé. Vous voyez, je l'ai trouvée tout seul.

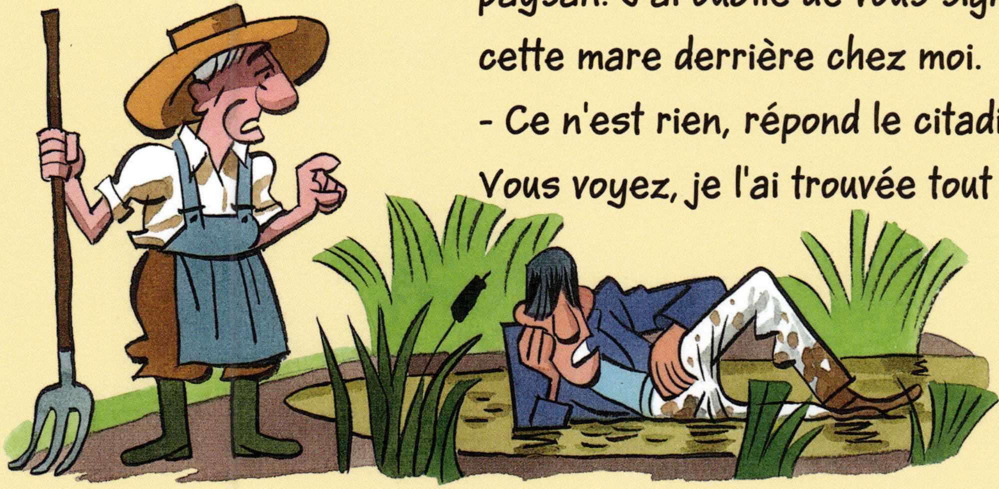

Histoire drôle

16

Janvier

Le maître demande à Laura :

- Conjugue-moi le verbe « marcher » au présent.

- Je marche... Tu marches... Il marche...

- Plus vite, Laura, tu traînes !

- Nous courons, vous courez, ils courent !

Histoire drôle

17

Janvier

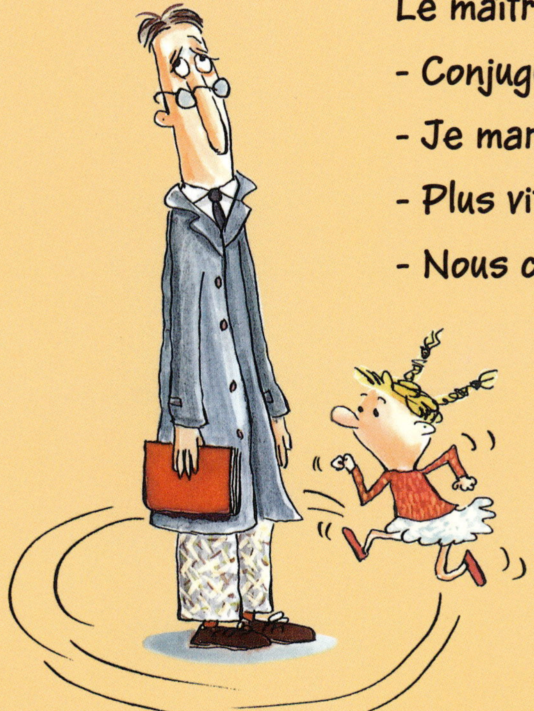

Histoire drôle

18

Janvier

Dans une grande entreprise, le directeur demande à un jeune employé :

- Comment vous appelez-vous, mon garçon ?
- Thomas. Et vous ?

Le directeur est furieux.

- Mon petit bonhomme, s'écrie-t-il, je ne sais pas d'où vous arrivez, mais dans mon entreprise, on n'appelle pas les gens par leur prénom, mais par leur nom ! Si vous vous appelez Thomas Tartempion, je vous appellerai « Tartempion », pas Thomas ! Alors, c'est quoi, votre NOM DE FAMILLE ?

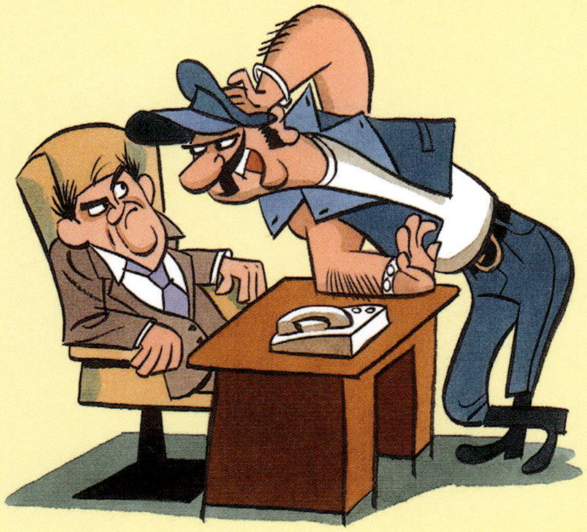

- Mon nom est « Monchéri ».
- Très bien, THOMAS, au travail.

Histoire drôle

19

Janvier

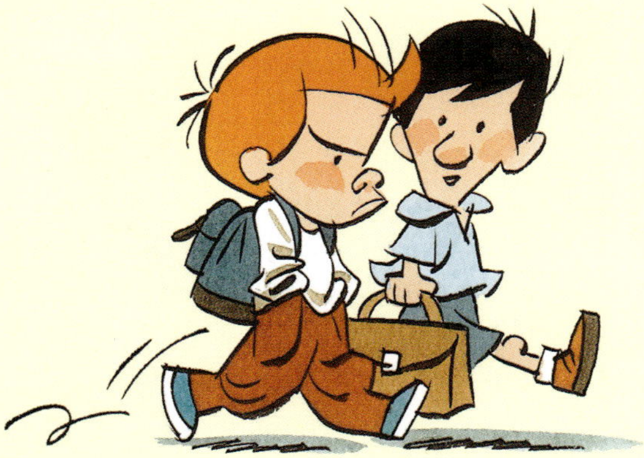

- Maman me dispute pour une chose que je n'ai même pas faite, se plaint Julien.
- Ah bon ? Qu'est-ce que c'est ?
- Mes devoirs.

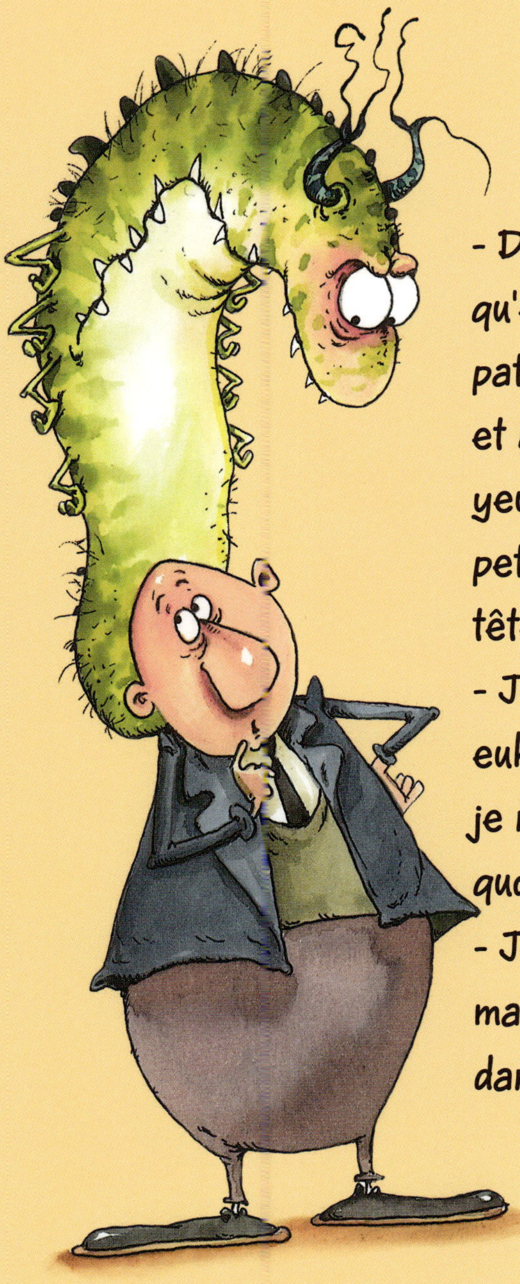

- Dis, papa, qu'est-ce qui a huit pattes, qui est vert et bleu avec des yeux rouges et deux petites pinces sur la tête ?
- Je ne sais pas... euh... non, vraiment, je ne vois pas. C'est quoi ?
- Je n'en sais rien, mais tu en as un dans le cou.

Histoire drôle

20

Janvier

Histoire drôle

21

Janvier

Un myope se fait accompagner chez l'ophtalmologiste.
- Docteur, dit-il, je ne vois rien du tout, il faut absolument me soigner...

L'ophtalmologiste hoche la tête.
- Voyons ça : lisez-moi les lettres qui sont sur le tableau, au mur.
- Quel tableau ?

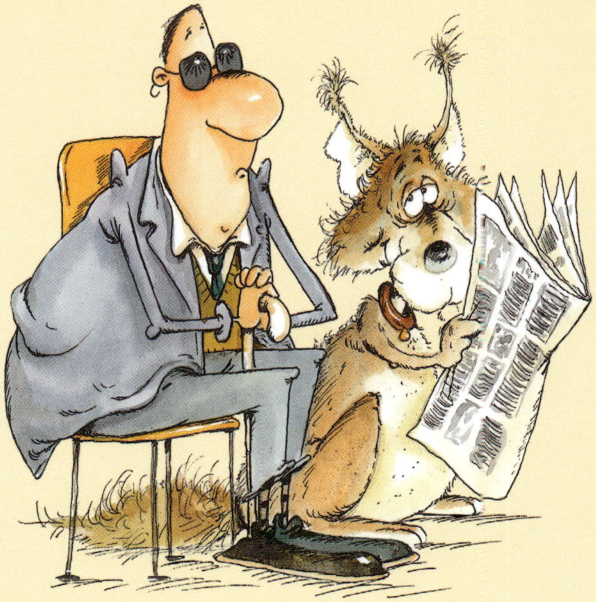

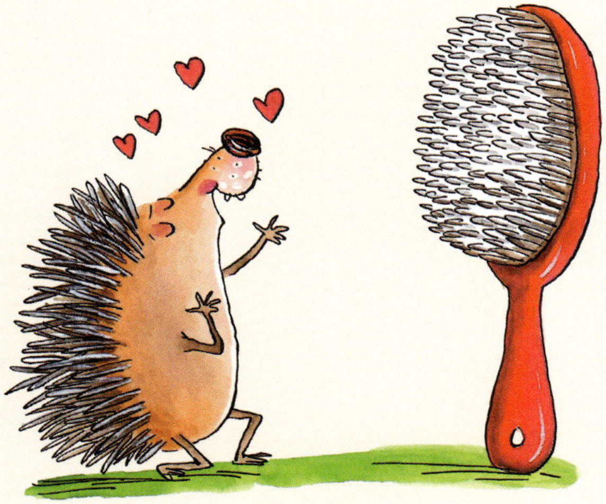

Que dit un hérisson qui vient de discuter pendant trente minutes avec une brosse à cheveux ?
- Tout le monde peut se tromper...

Histoire drôle
22
Janvier

Trois souris sont assises devant un morceau de fromage, discutant de tout et de rien. Soudain, l'une d'elles s'exclame :
- Moi, je suis très forte, sans vouloir me vanter ! J'arrive à déjouer les pièges à souris en les soulevant avec mes pattes arrière. Ça fait tomber le bout de fromage, et le tour est joué !
- Moui ! dit sa copine, mais moi, je suis plus forte encore. Les grains de blé empoisonné que les hommes mettent dans les caves ne me font rien du tout : J'en mange chaque midi et chaque soir, et je suis complètement immunisée.

Histoire drôle
23
Janvier

La troisième se lève en s'excusant :
- Vous êtes très fortes, effectivement... Je dois vous laisser, c'est l'heure de mon cours de boxe avec le chat.

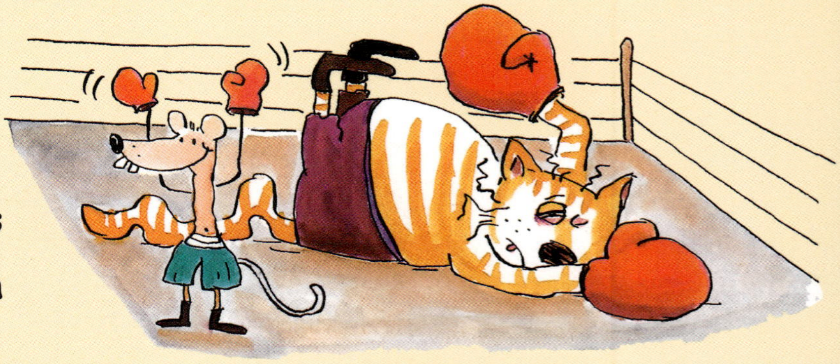

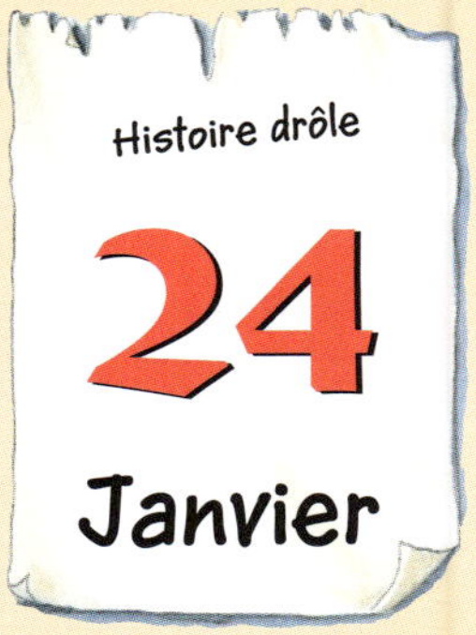

Un gars rend visite à un copain et le trouve en train de jouer aux échecs avec son chien.
- Je n'en crois pas mes yeux ! Ton chien joue aux échecs ! C'est le chien le plus intelligent de la terre !
- Bof ! répond l'autre. Intelligent, c'est vite dit. Je l'ai battu trois fois sur les cinq parties que l'on a jouées ensemble aujourd'hui.

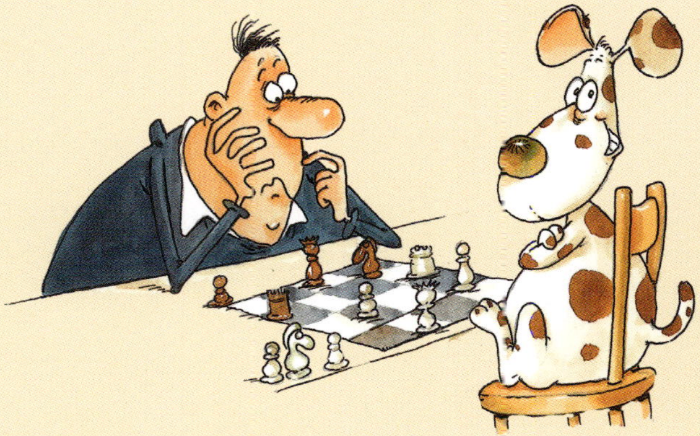

Une dame trouve un chat dans son réfrigérateur. Le chat est en train de se bâfrer de beurre, de lait et de crème Chantilly. Elle essaye de le sortir du frigo, mais, miaou ! grr ! le chat ne se laisse pas faire et la griffe au bras. Désespérée, elle appelle son mari.
- Chéri ! Il y a un chat dans notre frigo, il m'a griffée !
Le mari arrive, l'air renfrogné, et essaye à son tour d'enlever le chat du réfrigérateur. Mais, là encore, miaou ! grr ! le chat se rebiffe. Alors, le mari se jette sur le chat, MIAOU ! GRR ! qui griffe, crache et mord là où il peut. Finalement, l'homme réussit à passer la porte d'entrée, MIAOUU ! GRRR ! avec le chat, et la porte claque. Son épouse va dans la cuisine et entreprend de réparer les dégâts. Peu après, la porte d'entrée claque à nouveau.
- Alors, chéri, tu as réussi à te débarrasser de ce chat enragé ?
Et là, une petite voix répond : - Miaou ! grr !

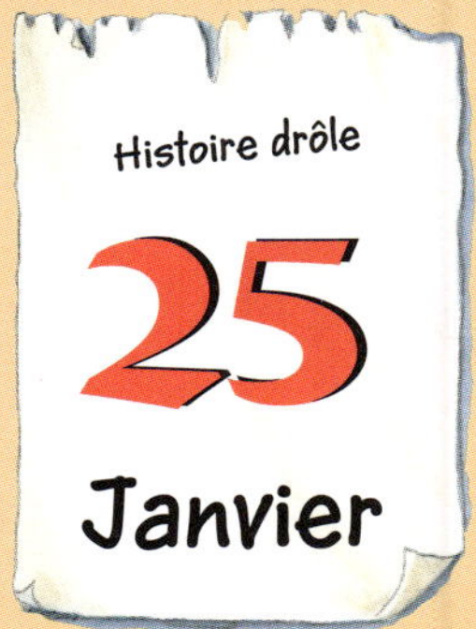

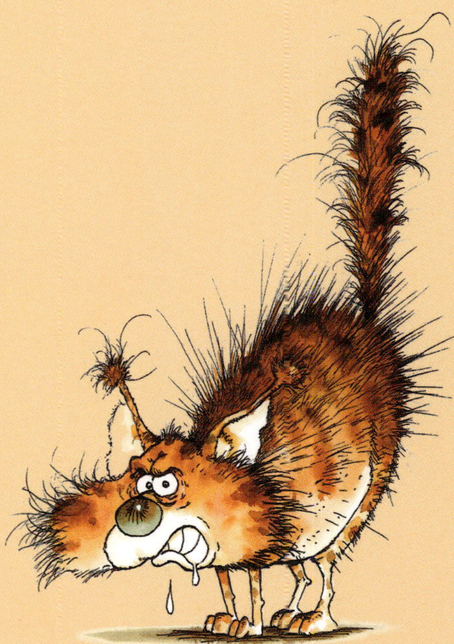

Histoire drôle

26 Janvier

Un gars essaye de vendre son chien à un de ses copains.

- Achète-le, c'est une affaire ! C'est un chien qui parle ! Je te le vends pour 10 euros.

- Un chien qui parle ? À 10 euros ? Tu te fiches de moi !

Or, le chien lève le museau et se met à parler.

- S'il vous plaît, supplie-t-il, achetez-moi, je ne veux plus rester avec cet homme cruel qui me bat et qui ne me donne jamais à manger... Je vous en prie, je vous ferai la vaisselle, j'irai faire vos courses, mais ne me laissez pas avec ce monstre !

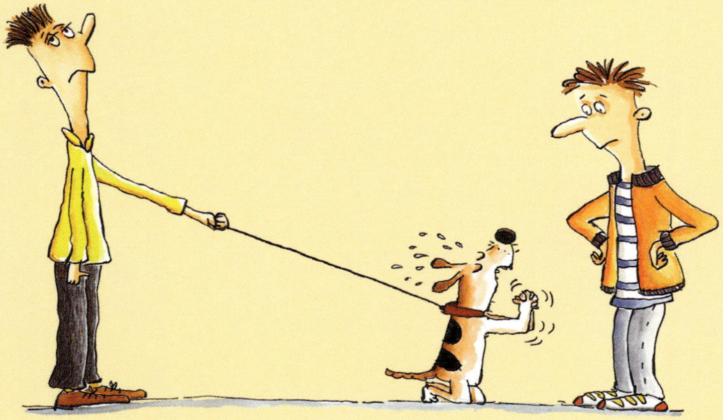

Le copain est estomaqué.

- Mais c'est un chien qui parle ! Il parle vraiment ! T'es fou de le vendre 10 euros, il vaut une fortune ! Pourquoi tu veux t'en débarrasser ?

- Parce que j'en ai marre : il ne peut pas s'empêcher de mentir !

Devinette

27 Janvier

Pourquoi les éléphants n'ont-ils pas d'ordinateur ?

(réponse : parce qu'ils ont peur des souris.)

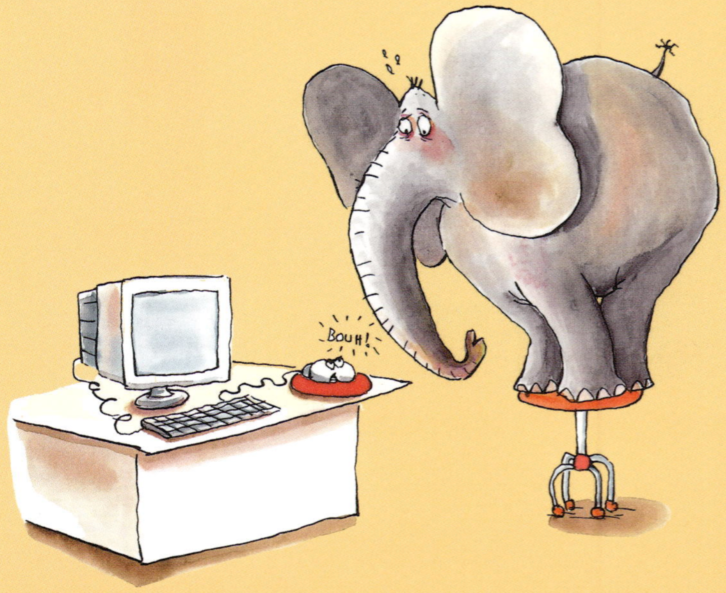

Histoire drôle

28

Janvier

Une femme passe son permis de conduire pour la dixième fois, et malgré ça, continue à enchaîner erreur sur erreur. Une fois la voiture arrêtée, l'examinateur lui explique sa décision.

- Je suis désolé, mademoiselle, mais je suis obligé de vous refuser le permis de conduire. Vous êtes beaucoup trop dangereuse, vous grillez les feux rouges, vous manquez de renverser les passants, vous prenez l'autoroute dans le mauvais sens et vous vous garez au milieu de la route !

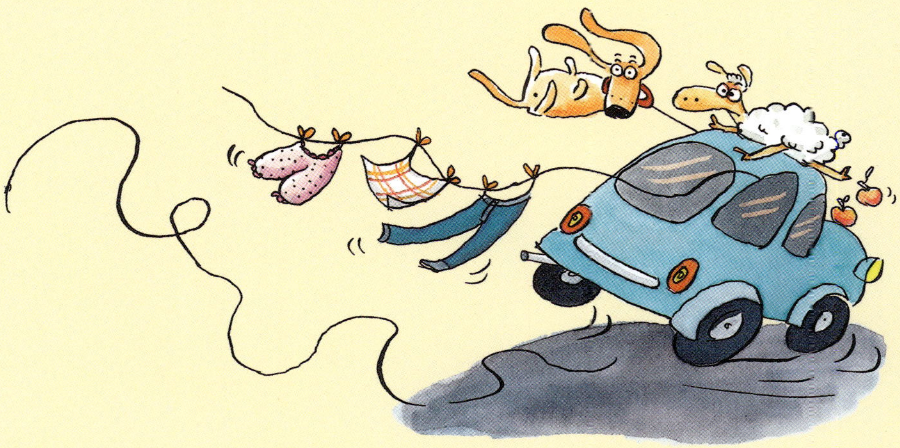

La demoiselle se fâche :

- C'est injuste ! Injuste ! Je n'ai blessé personne, cette fois !

Histoire drôle

29

Janvier

Un enfant observe attentivement sa petite sœur qui vient juste de naître.

- Dis, papa, ça marche avec combien de piles, ce truc-là ?

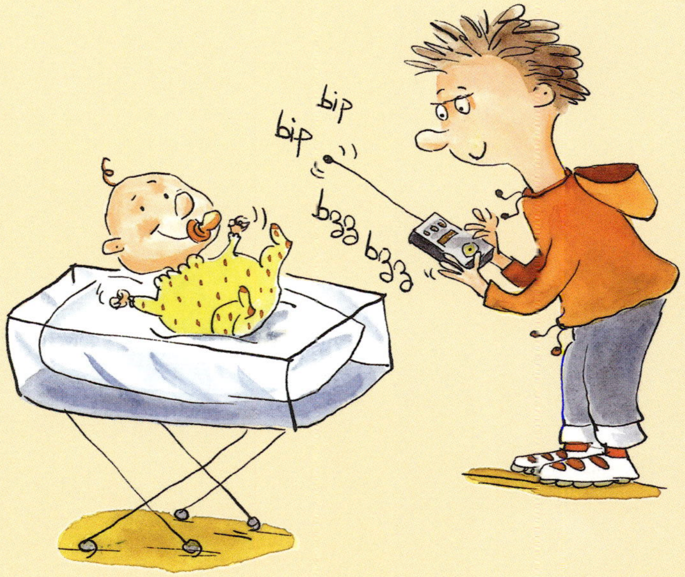

Histoire drôle

30

Janvier

Deux canards sont sur un lac. L'un dit « Coin-coin ». Immédiatement, l'autre le bouscule violemment en s'écriant : « Copieur ! J'allais le dire ! ».

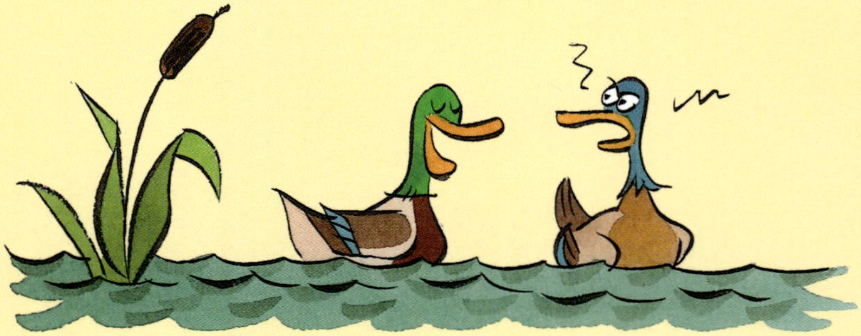

Deux crocodiles sont sur un lac. L'un dit « Coin-coin ». Immédiatement, l'autre le bouscule violemment en s'écriant : « Imbécile ! T'es pas un canard ! ».

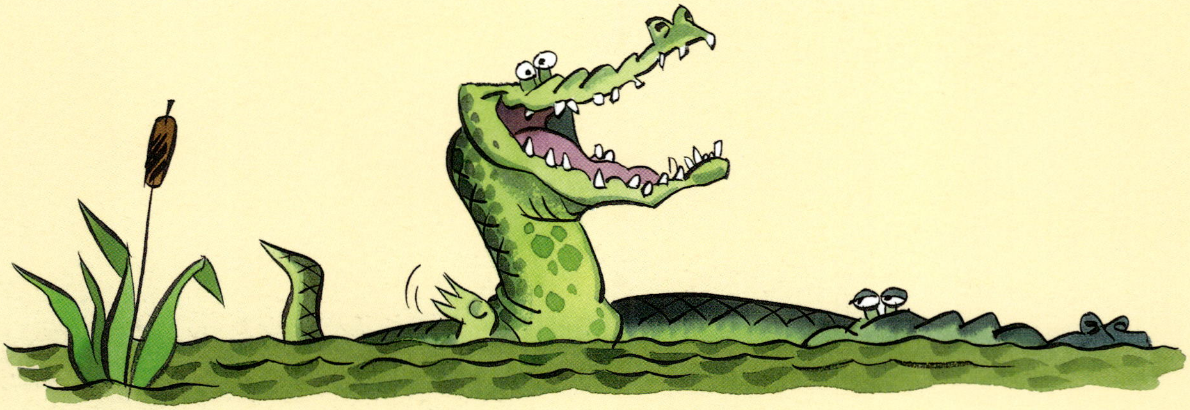

Histoire drôle

31

Janvier

Histoire drôle

1

Février

Deux amis se rencontrent au retour des vacances.

- Alors, tu étais où ?

- Oh ! la première semaine, j'étais dans les Alpes, et la seconde, j'étais dans le plâtre.

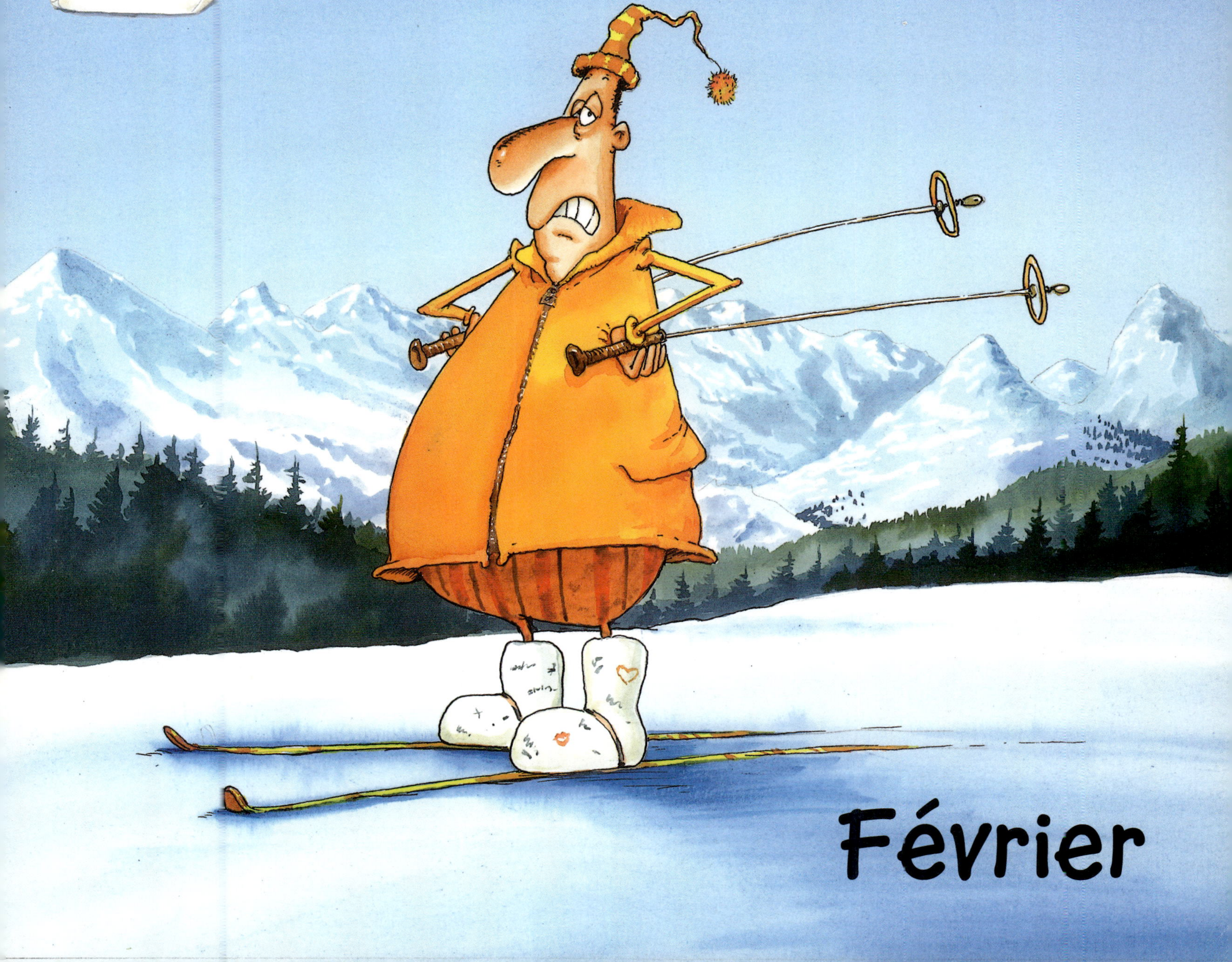

Février

Devinette

2

Février

A) Combien d'actions sont nécessaires pour faire entrer un éléphant dans un réfrigérateur ?

Réponse : trois actions.

1. Ouvrir le réfrigérateur. 2. Mettre l'éléphant. 3. Fermer le réfrigérateur.

B) Maintenant, combien d'actions sont nécessaires pour faire entrer une girafe dans un réfrigérateur ?

Réponse : quatre actions. 1. Ouvrir le réfrigérateur. 2. Enlever l'éléphant. 3. Mettre la girafe. 4. Fermer le réfrigérateur.

C) Le lion décide de manger tous les animaux de la jungle. Il les chasse sauvagement et finit par tous les manger. Tous, sauf un. Lequel ?

Réponse : la girafe ! Elle est dans le réfrigérateur !

D) Pourquoi les éléphants ont-ils la grippe ?

Réponse : parce que des imbéciles les mettent dans les frigos !

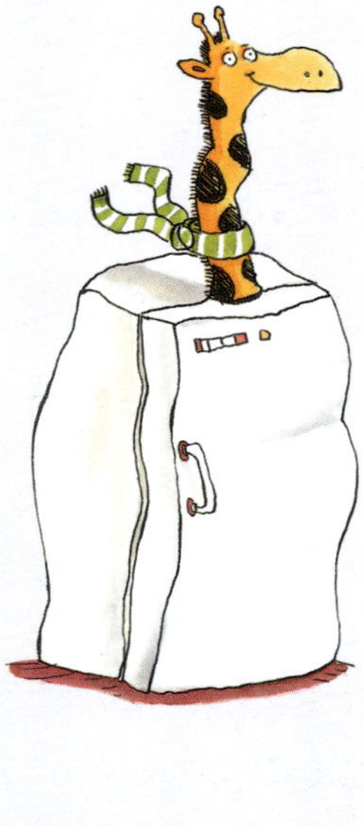

Petite annonce

3

Février

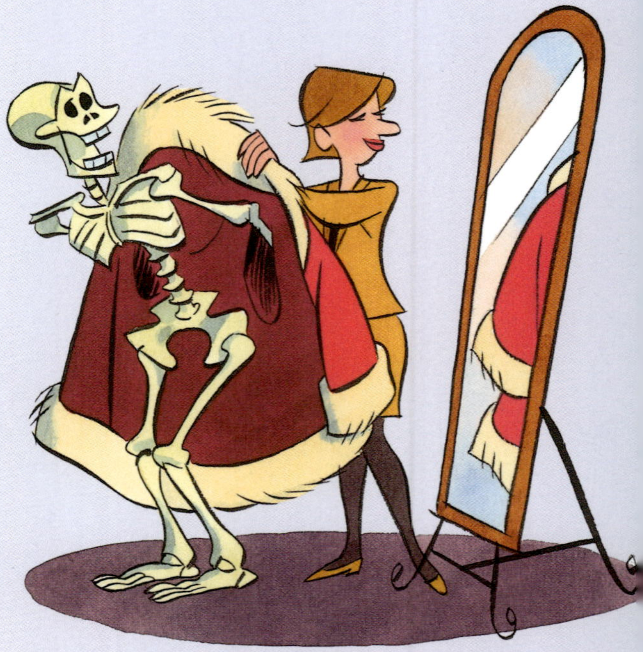

GEL : squelette frileux achète vêtements chauds pour l'hiver.

Dans un bel igloo tout rond, un esquimau raconte l'histoire du Petit Poucet à son fils.
- Alors, l'ogre, qui avait chaussé les bottes de sept lieues, se mit à courir, et le Petit Poucet, effrayé, se réfugia dans le coin le plus sombre de la maison.
- Papa, dit le petit garçon en regardant avec attention l'intérieur de l'igloo. Je voudrais savoir...
- Ce qu'est un ogre ?
- Non, ce qu'est un coin.

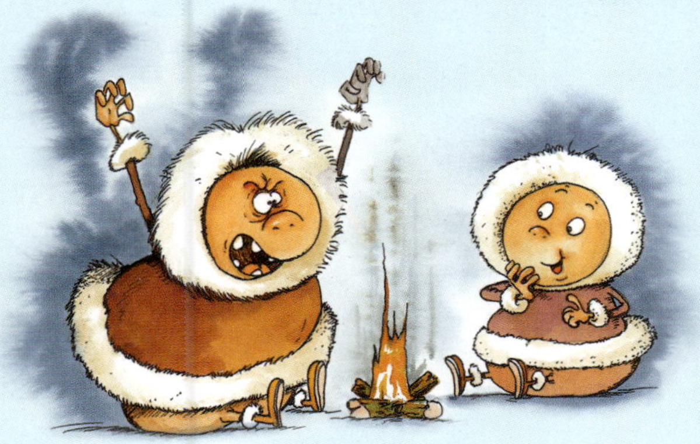

Histoire drôle
4
Février

Dans un train reliant Paris à Marseille, un fou se penche constamment à la fenêtre pour jeter des pincées de sel. Son voisin, étonné, lui demande :
- Pourquoi faites-vous cela ?
- Pour éviter d'être attaqué par des tigres, répond le fou.
- Mais enfin ! Il n'y a pas de tigre en France !
- Ben oui, puisque je lance du sel ! Vous voyez bien que ça marche !

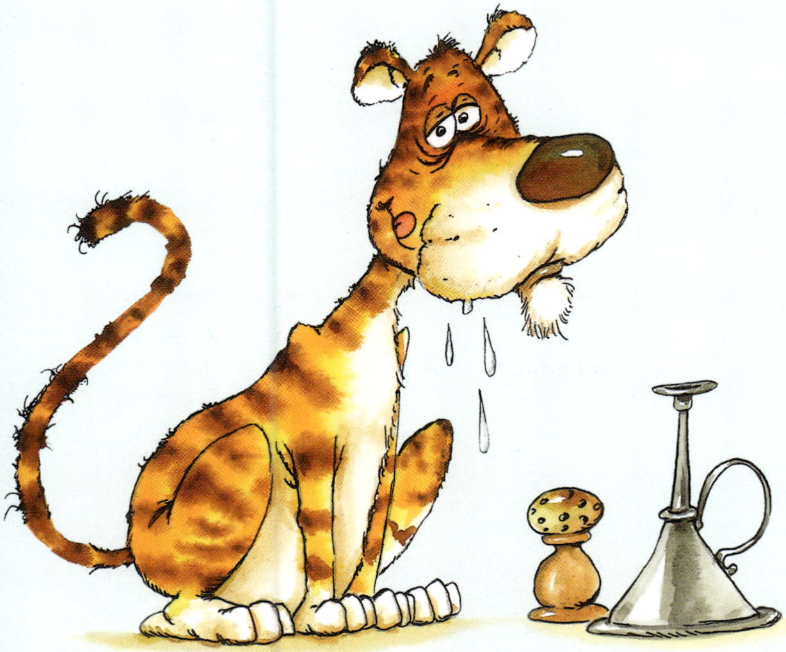

Histoire drôle
5
Février

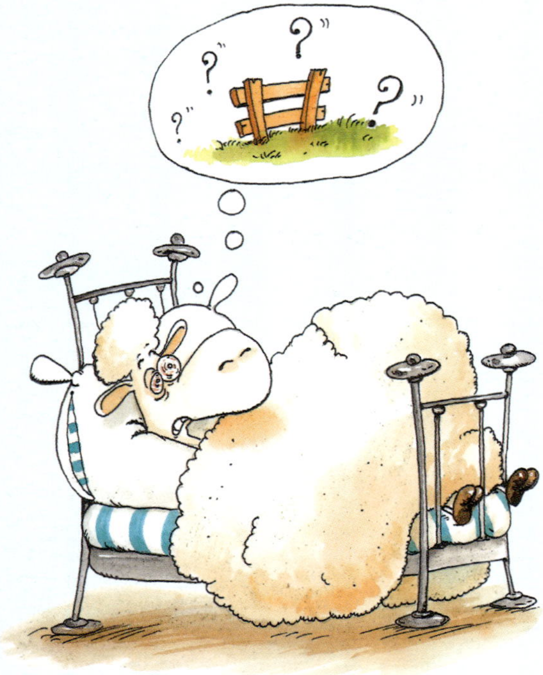

Devinette

6

Février

Les enfants français, couchés dans leurs lits, comptent les moutons pour s'endormir. Mais, en inde, que comptent les enfants fakirs, couchés sur leurs planches à clous ?

(Réponse : un hérisson... deux hérissons... trois hérissons...)

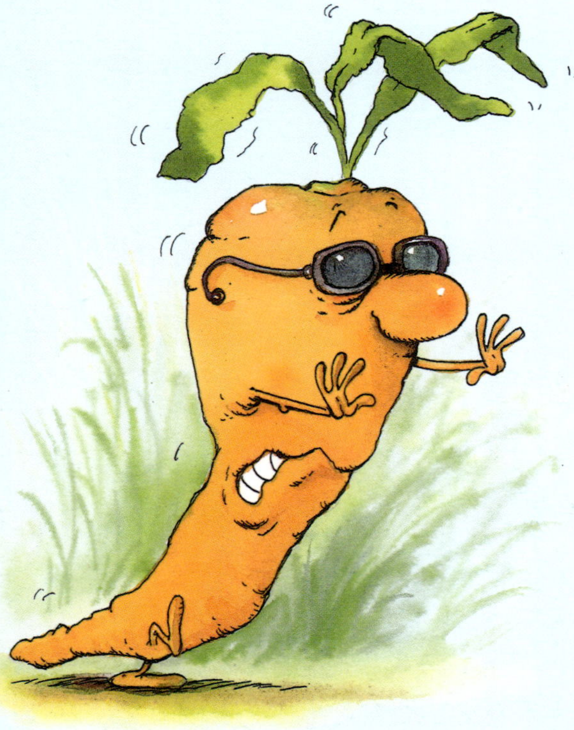

Les carottes sont-elles bonnes pour la vue ?

(Réponse : oui. Vous avez déjà vu un lapin avec des lunettes ?)

Devinette

7

Février

Histoire drôle

8

Février

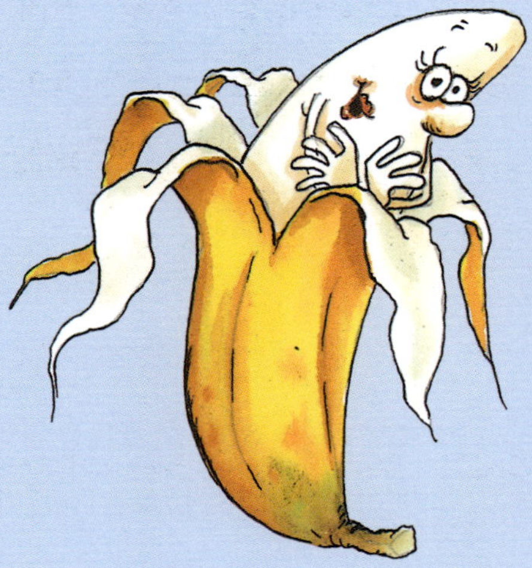

Une maman vient d'apprendre à son fils à éplucher une banane. Tout fier, il regarde la peau de banane dans sa main.

- Qu'est-ce que j'en fais, maintenant, du manteau de la banane ?

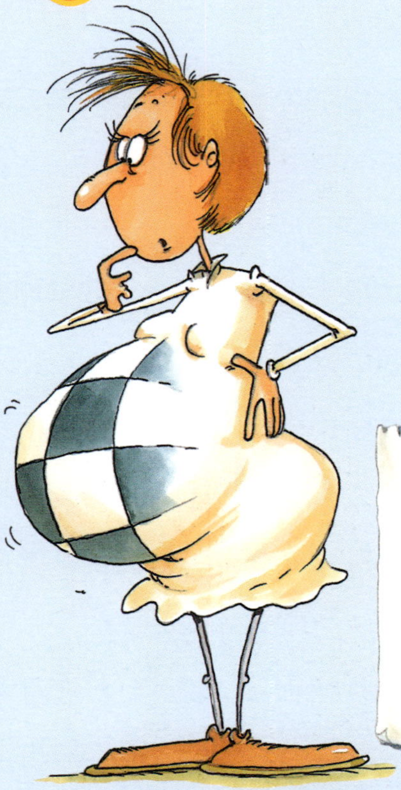

Une future maman dit à sa petite fille de quatre ans :

- Touche mon ventre. Tu sens les petits coups ?

C'est ton petit frère qui donne des coups de pied.

- Pourquoi ? s'étonne la petite fille.

- Je ne sais pas, peut-être qu'il s'ennuie là-dedans. Alors, pour jouer, il donne des coups.

- Bah, c'est simple alors : tu n'as qu'à avaler une balle pour qu'il s'amuse avec !

Histoire drôle

9

Février

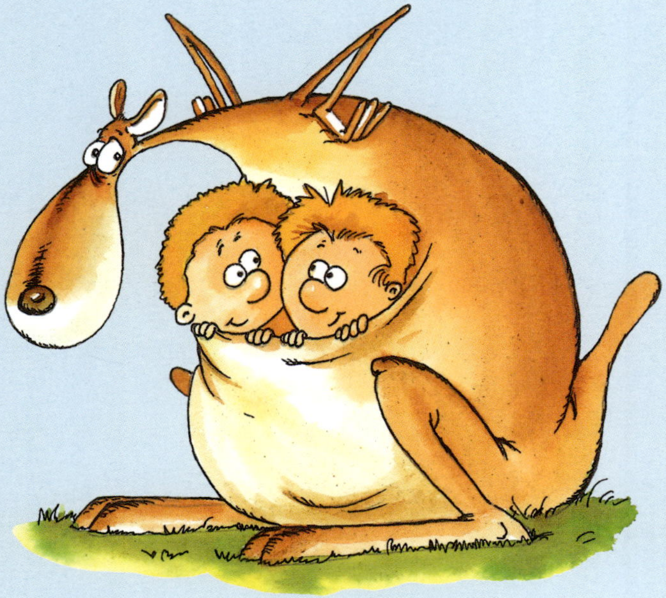

La maman de deux bébés jumeaux dit à son mari :

- La baby-sitter ne pouvait pas venir ce soir pour que nous allions au bal costumé. Alors, j'ai commandé deux costumes de kangourous, et nous mettrons chacun un bébé dans une poche.

Histoire drôle

10

Février

Histoire drôle

11

Février

Au supermarché, avant de passer à la caisse, Thomas et son père font la queue. Ils se trouvent derrière une très grosse dame.

- T'as vu la dame, dit Thomas. On dirait un camion !

- Veux-tu te taire ! rougit le père. Ce n'est pas gentil de dire ça !

À ce moment, le téléphone portable de la dame se met à sonner.

- Tu vois que j'avais raison ! s'exclame le petit garçon. Elle klaxonne !

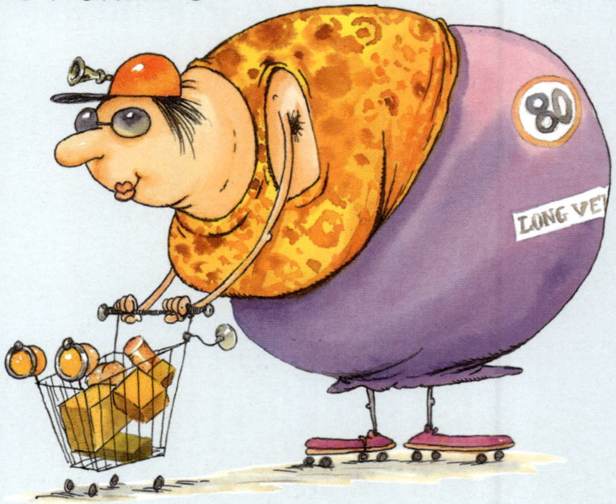

Histoire drôle

12

Février

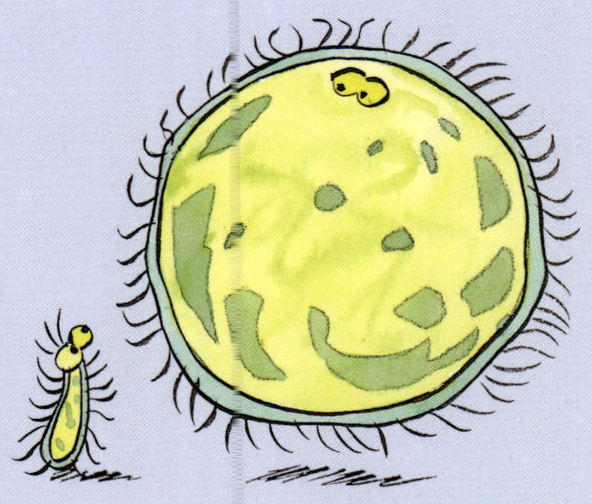

Deux microbes se rencontrent.

- Qu'est-ce qu'il t'arrive ? Tu es tout pâlichon !

- Je suis malade. J'ai avalé une aspirine...

Histoire drôle

13

Février

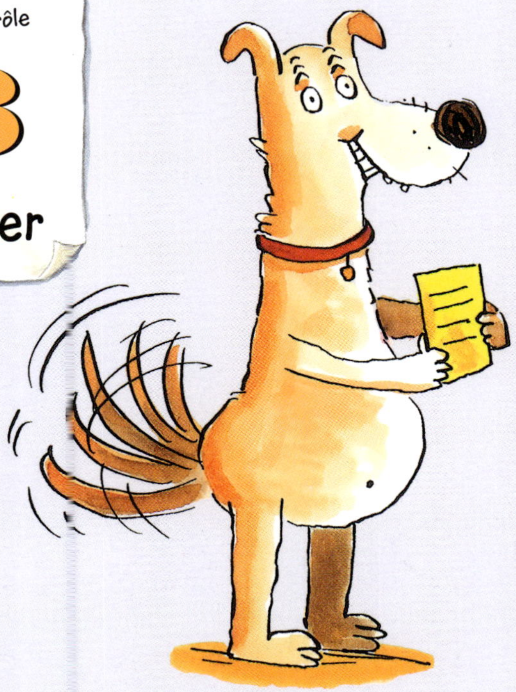

Un chien entre dans un bureau de poste, prend un formulaire pour les télégrammes et le remplit soigneusement.

« Woof...Woof Woof... Woof, Woof Woof Woof... Woof. »

L'employé des postes prend le télégramme en main et dit au chien :

- Il y a seulement huit mots. Vous pouvez mettre deux autres « Woof » pour le même prix.

- Quoi ? Mais ça ne voudrait plus rien dire !

Histoire drôle

14 Février

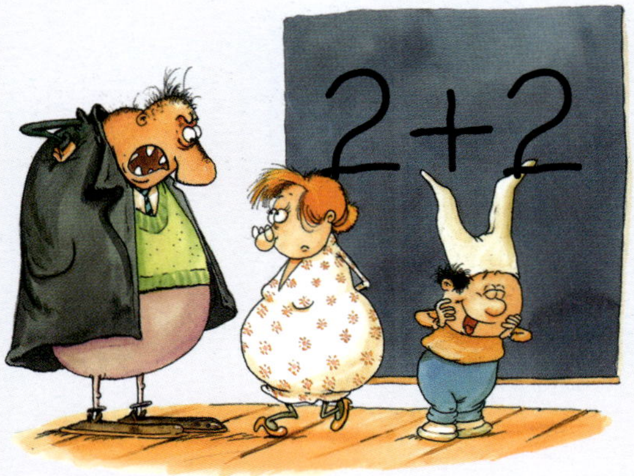

Maxime rend son livret à son papa.

- Maxime ! C'est une catastrophe ! Tu as des zéros partout !
- C'est pas ma faute, papa, c'est la maîtresse, elle me déteste. Elle fait exprès de me poser des questions trop difficiles pour que j'aie des mauvaises notes.

Indigné, le père va voir la maîtresse le lendemain matin, accompagné de son fils.

- Alors, madame, dit-il furieusement, il paraît que vous détestez Maxime et que vous lui posez des questions trop dures pour son âge ?
- Mais pas du tout, monsieur, répond la maîtresse, très impressionnée. Enfin, voyons ! euh... Maxime, combien font 2 + 2 ?

Là, Maxime se tourne vers son père.

- Tu vois, ce que je te disais ? Elle recommence !

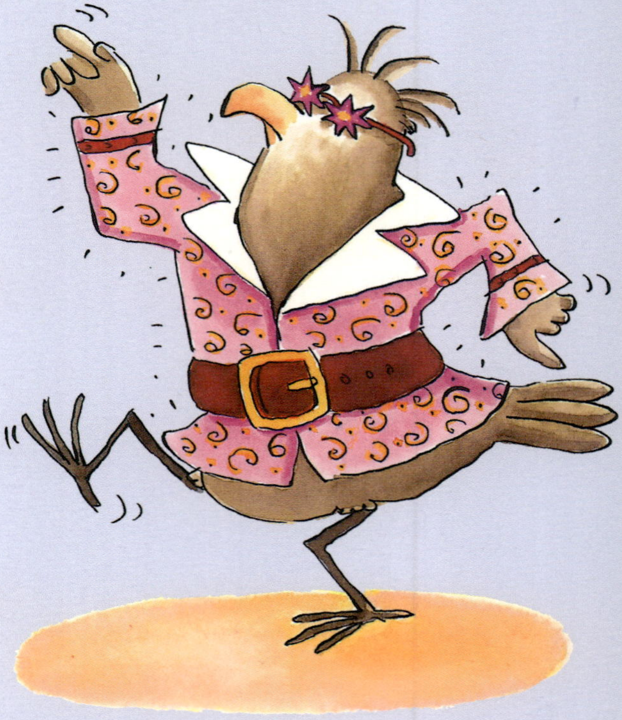

DANSE :
hibou cherche boîte de nuit.

Petite annonce

15 Février

Le père de Julie se fâche :

- Julie ! Ne traite pas ton frère d'idiot ! Allez, dis-lui tout de suite que tu regrettes, et plus vite que ça !

- Rémi, dit Julie en baissant la tête, je regrette que tu sois un idiot.

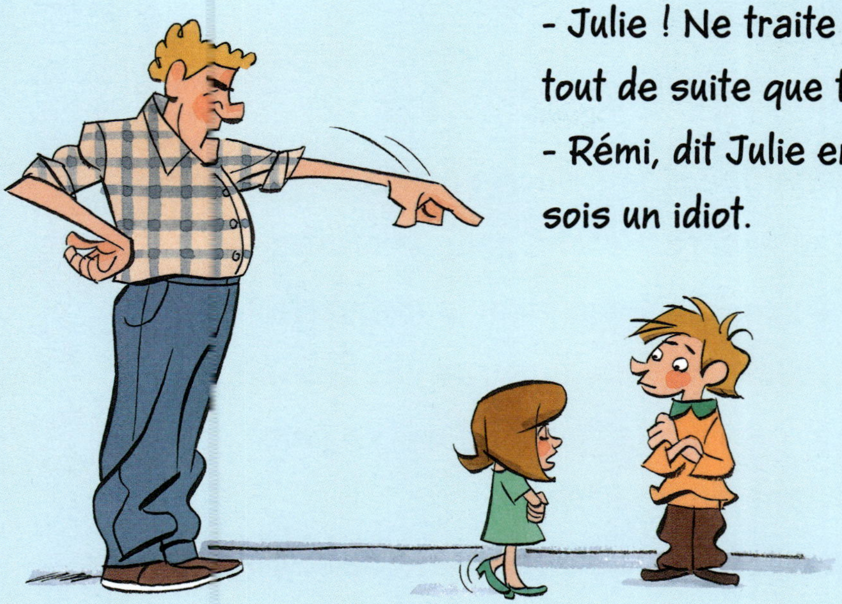

Histoire drôle

16

Février

C'est le déluge, aux premiers temps de la Terre et de l'humanité. Les animaux s'embarquent précipitamment sur l'arche de Noé. Soudain, l'éléphant barrit violemment.

- Arrête de pousser ! dit-il à une puce.

- Excuse-moi, je ne t'avais pas vu...

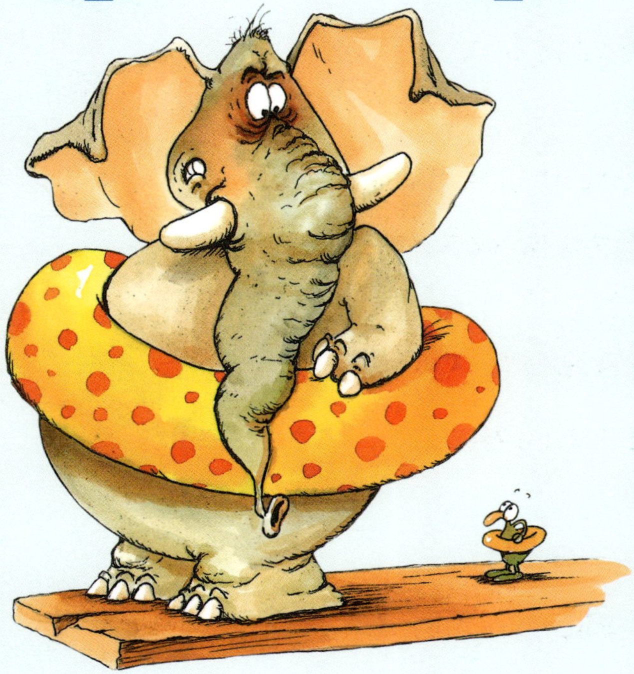

Histoire drôle

17

Février

Histoire drôle

18

Février

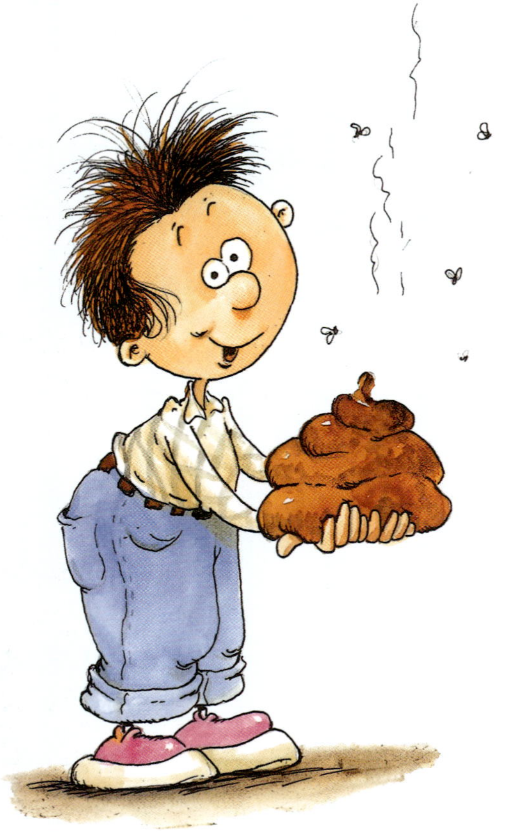

- Jean-Jacques ! s'écrie maman.
Tu as encore marché dans la crotte de chien ! Il y en a plein la moquette !
La prochaine fois, tu auras une fessée, ça t'apprendra à faire attention. Va jouer dehors pendant que je nettoie !
Jean-Jacques sort et revient deux minutes plus tard avec une crotte de chien dans la main.
- Maman ! Regarde dans quoi j'ai failli marcher !

Deux œufs sont dans une poêle.
L'un dit : « Pfou ! Il fait chaud ici ! »
L'autre saute en l'air, en hurlant :
« Au secours ! Un œuf qui parle ! »

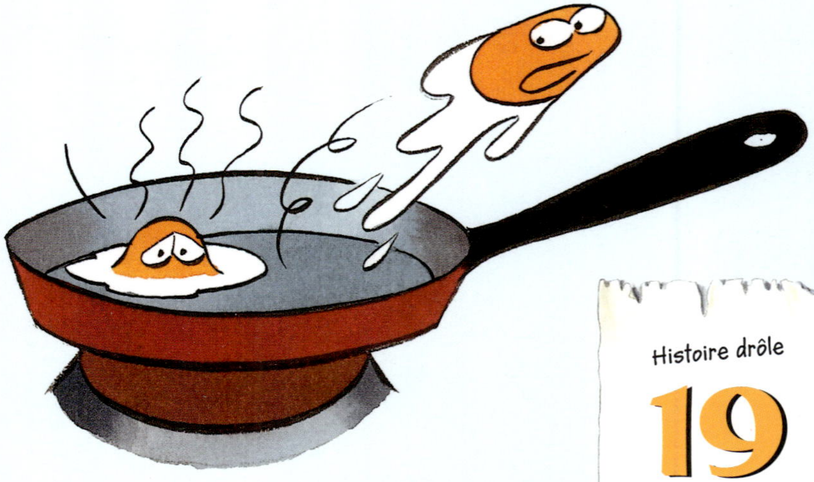

Histoire drôle

19

Février

Histoire drôle

20

Février

Un fou entre dans une boulangerie. Il est rempli de tics et s'exprime difficilement. Il commande un énorme gâteau d'anniversaire.

La boulangère lui fait la conversation :

- *Il est pour qui, ce beau gâteau ?*
- C'est pour ma p'tite sœur, elle a 12 ans au... au... aujourd'hui !
- Et comment s'appelle-t-elle, votre petite sœur ?
- Elle s'appelle Pétale !
- Pétale ! Quel joli prénom ! s'exclame la boulangère.
- Oui, on l'a appelée comme ça parce que... que... que le jour où elle est née, alors qu'elle dormait dans... dans... dans son berceau, un pétale de rose poussé par le vent est venu se poser délica-ca-catement sur elle. Alors, on l'a appelée Pétale...
- Et vous, comment vous appelez-vous ?
- Moi, on m'appelle Poutrelle !

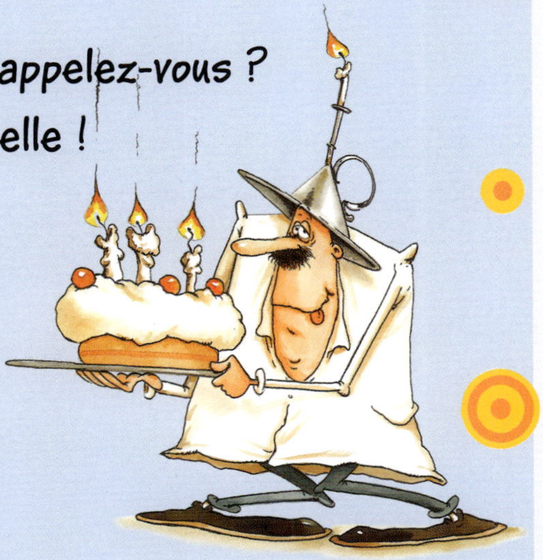

Petite annonce

21

Février

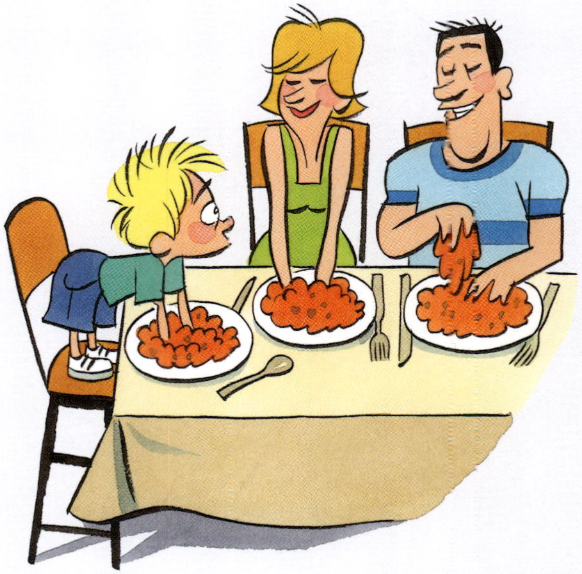

VIE COMMUNE : enfant indiscipliné cherche parents compréhensifs.

Deux fous dans une voiture.

L'un : « Au secours, il n'y a plus de freins ! »

L'autre : « Ne t'inquiète pas, il y a un panneau Stop en bas de la rue. »

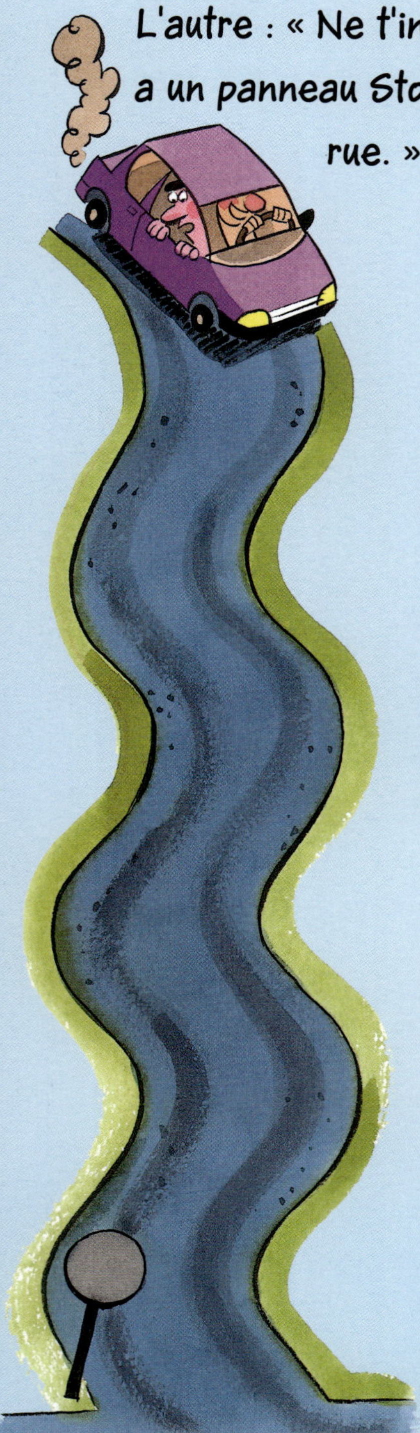

Histoire drôle

22

Février

Histoire drôle

23

Février

- Garçon ! Apportez-moi une douzaine de fautes d'orthographe, s'il vous plaît !
- Mais nous n'en avons pas !
- Ah bon ? Pourtant, il y en a plein dans le menu !

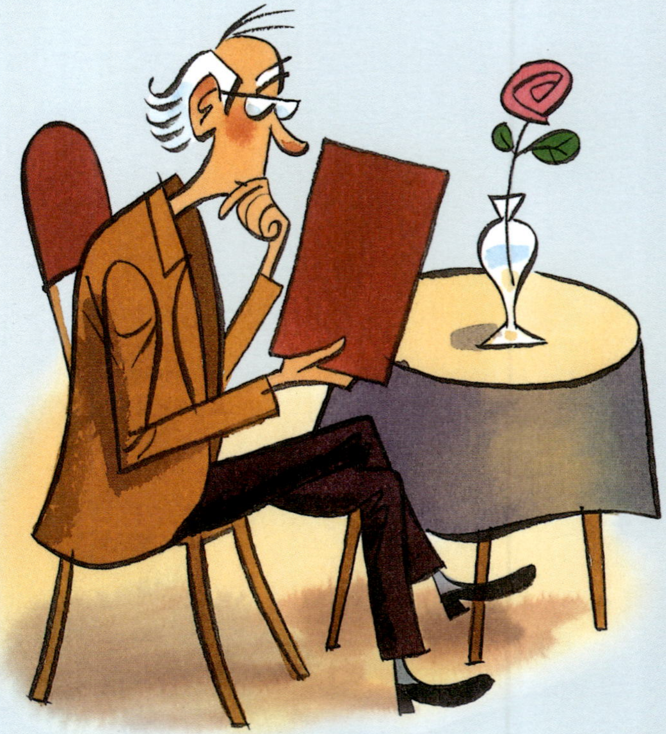

Un citadin s'installe à la campagne.

Pour essayer de gagner du temps pour aller au travail le matin, il va voir son voisin, un paysan.

- Pourrais-je traverser votre champ le matin, pour avoir le bus de 7h ?
- Bien sûr, répond le paysan, et si mon taureau vous voit, vous pourrez même avoir le bus de 6h30.

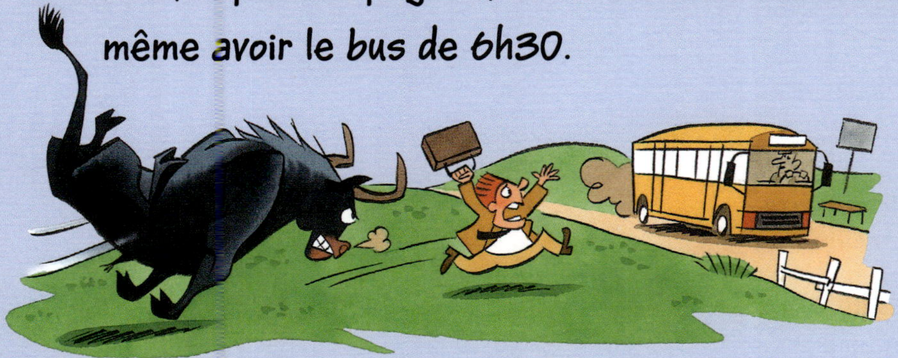

Histoire drôle

24

Février

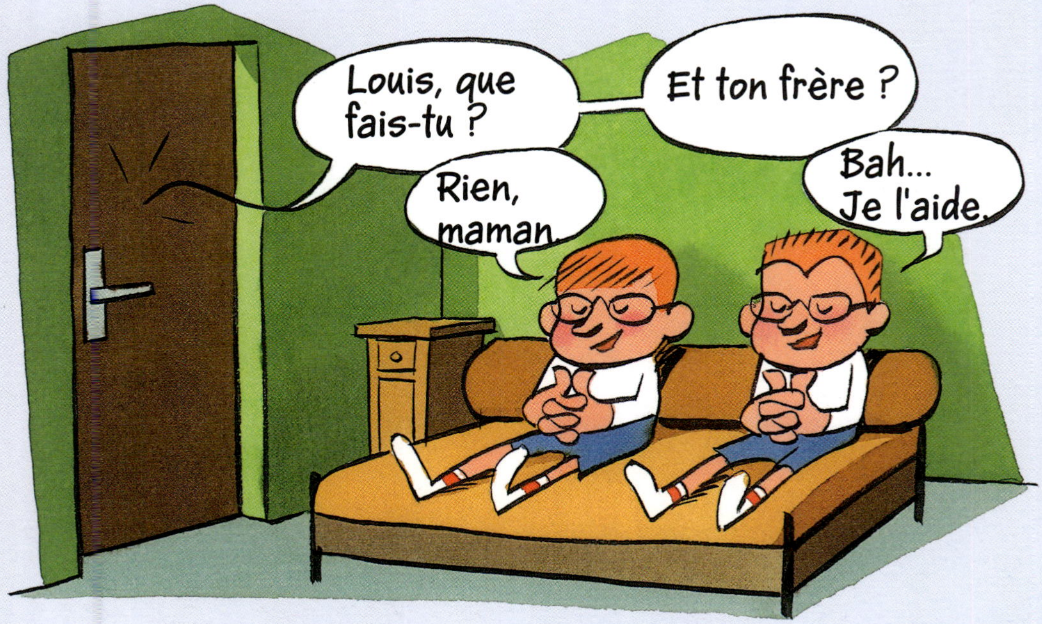

Histoire drôle

25

Février

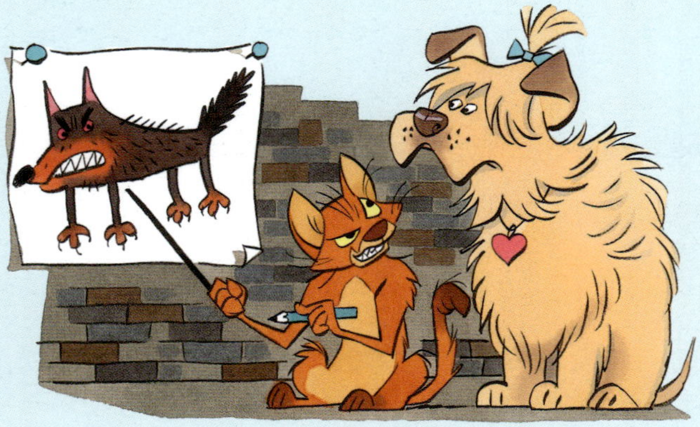

PSYCHOLOGIE : chat méchant donne cours à chien gentil.

Petite annonce

26

Février

Histoire drôle

27

Février

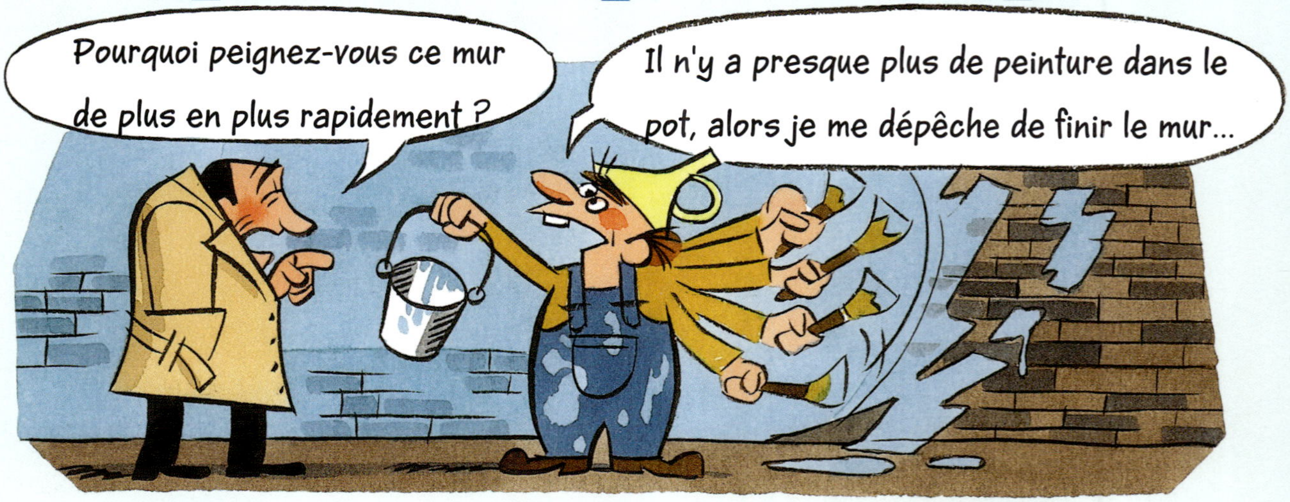

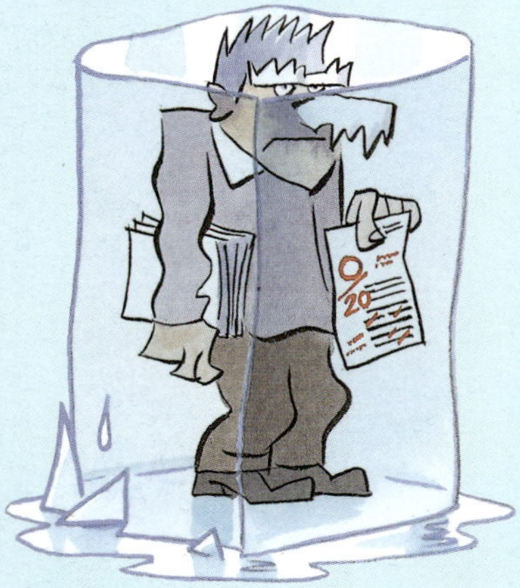

Quelle est la ressemblance entre un thermomètre et un maître d'école ?

(Réponse : quand ils marquent zéro, on tremble.)

Devinette

28

Février

Histoire drôle

1

Mars

Un homme pêche depuis une heure sous une pluie battante.
Sa femme, inquiète, lui apporte un parapluie.
- Ça va ? demande-t-elle. Tu as attrapé quelque chose ?
- Ouais, répond le pêcheur. Un rhume !

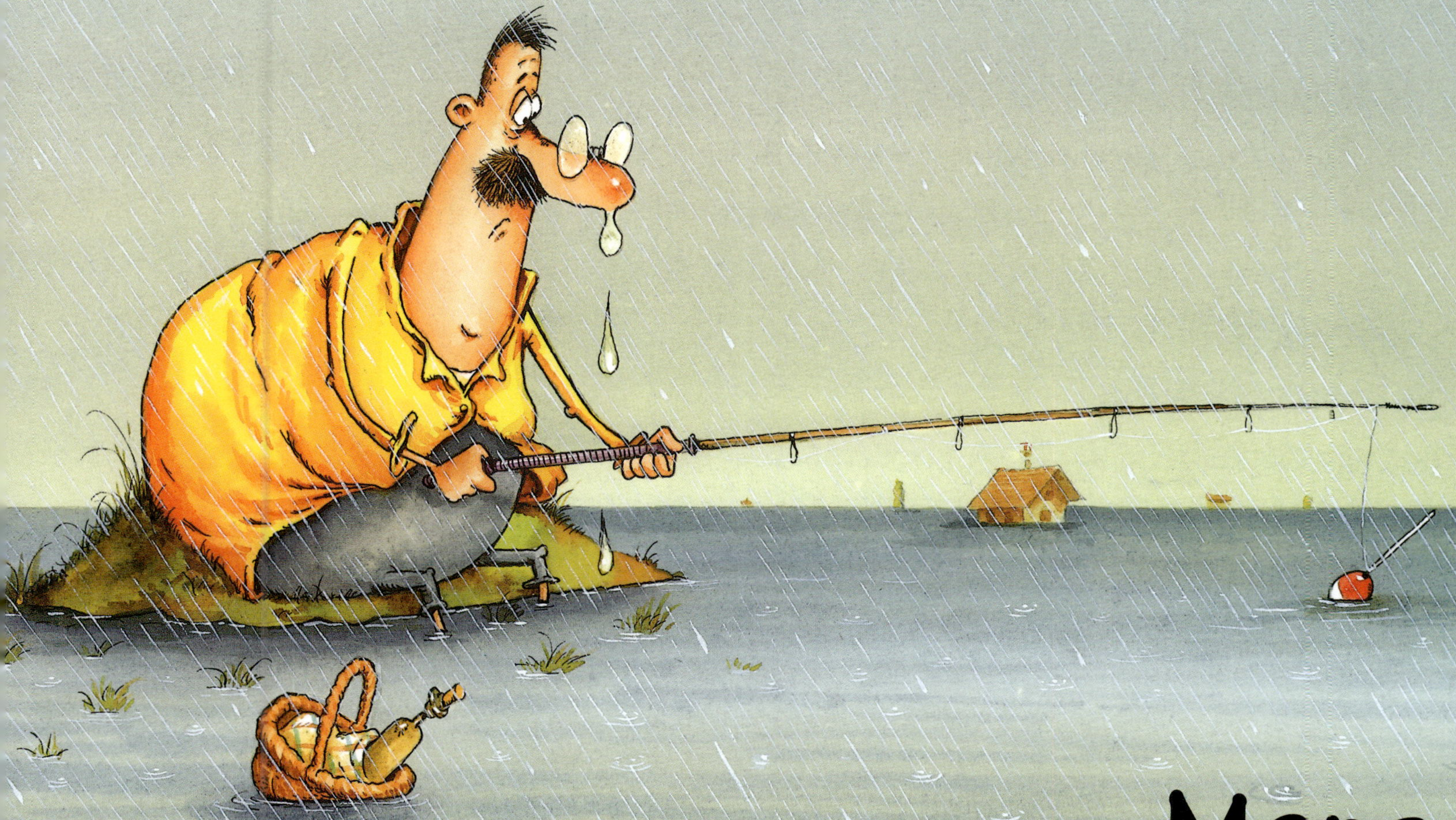

Mars

La maîtresse :

- Je vous rappelle que dans une fable, il y a toujours une morale à la fin, qui nous dit quelle leçon tirer de l'histoire. Qui pourrait me raconter une histoire, avec une leçon à tirer à la fin ? Frédéric ?

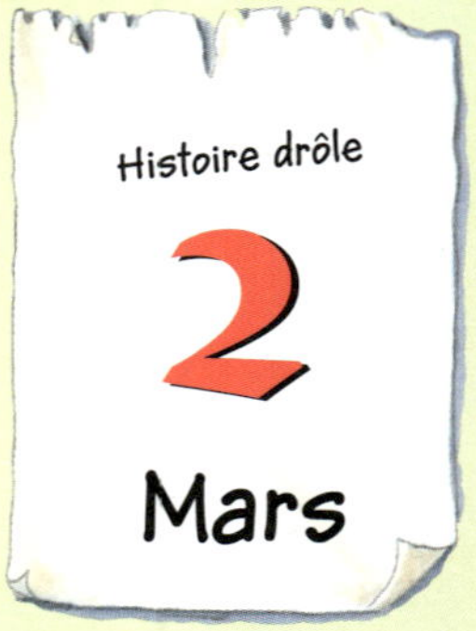

Frédéric ne se fait pas prier.

- C'est l'histoire de Superman qui vole dans le ciel, quand tout à coup un méchant géant vert fonce sur lui en hélicoptère pour l'embêter. Alors, Superman attrape le géant vert, et pif ! paf ! dans la figure, il envoie le géant vert sur la planète Mars.

Tous les élèves éclatent de rire.

- C'est bien, Frédéric, mais il n'y a pas de morale.

- C'est parce que c'est pas fini. Après, Superman se pose sur un immeuble de trois cents étages, en plein milieu de Los Angeles, et des cambrioleurs foncent sur lui pour l'embêter. Alors, Superman attrape les cambrioleurs, et pif ! paf ! dans la figure, il les envoie sur la planète Mars.

De nouveau, tout le monde rigole.

- Voyons, Frédéric...

- Attendez, je termine. Après, Superman descend dans la rue, mais là, il y a cent mille gangsters qui foncent sur lui pour l'embêter. Mais Superman les attrape, et pif ! paf ! dans la figure, il les envoie sur la planète Mars. Voilà.

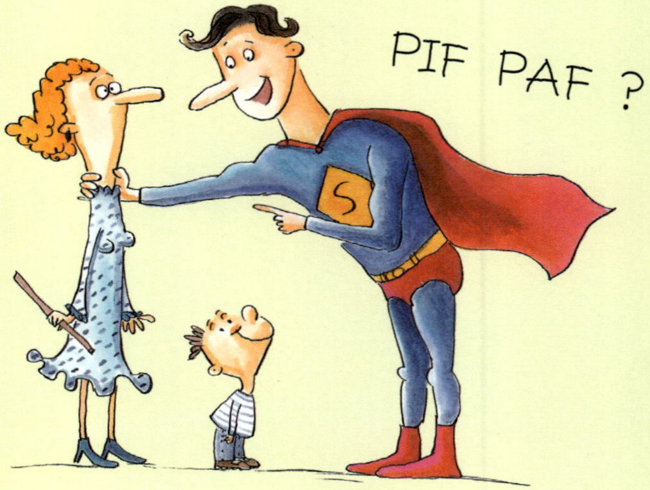

- Il n'y a pas de leçon à tirer de ton histoire, Frédéric ! gronde la maîtresse.

- Si, madame, la leçon, c'est qu'il ne faut pas embêter Superman, sinon pif ! paf ! dans la figure, et on se retrouve sur Mars.

Histoire drôle

3

Mars

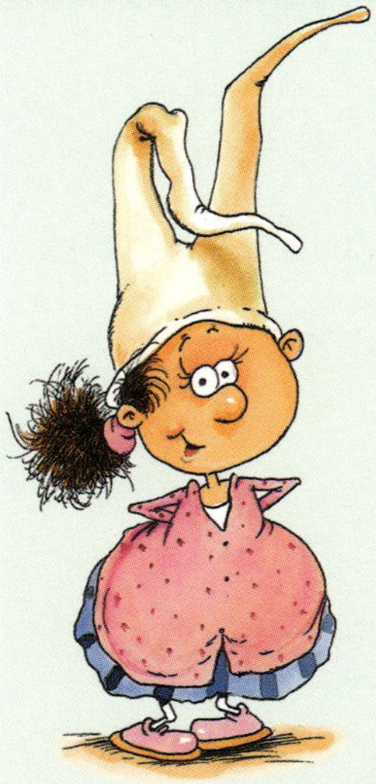

Une petite fille rentre de l'école et demande à son père :

- Tu connais la dernière ?

Le père est intrigué.

- La dernière ? Euh... non.
- Bah, c'est moi !

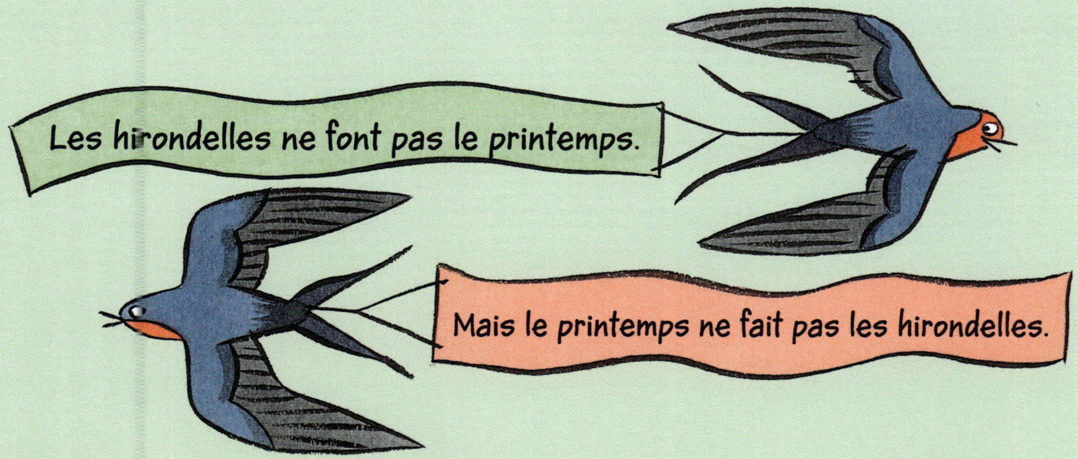

Petite annonce

4

Mars

Petite annonce

5

Mars

COURRIER : fou subtil achète enveloppes timbrées.

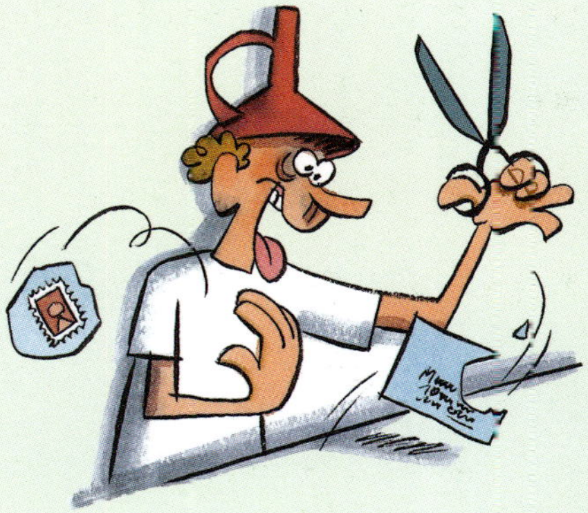

Histoire drôle

6

Mars

Il a plu toute la nuit, la terre est trempée. Lenny joue avec ses copains dans les flaques de boue du jardin, au grand désespoir de sa maman.

- Lenny, viens immédiatement prendre une douche !

- J'arrive, maman ! crie l'enfant.

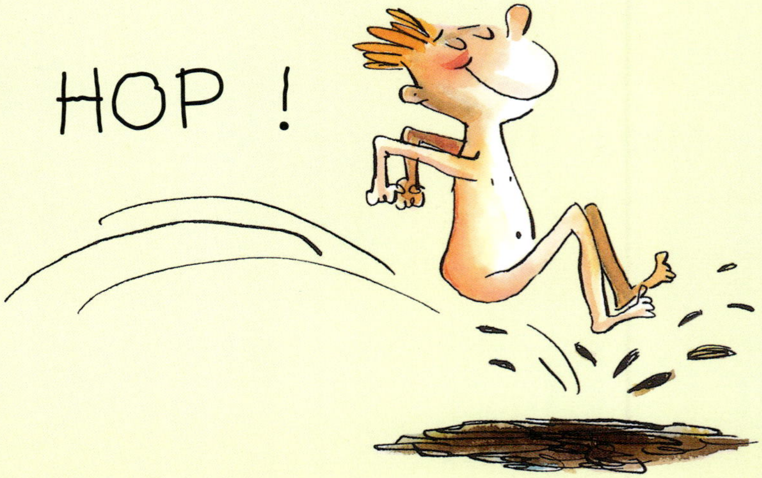

Puis il se tourne vers ses copains :

- Bon, je vais prendre ma douche et puis je reviens tout de suite jouer dans la gadoue avec vous.

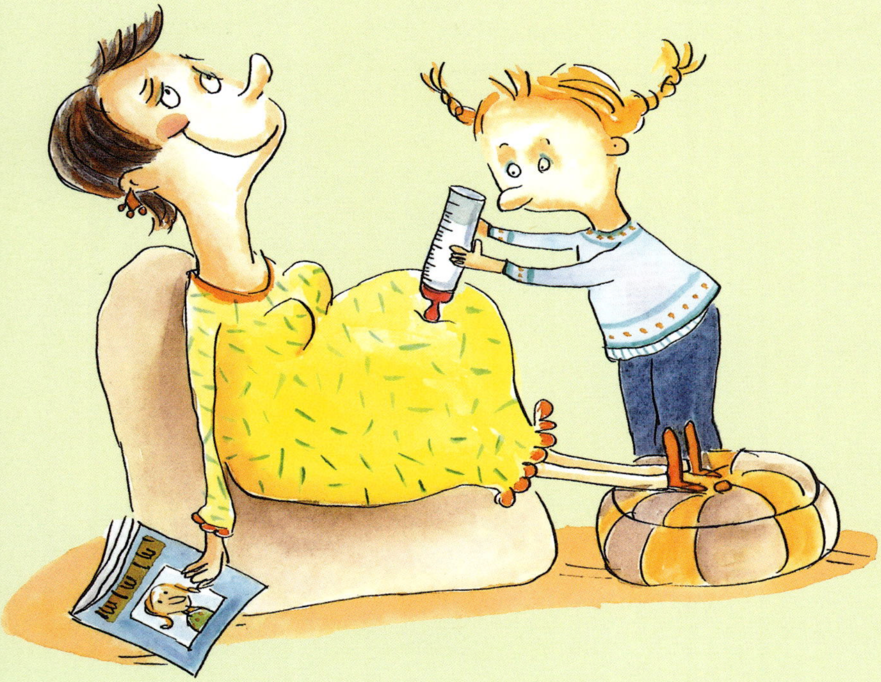

Une petite fille s'étonne du gros ventre de sa maman.

- Maman, pourquoi tu as un gros ventre ?

- Parce que j'attends un bébé, ma chérie.

- Et il est où, ce bébé ?

- Ici, tout près de mon cœur, répond la maman.

- Ah oui ! et dans le ventre, il y a la poussette ?

Histoire drôle

7

Mars

Histoire drôle

8

Mars

Nicolas est au musée avec ses parents, et il s'ennuie fermement.
Alors que son père contemple depuis dix minutes le même tableau, il demande :
- Papa ! elle est où, la télécommande, que je change de chaîne ?

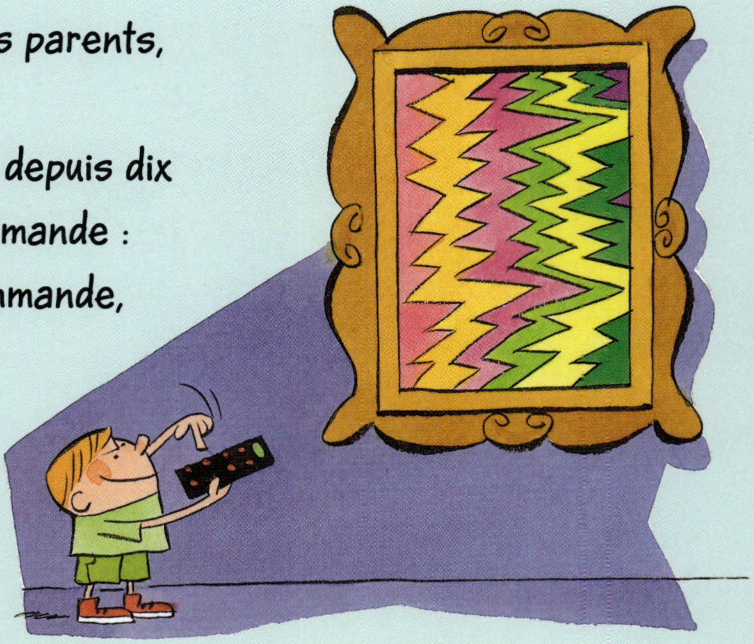

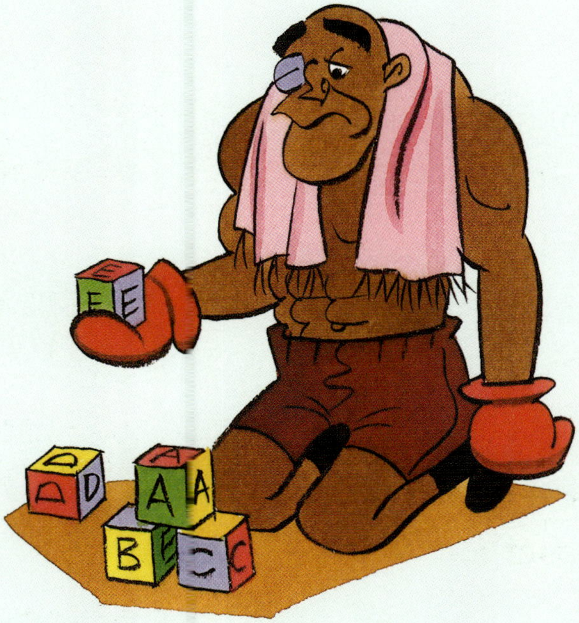

Quelles sont les deux lettres qui conviennent aux deux boxeurs à la fin d'un combat ?

(Réponse : le « O » et le « K ». À la fin du combat, l'un d'eux est O.K., l'autre est K.O. !)

Devinette

9

Mars

Devinette

10

Mars

Quel animal mange avec sa queue ?

(Réponse : tous les animaux qui ont une queue mangent avec leur queue ! Ils ne peuvent pas l'enlever pour manger !)

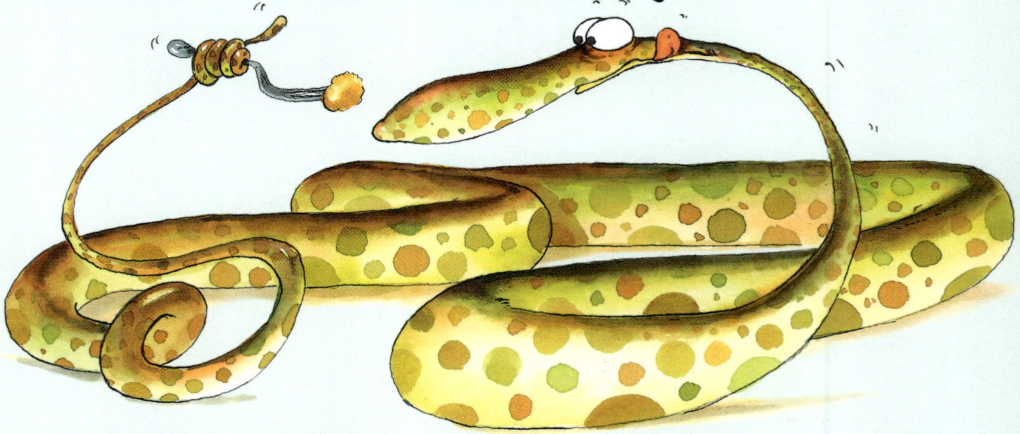

Un médecin fait entrer un patient dans son cabinet.

- Alors, qu'est-ce qui ne va pas ? demande-t-il.

Le patient ne répond rien. Il s'assied par terre, met le nez sur le sol, se tord la jambe droite, la passe par-dessus sa tête et la cale bien sur sa nuque. Puis il se tord la jambe gauche, la met sous la jambe droite, autour de son cou.

Histoire drôle

11

Mars

- Vous voyez, docteur, gémit-il, quand je fais ça, j'ai mal partout !

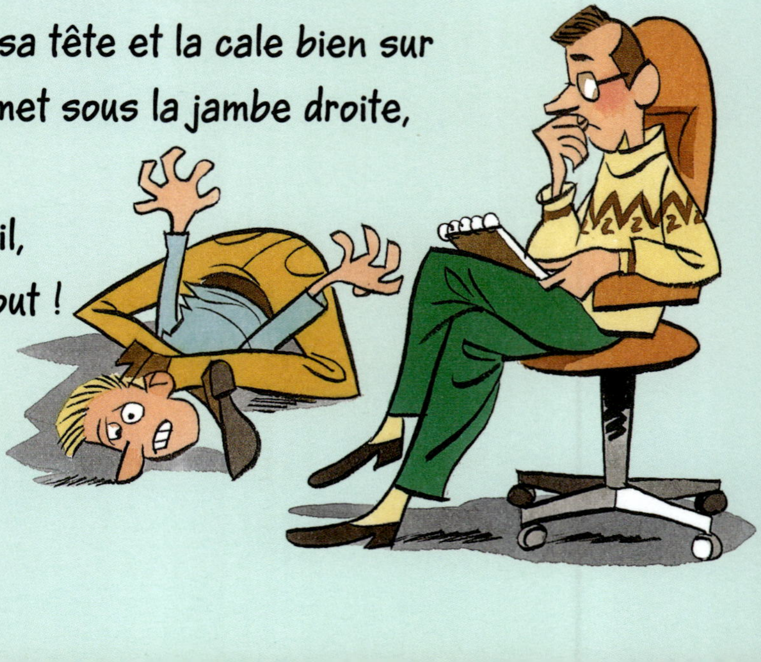

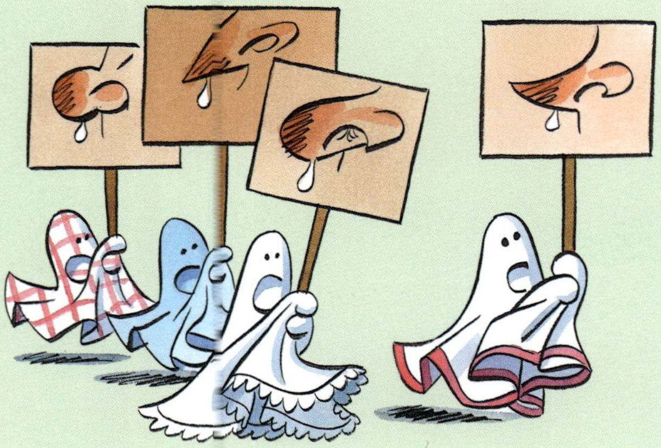

ENNUI : mouchoir sans emploi cherche nez enrhumé.

Petite annonce
12
Mars

Petite annonce
13
Mars

SPORT : M. Gorille vient de remporter les Championnats du Monde de boxe, catégorie poids lourds.

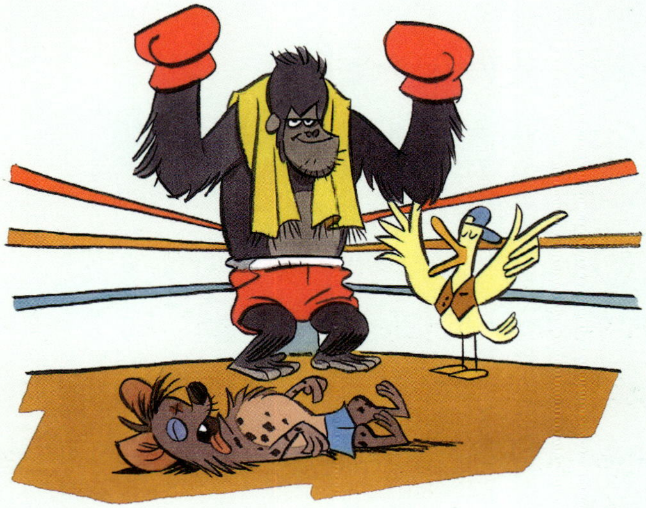

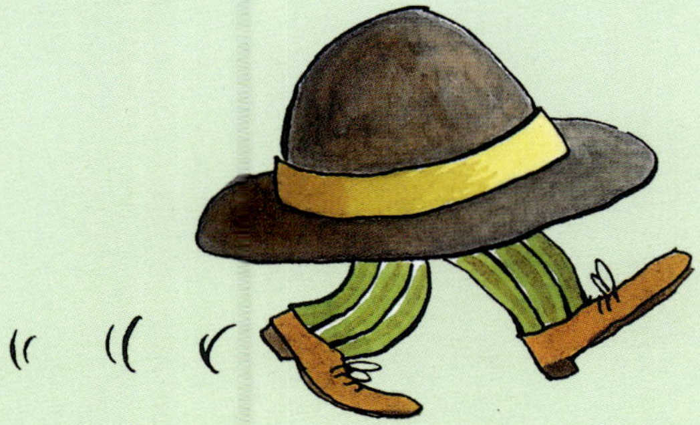

INFO : le marchand de chapeaux a perdu la tête.

Petite annonce
14
Mars

Histoire drôle

15

Mars

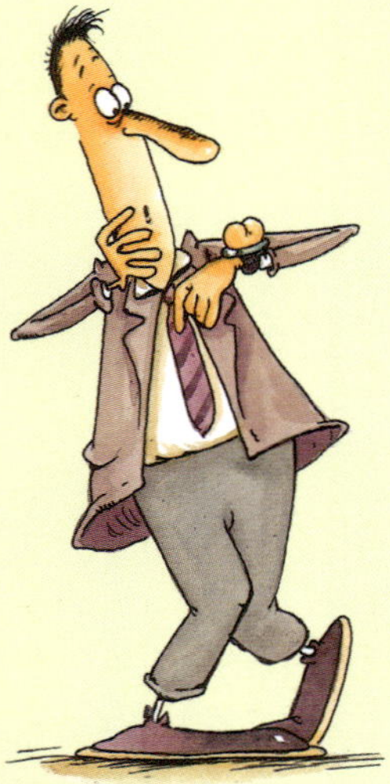

- Pardon, monsieur ! demande un garnement à un passant. Pourriez-vous me donner l'heure, je vous prie ?
- Bien sûr, mon petit. Il est 16h10.
- Merci, monsieur. À 16h30, vous pourrez embrasser mon derrière !

Et le gamin détale en courant. Le monsieur, outré, se met à poursuivre le gosse, mais, au bout de quelques mètres, il se heurte à un policier.

- Holà ! s'indigne le policier. Où allez-vous d'un pas si pressé ?
- Je poursuis ce garnement, qui m'a dit qu'à 16h30 je pourrais embrasser son derrière !

Le policier regarde sa montre.

- Pas besoin de courir ! Il vous reste quinze minutes !

Petite annonce

16

Mars

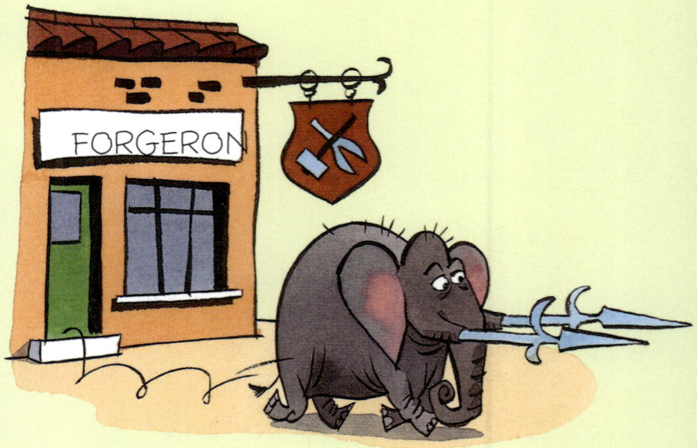

ENTRAIDE : éléphant sans défenses recherche protection contre chasseur aux dents longues.

Histoire drôle

17

Mars

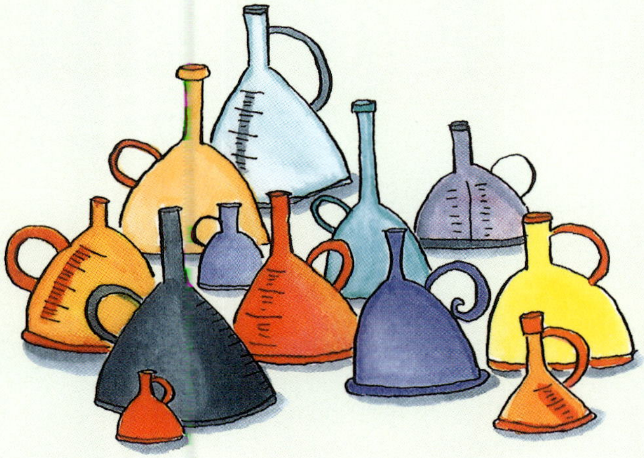

Un fou vient d'être amené à l'asile par deux infirmiers. À peine entré, il s'écrie :
- Dites donc ! Il y a un monde fou, là-dedans !

Histoire drôle

18

Mars

Un automobiliste distrait grille un feu rouge.
Un agent le siffle.
- Eh bien ! mon gaillard, vous n'avez pas vu le feu ?
- Qu'est-ce que vous voulez que j'y fasse ? Appelez les pompiers !

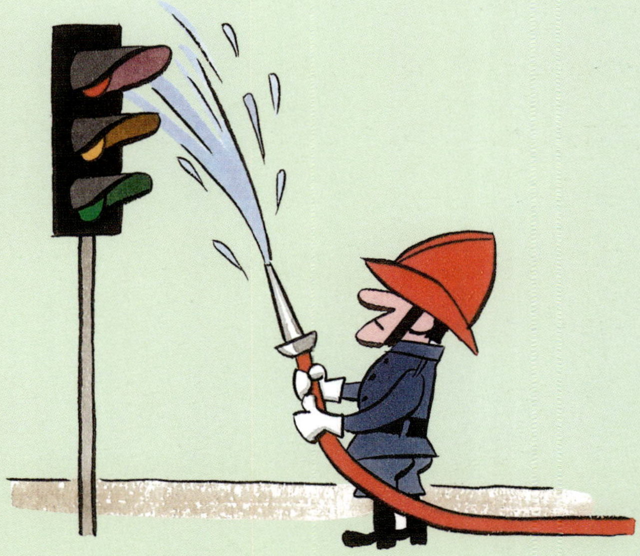

Histoire drôle

19

Mars

C'est l'anniversaire des douze ans de Jean.
- Tu vois, explique sa grand-mère, ce soir, tu auras un énorme gâteau avec douze bougies.
- C'est chouette, mamie. Mais je préférerais douze énormes gâteaux avec une seule bougie.

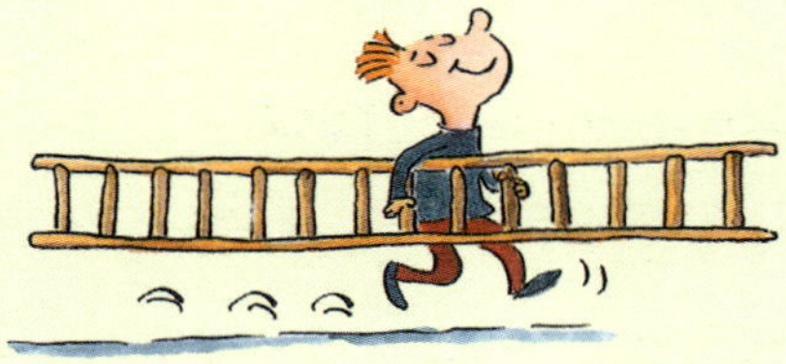

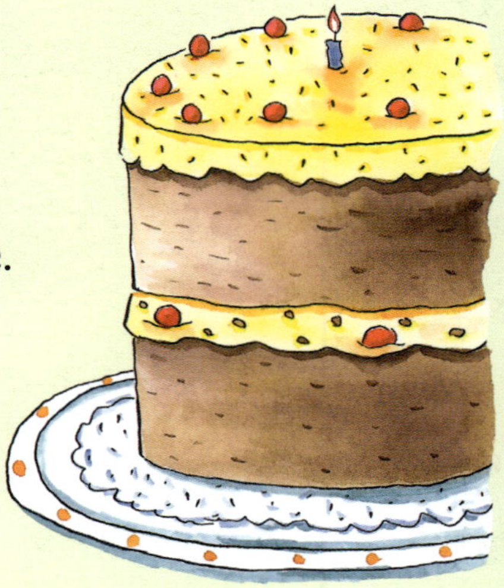

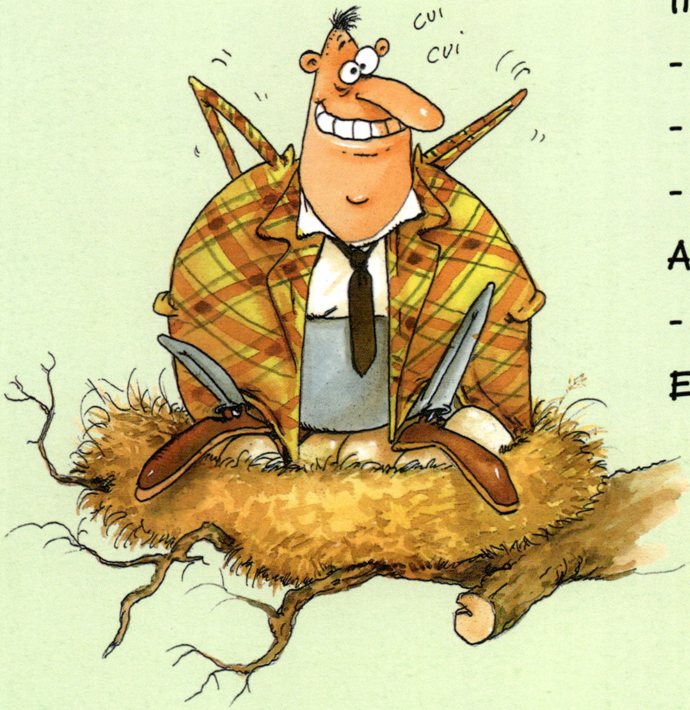

Un directeur de cirque passe des auditions pour trouver de nouveaux spectacles.
- Alors, dit-il à un artiste, que savez-vous faire ?
- J'imite les oiseaux, répond timidement l'artiste.
- Aucun intérêt, tranche le directeur du cirque. Au suivant!
- Je regrette ! Au revoir, salue l'artiste.
Et il s'envole par la fenêtre.

Histoire drôle

20

Mars

Devinette

21

Mars

Que mange le superbébé de Superman ?
- Des superbiberons.
Pourquoi le superbébé de Superman a-t-il besoin de supercouches ?
- Parce qu'il fait des superpipis et des supercacas.
Pourquoi le superbébé de Superman a-t-il été puni par la maîtresse ?
- Parce qu'un copain avait foncé sur lui pour l'embêter, alors superbébé l'a attrapé, et pif ! paf ! dans la figure, il l'a envoyé sur la planète Mars.

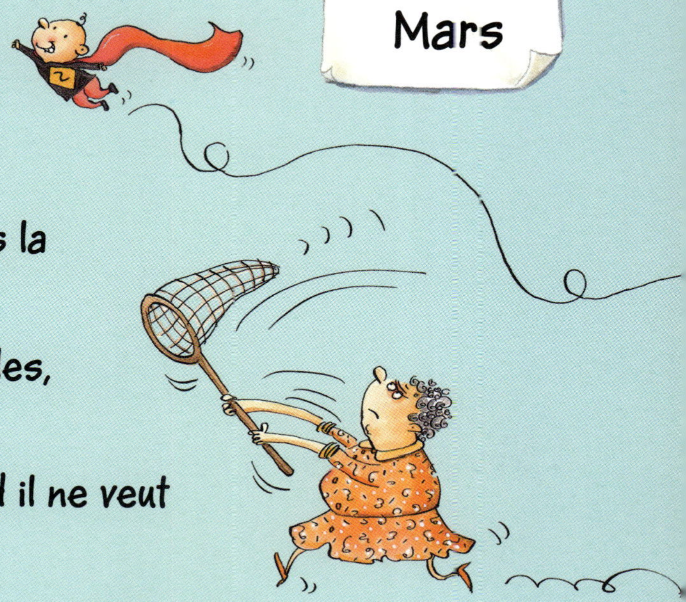

Pourquoi Superman est-il obligé de se boucher les oreilles, le soir ?
- Parce que son superbébé pousse des supercris quand il ne veut pas aller dormir.
Qui garde le superbébé de Superman ?
- Une supernourrice, habituée aux enfants qui font des supercolères, qui donnent des supercoups de pied quand ils ne sont pas contents, et qui volent dans la maison lorsqu'ils ne veulent pas prendre leur bain.
Pourquoi ne fête-t-on jamais l'anniversaire du superbébé de Superman ?
- Parce qu'à chaque fois, le gâteau se retrouve collé au mur quand le superbébé supersouffle les bougies.
Qu'y a-t-il de pire qu'un superbébé garçon de Superman ?
- Un superbébé fille.
Qu'y a-t-il de pire qu'un superbébé fille de Superman ?
- Deux superbébés filles.

Histoire drôle

22

Mars

Un voyou entre en trombe dans un commissariat.

- Mettez-moi en prison, vite, vite !
- Pour quelle raison ?
- J'ai tiré sur un gros musclé avec un revolver et je l'ai manqué ! Vite !

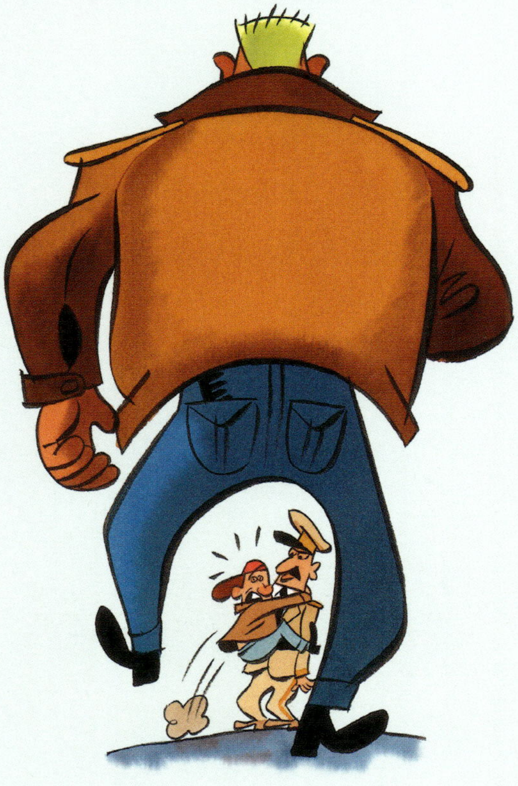

Histoire drôle

23

Mars

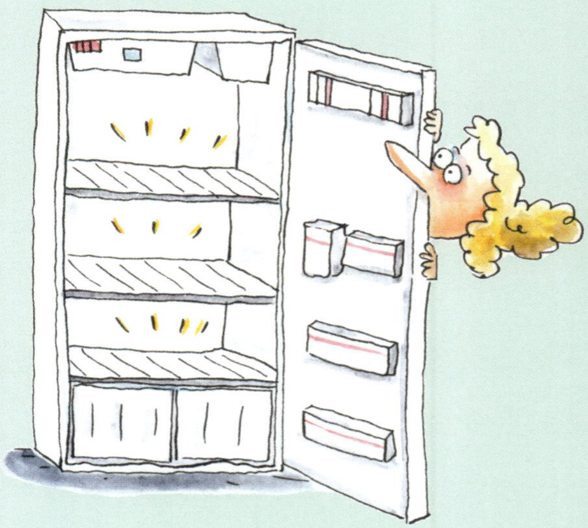

Une maman dit à sa fille :

- Si j'avais du gruyère, je te ferais une omelette au gruyère, mais, de toute façon, je n'ai pas d'œufs.

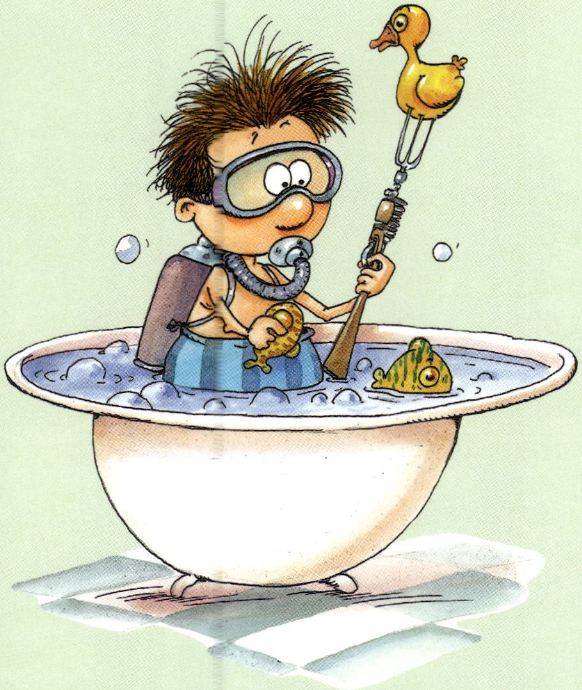

Histoire drôle

24

Mars

Un petit garçon interroge sa maman.
- Maman, dis-moi ! Ça te fait plaisir, chaque jour, de me donner deux bains, de me laver les oreilles, le nez, de me couper les ongles ou les cheveux, de m'habiller avec de beaux vêtements ou de beaux pyjamas ?
- Bien sûr ! répond la mère en souriant.
- Et qu'est-ce que tu faisais, quand je n'étais pas né, pour t'amuser ?

AVIS : attent on, aujourd'hui, M. Mouton s'est fait tondre, on lui a pris toute sa laine et il a les nerfs en pelote.

Petite annonce

25

Mars

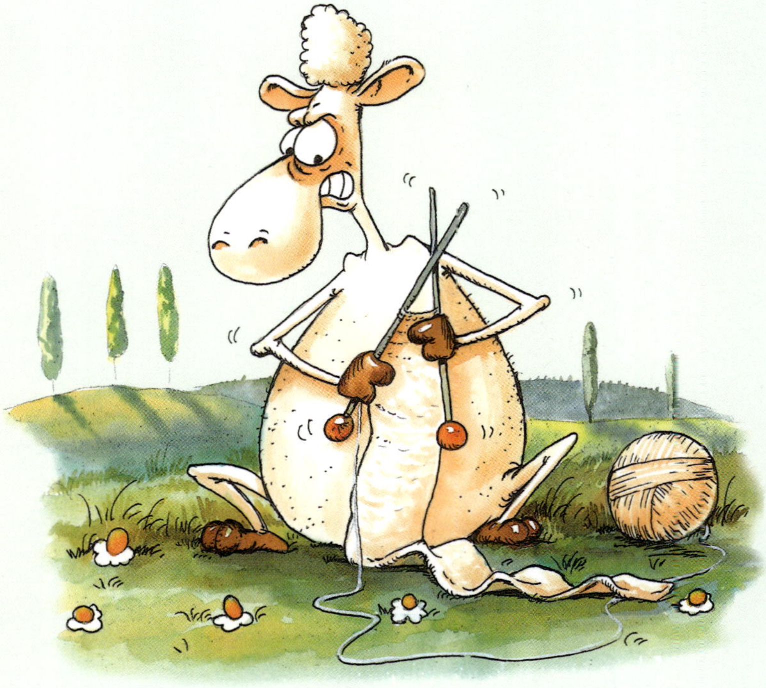

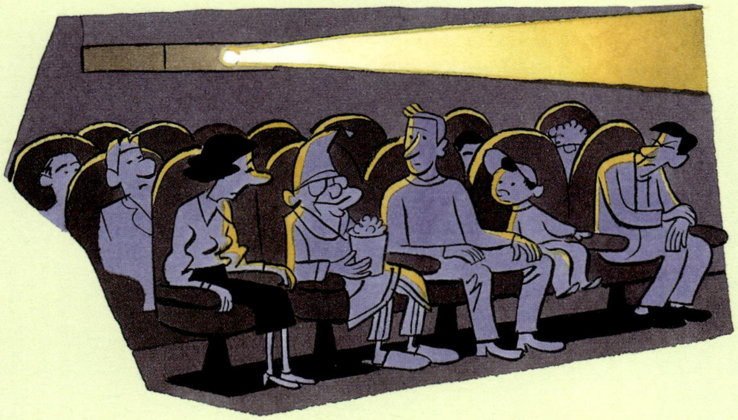

Histoire drôle

26

Mars

Une dame s'étonne en voyant son mari se mettre au lit avec ses lunettes sur le nez.

- Eh bien ? Tu n'enlèves plus tes lunettes pour dormir ?

- Ah, non ! répond le mari. La nuit dernière, je les avais enlevées, et j'ai rêvé que j'allais au cinéma. Et évidemment, sans mes lunettes, je n'ai pas pu voir le film !

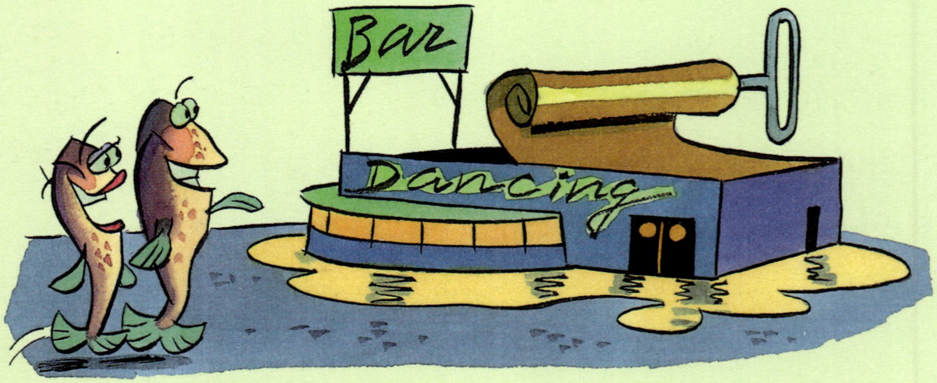

Petite annonce

27

Mars

DANCING : sardines cherchent boîte sympa.

Histoire drôle

28 Mars

Un gangster rentre chez lui après avoir accompli trois attaques à main armée.

- Tu vas être fier, lui annonce son épouse. Notre petit garçon vient de prononcer ses premiers mots !

- Lesquels ?

« Papa ? Maman ?»

- Non. « Haut les mains » !

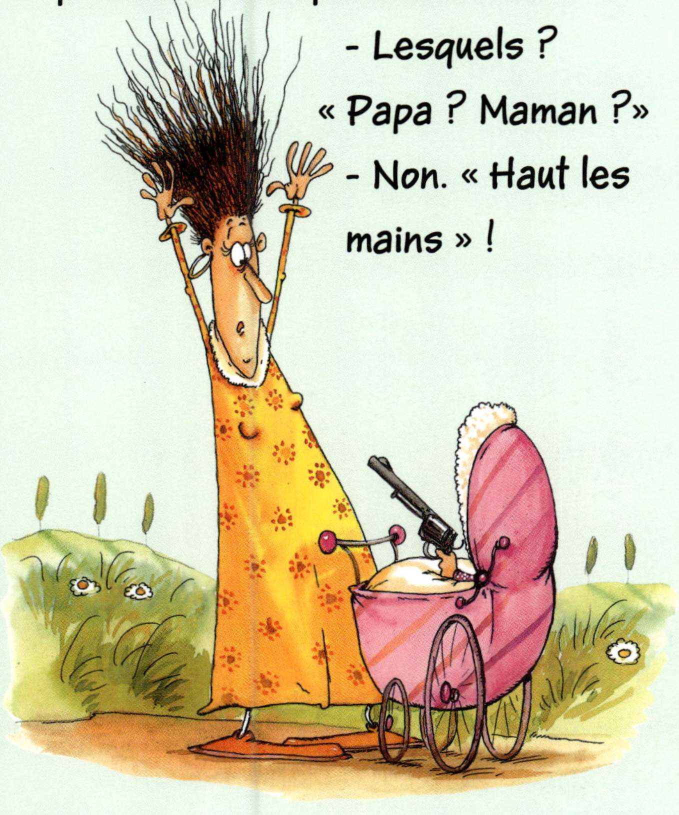

Histoire drôle

29 Mars

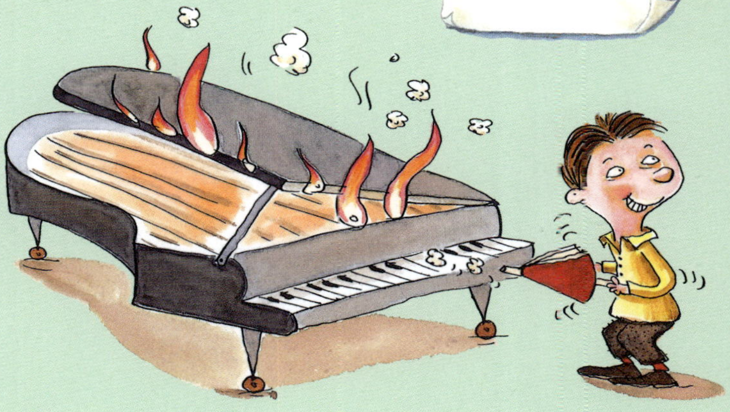

- Au feu ! Au feu ! crie le professeur de musique à son élève, pendant le cours de piano. Vite, appelle les pompiers !

Voyant que son élève ne bouge pas, elle répète :

- Va vite appeler les pompiers, pendant que je sauve les partitions !

- J'y vais, répond l'élève, j'y vais... J'attends juste que cette saleté de piano ait brûlé avant.

Devinette

30 Mars

Comment appelle-t-on une pomme de terre poilue qui se promène dans les bois un soir de pleine lune ?

(Réponse : une patate-garou.)

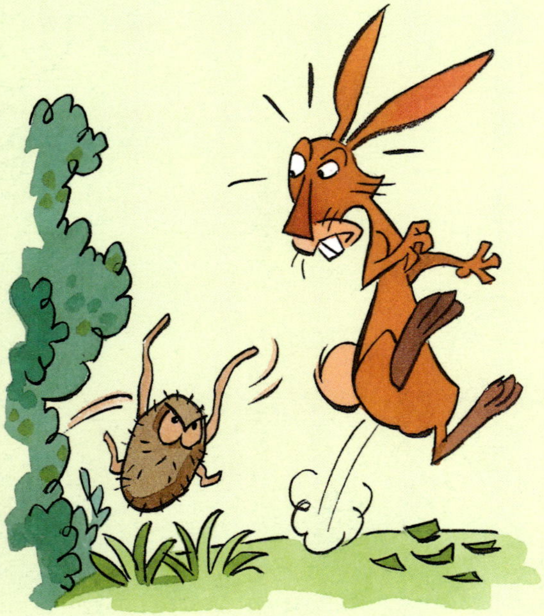

Histoire drôle

31 Mars

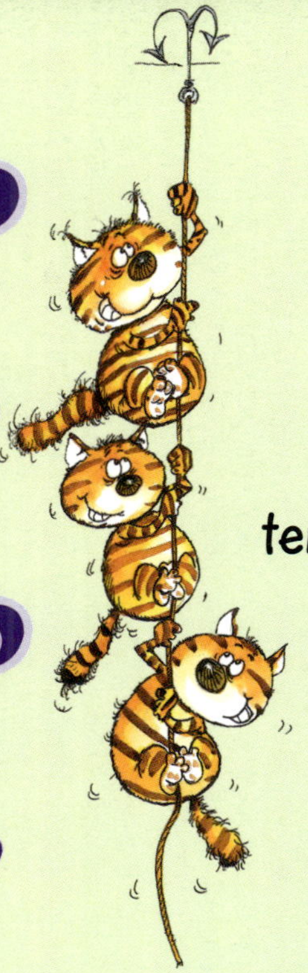

Trois prisonniers tentent de s'échapper d'une prison. Ils coupent les barbelés sur le mur et entreprennent de l'escalader. Mais le bruit attire un garde.

- Qui va là ? hurle le surveillant, en pointant un fusil vers le mur.
- Miaou ! fait le premier prisonnier.
- Saleté de chat ! dit le garde.

Le second prisonnier essaye à son tour de passer par-dessus le mur.

- Qui va là ? hurle à nouveau le garde.
- Miaou, miaou !
- Encore ce sale chat ! peste le surveillant.

Le troisième prisonnier monte à son tour.

- Qui va là ?

Et le prisonnier de répondre :

- Ne vous inquiétez pas, c'est encore cette saleté de chat !

Devinette

1

Avril

Un soir de pleine lune, une grenouille verte en maillot de bain rose tombe du ciel, on ne sait trop comment, et va bientôt plonger dans la mer. Quel bruit va-t-elle faire en entrant dans l'eau, sachant que la mer est turquoise et que le maillot de bain rose de la grenouille est un peu trop grand pour elle ?

(Réponse : elle va faire PLOUF !)

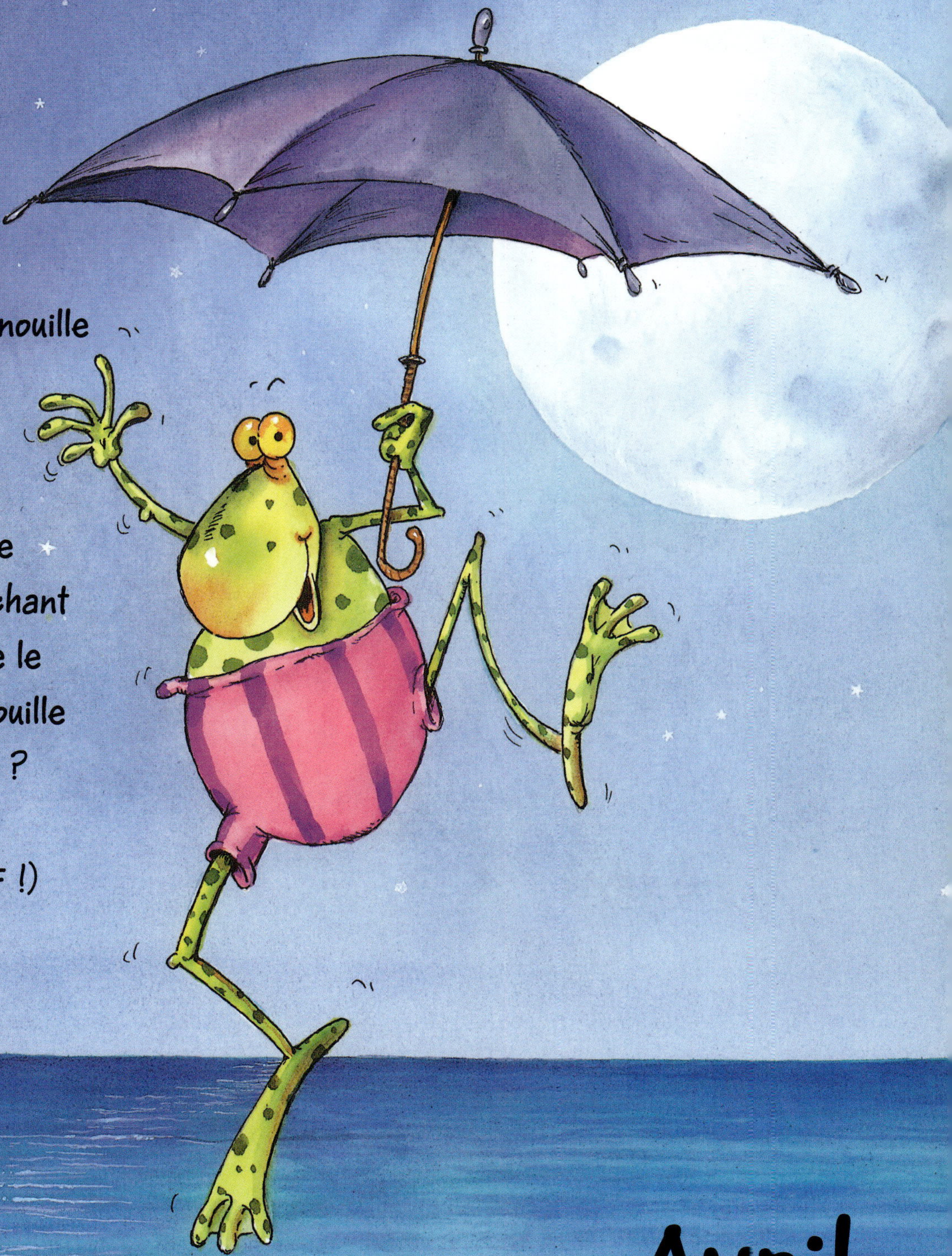

Avril

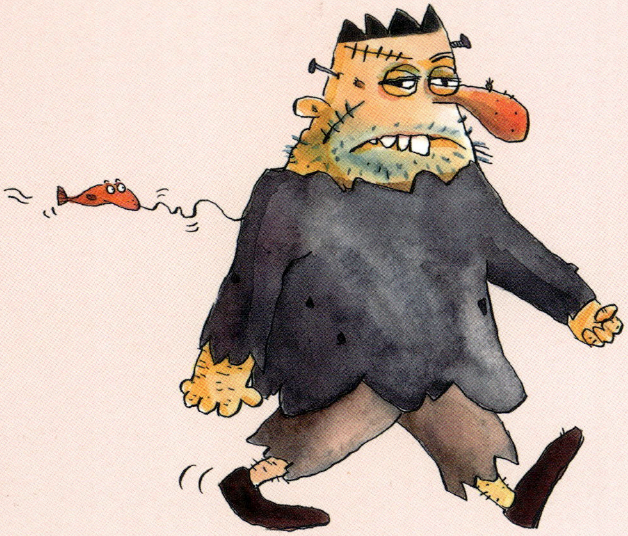

Petite annonce
2
Avril

AMI : poisson d'avril
cherche dos accueillant.

Histoire drôle
3
Avril

Paul va chez le boucher.

- Bonjour, je voudrais cinq kilos de viande de bœuf, sept kilos d'escalopes de dinde, huit kilos de gigot d'agneau et sept entrecôtes de 150 grammes chacune, s'il vous plaît.
- Eh bien, s'exclame le boucher, tu as un solide appétit !
- Euh, pour dire vrai, ce qui m'intéresse, c'est le poids de toute cette viande. C'est pour résoudre un problème que nous a donné notre maîtresse !

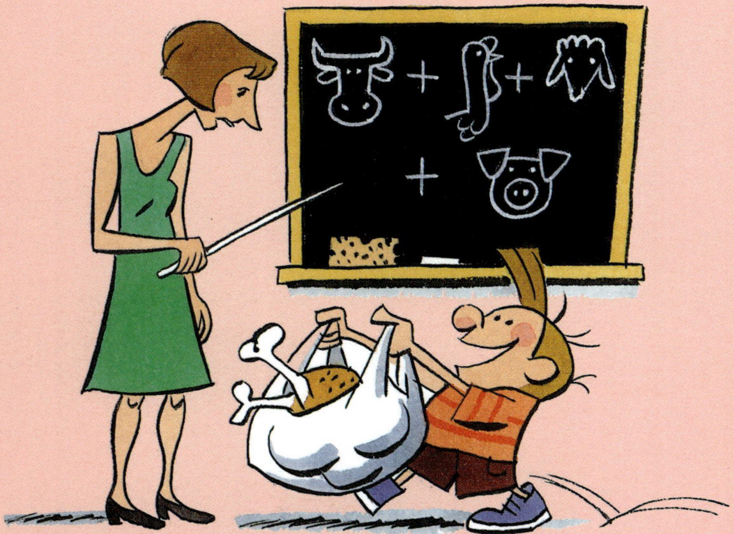

Petite annonce

4 Avril

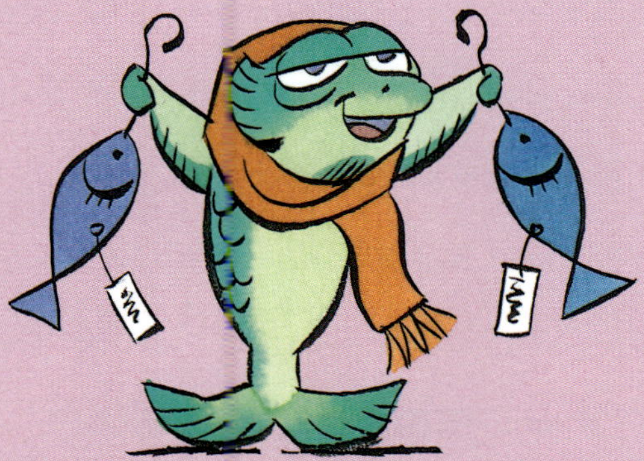

Mois d'avril fatigué vend poissons farceurs.

Histoire drôle

5 Avril

Deux vaches anglaises broutent dans un pré.

- Ça ne t'inquiète pas, ces histoires de vache folle ? demande l'une.

- Pourquoi ça m'inquiéterait ? s'étonne l'autre. Ça ne me concerne pas, je ne suis pas une vache, je suis une poule !

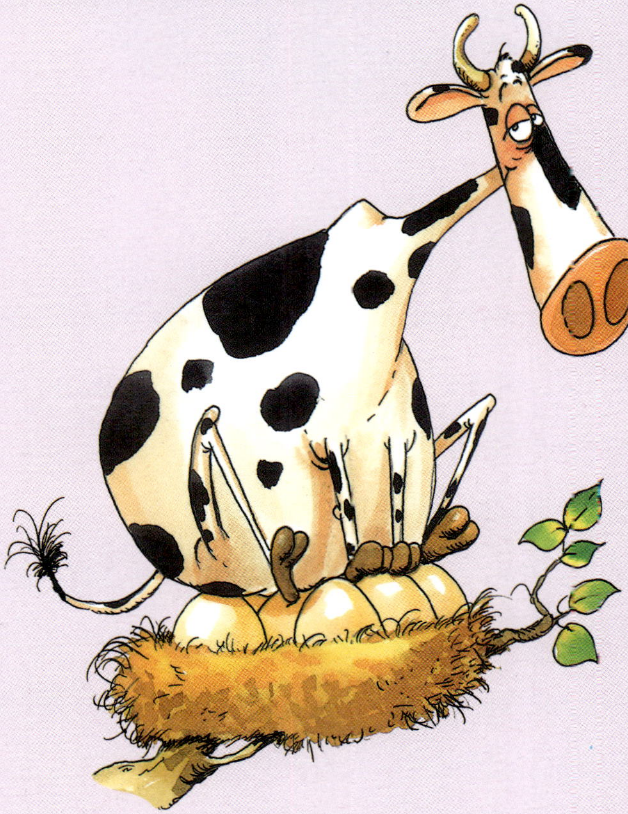

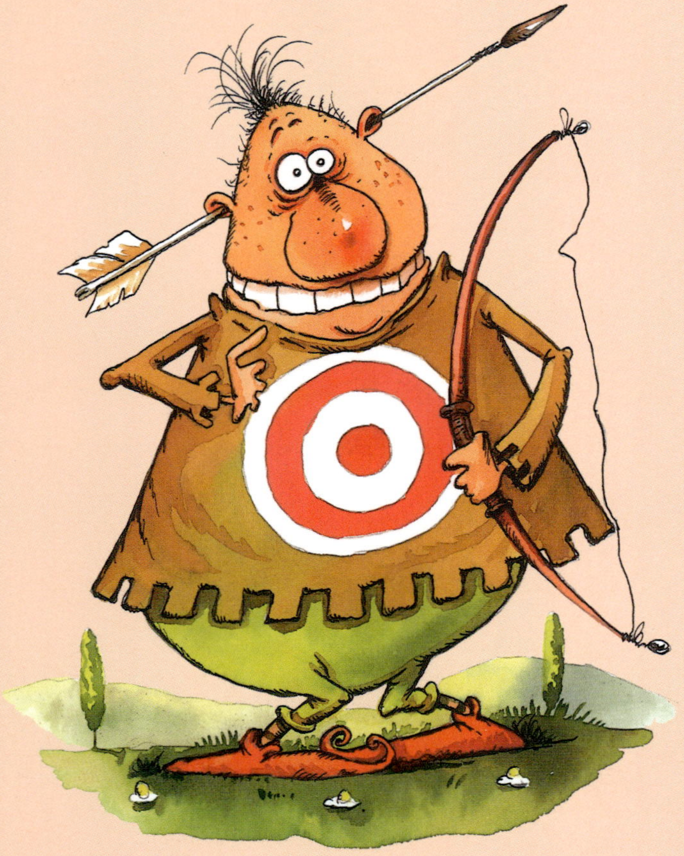

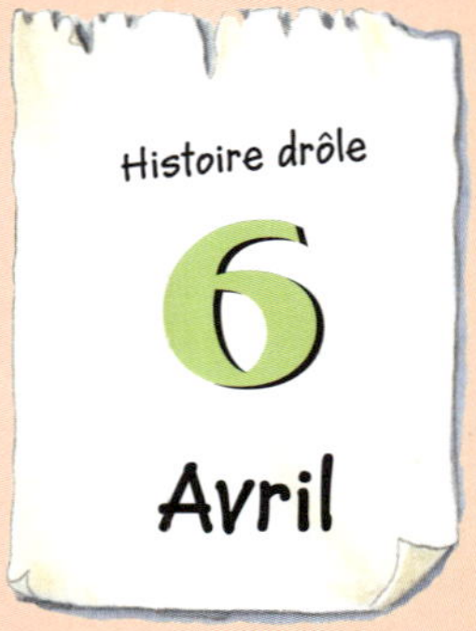

À un concours de tir à l'arc, trois compétiteurs s'affrontent. L'épreuve est simple : il faut tirer sur une pomme qui est placée sur la tête d'un jeune homme, à 50 mètres de distance.
Le premier concurrent se place, tend son arc, ferme un œil pour viser et tire. La flèche tourne dans l'air à la vitesse du vent et se plante en plein dans la pomme. Le concurrent regarde ses adversaires en souriant.
- Je suis... Guillaume Tell.
Le second compétiteur se place, tend son arc, ferme un œil et tire. La flèche tournoie dans l'air et se plante, là encore, au milieu de la pomme. L'archer regarde ses adversaires en souriant.
- Moi, je suis... Robin des Bois.
Le troisième concurrent se place, tend son arc, ferme un œil et tire. La flèche dévie de sa trajectoire et se plante dans le pied du jeune homme qui tient la pomme sur sa tête. Le concurrent regarde ses adversaires d'un air malheureux.
- Je suis... désolé.

Petite annonce

7

Avril

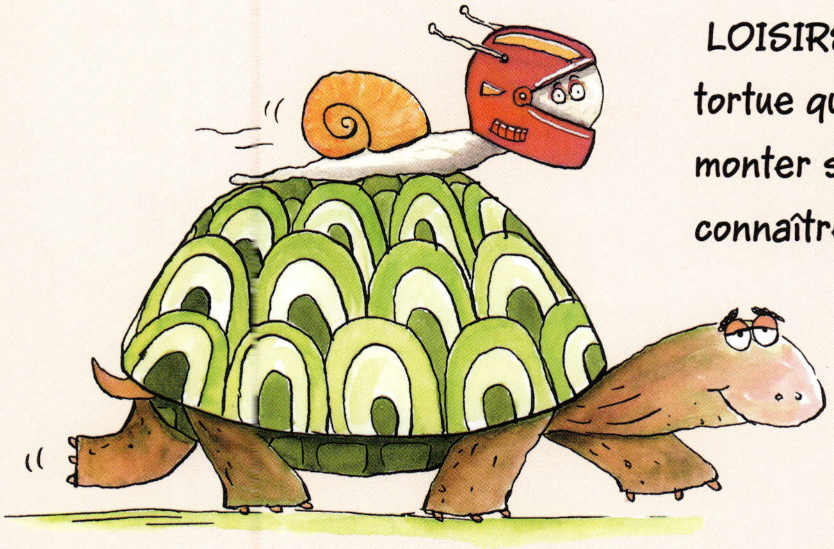

LOISIRS : escargot cherche tortue qui accepte de le laisser monter sur sa carapace, pour connaître l'ivresse de la vitesse.

Histoire drôle

8

Avril

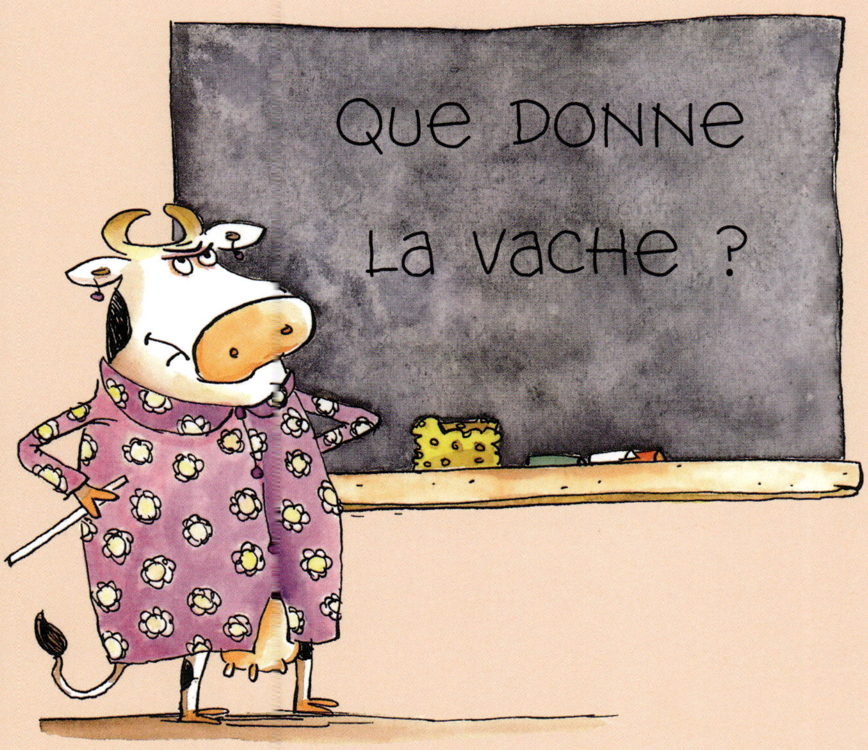

La maîtresse vérifie que la leçon sur les animaux est bien connue de tous les enfants.

- Voyons, les enfants : que donne le mouton ?
- Les moutons nous donnent de la laine.
- Très bien. Que donne la poule ?
- La poule nous donne des œufs.
- Parfait. Que donne la vache ?
- La vache nous donne des devoirs.

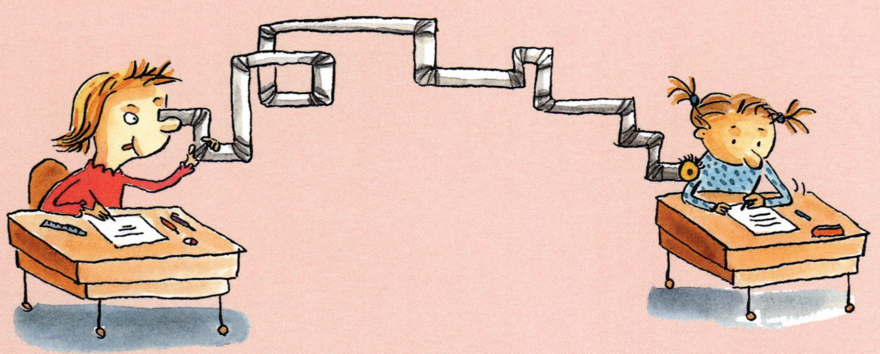

Histoire drôle

9

Avril

Cette fois, la maîtresse en a assez :

- Martine ! Cesse immédiatement de copier ton problème sur ta voisine !

- Mais je ne copie pas le problème, maîtresse. Je ne copie que la solution !

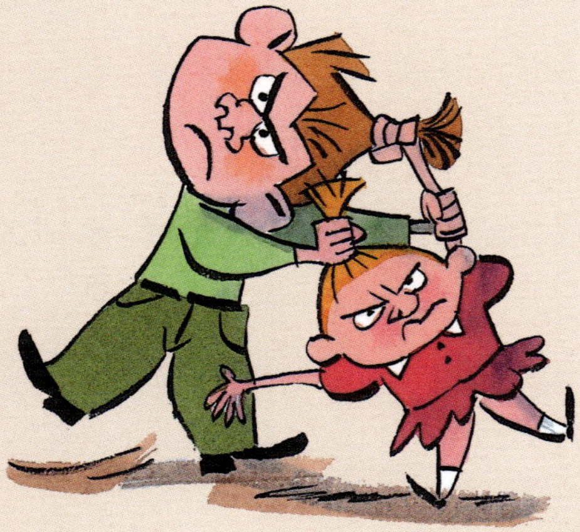

- Maman, il y a Mélanie qui m'a tiré les cheveux.

- Allons, Pierre, elle n'a que trois ans ! Elle n'a pas voulu te blesser. Elle ne sait pas que ça fait mal.

Pierre quitte la pièce et, une minute plus tard, on entend Mélanie hurler.

Pierre revient voir sa mère.

- Maintenant, elle sait.

Histoire drôle

10

Avril

Histoire drôle

11 Avril

Un fou entre dans un café à Paris.
- Garçon ! Une limonade avec une rondelle de citron, je vous prie.
Le garçon lui apporte la limonade dans un grand verre et la rondelle de citron dans une petite soucoupe en porcelaine. Le fou trempe la rondelle de citron dans la limonade avant de boire. Puis il mange la soucoupe en porcelaine.
- Garçon, la même chose !
Le garçon, à nouveau, lui apporte la limonade dans un grand verre, et la rondelle de citron dans une soucoupe.

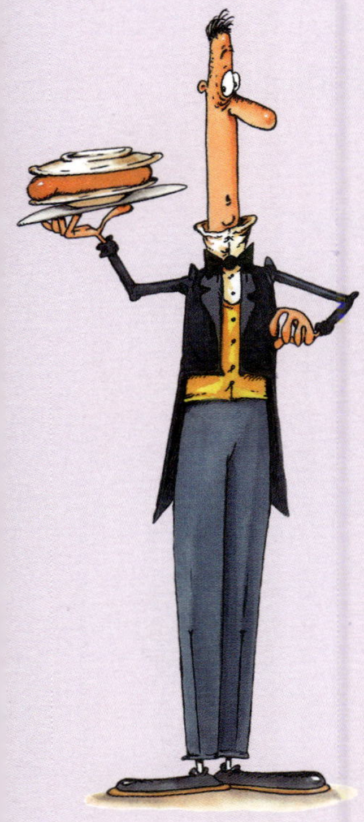

Le fou trempe une nouvelle fois sa rondelle de citron dans la limonade avant de boire, puis mange la soucoupe en porcelaine. Au moment de payer l'addition, il dit au garçon :
- Vous savez, votre limonade est vraiment excellente, mais, sans vouloir critiquer, vos sandwichs sont presque immangeables...

Petite annonce

12 Avril

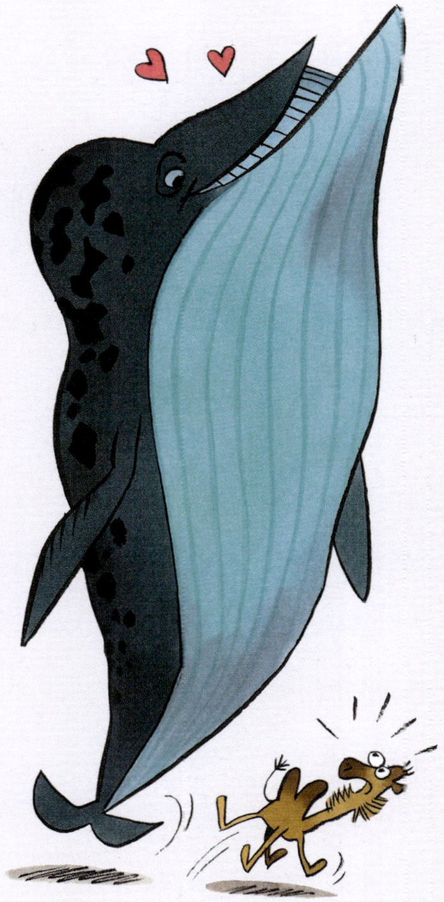

AMITIÉ : baleine à bosse cherche chameau sympa.

La pensée du jour :

« C'est dingue, quand on y pense : Pâques tombe toujours un dimanche et Noël le 25 décembre ! »

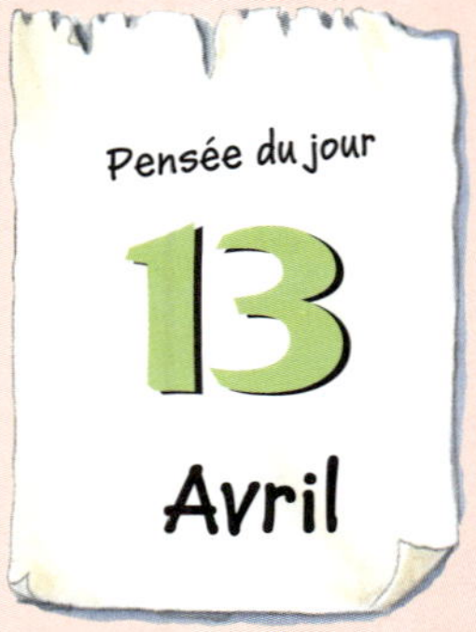

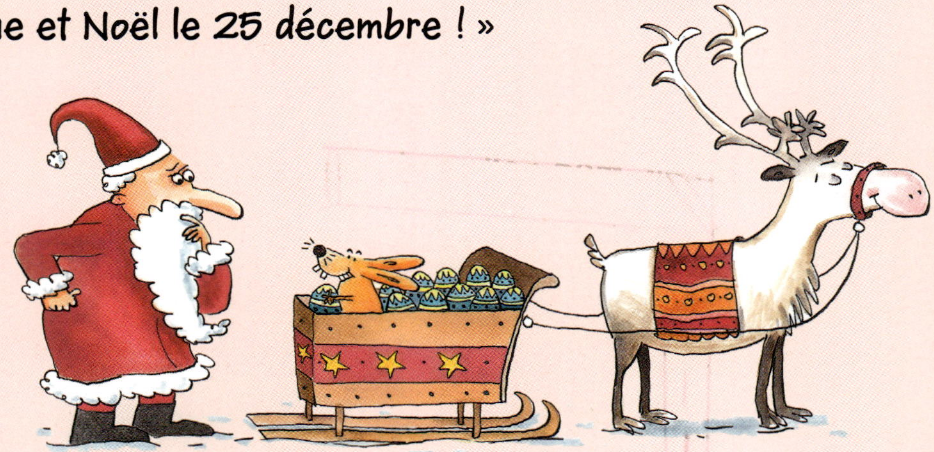

Un homme est au cinéma. Devant lui sont assis un monsieur à lunettes et son chien. Or, chose curieuse, le chien semble parfaitement comprendre le film : il pleure quand c'est émouvant et aboie quand c'est drôle.

À la fin de la projection, l'homme va voir le monsieur à lunettes et son chien extraordinaire.

- C'est incroyable : on dirait que votre chien a vraiment aimé le film !
- Oui, c'est incroyable, répond le monsieur à lunettes, parce qu'il n'avait pas du tout aimé le livre.

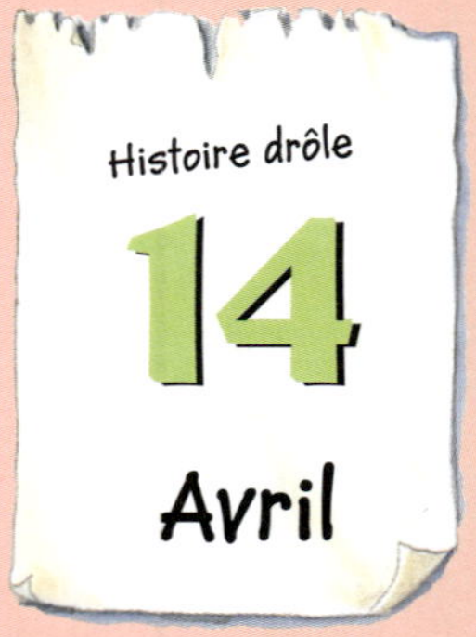

Histoire drôle

15

Avril

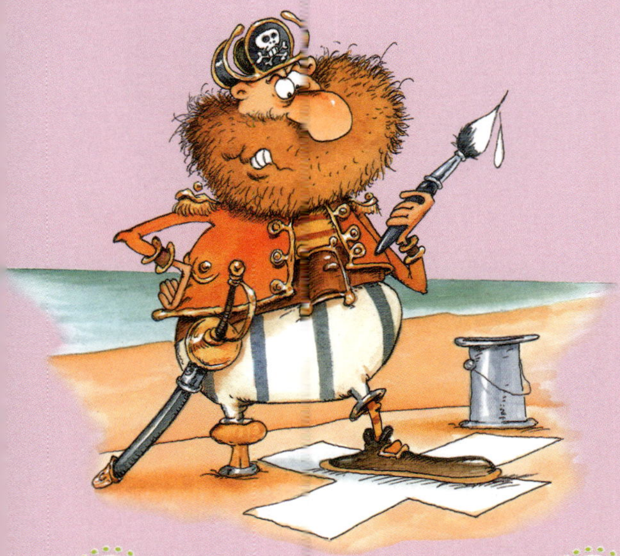

Un marin raconte sa chasse au trésor.

- J'avais en ma possession l'authentique carte du trésor du capitaine Cook. C'était une très belle carte, et le trésor y était indiqué d'une croix noire. J'ai pris mon bateau, mes pelles et mes pioches, et je me suis rendu sur l'île, à 6000 km d'ici. Et là-bas, j'ai trouvé...

- Le trésor ? demande un auditeur passionné par le récit.

- Non, répond le marin. J'ai trouvé la croix noire.

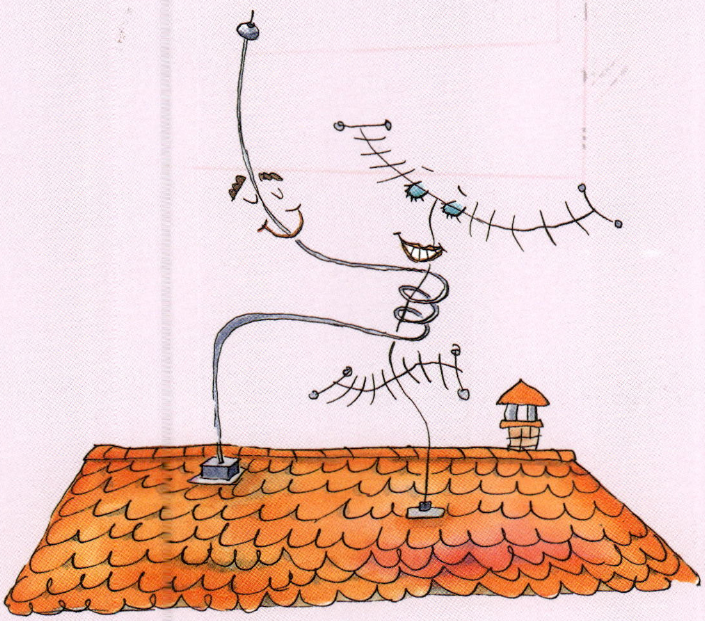

INFO : Mlle Antenne a eu un coup de foudre pour M. Paratonnerre.

Petite annonce

16

Avril

Devinette

17

Avril

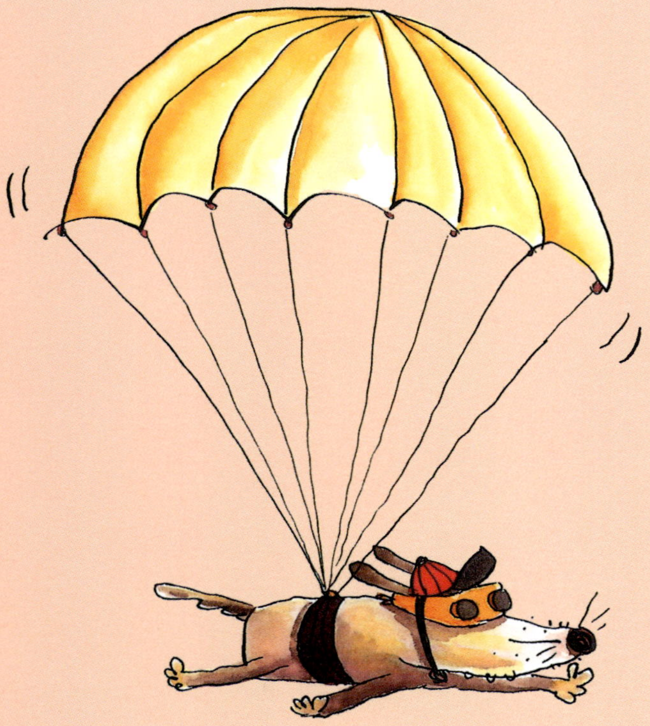

Comment les fous font-ils pour chasser le canard sans fusil ?

(Réponse : ils lancent leurs chiens de chasse très haut.)

Histoire drôle

18

Avril

Maman interroge son fils.
- Théo, peux-tu m'expliquer pourquoi il ne reste plus qu'un paquet de gâteaux dans le buffet, alors qu'hier il y en avait deux ?
- Il en reste un parce que je ne l'avais pas vu, sinon je l'aurais mangé aussi.

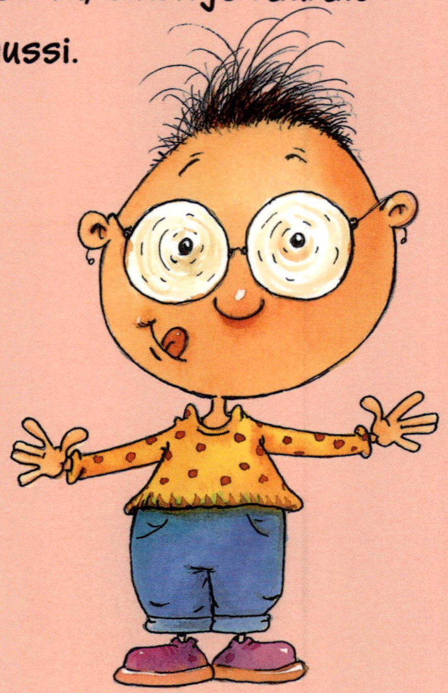

Histoire drôle

19

Avril

Furieux d'avoir reçu une fessée de son père parce qu'il avait fait tomber le vase de grand-mère sur le chat, Jérémie raconte à son meilleur copain :

- J'avais d'abord rêvé, pour me venger, de faire sauter la maison avec de la dynamite, mais j'ai trouvé que cette punition n'était pas assez forte pour eux. Alors j'ai volé la télécommande du téléviseur et je l'ai enterrée dans le jardin.

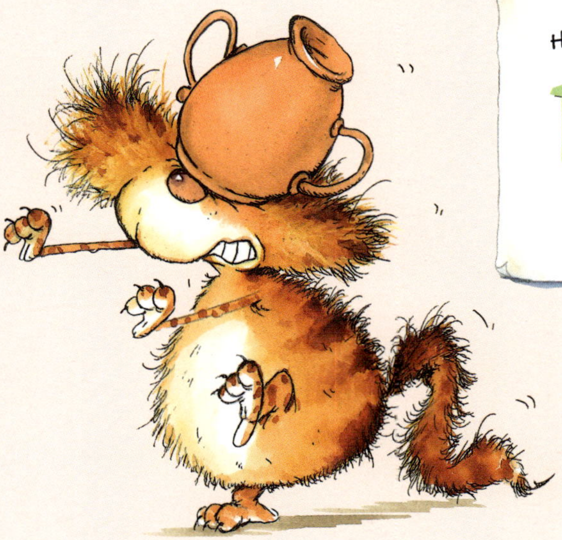

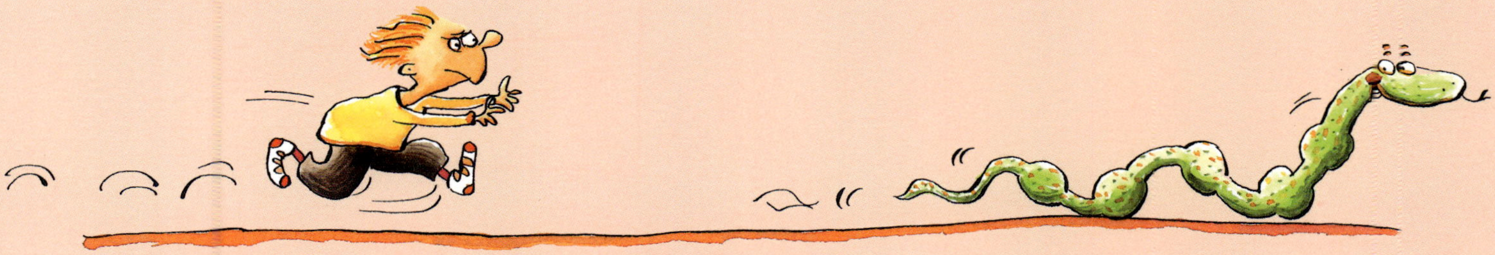

Petite annonce

20

Avril

LE SAVIEZ-VOUS ? à Pâques, les serpents gobent des œufs en chocolat.

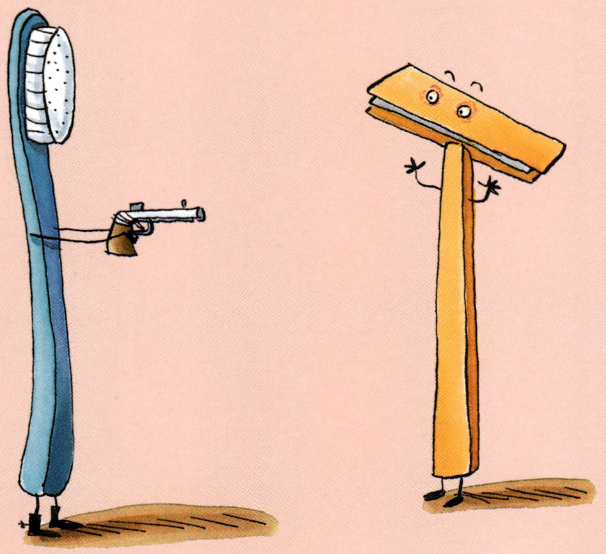

Histoire drôle

21

Avril

PRISON : Mme Moustache vient d'être arrêtée par la police. Elle avait chargé un tueur à gages d'assassiner M. Rasoir.

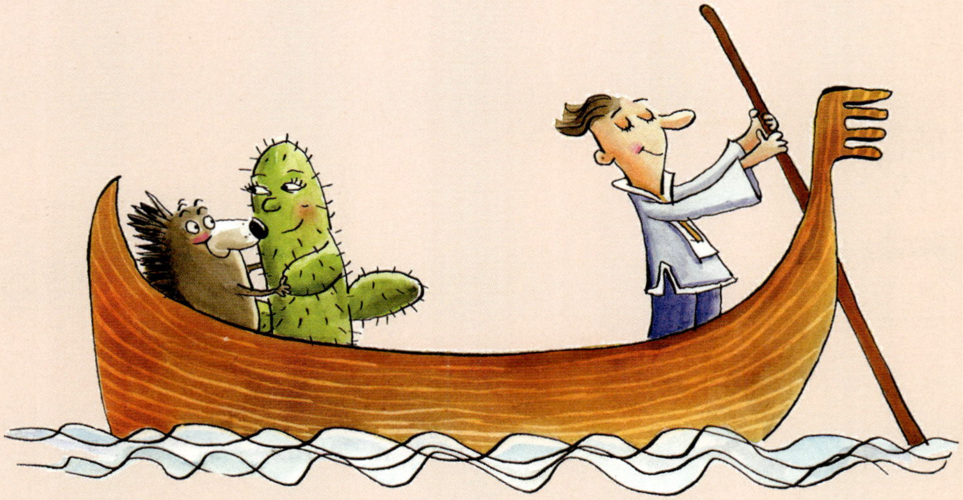

Que dit un hérisson quand il se cogne contre un cactus ?

(Réponse : il dit : « Comment faites-vous pour avoir la peau aussi douce ? »)

Devinette

22

Avril

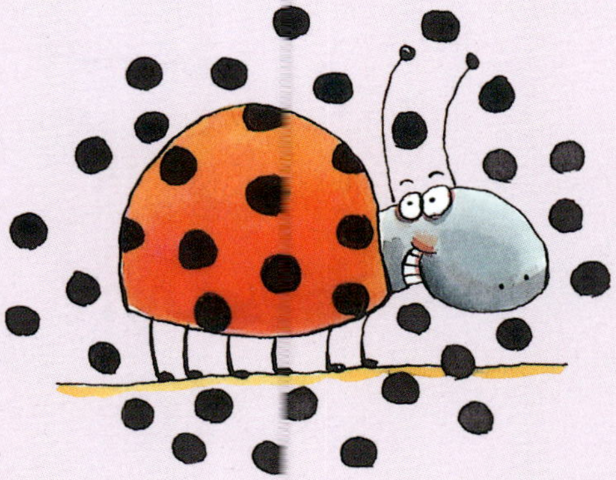

Histoire drôle

23

Avril

Deux amis se rencontrent.

- Je suis inquiet, dit l'un. Mes yeux me font mal et je vois des points noirs.

- Il faut que tu te soignes, dit l'autre. Quand est-ce que tu vois l'ophtalmologue ?

- Jamais. Je vois juste des points noirs.

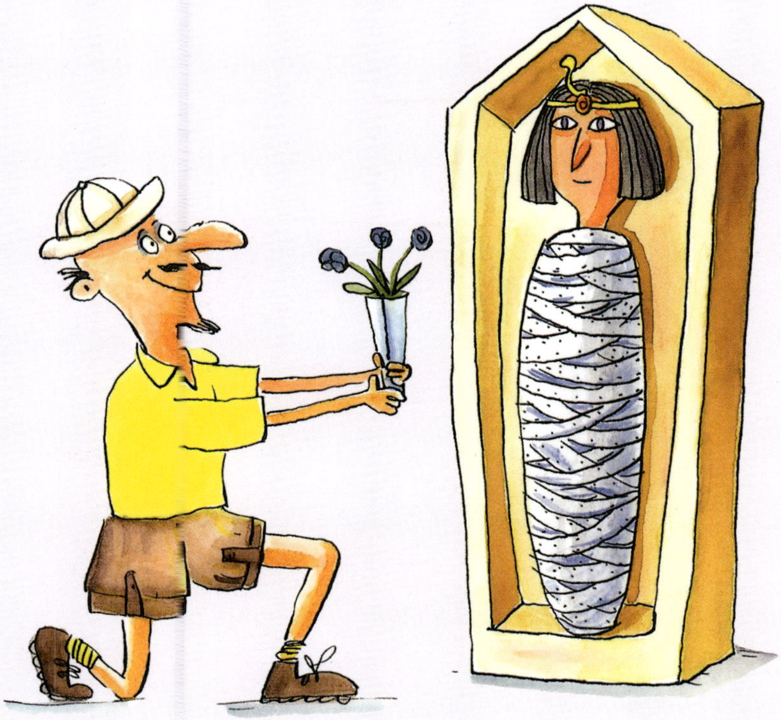

NOCES : archéologue cherche à épouser femme très âgée.

Petite annonce

24

Avril

Histoire drôle

25 Avril

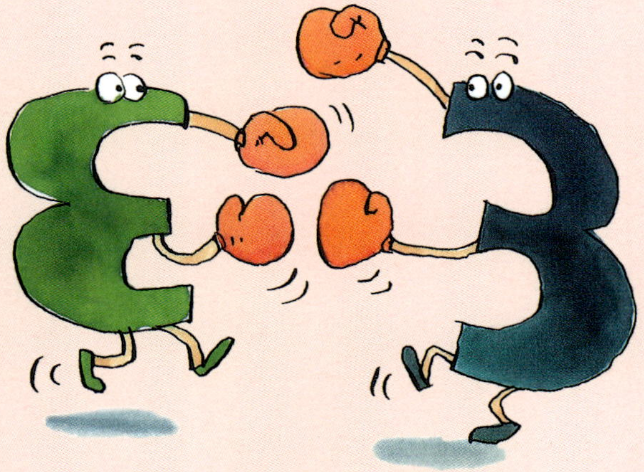

La maîtresse interroge Julien :

- Combien font 3 et 3 ?

- Match nul, maîtresse.

Petite annonce

26 Avril

CONSEIL : Mme Allumette interdit formellement à ses enfants de se gratter la tête.

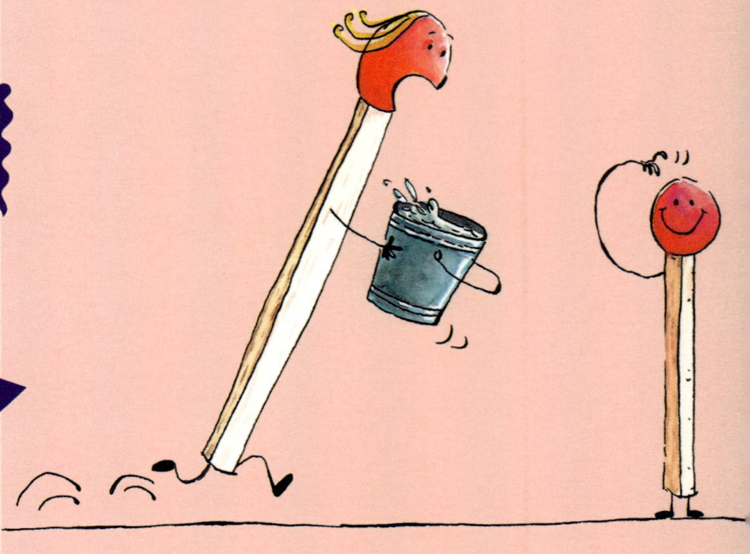

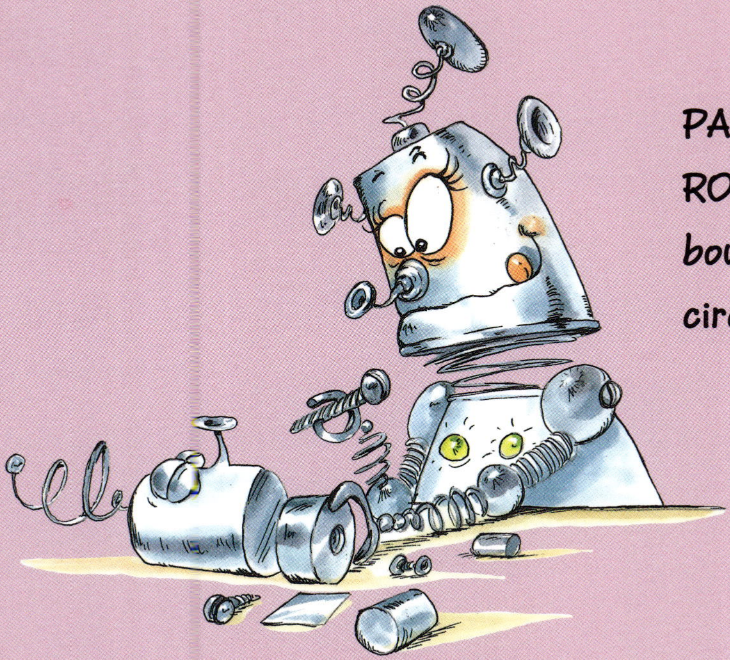

PARENTS : M. et Mme ROBOT cherchent tôles, boulons, écrous, vis et circuits pour faire un enfant.

Petite annonce

27

Avril

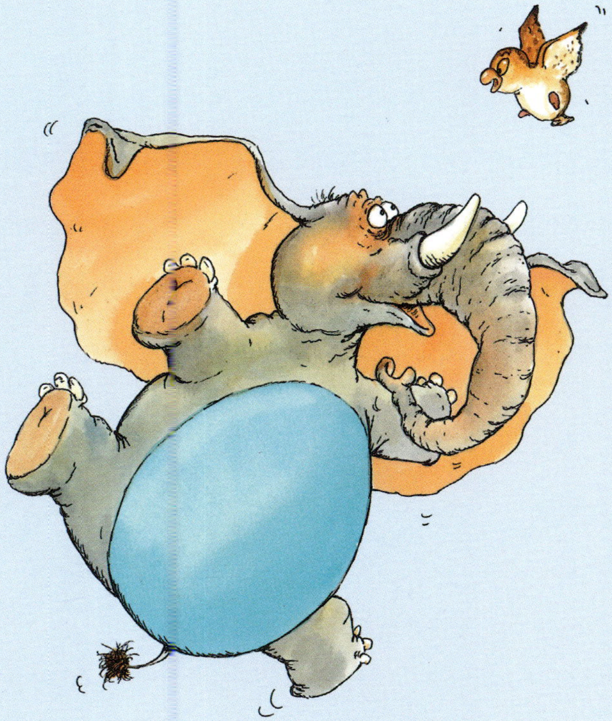

Pourquoi ne voit-on pas les éléphants voler dans le ciel ?

(Réponse : parce qu'ils se peignent le ventre en bleu avant de s'envoler pour qu'on ne puisse pas les repérer.)

Devinette

28

Avril

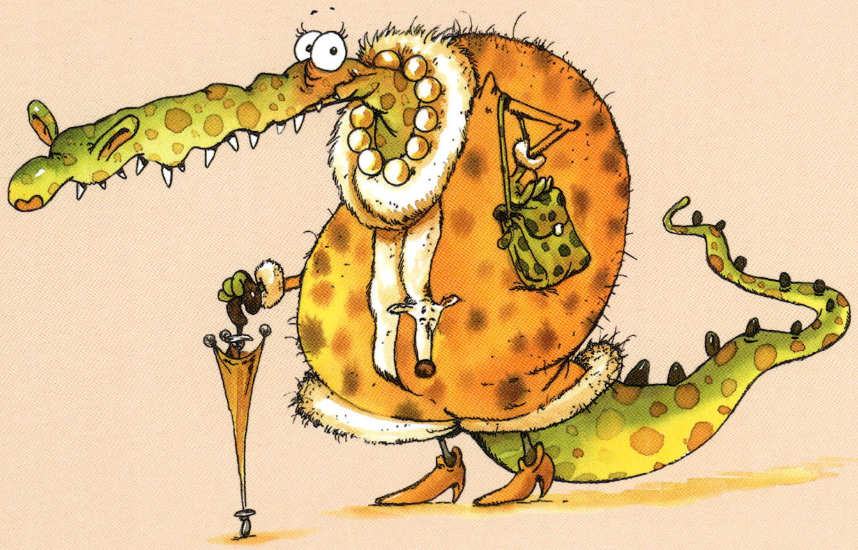

Petite annonce

29

Avril

PROVERBE : Quand les crocodiles achèteront des sacs à main, les chiens achèteront des sacs à puce.

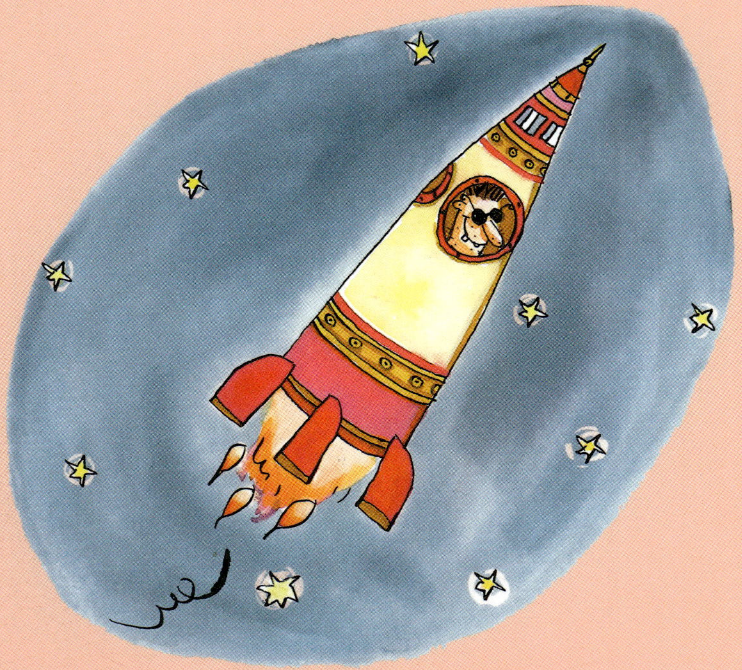

Un savant fou a décidé d'aller en fusée se poser sur le Soleil. D'autres savants lui ont expliqué que c'était impossible à cause de la chaleur. Alors le savant fou a déclaré qu'il s'y poserait la nuit.

Histoire drôle

30

Avril

Histoire drôle

1

Mai

Un motard tombe en panne sur une route de campagne. Il s'arrête, descend de sa moto et essaye d'identifier l'origine de la panne. Une vache s'approche de lui, l'observe un instant et dit :

- Je parie que ça vient du carburateur.

Étonné, le motard va voir le fermier.

- Votre vache vient de me parler ! Elle m'a dit que la panne de ma moto provenait du carburateur !

Le fermier secoue la tête.

- Ne l'écoutez pas. Elle n'y connaît rien, aux motos.

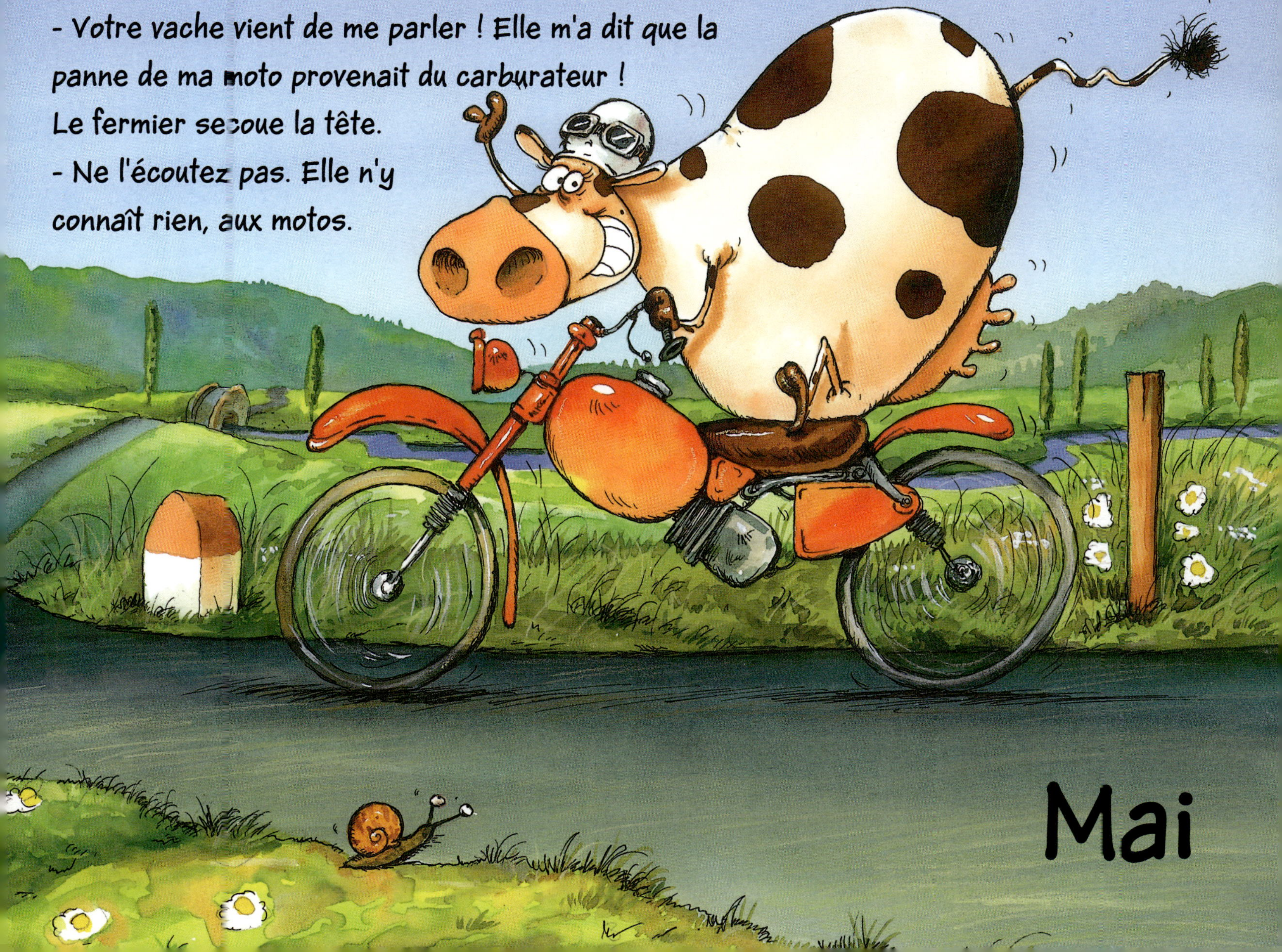

Mai

Devinette

2

Mai

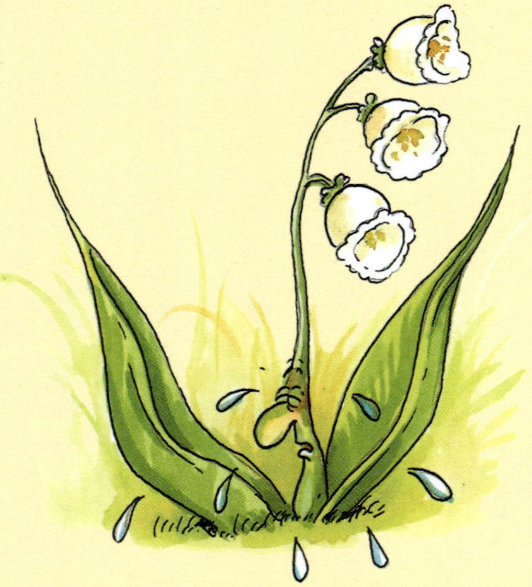

Pourquoi le bébé muguet pleurait-il ce matin ?

(Réponse : parce qu'il s'est fait sonner les clochettes par son papa.)

Une coccinelle, un mille-pattes et un papillon se sont donné rendez-vous.
La coccinelle et le papillon arrivent à l'heure, mais le mille-pattes se fait attendre.
- Mais qu'est-ce qu'il fait, bon sang ! s'énerve la coccinelle. Il devrait être là depuis une demi-heure !
Soudain, le mille-pattes arrive, tout essoufflé.
- Excusez-moi, mais il y a un écriteau, là-bas, qui dit : « Essuyez vos pieds, s'il vous plaît. »

Histoire drôle

3

Mai

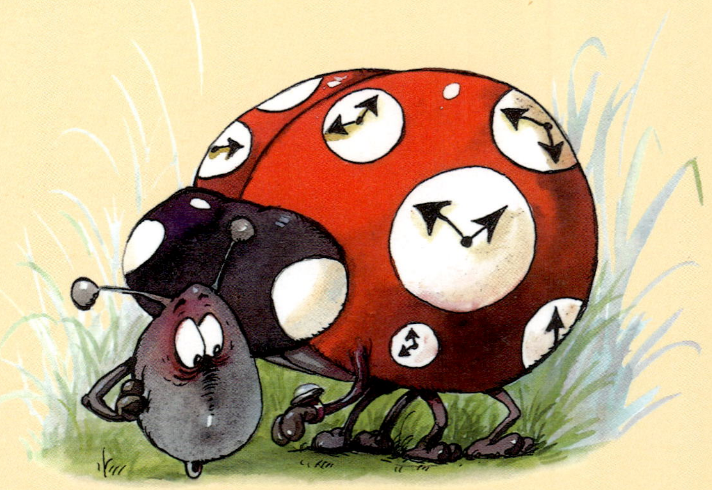

Histoire drôle

4

Mai

Un monsieur veut s'acheter un perroquet pour avoir de la compagnie. Il va donc dans une animalerie et voit trois très beaux perroquets.

- Celui-ci, dit le vendeur en montrant le premier oiseau, est à 100 euros. C'est une affaire : il parle le français, l'anglais et l'espagnol.

- Ça me paraît raisonnable, dit l'homme.

- Celui-ci, continue le vendeur en montrant le second perroquet, est à 200 euros. C'est un peu plus cher, parce qu'il parle le français, l'anglais, l'espagnol, l'allemand, le néerlandais, et qu'il sait calculer aussi bien qu'un ordinateur. Cet oiseau est un vrai bijou.

- Un peu cher, mais il les vaut, ces 200 euros, approuve l'homme.

- Enfin, dit le vendeur en montrant le troisième perroquet, celui-ci est à 400 euros.

- 400 euros ! s'exclame l'homme. Qu'est-ce qu'il fait, pour valoir ce prix-là ?

Le vendeur hausse les épaules.

- Il ne parle pas, ne compte pas et ne fait rien du tout, à ma connaissance, mais les deux autres l'appellent « chef »...

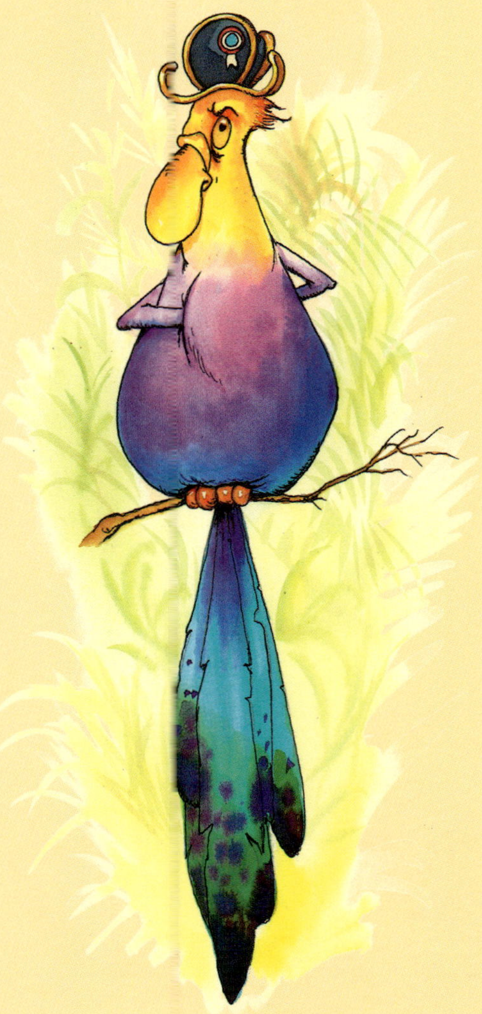

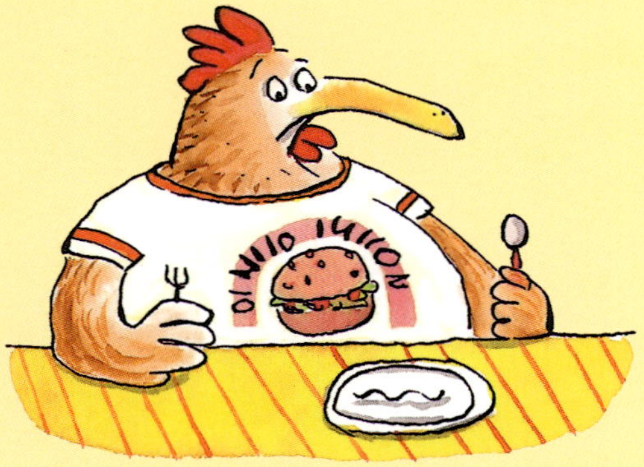

LIGNE : poule au régime cherche ver de terre allégé.

Petite annonce
5
Mai

Petite annonce
6
Mai

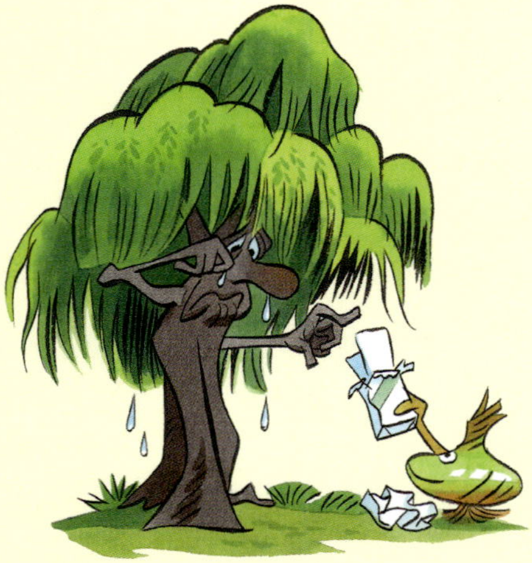

AMI : saule pleureur cherche oignon sympa.

LIGNE : bourdon un peu enveloppé échange pot de miel contre taille de guêpe.

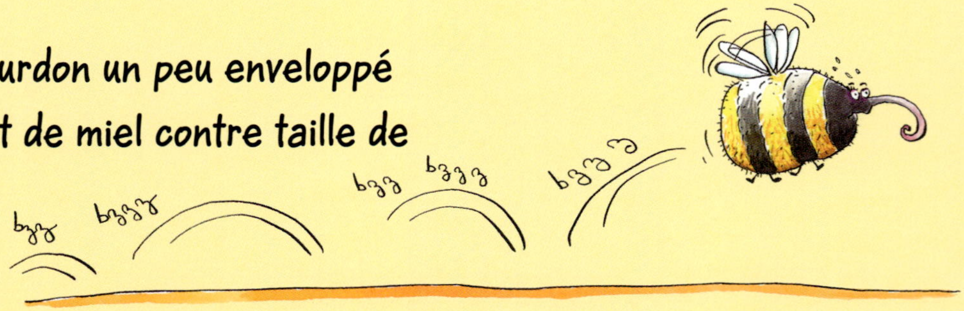

Petite annonce
7
Mai

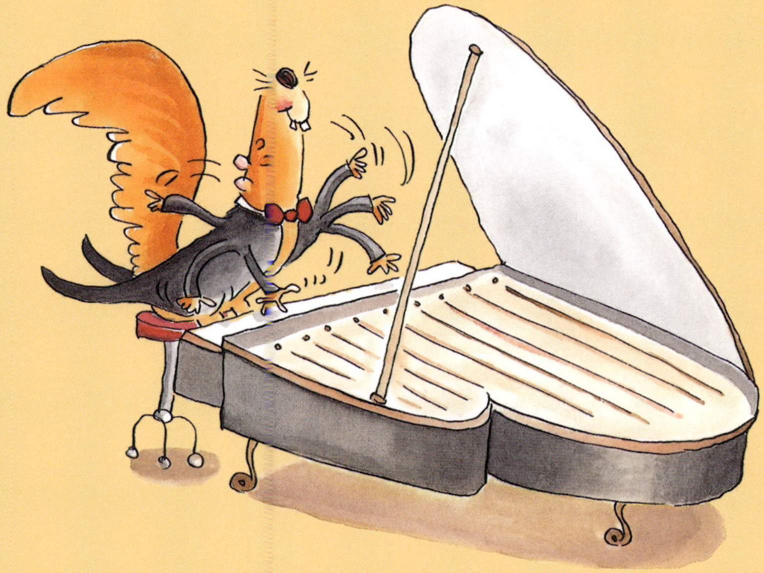

Devinette

8 Mai

Quelle est la différence entre un écureuil et un piano ?

- Il n'y en a pas. Ils montent tous les deux aux arbres, sauf le piano.

Aymeric doit garder sa petite sœur de cinq ans pendant que ses parents vont faire des courses.

Il décide de l'emmener pêcher dans le ruisseau qui coule devant chez lui.

Quand ses parents rentrent, la maman demande à Aymeric si tout s'est bien passé.

- Ouais, répond l'enfant, mais je n'emmènerai plus Nina à la pêche !

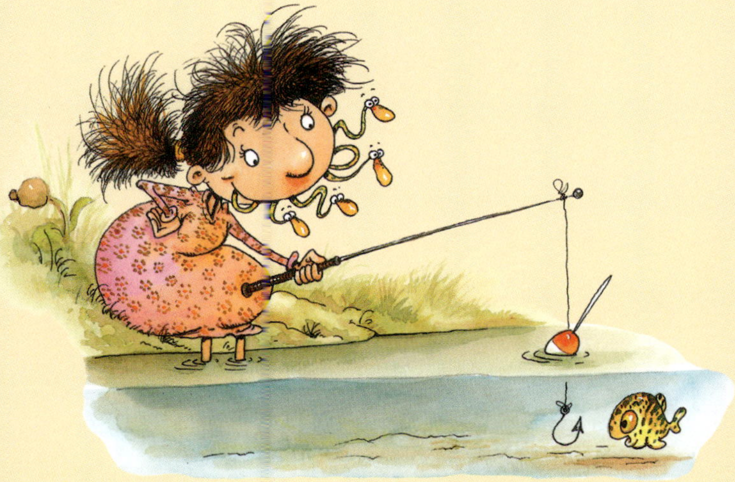

- Tu sais, explique la maman, il faut être patient avec ta sœur, elle est petite. Elle a effrayé les poissons en faisant du bruit ?

- Non, elle n'a fait aucun bruit. Elle était trop occupée à manger les asticots qui devaient me servir d'appâts !

Histoire drôle

9 Mai

Histoire drôle

10 Mai

La maîtresse interroge Bastien :
- Bastien, que veux-tu faire comme métier quand tu seras grand ?
- Agent de police, maîtresse, comme ça je pourrai jouer au milieu de la rue sans me faire disputer par maman !

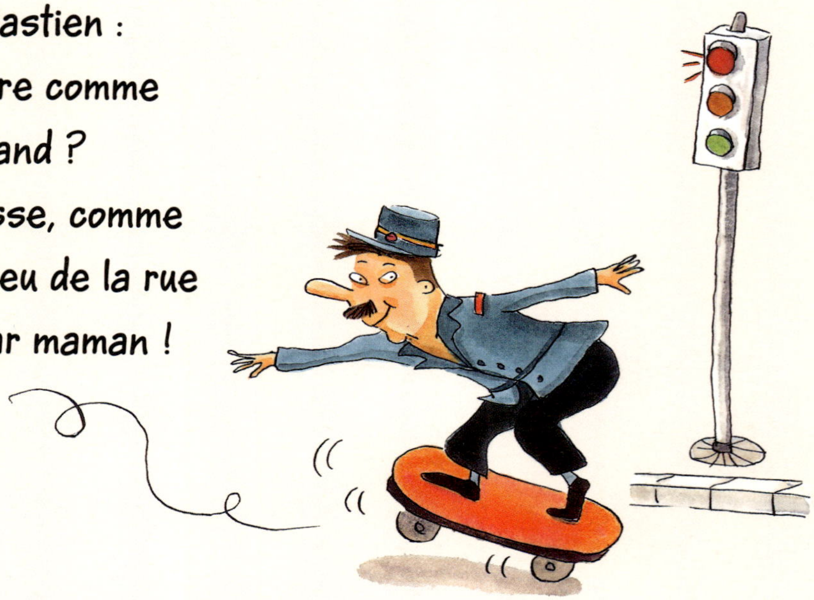

Histoire drôle

11 Mai

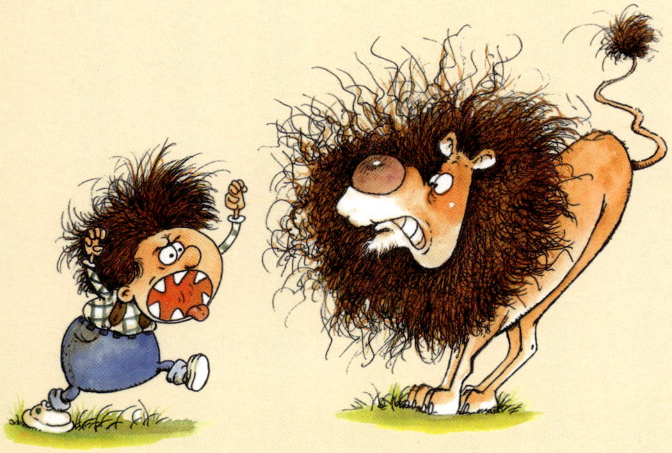

Un cirque vient de s'installer sur la place du village. Sitôt sortis de l'école, les enfants se précipitent vers la ménagerie, où sont gardés tous les animaux.
- Hé ! Oh ! s'écrie le gardien, ne vous approchez pas trop de la cage de ce lion, les enfants !
Un gamin hausse les épaules.
- Ne vous inquiétez pas, on ne va pas le manger, votre lion !

Histoire drôle

12 Mai

Dans un café, un client s'indigne.

- Garçon ! Il n'y a donc pas moyen d'être servi, ici ? Cela fait quinze fois que je commande un Coca, et vous ne m'avez toujours rien apporté !

- Je suis désolé, monsieur, je m'en occupe tout de suite.

Le serveur se tourne vers le bar et crie :

- Patron, quinze Coca pour ce monsieur ! Quinze !

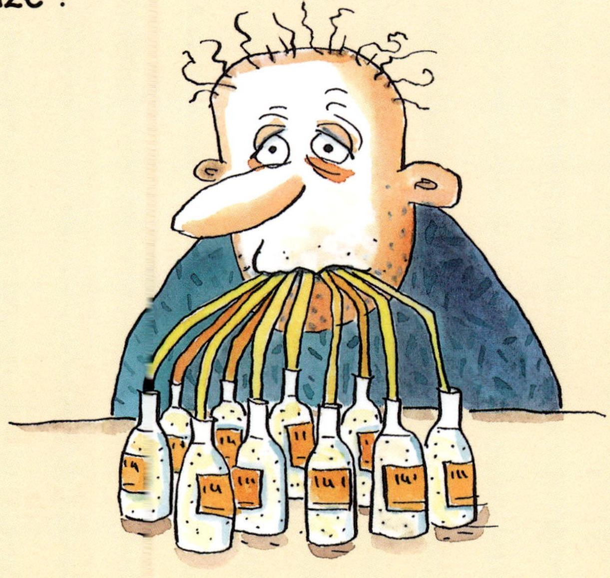

Devinette

13 Mai

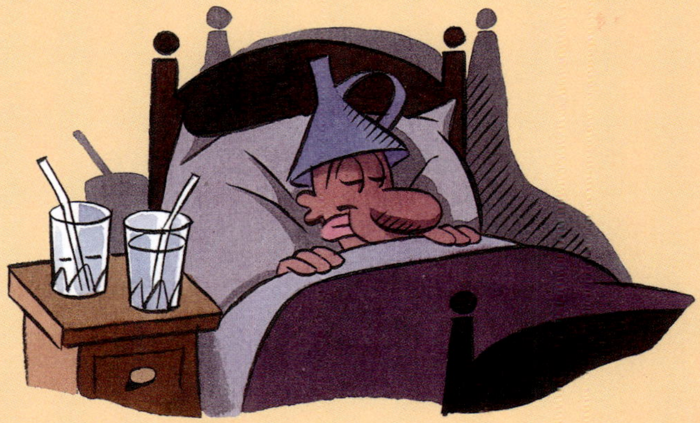

Pourquoi les fous ont-ils un verre d'eau vide et un verre d'eau plein sur leur table de nuit ?

(Réponse : parce que parfois, ils ont soif, et parfois, ils n'ont pas soif.)

Histoire drôle

14

Mai

Le chef d'une tribu de cannibales montre à des touristes son nouveau réfrigérateur.

- Vous voyez, on n'est plus des barbares ! On a l'électricité, l'eau courante, et le magasin d'électroménager vient de nous faire livrer ce magnifique frigo !

Un touriste fronce les sourcils.

- Et vous y avez mis quoi, dans ce frigo ?

Le chef cannibale éclate de rire.

- Nous y avons mis les livreurs du magasin d'électroménager !

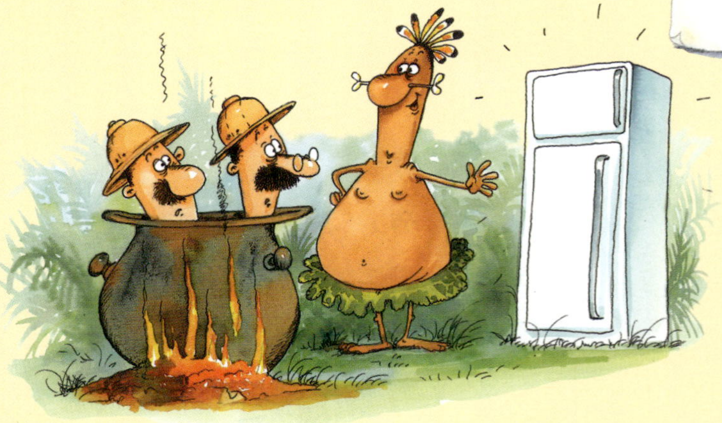

Qu'est-ce qui passe sous la terre à plus de 200 km/h ?

(Réponse : une taupe rapide, mais alors, rapide !)

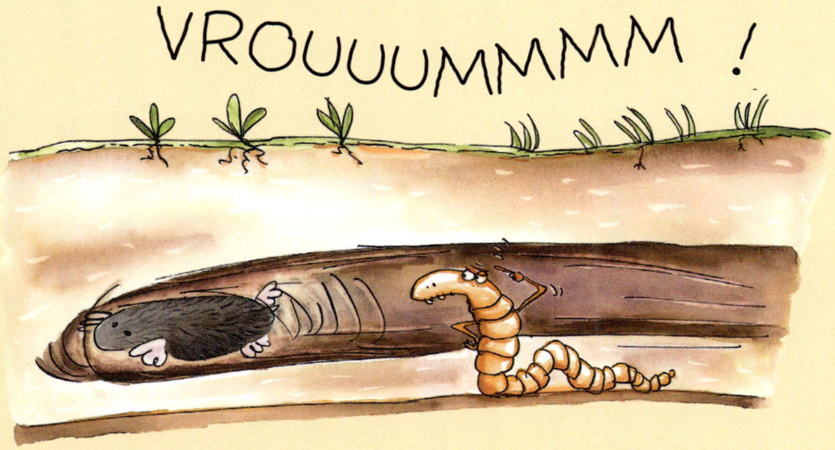

Devinette

15

Mai

Devinette

16

Mai

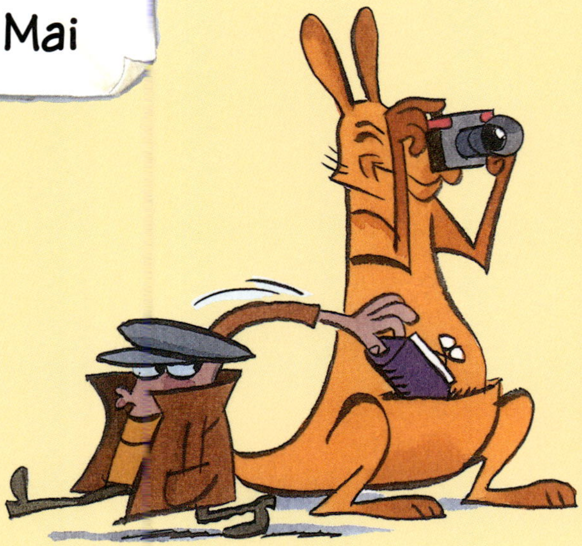

Que craignent le plus les kangourous ?

(Réponse : les pickpockets.)

Histoire drôle

17

Mai

Un couple vient d'emménager dans un immeuble neuf mais mal conçu.

- Écoutez, dit la dame au propriétaire, nous allons déménager. Voilà une semaine que nous sommes dans cet appartement, et les murs sont tellement minces que quand j'épluche des oignons, le voisin se met à pleurer !

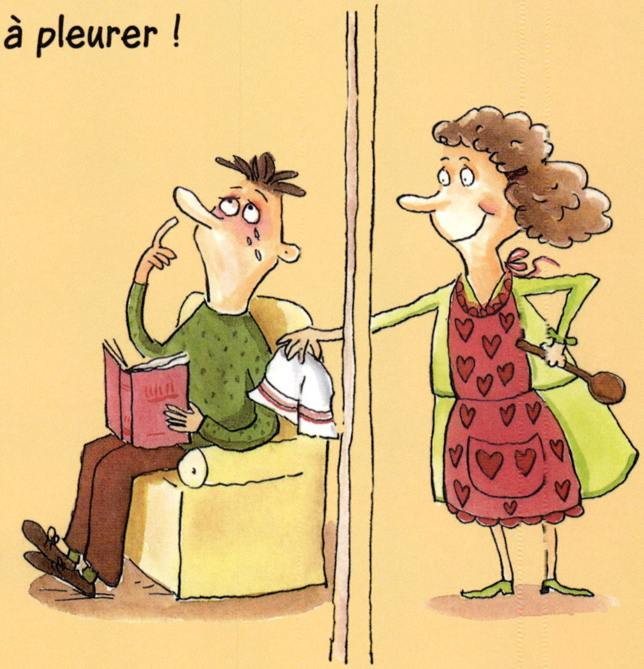

Histoire drôle

18

Mai

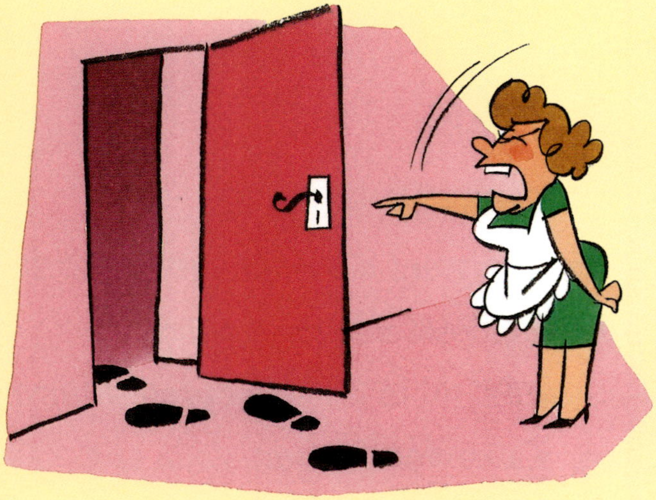

L'homme invisible se dispute depuis trois jours avec sa femme, quand celle-ci, excédée, s'écrie :

- Hors d'ici ! Je ne veux plus te voir !

DÉSESPOIR : pot de chambre traumatisé cherche bébé portant des couches.

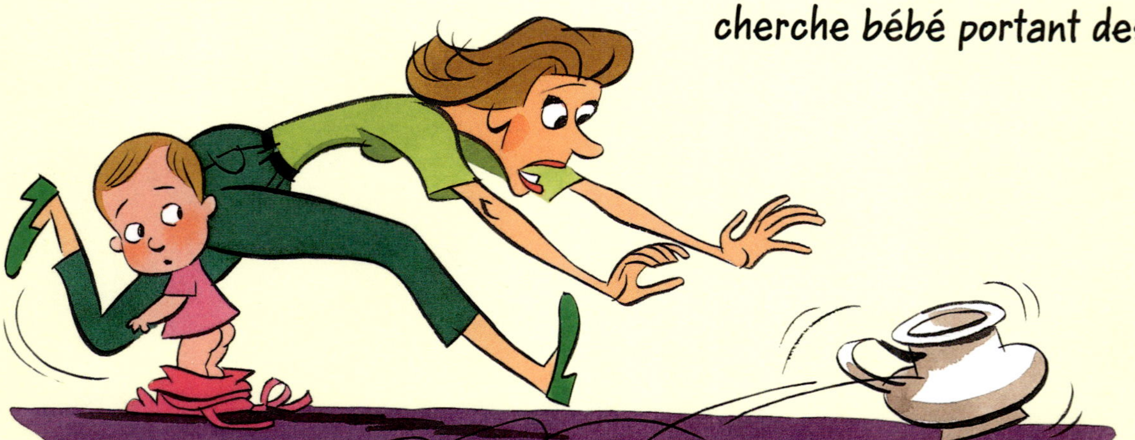

Petite annonce

19

Mai

Devinette

20

Mai

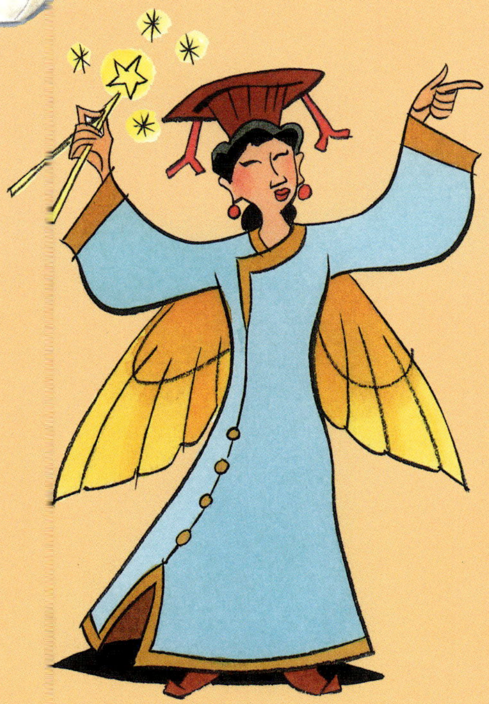

Pourquoi les fées chinoises sont-elles les meilleures fées ?

(Réponse : parce qu'elles ont deux baguettes.)

Histoire drôle

21

Mai

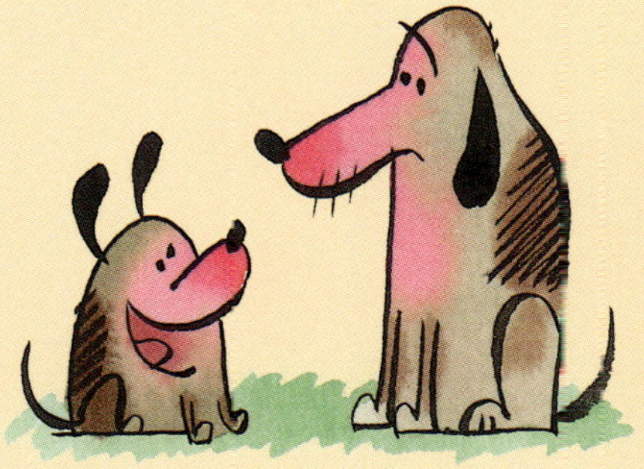

Un petit chiot demande à son père :

- Dis, papa, mon vrai nom, c'est « Assis » ou « Couché » ?

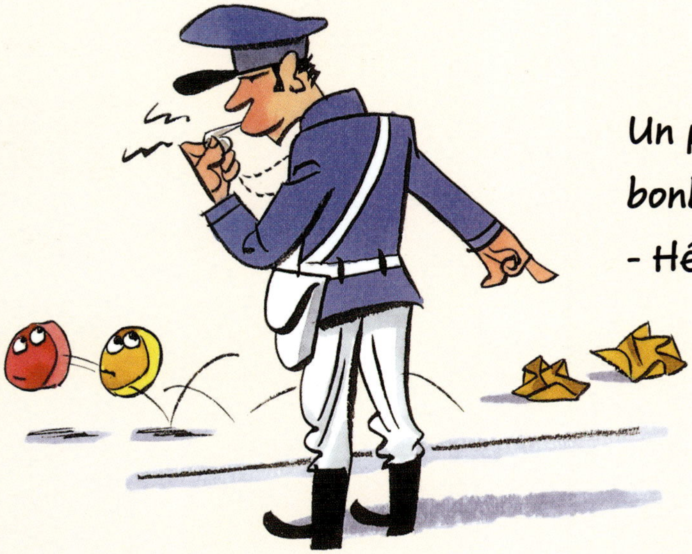

Histoire drôle

22

Mai

Un policier interpelle deux bonbons :

- Hé ! Vous ! Vos papiers !

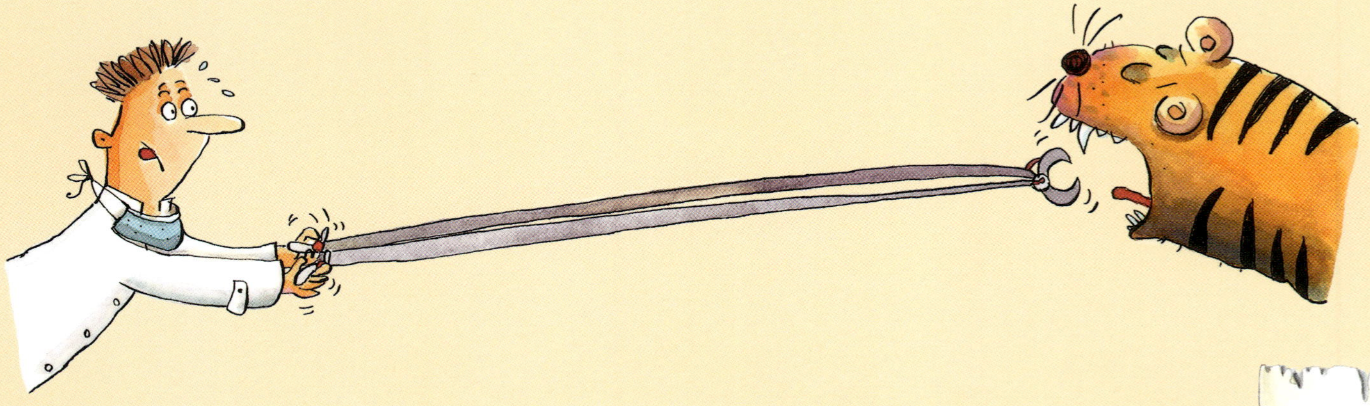

Petite annonce

23

Mai

URGENCE : tigre ayant une rage de dents cherche dentiste très courageux.

Histoire drôle

24

Mai

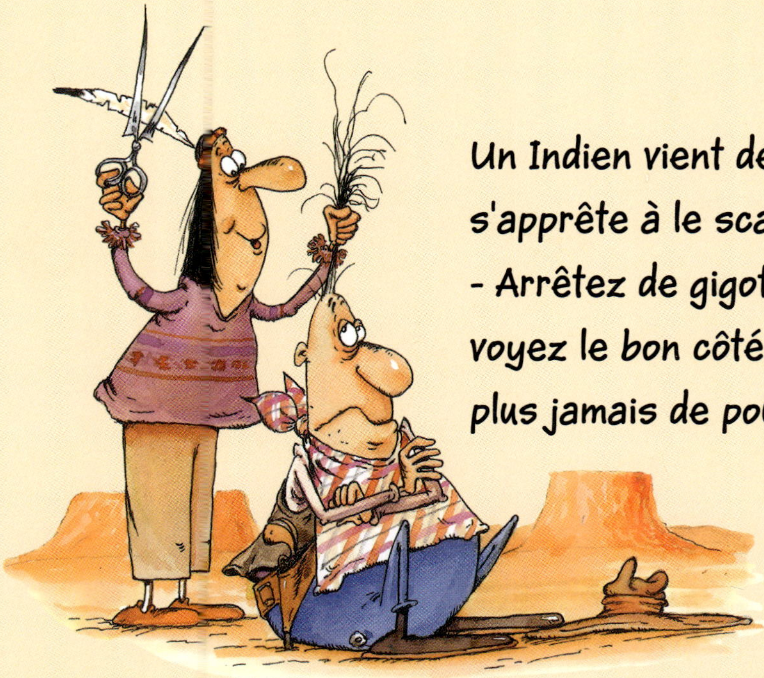

Un Indien vient de capturer un cow-boy et s'apprête à le scalper.

- Arrêtez de gigoter, dit-il à sa victime, et voyez le bon côté des choses : vous n'aurez plus jamais de poux !

Pourquoi les footballeurs portent-ils des shorts ?

(Réponse : vous croyez vraiment que le foot serait autorisé à la télé s'ils étaient en slip ?)

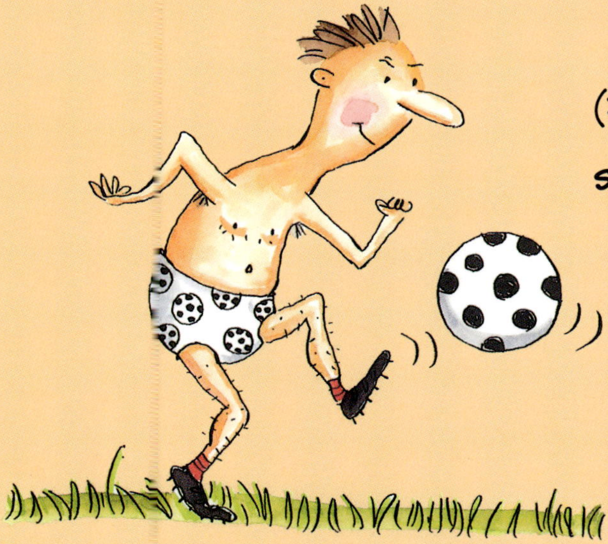

Devinette

25

Mai

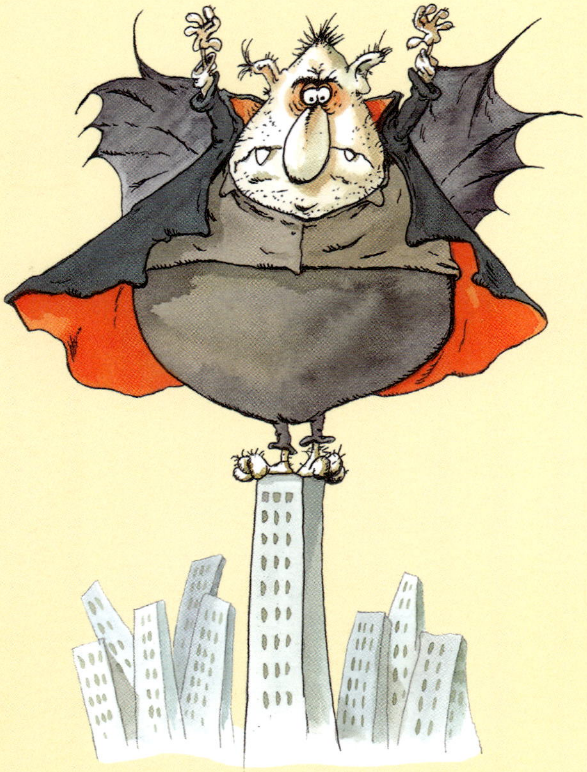

Devinette

26

Mai

Où Dracula loge-t-il lorsqu'il va à New York ?

(Réponse : il loge au Vampire State Building.)

Un homme rentre chez lui. La porte à peine passée, son chien, un énorme berger allemand, se jette sur lui, l'attrape par le col et le traîne jusque dans la penderie, avant de le lâcher.
L'homme se relève péniblement.
- Rex ! dit-il d'un ton las. Combien de fois faudra-t-il que je t'explique que tu dois m'apporter mes chaussons quand je rentre, pas m'emporter jusqu'à mes chaussons !

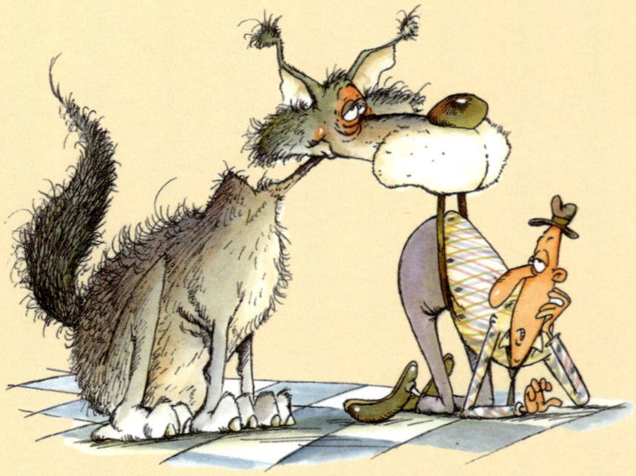

Histoire drôle

27

Mai

Petite annonce

28

Mai

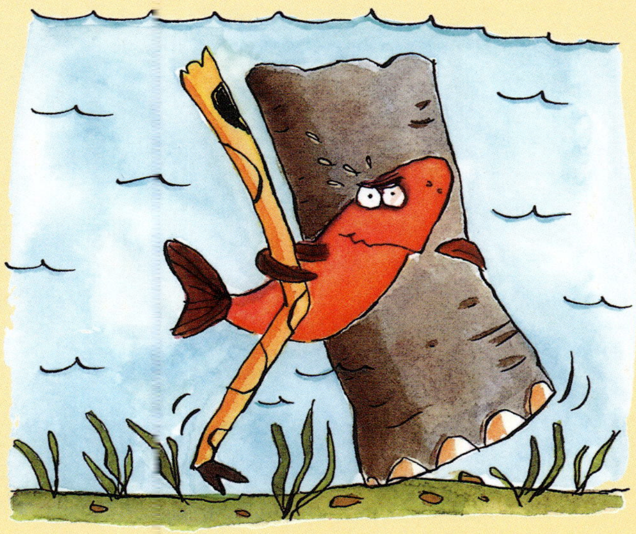

PROBLÈME : poisson désirant jouer au football cherche jambes solides.

Petite annonce

29

Mai

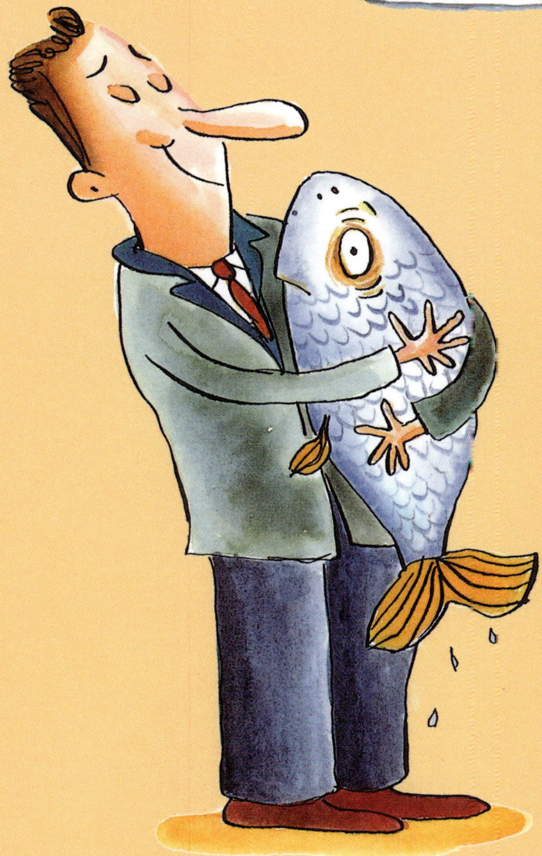

ANIMAUX : directeur de zoo excédé échange perroquet bègue contre une carpe.

Histoire drôle

30

Mai

Julien arrive à l'école, la tête tout enflée et pleine de pansements et de bandages. Ses copains se précipitent autour de lui.

- Que t'est-il arrivé ? s'écrient-ils, affolés.
- Oh, c'est rien ! répond Julien. C'est juste une guêpe qui s'est posée sur ma joue.
- Wouah ! Elle devait être énorme pour te piquer comme ça !
- Non, elle ne m'a pas piqué. Mon père avait une pelle dans les mains et il a voulu l'écraser pendant qu'elle était immobile sur ma joue.

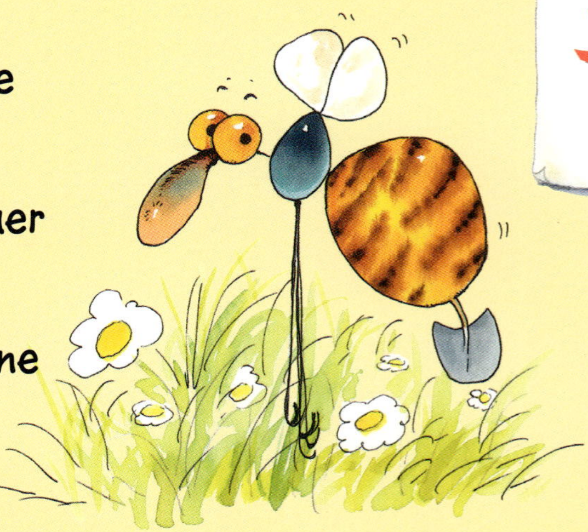

Deux enfants s'ennuient dans un square.

- J'ai une idée ! Ramassons deux escargots et faisons une course !
- Ne sois pas stupide. Tu sais très bien que c'est nous qui gagnerions !

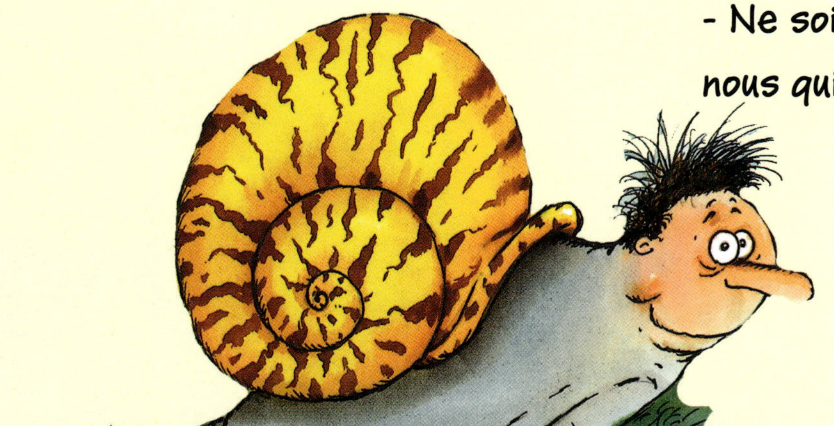

Histoire drôle

31

Mai

Histoire drôle

1

Juin

Julien et son papa se promènent au bord d'un lac.

- Dis, papa, pourquoi les grandes barques en bois elles flottent sur l'eau, et pas les petits cailloux ?

- Je ne sais pas, Julien.

Ils continuent leur promenade, et Julien voit des petits poissons qui frétillent au bord du lac.

- Dis, papa, comment ils font, les poissons, pour respirer sous l'eau ?

Le père hausse les épaules.

- Je n'en sais rien, Julien.

La promenade continue. Julien voit des oiseaux haut dans le ciel.

- Dis, papa, pourquoi le ciel est tout bleu ? Et comment les oiseaux font-ils pour voler si haut sans tomber ? Et les avions, qui sont tellement lourds, comment ça se fait qu'on arrive à les envoyer au-dessus des nuages ?

Le père soupire.

- Euh... Je ne sais pas, Julien.

Alors Julien s'arrête.

- Dis, papa, ça ne te dérange pas que je te pose tout le temps des questions ?

- Bien sûr que non, mon fils ! Si tu ne posais pas de questions, tu n'apprendrais jamais rien !

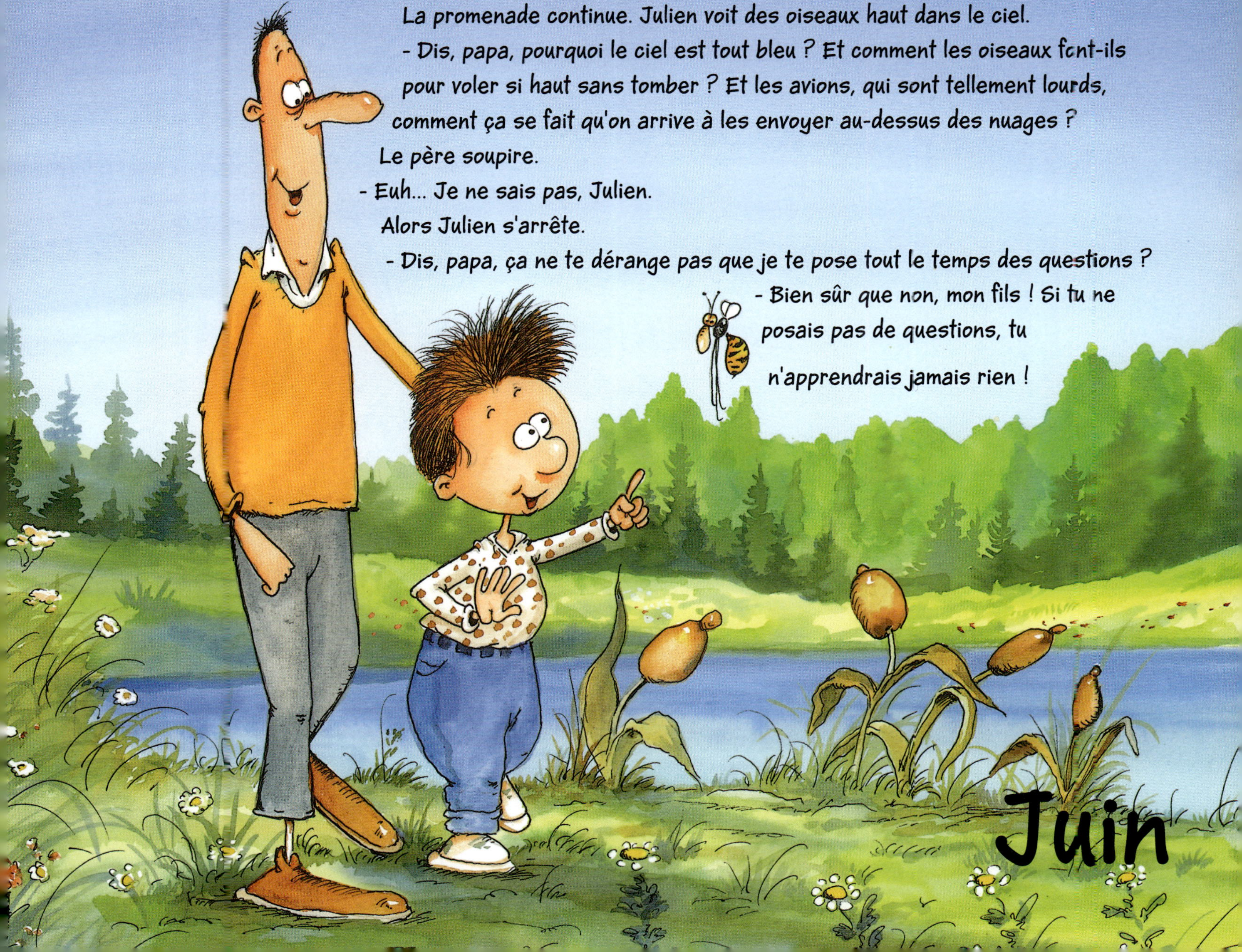

Juin

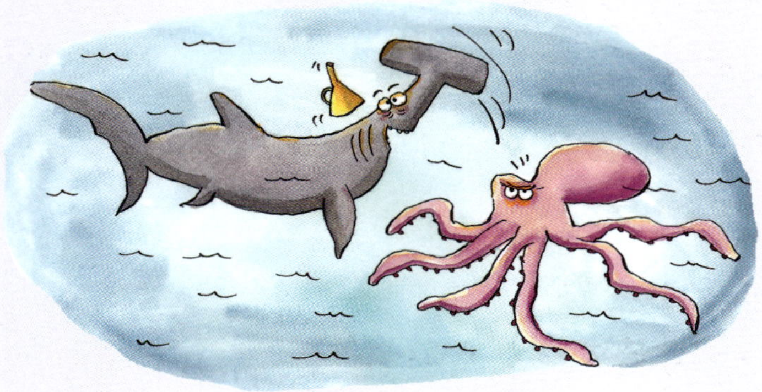

Petite annonce
2
Juin

FOLIE : asile aquatique cherche requin marteau.

Petite annonce
3
Juin

AMOUR : bourdon romantique cherche abeille noctambule pour lune de miel.

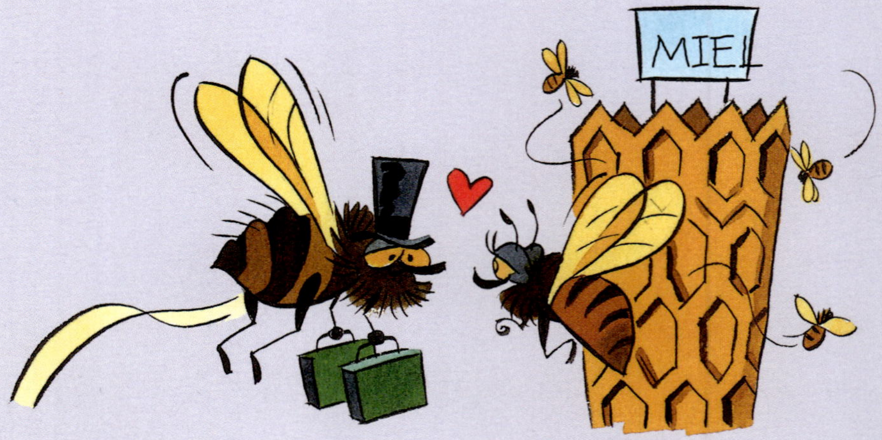

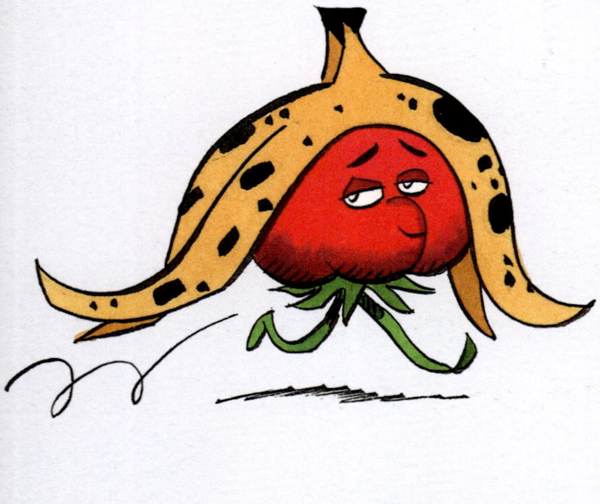

Devinette
4
Juin

Qu'est-ce qui est jaune et qui traverse les murs ?
(Réponse : une banane magique.)

Qu'est-ce qui est rouge et qui s'écrase contre un mur ? (Réponse : une tomate qui s'est prise pour une banane magique.)

Histoire drôle

5

Juin

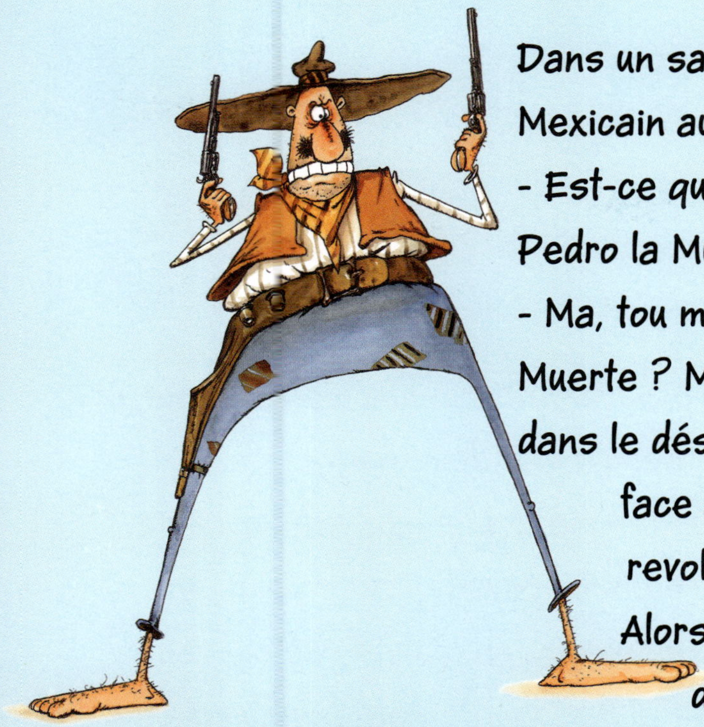

Dans un saloon, un cow-boy discute avec un Mexicain autour d'une bonne bouteille...

- Est-ce que par hasard tu ne connaîtrais pas Pedro la Muerte ?

- Ma, tou me démandes si zé connais Pedro la Muerte ? Ma... Un jour qué zé me promenais dans le désert sur mon ceval, tout à coup, zé me retrouve face à face avec Pedro la Muerte. Il avait deux gros revolvers ! Il m'a dit : « Tu descends de ton cheval ! » Alors, comme il avait deux gros revolvers, zé souis descendu dé mon ceval. Puis, Pedro la Muerte, il m'a dit : « Maintenant, tu enlèves tes bottes ! » Alors, comme il avait les revolvers, z'ai enlevé les bottes. Puis il a dit : « Maintenant, tu enlèves tes chaussettes ! » Qu'est-ce qué zé pouvais faire ? Z'ai enlevé les saussettes! Puis il a dit : « Maintenant, tu MANGES tes chaussettes ! » Alors, je lui ai dit : « Non, non, pitié, Pedro, pas les saussettes ! » Ma, zé pouvais rien faire, il avait les revolvers. Alors, z'ai MANZÉ mes saussettes... Tout à coup, Pedro a eu oun instant de distraction et zé lui ai piqué ses revolvers ! Et zé lui ai dit : « Maintenant, Pedro, tou enlèves tes bottes ! » Comme z'avais les deux gros revolvers, il a enlevé ses bottes. Puis zé lui ai dit : « Pedro, maintenant, tou enlèves tes saussettes ! » Il pouvait rien faire, z'avais les revolvers, alors, il a enlevé ses saussettes ! Puis zé lui ai dit : « Et maintenant, Pedro, tou vas MANZER tes saussettes ! » Il m'a dit : « Non, non, pitié, pas les chaussettes ! » Ma, il avait pas le choix, z'avais les revolvers, alors il a MANZÉ ses saussettes ! Et tou me demandes si zé connais Pedro la Muerte ? Ma, nous avons DÎNÉ ensemble !

Histoire drôle

6 Juin

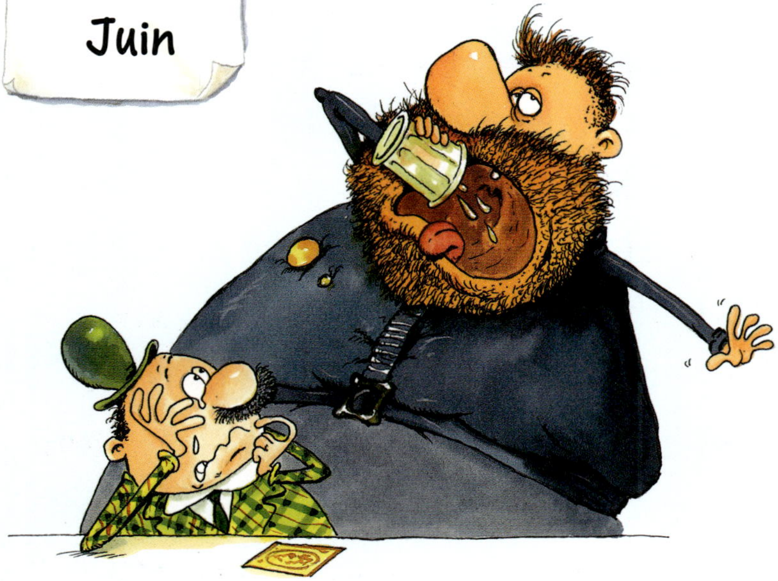

Un pauvre petit bonhomme est dans un bar depuis une demi-heure.
Il contemple tristement son verre de bière en soupirant. Tout à coup, un homme barbu en blouson de cuir entre dans le bar, voit le petit bonhomme, lui donne une grande claque dans le dos en riant, et lui boit sa bière.
Le petit homme triste se met à pleurer à chaudes larmes.
- Eh, oh ! lui dit le barbu, désolé. Ce n'était qu'une plaisanterie, je te prends une autre bière, je ne voulais pas te faire pleurer ! Garçon, une autre !
- Non, non, laissez ! dit le petit bonhomme. Je pleure parce que cette journée a été la plus terrible de ma vie. Ce matin, ma voiture tombe en panne, j'arrive en retard au travail. Mon patron m'annonce qu'il me renvoie. Quand je rentre à la maison, j'annonce ça à ma femme, qui me quitte en emmenant mes deux enfants. À peine partie, le four, dans lequel ma femme faisait cuire un rôti, explose, et la maison entière brûle. En sortant appeler les pompiers, je me fais renverser par une voiture. Le temps d'arriver à l'hôpital, ma maison était détruite... Alors, je viens dans ce bar pour mettre fin à mes jours, et voilà qu'un imbécile, qui se croit rigolo, vient me boire mon verre de poison !

Histoire drôle

7 Juin

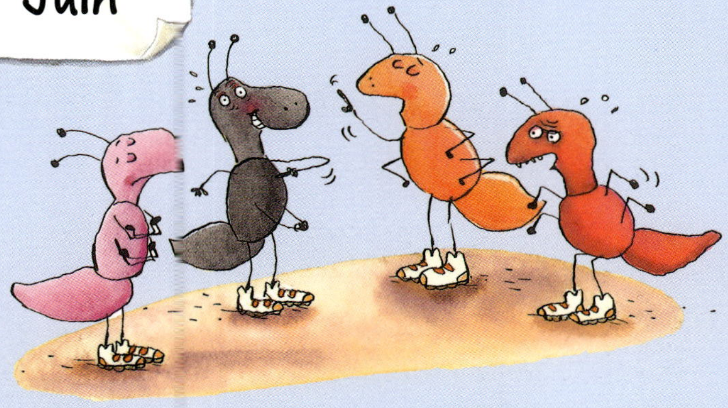

Quatre fourmis font une course sur un chemin de la grande forêt. Il y a une fourmi rouge, une fourmi rousse, une fourmi noire et une fourmi rose.

La fourmi rouge dit : « Je suis devant la rousse ! »
La fourmi rousse dit : « Je suis devant la noire ! »
La fourmi noire dit : « Je suis devant la rose ! »
La fourmi rose dit : « Je suis la première ! »
Comment est-ce possible ?
- La rose est une sale menteuse !

Histoire drôle

8 Juin

Un gars est en train de creuser un trou de belle taille dans son jardin. Son voisin, intrigué, lui demande :
- C'est pour quoi, ce trou ?
L'autre répond :
- C'est pour enterrer mon pauvre petit canari qui est mort ce matin.
- Mon Dieu ! Je suis vraiment navré pour vous. Mais... n'est-ce pas un bien grand trou pour un si petit oiseau ?
- C'est parce que mon « si petit oiseau » est dans le ventre de votre « si gros chat » !

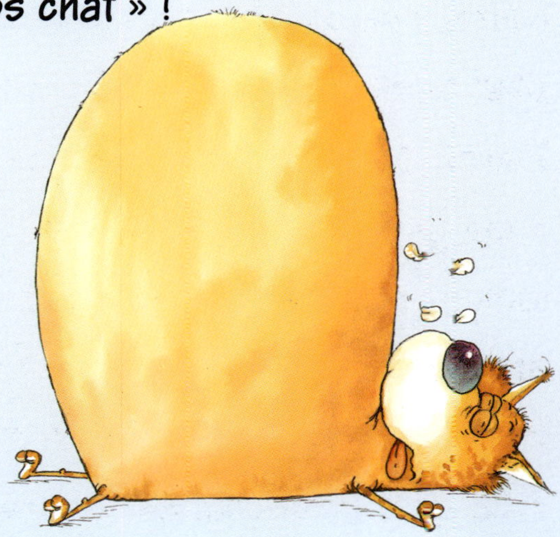

Histoire drôle

9

Juin

Un petit garçon regarde en souriant l'orage qui gronde au-dehors, la pluie qui bat les vitres et les éclairs rageurs qui déchirent le ciel.

- Pourquoi souris-tu comme ça ? lui demande sa maman, intriguée.

- Parce que Dieu me prend en photo !

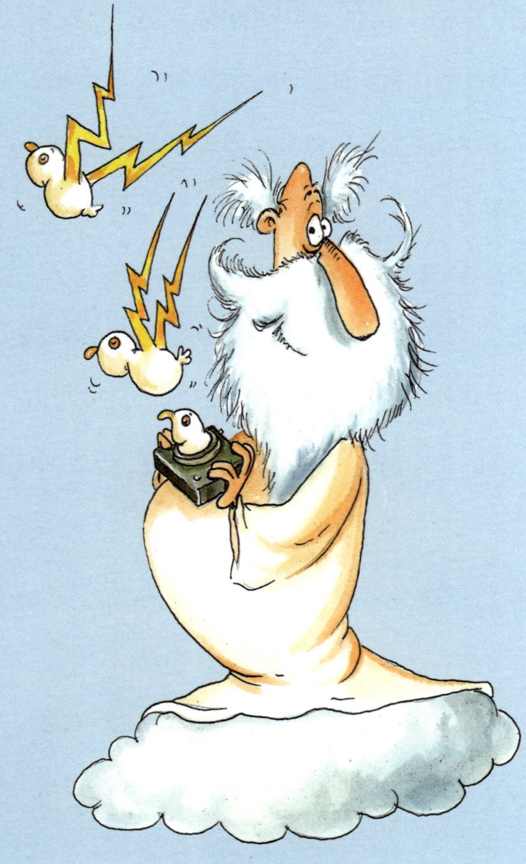

Histoire drôle

10

Juin

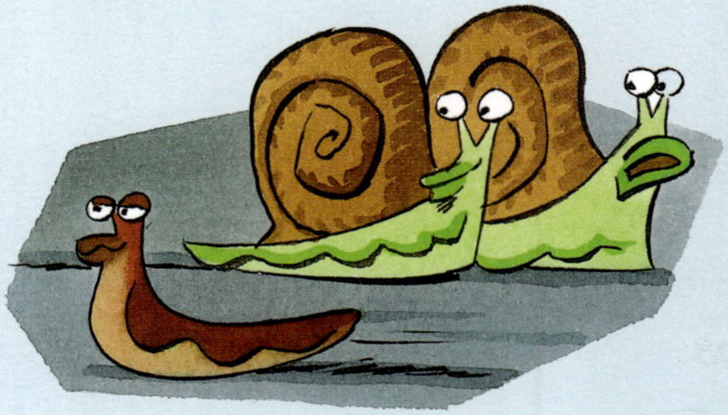

Deux escargots se promènent lorsqu'ils croisent des limaces.

- Vite, demi-tour, on est dans un champ de nudistes !

Histoire drôle

11 Juin

Une jeune fille, qui souhaite devenir infirmière, passe son examen de fin d'année.

- Citez-moi, dit l'examinateur, une maladie causée par l'eau.

- Euh... La noyade ?

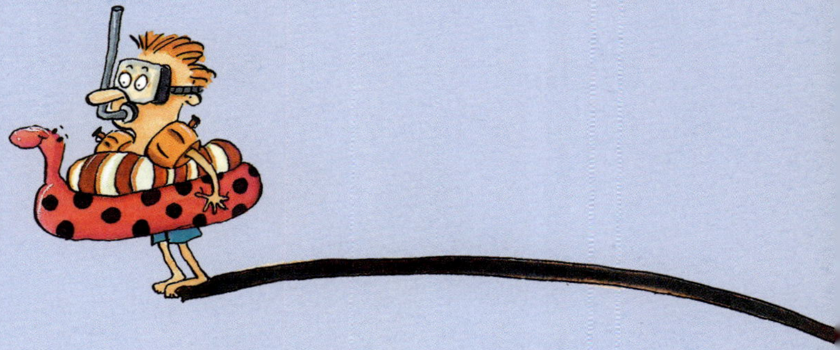

Un labrador passe des tests pour devenir chien policier. L'homme, chargé de lui faire passer les examens, lui dit :

- Pour devenir un chien policier, il faut savoir taper à la machine, au moins cinquante mots par minute.

Le labrador s'assied devant la machine et tape quatre-vingts mots à la minute.

- Parfait, dit l'homme. Vous devez aussi réussir le parcours d'obstacles en moins de dix minutes. Le labrador saute les obstacles un par un et termine en quatre minutes. Un vrai record.

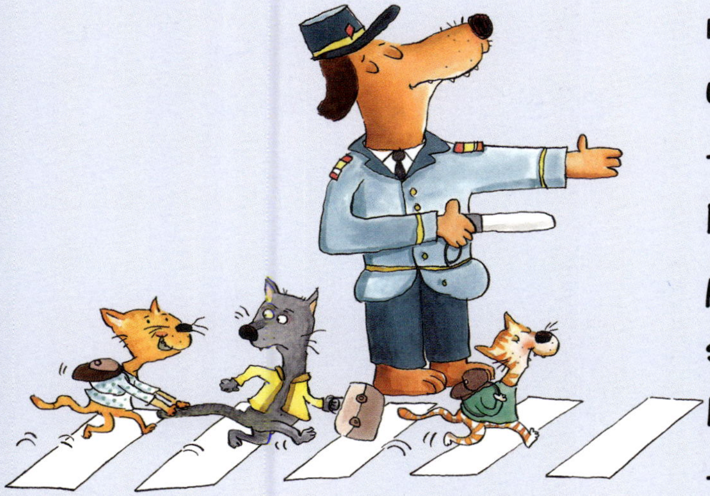

- Très bien, le félicite l'homme.

Mais il y a une dernière condition : pour devenir chien policier, il faut savoir parler deux langues.

Le labrador le regarde et dit :

- Miaou.

Histoire drôle

12 Juin

Histoire drôle

13 Juin

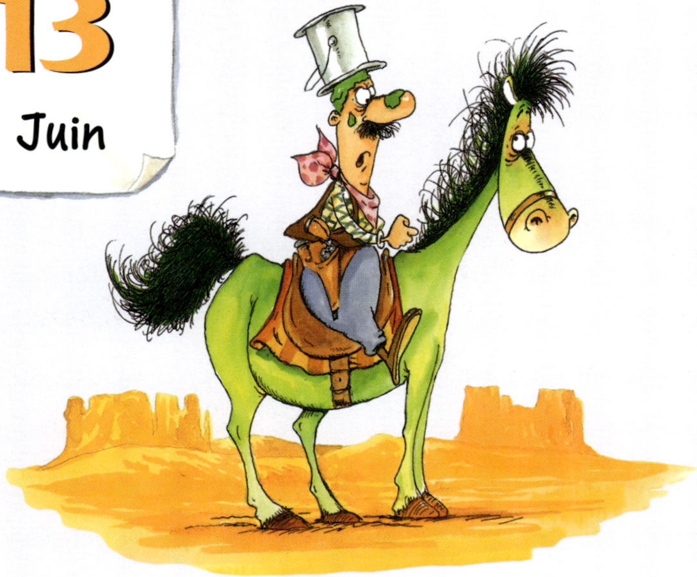

Jack le cow-boy, très en colère, entre dans un saloon en faisant claquer les portes à battants :

- Qui a peint mon cheval en vert ?

Joe la Montagne se lève d'une table, il fait deux mètres de haut, cent trente kilos, et possède des biceps gros comme des cuisses :

- C'est moi ! 'Y a un problème ?

- Euh... non, répond Jack, c'est juste pour savoir quand je peux mettre la deuxième couche...

Petite annonce

14 Juin

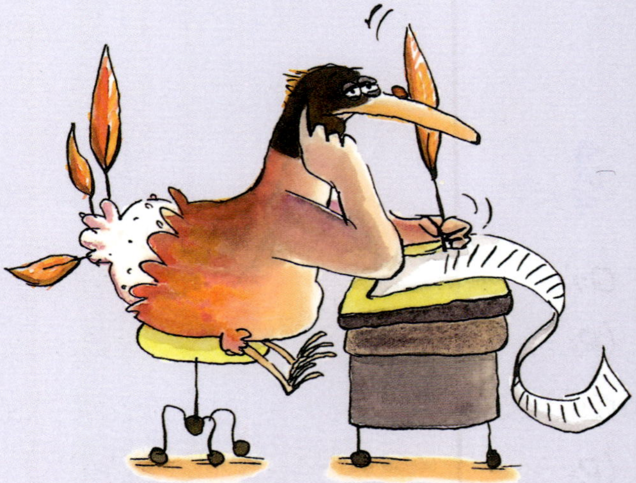

VOCATION : oiseau écrivain cherche stylo plume.

Petite annonce

15

Juin

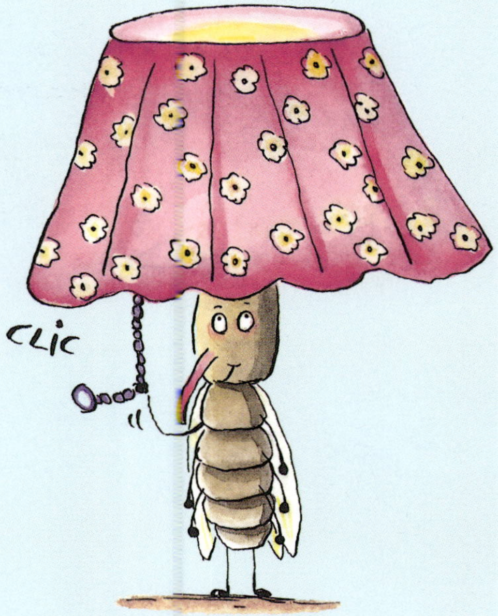

VOISINAGE : Mme Fourmi accepte que M. et Mme Luciole soient ses voisins, à condition qu'ils éteignent la lumière le soir.

Qu'a dit Tarzan en voyant arriver les éléphants ?
(Réponse : « Tiens, voilà les éléphants. »)
Qu'a dit Tarzan en voyant arriver les éléphants qui portaient des lunettes noires ?
(Réponse : « Qui c'est, ceux-là ? »)
Qu'a dit Tarzan quand les éléphants ont retiré leurs lunettes noires ?
(Réponse : « Ah, c'est vous ? Je ne vous avais pas reconnus. »)

Devinette

16

Juin

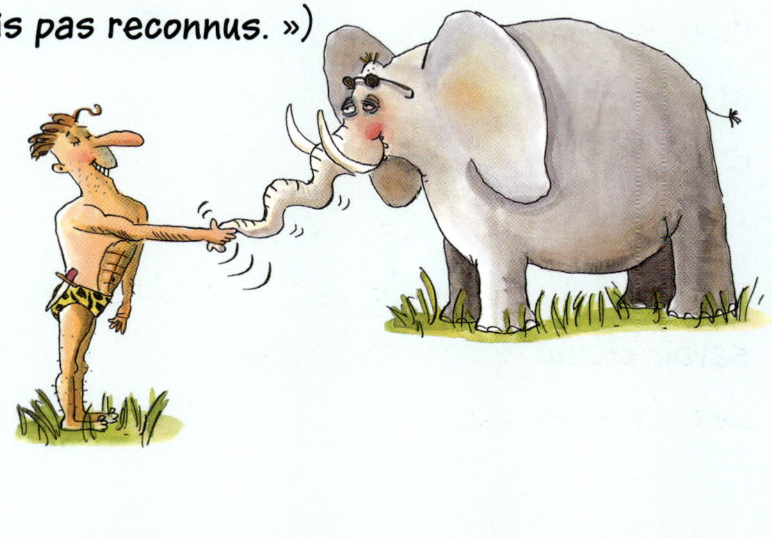

PRÉCISION : le docteur Soleil reçoit sur rendez-vous uniquement la journée. Pour les rendez-vous de nuit, voir avec le docteur Lune.

Petite annonce

17

Juin

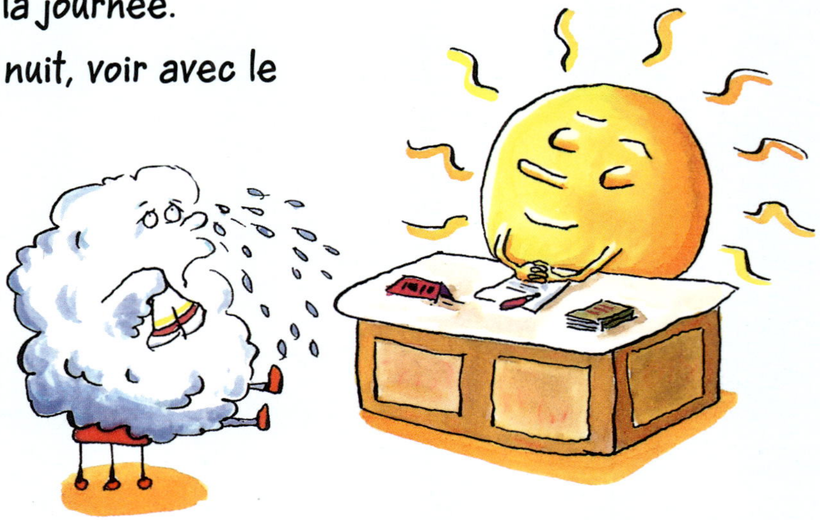

Que dit un dentiste à un policier qui refuse de se laisser soigner les dents ?

(Réponse : « Au nom de la loi ! Ouvrez cette bouche ! »)

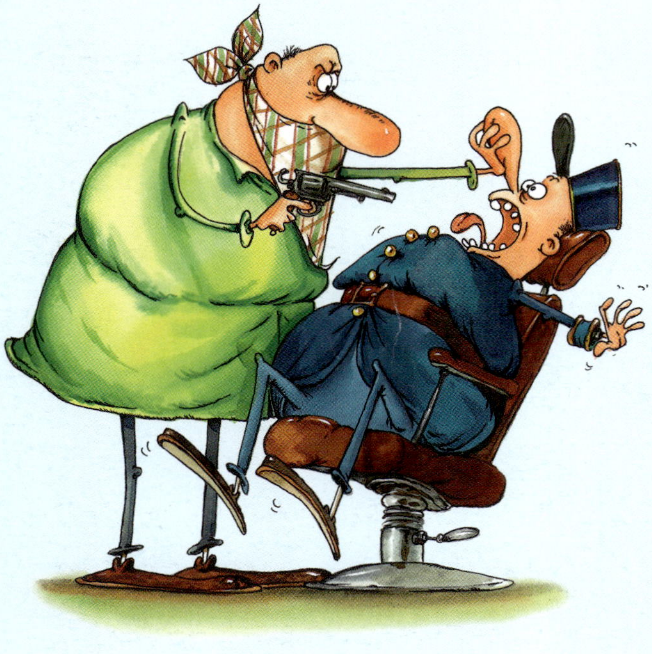

Devinette

18

Juin

Histoire drôle

19

Juin

Un monsieur entre chez le coiffeur avec un petit garçon. Il se fait couper les cheveux et dit au coiffeur :

- Coupez les cheveux de mon fils, je vais chercher des sous et je reviens.

Le coiffeur coupe les cheveux du gamin, mais au bout de trente minutes, le monsieur n'est toujours pas revenu.

- Eh bien ! dit-il à l'enfant, il en met un temps pour aller chercher des sous, ton père.

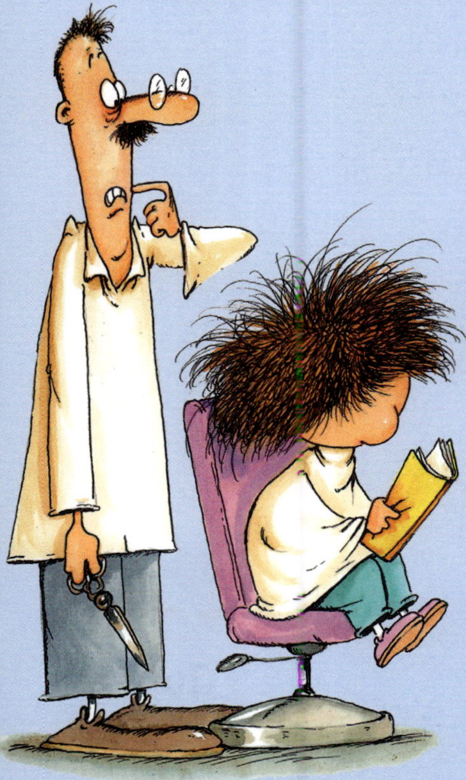

- Ce n'est pas mon père, dit l'enfant. C'est un monsieur qui m'a abordé dans la rue en me disant : « Viens, petit, on va aller se faire couper les cheveux gratuitement » !

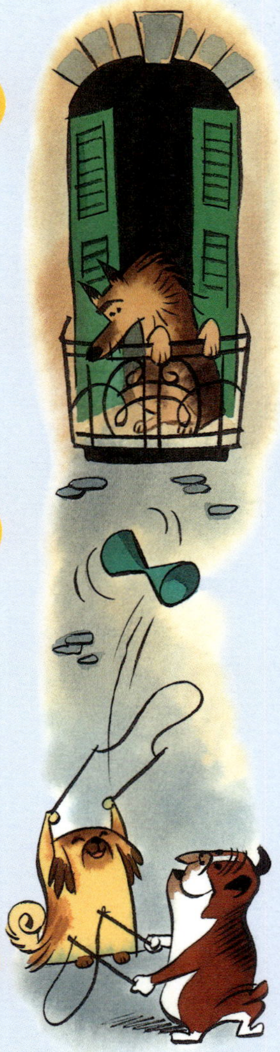

Histoire drôle

20

Juin

Un chien pékinois et un bouledogue jouent au bas d'un immeuble, quand ils voient un berger allemand, à un balcon du deuxième étage.

- Viens jouer avec nous ! On s'éclate, ici !

- Je ne peux pas, répond le berger allemand, ma maîtresse ne me laisse pas sortir seul.

- Tu t'en fiches ! Saute du balcon !

- C'est ça, dit le berger, c'est ça. Pour qu'après, j'aie le nez aussi écrasé que les vôtres !

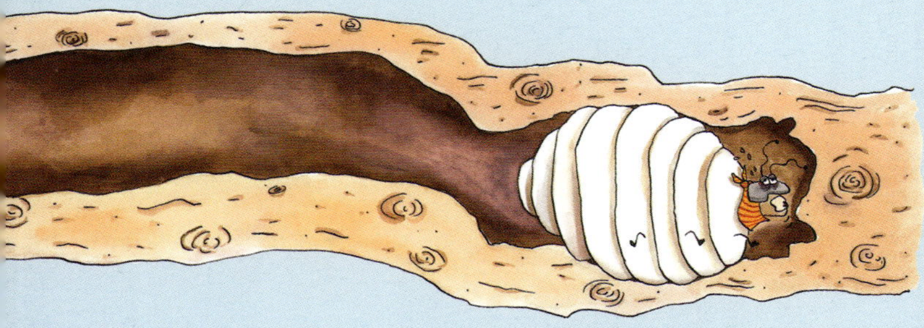

L'arche de Noé vient de s'échouer sur le mont Ararat.

Noé en fait sortir tous les couples d'animaux qu'il avait embarqués avant le déluge, puis demande à Mme Noé de le suivre pour reconstruire le Monde.

- On ne peut pas laisser l'arche comme ça, déclare Mme Noé, cela va polluer l'eau, tout ce bois.

Nous devons détruire l'arche avant de nous en aller.

- Ne t'en fais pas pour ça, répond Noé. L'arche n'encombrera pas longtemps le paysage et ne polluera rien du tout. Je laisse à bord le couple de termites, qui se chargera de la faire disparaître...

Histoire drôle

21

Juin

CONTE : loup déçu échange chaperon rouge contre chat peureux de n'importe quelle couleur.

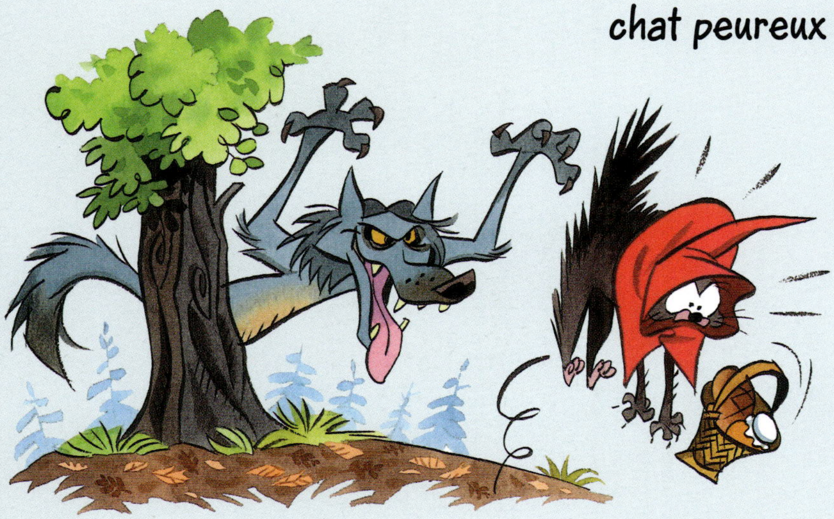

Petite annonce

22

Juin

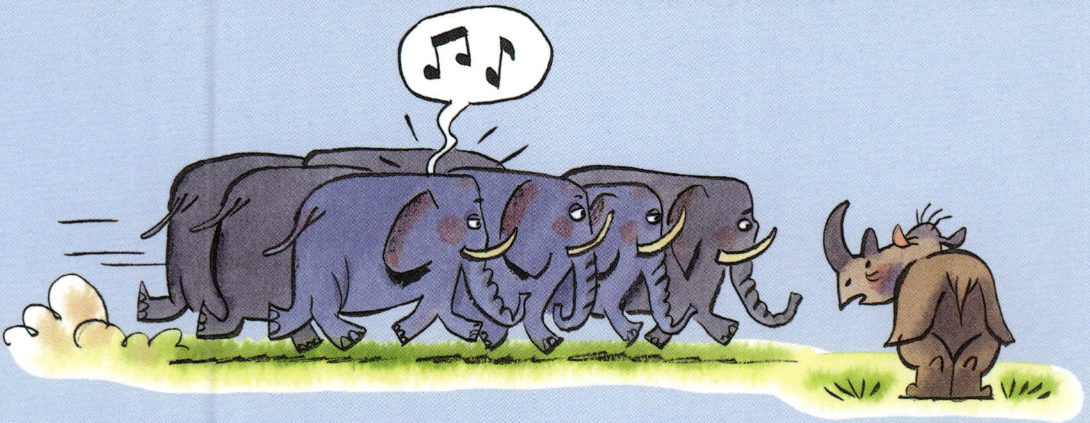

Devinette
23
Juin

Pourquoi les éléphants se déplacent-ils en troupeaux bien serrés ?

- Parce que celui du milieu a une bonne radio.

Pourquoi les rhinocéros se déplacent-ils en troupeaux bien serrés ?

- Pour faire croire aux éléphants qu'ils ont une radio, eux aussi.

Pourquoi l'éléphant du milieu sort-il du troupeau de temps en temps ?

- Pour changer les piles de la radio.

Devinette
24
Juin

Deux enfants se promènent dans la campagne.

- Ouaaah ! T'as vu la superforêt ?
- Non, j'vois rien : il y a plien d'arbres !

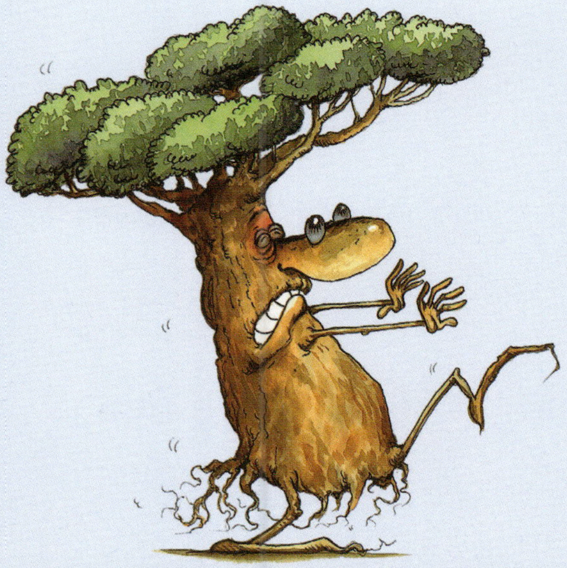

Petite annonce

25

Juin

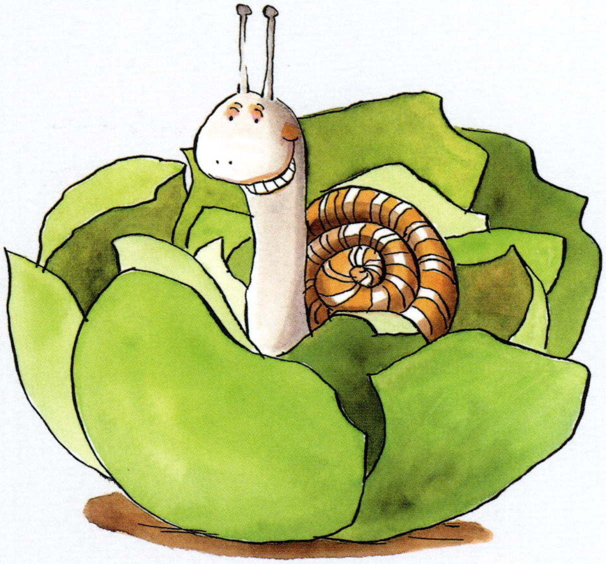

DÉMENTI : Monsieur Escargot ne raconte jamais de salades.

Un homme apprend à conduire à son fils.

- Mon garçon, c'est très simple : si tu respectes les trois règles, tu conduiras comme un as.

Règle n°1 : quand le feu est rouge, tu t'arrêtes. Compris ?

- Oui, papa.

- Très bien.

Règle n°2 : quand le feu est vert, tu passes. Compris ?

- Oui, papa.

- Parfait.

Règle n°3 : quand je deviens tout blanc, tu freines comme un fou, tu descends de la voiture et tu me laisses conduire. Compris ?

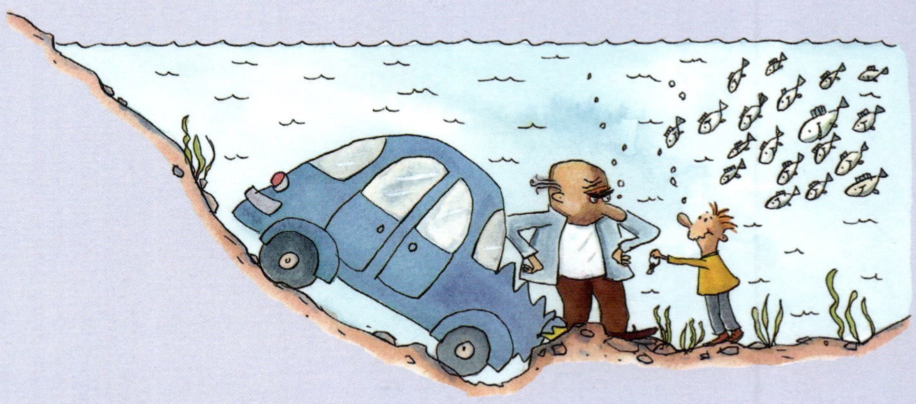

Histoire drôle

26

Juin

Petite annonce

27

Juin

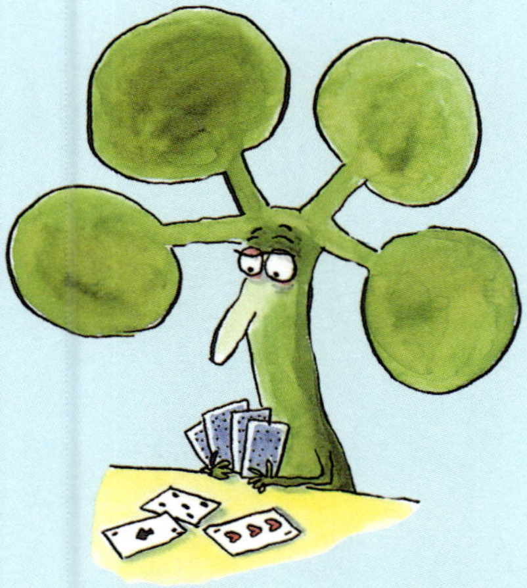

SUPERSTITION : M. Trèfle cherche quatre feuilles pour avoir de la chance.

Petite annonce

28

Juin

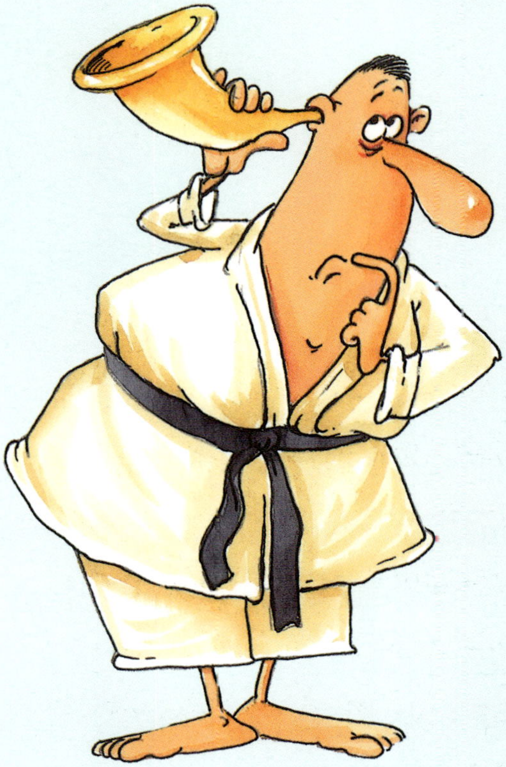

ARTS MARTIAUX : professeur de kung-fu cherche volontaire pour tester l'efficacité du « cri qui tue ». Sourds s'abstenir.

Histoire drôle

29

Juin

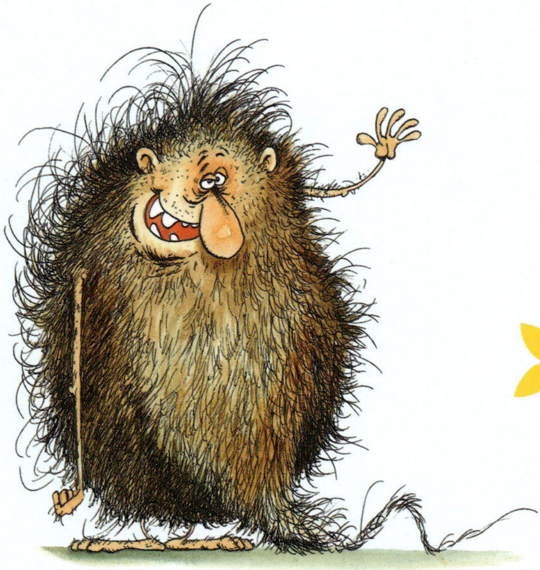

Un homme très poilu, avec des cheveux en bataille qui lui tombent jusqu'aux fesses, et une barbe qui lui arrive aux genoux, pénètre dans un salon de coiffure.

- Pour moi, dit-il au coiffeur, ce sera comme d'habitude.

Le coiffeur s'étonne.

- Comme d'habitude ? Et c'est comment, d'habitude ?

- Vous me rasez la tête et la barbe, comme la dernière fois, il y a cinq ans.

Devinette

30

Juin

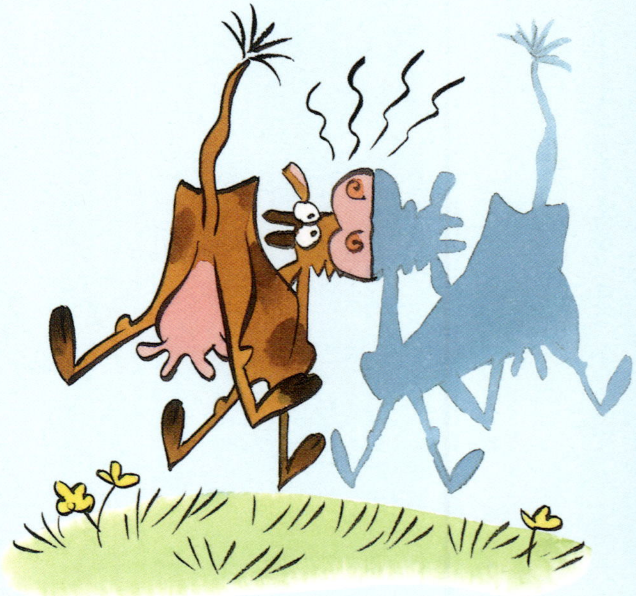

Qu'est-ce qui est transparent et qui court dans les prés ?

(Réponse : un troupeau de vitres.)

Histoire drôle

1

Juillet

Un homme dit à son meilleur ami :

- Je sais ce qu'on va faire : on va ouvrir un bar au milieu du désert du Sahara !

- Mais on n'aura presque pas de clients ! C'est le désert !

- Ouais, répond l'autre, mais alors ceux qui viendront, qu'est-ce qu'ils auront soif !

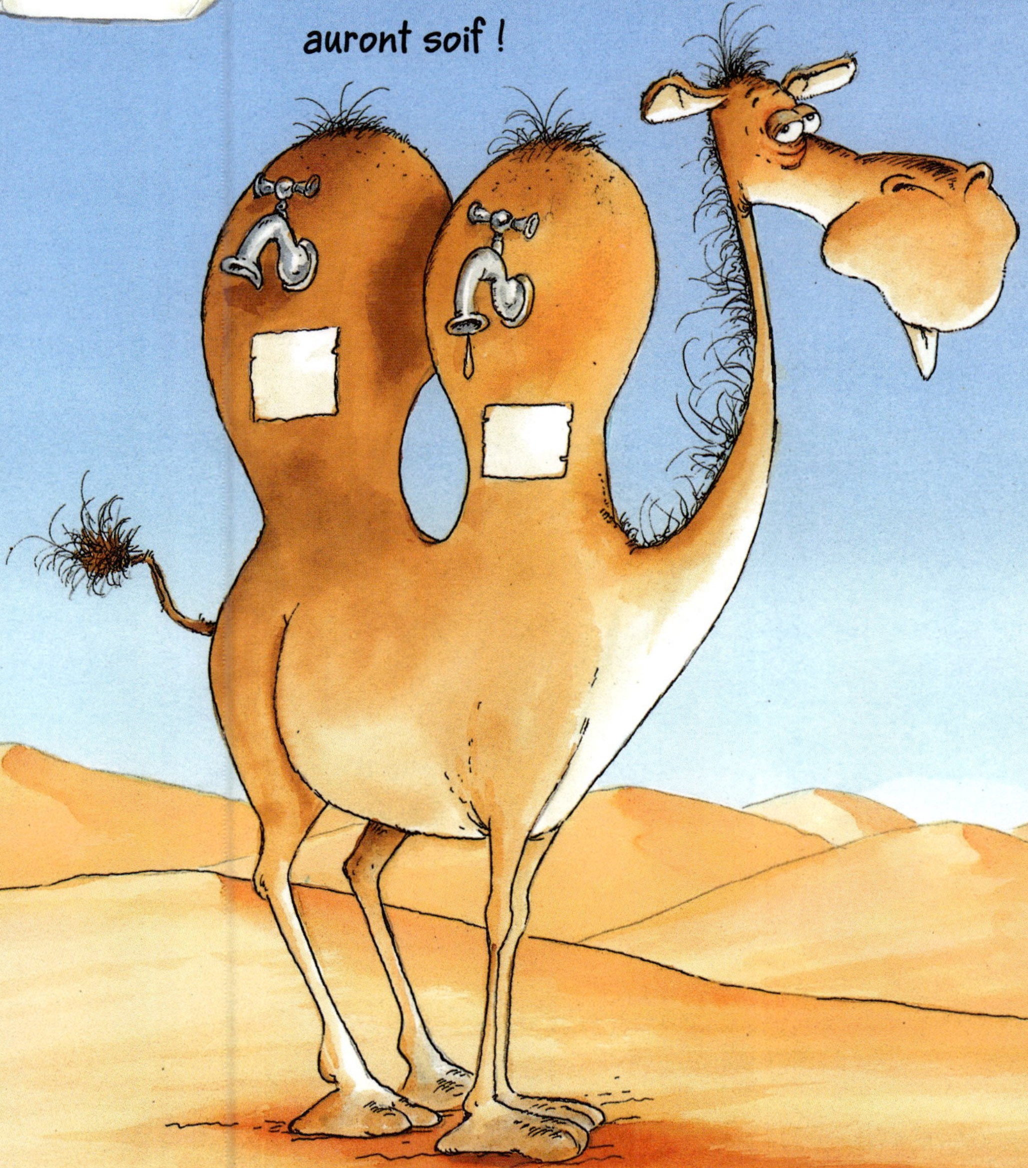

Juillet

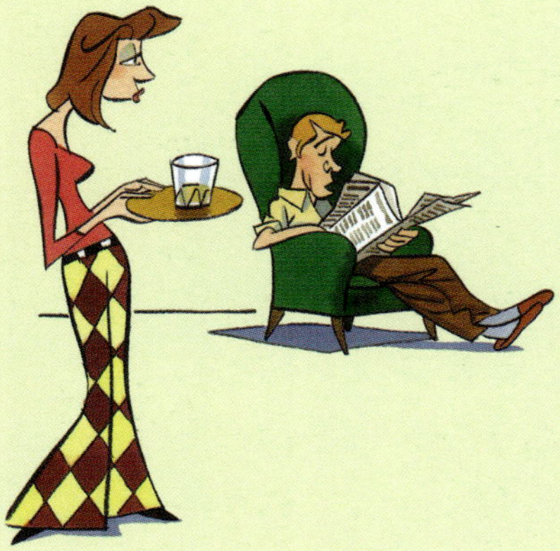

La maman de Yohan va voir son mari.

- Il va falloir appeler le médecin. Yohan dit qu'il a mal à la tête et au ventre.

- Laisse tomber ! répond le père. Il nous fait le coup au moins une fois par semaine pour ne pas aller à l'école.

- C'est vrai, mais c'est la première fois qu'il le fait le premier jour des vacances, alors qu'il n'y a pas école !

Histoire drôle
2
Juillet

Petite annonce
3
Juillet

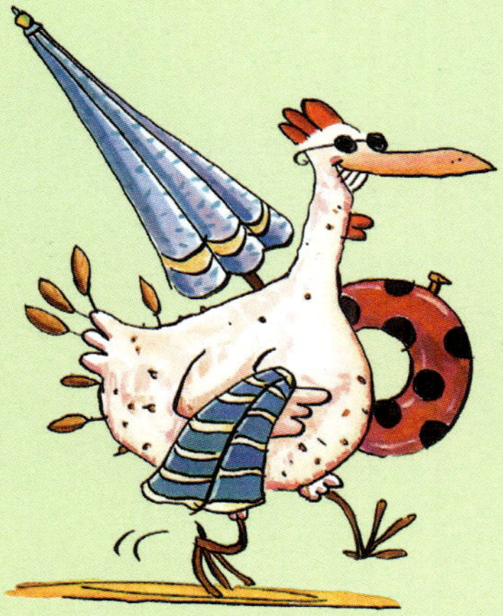

VACANCES : poulet fermier cherche camping sur la côte pour rôtir au soleil.

Des poissons font les fous au milieu de l'océan. Tout à coup, l'un d'eux aperçoit une étoile de mer qui vient dans leur direction.

- Attention, s'écrie-t-il, voilà le shérif !

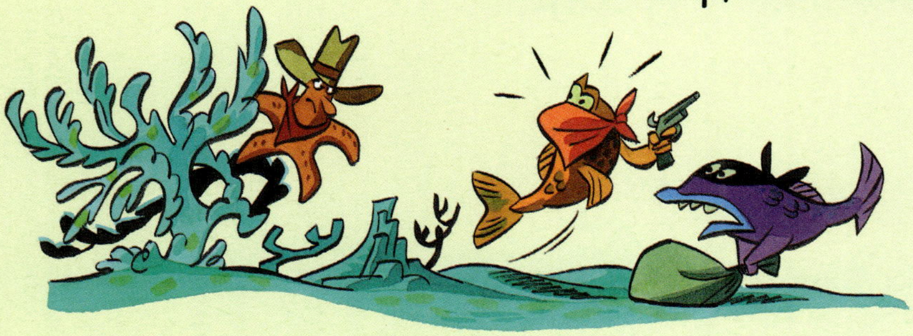

Histoire drôle
4
Juillet

Histoire drôle

5

Juillet

Après son mariage, un cow-boy rentre au ranch avec sa femme, qu'il a installée derrière lui, sur son cheval.

La femme est un peu forte, le cow-boy est bien enveloppé, bref, la charge est trop lourde pour l'animal, qui trébuche et s'écroule sur le sol.

Le cow-boy, projeté au sol, relève sa femme, brosse la poussière de sa robe de mariée, puis regarde le cheval droit dans les yeux en disant :

- Une fois.

Ils remontent sur le cheval, qui trotte à nouveau péniblement et trébuche une nouvelle fois. Le cow-boy et sa femme se relèvent, se nettoient, et le cow-boy regarde le cheval droit dans les yeux en disant :

- Deuxième fois.

Ils remontent sur le pauvre animal, qui trébuche à nouveau. Le cow-boy se relève, brosse la poussière de la robe de sa femme, regarde le cheval droit dans les yeux et dit :

- Troisième fois.

Il enlève ses gants et donne une terrible claque au cheval.

Sa femme s'étonne.

- Tu es trop sévère avec lui, il aurait fallu amener deux chevaux, plutôt que de monter à deux sur lui.

C'est de notre faute, pas la sienne !

Le cow-boy regarde sa femme droit dans les yeux et dit :

- Une fois.

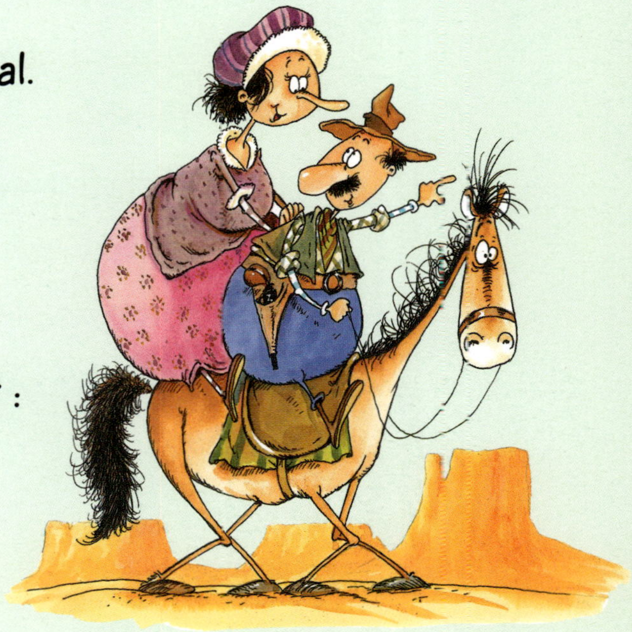

Histoire drôle

6

Juillet

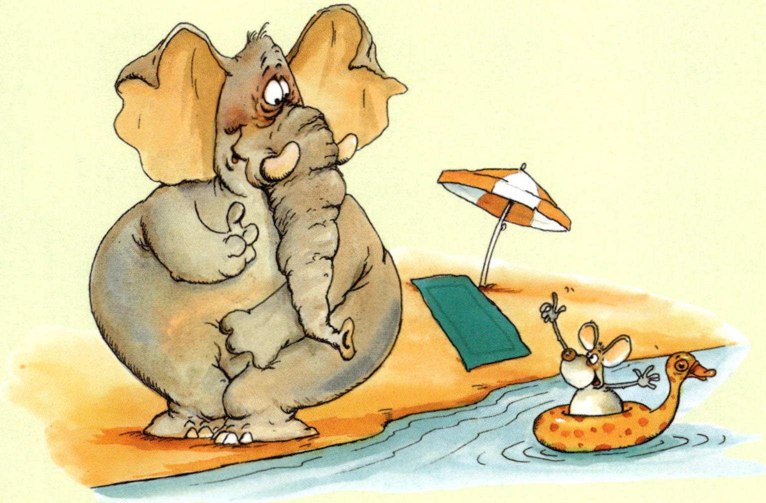

Une souris se baigne dans un grand lac.

Son copain l'éléphant arrive.

- Hé, dit la souris, viens te baigner, elle est bonne !

- Je ne peux pas, répond le pachyderme, je n'ai pas mon maillot de bain...

- C'est pas grave, je te prête le mien !

Histoire drôle

7

Juillet

Un paresseux va chez le médecin.

- En ce moment, j'ai des insomnies terribles. Je n'arrive plus à dormir normalement.

- Vous vous réveillez souvent ? interroge le docteur.

- Oh oui ! Tous les trois jours.

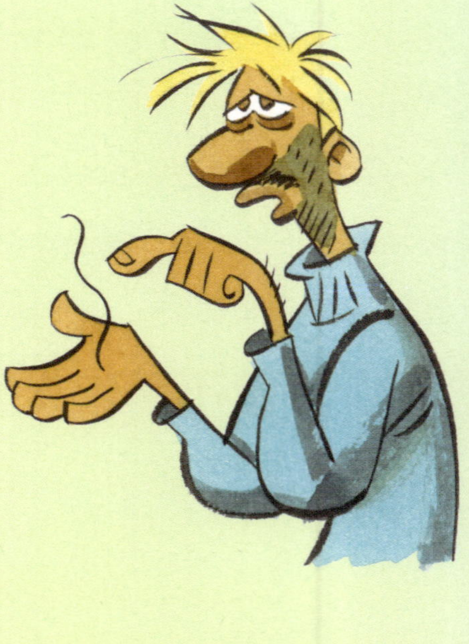

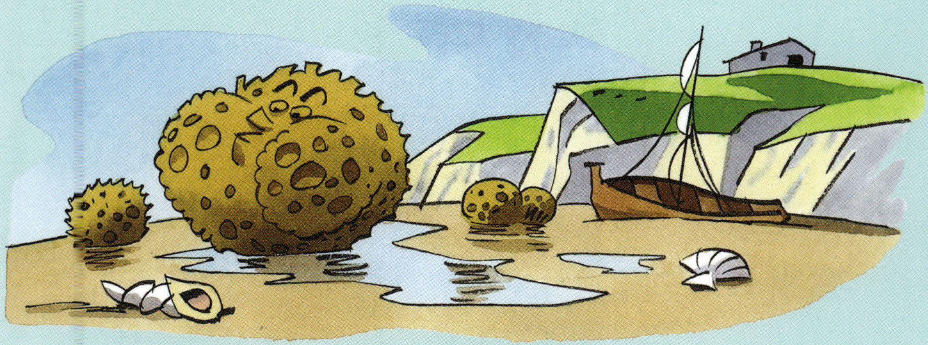

Devinette

8 Juillet

Pourquoi les fleuves débordent-ils de temps en temps, alors que la mer ne déborde jamais ?

(Réponse : parce que dans la mer, il y a des éponges...)

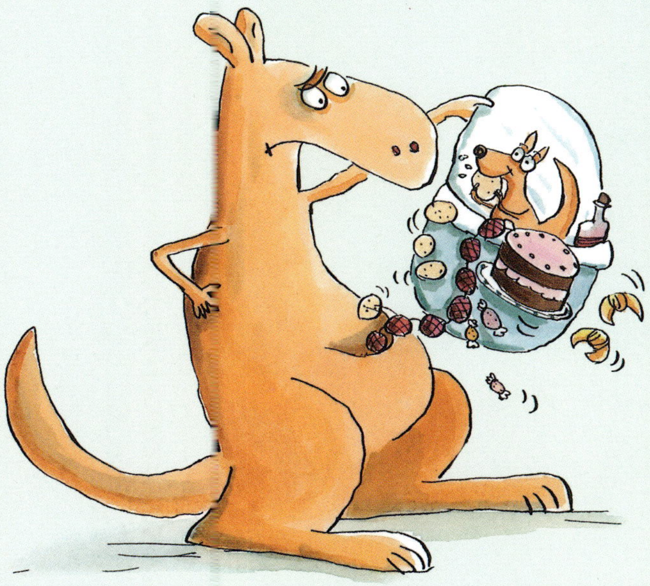

Maman kangourou saute à travers champs, gaiement. Soudain, elle s'arrête, se gratte le ventre, puis repart en sautillant. Mais, quelques mètres plus loin, elle s'arrête de nouveau, se gratte le ventre, puis repart, avant de s'arrêter à nouveau. Furieuse, elle se gratte à nouveau le ventre, puis sort son fils de sa poche et lui donne une grosse fessée.

- Ça t'apprendra à manger des biscottes dans ton lit !

Histoire drôle

9 Juillet

Une souris et un éléphant font du jogging dans la jungle. La souris, peu habituée à courir si vite, commence à s'essouffler.

- Si tu veux, propose l'éléphant, tu peux monter sur mon dos, pour te reposer.
- D'accord, répond la souris, soulagée, mais après, on échange.

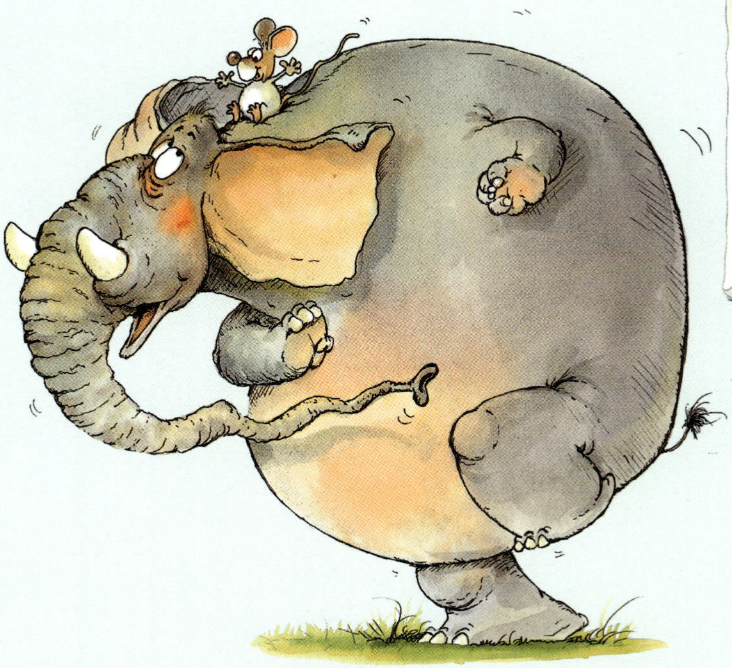

Histoire drôle

10

Juillet

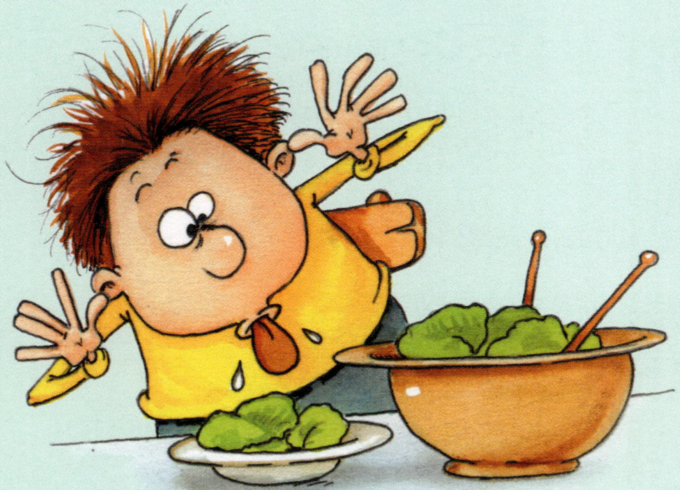

Maman se fâche.

- Denis ! Ne prends pas avec les doigts dans le saladier sans demander ! Tu as une langue, nom d'une pipe !
- Oui, mais elle n'est pas assez longue !

Histoire drôle

11

Juillet

Histoire drôle

12 Juillet

Un portier à l'air très fatigué ouvre la porte d'un grand hôtel à une dame très chic.

- Cela doit être épuisant d'ouvrir et de fermer cette porte tout le temps, lui dit-elle.
- Oui, madame.
- Cela fait mal au bras ?
- Non, madame.
- Vous aimez mieux ouvrir la porte ou la fermer ?
- Je n'ai pas de préférence, madame.
- Alors c'est la chaleur qui vous fatigue ?
- Non, madame.
- Quoi alors ?
- Les questions qu'on me pose, madame.

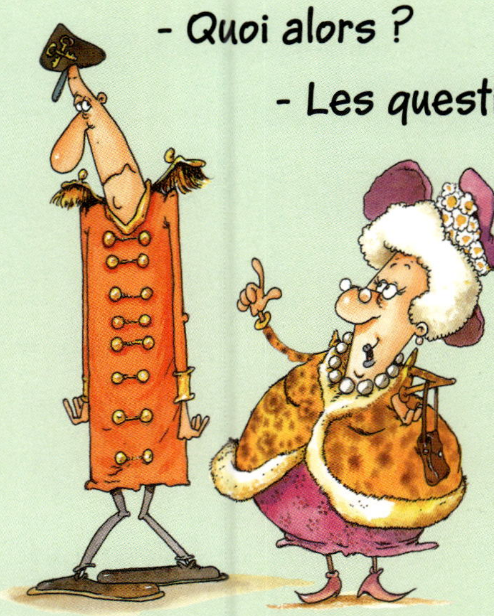

Petite annonce

13 Juillet

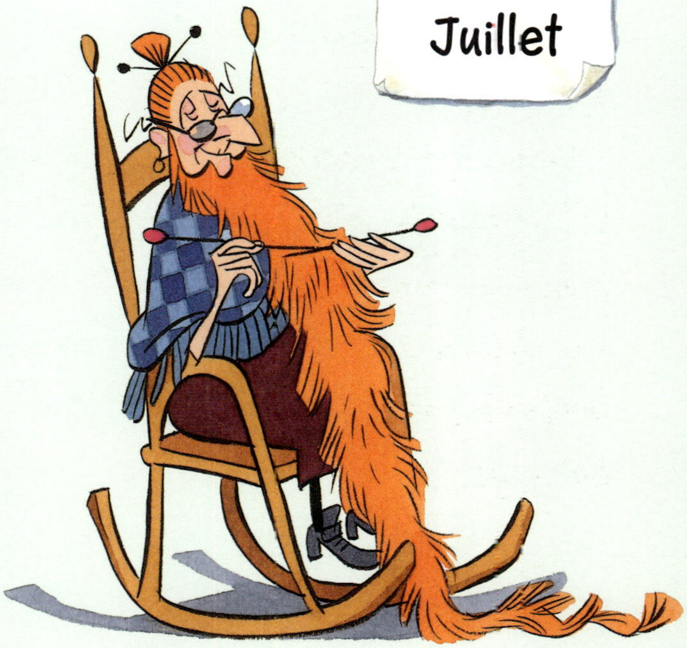

ESTHÉTIQUE : femme à barbe achète rasoir de toute urgence.

Histoire drôle

14

Juillet

Un petit lapin et un gros lion entrent dans un restaurant. Ils s'attablent et le lapin passe la commande.

- Pour moi, ce sera une laitue, des carottes et un grand jus de tomate ; et pour mon ami, juste un verre d'eau.

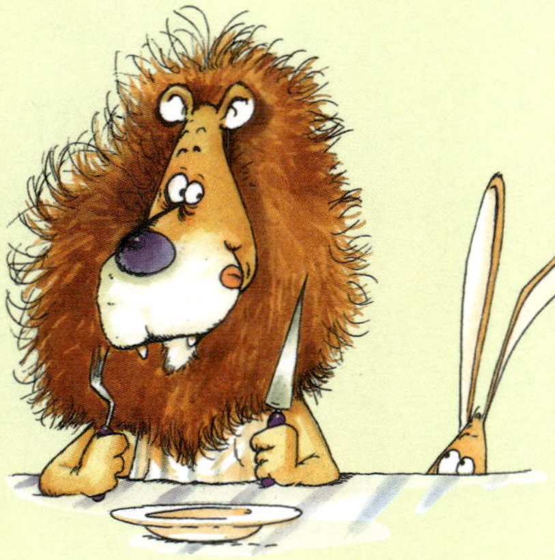

- Ah ? s'étonne le garçon. Il n'a pas faim ?
- C'est ça, répond le lapin, il n'a pas faim.
- Vous êtes sûr qu'il ne veut pas grignoter un petit quelque chose ?
- N'insistez pas ! s'énerve le lapin. Vous pensez bien que si mon ami le lion avait faim, je ne serais pas venu dîner avec lui !

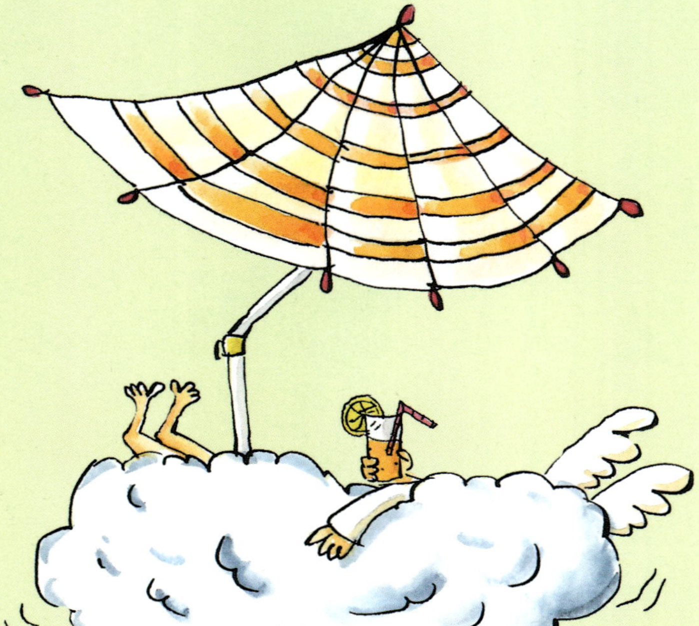

PARADIS : ange voulant déménager cherche nuage confortable en location.

Petite annonce

15

Juillet

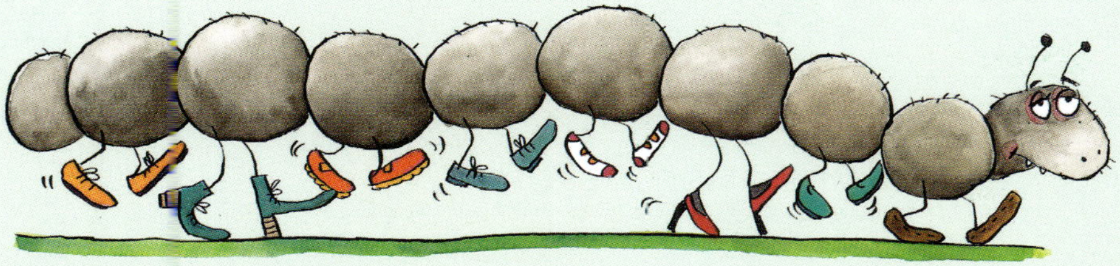

Petite annonce

16

Juillet

COMMERCE : mille-pattes cherche chaussures en solde.

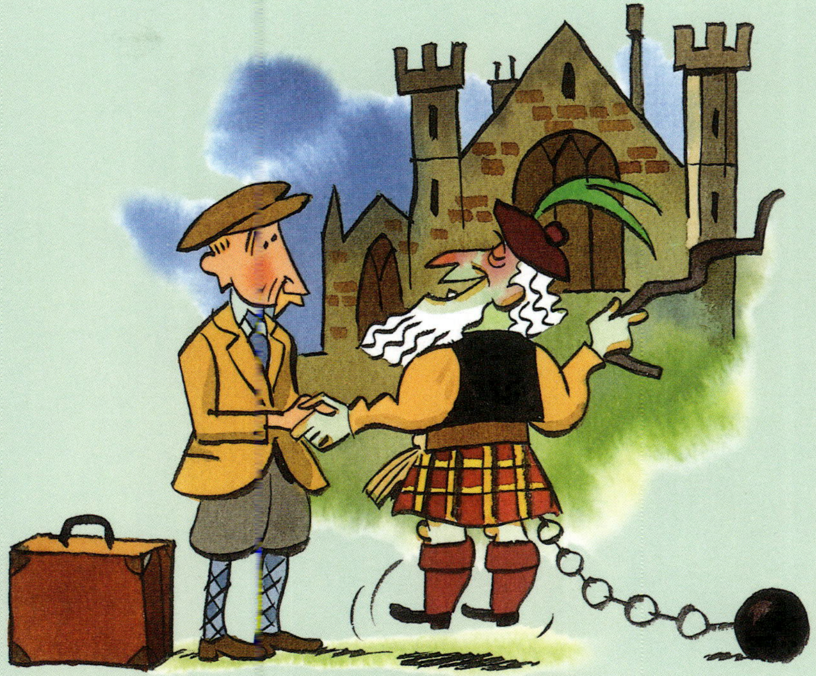

Un touriste va passer une nuit dans un château écossais. Méfiant, il demande tout de même au propriétaire :

- Dites-moi, il n'y a pas de fantômes, au moins, dans votre château ?

Le propriétaire éclate de rire.

- Des fantômes ?
Dans mon château ?
Vous plaisantez !
Je n'ai rien entendu de plus stupide depuis quatre cents ans que j'habite ici !

Histoire drôle

17

Juillet

Histoire drôle

18

Juillet

Un cactus se vante :

- Moi, je sais parler le langage des humains !
- Ah bon ? s'étonne un de ses congénères.
- Oui. D'ailleurs, ce n'est pas très compliqué, ils ne disent que deux mots :

« Aïe » et « Ouille » !

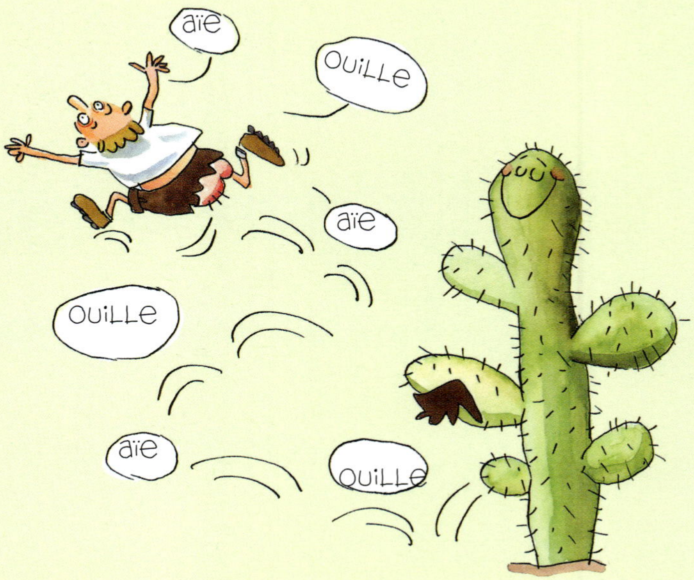

Histoire drôle

19

Juillet

Un petit garçon se précipite vers un policier.

- Vite, monsieur l'agent, un voyou se bat avec mon frère depuis une demi-heure !
- Une demi-heure ! Et tu ne viens me prévenir que maintenant ?
- Bah oui, jusqu'à présent, c'était mon frère qui gagnait !

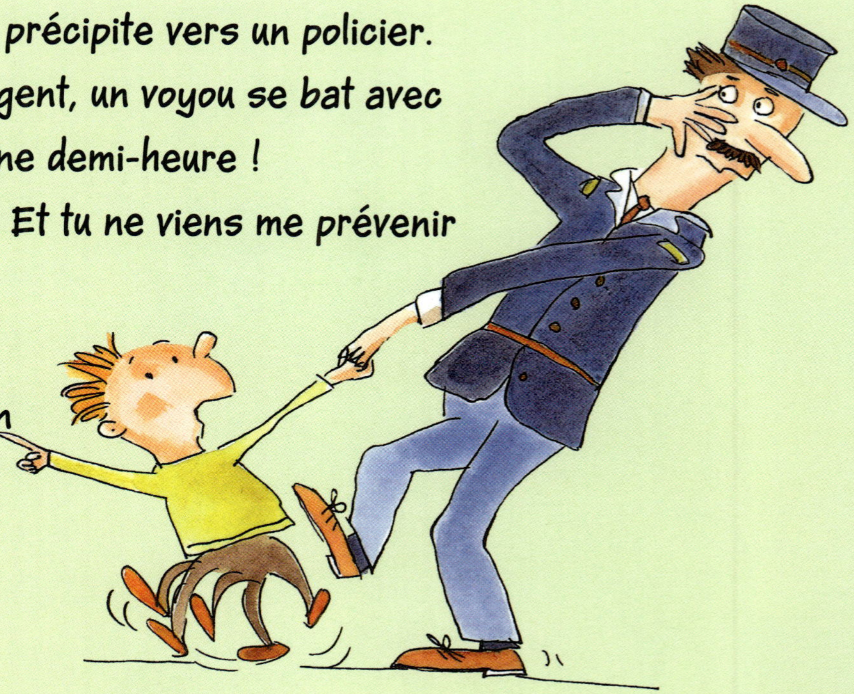

Histoire drôle

20

Juillet

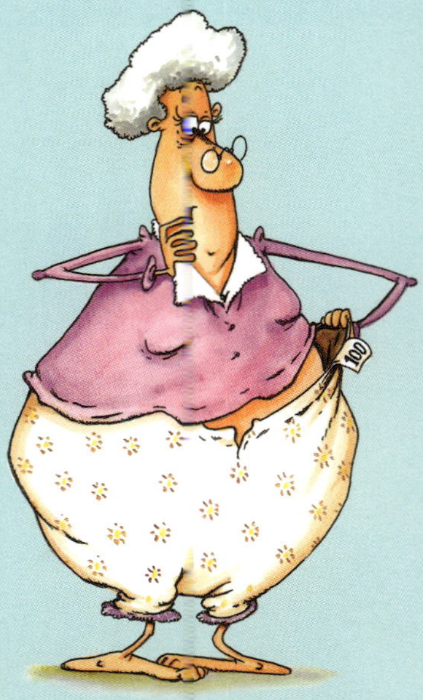

Sophie, six ans, demande à sa grand-mère :

- Tu as quel âge, toi, mamie ?
- Oh, tu sais, je suis très vieille, tellement vieille que je ne me souviens plus de mon âge...
- Eh bien, regarde sur ta culotte ! Moi, sur la mienne, il y a une étiquette où c'est marqué « 6 ans » !

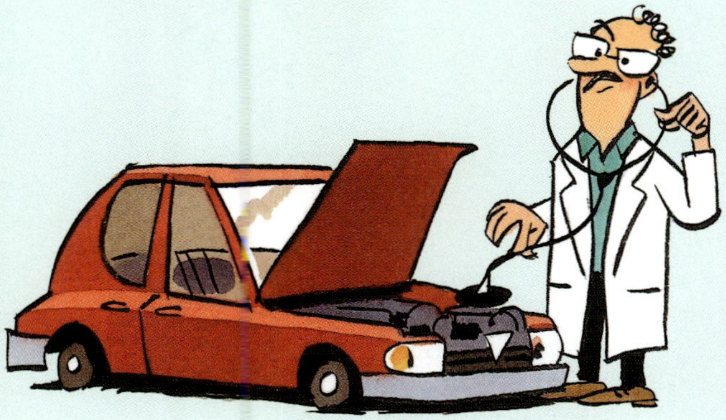

Quand les pneus vont-ils chez le médecin ?

(Réponse : quand ils sont crevés.)

Dev nette

21

Juillet

Histoire drôle

22 Juillet

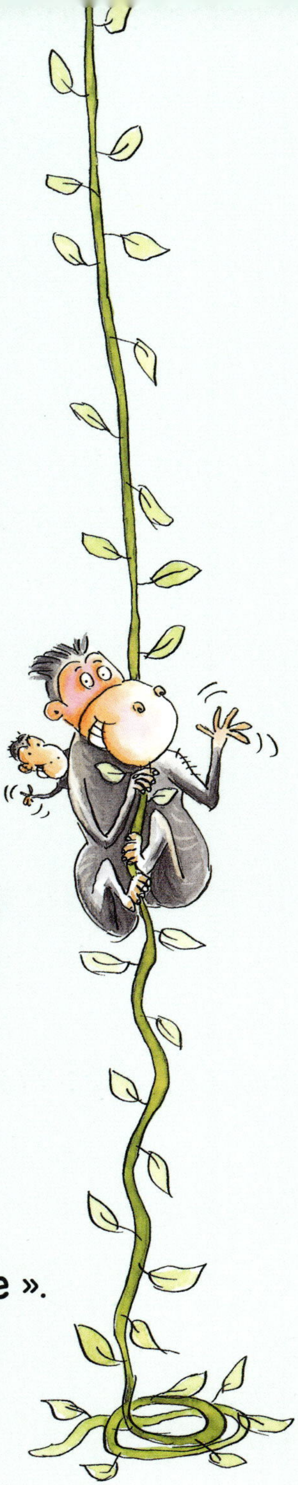

Maman demande :

- Alors, Solène, tu as vu quels animaux, au zoo ?
- Un loup et un singe.
- Oui, c'est bien... Et quoi d'autre ?
- Un singe.
- Tu l'as déjà dit, « singe ».
- Oui, mais il y en avait deux !

Devinette

23 Juillet

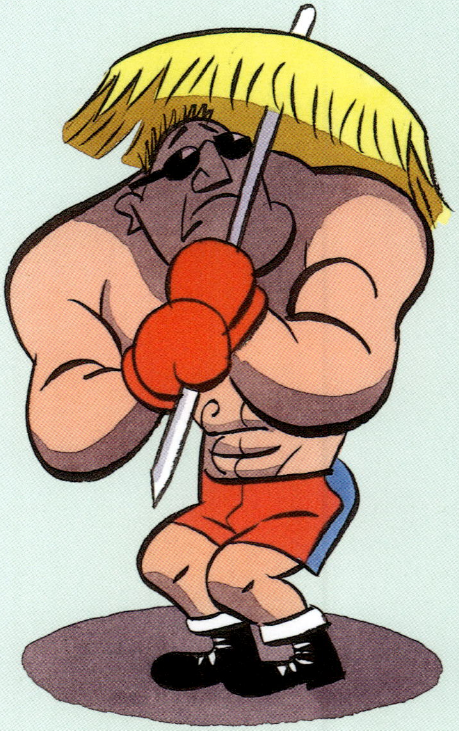

Quels sont les coups auxquels même un boxeur ne peut pas résister ?

(Réponse : les coups de soleil.)

Petite annonce

24

Juillet

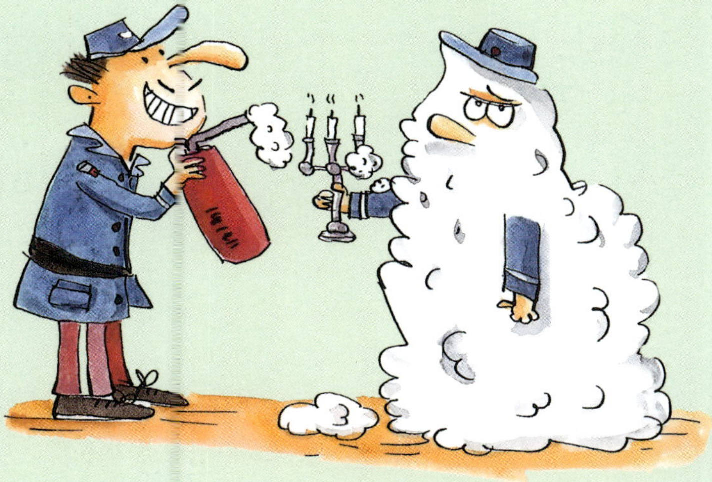

AVIS : les extincteurs doivent obligatoirement être vérifiés une semaine avant chaque incendie.

Un acteur doit entrer dans la cage d'un lion pour les besoins d'un film, mais il refuse.

- Mais enfin ! s'emporte le metteur en scène, vous ne risquez rien ! Ce lion a été élevé au biberon !

- Moi aussi, rétorque l'acteur, j'ai été élevé au biberon. Et pourtant, aujourd'hui, je mange des steaks !

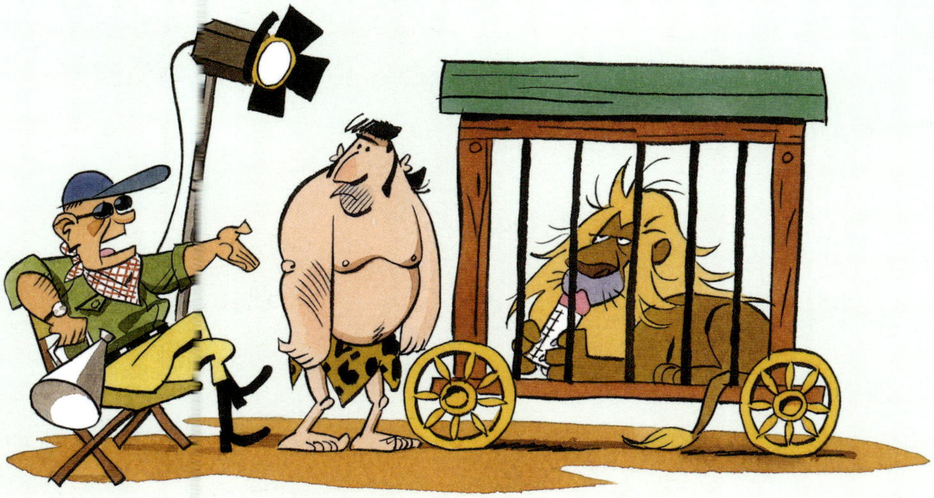

Histoire drôle

25

Juillet

Petite annonce

26

Juillet

CHIRURGIE : crocodile brûlé cherche sac à main pour greffe de peau.

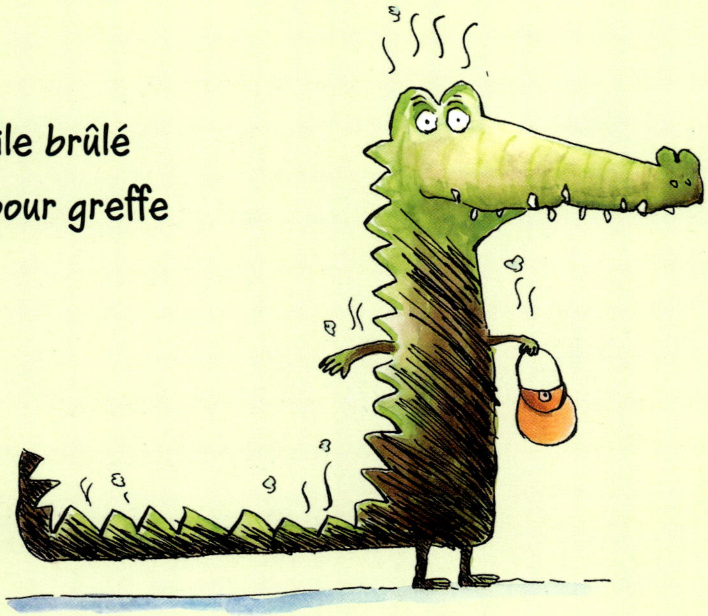

- La nuit dernière, dit un monsieur à sa femme, il y avait un chat en bas de chez nous qui m'empêchait de dormir, en poussant des petits « miaou ».

- Et alors ?

- Bah ! comme j'étais très énervé, je lui ai lancé un de mes chaussons par la fenêtre pour le faire taire.

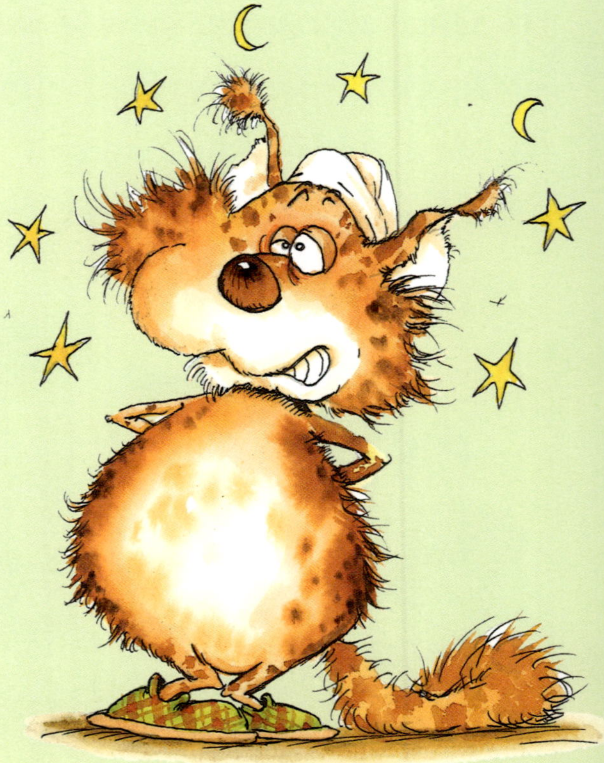

Histoire drôle

27

Juillet

- Et tu l'as touché ?

- Je le pense, oui. Ça ne l'a pas fait taire, mais il a passé le reste de la nuit à hurler « mi-aïe-aïe-ou ».

Histoire drôle
28
Juillet

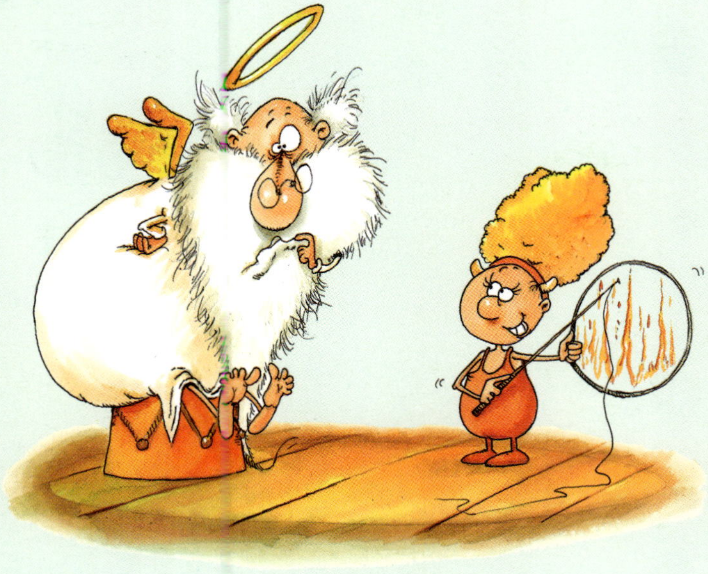

Une maman explique à sa petite fille que si elle est sage, elle ira au paradis, et que si elle fait des bêtises, elle ira en enfer. La petite réfléchit et demande :

- Et pour aller au cirque, qu'est-ce que je dois faire ?

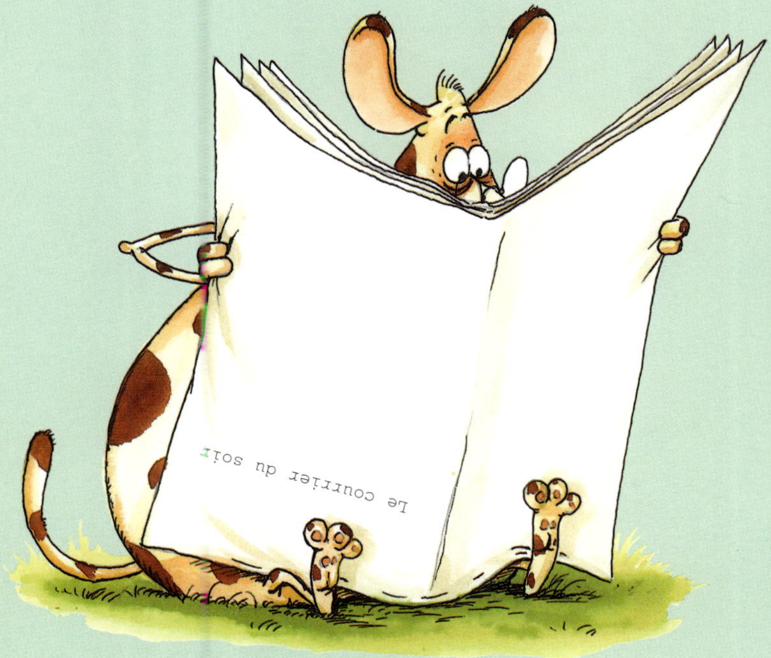

- J'ai perdu mon chien.

- Mets une annonce dans le journal !

- Non, ça ne sert à rien, il ne sait pas lire.

Histoire drôle
29
Juillet

Histoire drôle

30 Juillet

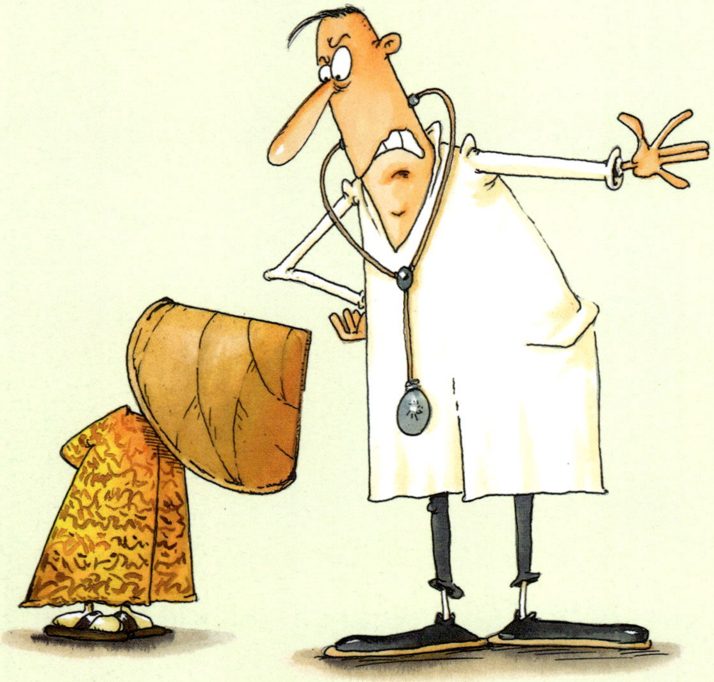

Un médecin désolé dispute son patient :
- Voilà trois semaines que je vous soigne pour votre jaunisse, et c'est seulement aujourd'hui que vous me dites que vous êtes chinois !

Devinette

31 Juillet

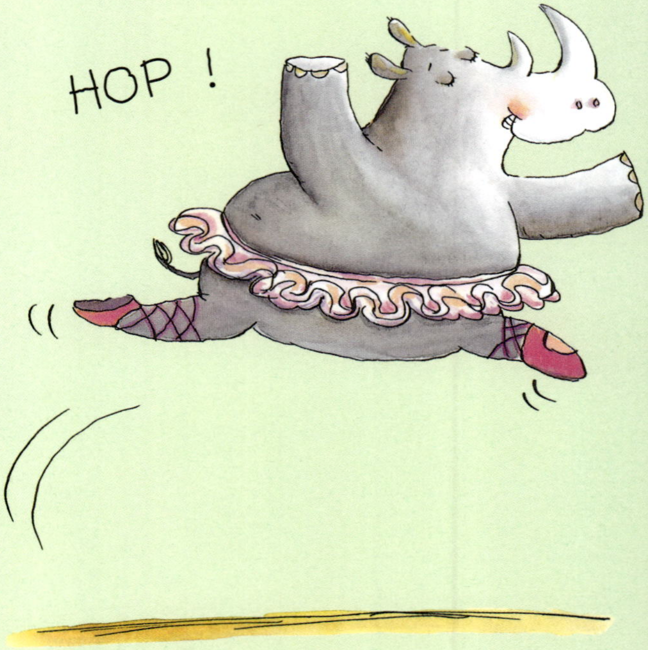

Quel animal peut sauter plus haut qu'une maison ?

(Réponse : tous les animaux peuvent sauter plus haut qu'une maison ! Vous avez déjà vu une maison sauter, vous ?)

Devinette

1

Août

Comment distingue-t-on une fourchette d'un requin ?

(Réponse : vous les mettez tous les deux dans la mer, et celui qui essaye de vous manger, c'est le requin.)

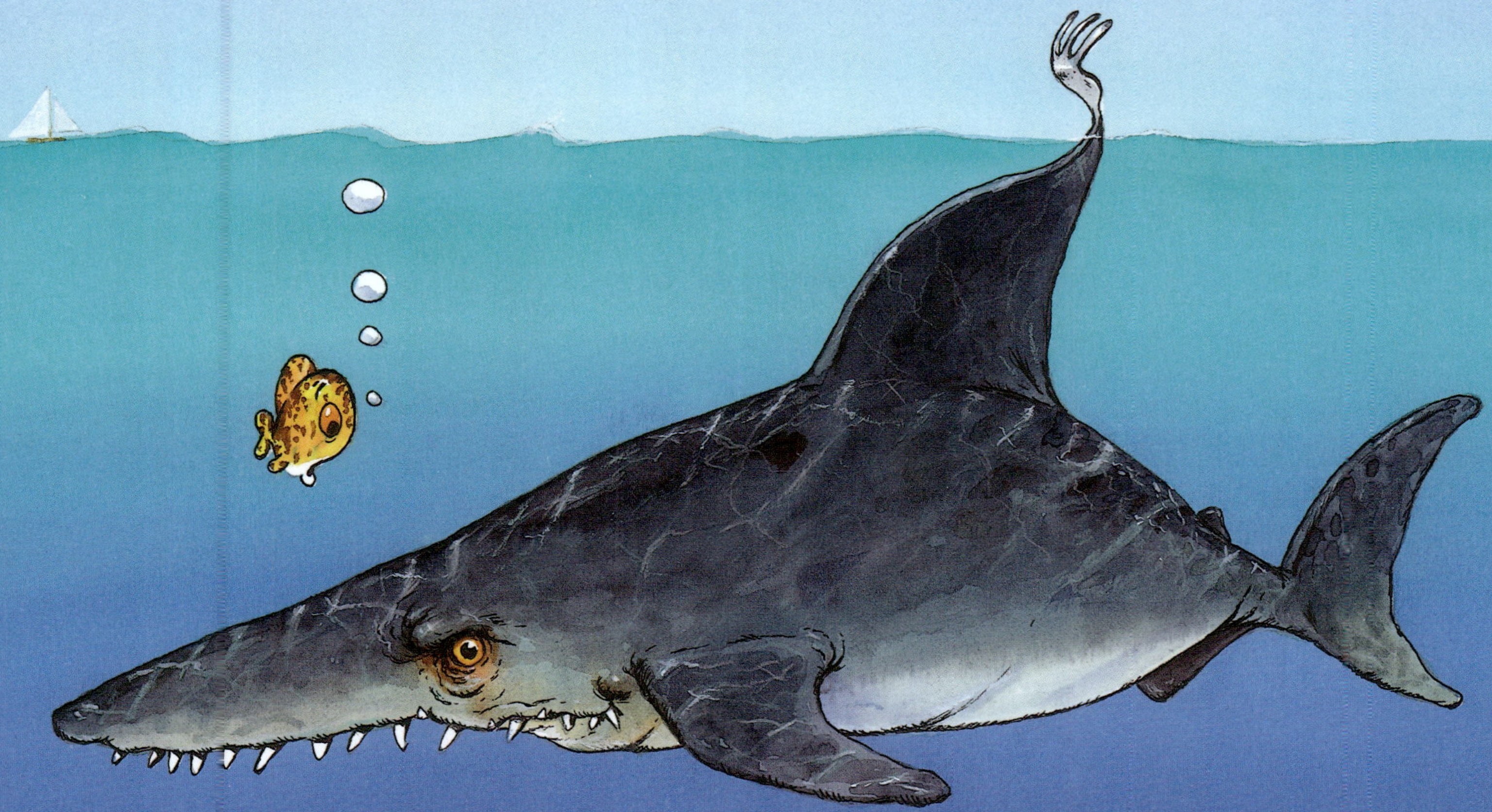

Août

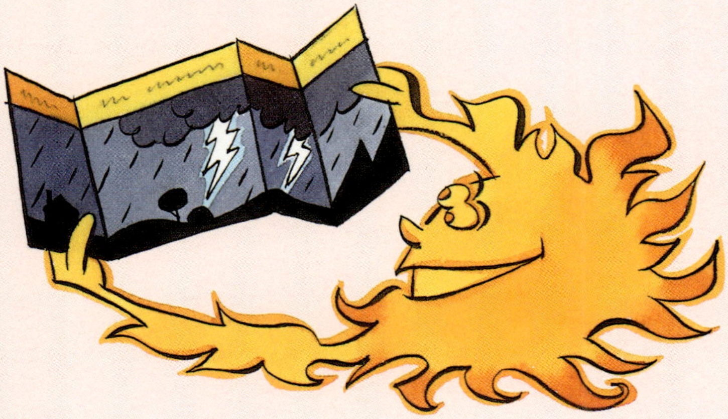

Petite annonce

2

Août

JUILLET-AOÛT : Soleil cherche endroit sympa pour les vacances.

Histoire drôle

3

Août

Dans un grand bar de Paris, un touriste américain appelle le garçon.

- On étouffe, ici ! Mettez en marche l'air conditionné, je vous prie !

- Bien, monsieur. Dix minutes plus tard, l'Américain rappelle le garçon.

- Maintenant, je gèle ! Arrêtez l'air conditionné, je vous prie !

- Bien, monsieur, répond poliment le garçon.

Il ne s'écoule pas cinq minutes avant que l'Américain ne hèle de nouveau le serveur.

- Garçon ! Il fait cent fois trop chaud ! Remettez l'air conditionné, je vous prie !

Un autre touriste, assis à une table voisine, dit au garçon :

- Je vous trouve vraiment patient avec cet Américain ! Moi, je l'aurais mis dehors, lui et son air conditionné !

Le garçon hausse les épaules.

- Oh ! vous savez, l'essentiel est qu'il soit content. De toute façon, nous ne l'avons pas, ici, l'air conditionné !

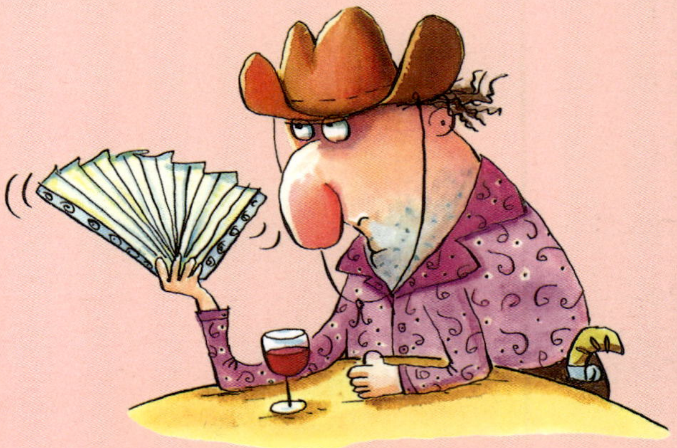

Histoire drôle

4 Août

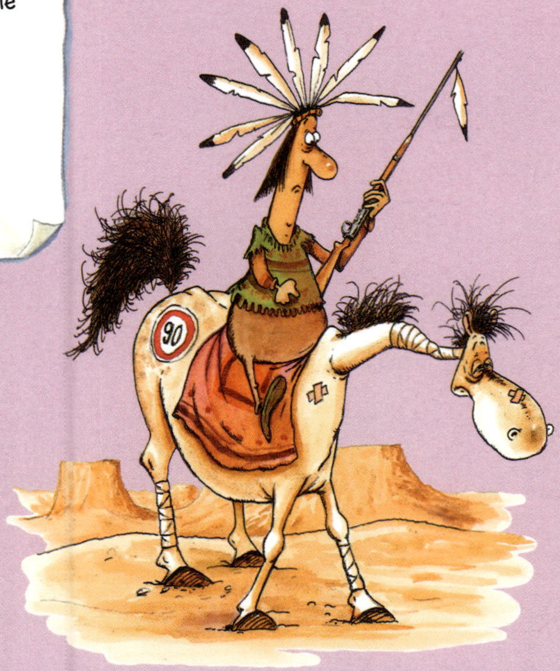

Au Far-West, Joe le cow-boy galope sur son cheval à travers la plaine. Il croise Œil-de-lynx l'Indien, qui lui aussi galope sur la plaine, mais son cheval est couvert de bosses et de plaies.

Les deux hommes se saluent et Joe demande :

- Qu'est-il arrivé à ton cheval pour qu'il soit amoché de la sorte ?

- Ne m'en parle pas, répond l'Indien. C'est ma squaw qui apprend à conduire !

Petite annonce

5 Août

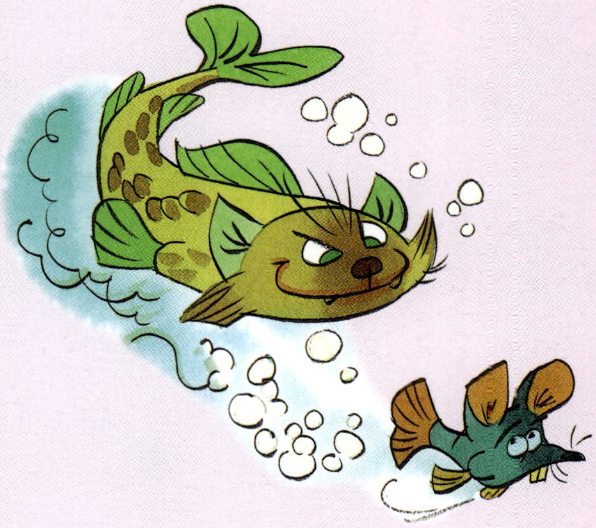

COPAINS : poisson-chat déprimé cherche poisson-souris.

Une jeune femme et son mari viennent de rentrer de l'hôpital avec leur premier bébé. - Chéri, dit la jeune maman, le bébé est mouillé, il faut le changer. Tu veux que je t'apprenne ?

- Je le ferai la prochaine fois, promet le mari, je regarde le match de foot.

Deux heures plus tard, le bébé est à nouveau mouillé.

- Chéri, appelle la jeune maman, je vais changer le bébé. Tu viens ?

Histoire drôle

6

Août

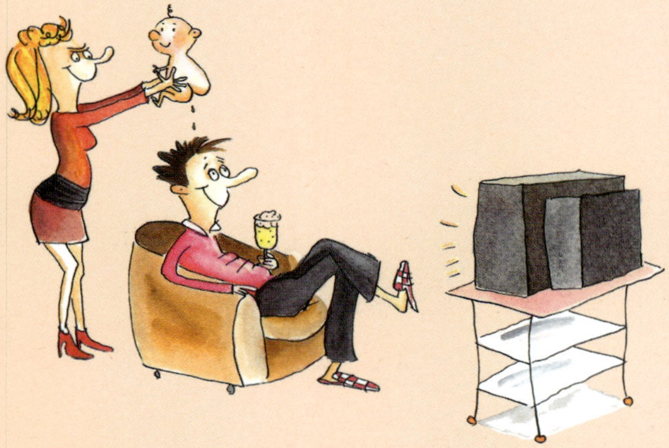

- La prochaine fois, répond à nouveau le mari, je regarde le match de rugby à la télé. Cette fois, la jeune femme se fâche.

- Tu m'as déjà dit tout à l'heure que tu apprendrais la prochaine fois ! Tu exagères !

- Mais non, ma chérie, explique le mari, tu as mal compris : je voulais dire que j'apprendrai la prochaine fois que nous aurons un bébé !

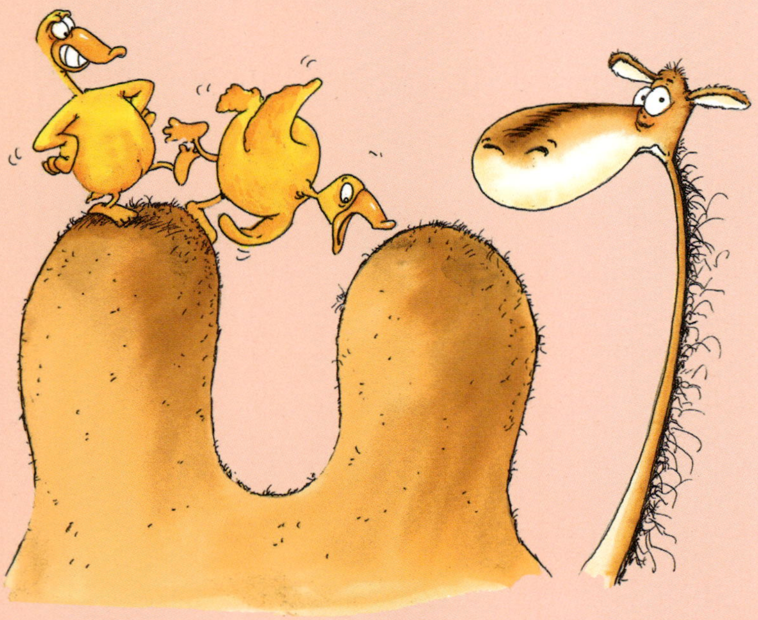

Deux canards marchent dans le désert. L'un des deux fait un croc-en-jambe à l'autre pour s'amuser. Le pauvre canard tombe la tête la première dans le sable, puis se relève.

- M'en fiche : je sais qui c'est !

Histoire drôle

7

Août

Les fourmis sont excédées. Depuis une semaine, un énorme éléphant vient manger des feuilles de l'arbre situé juste au-dessus de leur fourmilière, causant à chaque passage des dégâts énormes. La reine convoque tous ses sujets.

- Mes fils, mes filles, cela commence à bien faire ! La prochaine fois que cet éléphant viendra, nous l'attaquerons toutes et nous obtiendrons la victoire ! À bas les éléphants écraseurs de fourmilières !

- Hourra ! hurlent les fourmis. Vive la reine ! À bas les éléphants écraseurs de fourmilières !

Quelques heures plus tard, l'éléphant arrive pour manger les feuilles de l'arbre du dessus de la fourmilière, et, comme prévu, des centaines de milliers de fourmis se jettent sur lui, le piquant, le brûlant à l'acide formique, le mordant partout où elles le peuvent. L'énorme animal s'ébroue, chassant d'un coup de trompe toutes les fourmis loin de lui. Toutes, sauf une, accrochée à l'oreille du mastodonte, qui essaye tant bien que mal de ne pas tomber. Et là, une petite voix se fait entendre, venant des milliers de fourmis blessées durant le bref combat. - Vas-y, tu le tiens ! Étrangle-le !

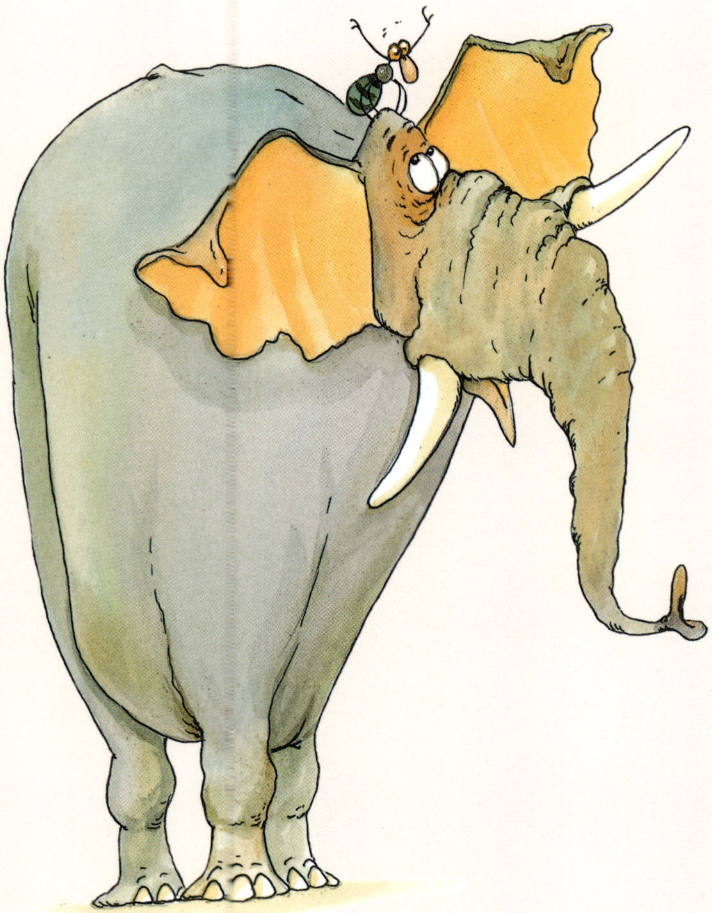

Histoire drôle

8

Août

Histoire drôle
9
Août

Un gros orage gronde dehors. Maman couche Noélie, lui fait une bise et éteint la lumière.
- Bonne nuit, ma chérie. N'aie pas peur de l'orage, la maison nous protège bien.
- Je peux dormir dans ton lit ? demande Noélie, un peu effrayée.
- Non, ma grande. Maman doit dormir à côté de papa.
Il y a un long silence, puis Noélie éclate de rire.
- Pfff ! Quel gros bébé !

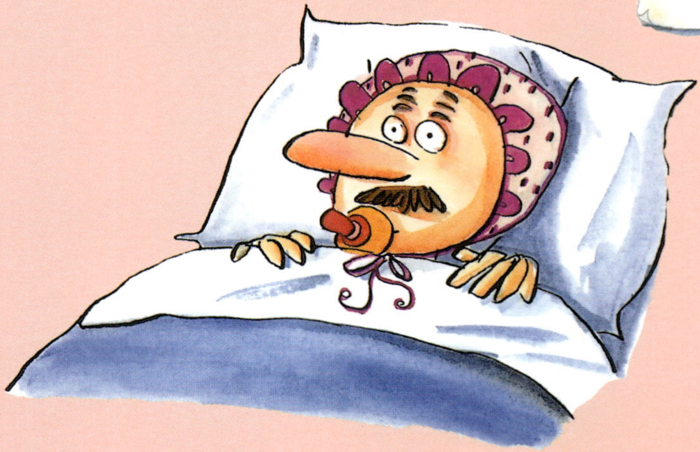

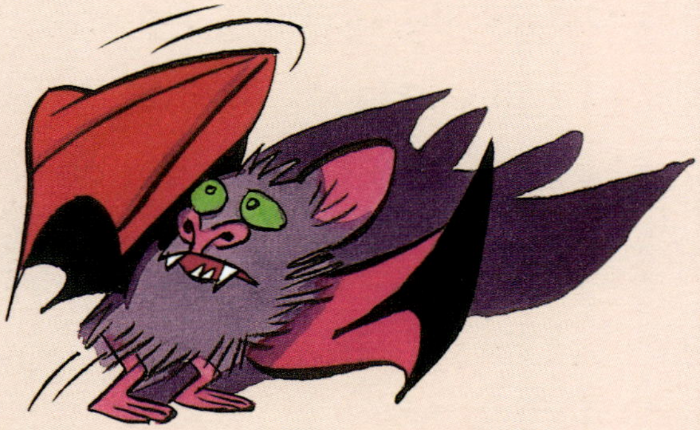

Qu'est-ce qui ne fait pas de bruit en se levant, mais qui réveille tout le monde ?

(Réponse : le soleil.)

Devinette
10
Août

Histoire drôle

11

Août

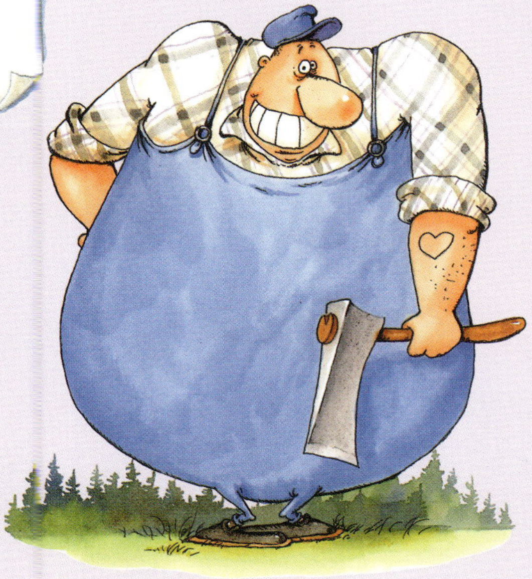

Un gars énorme, musclé comme un taureau, se présente pour une place de bûcheron, au Canada.

- Vous avez déjà travaillé comme bûcheron ? lui demande le chef du personnel.

- Ouais, répond le musclé. J'ai bossé dix ans dans le Sahara.

- Vous vous fichez de moi ! s'indigne le chef. Il n'y a pas d'arbres, dans le Sahara !

- Il n'y a PLUS d'arbres ! sourit le musclé. Nuance !

Devinette

12

Août

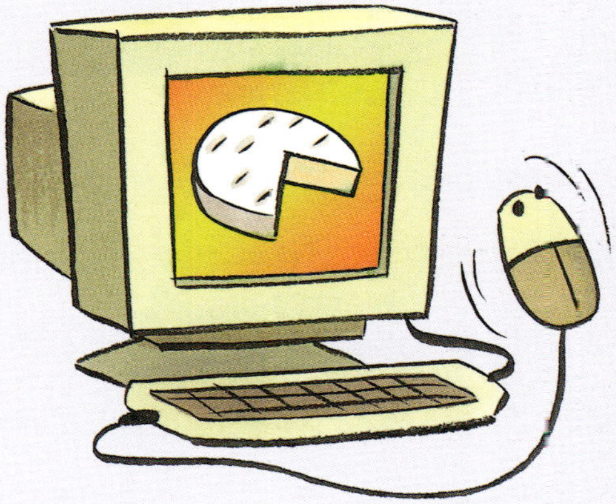

Comment savoir si un fou a utilisé un ordinateur ?

(Réponse : il y a du fromage à côté de la souris.)

Histoire drôle

13

Août

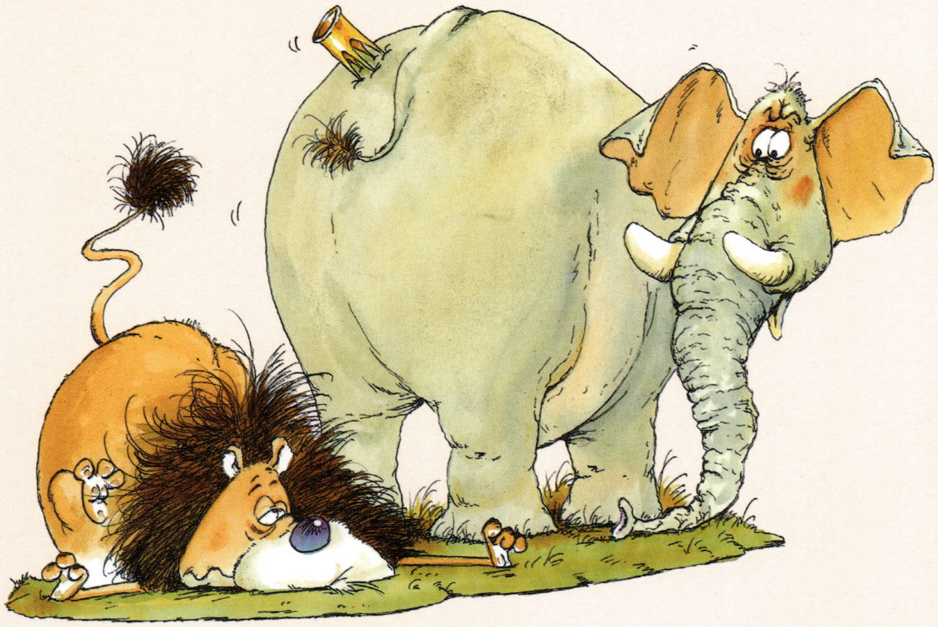

Un beau gros lion, tout fier de son allure et de sa musculature, se promène dans la jungle. Il rencontre une antilope.

- Hé, l'antilope ! Qui est le roi des rois de la jungle ?

- Oh ! Seigneur, c'est vous, bien sûr, vous êtes le plus beau des rois de la jungle, bafouille l'antilope, tout effrayée.

- C'est bien, dit le lion en reprenant son chemin, plus fier qu'un coq.

Il croise bientôt un orang-outan.

- Hé, toi, l'orang-outan ! Qui est le roi des rois de la jungle ?

- Euh… c'est toi, Seigneur, bien évidemment ! Tu es le plus fort des animaux de ce royaume, répond l'orang-outan en tremblant de peur.

- C'est très bien, dit le lion en reprenant son chemin, la tête haute.

Il tombe soudain sur un éléphant.

- Hé, l'éléphant ! Qui est le roi des rois de la jungle ?

L'éléphant baisse la tête, attrape notre lion avec sa trompe, le secoue un peu, le laisse tomber au sol et l'écrase avec chacune de ses pattes, puis il s'en va sans rien dire.

Le lion se relève difficilement.

- Eh bien ! bougonne-t-il, si on peut même plus se renseigner…

Histoire drôle

14

Août

Un homme et sa femme sont devant un ascenseur.

L'homme est chargé de paquets, il ne peut pas appuyer sur le bouton.

- Chérie, est-ce que tu peux appeler l'ascenseur, s'il te plaît ?

Sa femme sourit et crie :

- HÉ OH ! ASCENSEUR, ON T'ATTEND !

Stupéfait, le mari la regarde et lui dit :

- Mais pas comme ça, imbécile ! Appelle-le avec le doigt !

Alors la femme met un doigt dans sa bouche et crie :

- HÉ OH ! ASCHENSHEUR, ON T'ACHTEND !

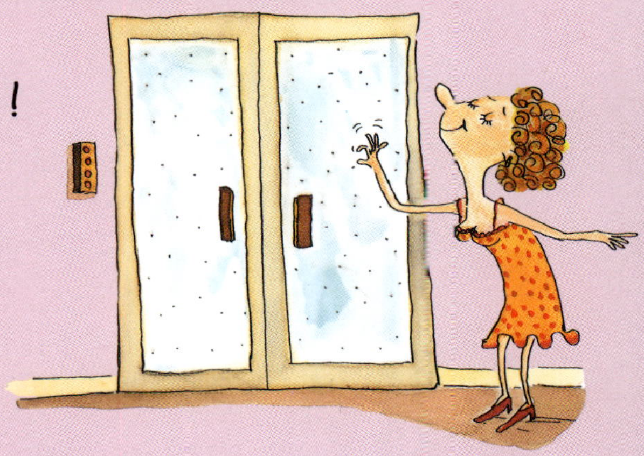

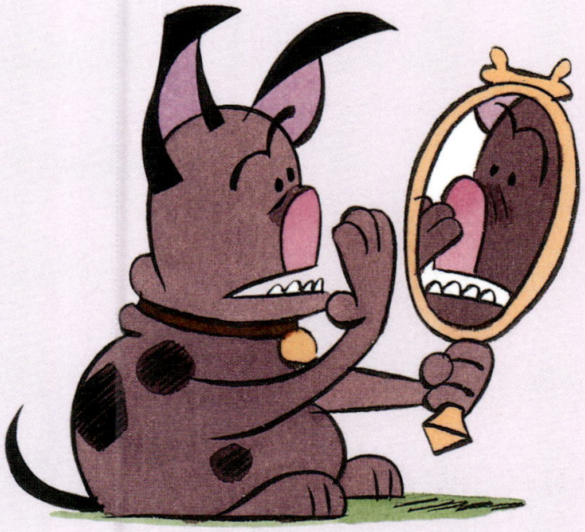

Mon chien n'a pas de nez, comment sent-il ?

(Réponse : il sent mauvais.)

Devinette

15

Août

Histoire drôle

16

Août

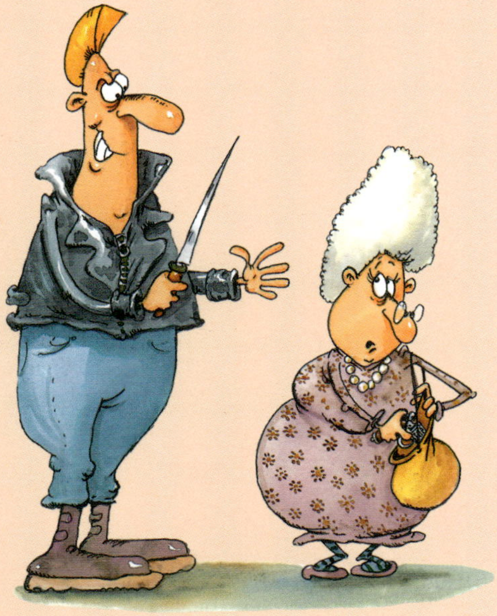

Dans la rue, un jeune homme bizarre demande à une dame :

- Excusez-moi, madame, auriez-vous vu un policier, dans le coin ?
- Ah ! non, jeune homme, je suis désolée.
- Pas moi, dit le garçon. Donnez-moi votre sac à main !

Devinette

17

Août

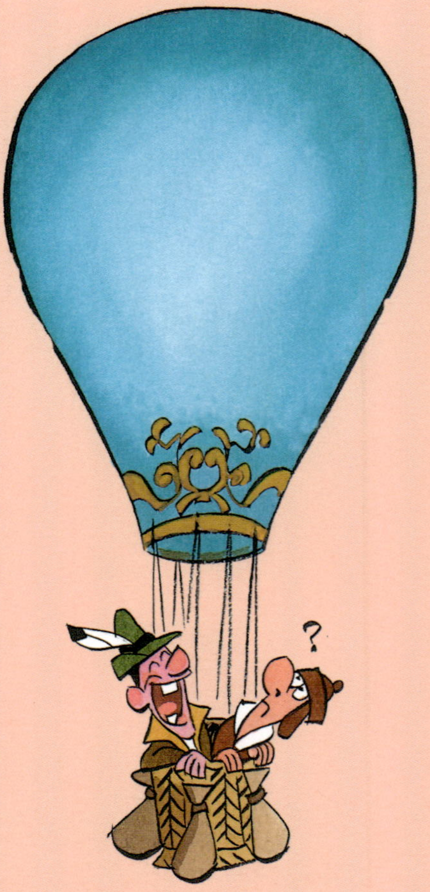

Pourquoi ne doit-on pas raconter de blagues à un ballon ?

(Réponse : il pourrait éclater de rire.)

Histoire drôle

18 Août

Un homme boit de l'alcool à un bar. Sur le comptoir, il y a une petite souris qui ingurgite toutes les gouttes que l'ivrogne renverse. À deux heures du matin, complètement ivres, le client et la souris sortent du bar en chantant à tue-tête. Ils chantent si fort qu'un type furieux ouvre sa fenêtre pour se plaindre.

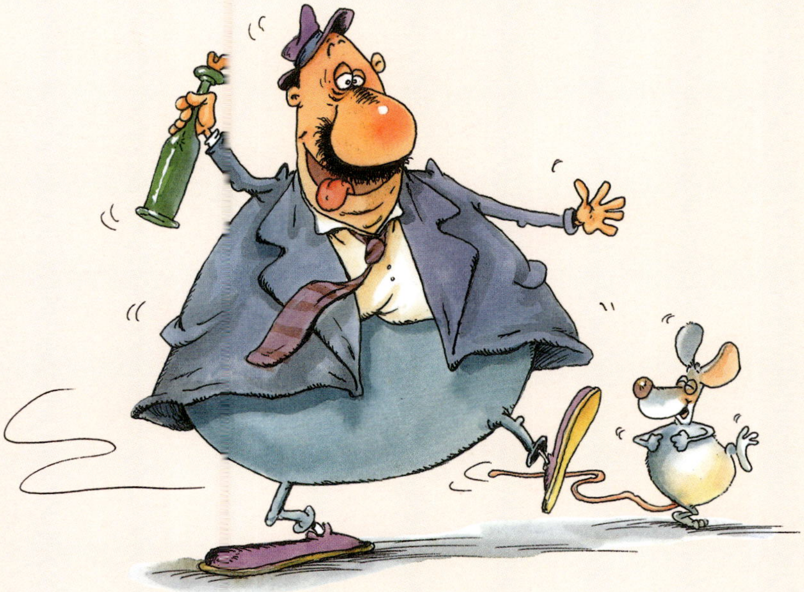

- C'est pas fini ce raffut ! Je vais appeler la police !

L'ivrogne lève son poing.

- Qu'est-ce qu'y a ? T'es pas content ? Descends, si t'es un homme !

Et la petite souris ajoute :

- Ouais, descends ! Et amène ton chat, que je lui fasse sa fête !

Devinette

19 Août

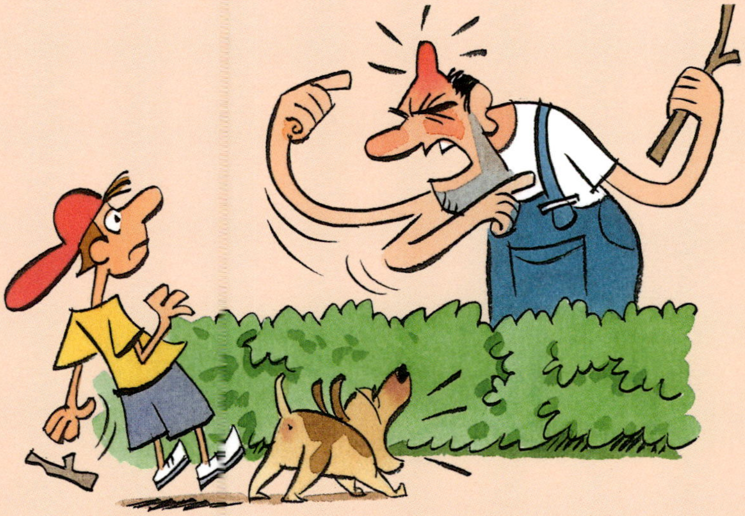

Comment appelle-t-on un boomerang qui ne revient pas ?

(Réponse : un bout de bois.)

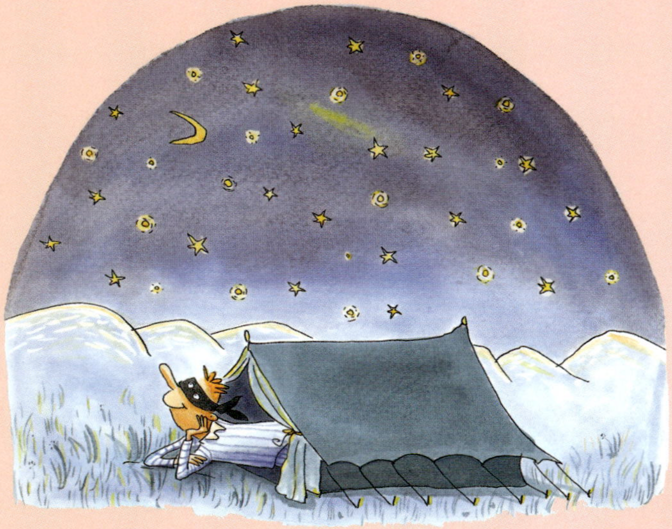

Histoire drôle

20

Août

Sherlock Holmes et le Dr Watson sont au camping. Après un bon repas et une bouteille de vin, ils gagnent leur sac de couchage pour la nuit et s'endorment.
Quelques heures plus tard, Holmes se réveille et aussitôt secoue son compagnon :

- Watson, regardez le ciel et dites-moi ce que vous voyez.
- Je vois des millions et des millions d'étoiles.
- Qu'est-ce que cela évoque pour vous ?
- Astronomiquement, répond Watson, cela me dit qu'il y a des millions de galaxies et potentiellement des milliards de planètes. Astrologiquement, j'observe que Saturne est en Lion. Horairement, j'en déduis qu'il est environ 3h 15. Théologiquement, je vois que Dieu est tout-puissant et que nous sommes petits et insignifiants. Météorologiquement, je pense que nous aurons une belle journée demain.

Et vous, Holmes ?

Sherlock Holmes reste silencieux une minute, puis déclare :

- Watson, vous êtes un abruti. Des voleurs nous ont fauché la tente.

Histoire drôle

21

Août

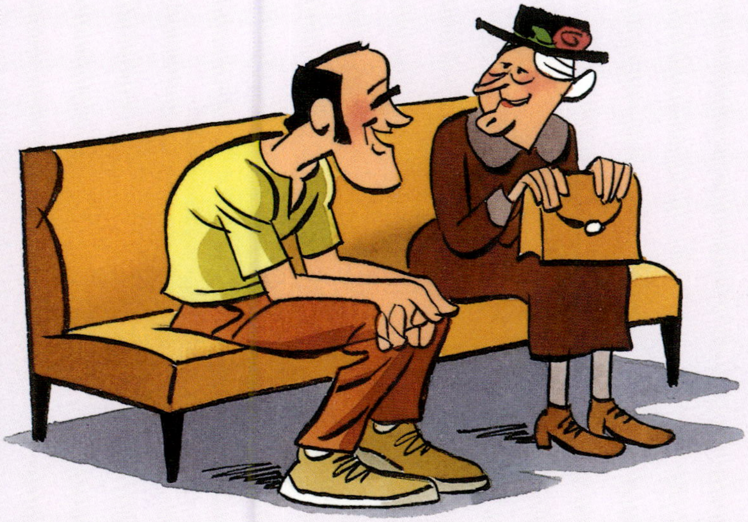

- Mon fils est né hier.
- Félicitations. Comment s'appelle-t-il ?
- Je ne sais pas, il ne parle pas encore.

Histoire drôle

22

Août

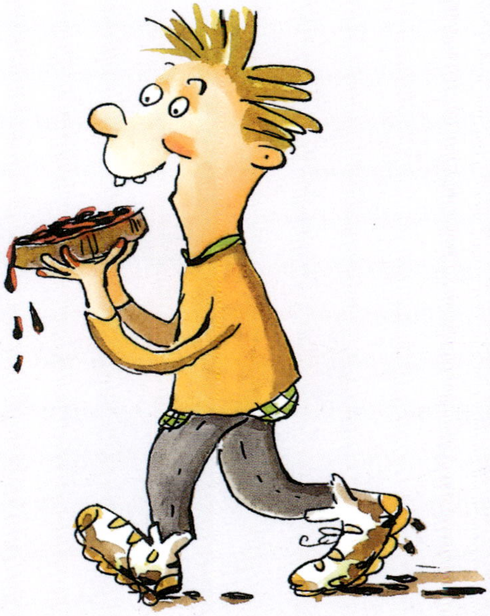

La maman dit à son fils :

- Tu as encore mis tes doigts sales sur la porte !
- C'est pas vrai ! Moi, justement, je l'ai ouverte avec le pied !

Histoire drôle

23 Août

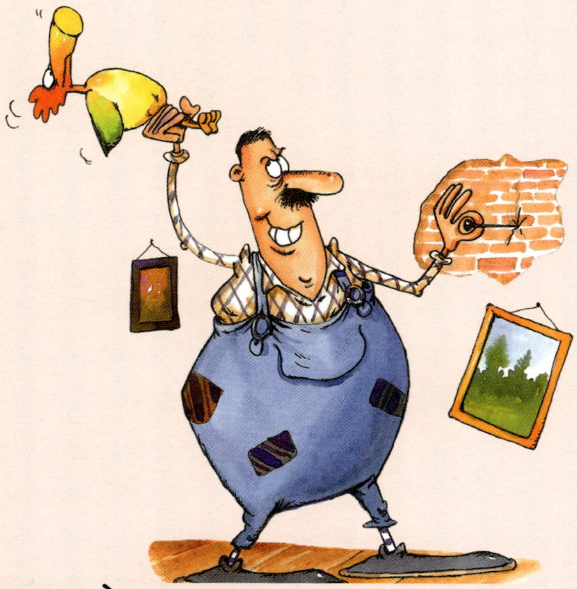

Un homme à son voisin :

- Depuis que ma femme a acheté un perroquet, je ne peux plus planter un clou à la maison.
- Ah bon ? s'étonne le voisin. À cause du bruit ?
- Non. Cette sale bête répète tous les gros mots que je dis quand je me tape sur les doigts !

Devinette

24 Août

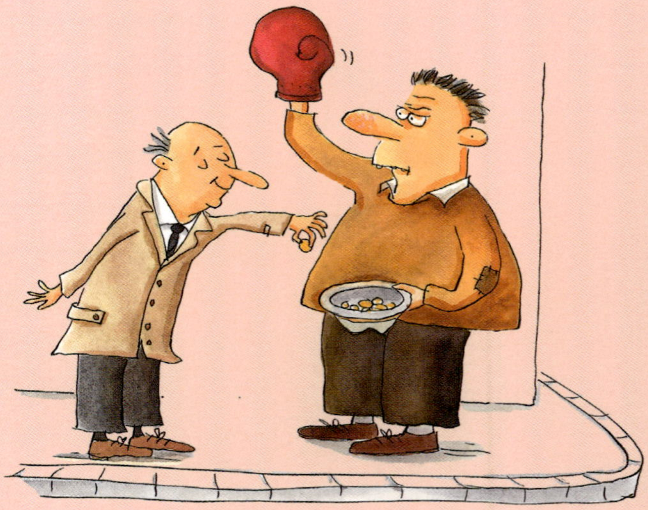

Qui préfère donner que recevoir ?

(Réponse : les boxeurs.)

Histoire drôle

25

Août

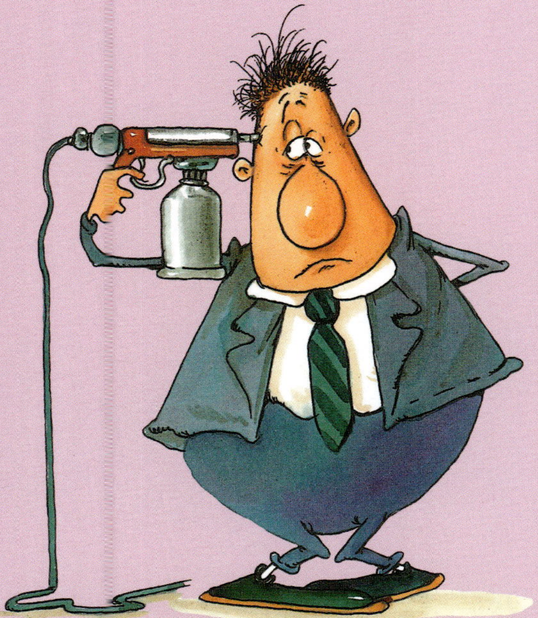

Un homme aux cheveux verts s'adresse à son magasin de bricolage favori.
- Bonjour, dit-il, je voudrais échanger mon pistolet à peinture contre un autre que je ne puisse pas confondre avec mon sèche-cheveux.

Devinette

26

Août

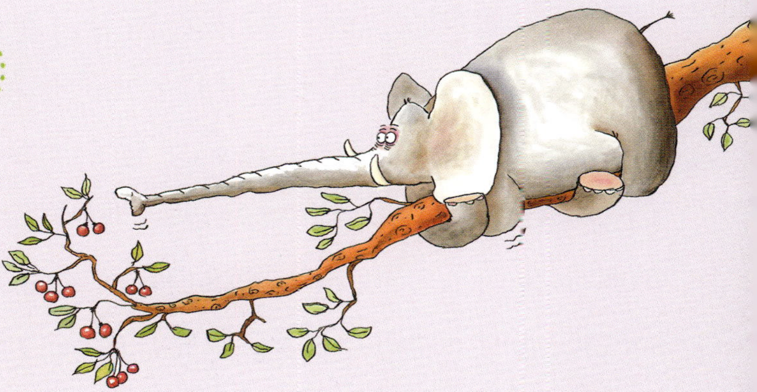

Pourquoi les éléphants montent-ils dans les cerisiers ?

(Réponse : parce qu'ils adorent manger des cerises.)

Histoire drôle

27

Août

Un homme entre dans un café avec un super berger allemand, et montre son chien avec beaucoup de fierté, décrivant ses muscles puissants, ses dents aiguisées et tranchantes, et son poil si doux. Bientôt un petit homme entre à son tour, accompagné d'un grand chien jaune tout maigre avec des grosses pattes. L'homme au berger allemand sourit ironiquement, mais le chien jaune se jette sur son beau berger et l'assomme en dix secondes.

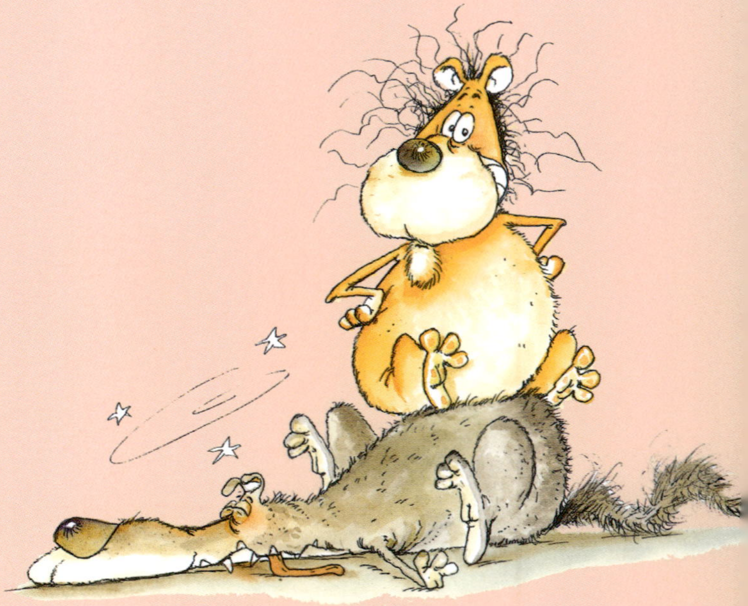

- Que... QUOI ? Votre chien jaune à grosses pattes a assommé mon beau chien musclé ? Il me le payera ! Attendez ici, je reviens !

Effectivement, dix minutes plus tard, il revient avec deux gros rottweillers qui attaquent le chien jaune sans ménagement, mais, pif ! paf ! les deux rottweillers sont assommés à leur tour sans difficulté par le chien jaune tout maigre.

- Quoi ! Votre chien jaune à grosses pattes a battu mes chiens ? Attendez-moi ici, je vais lui faire avaler sa queue, moi !

Il revient encore dix minutes plus tard avec deux dobermans enragés qui fondent sur le chien jaune et qui, pif ! paf ! sont assommés eux aussi en dix secondes par le chien jaune à grosses pattes. Cette fois, le propriétaire des chiens s'approche du petit homme au chien jaune et demande :

- C'est quoi, la race de ce chien ? Il est très fort !

- Je n'en sais rien, dit le petit homme. Tout ce que je peux vous dire, c'est qu'il était bien plus fort quand il avait sa crinière.

Petite annonce

28 Août

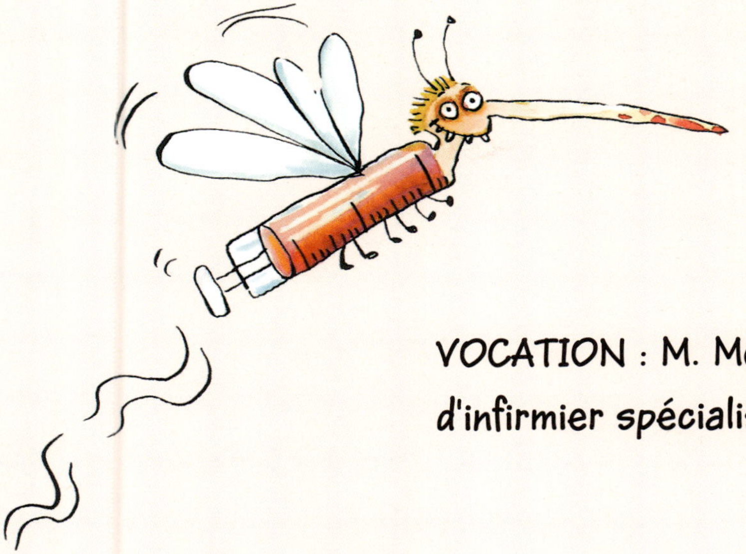

VOCATION : M. Moustique cherche place d'infirmier spécialiste des prises de sang.

Histoire drôle

29 Août

Un homme catastrophé entre dans une pharmacie.

- Je voudrais un remède radical contre le hoquet !

- Vraiment radical ? demande le pharmacien.

- Oui, c'est ça, ra-di-cal.

Le pharmacien lui donne alors une énorme paire de claques sur la figure.

- Eh bien ! dit-il en souriant, il est passé votre hoquet, maintenant ?

L'homme, tout penaud, se frotte les joues en répondant :

- C'est-à-dire que le remède, c'était pour ma femme, qui attend dans la voiture...

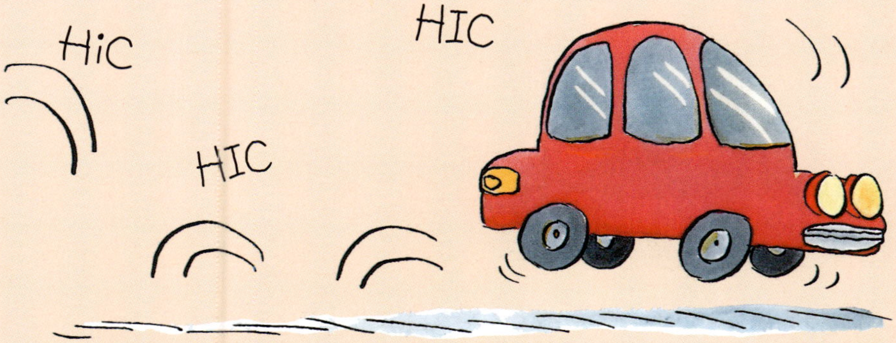

Petite annonce

30 Août

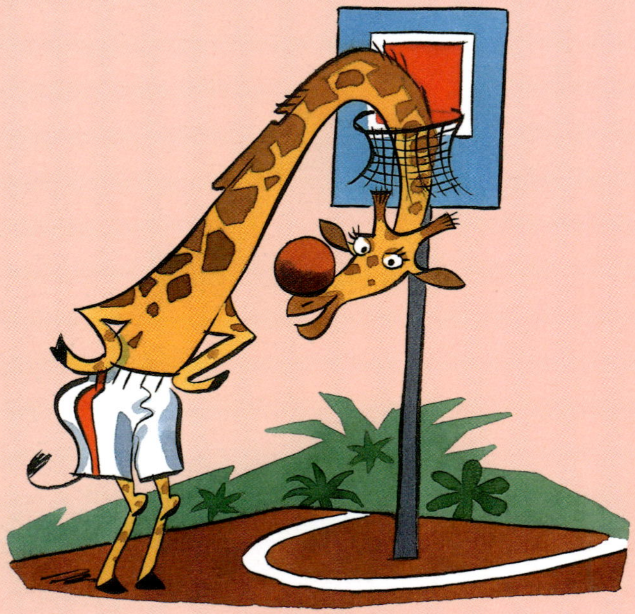

SPORT : Mlle Girafe est sélectionnée pour le championnat du monde de basket-ball.

Devinette

31 Août

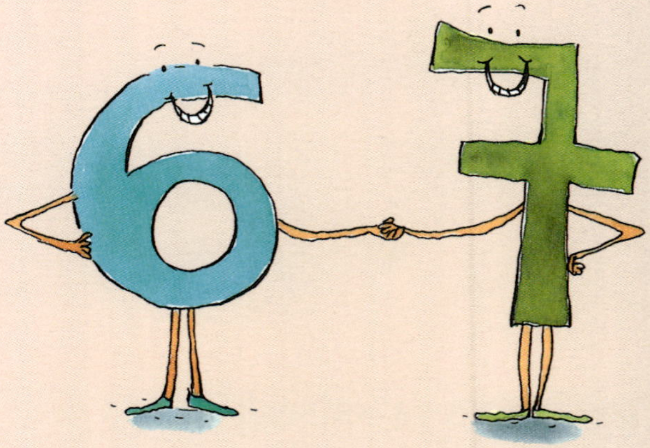

Faut-il dire 6 et 7 font « onze », ou 6 et 7 font « t-onze » (avec la liaison) ?

(Réponse : ni l'un ni l'autre ; ça fait treize.)

Histoire drôle

1

Septembre

Sur une plage, un vacancier ramasse un coquillage et le porte à son oreille pour entendre la mer. Mais au lieu du doux reflux, il entend :

- Bonjour, vous êtes bien sur le répondeur de la mer Méditerranée. Je suis absente pour le moment, mais vous pouvez laisser un message après le bip.

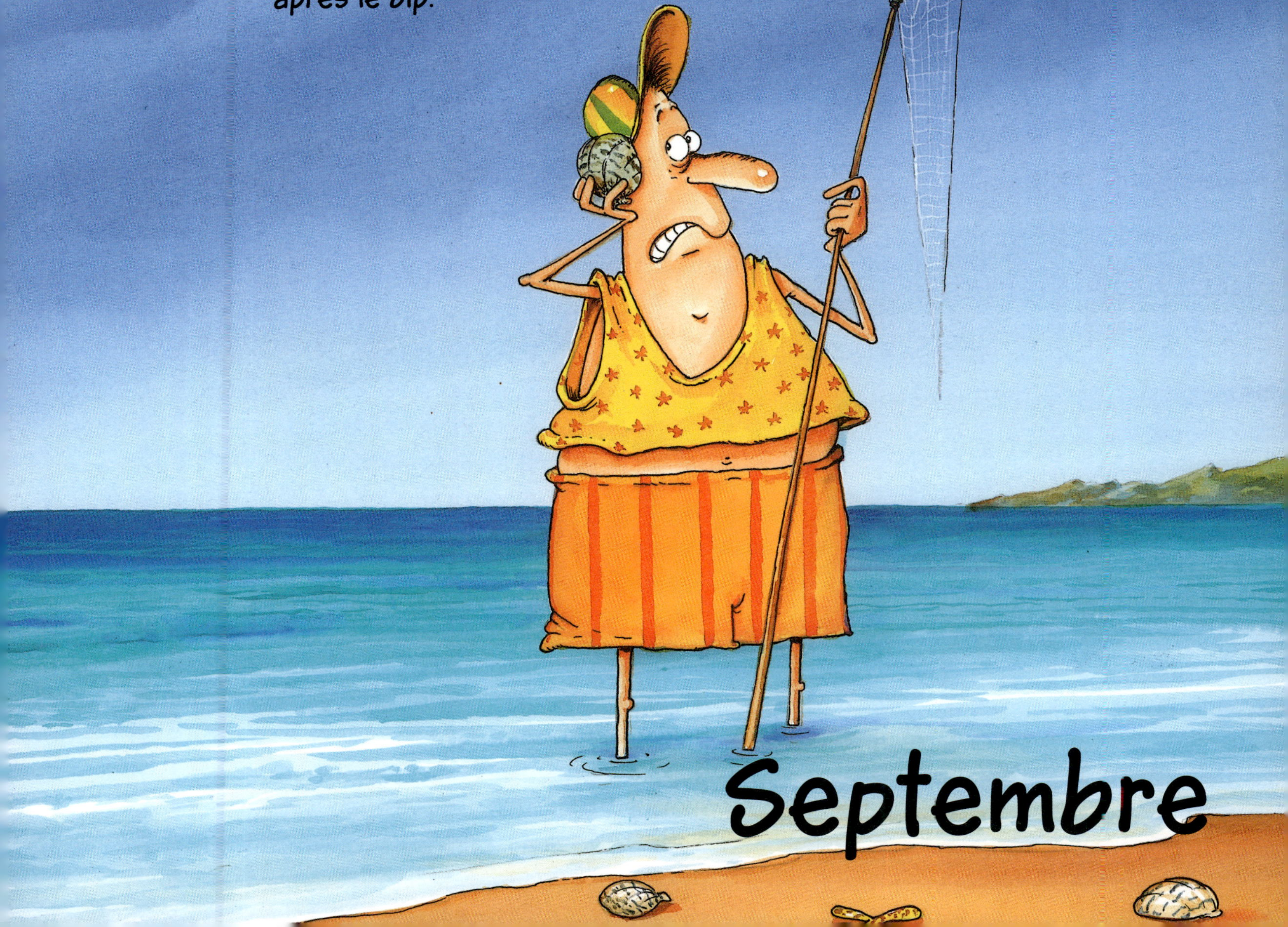

Septembre

Histoire drôle

2 Septembre

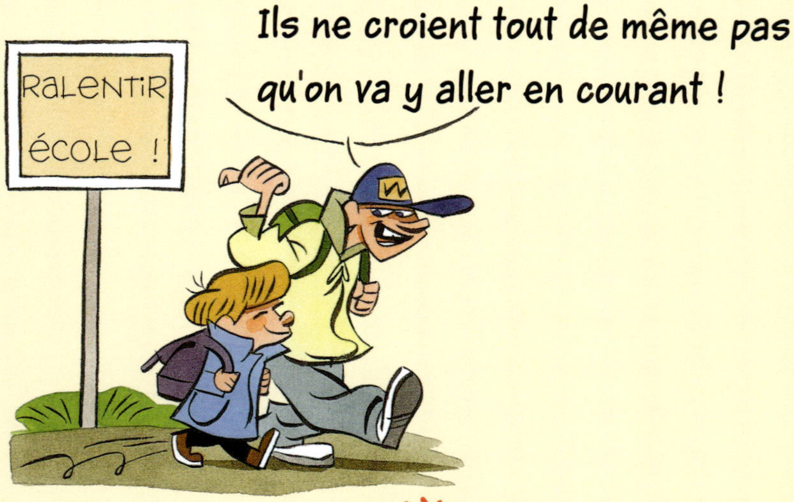

Petite annonce

3 Septembre

SERVICE : ogre sympathique débarrasse gratuitement maîtres et maîtresses d'école de leurs enfants turbulents.

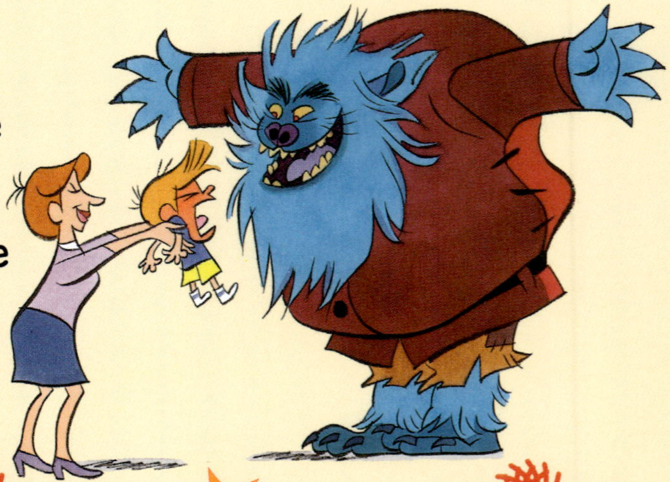

Devinette

4 Septembre

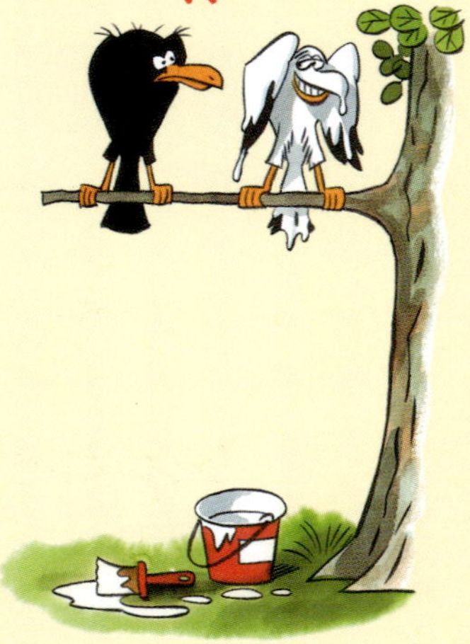

Qu'est-ce qui est noir quand il est propre,
et blanc quand il est sale ?

(Réponse : le tableau noir du maître d'école.)

Un pâtissier ouvre sa pâtisserie. Un enfant entre et demande :

- Bonjour, monsieur. Vous avez des tartes aux épinards ?
- Non, mon petit, répond le pâtissier, navré.

Le lendemain, à l'ouverture de la pâtisserie, deux enfants entrent.

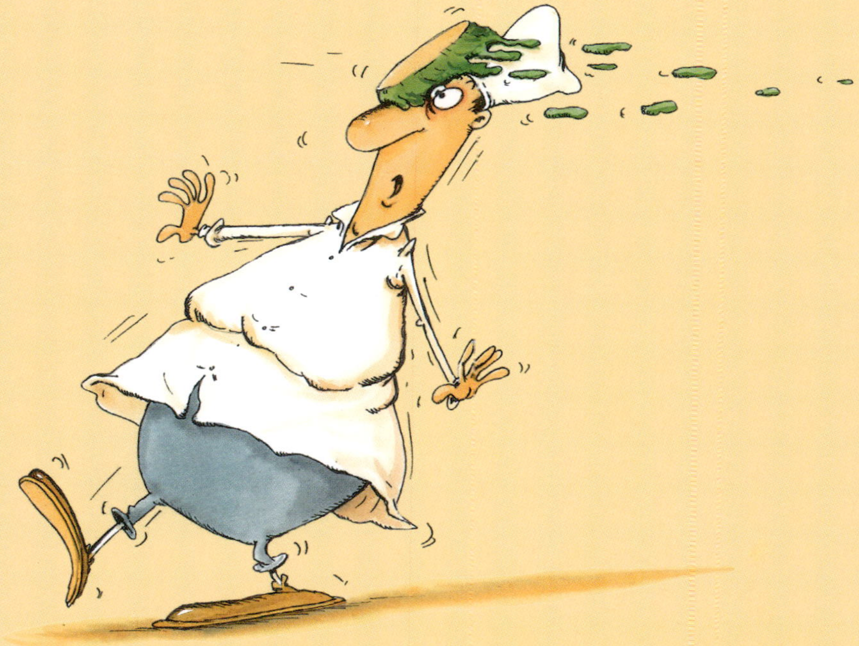

- Bonjour, monsieur. Vous avez des tartes aux épinards ?
- Non, mes enfants, je suis désolé, je ne fais pas de tartes aux épinards.

Le lendemain, à l'ouverture de la pâtisserie, trois enfants entrent.

- Bonjour, monsieur. Vous avez des tartes aux épinards ?
- NON ! se fâche le pâtissier, je n'en ai pas ! Fichez le camp !

Ainsi, chaque matin, 4, 5, 6, 7, 10, 15, 20 enfants viennent dans la pâtisserie demander, devinez quoi ? des tartes aux épinards !

Le 23ème jour, cette fois, le pâtissier a préparé tout un stock de tartes aux épinards, pour clouer le bec à tous ces gamins qui lui gâchent la vie depuis si longtemps.

Et ça ne rate pas : à l'ouverture de la pâtisserie, vingt-trois enfants entrent et demandent :

- Bonjour, monsieur. Vous avez des tartes aux épinards ?
- OUI ! OUI ! J'en ai ! Une montagne de tartes aux épinards !

Et là, les enfants éclatent de rire en s'écriant :

- C'est pas bon, hein !

Histoire drôle

5

Septembre

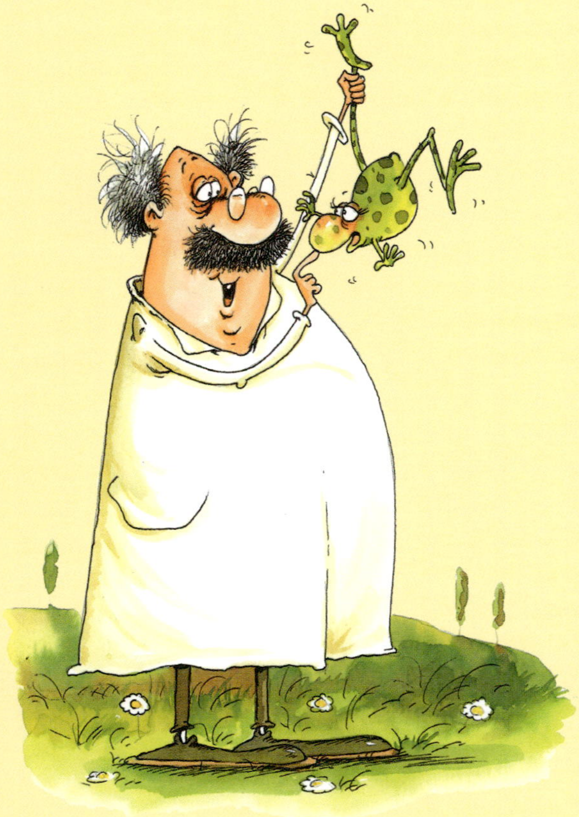

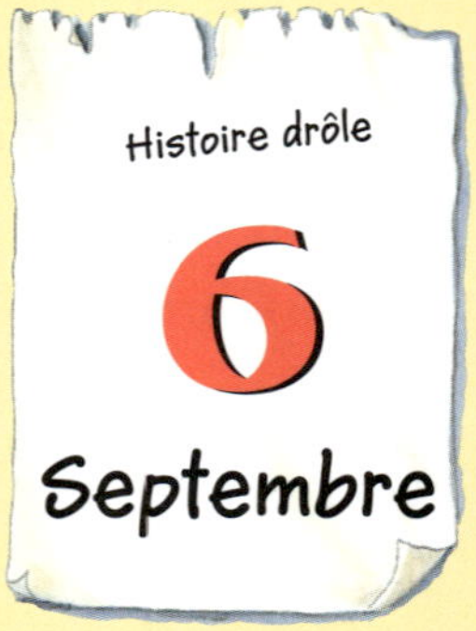

Un mathématicien se promène dans un village, lorsqu'il entend une grenouille l'appeler.

- Hé ! jeune homme, si tu m'embrasses, je deviendrai une magnifique princesse.

Le mathématicien se baisse, ramasse la grenouille, la regarde et la met dans sa poche en souriant.

La grenouille commence à s'impatienter.

- Hé ! jeune homme, si tu m'embrasses, je deviendrai une magnifique princesse et je resterai avec toi pendant trois mois.

Le mathématicien prend la grenouille dans sa main, la regarde en souriant et la remet dans sa poche sans rien dire. La grenouille s'énerve.

- Hé ! jeune homme, si tu m'embrasses, je deviendrai une magnifique princesse, et je resterai avec toi pendant trois mois et je ferai ton ménage, ton repassage, ta vaisselle, tout ce qui t'ennuie. Le mathématicien sort la grenouille de sa poche, l'observe un instant et l'y remet à nouveau. Cette fois, la grenouille n'en peut plus.

- QUOI ! s'écrie-t-elle, je te propose de me transformer en princesse, de rester avec toi et de faire toutes tes corvées, et tu ne m'embrasses toujours pas ? Qu'est-ce qu'il faut que je te promette pour que tu te décides ?

- Vois-tu, répond le mathématicien en prenant la grenouille, mon métier est passionnant, mais il me prend trop de temps pour avoir en plus une petite amie. Par contre, une grenouille qui parle, ça, c'est vachement chouette !

Histoire drôle

7

Septembre

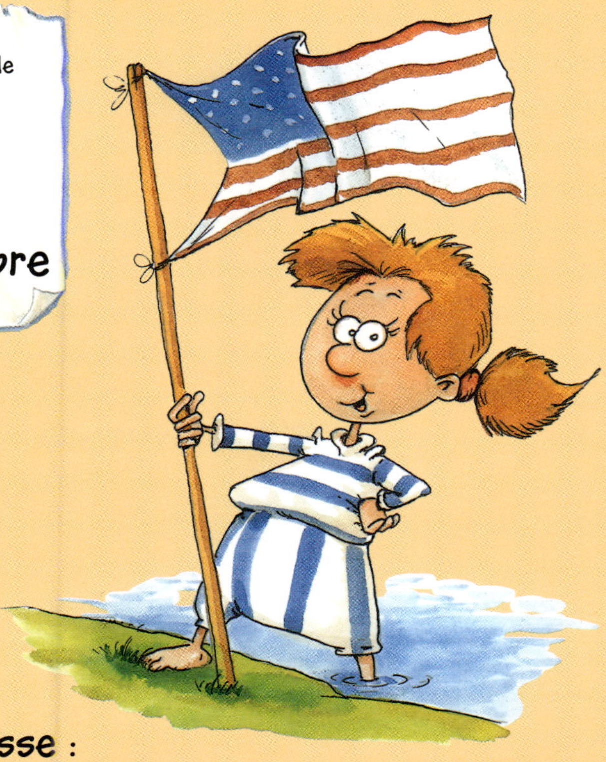

La maîtresse :

- Laura ! va au tableau.

Laura se lève et va devant le tableau.

- Très bien. Maintenant, montre-nous sur la carte du monde à quel endroit se trouve l'Amérique du Nord.

Laura prend la grande règle jaune et indique parfaitement le continent américain.

- C'est bien, la félicite la maîtresse. Maintenant, qui, dans la classe, peut me dire qui a découvert l'Amérique ?

Lydia lève la main.

- C'est Laura, maîtresse !

Histoire drôle

8

Septembre

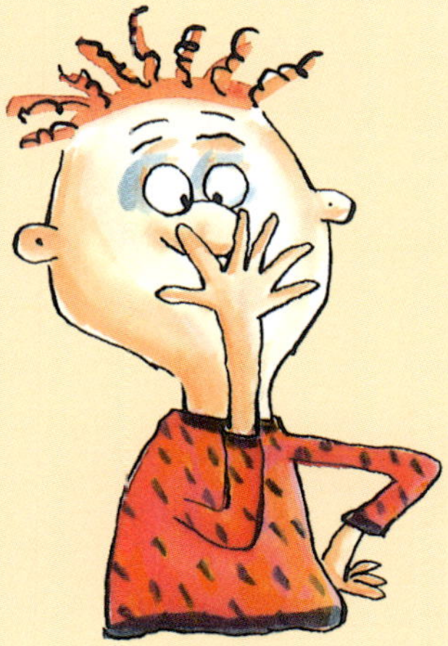

David rentre de l'école avec ses copains.

- Je vais avoir un zéro au contrôle de maths.

- Tu es sûr ?

- Aussi sûr que deux et deux font cinq.

Histoire drôle

9

Septembre

La maîtresse demande à Sébastien :

- Quels sont les os qui constituent le crâne ?

- Euh... J'ai oublié leurs noms, mais je peux vous assurer qu'hier je les avais tous en tête.

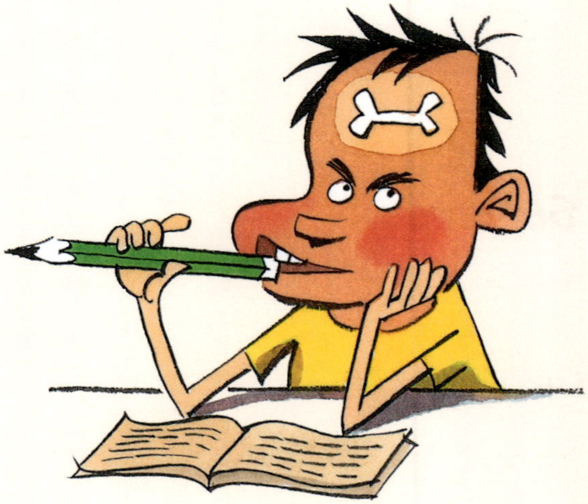

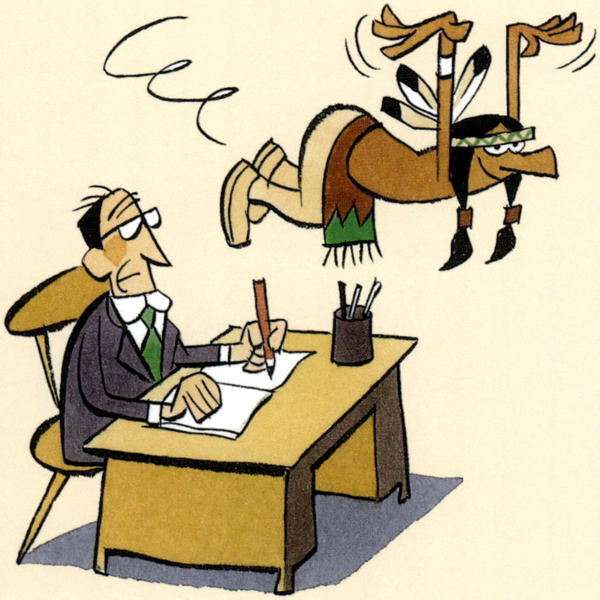

Un Indien se présente au bureau de l'état civil et déclare vouloir changer de nom.

- Comment vous nommez-vous ? demande l'employé.

- Je m'appelle « Petit Oiseau Qui Vole Dans L'Air Calme Du Matin En Chantant Dans L'Azur ».

- Et comment souhaitez-vous vous nommer ?

- « Cui Cui ».

Histoire drôle

10

Septembre

Histoire drôle

11
Septembre

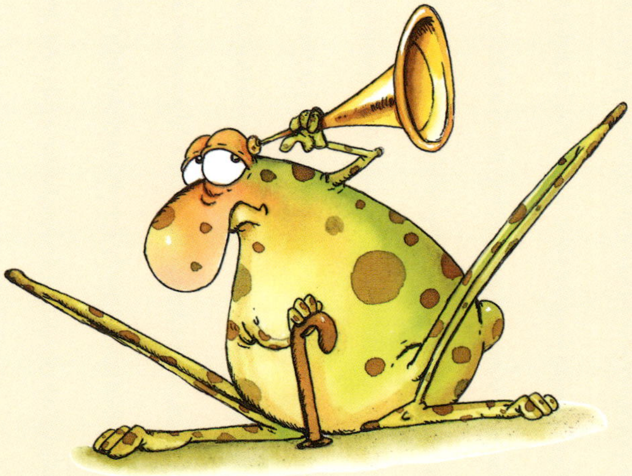

Un savant fou réalise une expérience sur une grenouille. Il lui attache une patte dans le dos et lui demande de sauter. La grenouille saute. Ensuite, il lui attache une deuxième patte dans le dos et lui demande de sauter. La grenouille saute. Il lui attache une troisième patte dans le dos, lui demande de sauter, et, tant bien que mal, la grenouille parvient à sauter. Enfin, il lui attache la quatrième patte dans le dos et lui demande de sauter. Bien évidemment, la grenouille ne saute pas. Il lui redemande en parlant un peu plus fort, toujours pas de saut, puis se met carrément à crier, mais la grenouille, les quatre pattes attachées, ne peut pas sauter. Le savant fou téléphone donc à un ami scientifique.

- J'ai les résultats, dit-il : Si on attache les quatre pattes d'une grenouille dans son dos, elle devient totalement sourde.

Petite annonce

12
Septembre

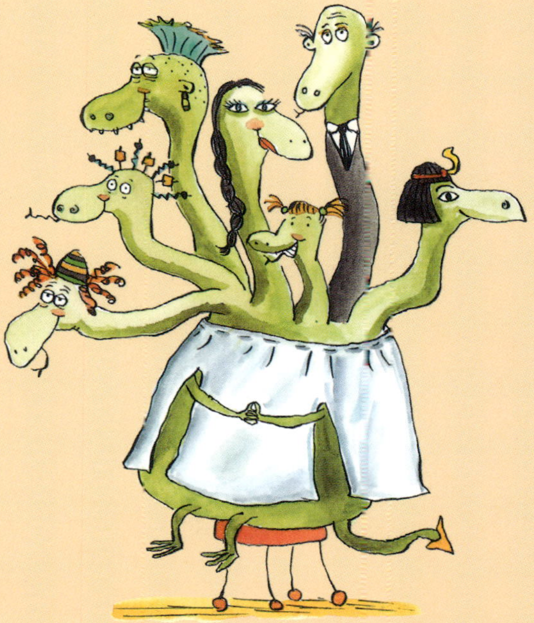

COMMERCE :
monstre à sept têtes
cherche coiffeur à
quatorze bras.

Histoire drôle

13

Septembre

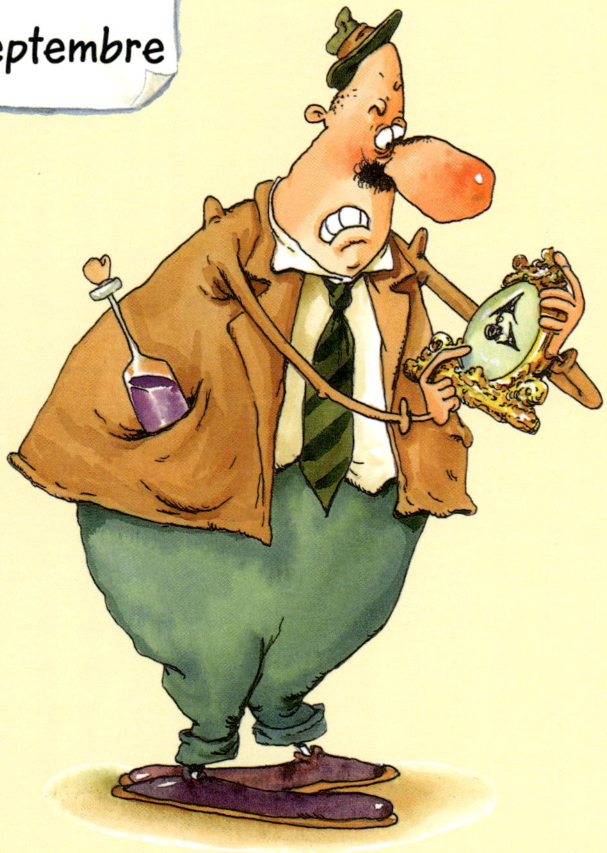

Un homme ivre rentre chez lui tard dans la nuit, au moment où son horloge sonne trois coups.

Il la regarde d'un air mauvais en pestant :

- Je sais qu'il est une heure, pas besoin de le répéter trois fois !

Histoire drôle

14

Septembre

Un paresseux va consulter son médecin pour des insomnies.

- Je ne comprends pas pourquoi je n'arrive pas à dormir la nuit, alors que, toute la journée, je dors si bien à mon travail !

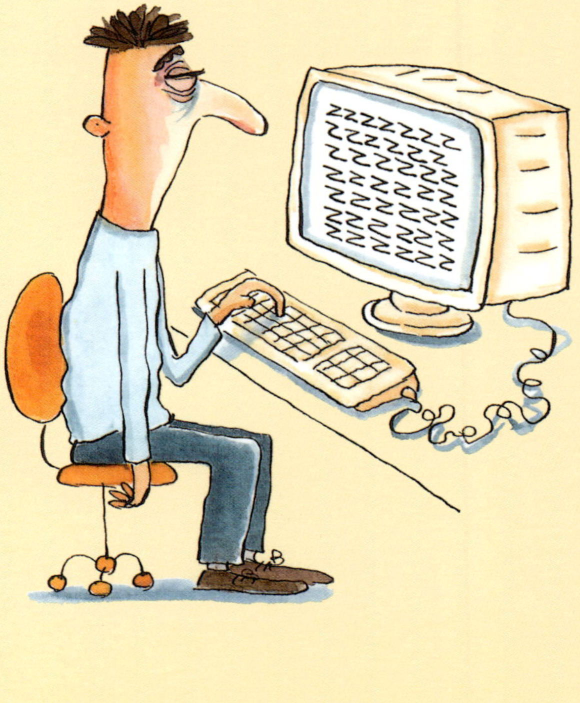

Histoire drôle

15

Septembre

Un fou prend le bus tous les matins et, chaque fois, il achète deux tickets pour le même trajet. Comme cela tous les matins. Au bout d'une semaine, le contrôleur, très intrigué, lui demande :

- Écoutez, pourquoi donc achetez-vous deux tickets alors qu'un seul suffit ?
- C'est très simple, lui répond le fou. Je mets un ticket dans ma poche droite et l'autre dans ma poche gauche. Si je perds le ticket de la poche droite, il me reste celui de la poche gauche. Si je perds celui de la poche gauche, j'ai encore celui de la poche droite !
- Ah oui ? Et si vous les perdez tous les deux en même temps ?
- Ce n'est pas grave, lui répond le fou, j'ai un abonnement !

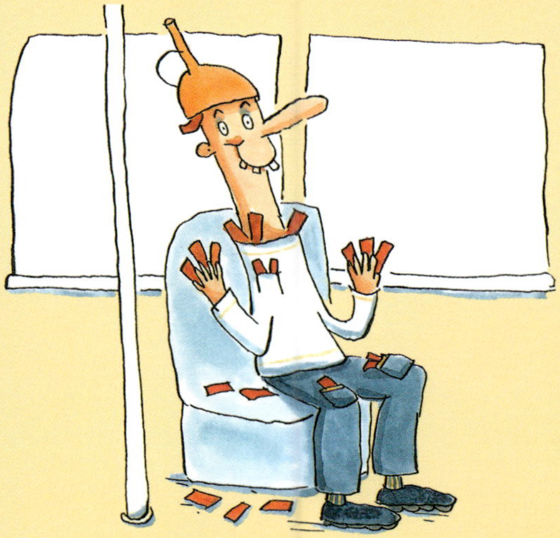

Petite annonce

16

Septembre

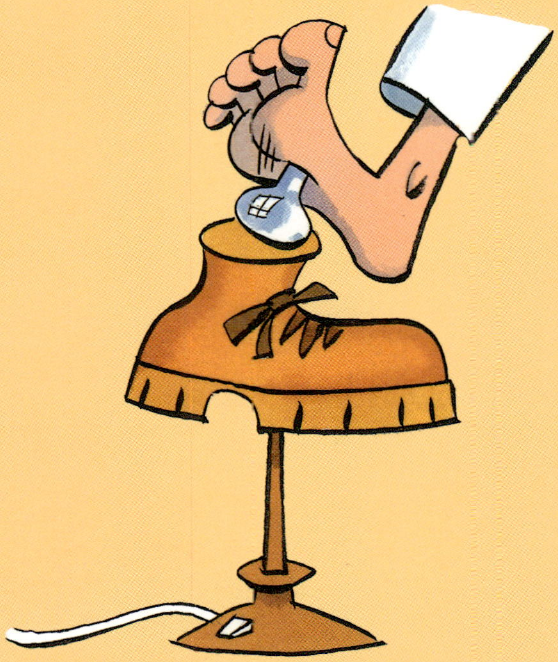

LUMIÈRE : ampoule au pied cherche lampe-chaussure.

Histoire drôle

17 Septembre

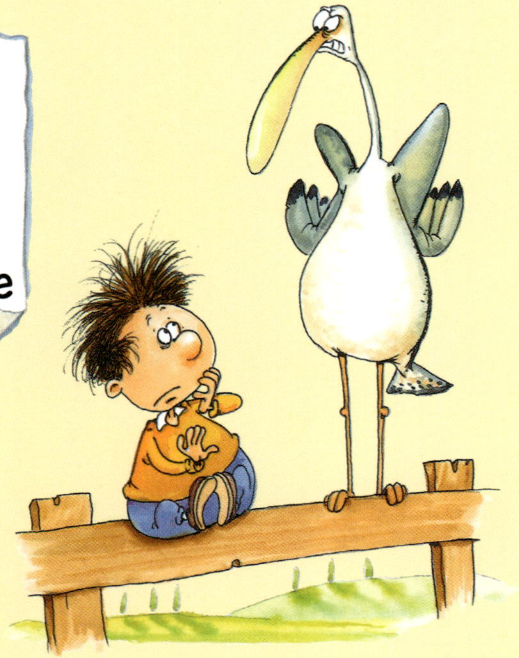

Un petit garçon, à la campagne, un peu rêveur, vient s'asseoir sur une clôture en bois, lève la tête, regarde le ciel et crie :
« Tapon, tapon ...tapon ! »
Rien ne se produit. Alors il insiste en scrutant le ciel de tous côtés :
«Tapon ...tapon ...tapon ! »
Soudain, un grand oiseau apparaît dans le ciel, il descend vers le petit garçon en planant majestueusement. Il vient se poser près de lui sur la clôture et lui dit :
- Héron, héron, petit, pas tapon !

Petite annonce

18 Septembre

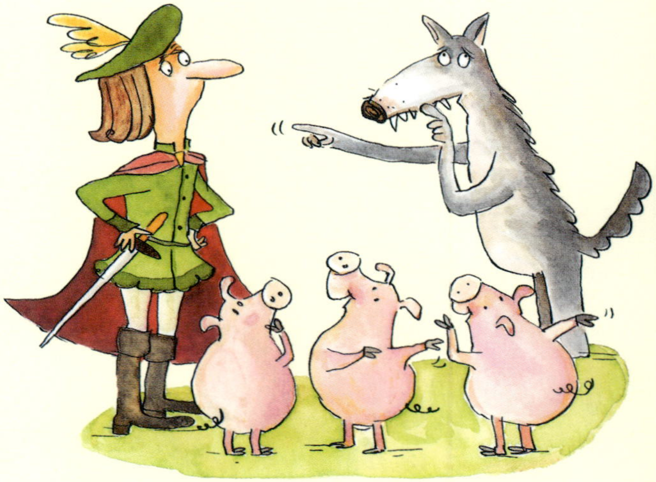

URGENT : prince charmant égaré cherche une bonne carte du pays des contes pour retrouver le château de la Belle au bois dormant.

Petite annonce
19
Septembre

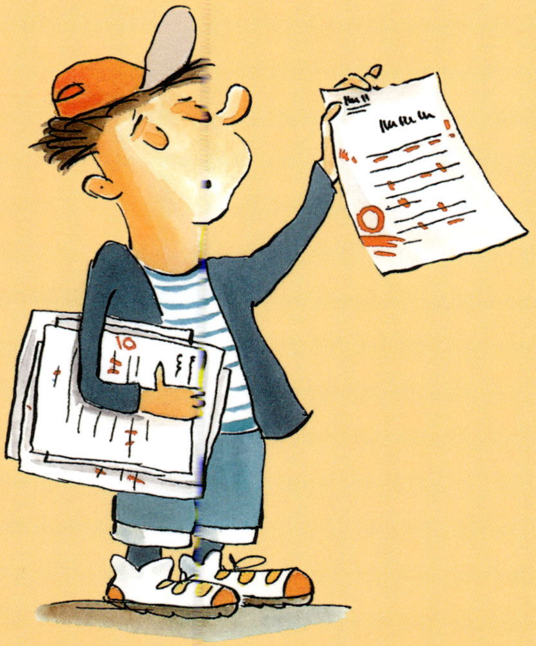

ÉCOLE : élève généreux donne tous ses devoirs gratuitement.

Dans un restaurant, un homme passe sa commande :

- Je voudrais une salade pas trop croquante, un steak pas trop cuit, des frites pas trop salées, et comme dessert... une poire pas trop mûre et un café pas trop fort.

Le garçon note tout très fidèlement et lui demande :

- Et comme boisson ? Vous préférez une limonade avec pas trop de bulles, ou de l'eau pas trop mouillée ?

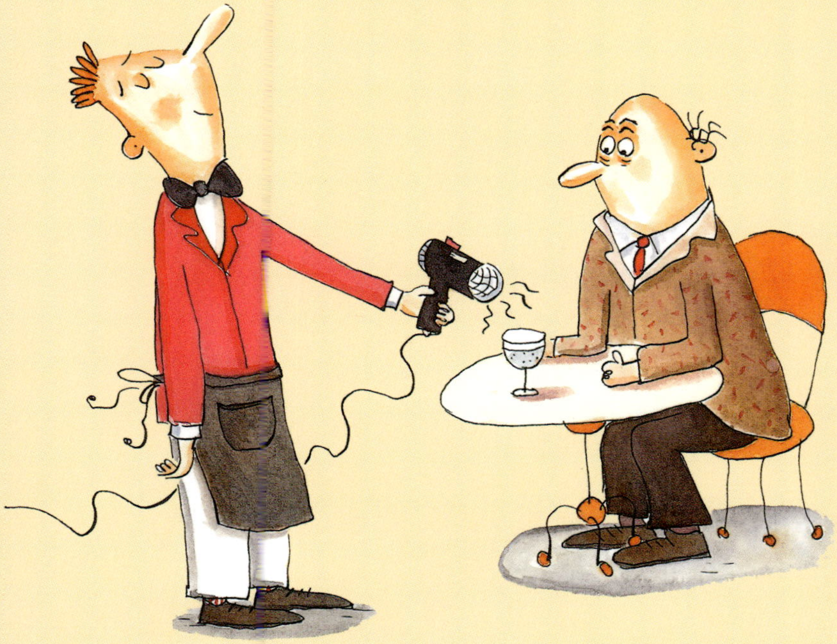

Histoire drôle
20
Septembre

Histoire drôle
21
Septembre

Un pou en rencontre un autre.

- Tu es malade ?

- Non, j'ai juste reçu un coup de peigne, ce matin.

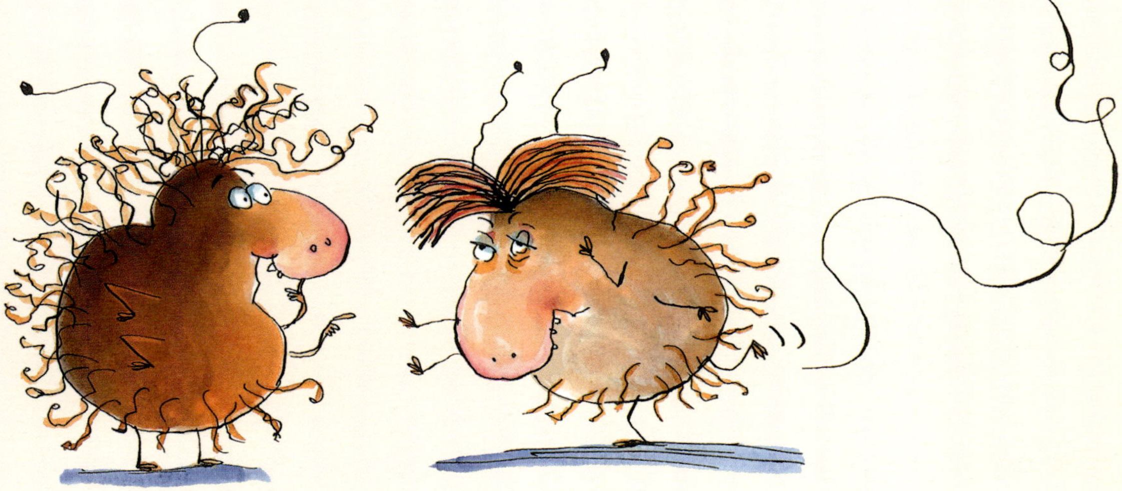

Pierre demande à sa sœur :

- Ça a des pattes, une olive noire ?

- Bien sûr que non, idiot !

- Bon, alors j'ai dû avaler un scarabée.

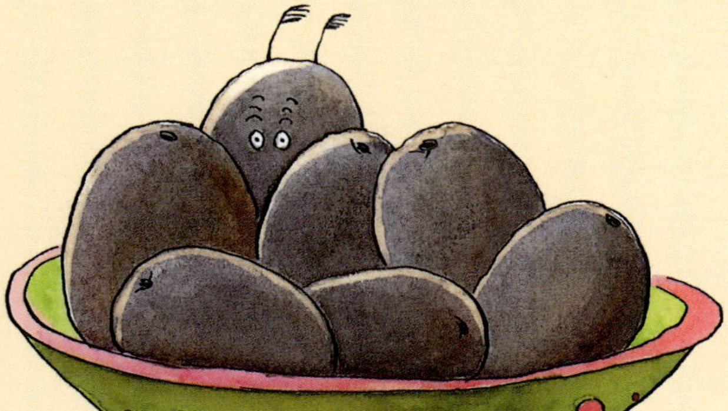

Histoire drôle
22
Septembre

Histoire drôle

23 Septembre

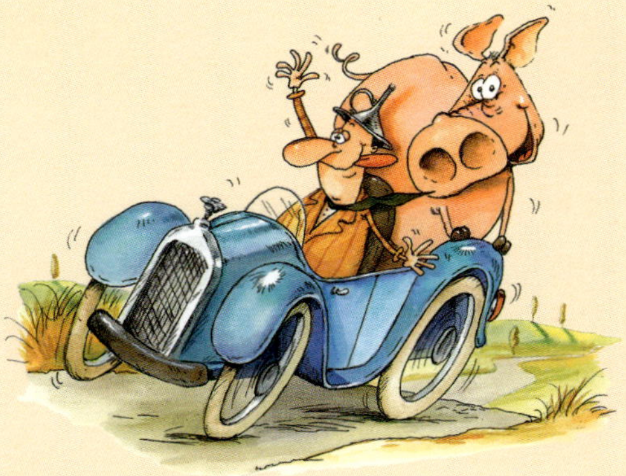

Un homme se promène en voiture en pleine campagne, lorsqu'il aperçoit un jeune cochon sauvage abandonné au milieu de la route.
Il décide de prendre l'animal à bord de sa voiture et regagne la ville. Un policier l'arrête à un carrefour.
- Vous ne pouvez pas garder ce cochon dans votre véhicule. C'est interdit. Vous feriez mieux de l'emmener au zoo.
- C'est une bonne idée, réplique l'homme, ravi.
Le lendemain, au même carrefour, le même agent aperçoit le même cochon, dans la même voiture avec le même conducteur.
- Qu'est-ce que vous faites encore là avec cet animal ? Je vous ai dit de l'emmener au zoo !
- C'est ce que j'ai fait, répond l'automobiliste.
Il a beaucoup aimé la visite. Et maintenant, je l'emmène voir un film au cinéma.

Petite annonce

24 Septembre

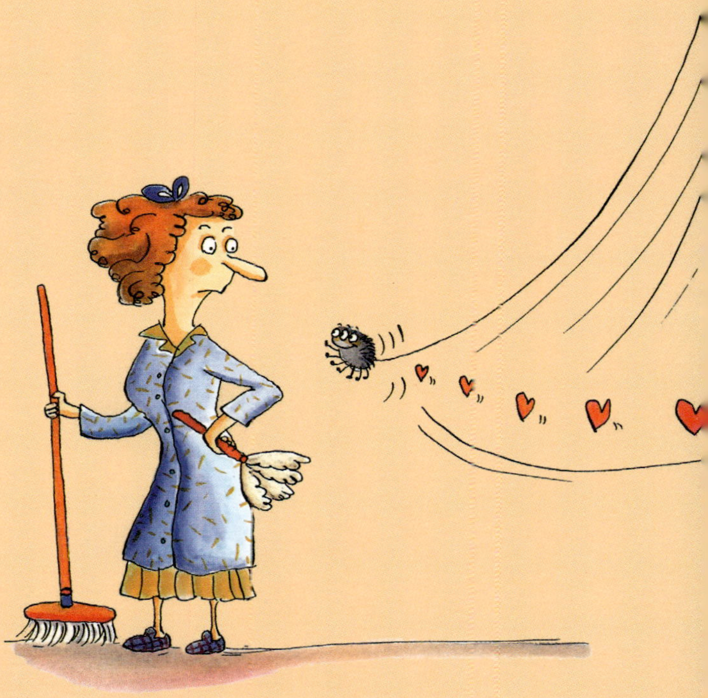

MÉDECINE : araignée myope à huit yeux cherche opticien pas cher.

Histoire drôle

25

Septembre

- Patrick, dit un père à son jeune fils, cette passion que tu as pour les westerns ne doit pas t'empêcher de faire tes devoirs. Si tu n'éteins pas immédiatement cette télé, je descends de mon cheval, je pose mes revolvers, j'enlève mes éperons et mes bottes, et je te donne une fessée !

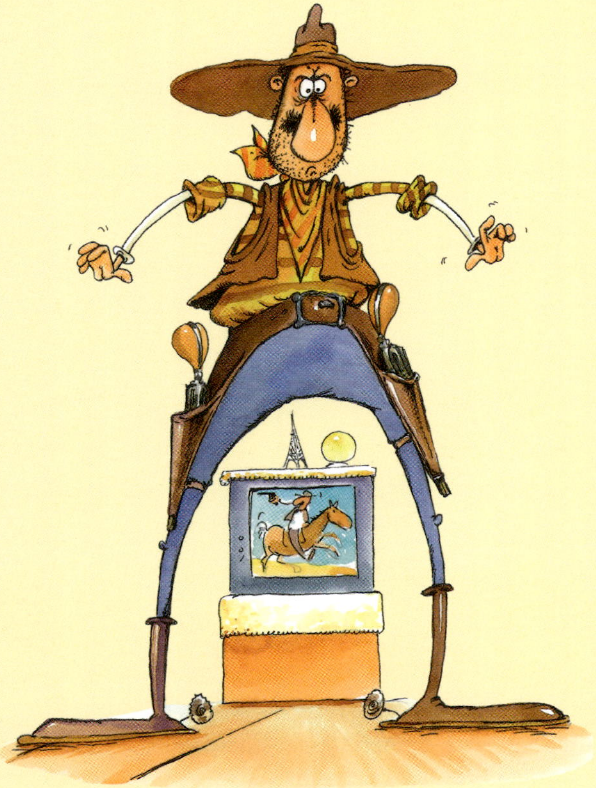

Devinette

26

Septembre

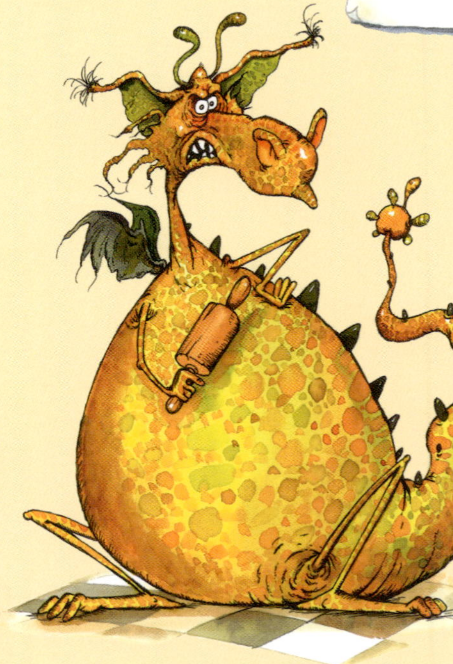

Quelle est la différence entre une maman très en colère et un dragon enragé ?

- Vous avez déjà vu un dragon avec du rouge à lèvres ?

Histoire drôle

27

Septembre

Bastien va voir sa mamie.

- Mamie, si tu devines combien j'ai de bonbons dans la main, je te les donne tous les deux.

- Tu en as deux, répond la mamie.

- Oh ! Comment as-tu deviné ?

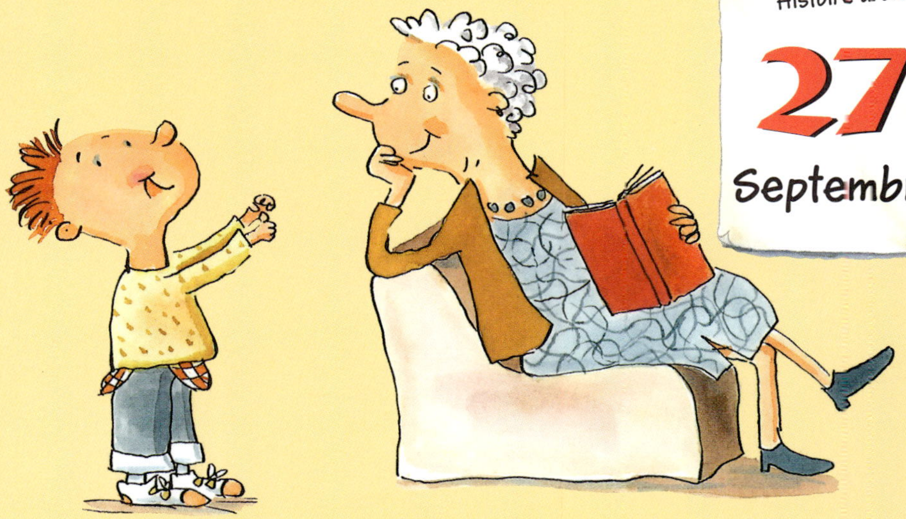

Une dame dispute son mari.

- Tu es vraiment fou de ta télé ! Tu ne penses plus qu'à ça !

- C'est faux, se défend le mari, je ne vois pas du tout pourquoi tu me dis ça !

- Parce que je viens de te dire à l'instant : « Viens voir le magnifique arc-en-ciel », et que tu m'as répondu : « Sur quelle chaîne ? ».

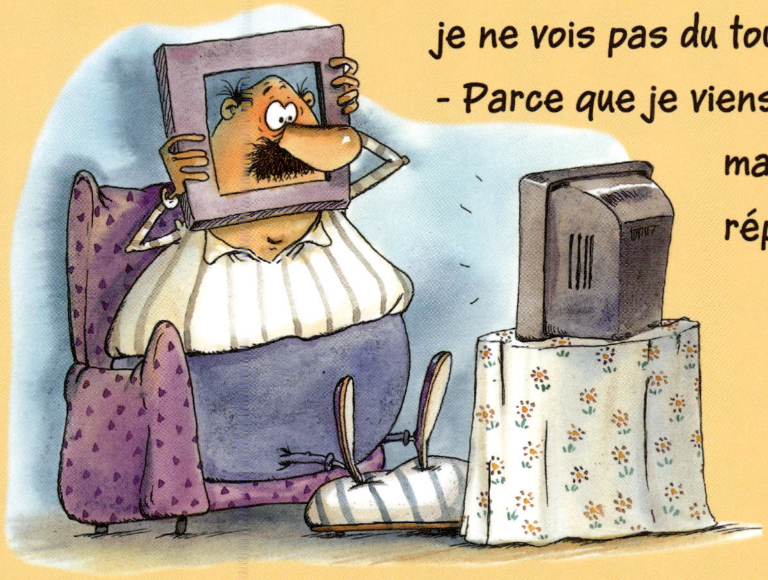

Histoire drôle

28

Septembre

Histoire drôle

29

Septembre

Une petite fille de six ans se met à crier en pleine nuit :

- Maman ! Maman !

Tirée de son sommeil par ces cris, la maman accourt, complètement affolée.

- Qu'est-ce qu'il y a, ma chérie ? Tu as fait un cauchemar ? Tu as mal quelque part ?

- Non, maman, j'ai juste soif. Tu peux m'apporter de l'eau ?

Très mécontente, la mère sermonne l'enfant.

- Tu n'as pas honte de me faire une peur pareille en pleine nuit, juste pour un peu d'eau ?

- C'est vrai, maman, excuse-moi. Tu peux m'apporter un Coca ?

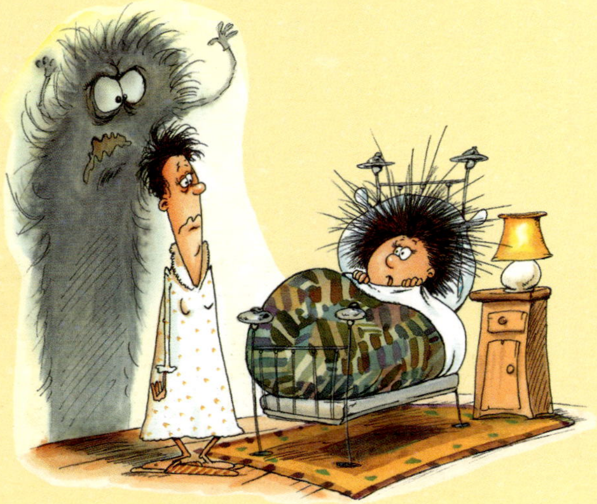

Petite annonce

30

Septembre

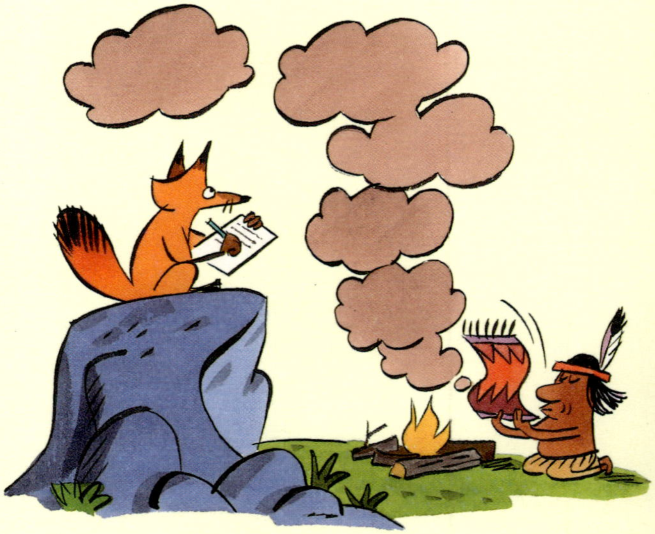

ENTRE PROS : renard échange ruses avec Sioux.

Un jeune trappeur est parti s'installer dans le Grand Nord canadien, mais il manque d'expérience. Il a un peu peur de l'hiver qui approche. Il ne sait pas si la réserve de bois qu'il a coupé est suffisante pour tenir tout l'hiver. Alors, il va voir un vieil Indien sur la colline pour lui demander conseil.

Le vieil Indien plisse les yeux, scrute l'horizon au loin dans la vallée, et dit :

- Hiver sera froid ! Le petit trappeur redescend vite dans la vallée et retourne à sa cabane couper plus de bois. Quand il en a coupé une bonne quantité supplémentaire, il remonte sur la colline et demande à nouveau conseil au vieil Indien pour être rassuré. Le vieil Indien plein de sagesse plisse les yeux, scrute l'horizon au loin dans la vallée, et dit : - Hiver sera très froid !

Alors, le petit trappeur redescend vite à sa cabane, couper encore plus de bois avant les premiers flocons. Il en a maintenant un tas énorme. Pour être vraiment rassuré, il remonte sur la colline voir le vieil Indien. Celui-ci à nouveau se concentre, plisse les yeux, scrute l'horizon au loin dans la vallée, et dit :

- Hiver sera très très froid !

Et le petit trappeur de s'exclamer : - Mais enfin, grand chef, comment pouvez-vous savoir que l'hiver sera si froid ?

- Nous avons chez nous un dicton, lui répond le vieil Indien : « Plus trappeur coupe du bois, plus hiver sera froid ! »

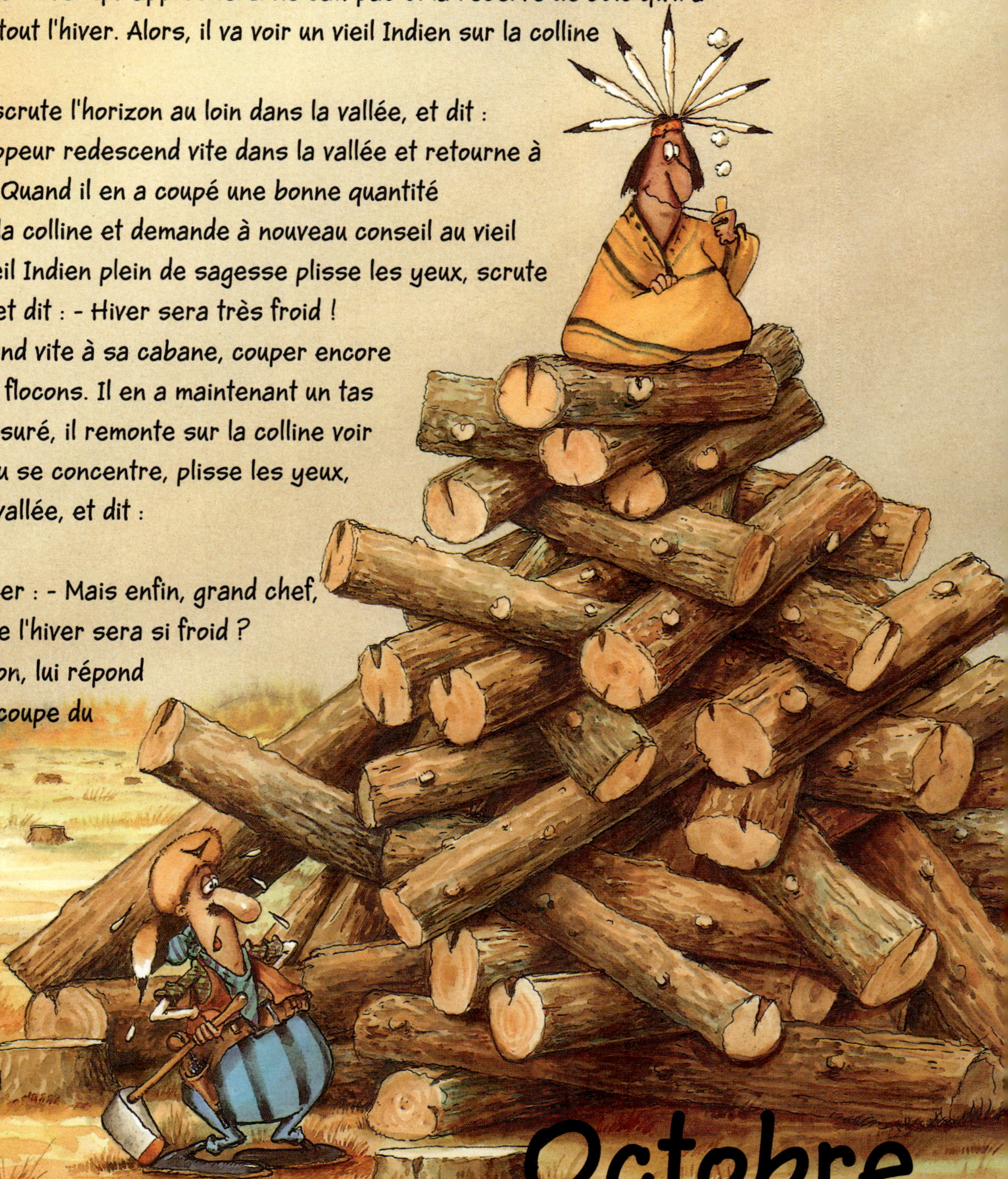

Histoire drôle

1

Octobre

Octobre

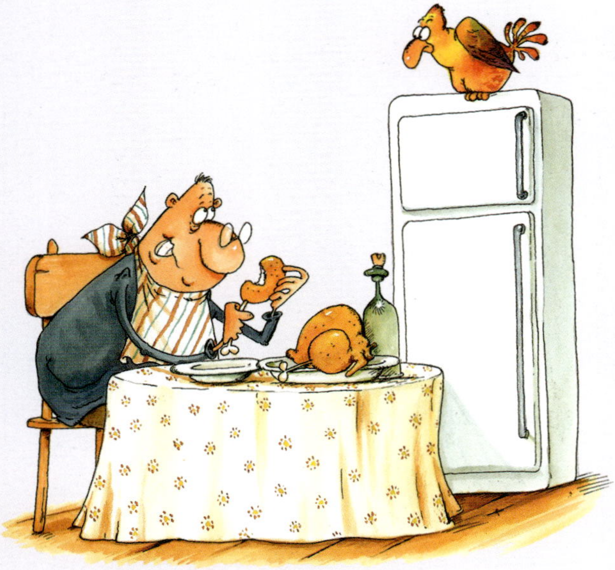

Un jeune homme a acheté un perroquet pas très cher dans une animalerie. Arrivé chez lui, il se rend compte que le perroquet sait très bien parler, mais qu'il ne dit que des horribles gros mots chaque fois qu'il ouvre la bouche.

Histoire drôle

2

Octobre

Au début, c'est supportable, mais, au fil des jours, le jeune homme n'en peut plus.

- Si tu ne cesses pas de dire des gros mots, je t'enferme dans le placard à chaussures ! Le perroquet s'en fiche. Le jeune homme l'enferme donc trois heures dans le placard à chaussures, mais rien ne change.

- Si tu ne cesses pas de dire des gros mots, je te mets sur le balcon, sous la neige, pendant toute la nuit !

Le perroquet s'en fiche, le jeune homme le met donc sur le balcon toute la nuit, dans le froid hivernal. Mais rien ne change. Le perroquet continue à dire des gros mots.

Cette fois, le jeune homme, excédé, attrape le perroquet et l'enferme une journée entière dans son réfrigérateur. Or, surprise, lorsque le perroquet ressort du frigo, il ne dit plus de gros mots, au contraire : - Je vous prie de bien vouloir m'excuser de mes grossièretés passées, je me rends bien compte maintenant qu'il n'est pas digne de vous de garder un oiseau qui ne sait qu'injurier les gens à longueur de journée. Vous pouvez me faire confiance, désormais je saurai me tenir. Le jeune homme est médusé.

- Comment se fait-il que tu aies changé aussi vite ? demande-t-il à l'oiseau parleur.

- Eh bien ! dans le réfrigérateur, j'ai beaucoup réfléchi, surtout lorsque j'ai vu ce que vous avez fait à ce pauvre poulet. Puis-je savoir ce qu'il vous avait fait, pour que vous le fassiez rôtir et que vous le mangiez à moitié ?

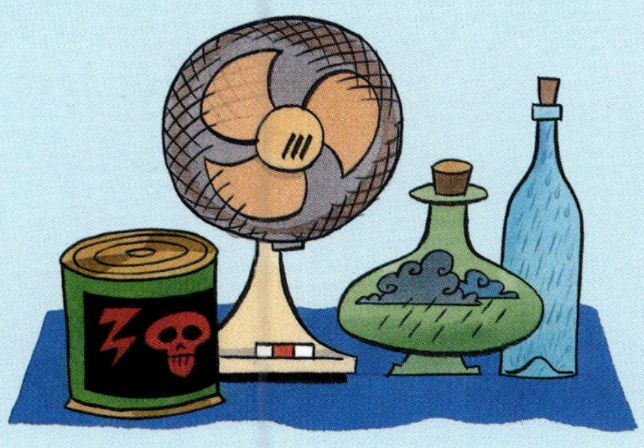

Petite annonce
3
Octobre

TEMPÊTE : ouragan venant de se faire cambrioler cherche d'urgence stock de vents forts, d'éclairs fulgurants, de nuages noirs, de pluies violentes et de grêlons gros comme des pastèques.

Petite annonce
4
Octobre

RESTAURANT : puce affamée cherche gros chien pour dîner.

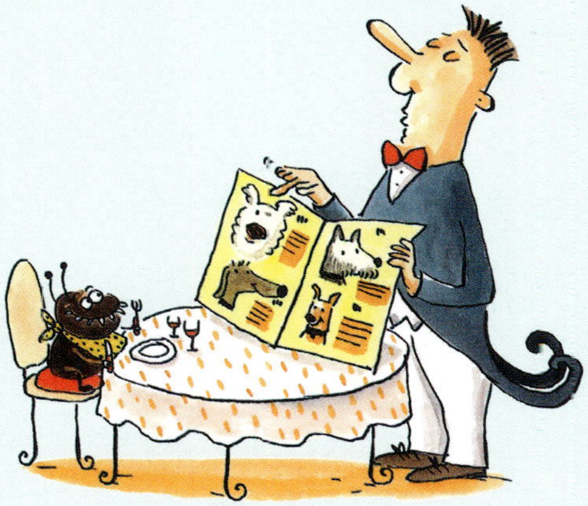

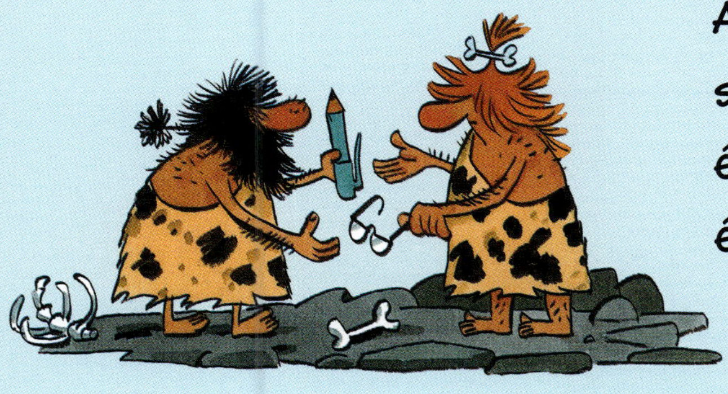

ASSOCIATION : lecteur ne sachant pas écrire recherche écrivain ne sachant pas lire pour échange de services.

Petite annonce
5
Octobre

Histoire drôle

6 Octobre

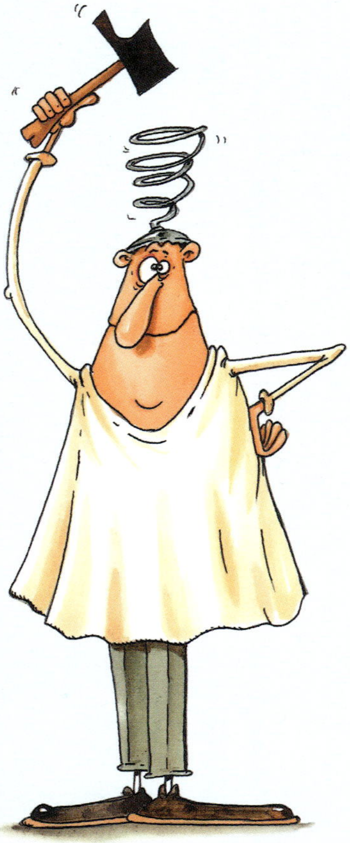

Le directeur d'un asile de fous parle à un de ses pensionnaires.

- Alors, mon ami, il paraît que vous vous tapez sur la tête avec un marteau douze heures par jour ?
- C'est vrai, répond le fou, mais j'utilise un marteau en caoutchouc.
- Ah bon ? Et pour quelles raisons ?
- Parce que, sinon, ça ferait trop mal ! Je suis peut-être fou, mais je ne suis pas idiot !

Histoire drôle

7 Octobre

Papa est très concentré, sur son bureau de la salle à manger.
Ses deux fils s'approchent prudemment.

- Euh... papa ?
- Mmmh ?
- Est-ce qu'on doit attendre que tu aies fini de faire nos devoirs avant d'allumer la télé ?

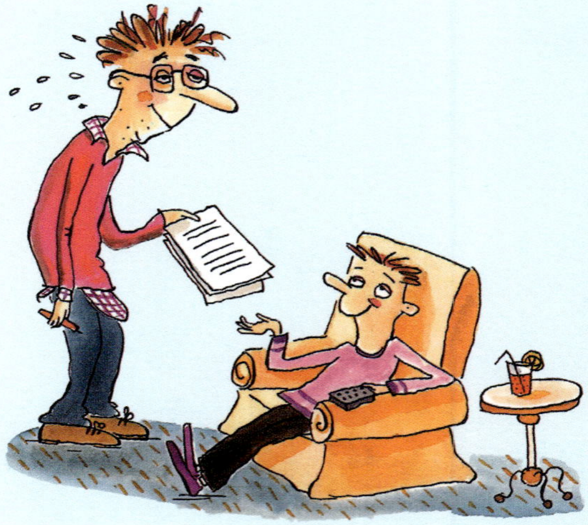

Histoire drôle

8 Octobre

Deux escargots arpentent un chemin.

- Si on allait cueillir des cerises, propose l'un.
- Idiot ! dit l'autre. On est en plein hiver, il n'y a pas de cerises !
- Oui, rétorque le premier, mais le temps d'arriver au cerisier, ce sera l'été !

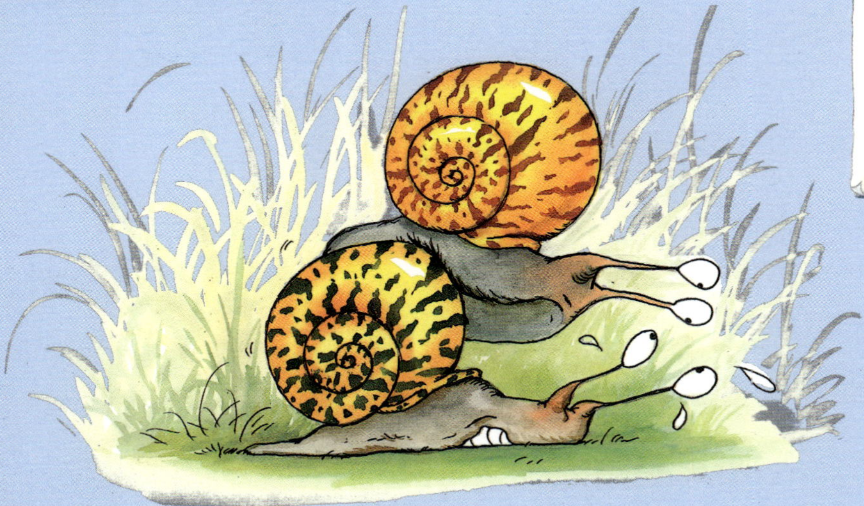

- Maman, tu peux m'apporter un verre d'eau ?
- Tais-toi, et dors ! Il est minuit !
- Mais j'ai soif !
- Tais-toi, ou je viens te donner une fessée !
- Maman, quand tu viendras me donner une fessée, tu pourras m'apporter un verre d'eau ?

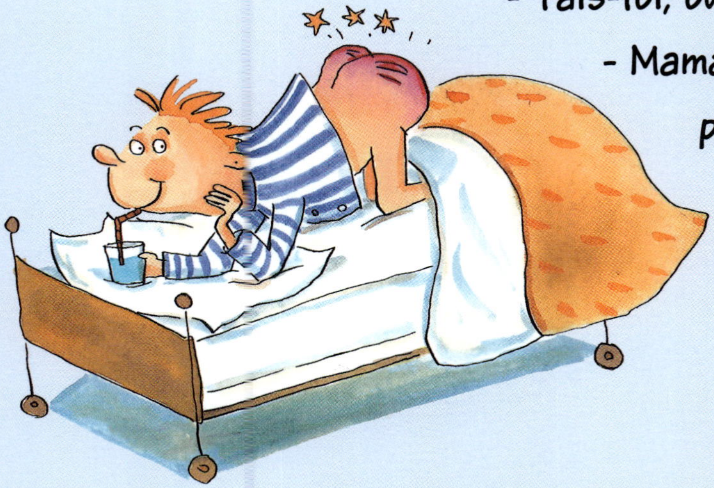

Histoire drôle

9 Octobre

Histoire drôle

10 Octobre

Une voyante va dans un commissariat.

- Je viens porter plainte pour cambriolage.

- Quel jour a eu lieu le vol ? demande l'agent.

- Il aura lieu demain, répond la voyante. Je l'ai lu dans ma boule de cristal !

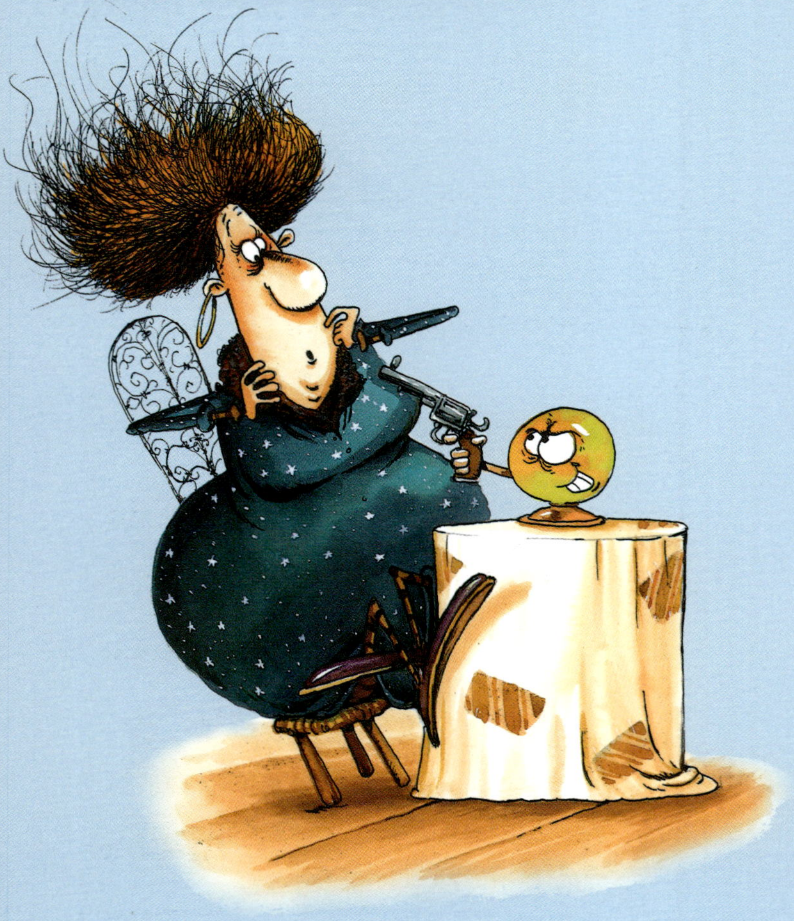

Histoire drôle

11 Octobre

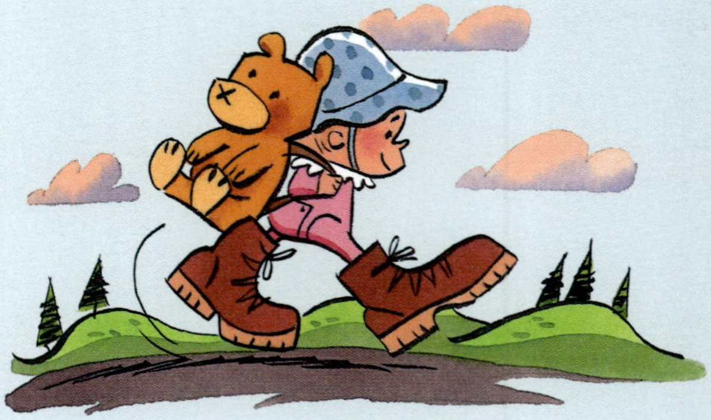

Une dame, très fière, parle à un fou.

« Mon bébé marche depuis trois mois, déjà. »

Le fou hausse les sourcils de surprise. « Depuis trois mois ! Il doit être loin, maintenant. »

Histoire drôle

12 Octobre

Deux élèves assis côte à côte viennent de faire un contrôle de maths.

- Qu'as-tu répondu au problème de robinets ? demande l'un.
- Je n'ai rien répondu, dit l'autre. Et toi ?
- Moi non plus. La maîtresse va croire qu'on a copié l'un sur l'autre...

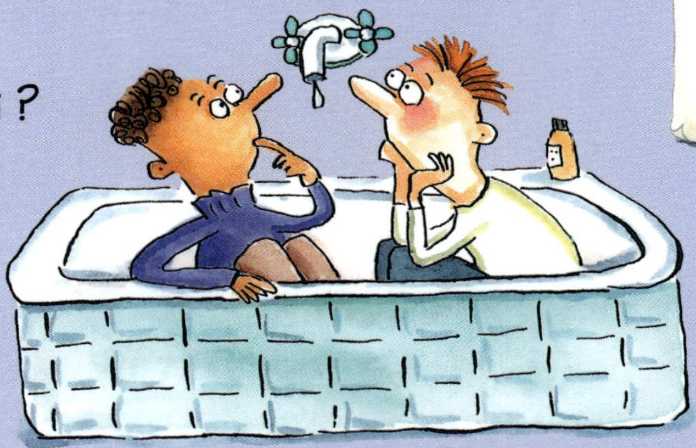

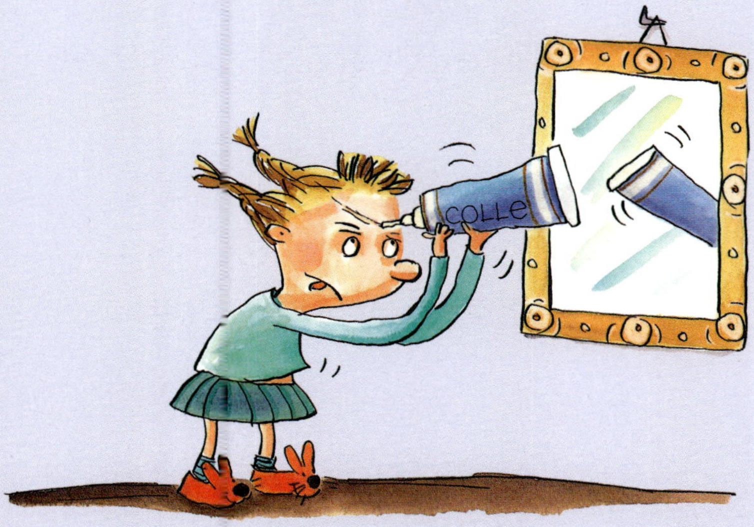

Une petite fille de quatre ans glisse sur le carrelage de la cuisine et se cogne le front. Elle se relève, un peu sonnée.

- Eh bien ! Heureusement que je n'étais pas une assiette, sinon je me serais cassée !

Histoire drôle

13 Octobre

Histoire drôle

14 Octobre

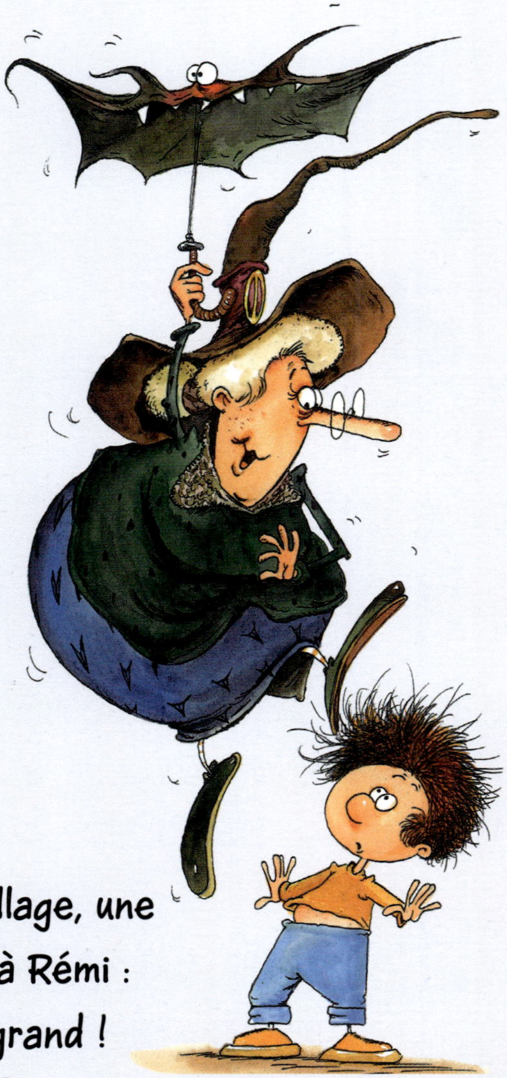

À une fête de village, une dame demande à Rémi :

- Comme tu es grand !

Tu as quel âge ?

- J'ai quatre ans.

- Quatre ans !

Tu es très grand, regarde, tu es plus grand que mon parapluie !

- Ah bon ? Il a quel âge, votre parapluie ?

Petite annonce

15 Octobre

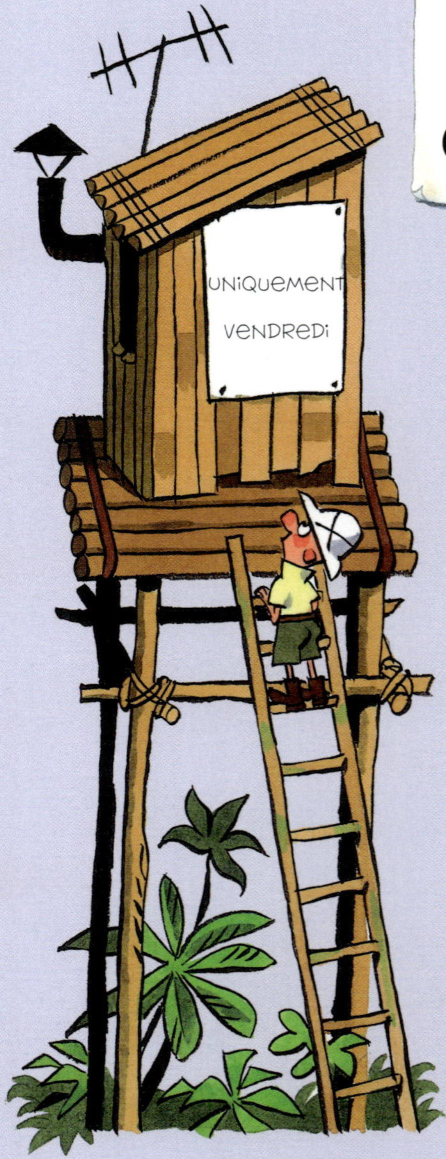

MONDANITÉS : M. Robinson Crusoë ne reçoit que le vendredi.

Histoire drôle

16 Octobre

- Pépé, dit fièrement Olivier. Aujourd'hui, à l'école, le maître nous a appris que lorsque quelqu'un nous pose une question, il ne faut pas répondre « Ouais », mais « Oui ».

- Ah ! C'est très bien, ça ! Et tu as bien compris cette leçon ?

- Ouais, ouais !

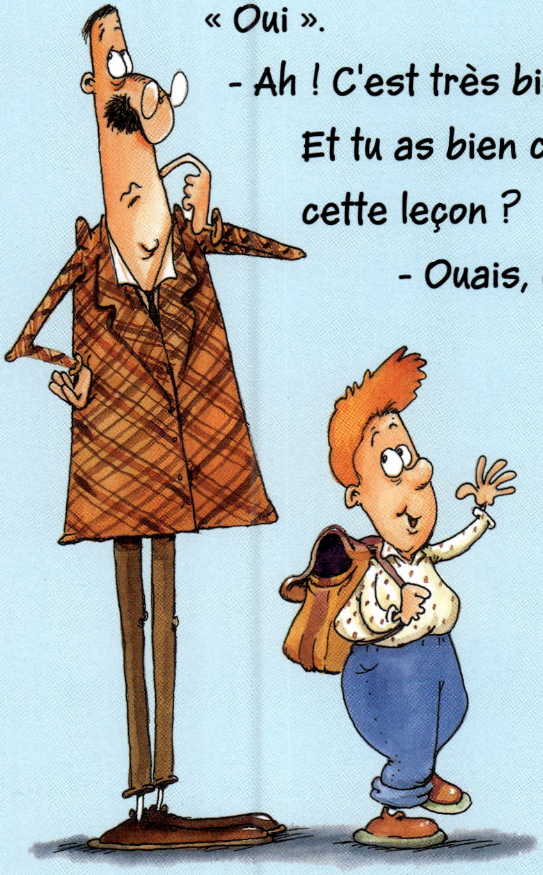

Devinette

17 Octobre

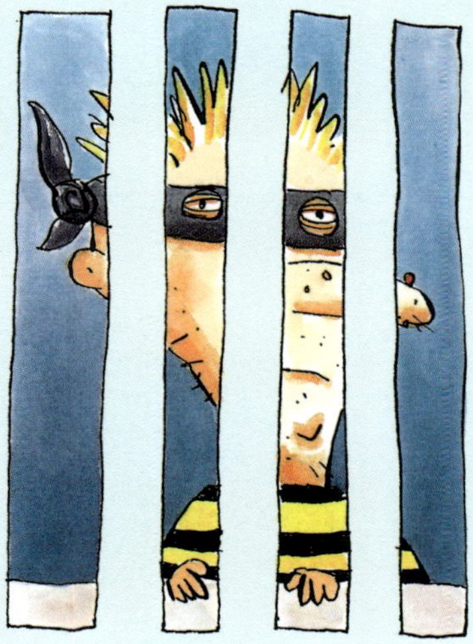

Dans la phrase : « Le voleur a été arrêté hier », où se trouve le sujet ?

(Réponse : en prison.)

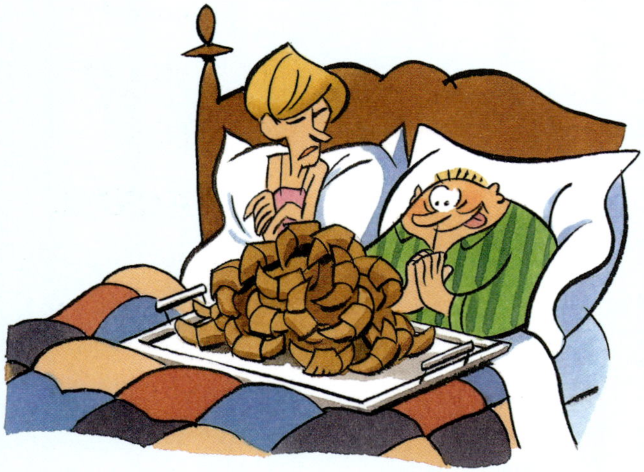

Un homme dit à son médecin :

- Ma femme dit que je suis fou parce que j'aime les croissants.

- Ah ? s'étonne le médecin. Pourtant, beaucoup de gens aiment les croissants. Moi-même, j'adore les croissants !

- Dans ce cas, venez chez moi, j'en mange deux mille par jour, je peux bien vous en offrir une centaine.

Histoire drôle

18

Octobre

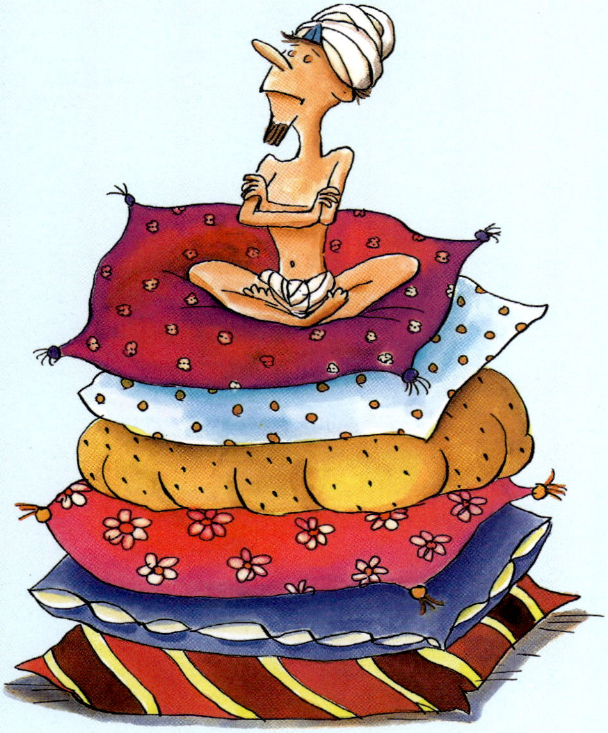

- Le fakir démissionne ! s'indigne un directeur de cirque. Et pourquoi, il démissionne ?

- Parce qu'il ne veut plus travailler pour des clous.

Histoire drôle

19

Octobre

Histoire drôle

20 Octobre

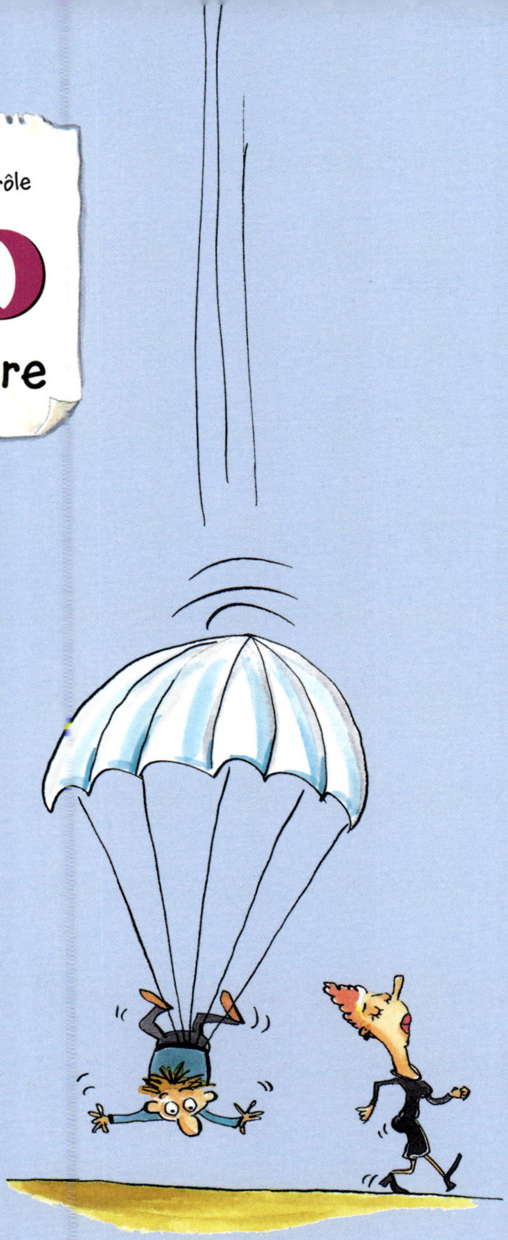

Une jeune femme à une autre :

- Alors, toujours amoureuse de ton parachutiste ?

- Oh ! non, je l'ai laissé tomber.

Histoire drôle

21 Octobre

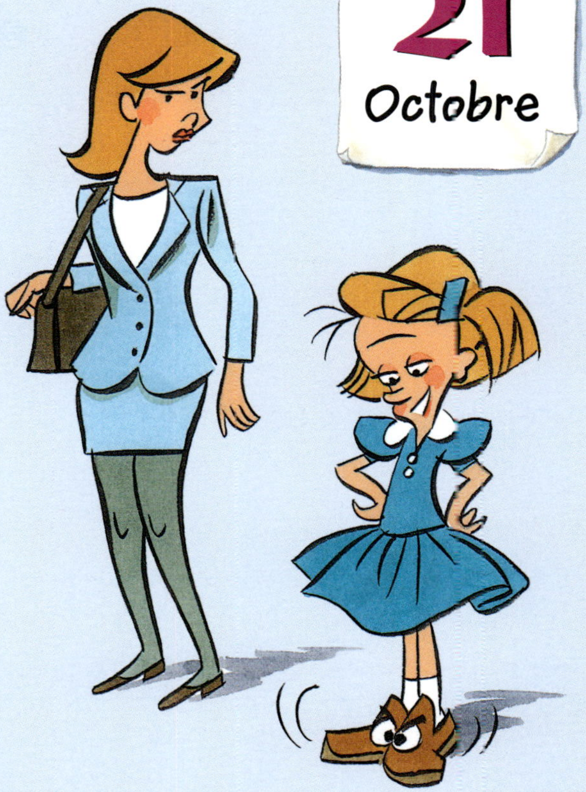

- Sophie, tu as encore mis tes chaussures à l'envers, dit une maman à sa petite fille de cinq ans.

- C'est pas vrai, c'est juste mes chaussures qui louchent !

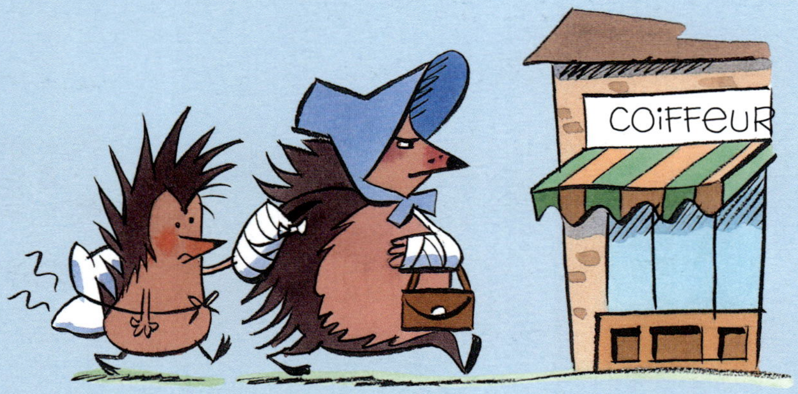

Devinette

22

Octobre

Pourquoi maman hérisson a-t-elle emmené son fils chez le coiffeur ?

(Réponse : parce qu'à chaque fois qu'elle lui donnait une fessée, elle se piquait les pattes.)

Un papa annonce une grande nouvelle à son fils :

- Paul, cette nuit, un ange a déposé une petite sœur pour toi. Tu veux la voir ?

- Non, non ! Mais j'aimerais bien voir l'ange, par contre.

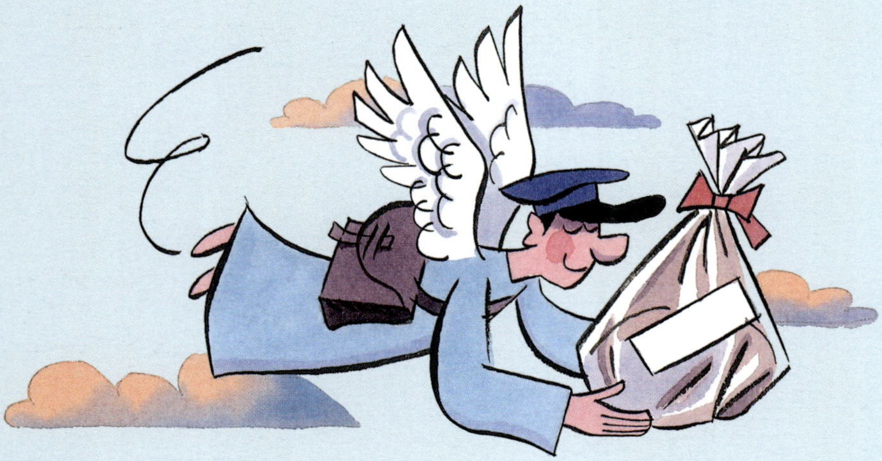

Histoire drôle

23

Octobre

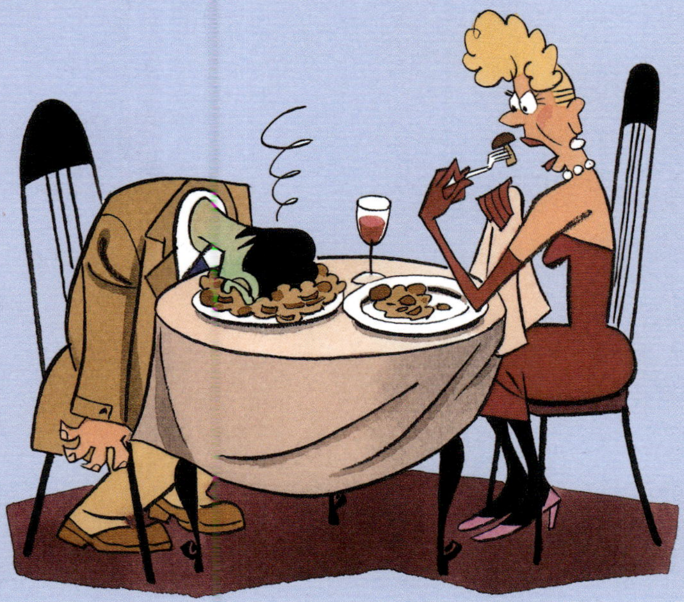

Dans un restaurant, un homme a très envie de prendre l'omelette aux champignons, mais il se demande s'ils ne sont pas empoisonnés.

Il appelle la serveuse.

- Mademoiselle, dites-moi : comment puis-je être sûr que je ne tomberai pas malade avec vos champignons ?

- En commandant autre chose, monsieur.

Histoire drôle

24 Octobre

Un enfant rentre de sa première journée d'école maternelle.

- Ça y est, maman, je sais compter sur les doigts !

- Oh, c'est bien ! Montre-moi.

- Regarde : un doigt, un doigt, un doigt, un doigt et un autre doigt.

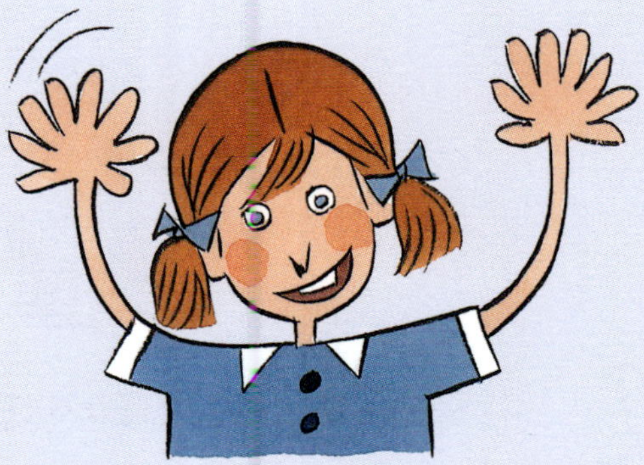

Histoire drôle

25 Octobre

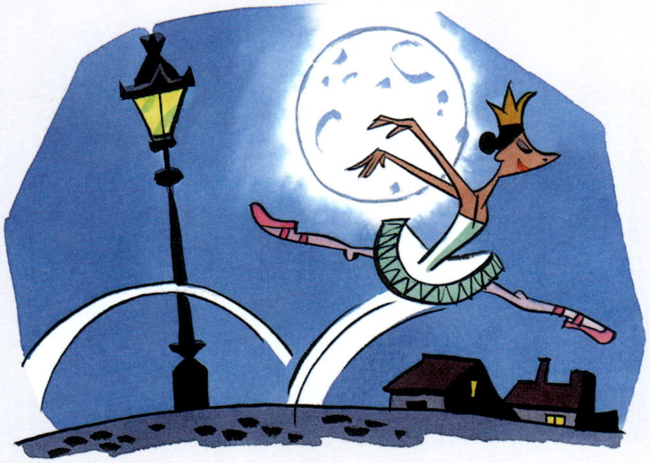

Devinette

26

Octobre

Comment une danseuse étoile rentre-t-elle chez elle, tard le soir ?

(Réponse : sur la pointe des pieds.)

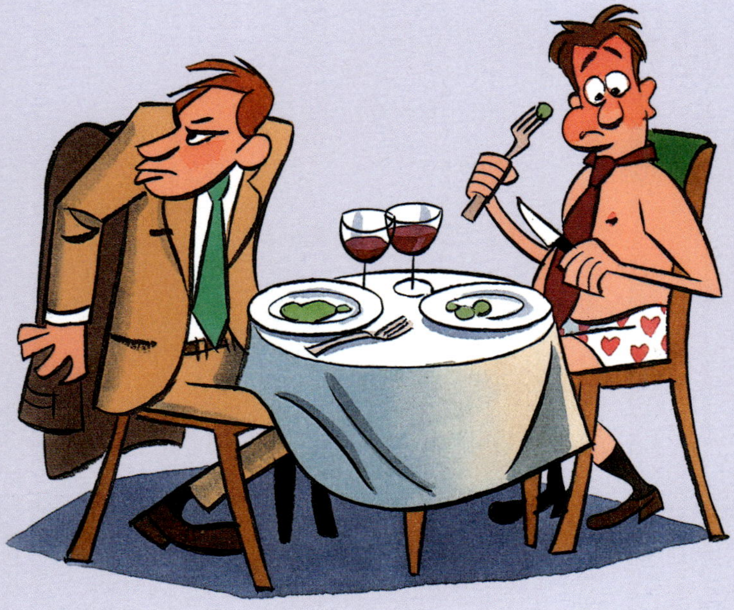

Deux amis sont au restaurant.

- Eh bien, tu ne manges plus ? s'étonne le premier.

- Non, répond l'autre, je surveille mon manteau.

- Mais pourquoi ?

- Parce que l'on vient de voler le tien.

Histoire drôle

27

Octobre

Histoire drôle

28

Octobre

Un fou va à l'hôtel. En pleine nuit, il descend à la réception pour demander un verre d'eau. On lui donne, il remonte dans sa chambre, puis revient demander un autre verre d'eau deux minutes plus tard. On lui donne, il remonte dans sa chambre, puis vient de nouveau demander un verre d'eau. Au bout de la dixième fois, le réceptionniste se fâche.

- Ça va durer encore longtemps, ce petit manège ? Qu'est-ce que vous fichez avec tous ces verres d'eau, nom d'une pipe en bois ?

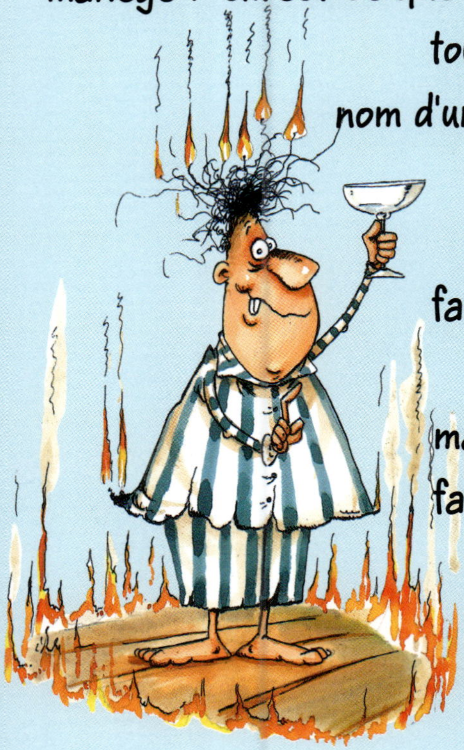

- C'est pas ma faute, explique le fou. Il y a le feu dans ma chambre, il faut bien que je l'éteigne !

Devinette

29

Octobre

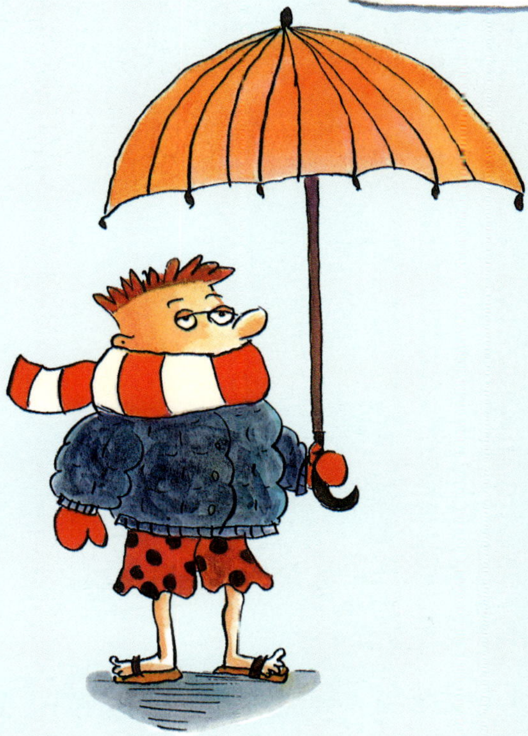

La maîtresse demande à Nicolas :

- Conjugue-moi le verbe « savoir » à tous les temps.

- Facile ! Je sais qu'il pleut, je sais qu'il neige, je sais qu'il fait beau.

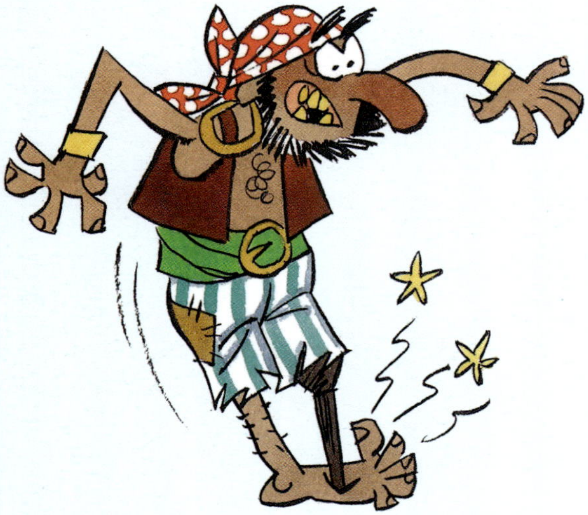

Qu'est-ce que je ne peux pas écraser avec mon pied gauche ?

(Réponse : avec mon pied gauche, je ne peux pas écraser mon pied gauche !)

Histoire drôle

30

Octobre

Un inventeur explique sa dernière trouvaille à son patron.

- C'est très simple : j'ai inventé un ordinateur miniature de la taille d'un cachet d'aspirine.

- Formidable ! Montrez-moi cette merveille !

Où est-il, cet ordinateur fabuleux ?

- Bah ! c'est là le problème...

Je ne le retrouve plus depuis que ma femme a eu mal à la tête, avant-hier.

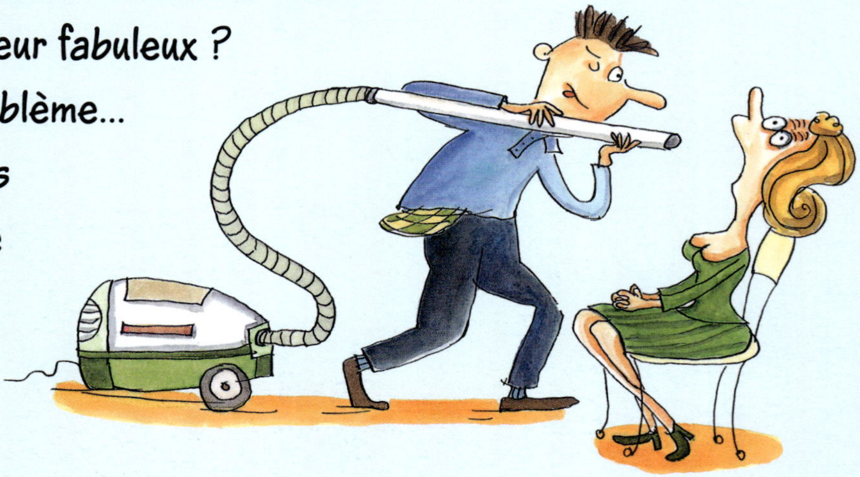

Histoire drôle

31

Octobre

Histoire drôle

1

Novembre

Un pingouin creuse un trou dans la glace pour pêcher son repas de midi.

- IL N'Y A PAS DE POISSONS ICI ! s'exclame une grosse voix.

Le pingouin est un peu étonné, mais il continue à pêcher comme si de rien n'était.

- VOUS ÊTES SOURD ? IL N'Y A PAS DE POISSONS ICI, NOM D'UN CHIEN ! s'exclame à nouveau la grosse voix.

- Qui me parle ? demande le pingouin en tremblant. C'est Vous, mon Dieu ?

- Non, répond la voix, c'est le directeur de cette patinoire !

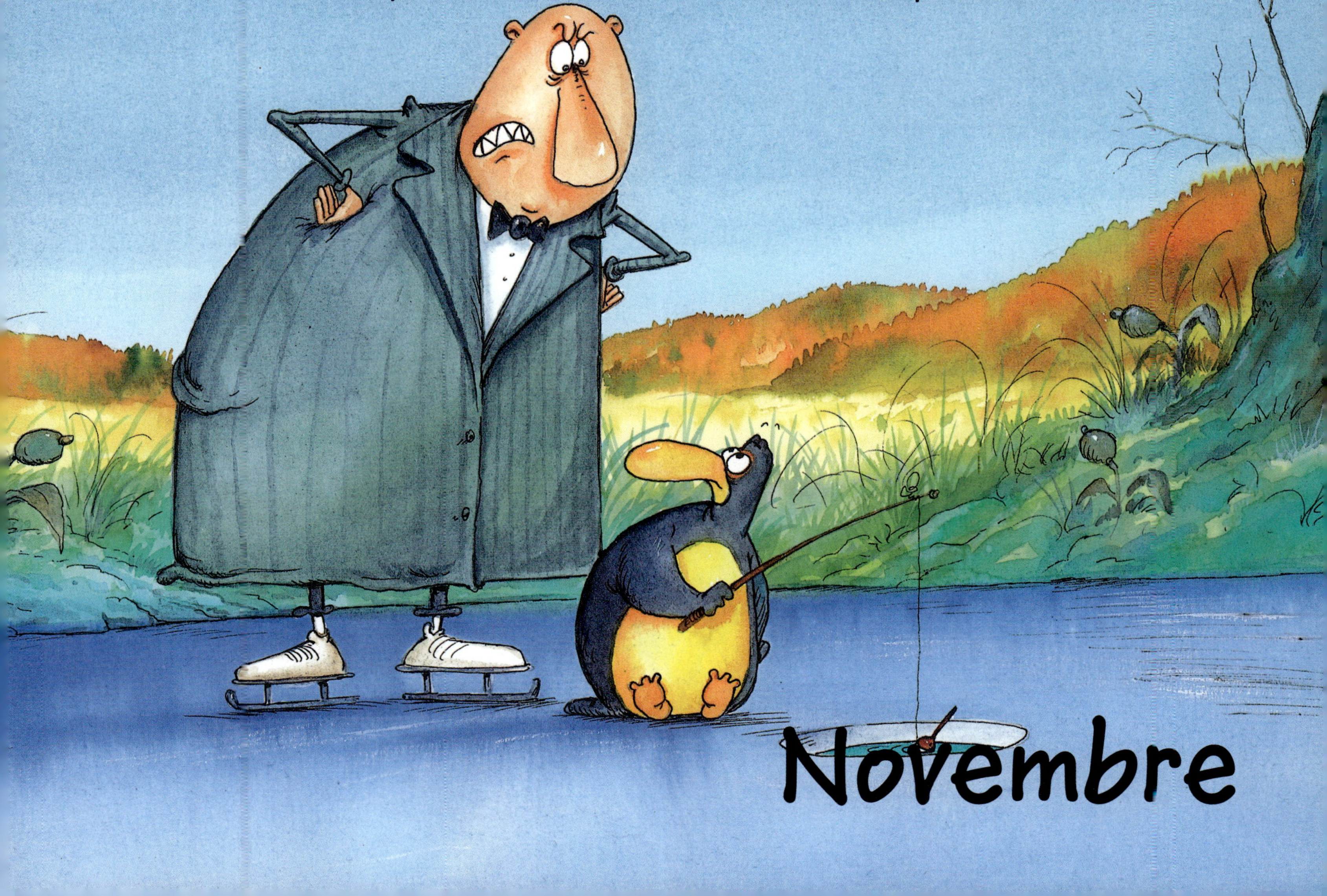

Novembre

Histoire drôle

2

Novembre

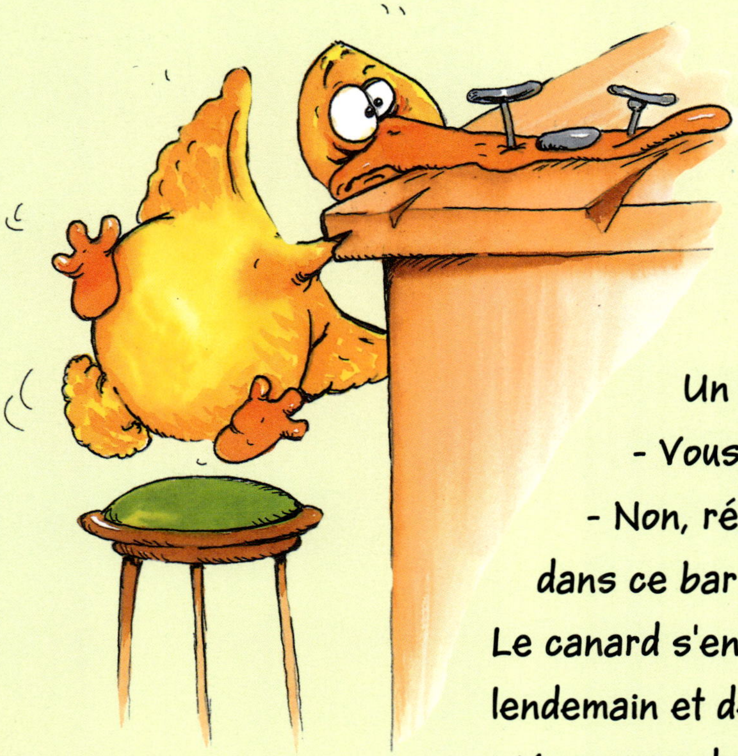

Un canard entre dans un bar et lance :

- Vous avez des cacahuètes ?

- Non, répond le patron, pas de cacahuètes dans ce bar.

Le canard s'en va sans rien dire, mais il revient le lendemain et demande à nouveau :

- Vous avez des cacahuètes ?

- Non ! s'exclame le patron, un peu énervé. Je vous ai déjà dit que je ne vends pas de cacahuètes !

Le canard s'en va et revient le lendemain.

- Vous avez des cacahuètes ?

Cette fois, le patron attrape le canard par le cou, en hurlant :

- NON ! Pas de cacahuètes, ici ! Si tu reviens demain, je prends deux clous et un marteau et je te cloue le bec sur le comptoir !

Le canard s'en va et revient le lendemain.

- Bonjour. Vous avez des clous ?

- Non, dit le patron. Pas de clous.

- Bon ! dit le canard. Alors, vous avez des cacahuètes ?

Petite annonce

3

Novembre

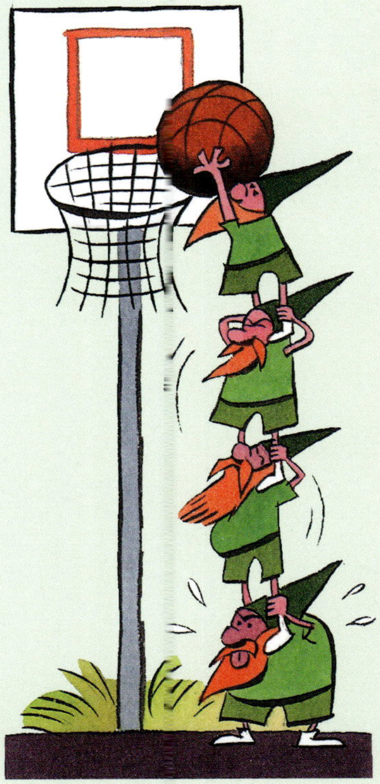

SPORTS : lutin sportif cherche quatre nains pour former équipe de basket-ball.

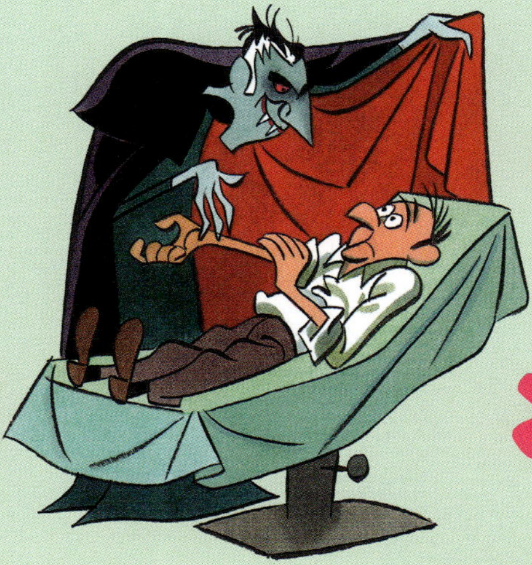

BROCANTE : vampire délicat reprend vos vieilles seringues contre une prise de sang gratuite.

Petite annonce

4

Novembre

Petite annonce

5

Novembre

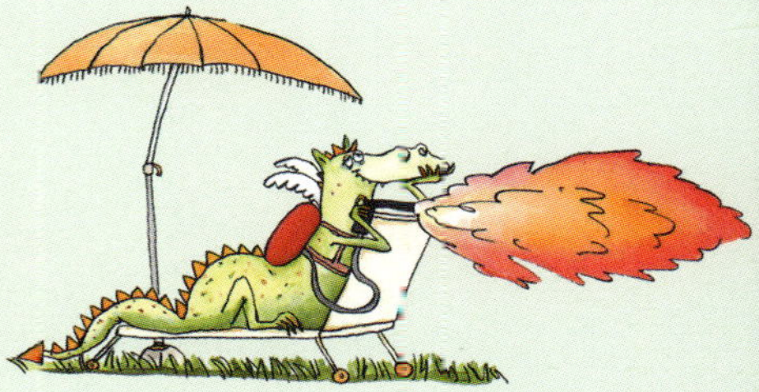

VIE PRATIQUE : dragon paresseux achète lance-flammes.

Histoire drôle

6 Novembre

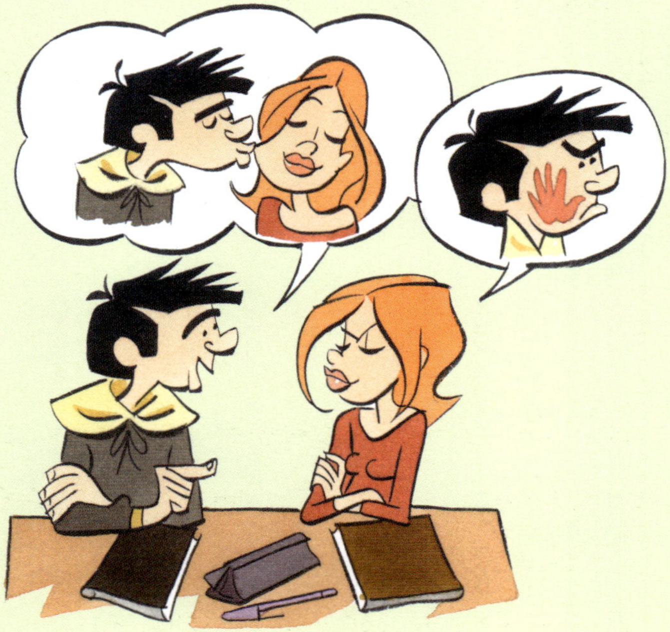

Un élève dit à sa meilleure copine :

- Cette nuit, j'ai rêvé que j'embrassais la plus belle fille du monde sur la joue.

- Je te donnais une claque, j'espère !

Histoire drôle

7 Novembre

La maîtresse demande :

- Par quelle lettre commence le mot « hier » ?

Jonathan lève la main.

- Par un « d », maîtresse.

- Non, Jonathan, ce n'est pas la bonne réponse.

- Si, maîtresse. Hier, on était dimanche, et « dimanche », ça commence par un « d » !

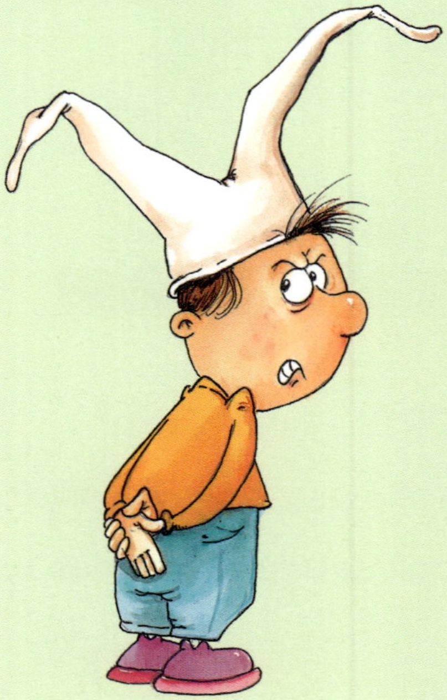

Histoire drôle

8 Novembre

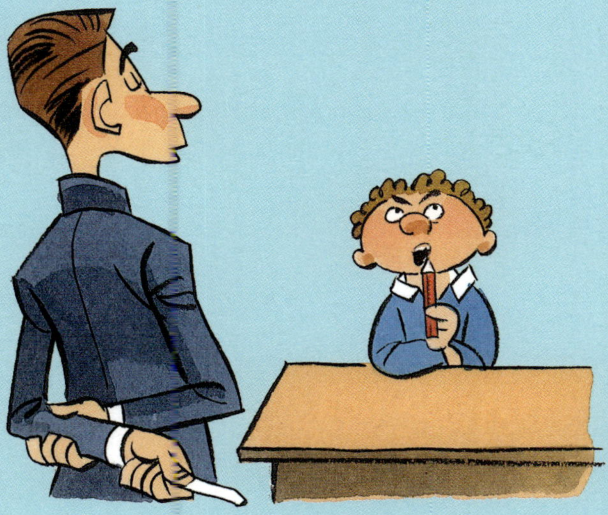

Le maître de la classe demande :

- Thierry, cite-moi cinq animaux qui vivent en Afrique centrale.

- Facile, maître : quatre éléphants et un lion.

À vingt-deux heures, un homme frappe avec insistance à la porte de son médecin. Lassé, celui-ci vient ouvrir en ronchonnant.

- Vous savez pourtant, proteste-t-il, que je ne reçois que jusqu'à 18 heures !

- Oui, répond l'homme, mais le chien qui m'a mordu la jambe ne le savait pas, lui !

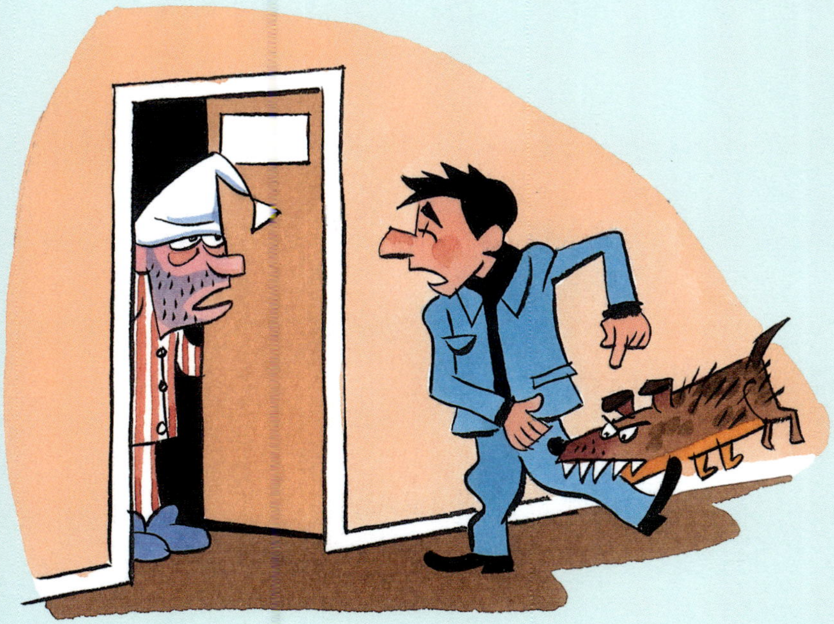

Histoire drôle

9 Novembre

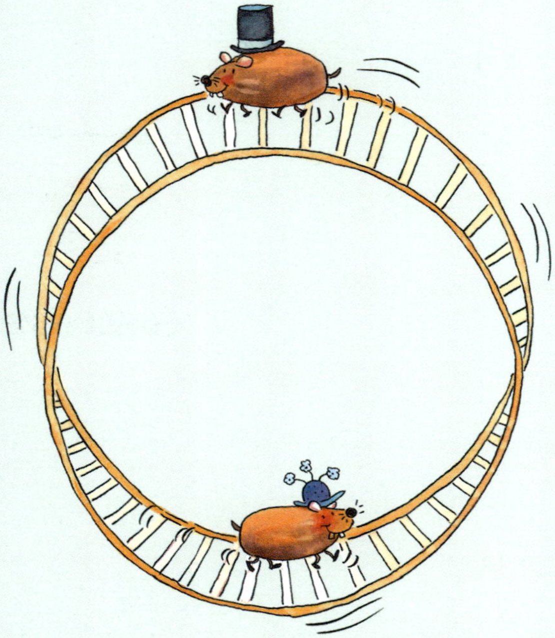

Devinette

10

Novembre

Comment savoir si votre hamster est un hamster mâle ou un hamster femelle ?

- C'est simple : vous l'appelez. S'IL vient, c'est un mâle. Si ELLE vient, c'est une femelle.

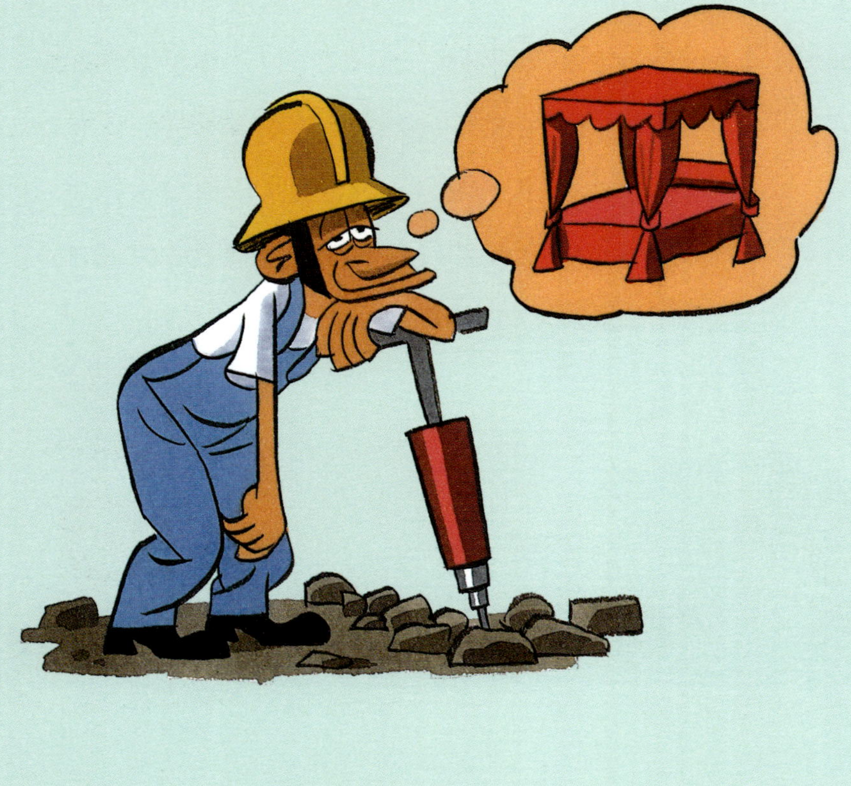

Quel est le futur de la phrase : « Je suis très fatigué » ?

(Réponse : « Je dors. »)

Devinette

11

Novembre

Histoire drôle

12

Novembre

Le dentiste prévient son patient :

- C'est une petite carie. Je vais creuser la dent avec la roulette, alors surtout, criez très fort ! Le patient devient tout pâle.

- Ça... ça va faire si mal que ça ?

- Non, répond le dentiste, vous ne sentirez absolument rien, mais il y a au moins dix personnes dans la salle d'attente, et je n'ai pas envie de louper le match de foot à la télé.

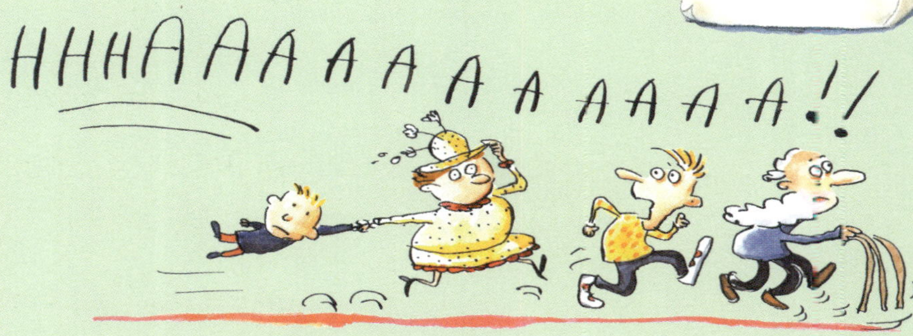

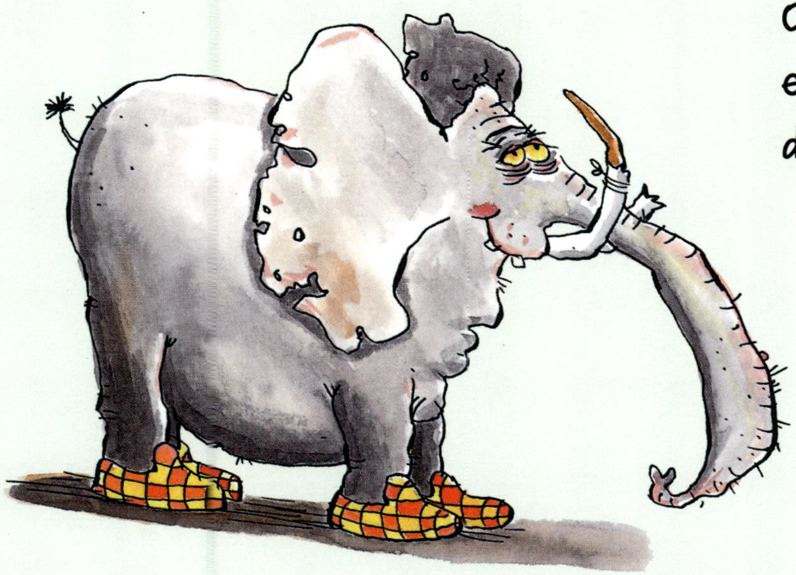

Petite annonce

13

Novembre

OFFRE D'EMPLOI : cirque peu fortuné engage éléphant prêt à travailler pour des cacahuètes.

Histoire drôle

14 Novembre

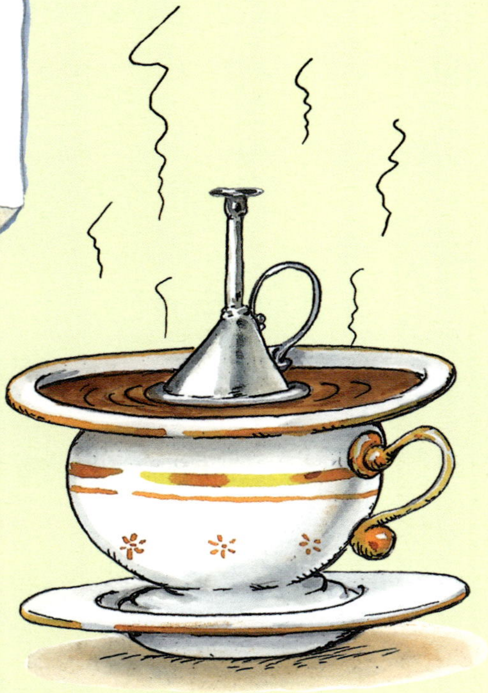

Un fou dans un café demande s'il peut avoir un morceau de sucre.

- Encore ! s'exclame le barman. C'est au moins le dixième sucre que je vous donne !
- C'est vrai, répond le fou, ennuyé, mais ils fondent tous dans mon thé !

Petite annonce

15 Novembre

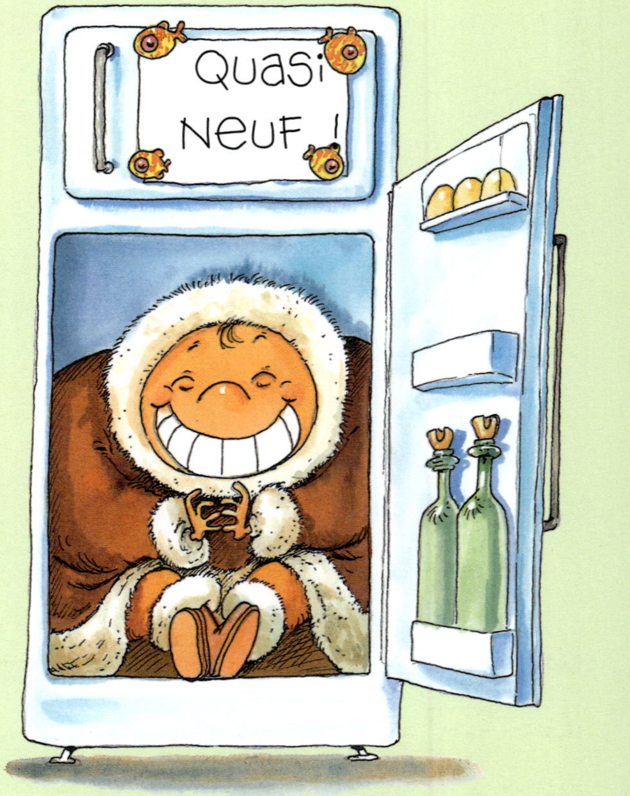

ÉLECTROMÉNAGER : esquimau vend réfrigérateur ayant très peu servi.

Histoire drôle

16 Novembre

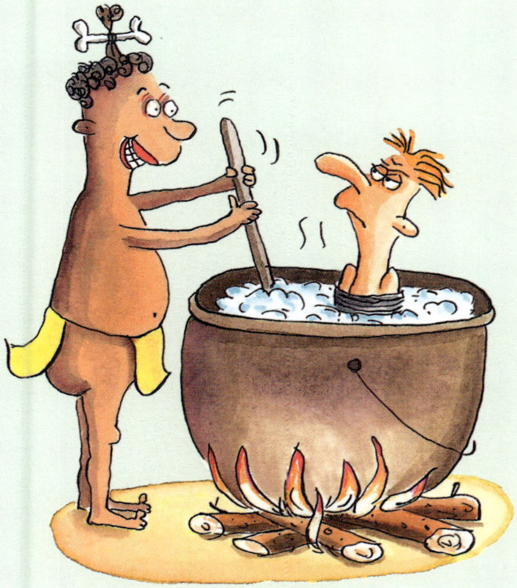

Un chef cannibale vient de jeter un homme dans une marmite immense pour le faire cuire et le manger.

- Vous n'allez pas me faire cuire dans ce chaudron ! s'indigne le pauvre prisonnier.

- Je suis désolé, explique le chef cannibale, mais je suis obligé. Le four micro-ondes est en panne.

Petite annonce

17 Novembre

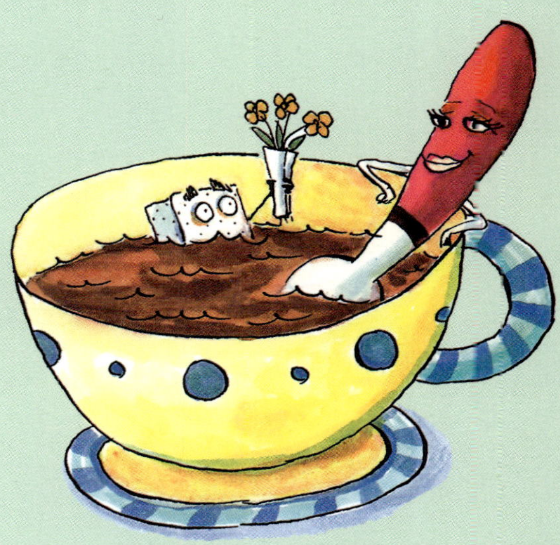

FLIRT : M. Morceau de Sucre donne rendez-vous à Mlle Petite Cuillère dans un café.

Histoire drôle

18 Novembre

L'air désespéré, un paysan dit à sa femme :

- Nous allons devoir accueillir une vache sous notre toit pendant une semaine.

- Comment ! C'est hors de question ! s'exclame la paysanne.

- Nous n'avons pas le choix, soupire le paysan.

- C'est la vache qui n'a pas le choix ! tempête la paysanne. Il est hors de question qu'une vache dorme chez moi ! Elle ira au champ, un point c'est tout.

- Elle ne sera pas d'accord.

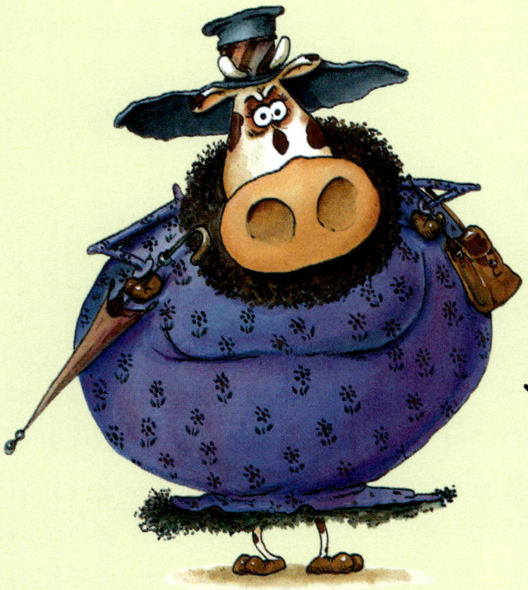

- Ah bon ! Et pourquoi ça ?

- C'est ta mère qui arrive demain, et elle n'acceptera jamais d'aller dormir dans un champ.

Devinette

19 Novembre

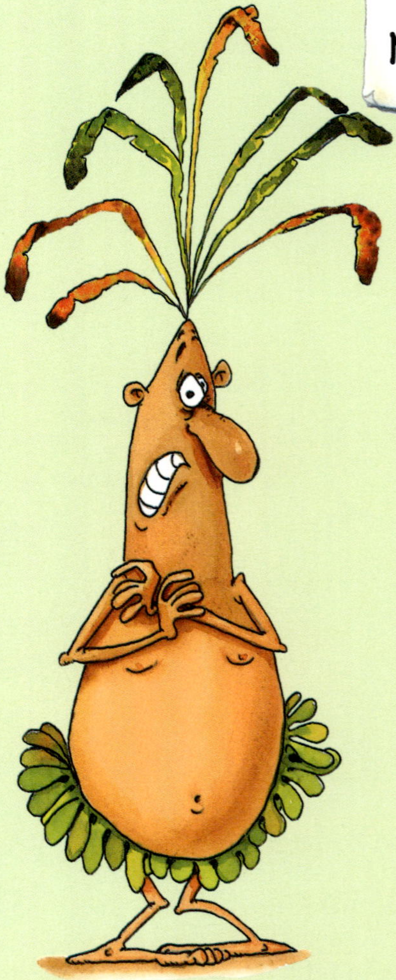

Pourquoi les Indiens d'Amérique ont-ils froid depuis 1492 ?

(Réponse : parce que Christophe Colomb les a découverts.)

Histoire drôle

20

Novembre

Un fou se jette du haut de la tour Eiffel et s'écrase sur le sol.
Tout de suite, un attroupement de curieux se forme.
Un policier arrive :
- Qu'est-ce qui se passe, ici ?
Le fou relève la tête :
- Je n'en sais rien, je viens d'arriver !

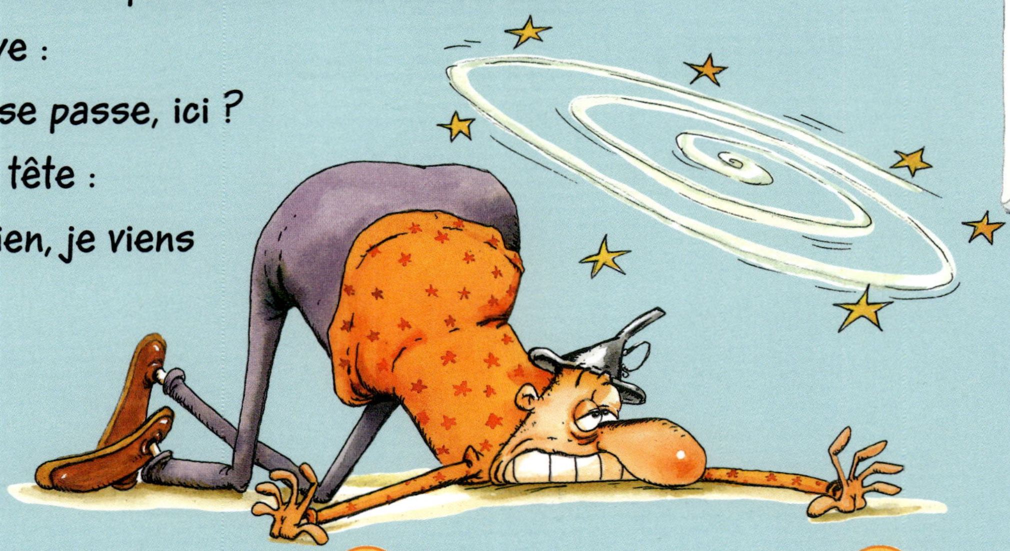

Petite annonce

21

Novembre

IMMOBILIER : mille-pattes cherche appartement dans résidence avec ascenseur.

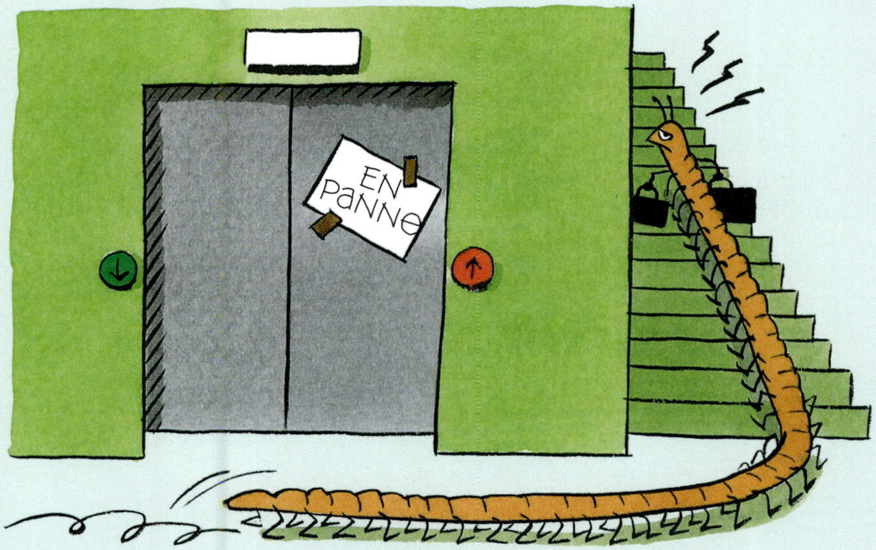

Devinette
22
Novembre

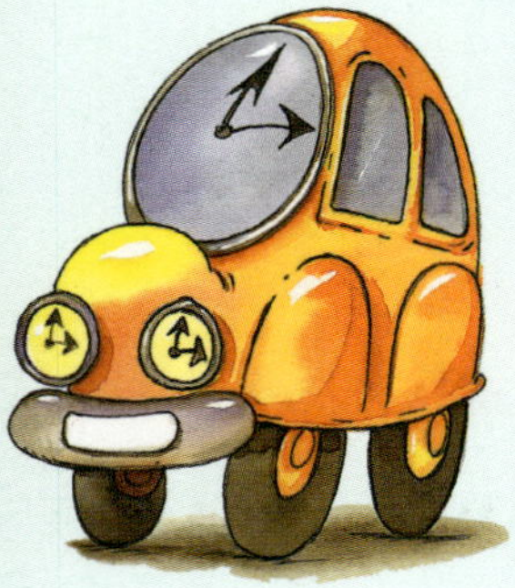

Un automobiliste s'arrête pour faire la sieste dans une station-service sur l'autoroute. Il s'installe confortablement dans sa voiture, mais à peine a-t-il fermé les yeux que quelqu'un le réveille :

- Vous avez l'heure ?
- Hmmm ? 14h.

Alors qu'il se rendort, une autre personne frappe à sa vitre :

- Vous avez l'heure ?
- Hmmm ? 14h10.

Énervé, il inscrit sur un papier « JE N'AI PAS L'HEURE ! », le colle sur la vitre et se rendort. Une minute plus tard, quelqu'un frappe à la vitre en criant :

- IL EST 14h30.

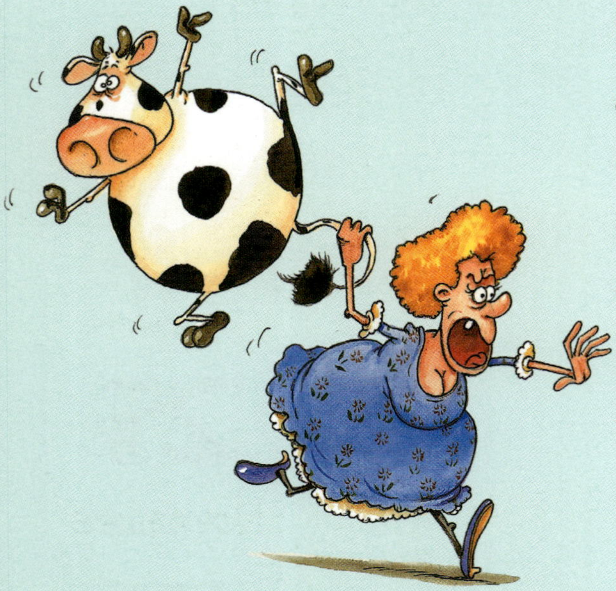

L'infirmier interroge l'homme qui vient d'être admis aux urgences avec une fracture du crâne.

- Que s'est-il passé ?
- Ma femme n'a pas apprécié que je lui dise que son steak était dur comme du bois.
- Et alors ?
- Elle m'a frappé la tête avec le steak !

Devinette
23
Novembre

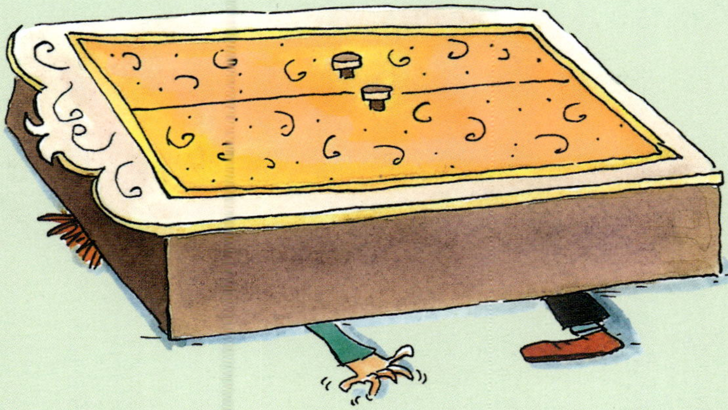

Histoire drôle

24

Novembre

Rémi arrive dans la cuisine en catastrophe.

- Maman ! L'armoire est tombée !

- Mon Dieu ! Vite, préviens ton père immédiatement !

- Il le sait déjà, maman, il est en dessous.

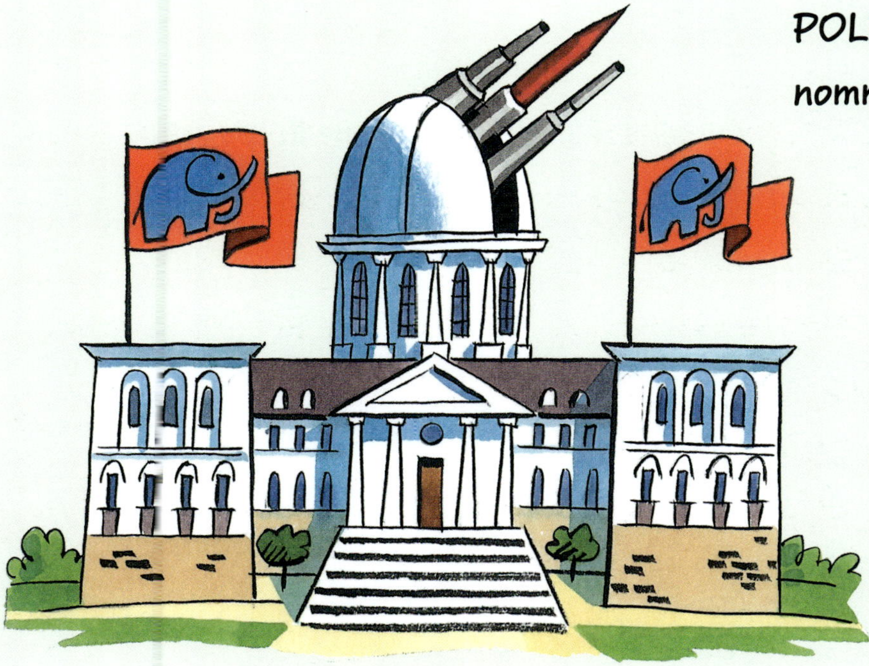

POLITIQUE : M. Éléphant vient d'être nommé ministre de la Défense.

Petite annonce

25

Novembre

Histoire drôle

26

Novembre

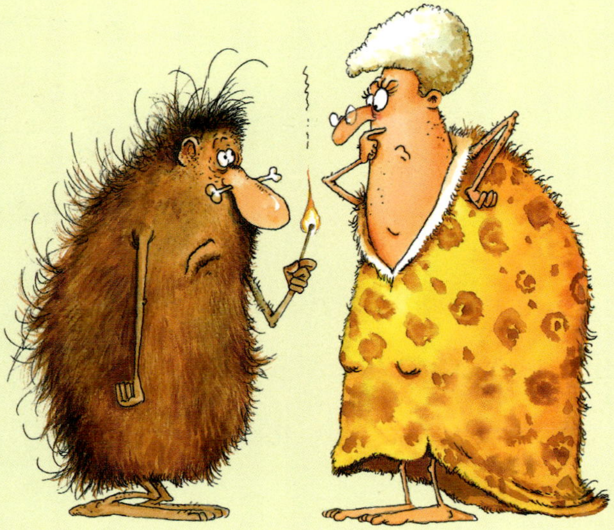

Un homme préhistorique annonce à sa femme :

- Ça y est ! J'ai découvert le feu ! Tu vas pouvoir nous cuisiner plein de plats tout chauds !

- Non. Pas avant que tu n'aies découvert le lave-vaisselle.

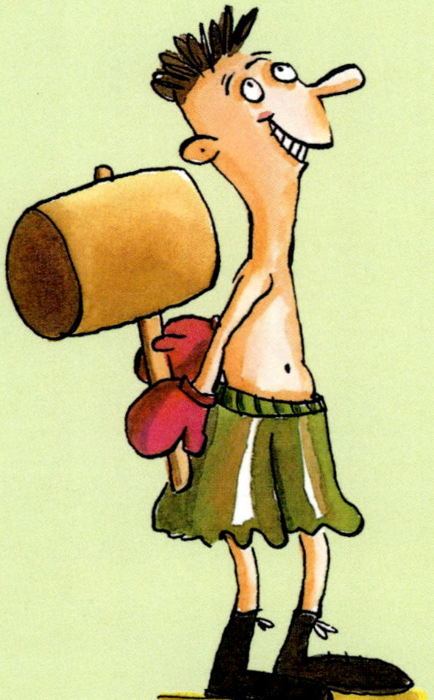

TRICHE : boxeur nul cherche arme de poing.

Petite annonce

27

Novembre

Histoire drôle

28

Novembre

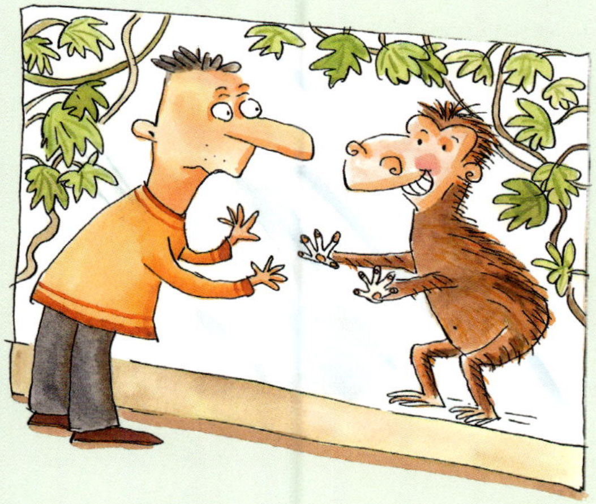

- Ainsi, s'étonne un juge dans un tribunal, vous portez plainte contre votre voisin parce qu'il vous a traité de macaque il y a trois ans ?
- Oui, monsieur le Juge.
- Mais pourquoi avoir attendu tout ce temps pour vous plaindre ?
- Parce qu'hier, je suis allé au zoo pour la première fois, et j'ai vu ce que c'était, un macaque !

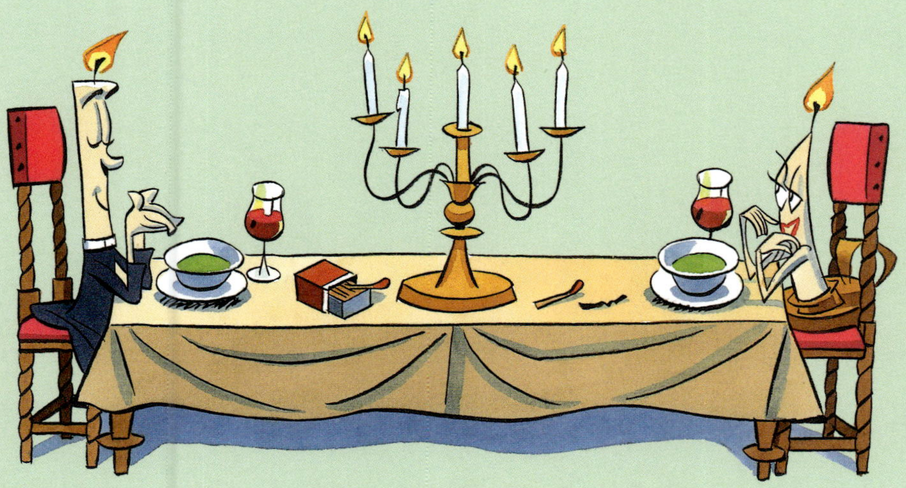

Petite annonce

29

Novembre

ROMANTIQUE : M. Cierge invite Mlle Bougie à dîner aux chandelles.

Histoire drôle

30 Novembre

Un monsieur veut s'acheter un chien. Il va donc dans une animalerie et voit un magnifique chien, très racé et musclé, qui n'arrête pas d'aboyer. Il demande au vendeur quel est le prix de l'animal.

- Ce chien vaut mille euros.
- Mille euros ! C'est très cher pour un chien qui n'arrête pas d'aboyer !
- Oui, dit le vendeur, mais ce chien n'est pas ordinaire : il est ceinture noire de karaté.
- Ceinture noire de karaté ?
- Je vais vous montrer.

Le vendeur s'approche du chien et lui dit :

- Allez, Jimmie, tu me casses cette table !

Et le chien, « YAAAH », casse la table en mille morceaux en dix secondes. Puis il se remet à aboyer comme un fou.

- Allez, Jimmie, continue le vendeur, tu me casses cette porte !

Et le chien, « YAAAH », casse la porte en mille morceaux en dix secondes. Puis il se met de nouveau à aboyer comme un fou.

- Je l'achète, dit l'homme, ce chien vaut de l'or.

Arrivé à la maison, le chien inspecte toutes les pièces, en aboyant de plus en plus fort. Son nouveau propriétaire met un doigt sur sa bouche en disant :

- Chut, Jimmie, tu me casses les oreilles !

Et le chien, « YAAAAH »...

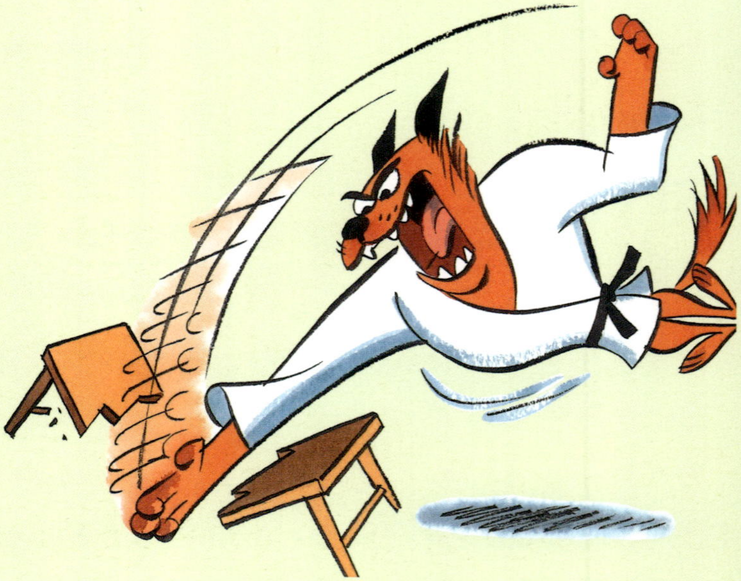

Un enfant paysan raconte le soir de Noël à ses nouveaux copains de l'immeuble où il habite maintenant.

- À Noël, on met ses chaussures devant la cheminée, et c'est par là que le père Noël va descendre pour distribuer ses cadeaux au pied du sapin.

- Je suis sûr, dit un grand, que ça n'existe même pas !

- De quoi ? Le père Noël ?

- Non. Les cheminées.

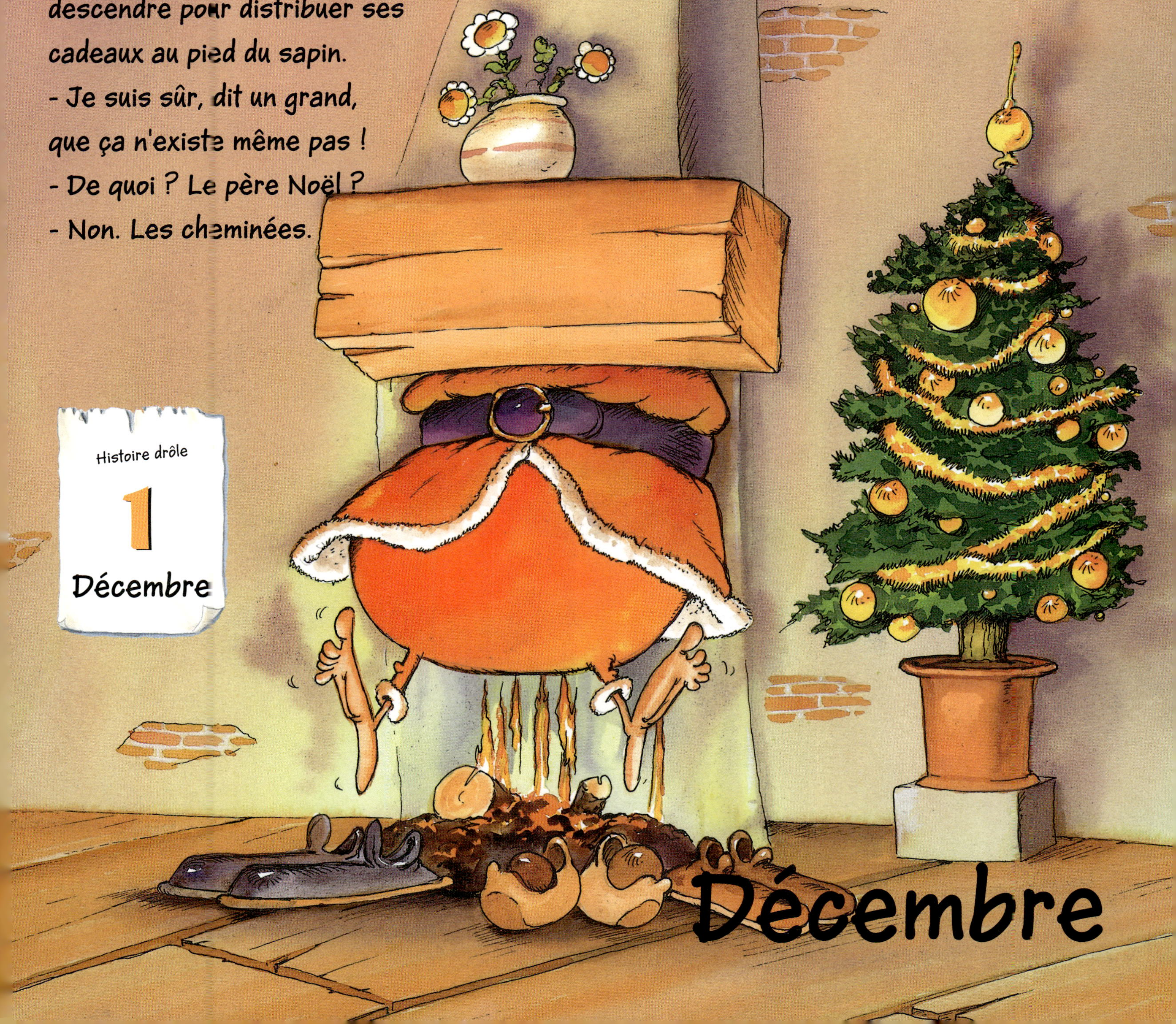

Décembre

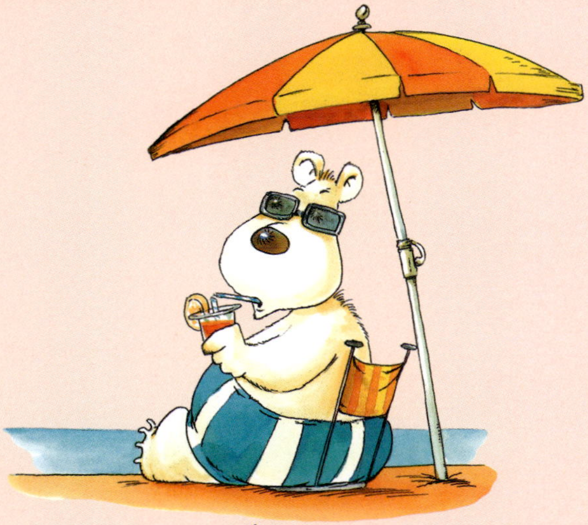

VACANCES : ours polaire frileux vend villa réfrigérée très confortable sur la banquise contre logement, même petit, dans les mers du Sud.

Petite annonce
2
Décembre

Petite annonce
3
Décembre

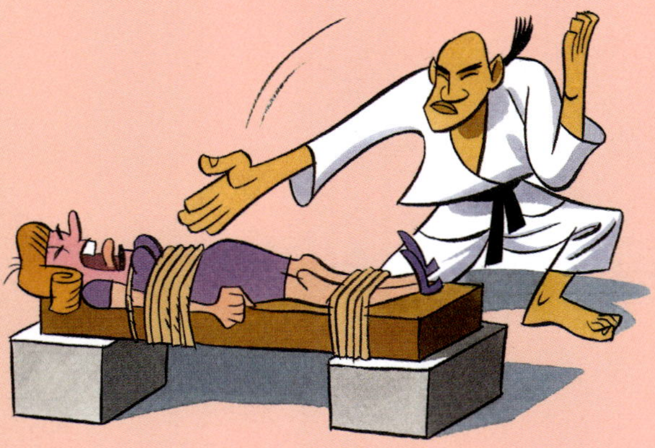

DOULEUR : femme au cœur brisé par un karatéka cherche judoka possédant un bon tube de colle.

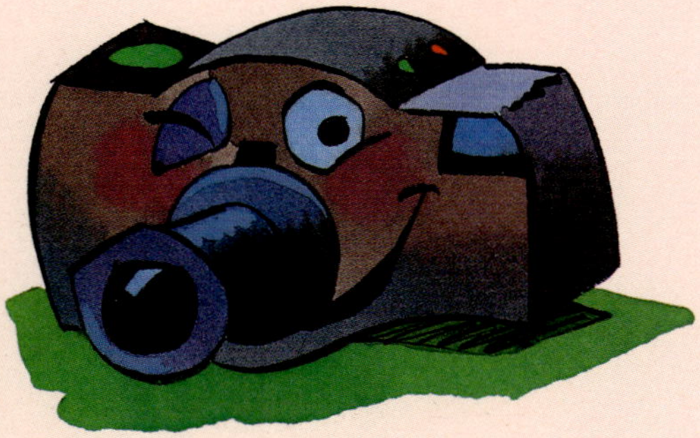

Connaissez-vous l'histoire de la pellicule ?

(Réponse : non, et c'est normal ; elle n'est pas encore développée.)

Devinette
4
Décembre

Petite annonce

5

Décembre

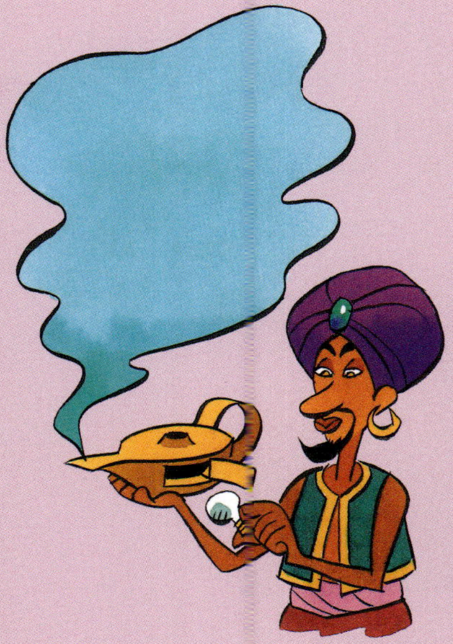

GRILLÉ : génie de la lampe achète ampoules neuves.

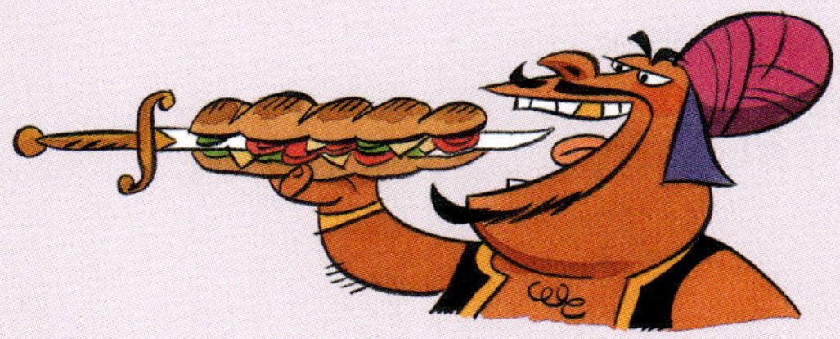

Que mange un avaleur de sabres au régime ?

(Réponse : des clous.)

Devinette

6

Décembre

Devinette

7

Décembre

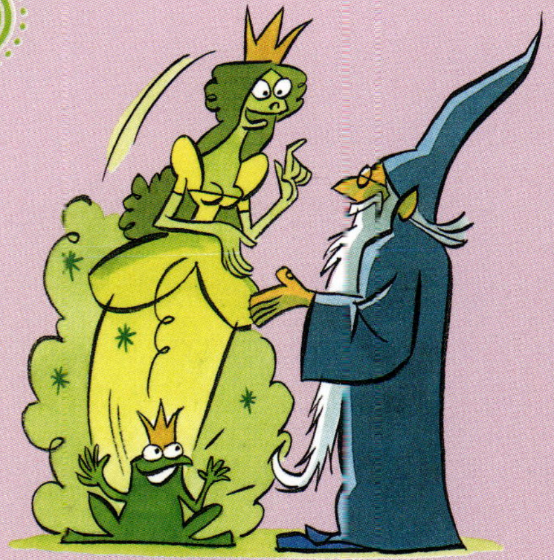

Que dit-on à Merlin quand il se présente ?

(Réponse : on lui dit : « Je suis enchanté de faire votre connaissance. »)

Histoire drôle

8

Décembre

Un médecin examine un patient que l'on vient d'opérer des deux jambes.

- Vos résultats sont très bons. D'ici un mois, vous pourrez danser le rock sans problème.

- Quoi ? C'est un miracle ! s'exclame le patient.

- Pourquoi donc ?

- Eh bien, parce qu'avant mon opération, je ne savais pas danser le rock !

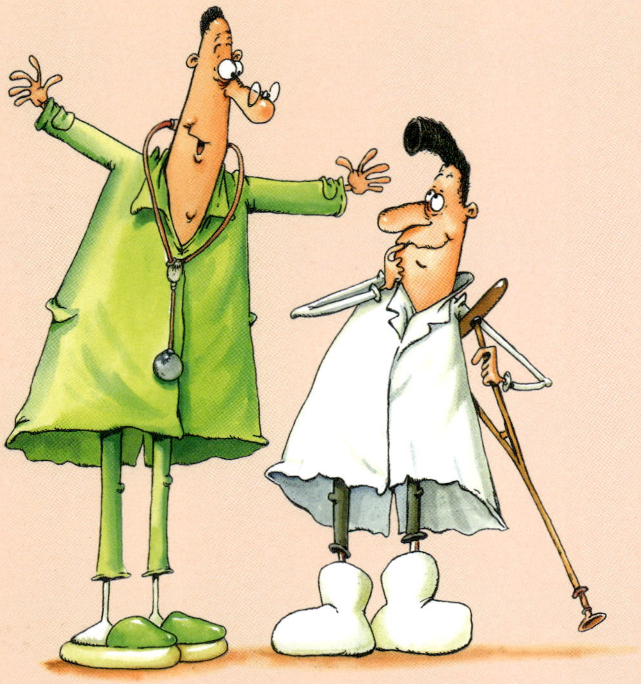

Devinette

9

Décembre

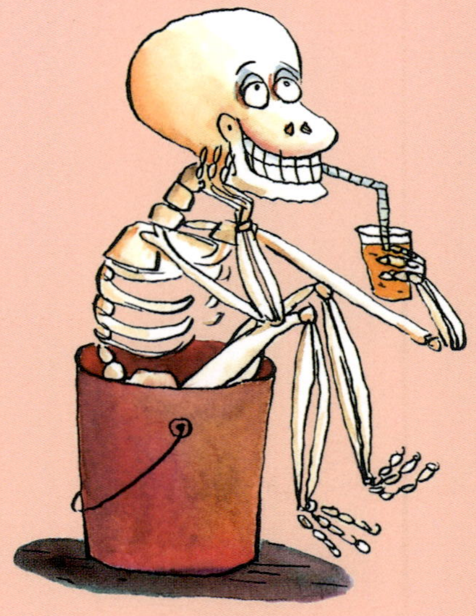

Que dit un squelette qui rentre dans un bar ?

(Réponse : je voudrais une limonade et une serpillière.)

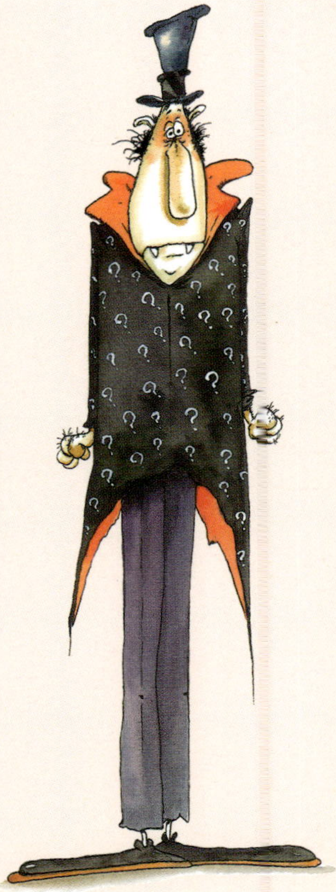

Histoire drôle

10 Décembre

ÉNIGME : un homme habillé tout en noir se promène sur une route. Il n'y a pas de lune, pas d'étoiles, les lampadaires le long de la route sont éteints. L'homme habillé tout en noir est en plein milieu de la route. Une voiture arrive, phares éteints, et pourtant, elle s'arrête et n'écrase pas l'homme habillé tout en noir. Pourquoi ?

(Réponse : il n'y a pas d'étoiles, pas de lune, les phares de la voiture sont éteints. Et pourtant, la voiture s'arrête. C'est normal : il fait jour !)

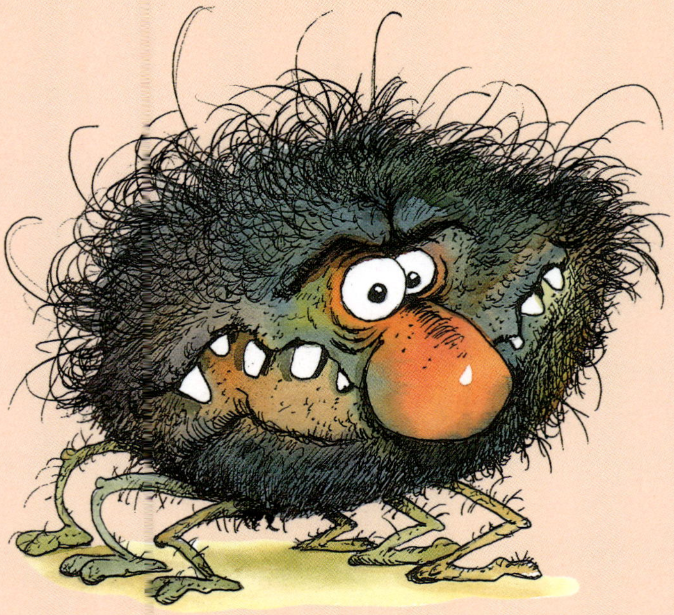

MODE : affreux pou désirant changer de tête cherche chevelure de chirurgien esthétique.

Petite annonce

11 Décembre

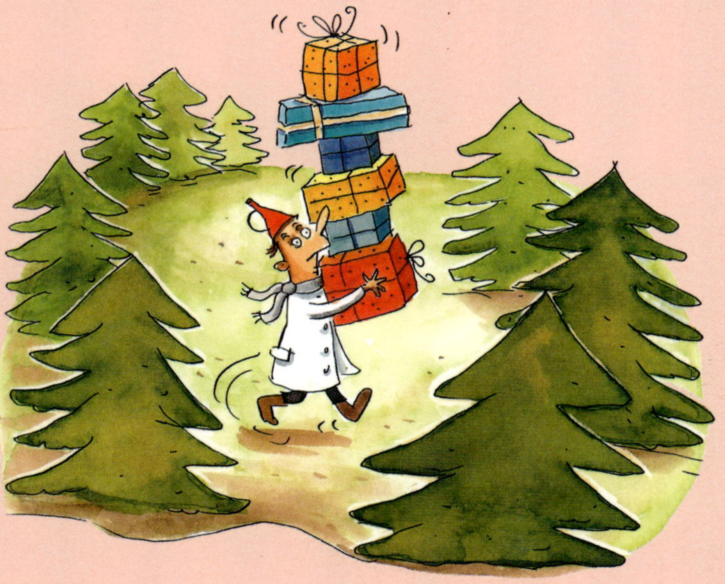

Un fou rentre de la forêt, l'air tout triste.

- Qu'est-ce qu'il t'arrive ? lui demande son meilleur ami.

- Je suis allé chercher un sapin de Noël dans la forêt, explique le fou en pleurant, mais je n'en ai trouvé aucun qui avait des boules et des guirlandes !

Histoire drôle

12

Décembre

Deux chiens se rencontrent.

- Tu as vu le nouveau trottoir ! Tout propre, tout neuf !

- Ouais, ça s'arrose !

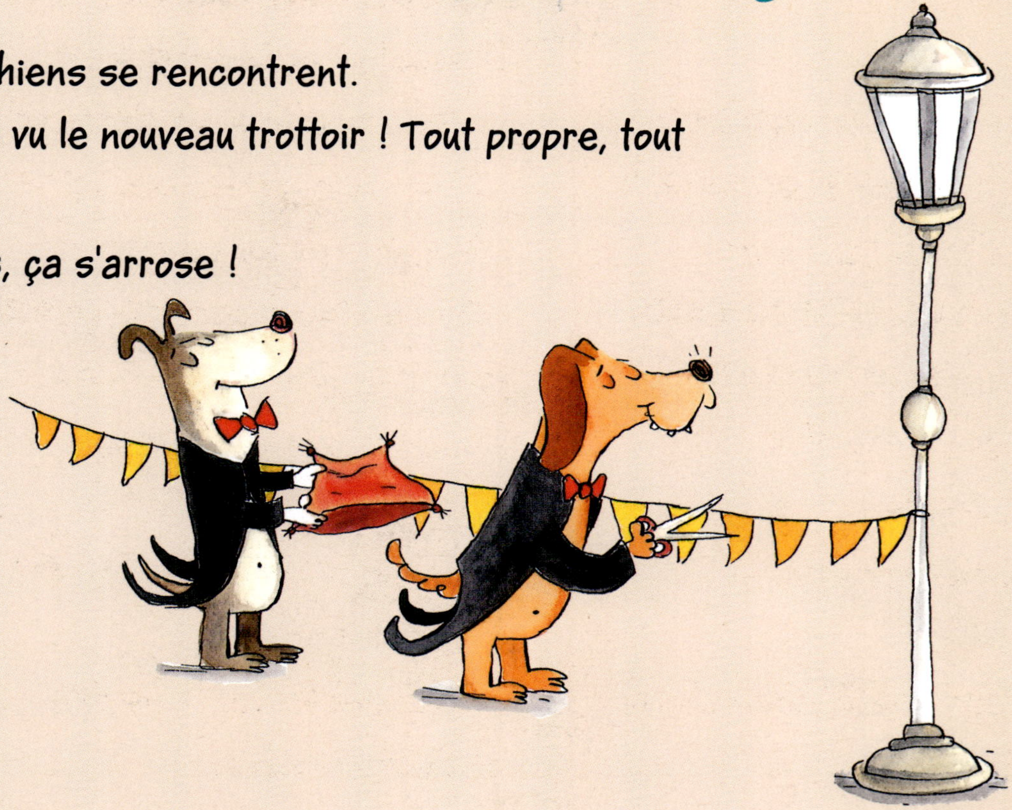

Histoire drôle

13

Décembre

Histoire drôle

14 Décembre

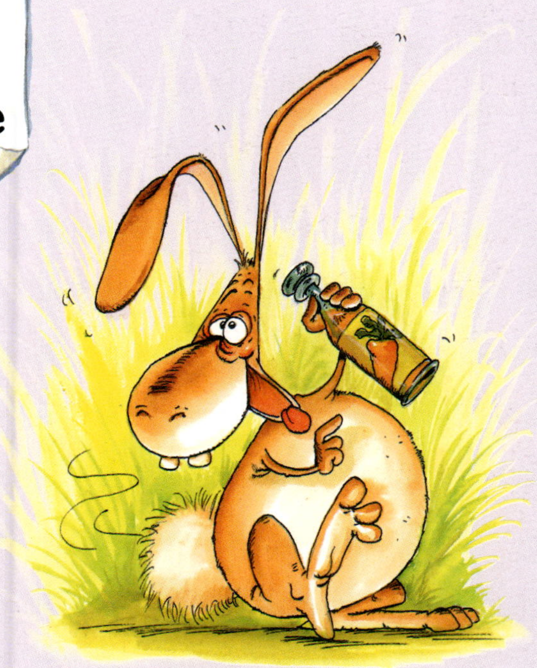

Un inspecteur de police rend son rapport après un hold-up dans un grand supermarché.

- Le vol qui a eu lieu cette nuit est très curieux : le cambrioleur a dérobé trois cents kilos de carottes, huit cents salades et cinq cents litres de vin rouge.

Le commissaire hoche la tête.

- Et vous recherchez quelqu'un en particulier ?

- Oui, répond l'inspecteur. Nous recherchons un lapin complètement ivre.

Histoire drôle

15 Décembre

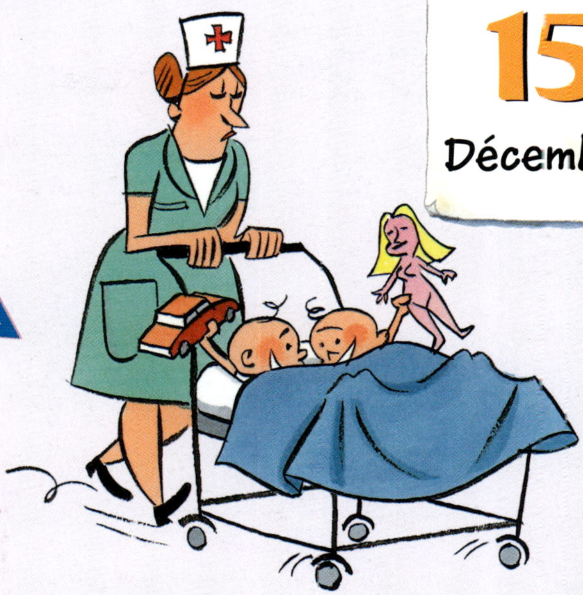

Deux bébés viennent de naître à l'hôpital. L'un dit à l'autre :

- T'es une fille ou un garçon ?

- J'suis une petite fille. Et toi ?

- Moi, je ne sais pas.

- Baisse ton drap, dit la petite fille, je vais te dire ce que tu es.

Le bébé baisse son drap.

- Plus bas, je ne vois rien.

Le bébé baisse encore le drap, et la petite fille sourit.

- T'es un garçon, tu as des chaussons bleus.

Devinette

16

Décembre

Quelle est la différence entre l'abominable homme des neiges et l'abominable femme des neiges ?

(Réponse : une abominable moustache.)

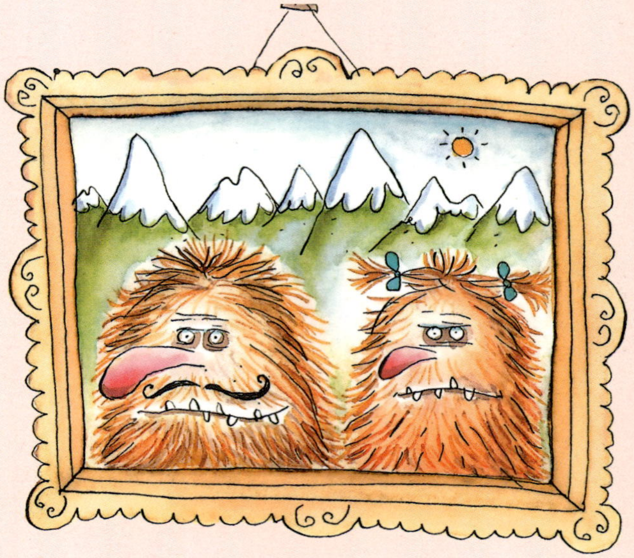

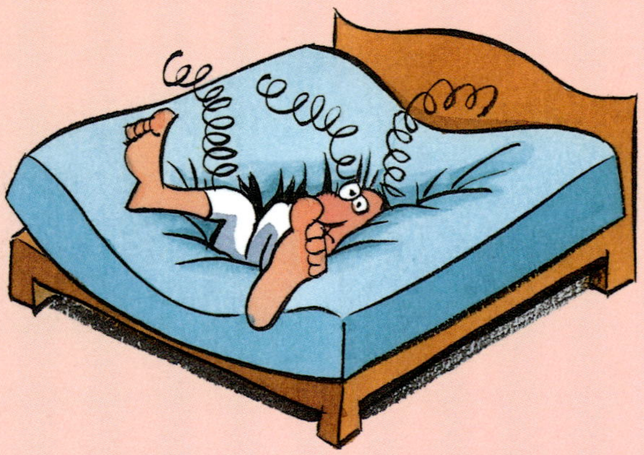

Petite annonce

17

Décembre

INSOMNIE : homme au sommeil lourd achète lit très solide.

Devinette

18

Décembre

Qu'est-ce qui est blanc et posé dans un coin ?

(Réponse : un frigo que l'on a puni.)

Qu'est-ce qui est blanc et qui se cache dans un buisson ?

(Réponse : un frigo puni qui a fait une fugue.)

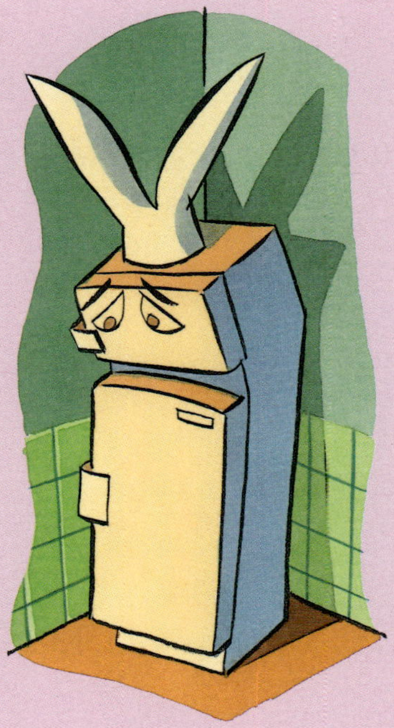

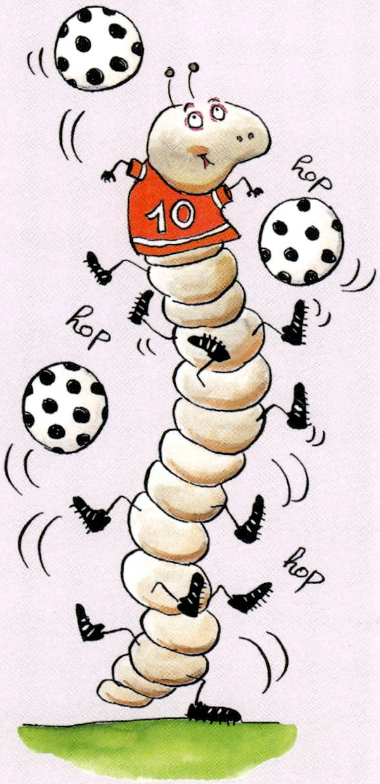

Petite annonce

19

Décembre

SPORT : M. Mille-pattes vient d'être sélectionné pour la Coupe du Monde de football.

Histoire drôle

20

Décembre

Un enfant appelle son père à son bureau.

- Papa, est-ce que tu pourrais me trouver l'adresse e-mail du père Noël, sur Internet ?

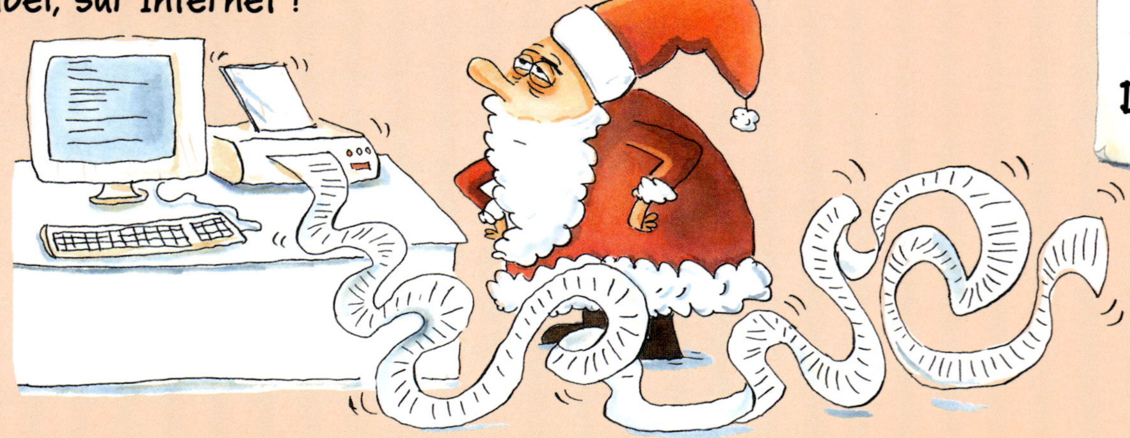

La maîtresse explique aux élèves la manière de conserver les aliments afin qu'ils ne pourrissent pas.

- Parlons maintenant du lait. Qui sait quel est le moyen le plus sûr de conserver le lait ?

- Moi, je sais, répond un élève. Le moyen le plus sûr pour conserver le lait, c'est de le laisser dans la vache.

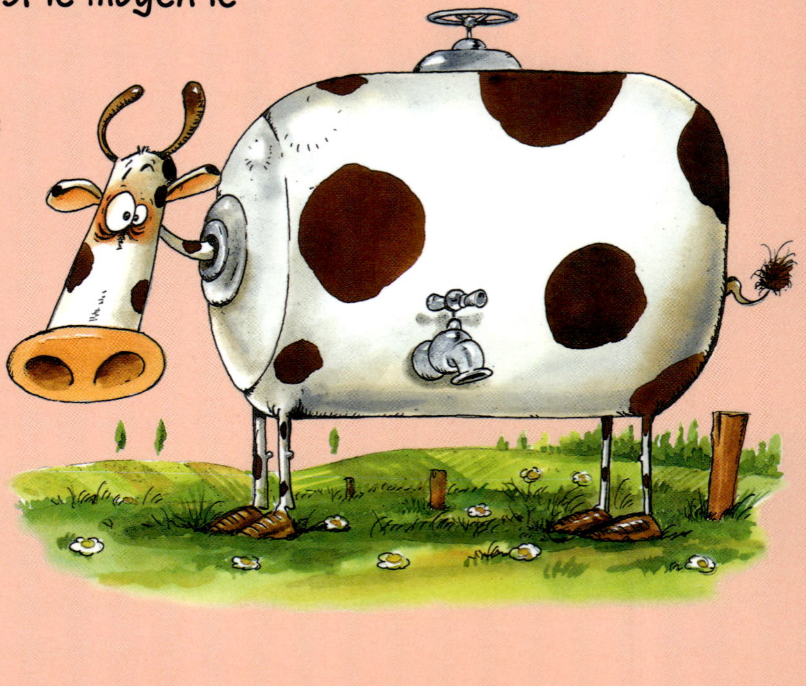

Histoire drôle

21

Décembre

Histoire drôle

22

Décembre

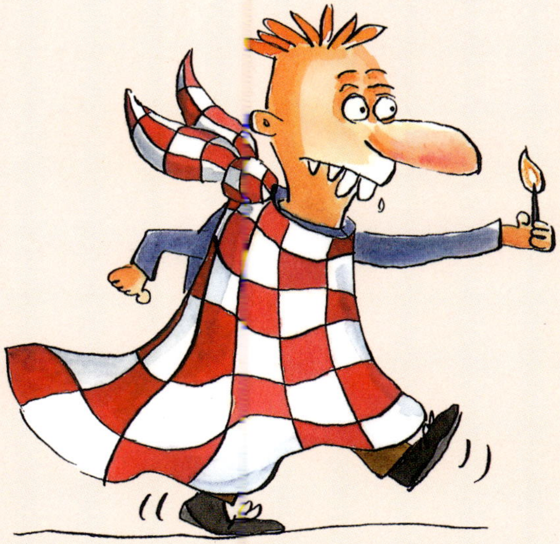

ÉNIGME : un homme entre dans une pièce avec une allumette à la main. Dans cette pièce, il y a une bougie, une cheminée et une cuisinière à gaz. Il a très faim. Qu'allume-t-il en premier ?

(L'allumette, bien sûr !)

Histoire drôle

23

Décembre

Maman demande à Julien :

- Ta sœur m'a dit que tu t'étais levé cette nuit pour guetter le père Noël ?
- Oui, m'man.
- Et tu l'as entendu ?
- Oui. J'ai surtout bien entendu tous les gros mots qu'il a dits quand il s'est cogné contre la table basse du salon !

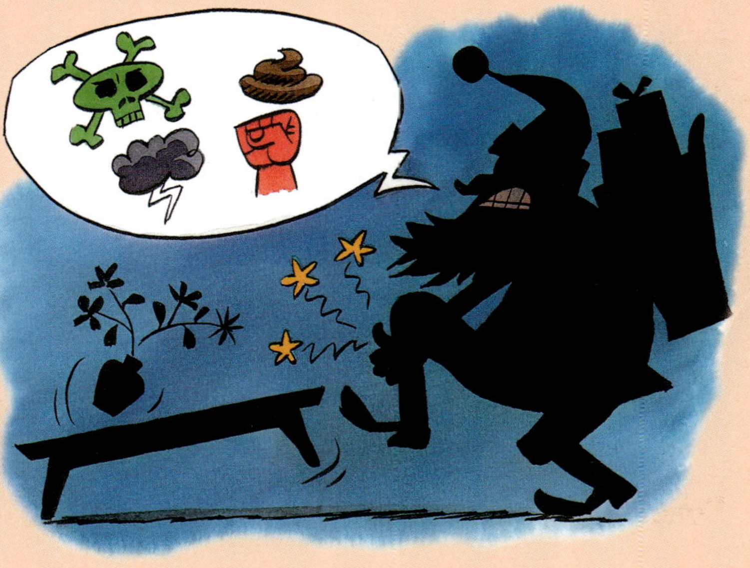

Histoire drôle

24

Décembre

Un gendarme arrête un automobiliste qui vient de griller un feu rouge.

- Alors, mon bonhomme, vous n'aviez pas vu le feu ?

- Si, si. C'est vous que je n'avais pas vu...

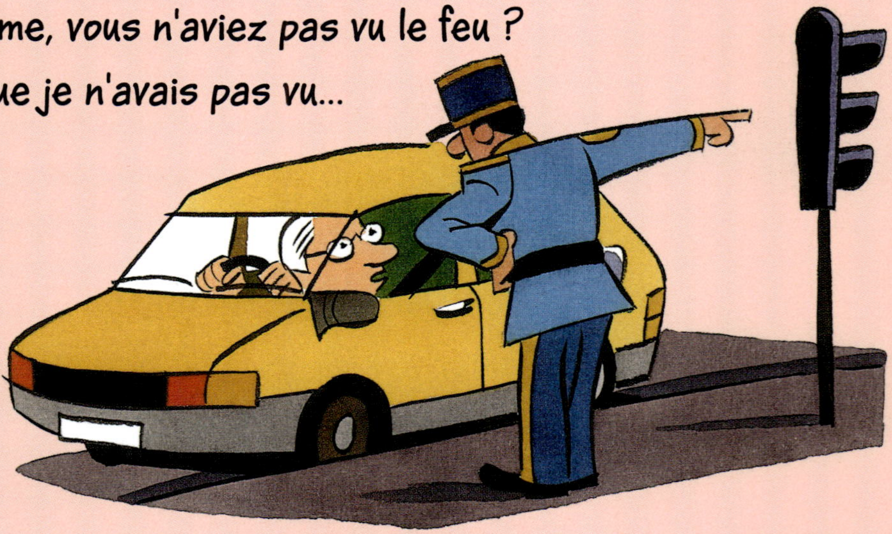

Deux pneus font le concours de la blague la plus drôle.

- Le premier qui éclate de rire a perdu !

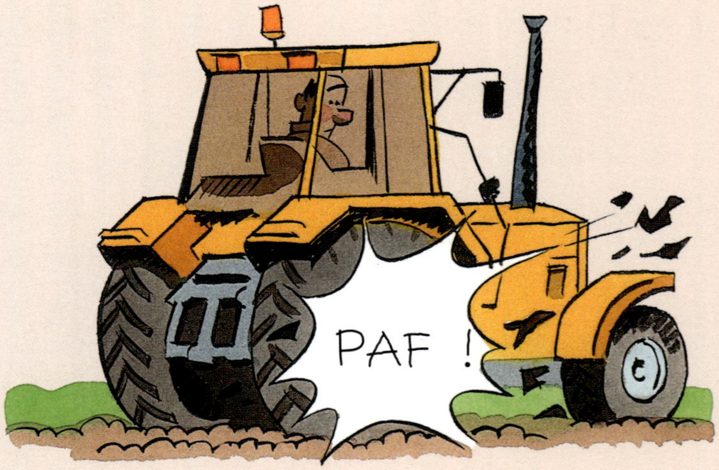

Histoire drôle

25

Décembre

Deux balles de tennis regardent un ballon de basket qui passe devant elles en roulant des mécaniques.

- Wouah, les muscles ! s'exclame l'une.

- Pff ! tout ça c'est de la gonflette, rétorque l'autre.

Histoire drôle

26

Décembre

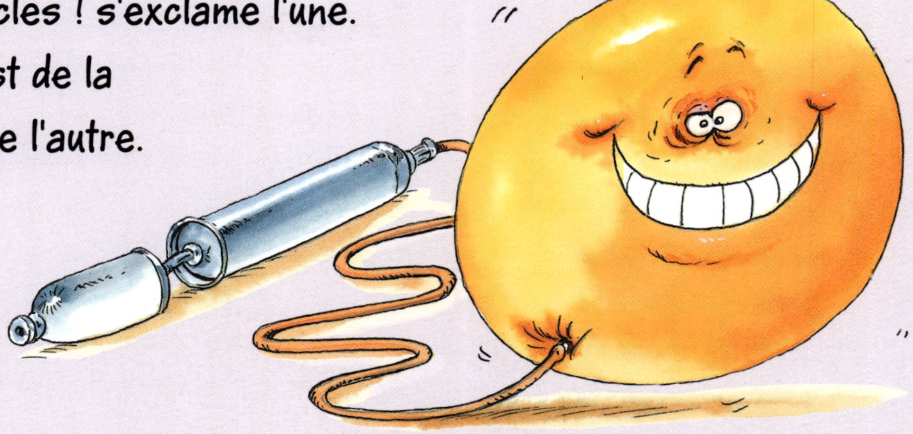

Un petit garçon veut réveiller son père qui fait tranquillement la sieste.

Il le secoue, sans arriver à le réveiller, puis lui soulève une paupière et voit son œil.

- Je ne comprends pas, dit-il à sa mère. Il ne répond pas, et pourtant, j'ai regardé à l'intérieur, et il est là !

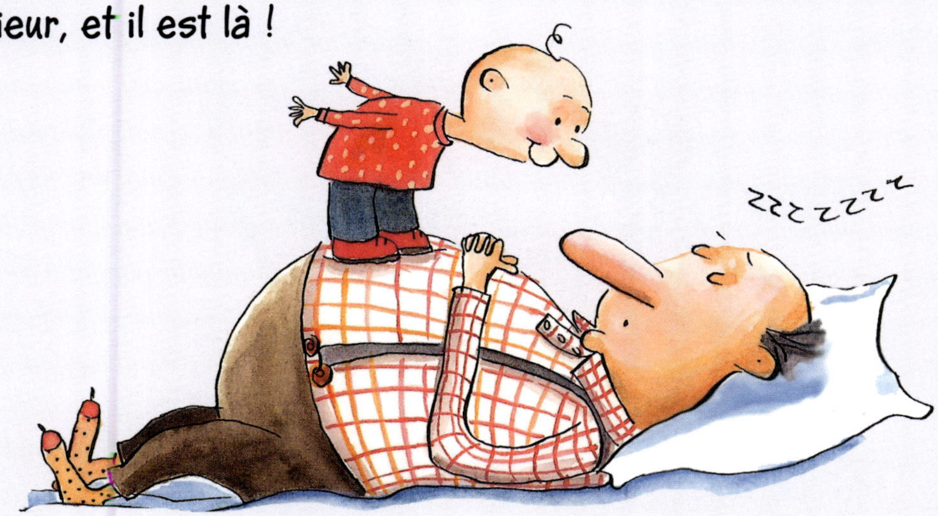

Histoire drôle

27

Décembre

Histoire drôle
28
Décembre

Pendant que son bébé joue avec le chien de la maison, comme il en a l'habitude, une maman toute contente appelle son mari.

- Chéri, bébé a prononcé ses premiers mots en jouant avec Rex !

Le mari accourt, tout heureux.

- Qu'est-ce qu'il a dit ? « Papa »? « Maman » ?
- Non. Il a dit « Ouaf, ouaf ».

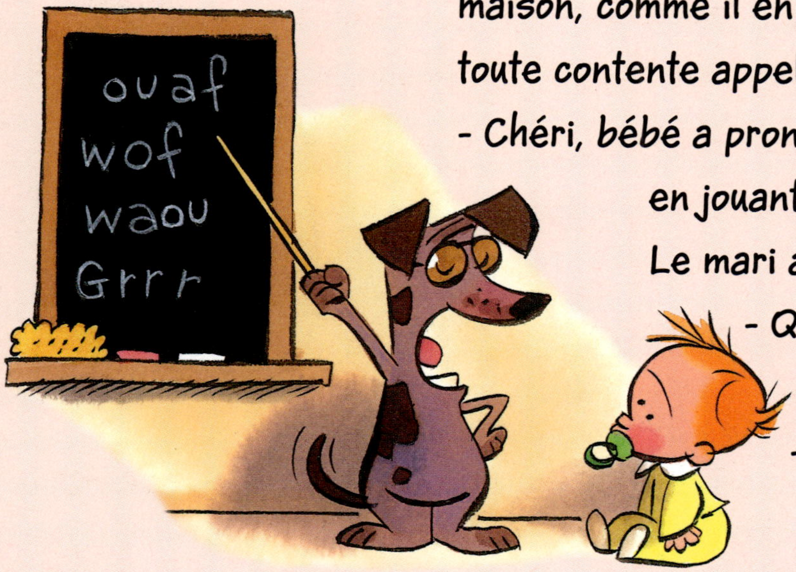

Un vétérinaire vient de terminer d'examiner un perroquet atteint d'une angine depuis quelques jours.

- Bon, dit-il à l'animal, en désignant un tas de plumes par terre, j'ai fini. Vous pouvez vous rhabiller.

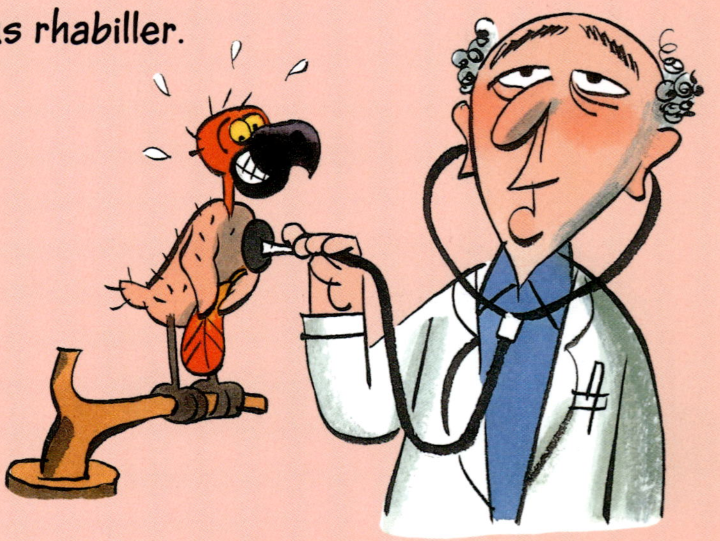

Histoire drôle
29
Décembre

Dans la jungle, un chimpanzé bouscule par mégarde un gorille qui tombe dans une énorme flaque de boue. Le chimpanzé s'enfuit tandis que le gorille, furieux, le poursuit. Le chimpanzé rentre précipitamment dans un bar, il prend un journal, s'assied à une table et fait semblant de le lire. Le gorille entre à son tour, l'air furibard.

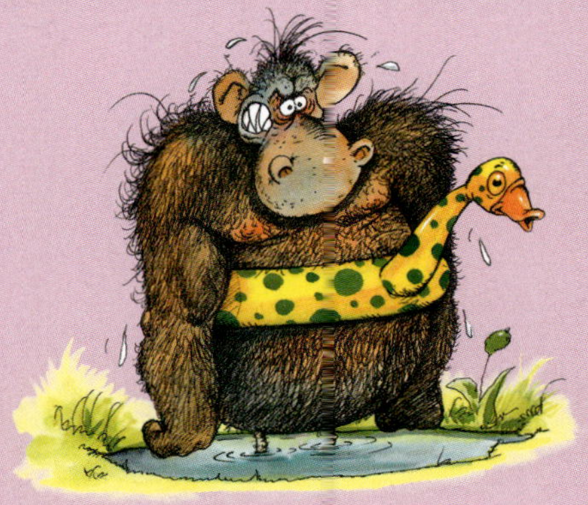

- Quelqu'un a-t-il vu un singe qui se sauvait, par ici ?

Le chimpanzé lève la tête de sa lecture.

- Celui qui a poussé un gorille dans la boue ?

Le gorille s'approche de lui, l'air étonné.

- C'est déjà dans le journal ?

Histoire drôle

30

Décembre

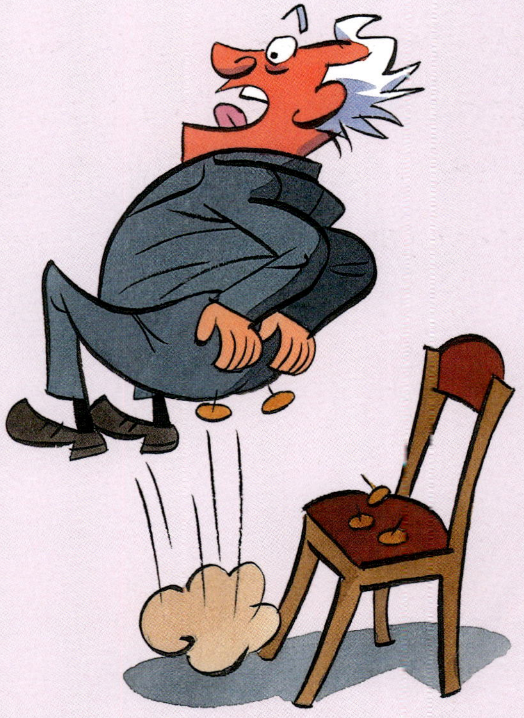

Julien rentre de l'école, tout fier.

- J'ai été le seul à savoir répondre à la question du maître, aujourd'hui !

- Ah oui ! s'étonne sa maman. Et c'était quoi, cette question ?

- Euh... c'était... euh... « Qui a posé ces punaises sur ma chaise ? »

Histoire drôle

31

Décembre

Imprimé en Belgique.

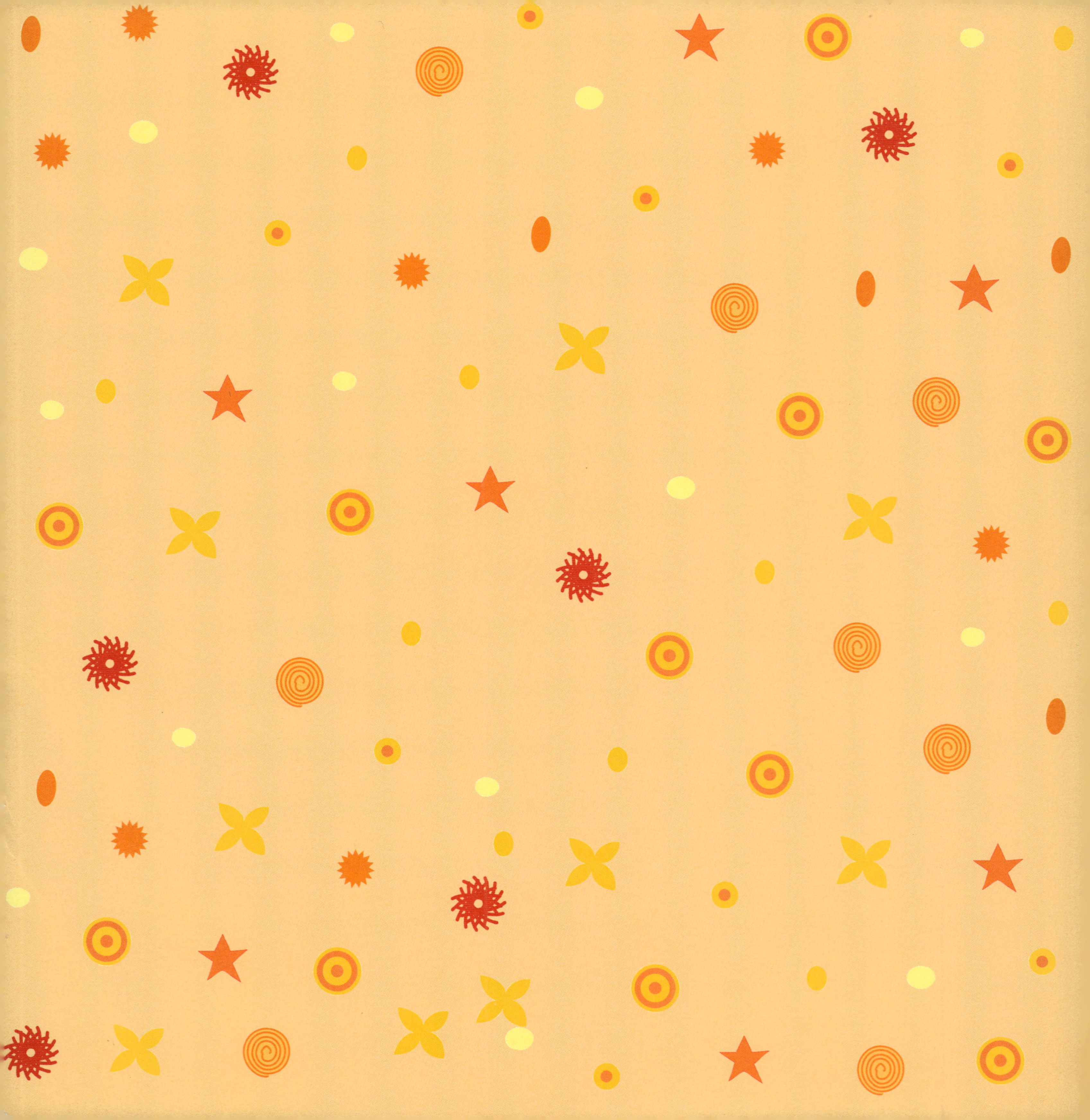

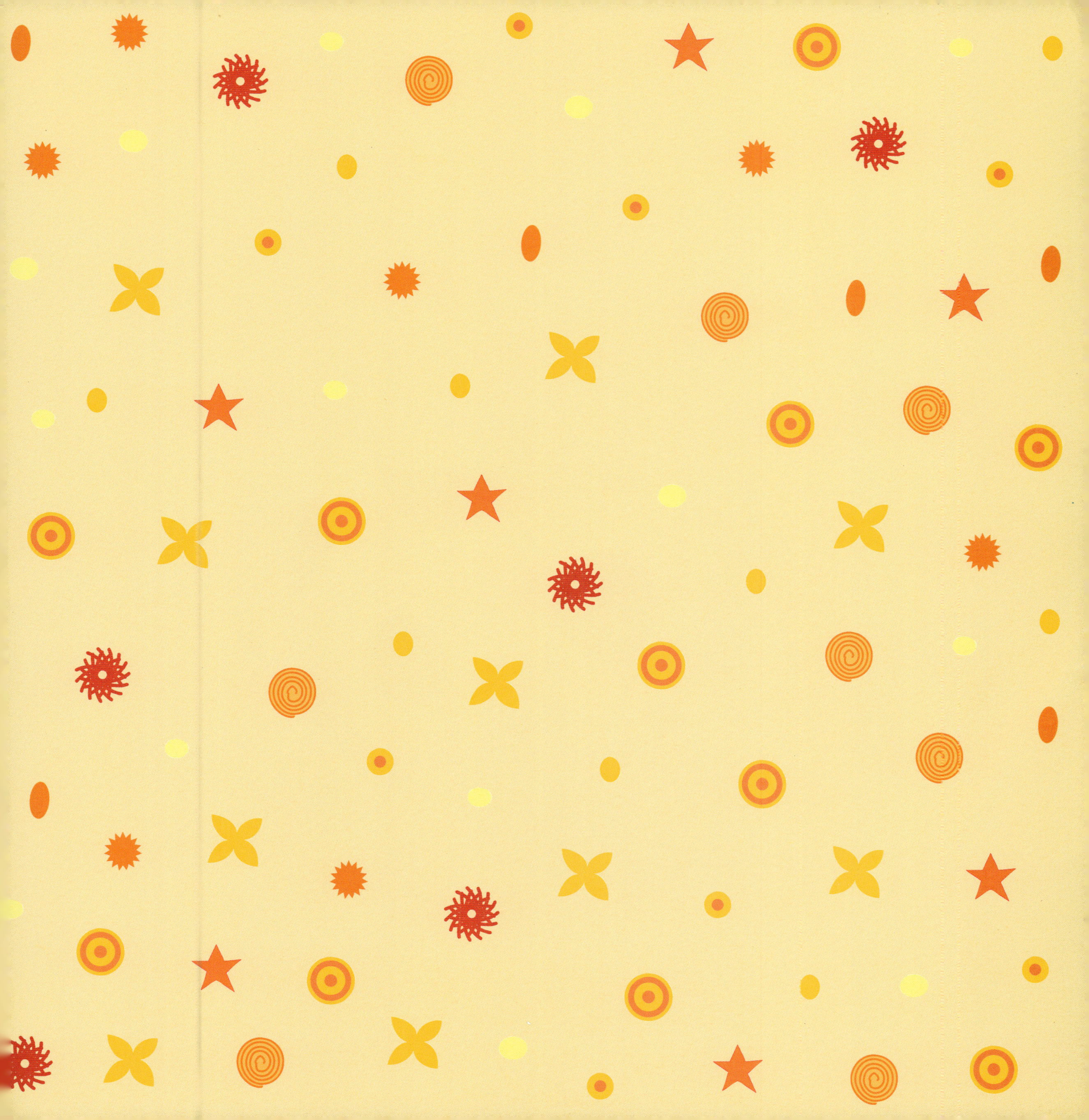

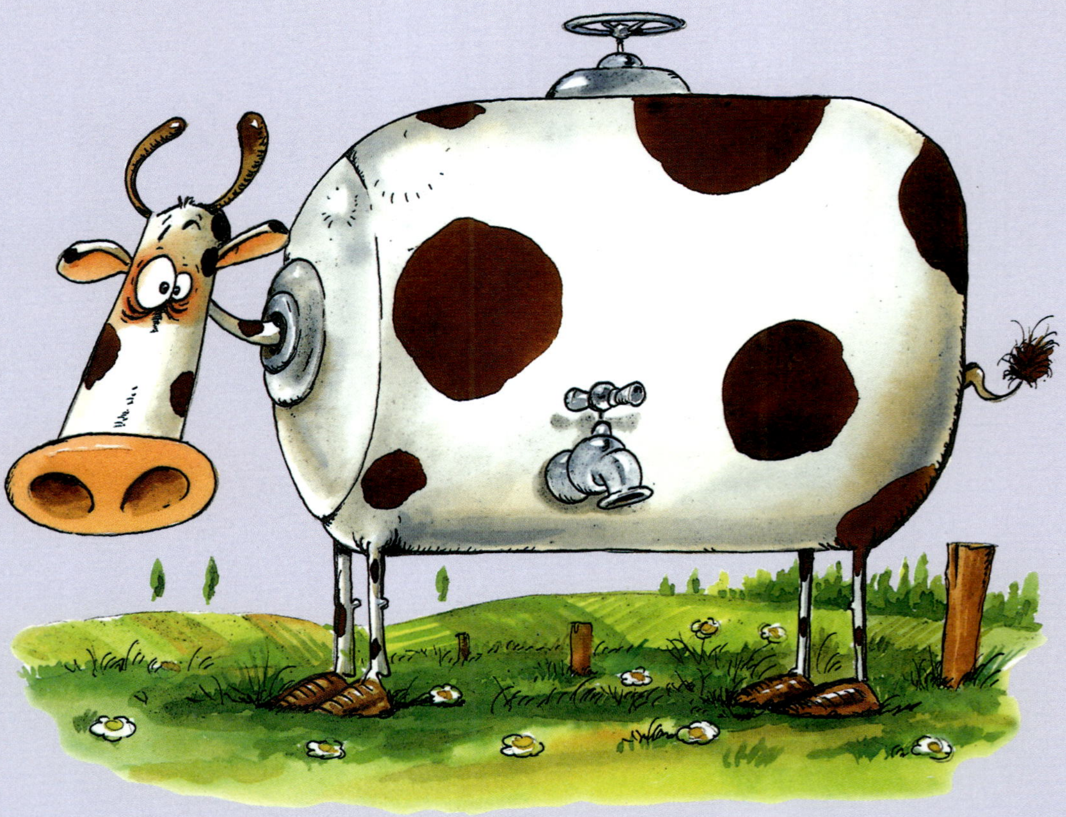